GLORY
TO GOD

© 2013 Westminster John Knox Press

First edition
Published by Westminster John Knox Press
Louisville, Kentucky

14 15 16 17 18 19 20 21 22—10 9 8 7 6 5 4 3

PRINTED IN THE UNITED STATES OF AMERICA

♾ The paper used in this publication meets the minimum requirements of the American National Standard for Information Sciences—Permanence of Paper for Printed Library Materials, ANSI Z39.48-1992.

978-0-664-50304-8	(Pew, Presbyterian seal, red)
978-0-664-50313-0	(Pew, Presbyterian seal, purple)
978-0-664-23896-4	(Pew, Ecumenical edition, red)
978-0-664-23897-1	(Pew, Ecumenical edition, purple)
978-0-664-50312-3	(Hymnal companion)
978-0-664-50314-7	(Accompaniment edition, red)
978-0-664-50321-5	(Accompaniment edition, purple)
978-0-664-50323-9	(Enlarged print, loose leaf)
978-0-664-50324-6	(Gift edition)
978-0-664-50322-2	(Enlarged print, text edition, bound)

CONTENTS

INTRODUCTION

The 216th General Assembly (2004) of the Presbyterian Church (U.S.A.) gave authorization to the Presbyterian Publishing Corporation (PPC) to research the feasibility of a new hymnal, in cooperation with the denomination's Office of Theology and Worship (TAW) and the Presbyterian Association of Musicians (PAM). The results of this study were reported to the 217th General Assembly (2006), which authorized the publishing company to proceed with preparing a new hymnal in consultation with these denominational bodies. The collection was presented to the 220th General Assembly (2012), which commended it for use in the church.

The process to develop a new hymnal began in 2008 with the hiring of an editor and the forming of the Presbyterian Committee on Congregational Song (PCOCS). Over the next three and a half years the committee met and considered thousands of hymns and songs. It was a rich and rewarding time, filled with deep and significant conversations. Each item under consideration was sung and thoroughly discussed. We reviewed every entry anonymously, with all author, composer, and copyright information blocked. When the committee felt ready to make a decision, a vote was taken and, if a two-thirds majority approved, the hymn or song moved forward. *Glory to God* is the culmination of this multiyear endeavor.

The PCOCS presents this collection with a great deal of excitement. We are eager for current and future generations to sing the hymns and songs, get to know the collection, and enjoy the rich diversity of gifts present here. Every member of the PCOCS desires that *Glory to God* will serve as an instrument of God's grace.

This we know:
We know this hymnal will change lives.
We know this hymnal will inspire the church.
We know these songs will enliven worship in powerful ways.
We know the familiar songs will sing anew.
We know the new songs will speak truth.

This we pray:
We pray that as we sing together from this hymnal, we will come to
 have a deeper sense of our unity in the body of Christ.
We pray that the Holy Spirit will bring surprises and breathe new life
 into our churches through this hymnal.

This we hope:
We hope the cover imprint fades from greasy fingers.
We hope the pages become wrinkled and torn from constant use.
We hope our children will sing from this hymnal—
    we hope our grandchildren will too.

We praise!
We praise God for this resource of song and give God the glory!

Mary Louise Bringle, *Chair*
Adam Copeland
Alfred Fedak
Stephen Fey
Charles Frost
Karen Hastings-Flegel
Beverly Howard
Paul Junggap Huh

Mary Beth Jones
Eric Myers
Chelsea Stern
Edwin Chr. van Driel
Michael Waschevski
Barbara Wheeler
Chi Yi Chen Wolbrink

David Eicher, *Editor*
Alan Barthel, *PAM ex-officio*
William McConnell, *PAM ex-officio*
David Gambrell, *TAW ex-officio*
David Maxwell, *PPC ex-officio*
Robin Howell, *Hymnal Project Coordinator*
Mary Margaret Flannagan, *Hymnal Advocacy and Relations Coordinator*

SERVICES OF WORSHIP

These worship resources are intended for use in conjunction with the *Book of Common Worship* (BCW) and in accordance with the Presbyterian Church (U.S.A.) Directory for Worship; see also the *Book of Common Worship: Pastoral Edition* (BCW—P), *Book of Common Worship: Daily Prayer* (BCW—DP), and *Book of Occasional Services* (BOS). At certain places in these liturgies, page numbers in those service books are cited for other appropriate texts.

THE SERVICE FOR THE LORD'S DAY

Christians meet for worship on the first day of the week, the day Christ Jesus rose from the dead. We gather to praise the triune God, confess our sin, and seek God's grace. We hear the good news of the gospel and celebrate the Lord's Supper. We go forth to glorify God through the service of daily living.

The Service for the Lord's Day is a service of Word and Sacrament. Together they form a unified liturgy; one is incomplete without the other.

GATHERING

Instrumental music, congregational song, or contemplative silence may precede the service.

CALL TO WORSHIP

All may stand as one of the following, or another verse from Scripture appropriate to the season or day (BCW 49–50, 165–400), is said.

A Our help is in the name of the Lord,
    maker of heaven and earth.
                                     Ps. 124:8

B This is the day that the Lord has made;
    let us rejoice and be glad in it.
                                    Ps. 118:24

C Cry out with joy to the Lord, all the earth.
    Worship the Lord with gladness.
    Come into God's presence with singing!
                                    Ps. 100:1–2

The grace of the Lord Jesus Christ 2 Thess. 3:18
be with you all.
And also with you.

Let us worship God.

HYMN, PSALM, OR SPIRITUAL SONG

OPENING PRAYER

*An Opening Prayer (BCW 50–52), such as the following, or the Prayer of the Day
(BCW 165–400) may be said from the baptismal font.*

A God of all glory,
on this first day you began creation,
bringing light out of darkness.

On this first day you began your new creation,
raising Jesus Christ from the darkness of death.

On this Lord's Day grant that we,
the people you create by water and the Spirit,
may be joined with all your works
in praising you for your great glory.
Through Jesus Christ,
in union with the Holy Spirit,
we praise you now and forever. **Amen.**

B Almighty God,
to whom all hearts are open,
all desires, known,
and from whom no secrets are hid:
Cleanse the thoughts of our hearts
by the inspiration of your Holy Spirit,
that we may perfectly love you
and worthily magnify your holy name;
through Christ our Lord. **Amen.**

CONFESSION AND PARDON

Water may be poured into the baptismal font. The minister leads the Call to Confession (BCW 52–53).

A The grace of God overflows for us   1 Tim. 1:14–15
through Christ Jesus
who came into the world to save sinners.

B The proof of God's amazing love is this: Rom. 5:8; Heb. 4:16
While we were sinners Christ died for us.
Because we have faith in him,
we dare to approach God with confidence.

C If we say we have no sin,   1 John 1:8–9
we deceive ourselves,
and the truth is not in us.
But when we confess our sins,
God who is faithful and just
will forgive us our sins
and cleanse us from all unrighteousness.

The minister continues:

Trusting in God's grace, let us confess our sin.

Following silent personal examination, all pray together the following or another Prayer of Confession (BCW 53–54, 87–89, 165–400).

A **Merciful God,**
we confess that we have sinned against you
in thought, word, and deed,
by what we have done,
and by what we have left undone.
We have not loved you
with our whole heart and mind and strength.
We have not loved our neighbors as ourselves.

In your mercy, forgive what we have been,
help us amend what we are,
and direct what we shall be,
that we may delight in your will
and walk in your ways,
to the glory of your holy name.

B Holy and merciful God,
in your presence we confess
our failure to be what you created us to be.
You alone know how often we have sinned
in wandering from your ways,
in wasting your gifts,
in forgetting your love.

By your loving mercy,
help us to live in your light
and abide in your ways,
for the sake of Jesus Christ our Savior.

The "Kyrie Eleison" ("Lord, Have Mercy," nos. 551–609) or "Agnus Dei"
("Lamb of God," nos. 551–609) may be sung.

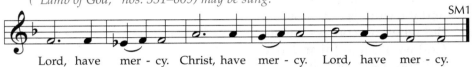

SM1

Lord, have mer - cy. Christ, have mer - cy. Lord, have mer - cy.

The minister may lift water from the font, declaring the good news of God's grace
(BCW 56–57).

A The mercy of the Lord   Ps. 103:17
is from everlasting to everlasting.
I declare to you, in the name of Jesus Christ,
we are forgiven. **Amen.**

B Anyone who is in Christ is a new creation.   2 Cor. 5:17
The old life has gone; a new life has begun.
Know that you are forgiven and be at peace. **Amen.**

A song of praise, such as "Gloria in Excelsis" ("Glory to God," nos. 551–609)
or "Gloria Patri" ("Glory Be to the Father," nos. 551–609), may be sung.

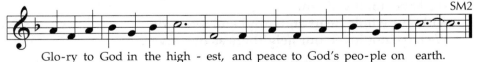

SM2

Glo-ry to God in the high - est, and peace to God's peo-ple on earth.

A summary of the Law of God (p. 36) or a call to faithfulness (BCW 57) may also
be included here.

Worshipers may share signs of Christ's peace and reconciling love here or after the
Prayers of the People. The people are then seated.

WORD

PRAYER FOR ILLUMINATION

A Prayer for Illumination (BCW 60, 90–91), such as the following, or the Prayer of the Day (BCW 165–400) is said.

Lord, open our hearts and minds
by the power of your Holy Spirit,
that as the Scriptures are read
and your Word is proclaimed,
we may hear with joy
what you say to us today. **Amen.**

The reader may then say:

A Hear the Word of the Lord.

B Hear what the Spirit is
saying to the church.   Rev. 2:7

SCRIPTURE

Readings from the Old and New Testaments are normally included.

The Revised Common Lectionary (BCW 1035–1048) provides three readings and a psalm: (1) the First Reading, from the Old Testament or Acts (in Easter); the Psalm, sung as a response to the First Reading; (2) the Second Reading, from a New Testament epistle; and (3) the Gospel Reading.

Before each reading:

A reading from _____.

After each reading:

A The Word of the Lord.
Thanks be to God.

B Holy wisdom, holy Word.
Thanks be to God.

An anthem, a Gospel acclamation, or an alleluia (nos. 551–609) may be sung before the reading of the Gospel.

The reading of the Gospel may be announced by saying:

The Gospel of our Lord Jesus Christ according to _____.
Glory to you, O Lord.

After the reading of the Gospel, the following may be said:

The Gospel of the Lord.
Praise to you, O Christ.

Silence for reflection may follow the readings from Scripture.

SERMON

An Ascription of Praise (BCW 62–63, 91–92) may conclude the Sermon.

Blessing and glory and wisdom   Rev. 7:12
and thanksgiving and honor
and power and might
be to our God forever and ever! **Amen.**

Silence for reflection may follow.

*An Invitation to Discipleship (BCW 92–93) may take place here, giving
opportunity for any who wish to make a personal commitment to Christ or to live
more fully into their baptismal calling.*

HYMN, PSALM, OR SPIRITUAL SONG

*All may stand. If Baptism or a pastoral rite of the church follows, candidates may
come forward during the singing.*

AFFIRMATION OF FAITH

*The Nicene Creed (p. 34) is particularly appropriate for the celebration of the
Lord's Supper. When the Sacrament of Baptism (p. 14) is to be celebrated, however,
the Apostles' Creed (pp. 17, 35) is used within the baptismal liturgy.*

BAPTISM OR PASTORAL RITE OF THE CHURCH

*The Sacrament of Baptism (p. 14; BCW 403–429) appropriately follows the
Proclamation of the Word. Pastoral rites associated with Baptism—reaffirmation
of the baptismal covenant (p. 20; BCW 431–454), reception of new members
(BCW 455–462), marriage (BCW 841–902), ordination or installation
(BOS 5–118)—also may take place here.*

PRAYERS OF THE PEOPLE

*It is particularly appropriate for a deacon or elder to lead the Prayers of the People
(BCW 99–120) from the midst of the congregation or from the Lord's Table.*

Intercessions are made for:

> *the church universal;*
> *the local congregation;*
> *the well-being of the earth;*
> *peace and justice in the world;*
> *nations and leaders;*
> *the local community;*
> *the poor and oppressed;*
> *the sick, bereaved, and lonely;*
> *all who suffer in body, mind, or spirit;*
> *other special needs.*

Those who have died are remembered with thanksgiving.

Worshipers may respond with specific prayers, aloud or in silence, as bidden. After each petition, one of the following may be said.

A Lord, in your mercy:
hear our prayer.

B We pray to you, O Lord:
Lord, have mercy.

Sharing the Peace of Christ is included here, if not earlier in the service.

The peace of our Lord Jesus Christ be with you.
And also with you.

The people may exchange signs of Christ's peace and reconciling love.

EUCHARIST

OFFERING

One of the following, or another Invitation to Offering (BCW 67), may be said.

A The earth is the Lord's, and all that is in it,
the world, and those who live in it.

Ps. 24:1

B Freely you have received, freely give.

Matt. 10:8

Let us return to God the offerings of our life
and the gifts of the earth.

As offerings are gathered, an anthem may be sung or other appropriate music may be offered. The minister and elders or deacons prepare the table. The people's offerings, which may include food for the hungry, are brought to the table. A song of praise may be sung.

All that is in the heavens and on the earth   1 Chr. 29:11, 14
is yours, O Lord,
and of your own we give you.

An elder or deacon may then say:

Blessed are you, O God, maker of all things.
Through your goodness you have blessed us with these gifts:
our selves, our time, and our possessions.
Use us, and what we have gathered,
in feeding the world with your love;
through the one who gave himself for us,
Jesus Christ our Savior and Lord. **Amen.**

*The norm of Christian worship is to celebrate the Lord's Supper on each Lord's
Day. If the Lord's Supper is omitted, the service may include a prayer of
thanksgiving (BCW 80–81, 158–159, 165–400), concluding with the Lord's
Prayer (pp. 11, 35; no. 464). The service then continues at the closing hymn.*

INVITATION TO THE LORD'S TABLE

The minister may say these or similar words (BCW 68–69, 125):

This is the joyful feast of the people of God!

People will come from north and south   Luke 13:29
and from east and west
to sit at table in the kingdom of God.

According to Luke,   Luke 24:30–31
when our risen Lord was at table with his disciples,
he took the bread, blessed and broke it,
and gave it to them.
Their eyes were then opened,
and they recognized him.

This is the Lord's table.
Our Savior invites those who trust him
to share the feast that he has prepared.

GREAT THANKSGIVING

All may stand for the Great Thanksgiving (BCW 69–73, 126–156, 165–400).
The introductory dialogue may be spoken or sung.

Minister/Leader · People · SM3

The Lord be with you. **And al - so with you.**

Minister/Leader · People

Lift up your hearts. **We lift them to the Lord.**

Minister/Leader

Let us give thanks to the Lord our God.

People

It is right to give our thanks and praise.

Thanks and praise is given for:

> *God's work in creation, providence, and covenant history;*
> *the witness of the prophets;*
> *God's steadfast love in spite of human sin;*
> *the ultimate gift of Christ;*
> *the festival or season of the Christian year.*

With heavenly choirs and the faithful of every time and place, the people sing the
Sanctus, "Holy, holy, holy" (nos. 551–609).

Isa. 6:3, Rev. 4:8; Ps. 118:25–26
SM4

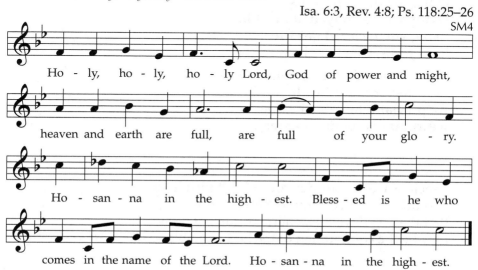

Ho - ly, ho - ly, ho - ly Lord, God of power and might,
heaven and earth are full, are full of your glo - ry.
Ho - san - na in the high - est. Bless - ed is he who
comes in the name of the Lord. Ho - san - na in the high - est.

The prayer continues, thankfully remembering:

> *the Word made flesh;*
> *Jesus' life and ministry;*
> *his death and resurrection;*
> *the promised coming of his reign;*
> *the gift of the sacrament.*

We give you thanks that the Lord Jesus,
on the night before he died, took bread,
and after giving thanks to you, he broke it,
and gave it to his disciples, saying:
Take, eat. This is my body, given for you.
Do this in remembrance of me.

In the same way Jesus took the cup, saying:
This cup is the new covenant sealed in my blood,
shed for you for the forgiveness of sins.
Whenever you drink it, do this in remembrance of me.

The prayer continues, thankfully remembering our salvation in Christ and offering our lives to God in service and praise as we celebrate this meal.

A Memorial Acclamation (nos. 551–609) is sung or said.

A Great is the mystery of faith:

Christ has died, Christ is ris - en, Christ will come a - gain.

B Praise to you, Lord Jesus:
**Dying you destroyed our death,
rising you restored our life.
Lord Jesus, come in glory.**

C According to Christ's commandment:
**We remember his death,
we proclaim his resurrection,
we await his coming in glory.**

The prayer continues:

Gracious God, pour out your Holy Spirit upon us
and upon these your gifts of bread and wine,
that the bread we break and the cup we bless
may be the communion of the body and blood of Christ.

Calling on the power of the Holy Spirit, we pray:

> *that we may be made one with the risen Christ and with all God's people;*
> *that we may be faithful as Christ's body in ministry in the world;*
> *that we may live in anticipation of the fullness of God's realm.*

The prayer concludes with praise to the triune God, and the Great Amen (nos. 551–609).

Through Christ, with Christ, in Christ,
in the unity of the Holy Spirit,
all glory and honor are yours, almighty God, now and forever.

SM6

A - men,   a - men,   a - men.

LORD'S PRAYER

The Lord's Prayer (no. 464) is sung or spoken (see also p. 35).

Our Father in heaven,
    hallowed be your name,
    your kingdom come,
    your will be done, on earth as in heaven.
Give us today our daily bread.
Forgive us our sins
    as we forgive those who sin against us.
Save us from the time of trial
    and deliver us from evil.
For the kingdom, the power,
    and the glory are yours
    now and forever. Amen.

BREAKING OF THE BREAD

The minister lifts and breaks the bread, saying:

Jesus said: I am the bread of life.   John 6:35

The minister pours and/or lifts the cup, saying:

Jesus said: I am the vine, you are the branches.   John 15:5

Come to me and never be hungry;   John 6:35
believe in me and never thirst.

Extending the bread and cup to the people, the minister says:

The gifts of God for the people of God.
Thanks be to God.

COMMUNION OF THE PEOPLE

During the Communion of the People, hymns, psalms, and spiritual songs may be sung (nos. 494–538), or other appropriate music may be offered.

In giving the bread, the server says:

A The bread of heaven.
Amen.

B The body of Christ,
given for you. **Amen.**

In giving the cup, the server says:

A The cup of salvation.
Amen.

B The blood of Christ,
given for you. **Amen.**

PRAYER AFTER COMMUNION

One of the following or another Prayer after Communion (BCW 76–77, 157–158) is said. Option A may be sung (no. 535).

A Bless the Lord, O my soul;   Ps. 103:1–2
**and all that is within me,
bless God's holy name.**

Bless the Lord, O my soul;
and forget not all God's benefits.

B God of abundance,
with this bread of life and cup of salvation
you have united us with Christ,
making us one with all your people.

Now send us forth in the power of your Spirit
that we may proclaim your redeeming love to the world
and continue forever in the risen life
of Jesus Christ, our Lord. **Amen.**

Deacons and/or elders may be commissioned to extend the celebration of the Lord's Supper to those unable to gather with the worshiping community.

We send you out with this bread and cup
to share the feast of the risen Lord.
We who are many are one body,   1 Cor. 10:17
for we all partake of the one bread.

Those commissioned for the extended serving of communion depart immediately.

Sending

If the Lord's Supper is omitted, the service concludes with the sending.

Brief announcements related to the church's mission may be mentioned here.

Hymn, Psalm, or Spiritual Song

Blessing and Charge

The minister speaks the Blessing (BCW 78, 161) to the congregation.

A The grace of the Lord Jesus Christ,   2 Cor. 13:13
the love of God,
and the communion of the Holy Spirit
be with you all. **Alleluia!**   *or* **Amen.**

B The Lord bless you and keep you.   Num. 6:24–26
The Lord be kind and gracious to you.
The Lord look upon you with favor
and give you peace. **Alleluia!**   *or* **Amen.**

A deacon or elder may give the Charge (BCW 78, 159–160) from the font, table, or door of the church.

A Go in peace to love and serve the Lord. **Amen.**

B Go out into the world in peace;
have courage;
hold on to what is good;
return no one evil for evil;
support the weak;
help the suffering;
honor all people;
love and serve the Lord,
rejoicing in the power of the Holy Spirit. **Amen.**

C Go in peace
and in the name of Christ,
remember the poor. **Amen.**

Instrumental music may follow the Charge.

The Sacrament of Baptism

Through Baptism we are incorporated into the universal church. Ecumenical representatives may be invited to share in presiding in this liturgy wherever the role of a minister is indicated.

If the Easter Vigil is part of the liturgical practice of the congregation, the paschal candle is lighted and placed by the font at the beginning of the Service for the Lord's Day.

Following the sermon, an appropriate hymn is sung as the candidates, sponsors, and parents assemble at the baptismal font or pool. An elder or another representative of the congregation may carry a large pitcher of water to the place of baptism.

Presentation

The minister addresses all present:

Hear the words of our Lord Jesus Christ: Matt. 28:18–20

All authority in heaven and on earth
has been given to me.
Go therefore and make disciples of all nations,
baptizing them in the name of the Father,
and of the Son,
and of the Holy Spirit,
teaching them to obey everything that I have commanded you.
And remember, I am with you always, to the end of the age.

A member of the congregation or ecumenical representative may speak these or similar words (BCW 403–404; BCW—P 8–9; see also Ezek. 36:25–27; John 3:3, 5; and Titus 3:4–7) from the midst of the people.

A   There is one body and one Spirit,   Eph. 4:4–6
just as you were called
to the one hope of your calling,
one Lord, one faith, one Baptism,
one God and Father of all,
who is above all and through all and in all.

B   As many of you as were baptized into Christ   Gal. 3:27–28
have clothed yourselves with Christ.
There is no longer Jew or Greek;
there is no longer slave or free;
there is no longer male or female;
for all of us are one in Christ Jesus.

An elder presents each candidate for Baptism, using the appropriate forms.

For adults and older children:

A   On behalf of the session,
I present N. and N.
to receive the Sacrament of Baptism.

For infants and younger children:

B   On behalf of the session,
I present N., [*son/daughter*] of N. and N.,
to receive the Sacrament of Baptism.

The minister addresses candidates for Baptism who are adults and older children:

A   Putting your whole trust
in the grace and love of Jesus Christ,
N. and N., do you desire to be baptized?
I do.

The minister addresses parents presenting children for Baptism:

B   Do you desire that N. and N. be baptized?
I do.

Relying on God's grace
do you promise to nurture N. and N.
in the life and faith of the Christian community?
I do.

The minister addresses sponsors (if any are present) for each candidate:

Will you, by your prayers and witness,
help N. and N. to grow into the full stature of Christ?
I will.

The minister addresses the congregation:

Do you, as members of the church of Jesus Christ,
promise to guide and nurture N. and N.
by word and deed,
with love and prayer?
We do.

Will you encourage *them* to know, trust, and follow Christ,
and to be faithful *members* of his church?
We will.

PROFESSION OF FAITH

Through the Sacrament of Baptism we enter the covenant
God has established in Jesus Christ.

Within this covenant God gives us new life,
guards us from evil, and nurtures us in love.

Through this covenant, we choose whom we will serve
by turning from evil and turning to Jesus Christ.

*The minister asks the following questions of the candidates for Baptism and/or the
parents or guardians of children being presented for Baptism.*

Trusting in the gracious mercy of God,
do you turn from the ways of sin
and renounce evil and its power in the world?
I renounce them.   *or*   **I do.**

Who is your Lord and Savior?
Jesus Christ is my Lord and Savior.

Will you be Christ's faithful disciple,
obeying his word and showing his love?
I will, with God's help.

*The minister asks the following question to those being baptized on public
profession of faith.*

Will you devote yourself   Acts 2:42
to the church's teaching and fellowship,
to the breaking of bread and the prayers?
I will, with God's help.

The people may stand.

All profess their faith in the words of the Apostles' Creed (see also p. 35).
The question-and-answer form ("Do you believe in God?") may also be used.

With the whole church, let us confess our faith.

I believe in God, the Father almighty,
creator of heaven and earth.

I believe in Jesus Christ, God's only Son, our Lord,
who was conceived by the Holy Spirit,
born of the Virgin Mary,
suffered under Pontius Pilate,
was crucified, died, and was buried;
he descended to the dead.
On the third day he rose again;
he ascended into heaven,
he is seated at the right hand of the Father,
and he will come to judge the living and the dead.

I believe in the Holy Spirit,
the holy catholic church,
the communion of saints,
the forgiveness of sins,
the resurrection of the body,
and the life everlasting. Amen.

THANKSGIVING OVER THE WATER

Water is poured visibly and audibly into the font.

The minister leads the people in the Thanksgiving Over the Water
(BCW 410–412, 422–425; BCW—P 16–18, 28–32).

The Lord be with you.
And also with you.

Let us give thanks to the Lord our God.
It is right to give our thanks and praise.

Thanks and praise is given for:

> *God's covenant faithfulness;*
> *the cleansing and rebirth in the flood in the time of Noah;*
> *the exodus through the waters of the sea;*
> *Jesus' baptism in the Jordan;*
> *the baptism of Jesus' death and resurrection.*

The power of the Holy Spirit is called upon:

> *to attend and empower the baptism;*
> *to make the water a place of redemption and rebirth;*
> *to equip the church for faithfulness.*

The prayer concludes with praise to the triune God.

To you be all praise, honor, and glory;
through Jesus Christ our Savior,
who, with you and the Holy Spirit,
lives and reigns forever. **Amen.**

BAPTISM

The people may be seated. Candidates (other than infants) may kneel; if candidates are to be immersed, they may walk down into the water.

Calling each candidate by his or her Christian (first or first and middle) name, the minister shall pour water visibly and generously on the candidate's head or immerse the candidate in water, while saying:

N., I baptize you
in the name of the Father,
and of the Son,
and of the Holy Spirit. **Amen.**

The minister lays hands on the head of each person baptized, while saying:

O Lord, uphold N. by your Holy Spirit.   Isa. 11:2
Give *him/her* the spirit of wisdom and understanding,
the spirit of counsel and might,
the spirit of knowledge and the fear of the Lord,
and the spirit of joy in your presence,
both now and forever. **Amen.**

The minister may mark the sign of the cross with oil on the forehead of each of the newly baptized while saying:

N., child of the covenant,
you have been sealed by the Holy Spirit in Baptism
and marked as Christ's own forever. **Amen.**

The minister addresses all who have been baptized:

God who began a good work in you   Phil. 1:6
will bring it to completion
by the day of Jesus Christ. **Amen.**

Candidates who have been kneeling will stand.

WELCOME

An elder or ecumenical representative may say:

N. and N. *have* been received
into the one holy catholic and apostolic church
through Baptism.

By the power of the Holy Spirit,
they have become *members* of the household of God,
to share with us in the priesthood of Christ.

Welcome to the family of God,
and to Christ's ministry with us!
Amen. Alleluia!

A baptismal candle may be lighted from the paschal candle and given to each of the baptized by a sponsor or an elder.

Live as a child of the light   Matt. 5:16; Eph. 5:8
and let your light shine before others. **Amen.**

The minister says:

The peace of Christ be with you.
And also with you.

An Ascription of Praise (nos. 551–609) may be sung.

Those who have been baptized are welcomed in a manner appropriate to the congregation. The people may exchange signs of Christ's peace, greeting those who have been baptized.

The service continues with the Prayers of the People, which include petitions for the newly baptized and for those who will nurture them in faith (BCW 416–417; BCW—P 22–23).

It is appropriate for the newly baptized to receive communion first.

REAFFIRMATION OF THE BAPTISMAL COVENANT

This liturgy is for persons who were baptized as infants and nurtured in the church, and who now are making a public profession of faith.

The liturgy takes place at the baptismal font or pool, which shall be filled with water. Following the sermon, an appropriate hymn is sung as those making a public profession of faith gather at the place of Baptism.

PRESENTATION

An elder presents the candidates.

N. and N. *are* presented by the session
for the reaffirmation of the baptismal covenant.

They now *desire* to profess publicly *their* faith
and to assume greater responsibility
in the life of the church
and God's mission in the world.

Addressing the candidates, the minister says:

We rejoice that you now desire to declare your faith
and to share with us in our common ministry.

In Baptism you were joined to Christ
and made *members* of his church.

In the community of the people of God
you have learned of God's purpose for you
and for all creation.

You have been nurtured at the table of our Lord
and called to witness to the gospel of Jesus Christ.

A member of the congregation or ecumenical representative may speak these or similar words (BCW 448; BCW—P 60–61) from the midst of the people.

You are citizens with the saints   Eph. 2:19–20
and members of the household of God,
built upon the foundation of the apostles and prophets,
with Christ Jesus himself as the cornerstone.

PROFESSION OF FAITH

*The minister asks the following questions (BCW 449–450; BCW—P 61–62)
of those who are reaffirming the baptismal covenant.*

Trusting in the gracious mercy of God,
do you turn from the ways of sin
and renounce evil and its power in the world?
I renounce them.   *or*   **I do.**

Who is your Lord and Savior?
Jesus Christ is my Lord and Savior.

Will you be Christ's faithful disciple,
obeying his word and showing his love?
I will, with God's help.

*The minister asks the following question (BCW 451; BCW—P 64) to those
making a public profession of faith.*

Will you devote yourself   Acts 2:42
to the church's teaching and fellowship,
to the breaking of bread and the prayers?
I will, with God's help.

*The people may stand. All profess their faith in the words of the Apostles' Creed
(pp. 17, 35). The creed in question-and-answer form may be used.*

The minister then offers the following, or a similar prayer.

Those reaffirming the baptismal covenant may touch the water of the font.

Gracious God, by water and the Spirit
you claimed us as your own,
cleansing us from sin and giving us new life.

You made us members of your body, the church,
calling us to be your servants in the world.

Renew in N. and N. the covenant you made in *their* Baptism.

Continue the good work you have begun in *them*.

Send *them* forth in the power of your Spirit
to love and serve you with joy,
and to strive for justice and peace in all the earth,
in the name of Jesus Christ our Lord. **Amen.**

Laying On of Hands

The candidates kneel. The minister lays both hands on the head of each of the candidates in turn, while offering the following or a similar prayer. The sign of the cross may be marked with oil on the forehead of each candidate.

O Lord, uphold N. by your Holy Spirit.
Daily increase in *him/her* your gifts of grace: Isa. 11:2
the spirit of wisdom and understanding,
the spirit of counsel and might,
the spirit of knowledge and the fear of the Lord,
the spirit of joy in your presence,
both now and forever. **Amen.**

After each candidate has received the laying on of hands, the minister prays:

Ever-living God, guard *these* your *servants*
with your protecting hand,
and let your Holy Spirit be with *them* forever.
Lead *them* to know and obey your Word,
that *they* may serve you in this life
and dwell with you forever in the life to come;
through Jesus Christ our Lord. **Amen.**

Welcome

A representative of the session addresses those who have reaffirmed the baptismal covenant:

N. and N., by publicly professing your faith,
you have expressed your intention
to continue in the covenant God made with you
in your Baptism.

We welcome you as you join with us
in the worship and mission of the church.
Amen. Alleluia!

The minister says:

The peace of Christ be with you.
And also with you.

An Ascription of Praise (nos. 551–609) may be sung.

The people may exchange signs of Christ's peace, greeting those who have publicly professed their faith.

Daily Prayer

These services for Daily Prayer are intended for individual or family use, small-group meetings, retreats or conferences, and councils of the church.

Morning Prayer

Opening Sentences

All may stand.

O Lord, open my lips, Ps. 51:15
and my mouth shall proclaim your praise.

These or other Opening Sentences (BCW 491–492, 524–543; BCW—DP 27–28, 65–104) are said.

A The Lord's unfailing love and mercy never cease, Lam. 3:22–23
fresh as the morning and sure as the sunrise.

B The Lord is clothed with honor and majesty, Ps. 104:1–2
wrapped in light, as with a garment.

Morning Psalm or Hymn

A morning psalm, such as Psalm 95:1–7; 100; 63:1–8; or 51:1–12, or another morning hymn may be sung. All are then seated.

Psalm(s)

One or more additional psalms (BCW 611–783, 1050–1095; BCW—DP 181–390, 461–506) are sung or said. Silence for reflection follows each psalm, concluding with the appointed psalm prayer (BCW 611–783; BCW—DP 181–390).

Scripture Reading

A reading from Scripture (BCW 1050–1095; BCW—DP 461–506; or Revised Common Lectionary Daily Readings) follows. After the reading:

A The Word of the Lord.   B Holy wisdom, holy Word.
Thanks be to God.   **Thanks be to God.**

Silence follows for reflection on the meaning of the Scripture.

The Scripture may be briefly interpreted, or a nonbiblical reading may be read.

CANTICLE

The "Benedictus"("Song of Zechariah"; Luke 1:68–79; no. 109) or a hymn may be sung. All may stand.

THANKSGIVING AND INTERCESSION

See prayers for each day of the week: BCW 496–499; BCW—DP 33–37.

Satisfy us with your love in the morning,   Ps. 90:14
and we will live this day in joy and praise.

Thanks is given for:

> *the beauty of creation and the wonder of living;*
> *the love of family and friends;*
> *particular blessings of the day;*
> *opportunities for faithful service;*
> *the mission and ministry of the church.*

Intercessions are made for:

> *family, friends, and neighbors;*
> *those who are sick or suffering;*
> *those who are poor or vulnerable;*
> *peace and justice in the world;*
> *the church of Jesus Christ in every land.*

Other thanksgivings and intercessions may be offered. There may be silent prayer. A concluding prayer, such as the following, or another (BCW 500–501, 524–543; BCW—DP 37–39) is said.

As you cause the sun to rise, O God,
bring the light of Christ to dawn in our souls
and dispel all darkness.
Give us grace to reflect Christ's glory;
and let his love show in our deeds,
his peace shine in our words,
and his healing in our touch,
that all may give him praise, now and forever. **Amen.**

The Lord's Prayer is sung (no. 464) or said (pp. 11, 35).

A morning hymn (nos. 662–670) may be sung.

DISMISSAL

The leader dismisses the people using these or similar words (BCW 502–503; BCW—DP 40–41).

May the God of hope fill us with all joy and peace   Rom. 15:13
through the power of the Holy Spirit. **Amen.**

Bless the Lord.
The Lord's name be praised.

A sign of peace may be exchanged by all.

Midday Prayer

Opening Sentences

All may stand.

Our help is in the name of the Lord,   Ps. 124:8
maker of heaven and earth.

These or other Opening Sentences (BCW 545; BCW—DP 106–107) are said.

Like an eagle teaching her young to fly,   Deut. 32:11
the Lord keeps us from falling.

Praise the Lord.
The Lord's name be praised.

Hymn

A hymn may be sung. All are then seated.

Psalm(s)

One or more psalms (BCW 611–783, 1050–1095; BCW—DP 181–390, 461–506) are sung or said. Silence for reflection follows each psalm, concluding with the appointed psalm prayer (BCW 611–783; BCW—DP 181–390).

Scripture Reading

A reading from Scripture (BCW 1050–1095; BCW—DP 461–506; or Revised Common Lectionary Daily Readings) follows. After the reading:

A   The Word of the Lord.   B   Holy wisdom, holy Word.
Thanks be to God.   **Thanks be to God.**

Silence follows for reflection on the meaning of the Scripture.

PRAYERS

All may stand. There may be a brief time of prayer, spoken and/or silent.

The leader concludes with the following or a similar prayer (BCW 546–548; BCW—DP 108–110).

New every morning is your love, great God of light,
and all day long you are working for good in the world.
Stir up in us the desire to serve you,
to live peacefully with our neighbors,
and to devote each day to your Son,
our Savior, Jesus Christ the Lord. **Amen.**

The Lord's Prayer is sung (no. 464) or said (pp. 11, 35).

A hymn may be sung.

DISMISSAL

The leader concludes:

The God of peace be with us.   Phil. 4:9
Amen.

Bless the Lord.
The Lord's name be praised.

A sign of peace may be exchanged by all.

Evening Prayer

If a shorter service is required, the "Thanksgiving for Light" and "Evening Psalm" may be omitted. See BCW 513–515, 524–543; BCW—DP 53–54, 65–104. The service then continues with the additional psalms.

Opening Sentences

As the service begins, the room is dimly lit. A large candle is lighted.

All may stand as these or other Opening Sentences (BCW 505–507; BCW—DP 43–45) are said.

Jesus Christ is the light of the world,   John 1:5, 8:12
the light no darkness can overcome.

Stay with us, Lord, for it is evening,   Luke 24:29
and the day is almost over.

Let your light scatter the darkness
and illumine your church.

Evening Hymn

As the "Phos Hilaron"("Hymn to Christ the Light," nos. 671–673) is sung, other candles are lighted from the large candle and the lights in the room are turned up.

Thanksgiving for Light

See BCW 507–511; BCW—DP 46–51.

The Lord be with you.
And also with you.

Let us give thanks to the Lord our God.
It is right to give our thanks and praise.

Thanks and praise is given for:

> *God's creative work and gift of light;*
> *the light of Christ, shining in darkness;*
> *the illumination of the Spirit.*

The prayer concludes with praise to the triune God.

EVENING PSALM

The evening psalm, Psalm 141 (no. 674), is sung. Incense may be burned.

After a period of silent prayer, the psalm prayer is said.

Holy God,
let the incense of our prayer ascend before you,
and let your loving-kindness descend upon us,
that with devoted hearts we may sing your praises
with the church on earth and the whole heavenly host,
and glorify you forever and ever. **Amen.**

PSALM(S)

One or more additional psalms (BCW 611–783, 1050–1095; BCW—DP 181–390, 461–506) are sung or said. Silence for reflection follows each psalm, concluding with the appointed psalm prayer (BCW 611–783; BCW—DP 181–390).

SCRIPTURE READING

A reading from Scripture (BCW 1050–1095; BCW—DP 461–506; or Revised Common Lectionary Daily Readings) follows. After the reading:

A The Word of the Lord.   B Holy wisdom, holy Word.
Thanks be to God.   **Thanks be to God.**

Silence follows for reflection on the meaning of the Scripture.

The Scripture may be briefly interpreted, or a nonbiblical reading may be read.

CANTICLE

The "Magnificat"("Song of Mary"; Luke 1:46–55; nos. 99, 100) or a hymn may be sung. All may stand.

THANKSGIVING AND INTERCESSION

See prayers for each day of the week: BCW 517–520; BCW—DP 57–60.

To you, O Lord, I lift up my soul.   Ps. 25:1–2
O God, in you I trust.

Thanks is given for:

> *the life and work of the local congregation;*
> *the love of family and friends;*
> *particular blessings of the day;*
> *opportunities for faithful service;*
> *the good news of the gospel.*

Intercessions are made for:

> *family, friends, and neighbors;*
> *those who are sick or suffering;*
> *those who are poor or vulnerable;*
> *peace and justice in the world;*
> *the Spirit's power in the church.*

Other thanksgivings and intercessions may be offered. There may be silent prayer. A concluding prayer, such as the following or another (BCW 520–522, 524–543; BCW—DP 61–63, 65–104), is said.

As you have made this day, O God,
you also make the night.
Give light for our comfort.
Come upon us with quietness and still our souls,
that we may listen for the whisper of your Spirit
and be attentive to your nearness in our dreams.
Empower us to rise again in new life
to proclaim your praise,
and show Christ to the world,
for he reigns forever and ever. **Amen.**

The Lord's Prayer is sung (no. 464) or said (pp. 11, 35).

An evening hymn (nos. 675–678) may be sung.

DISMISSAL

The leader dismisses the people using these or similar words (BCW 523; BCW—DP 64).

May the peace of God,   Phil. 4:7
which surpasses all understanding,
guard our hearts and minds in Christ Jesus. **Amen.**

Bless the Lord.
The Lord's name be praised.

A sign of peace may be exchanged by all.

PRAYER AT THE CLOSE OF DAY

OPENING SENTENCES

All may stand.

O God, come to our assistance.
O Lord, hasten to help us.

The Lord grant us a restful night
and peace at the last. **Amen.**

Ps. 70:1

EVENING HYMN

A hymn appropriate to the end of the day may be sung.

CONFESSION AND PARDON

Almighty God, maker of all,
have mercy on us.

Jesus Christ, redeemer of the world,
have mercy on us.

Holy Spirit, giver of life,
have mercy on us.

There is a brief period of silence for self-examination.

I confess to God Almighty,
before the whole company of heaven,
and to you, my brothers and sisters,
that I have sinned in thought, word, and deed,
and pray God Almighty to have mercy on me.

May Almighty God have mercy on you,
pardon and deliver you from all your sins
and give you time to amend your life. Amen.

I confess to God Almighty,
before the whole company of heaven,
and to you, my brothers and sisters,
that I have sinned in thought, word, and deed,
and pray God Almighty to have mercy on me.

May Almighty God have mercy on you,
pardon and deliver you from all your sins
and give you time to amend your life. **Amen.**

All are seated.

Psalm

One of the following psalms is sung or said: Psalm 4, 23, 33, 34, 91, 121, 130, 134, 136, or 139. Silence for reflection follows each psalm, concluding with the appointed psalm prayer (BCW 611–783; BCW—DP 181–390).

Scripture Reading

One of the following, or another reading from Scripture (BCW 554–555; BCW—DP 116–117), is read.

A Jesus said: Come to me, all you that are weary   Matt. 11:28–30
and are carrying heavy burdens,
and I will give you rest.
Take my yoke upon you, and learn from me;
for I am gentle and humble in heart,
and you will find rest for your souls.
For my yoke is easy, and my burden is light.

B Jesus said: Peace I leave with you;   John 14:27
my peace I give to you.
I do not give to you as the world gives.
Do not let your hearts be troubled,
and do not let them be afraid.

C I am convinced that neither death, nor life,   Rom. 8:38–39
nor angels, nor rulers,
nor things present, nor things to come,
nor powers, nor height, nor depth,
nor anything else in all creation,
will be able to separate us from the love of God
in Christ Jesus our Lord.

After the reading:

A The Word of the Lord.   B Holy wisdom, holy Word.
Thanks be to God.   **Thanks be to God.**

Silence follows for reflection on the meaning of the Scripture.

PRAYER

A Into your hands, O Lord, I commend my spirit;   Ps. 31:5; 17:8, 15
for you have redeemed me, O Lord, O God of truth.

Keep us, O Lord, as the apple of your eye;
hide us under the shadow of your wings.

In righteousness I shall see you;
when I awake your presence shall give me joy.

B I will lie down in peace and take my rest,   Ps. 4:8
for in God alone I dwell unafraid.

Thanksgivings and intercessions may be offered. There may be silent prayer. Then a concluding prayer (BCW 556–560; BCW—DP 118–22) is said:

O Lord, support us all the day long
until the shadows lengthen
and the evening comes,
and the busy world is hushed,
and the fever of life is over,
and all our work is done.
Then, in your mercy,
grant us a safe lodging,
and a holy rest,
and peace at the last;
through Jesus Christ our Lord. **Amen.**

The Lord's Prayer is sung (no. 464) or said (pp. 11, 35).

CANTICLE

The "Nunc Dimittis"("Song of Simeon"; Luke 2:29–32; no. 545) or a hymn may be sung. All may stand. This refrain may be sung or spoken:

**Guide us waking, O Lord, and guard us sleeping;
that awake we may watch with Christ,
and asleep rest in his peace.**

DISMISSAL

May Almighty God bless, preserve, and keep us,
this night and forevermore. **Amen.**

Bless the Lord.
The Lord's name be praised.

A sign of peace may be exchanged by all.

OTHER TEXTS FOR WORSHIP

Nicene Creed

Let us confess the faith of the universal church.

We believe in one God,
    the Father, the Almighty,
    maker of heaven and earth,
    of all that is, seen and unseen.

We believe in one Lord, Jesus Christ,
    the only Son of God,
    eternally begotten of the Father,
    God from God, Light from Light,
    true God from true God,
    begotten, not made,
    of one Being with the Father;
    through him all things were made.
For us and for our salvation
    he came down from heaven,
    was incarnate of the Holy Spirit and the Virgin Mary
    and became truly human.
For our sake he was crucified under Pontius Pilate;
    he suffered death and was buried.
On the third day he rose again
    in accordance with the Scriptures;
    he ascended into heaven
    and is seated at the right hand of the Father.
He will come again in glory to judge the living and the dead,
    and his kingdom will have no end.

We believe in the Holy Spirit, the Lord, the giver of life,
    who proceeds from the Father and the Son,
    who with the Father and the Son
    is worshiped and glorified,
    who has spoken through the prophets.
We believe in one holy catholic and apostolic church.
We acknowledge one baptism for the forgiveness of sins.
We look for the resurrection of the dead,
    and the life of the world to come. Amen.

Apostles' Creed

Let us confess the faith of our Baptism.

I believe in God, the Father almighty,
Maker of heaven and earth,

and in Jesus Christ his only Son, our Lord;
who was conceived by the Holy Ghost,
born of the Virgin Mary,
suffered under Pontius Pilate,
was crucified, dead, and buried;
he descended into hell;
the third day he rose again from the dead;
he ascended into heaven,
and sitteth on the right hand
of God the Father Almighty;
from thence he shall come to judge the quick and the dead.

I believe in the Holy Ghost;
the holy catholic church;
the communion of saints;
the forgiveness of sins;
the resurrection of the body;
and the life everlasting. Amen.

See also common text (p. 17) and musical setting (no. 481).

Lord's Prayer

Our Father, who art in heaven,
hallowed be thy name,
thy kingdom come,
thy will be done,
on earth as it is in heaven.
Give us this day our daily bread;
and forgive us our debts,
as we forgive our debtors;
and lead us not into temptation,
but deliver us from evil.
For thine is the kingdom, and the power,
and the glory, forever. Amen.

See also common text (p. 11) and musical setting (no. 464).

The Law of God

God spoke all these words, saying,
    I am the Lord your God.

Exod. 20:1–17

You shall have no other gods before me.

You shall not make for yourself an idol
    whether in the form of anything that is in heaven above
        or that is on the earth beneath,
            or that is in the water under the earth.
            You shall not bow down to them or worship them.

You shall not make wrongful use
    of the name of the Lord your God.

Remember the sabbath day, and keep it holy.

Honor your father and your mother.

You shall not murder.

You shall not commit adultery.

You shall not steal.

You shall not bear false witness against your neighbor.

You shall not covet your neighbor's house;
    you shall not covet your neighbor's wife,
        or anything that belongs to your neighbor.

Summary of the Law

Our Lord Jesus said:
You shall love the Lord your God
    with all your heart,
        and with all your soul,
            and with all your mind.

Matt. 22:37–40

This is the greatest and first commandment.

And a second is like it:
You shall love your neighbor as yourself.

On these two commandments
    hang all the law and the prophets.

A BRIEF STATEMENT OF FAITH

1   In life and in death we belong to God.

Through the grace of our Lord Jesus Christ,
    the love of God,
        and the communion of the Holy Spirit,
we trust in the one triune God, the Holy One of Israel,
    whom alone we worship and serve.

2   We trust in Jesus Christ,
    fully human, fully God.

Jesus proclaimed the reign of God:
    preaching good news to the poor
        and release to the captives,
    teaching by word and deed
        and blessing the children,
    healing the sick
        and binding up the brokenhearted,
    eating with outcasts,
        forgiving sinners,
    and calling all to repent and believe the gospel.

Unjustly condemned for blasphemy and sedition,
    Jesus was crucified,
        suffering the depths of human pain
            and giving his life for the sins of the world.

God raised this Jesus from the dead,
    vindicating his sinless life,
        breaking the power of sin and evil,
            delivering us from death to life eternal.

3   We trust in God,
    whom Jesus called Abba, Father.

In sovereign love God created the world good
    and makes everyone equally in God's image,
        male and female, of every race and people,
        to live as one community.

But we rebel against God; we hide from our Creator.
    Ignoring God's commandments,
        we violate the image of God in others and ourselves,
        accept lies as truth,
            exploit neighbor and nature,
    and threaten death to the planet entrusted to our care.
We deserve God's condemnation.

Yet God acts with justice and mercy to redeem creation.

In everlasting love,
the God of Abraham and Sarah chose a covenant people
to bless all families of the earth.

Hearing their cry,
God delivered the children of Israel
from the house of bondage.

Loving us still,
God makes us heirs with Christ of the covenant.

Like a mother who will not forsake her nursing child,
like a father who runs to welcome the prodigal home,
God is faithful still.

4   We trust in God the Holy Spirit,
everywhere the giver and renewer of life.

The Spirit justifies us by grace through faith,
sets us free to accept ourselves
and to love God and neighbor,
and binds us together with all believers
in the one body of Christ, the Church.

The same Spirit who inspired the prophets and apostles
rules our faith and life in Christ through Scripture,
engages us through the Word proclaimed,
claims us in the waters of baptism,
feeds us with the bread of life and the cup of salvation,
and calls women and men to all ministries of the Church.

In a broken and fearful world
the Spirit gives us courage
to pray without ceasing,
to witness among all peoples to Christ as Lord and Savior,
to unmask idolatries in Church and culture,
to hear the voices of peoples long silenced,
and to work with others for justice, freedom, and peace.

In gratitude to God, empowered by the Spirit,
we strive to serve Christ in our daily tasks
and to live holy and joyful lives,
even as we watch for God's new heaven and new earth,
praying, "Come, Lord Jesus!"

5   With believers in every time and place,
we rejoice that nothing in life or in death
can separate us from the love of God
in Christ Jesus our Lord.

The concluding doxology may be sung (nos. 580–582):

6   Glory be to the Father,
and to the Son,
and to the Holy Spirit. Amen.

EL CREDO NICENO

Creemos en un solo Dios,
    Padre Todopoderoso,
Creador del cielo y de la tierra,
y de todas las cosas visibles e invisibles.

Y en un solo Señor Jesucristo,
    Hijo unigénito de Dios,
    engendrado del Padre antes de todos los siglos,
    Dios de Dios, luz de luz,
    verdadero Dios de verdadero Dios,
    engendrado, no hecho,
    siendo de una substancia con el Padre,
    por quien todas las cosas fueron hechas;
quien por nosotros los seres humanos y para nuestra salvación
    descendió del cielo, y fue encarnado por el Espíritu Santo de la
    virgen María,
    y se hizo hombre,
y fue crucificado por nosotros bajo Poncio Pilato.
    Padeció y fue sepultado
y al tercer día resucitó
    conforme a las Escrituras,
    ascendió al cielo
    y está sentado a la diestra del Padre.
Y vendrá otra vez en gloria
    para juzgar a los vivos y a los muertos;
    y su reino no tendrá fin.

Creemos en el Espíritu Santo, el Señor y Dador de la vida,
    quien procede del Padre y del Hijo,
    quien con el Padre y el Hijo
    debe ser adorado y glorificado,
    quien habló por medio de los profetas.
Creemos en una sola Iglesia, santa, universal y apostólica.
Reconocemos un solo bautismo para la remisión de los pecados;
y esperamos la resurrección de los muertos
    y la vida del mundo venidero. Amén.

EL CREDO APOSTÓLICO

Creo en Dios Padre Todopoderoso,
    Creador del cielo y de la tierra;

y en Jesucristo, su único Hijo, Señor nuestro;
    quien fue concebido por el Espíritu Santo,
    nació de la virgen María,
    padeció bajo el poder de Poncio Pilato,
    fue crucificado, muerto y sepultado;
descendió a los infiernos;
al tercer día resucitó de entre los muertos;
ascendió al cielo y está sentado a la diestra
    de Dios Padre Todopoderoso,
de donde vendrá a juzgar a los vivos y a los muertos.

Creo en el Espíritu Santo,
    la Santa Iglesia Universal,
    la comunión de los santos,
    el perdón de los pecados,
    la resurrección del cuerpo,
    y la vida perdurable. Amén.

EL PADRE NUESTRO

Padre nuestro que estás en los cielos,
    santificado sea tu nombre.
    Venga tu Reino.
    Hágase tu voluntad,
    como en el cielo, así también en la tierra.
El pan nuestro de cada día, dánoslo hoy.
Perdónanos nuestras deudas,
    como también nosotros perdonamos a nuestros deudores.
No nos metas en tentación,
    sino líbranos del mal,
porque tuyo es el Reino, el poder
    y la gloria, por todos los siglos. Amén.

LOS DIEZ MANDAMIENTOS

Habló Dios todas estas palabras:
    Yo soy el Señor, tu Dios,

Éxodo 20:1–17

No tendrás dioses ajenos delante de mí.

No te harás imagen
    ni ninguna semejanza de lo que esté arriba en el cielo,
    ni abajo en la tierra,
    ni en las aguas debajo de la tierra.
    No te inclinarás a ellas ni las honrarás.

No tomarás el nombre del Señor, tu Dios, en vano.

Acuérdate del sábado para santificarlo.

Honra a tu padre y a tu madre.

No matarás.

No cometerás adulterio.

No hurtarás.

No dirás contra tu prójimo falso testimonio.

No codiciarás la casa de tu prójimo:
    no codiciarás la mujer de tu prójimo,
    ni cosa alguna de tu prójimo.

EL GRAN MANDAMIENTO

Jesús le dijo:
Amarás al Señor tu Dios
    con todo tu corazón,
        con toda tu alma
            y con toda tu mente.

Mateo 22:37–40

Éste es el primero y grande mandamiento.

Y el segundo es semejante:
Amarás a tu prójimo como a ti mismo.

De estos dos mandamientos
    dependen toda la Ley y los Profetas.

Una Breve Declaración de Fe

1   En la vida como en la en muerte pertenecemos a Dios.

Por la gracia de nuestro Señor Jesucristo,
    el amor de Dios,
        y la comunión del Espíritu Santo,
confiamos en el Dios único y trino, el Santo de Israel,
    a quien sólo adoramos y servimos.

2   Confiamos en Jesucristo,
        plenamente humano, plenamente Dios.

Jesús proclamó el reinado de Dios:
    predicando buenas nuevas a los pobres
        y libertad a los cautivos,
    enseñando por medio de palabra y hechos.
        y bendiciendo a los niños,
    curando a los enfermos
        y sanando a los quebrantados de corazón,
    comiendo con los despreciados,
        perdonando a los pecadores,
    y llamando a todos a arrepentirse y a creer en el evangelio.

Condenado injustamente por blasfemia y sedición,
    Jesús fue crucificado,
        sufriendo la profundidad del dolor humano
        y dando su vida por los pecados del mundo.

Dios levantó a este Jesús de los muertos,
    vindicando su vida sin pecado,
        rompiendo el poder del pecado y del mal,
        rescatándonos de la muerte a la vida eterna.

3   Confiamos en Dios,
        a quien Jesús llamó Abba, Padre.

En amor soberano Dios creó al mundo bueno
    e hizo a cada uno igualmente a imagen de Dios,
        varón y hembra, de toda raza y pueblo,
            para vivir como una sola comunidad.

Pero nos rebelamos contra Dios; nos escondemos de nuestro Creador.
    Desconociendo los mandamientos de Dios,
        violamos la imagen de Dios en otros y en nosotros mismos,
        aceptamos las mentiras como verdad,
            explotamos al prójimo y a la naturaleza,
    y amenazamos de muerte al planeta confiado a nuestro cuidado.

Merecemos la condenación de Dios.

Sin embargo: Dios actúa con justicia y misericordia para redimir a la
    creación.

Con amor perdurable,
    el Dios de Abraham y Sara escogió a un pueblo del pacto
    para bendecir a todas las familias de la tierra.

Escuchando su clamor,
    Dios liberó a los hijos e hijas de Israel
    de la casa de servidumbre.

Amándonos aún,
    Dios nos hace, con Cristo, herederos del pacto.

Como madre resuelta a no abandonar a su niño de pecho,
    como padre que corre a dar al pródigo la bienvenida al hogar,
    Dios sigue aun siendo fiel.

4   Confiamos en Dios el Espíritu Santo,
    en todo lugar dador y renovador de vida.

El Espíritu nos justifica por la gracia mediante la fe,
    nos deja libres para aceptarnos,
        y para amar a Dios y al prójimo,
    y nos unifica con todos los creyentes
        en el cuerpo único de Cristo, la Iglesia.

El mismo Espíritu que inspiró a profetas y apóstoles
    norma nuestra fe y vida en Cristo por medio de la Escritura,
        nos compromete por medio de la Palabra proclamada,
    nos hace suyos en las aguas del bautismo,
        nos alimenta con el pan de vida y la copa de salvación,
    y llama a mujeres y hombres a todos los ministerios de la Iglesia.

En un mundo quebrantado y temeroso
    el Espíritu nos da valor
        para orar sin cesar,
    para testificar de Cristo como Señor y Salvador ante todos los pueblos,
        para desenmascarar idolatrías en la Iglesia y en la cultura,
    para oír las voces de pueblos por largo tiempo silenciados,
        y para laborar con otros por la justicia, la libertad y la paz.

En gratitud a Dios, dinamizados por el Espíritu,
    nos esforzamos por servir a Cristo en nuestras tareas diarias
        y por vivir vidas santas y gozosas,
    mientras aguardamos el nuevo cielo y la nueva tierra de Dios,
        orando: «¡Ven, Señor Jesús!»

5   Con creyentes en todos tiempos y lugares,
    nos gozamos de que nada en la vida o en la muerte
        puede separarnos del amor de Dios
        en Cristo Jesús, Señor nuestro.

6   Gloria sea al Padre,
    al Hijo,
        y al Espíritu Santo. Amén.

니케아 신조

우리는 전능하신 아버지이신 한 하나님을 믿는다.

> 그는 하늘과 땅을 지으신 이시요,
> 보이는 것이나 보이지 않는 모든 것을 지으신 분이다.

우리는 한주 예수 그리스도를 믿는다.
> 그는 하나님의 독생자이시며,
> 모든 세상이 있기전에 아버지로부터 나셨으며,
> 하나님의 하나님이시며, 빛의 빛이시며,
> 참하나님의 참하나님이시다.
> 그는 하나님께로부터 나셨고 지으심을 받은 것이 아니다.
> 그는 모든 것을 지으신 아버지와
> 한 실체를 가지셨다.

그는 우리 인간과 우리의 구원을 위하여
> 하늘에서 내려오셨고,
> 성령에 의하여 동정녀 마리아로 말미암아 몸을 입으시고,
> 참으로 사람이 되셨다.

그는 우리를 위하여 본디오 빌라도에 의하여 십자가형을 받으셨으며,
> 죽음의 고난을 당하시고 매장되셨다.

그는 성경의 말씀대로
> 사흘만에 부활하셨으며,
> 하늘에 오르사
> 아버지의 우편에 앉아계신다.

그는 영광 중에 다시 오셔서 산 자와 죽은 자를 심판하실 것이며,
> 그의 나라는 영원할 것이다.

우리는 주이시며 생명을 주시는 분인 성령을 믿는다.
> 그는 아버지와 아들로부터 나오셨고,
> 아버지와 아들과 함께
> 예배와 영광을 받으신다.
> 그는 예언자들을 통하여 말씀하셨다.

우리는 거룩하고 보편적이며 사도적인 하나의 교회를 믿는다.
우리는 죄사함을 위한 하나의 세례를 인정한다.
우리는 죽은 자의 부활과
> 내세의 삶을 고대한다. 아멘.

사도신경

나는 전능하신 아버지 하나님,
　　천지의 창조주를 믿습니다.

나는 그의 유일하신 아들, 우리 주 예수 그리스도를 믿습니다.
　　그는 성령으로　잉태되어
　　동정녀 마리아에게 나시고,
　　본디오 빌라도에게 고난을 받아
　　십자가에 못 박혀 죽으시고,
　　장사된 지 사흘만에 죽은 자 가운데서 다시 살아나셨으며,
하늘에 오르시어
　　전능하신 아버지 하나님 우편에 앉아 계시다가,
거기로부터 살아 있는 자와 죽은 자를 심판하러 오십니다.

나는 성령을 믿으며,
　　거룩한 공교회와
　　성도의 교제와
　　죄를 용서받는 것과
　　몸의 부활과 영생을 믿습니다. 아멘.

주기도문

하늘에 계신 우리 아버지,
　　아버지의 이름을 거룩하게 하시며,
　　아버지의 나라가 오게 하시며,
　　아버지의 뜻이 하늘에서와 같이
　　땅에서도 이루어지게 하소서.
오늘 우리에게 일용할 양식을 주시고,
우리가 우리에게 잘못한 사람을 용서하여 준 것 같이
　　우리 죄를 용서하여 주시고,
우리를 시험에 빠지지 않게 하시고,
　　악에서 구하소서.
나라와 권능과 영광이 영원히 아버지의 것입니다. 아멘.

십계명

하나님이 이 모든 말씀으로 말씀하여 이르시되   출애굽기20:1-17
　　나는 너를 애굽 땅, 종 되었던 집에서 인도하여 낸
　　네 하나님 여호와니라.

너는 나 외에는 다른 신들을 네게 두지 말라.

너를 위하여 새긴 우상을 말들지 말고,
　　또 위로 하늘에 있는 것이나,
　　아래로 땅에 있는 것이나,
　　땅 아래 물 속에 있는 것의
　　어떤 형상도 만들지 말며,
그것들에게 절하지 말며, 그것들을 섬기지 말라.

너는 네 하나님 여호와의 이름을 망령되게 부르지 말라.

안식일을 기억하여 거룩하게 지키라.

네 부모를 공경하라

살인하지 말라.

간음하지 말라.

도둑질하지 말라.

네 이웃에 대하여 거짓 증거하지 말라.

네 이웃의 집을 탐내지 말라.
　　네 이웃의 아내나, 그의 남종이나 그의 여종이나,
　　　그의 소나 그의 나귀나,
　　무릇 네 이웃의 소유를 탐내지 말라.

가장 큰 계명

예수께서 이르시되,   마태복음 22:37-40
　　**네 마음을 다하고 목숨을 다하고 뜻을 다하여
　　주 너의 하나님을 사랑하라 하셨으니,**

이것이 크고 첫째 되는 계명이요,

둘째도 그와 같으니,
네 이웃을 네 자신같이 사랑하라 하셨으니,

이 두 계명이 온 율법과 선지자의 강령이니라.

간추린 신앙고백

1 사나 죽으나 우리는 하나님의 것이다.

우리 주 예수 그리스도의 은혜와,
 하나님의 사랑과,
  성령의 교통하심으로,
우리는 오직 한 분 삼위일체 하나님, 이스라엘의 거룩하신 분을 믿으며,
그분만을 예배하고 섬긴다.

2 우리는 그리스도를 믿는다.
 그는 완전히 사람이셨고, 완전히 하나님이셨다.

예수는 하나님의 통치를 선포하셨으며,

 가난한 자에게 복음을 전하시고,
  포로된 자에게 해방을 선포하시고,
 말씀과 행위로써 가르치시고,
  어린이를 축복하시고,
 병든 자를 고치시고,
  마음 상한 자를 싸매어 주시고,
 버림받은 자와 함께 잡수시고,
  죄인을 용서하시고,
 모든 사람을 불러 회개하고 복음을 믿게 하셨다.

예수는 신성모독과 소요 선동죄로 부당하게 정죄되어,
 십자가에 못 박히시고,
  인간고를 깊이 겪으시며,
   세상 죄를 위하여 자기 생명을 내어 주셨다.

하나님은 이 예수를 죽은 자들 가운데서 살리시어,
 그의 죄 없는 삶을 입증하시고,
  죄와 악의 권세를 깨뜨려,
   우리를 죽음에서 건져 영생에 이르게 하셨다.

3 우리는 하나님을 믿는다.
 예수는 그를 아빠, 곧 아버지라 부르셨다.

하나님은 주권적 사랑으로 세상을 선하게 창조하셨으며,
 각 사람을 하나님의 형상대로 동등하게 지으시어,
  남자와 여자, 각 인종과 백성을,
   한 공동체로 살게 하셨다.

그러나 우리는 하나님을 배반하고, 우리의 창조자를 피하여 숨는다.
 하나님의 계명을 무시하고,
  다른 사람과 또 우리 자신 속에 있는 하나님의 형상을 깨뜨리며,
   거짓을 참이라고 받아들이고,
    이웃과 자연을 착취하며,
 우리에게 맡겨 돌보게 하신 지구를 죽음에 직면케 하고 있다.
우리는 하나님의 정죄를 받아 마땅하다.

그래도 하나님은 창조하신 세계를 구속하시려고 공의와 자비를 베푸신다.

영원하신 사랑으로,
  아브라함과 사라의 하나님은 언약의 백성을 택하시어,
    이 땅 만민이 복을 받게 하셨다.

그들의 울부짖음을 들으시고,
  하나님은 이스라엘 자손들을,
    종 되었던 집에서 구원해 주셨다.

지금도 우리를 사랑하셔서
  하나님은 그리스도와 더불어 우리를 언약의 상속자로 삼으신다.

마치 젖먹이를 물리치지 않는 어머니처럼,
  집으로 돌아오는 탕자를 맞으러 달려가는 아버지처럼,
    하나님은 여전히 신실하시다.

4 우리는 성령이신 하나님을 믿는다.
  그는 어디서나 생명을 주시고, 새롭게 하시는 분이시다.

성령은 은혜로 믿음을 통하여 우리를 의롭게 하시고,
  우리를 자유케하여 자신을 수용하게 하시며
    하나님과 이웃을 사랑하게 하시고,
  우리를 모든 믿는 자와 함께 묶어,
    하나인 그리스도의 몸 곧 교회되게 하신다.

바로 그 성령께서 일찍이 선지자와 사도들을 감동하셨고,
  이제는 성경을 통하여 그리스도 안에서
    우리의 신앙과 생활을 다스리시며,
      선포된 말씀을 통하여 우리를 붙드시고,
  세례의 물로 우리를 자기의 소유로 삼으시며,
      생명의 떡과 구원의 잔으로 우리를 먹이시고,
  여자와 남자를 교회의 모든 사역에 부르신다.

깨어지고 어두운 세상에서
  성령은 우리에게 용기를 주시어
    쉬지 않고 기도하게 하시고,
  모든 백성 중에서 그리스도를 주와 구세주로 증거하게 하시며,
    교회와 문화 속에 있는 우상 숭배를 폭로케 하시고,
  오랫동안 말 못하고 살던 사람들의 소리를 듣게 하시며,
    정의, 자유, 평화를 위하여 다른 사람들과 함께 일하게 하신다.

하나님께 감사하며, 성령이 주시는 힘으로,
  우리는 일상생활에서 그리스도를 섬기며,
    거룩하고 기쁘게 살기를 힘쓰고,
  하나님의 새 하늘과 새 땅을 깨어 기다리며
    '주 예수여 오시옵소서'하고 기도한다.

5 모든 시대와 장소의 믿는 자들과 더불어
  우리가 기뻐하는 것은, 사나 죽으나 그 아무것이라도
    우리 주 그리스도 예수 안에 있는 하나님의 사랑에서 우리를
      끊을 수 없기 때문이다.

6 성부와 성자와 성령께 영광을 돌릴지어다.아멘.

1 Holy, Holy, Holy! Lord God Almighty!

Descant

4 Ho - - - ly,

1 Ho - ly, ho - ly, ho - ly! Lord God Al - might - y!
2 Ho - ly, ho - ly, ho - ly! all the saints a - dore thee,
3 Ho - ly, ho - ly, ho - ly! though the dark - ness hide thee,
4 Ho - ly, ho - ly, ho - ly! Lord God Al - might - y!

ho - - - ly,

Ear - ly in the morn - ing our song shall rise to thee.
cast - ing down their gold - en crowns a - round the glass - y sea;
though the eye of sin - ful - ness thy glo - ry may not see,
All thy works shall praise thy name, in earth and sky and sea.

Much of the imagery of this hymn comes from Revelation 4:2–11, which its author, an Anglican bishop,
knew as a reading appointed for Trinity Sunday. The tune, written specifically for this text, reinforces the
Trinitarian theme by strong dependence on the D-major triad.

TEXT: Reginald Heber, 1827, alt.;
  Korean trans. The Christian Literature Society of Korea; Spanish trans. Juan B. Cabrera
MUSIC: John Bacchus Dykes, 1861; desc. David McKinley Williams, 1948
Korean Trans. The Christian Literature Society of Korea
Music Desc. © 1948, ren. H. W. Gray Co., Inc. (a div. of Belwin-Mills Publishing Corp.)

NICAEA
11.12.12.10

ho - - - ly,

Ho - ly, ho - ly, ho - ly! mer - ci - ful and might - y!
cher - u - bim and ser - a - phim fall - ing down be - fore thee,
on - ly thou art ho - ly; there is none be - side thee,
Ho - ly, ho - ly, ho - ly! mer - ci - ful and might - y!

God in three per - sons, bless - ed Trin - i - ty.

God in three per - sons, bless - ed Trin - i - ty!
who wert, and art, and ev - er - more shalt be.
per - fect in power, in love and pu - ri - ty.
God in three per - sons, bless - ed Trin - i - ty!

SPANISH

1 ¡Santo! ¡Santo! ¡Santo! Señor omnipotente,
siempre el labio mío loores te dará.
¡Santo! ¡Santo! ¡Santo! Te adoro reverente,
Dios en tres personas, bendita Trinidad.

2 ¡Santo! ¡Santo! ¡Santo! La inmensa muchedumbre
de ángeles que cumplen tu santa voluntad,
ante ti se postra, bañada de tu lumbre,
ante ti que has sido, que eres y serás.

3 ¡Santo! ¡Santo! ¡Santo! Por más que estés velado
e imposible sea tu gloria contemplar,
santo tú eres sólo y nada hay a tu lado,
en poder perfecto, pureza y caridad.

4 ¡Santo! ¡Santo! ¡Santo! La gloria de tu nombre
vemos en tus obras, en cielo, tierra y mar.
¡Santo! ¡Santo! ¡Santo! La humanidad te adore,
Dios en tres personas, bendita Trinidad.

KOREAN

1 거룩거룩거룩 전능하신 주여
이른아침우리주를 찬송합니다
거룩거룩거룩 자비하신 주여
성삼위일체 우리주로다

2 거룩거룩거룩 주의보좌 앞에
모든성도 금면류관 벗어드리네
천군천사 모두주께 굴복하니
영원히 위에 계신 주로다

3 거룩거룩거룩 주의 빛난 영광
모든죄인 눈어두워 보지못하네
거룩하신 이가 주님밖에 뉘뇨
권능과사랑 온전하셔라

4 거룩거룩거룩 전능하신 주여
천지만물 주의이름 찬송합니다
거룩거룩거룩 자비하신 주여
성삼위일체 우리주로다

2 Come, Thou Almighty King

1 Come, thou al - might - y King, help us thy name to sing; help us to praise: Fa - ther, all glo - ri - ous, o'er all vic - to - ri - ous, come, and reign o - ver us, An - cient of Days.

2 Come, thou in - car - nate Word, mer - ci - ful, might - y Lord, our prayer at - tend. Come, and thy peo - ple bless, and give thy word suc - cess; Spir - it of ho - li - ness, on us de - scend.

3 Come, ho - ly Com - fort - er, thy sa - cred wit - ness bear in this glad hour. Thou who al - might - y art, now rule in ev - ery heart, and ne'er from us de - part, Spir - it of power.

4 To thee, great One in Three, e - ter - nal prais - es be, hence ev - er - more! Thy sov - ereign maj - es - ty may we in glo - ry see, and to e - ter - ni - ty love and a - dore.

The author of this Trinitarian text is unknown, but this hymn has proved popular since the middle of the 18th century, partly because of its effective use of biblical metaphors, but also because of the strength of this tune, which was composed especially for these words.

TEXT: *Collection of Hymns for Social Worship*, 1757, alt.
MUSIC: Felice de Giardini, 1769, alt.

ITALIAN HYMN
6.6.4.6.6.6.4

Womb of Life and Source of Being 3

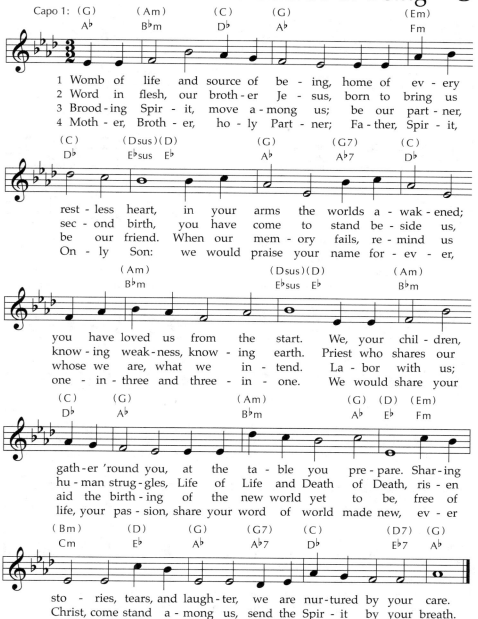

Capo 1: (G) (Am) (C) (G) (Em)
Ab Bbm Db Ab Fm

1 Womb of life and source of be - ing, home of ev - ery
2 Word in flesh, our broth - er Je - sus, born to bring us
3 Brood - ing Spir - it, move a - mong us; be our part - ner,
4 Moth - er, Broth - er, ho - ly Part - ner; Fa - ther, Spir - it,

(C) (Dsus)(D) (G) (G7) (C)
Db Ebsus Eb Ab Ab7 Db

rest - less heart, in your arms the worlds a - wak - ened;
sec - ond birth, you have come to stand be - side us,
be our friend. When our mem - ory fails, re - mind us
On - ly Son: we would praise your name for - ev - er,

(Am) (Dsus)(D) (Am)
Bbm Ebsus Eb Bbm

you have loved us from the start. We, your chil - dren,
know - ing weak - ness, know - ing earth. Priest who shares our
whose we are, what we in - tend. La - bor with us;
one - in - three and three - in - one. We would share your

(C) (G) (Am) (G) (D) (Em)
Db Ab Bbm Ab Eb Fm

gath - er 'round you, at the ta - ble you pre - pare. Shar - ing
hu - man strug - gles, Life of Life and Death of Death, ris - en
aid the birth - ing of the new world yet to be, free of
life, your pas - sion, share your word of world made new, ev - er

(Bm) (D) (G) (G7) (C) (D7) (G)
Cm Eb Ab Ab7 Db Eb7 Ab

sto - ries, tears, and laugh - ter, we are nur - tured by your care.
Christ, come stand a - mong us, send the Spir - it by your breath.
ser - vant, lord, and mas - ter, free for love and u - ni - ty.
sing - ing, ev - er prais - ing, one with all, and one with you.

Guitar chords do not correspond with keyboard harmony.

Old and new metaphors drawn from Psalm 23; John 1:14, 14:26, 20:19–23; Hebrews 5:1–10; and Genesis 1:1–2 combine here to express faith in and praise to the Triune God, identified as Source, Word, and Spirit. The second line of stanza two is adapted from Charles Wesley (see no. 119).

TEXT: Ruth Duck, 1986, 1990, alt.
MUSIC: Skinner Chávez-Melo, 1983
Text © 1992 GIA Publications, Inc.
Music © 1985, 1991 Skinner Chávez-Melo

RAQUEL
8.7.8.7.D

4 Holy God, We Praise Your Name

1 Ho - ly God, we praise your name; Lord of all, we
2 Hark! The glad ce - les - tial hymn an - gel choirs a -
3 All a - pos - tles join the strain as your sa - cred
4 Ho - ly Fa - ther, Ho - ly Son, Ho - ly Spir - it:

bow be - fore you. All on earth your scep - ter claim;
bove are rais - ing; cher - u - bim and ser - a - phim,
name they hal - low; proph - ets swell the glad re - frain,
three we name you, while in es - sence on - ly one;

all in heaven a - bove a - dore you. In - fi - nite your
in un - ceas - ing cho - rus prais - ing, fill the heavens with
and the bless - ed mar - tyrs fol - low, and from morn to
un - di - vid - ed God we claim you, and a - dor - ing,

vast do - main, ev - er - last - ing is your reign.
sweet ac - cord: "Ho - ly, ho - ly, ho - ly Lord!"
set of sun, through the church the song goes on.
bend the knee while we own the mys - ter - y.

Based on an 18th-century German metrical version of a celebrated 5th-century Latin hymn, *Te Deum laudamus*, this abbreviated 19th-century English paraphrase is sung by both Protestants and Roman Catholics. It is set here to the tune composed and named for the German version.

TEXT: Attr. Ignaz Franz, c. 1774; trans. Clarence Alphonsus Walworth, 1858, alt.
MUSIC: *Allgemeines Katholisches Gesangbuch*, c. 1774; harm. Johann Gottfried Schicht, 1819

GROSSER GOTT, WIR LOBEN DICH
7.8.7.8.7.7

God the Sculptor of the Mountains 5

1 God the sculp-tor of the moun-tains, God the
2 God the nui-sance of the Pha-raoh, God the
3 God the dress-er of the vine-yard, God the
4 God the un-ex-pect-ed in-fant, God the

mill-er of the sand, God the jewel-er of the
cleav-er of the sea, God the pil-lar in the
plant-er of the wheat, God the reap-er of the
calm, de-ter-mined youth, God the ta-ble-turn-ing

heav-ens, God the pot-ter of the land:
dark-ness, God the bea-con of the free:
har-vest, God the source of all we eat:
proph-et, God the res-ur-rect-ed truth:

you are womb of all cre-a-tion;
you are fount of all de-liv-erance;
you are host at ev-ery ta-ble;
you are pres-ent ev-ery mo-ment;

we are form-less; shape us now.
we are aim-less; lead us now.
we are hun-gry; feed us now.
we are search-ing; meet us now.

Despite the great sweep of these stanzas, each one ends by describing how our human condition needs God's help: formless, aimless, hungry, searching. Each of these adjectives is followed by a related three-syllable petition: shape us now, lead us now, feed us now, meet us now.

TEXT: John Thornburg, 1993, alt.
MUSIC: Amanda Husberg, 1995
Text © 1993 John Thornburg
Music © 1996 Abingdon Press (admin. The Copyright Company)

JENNINGS-HOUSTON
8.7.8.7.8.7

6 I Bind unto Myself Today

Capo 3:

1 I bind un-to my-self to-day the strong name
of the Trin-i-ty by in-vo-ca-tion
of the same, the Three in One and One in Three.

2 I bind this day to me for-ev-er, by power of
3 I bind un-to my-self to-day the vir-tues
4 I bind un-to my-self to-day the power of

faith, Christ's in-car-na-tion, his bap-tism in the
of the star-lit heav-en, the glo-rious sun's life-
God to hold and lead, God's eye to watch, God's

Jor-dan riv-er, his death on cross for my sal-
giv-ing ray, the white-ness of the moon at
might to stay, God's ear to heark-en to my

Guitar chords do not correspond with keyboard harmony.

This great Trinitarian text belongs to a Celtic style of hymn known as a *lorica,* from the Latin word for "armor" or "breastplate." In effect, it serves as both a statement of faith and a prayer for God's protection. The two tunes are named for an Irish saint and an Irish heroine.

TEXT: Attr. Patrick, 5th cent.; trans. Cecil Frances Alexander, 1889, alt.
MUSIC: ST. PATRICK: Irish melody; arr. Charles Villiers Stanford, 1902;
DEIRDRE: Irish melody; harm. Ralph Vaughan Williams, 1906

ST. PATRICK; DEIRDRE
LMD

va - tion, his burst - ing from the spic - ed tomb, his rid - ing
e - ven, the flash - ing of the light - ning free, the whirl - ing
need, the wis - dom of my God to teach, God's hand to

up the heaven - ly way, his com - ing at the
wind's tem - pes - tuous shocks, the sta - ble earth, the
guide, God's shield to ward, the word of God to

day of doom, I bind un - to my - self to - day.
deep salt sea a - round the old e - ter - nal rocks.
give me speech, God's heaven - ly host to be my guard.

5 Christ be with me, Christ with-in me, Christ be-hind me, Christ be-fore me,
Christ be-neath me, Christ a-bove me, Christ in qui - et, Christ in dan - ger,

Christ be - side me, Christ to win me, Christ to com - fort and re - store me.
Christ in hearts of all that love me, Christ in mouth of friend and strang - er.

continued

Mothering God, You Gave Me Birth 7

1 Moth - er - ing God, you gave me birth in the bright
2 Moth - er - ing Christ, you took my form, of - fer - ing
3 Moth - er - ing Spir - it, nur - turing one, in arms of

morn - ing of this world. Cre - a - tor, source of ev - ery
me your food of light, grain of life, and grape of
pa - tience hold me close, so that in faith I root and

breath, you are my rain, my wind, my sun.
love, your ver - y bod - y for my peace.
grow un - til I flower, un - til I know.

As the tune name hints, this text is derived from images in the writings of the English medieval mystic, Julian of Norwich. In 1393 she wrote down an account of her sixteen remarkable visions experienced twenty years earlier; they formed the basis of her theology of God's love.

TEXT: Jean Janzen, 1991
MUSIC: Carolyn Jennings, 1995
Text © 1991 Jean Janzen
Music © 1995 Augsburg Fortress

NORWICH
LM
(alternate tune: MARYTON)

8 Eternal Father, Strong to Save

1 E - ter - nal Fa - ther, strong to save, whose arm has bound the
2 O Sav - ior, whose al - might - y word the winds and waves sub -
3 O Ho - ly Spir - it, who did brood up - on the cha - os
4 O Trin - i - ty of love and power, all trav - elers guard in

rest - less wave, who bade the might - y o - cean deep its
mis - sive heard, who walked up - on the foam - ing deep, and
wild and rude, and bade its an - gry tu - mult cease, and
dan - ger's hour; from rock and tem - pest, fire and foe, pro -

own ap - point - ed lim - its keep: O hear us when we
calm a - mid its rage did sleep: O hear us when we
gave, for fierce con - fu - sion, peace: O hear us when we
tect them where - so - e'er they go; thus ev - er - more shall

cry to thee for those in per - il on the sea.
cry to thee for those in per - il on the sea.
cry to thee for those in per - il on the sea.
rise to thee glad praise from air and land and sea.

The year after this text was written for a student sailing to America, it was included in the most influential British hymnal of the 19th century. The tune especially composed for it preserves the ancient Roman name of the island where Paul was shipwrecked, now called Malta.

TEXT: William Whiting, 1860, alt.
MUSIC: John Bacchus Dykes, 1861

MELITA
8.8.8.8.8.8

The Play of the Godhead

1 The play of the God-head, the Trin-i-ty's dance, em-brac-es the
2 The warm mists of sum-mer, cool wa-ters that flow, turn crys-tal as
3 In God's gra-cious im-age of co-e-qual parts, we gath-er as

earth in a sa-cred ro-mance: with God the Cre-a-tor, and
ice when the win-try winds blow. The tap-root that nur-tures, the
danc-ers, u-nit-ing our hearts. Men, wom-en, and chil-dren, and

Christ the true Son, en-twined with the Spir-it, a web dai-ly
shoot grow-ing free, the life-giv-ing fruit, full and ripe on the
all liv-ing things, we join in the round of bright na-ture that

spun in span-gles of mys-ter-y, the great Three-in-One.
tree: more mys-tic and won-drous, the great One-in-Three.
rings with rap-ture and rhy-thm: cre-a-tion now sings!

This text gives life to the theological term *perichoresis*, a mutual, encompassing interaction, sometimes called "the threefold dance of the Trinity." Stanza two notes various "natural analogies" for the Trinity (steam / water / ice; root / shoot / fruit) that have been found inadequate.

TEXT: Mary Louise Bringle, 2000
MUSIC: William P. Rowan, 2000
Text © 2002 GIA Publications, Inc.
Music © 2000 William P. Rowan (admin. GIA Publications, Inc.)

PERICHORESIS
11.11.6.5.11.11

10 Sing Glory to the Name of God

(Psalm 29)

Unison

1 Sing glo-ry to the name of God, whose ho-ly splen-dor shines a-
2 The name of God is full of might: re-sound-ing thun-der, flash-ing
3 The name of God is wild and free, a-whirl in ho-ly mys-ter-
4 May God for-ev-er be our peace; may hymns of glo-ry nev-er

Harmony   *Unison*

broad.   En-throned a-bove the
light.   Al-le-lu – ia, al-le-lu – ia!   The wil-der-ness can-
y.   A se-cret wrapped in
cease: Let all the faith-ful

crash-ing waves, the God of grace and glo-ry saves.
not con-tain the ech-oes of the great re-frain:
smoke and fire, still chant-ed by the tem-ple choir:
peo-ple come; sing praise to God, the Three-in-One:

This sweeping paraphrase of Psalm 29 conveys a sense of the Jewish reverence for the sheer power of God's name, regarded as too holy for mortal tongues to pronounce. In keeping with its appointment for Trinity Sunday, the final stanza gives the psalm a Christian interpretation.

TEXT: David Gambrell, 2009
MUSIC: *Geistliche Kirchengesäng*, 1623, alt.; harm. Ralph Vaughan Williams, 1906
Text © 2011 David Gambrell (admin. Presbyterian Publishing Corp.)

LASST UNS ERFREUEN
LM with alleluias
(this tune in a higher key, 327)

Al - le - lu - ia, al - le - lu - ia! Al - le - lu - ia,

al - le - lu - ia, al - le - lu - ia!

11 Source and Sovereign, Rock and Cloud

1 Source and Sov-ereign, Rock and Cloud, For-tress, Foun-tain, Shel - ter, Light,
2 Word and Wis-dom, Root and Vine, Shep-herd, Sav-ior, Ser - vant, Lamb,
3 Storm and Still-ness, Breath and Dove, Thun-der, Tem-pest, Whirl-wind, Fire,

Judge, De - fend-er, Mer-cy, Might, Life whose life all life en-dowed:
Well and Wa - ter, Bread and Wine, Way who leads us to I AM:
Com - fort, Coun-selor, Pres-ence, Love, En-er - gies that nev - er tire:

May the church at prayer re - call that no sin-gle ho - ly name

but the truth be-hind them all is the God whom we pro - claim.

These scriptural names and images of the Triune God express a theological view reinforced by the structure:
the stanzas deal, in turn, with each Person of the Trinity and the refrain affirms their unity. The swirling
patterns of the Welsh tune add much energy to the text.

TEXT: Thomas H. Troeger, 1986
MUSIC: Joseph Parry, 1876
Text © 1986 Oxford University Press

ABERYSTWYTH
7.7.7.7.D

Immortal, Invisible, God Only Wise 12

1 Im - mor - tal, in - vis - i - ble, God on - ly wise,
2 Un - rest - ing, un - hast - ing, and si - lent as light,
3 To all, life thou giv - est, to both great and small.
4 Thou reign - est in glo - ry; thou dwell - est in light.

in light in - ac - ces - si - ble hid from our eyes,
nor want - ing, nor wast - ing, thou rul - est in might:
In all life thou liv - est, the true life of all.
Thine an - gels a - dore thee, all veil - ing their sight.

most bless - ed, most glo - rious, the An - cient of Days,
thy jus - tice, like moun - tains high soar - ing a - bove;
We blos - som and flour - ish like leaves on the tree,
All praise we would ren - der; O help us to see

al - might - y, vic - to - rious, thy great name we praise.
thy clouds, which are foun - tains of good - ness and love.
then with - er and per - ish; but naught chang - eth thee.
'tis on - ly the splen - dor of light hid - eth thee!

The opening line of this hymn was inspired by the three divine attributes listed in 1 Timothy 1:17 (King James Version), and it continues by considering how God's life exceeds our own finite existence. The text is well set to a Welsh melody shaped by many three-note units.

TEXT: Walter Chalmers Smith, 1867, alt.
MUSIC: Welsh folk melody; arr. *Caniadau y Cyssegr*, 1839

ST. DENIO
11.11.11.11

13 The Mighty God with Power Speaks
(Psalm 50)

1 The Might-y God with pow-er speaks, and all the world o-beys;
2 God comes not with a si-lent form, but rid-ing on the winds;
3 The heavens de-clare your jus-tice, Lord, as end-less as the sky;

from dawn un-til the set-ting sun, God's won-der earth dis-plays.
be-fore God's face, the rag-ing storm its blast of thun-der sends.
a-gainst the taunts of dis-be-lief, our God will tes-ti-fy.

The per-fect beau-ty all a-round from Zi-on's height shines forth;
All hail the Judge, in bold ar-ray, whose prom-ise is to bless;
Re-ceive my heart-felt gift of thanks, as hon-or to your might;

and stars a-cross the fir-ma-ment so bright-ly beam their worth.
who sees our sins, yet al-so feels our thirst for righ-teous-ness.
re-fresh my faith with each new day; pro-tect me through the night.

This paraphrase, set to a familiar English folk melody, focuses on the opening narrative section of Psalm 50 without attempting to summarize God's speeches in the latter portion of the psalm. Both parts bear witness to God's sovereignty, God's justice, and God's providence.

TEXT: Michael Morgan, 1999; rev. 2011
MUSIC: *English County Songs*, 1893; harm. Ralph Vaughan Williams, 1906
Text © 1999, 2011 Michael Morgan (admin. Faith Alive Christian Resources)

KINGSFOLD
CMD

For the Beauty of the Earth

14

1 For the beau-ty of the earth, for the glo-ry of the skies,
2 For the won-der of each hour of the day and of the night,
3 For the joy of ear and eye, for the heart and mind's de-light,
4 For the joy of hu-man love, broth-er, sis-ter, par-ent, child,
5 For thy-self, best gift di-vine to the world so free-ly given;

for the love which from our birth o-ver and a-round us lies:
hill and vale, and tree and flower, sun and moon, and stars of light:
for the mys-tic har-mo-ny link-ing sense to sound and sight:
friends on earth, and friends a-bove, for all gen-tle thoughts and mild:
for that great, great love of thine, peace on earth and joy in heaven:

Refrain

Lord of all, to thee we raise this our hymn of grate-ful praise.

In the course of many revisions, the original eucharistic emphasis of this text has shifted to a hymn of thanksgiving for a wide range of human experience, with a Christological summation. It is set here to the tune that is customary in North America, though not elsewhere.

TEXT: Folliott Sandford Pierpoint, 1864, alt.
MUSIC: Conrad Kocher, 1838; abr. William Henry Monk, 1861; harm. *The English Hymnal*, 1906

DIX
7.7.7.7.7.7

15 All Creatures of Our God and King

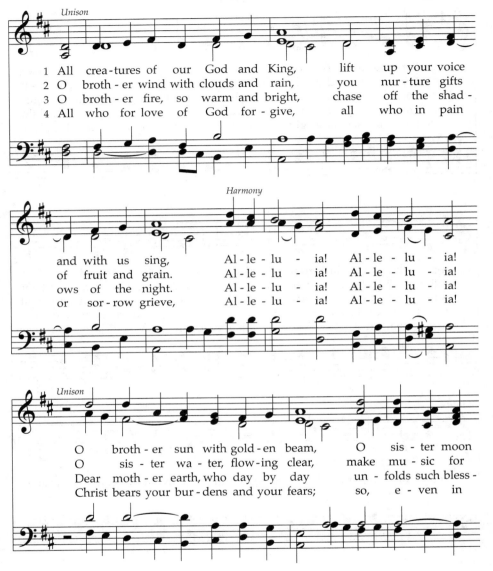

Unison

1 All crea-tures of our God and King, lift up your voice
2 O broth-er wind with clouds and rain, you nur-ture gifts
3 O broth-er fire, so warm and bright, chase off the shad-
4 All who for love of God for-give, all who in pain

Harmony

and with us sing, Al-le-lu - ia! Al-le-lu - ia!
of fruit and grain. Al-le-lu - ia! Al-le-lu - ia!
ows of the night. Al-le-lu - ia! Al-le-lu - ia!
or sor-row grieve, Al-le-lu - ia! Al-le-lu - ia!

Unison

O broth-er sun with gold-en beam, O sis-ter moon
O sis-ter wa-ter, flow-ing clear, make mu-sic for
Dear moth-er earth, who day by day un-folds such bless-
Christ bears your bur-dens and your fears; so, e-ven in

Sometimes called "The Canticle of the Sun," this cosmic roll call allows human beings to give voice to all creation. One of the earliest religious poems in the Italian language, it is made even more expansive by this broad, repetitive melody with interspersed "Alleluias."

TEXT: Francis of Assisi, 1225; trans. composite
MUSIC: *Geistliche Kirchengesäng*, 1623, alt.; harm. Ralph Vaughan Williams, 1906

LASST UNS ERFREUEN
LM with alleluias
(this tune in a higher key, 327)

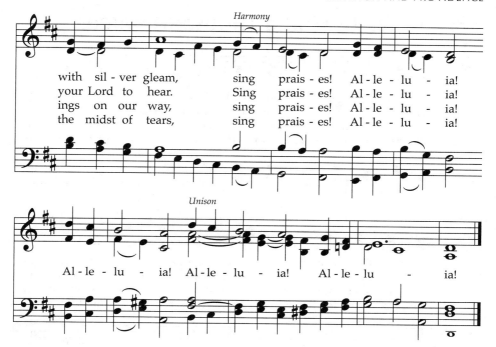

with sil-ver gleam, sing prais-es! Al-le-lu - ia!
your Lord to hear. Sing prais-es! Al-le-lu - ia!
ings on our way, sing prais-es! Al-le-lu - ia!
the midst of tears, sing prais-es! Al-le-lu - ia!

Al-le-lu - ia! Al-le-lu - ia! Al-le-lu - ia!

5 And you, most gentle sister death,
waiting to hush our final breath:
Alleluia! Alleluia!
Since Christ our light has pierced your gloom,
fair is the night that leads us home.
Sing praises! Alleluia!
Alleluia! Alleluia! Alleluia!

6 O sisters, brothers, take your part,
and worship God with humble heart.
Alleluia! Alleluia!
All creatures, bless the Father, Son,
and Holy Spirit, Three in One!
Sing praises! Alleluia!
Alleluia! Alleluia! Alleluia!

16 O That I Had a Thousand Voices

1 O that I had a thou-sand voic - es to praise my
2 Let ev - ery power in me im - plant - ed, a - rise, keep
3 You for - est leaves so green and ten - der that dance for
4 All crea-tures that have breath and mo - tion, that throng the

God with thou-sand tongues! My heart, which in the Lord re -
si - lence now no more; put forth the strength that God has
joy in sum - mer air; you mead - ow grass - es, bright and
earth, the sea, the sky, come, share with me my heart's de -

joic - es, would then pro - claim in grate-ful songs to all, wher -
grant - ed! Your no - blest work is to a - dore! O soul and
slen - der; you flowers so fra - grant and so fair: you live to
vo - tion; help me to sing God's prais - es high! My ut-most

ev - er I might be, what great things God has done for me!
bod - y, join to raise with heart-felt joy our Mak-er's praise!
show God's praise a - lone. Join me to make God's glo - ry known!
powers can nev - er quite de - clare the won - ders of God's might!

The German original of this hymn contained too many stanzas to sustain a unified theme. The four selected here place humankind in the midst of creation and form an effective song of praise to the Creator. As the tune name suggests, the music was later composed for these words.

TEXT: Johann Mentzer, 1704; trans. *The Lutheran Hymnal*, 1941, alt.
MUSIC: Attr. Johann B. König, 1738; *Harmonischer Liederschatz*, 1738
Text © 1941 Concordia Publishing House

O DASS ICH TAUSEND ZUNGEN HÄTTE
9.8.9.8.8.8

Sing Praise to God, You Heavens! 17
(Psalm 148)

1 Sing praise to God, you heav-ens! Sing praise, each shin-ing light!
2 Sing praise, O earth, sing prais-es! Sing prais-es, hill and plain,
3 Sing prais-es, all you crea-tures in whom God takes de-light:
4 Sing prais-es now, God's peo-ple; your gift of speech em-ploy

Sing, plan-ets in your or-bits; sing, stars all burn-ing bright!
you moun-tains thrust-ing sky-ward, you val-leys ripe with grain!
you whales that roam the o-ceans, you ea-gles in your flight!
to praise the Lord, your Mak-er, with thank-ful-ness and joy!

Sing praise, you winds and tem-pests, you driv-ing rain and snow!
Sing praise, each fra-grant flow-er; your fair-est hues dis-play.
Sing praise, you sheep on hill-sides, you cat-tle in the stall!
Sing with the whole cre-a-tion; a cos-mic cho-rus raise:

Sing, clouds that race and bil-low and shad-ow earth be-low!
Sing praise, you trees of au-tumn in glow-ing, glad ar-ray!
Though word-less, sing your prais-es to God who made you all!
"To God a-lone be glo-ry and ev-er-last-ing praise!"

This paraphrase of Psalm 148 reflects the spirit of praise linking Psalms 146–150. Of the two great themes found in these final five psalms—creation and deliverance—this psalm focuses on the former. The opening praise "from the heavens" is matched by praise "from the earth."

TEXT: Herman G. Stuempfle Jr., 1998
MUSIC: Johann Steurlein, 1575
Text © 2006 GIA Publications, Inc.

WIE LIEBLICH IST DER MAIEN
7.6.7.6.D

18 Hallelujah! Sing Praise to Your Creator

(Psalm 148)

1 Hal - le - lu - jah! Sing praise to your Cre - a - tor, sun, moon, and
2 Praise the Lord, all moun-tains and o - ceans, roll - ing thun - der and
3 Give to God all glo - ry and hon - or. From the depths to the

stars and an - gels a - bove. Praise the Lord, whose word es -
wind and storm clouds on high. Praise the Lord, your Mak - er,
heights let prais - es re - sound to the Lord, the source of

tab - lished the heav - ens, who up - holds all the earth in pow - er and
all liv - ing crea-tures, all the beasts in the fields and birds in the
strength and sal - va - tion for all peo - ple on whom God's fa - vor is

love. God reigns on high, let the heav - ens re - joice! (O)
sky. Both young and old, come and join in the song! (O)
found. Praise God, you saints who are claimed as God's own! (O)

This recent paraphrase of Psalm 148 expands our awareness of the breadth of God's creation by being set to a traditional Indonesian melody that has become the basis for one of the most widely known worship songs from Asia. It needs to be sung joyfully and at a lively tempo.

TEXT: Tilly Lubis, 2009; trans. David Diephouse, 2009
MUSIC: Batak melody; arr. H. A. Pandopo, 1999
Text © 2009 Faith Alive Christian Resources
Music Arr. © 1999 H. A. Pandopo (Harry van Dop)

NYANYIKANLAH NYANYIAN BARU
Irregular

God reigns on high, let the heav - ens re - joice!
Both young and old, come and join in the song!
Praise God, you saints who are claimed as God's own!

God of Great and God of Small 19

1 God of great and God of small, God of one and God of all,
2 God of land and sky and sea, God of life and des - ti - ny,
3 God of si - lence, God of sound, God by whom the lost are found,
4 God of heaven and God of earth, God of death and God of birth,

God of weak and God of strong, God to whom all things be - long,
God of nev - er - end - ing power, yet be - side me ev - ery hour,
God of day and dark - est night, God whose love turns wrong to right,
God of now and days be - fore, God who reigns for - ev - er - more,

Refrain

al - le - lu - ia, al - le - lu - ia, praise be to your name.

Although it uses remarkably simple language, this text affirms a great mystery: beyond all our powers of explanation, God holds together all the opposites that seem to pull us in one direction or another. Yet God is present to them all and also to us; for that we give praise.

TEXT: Natalie Sleeth, 1973
MUSIC: Natalie Sleeth, 1973; arr. Beverly A. Howard, 2012
Text and Music © 1973 Carl Fischer, Inc.

GOD OF GREAT AND SMALL
7.7.7.7 with refrain

20 All Things Bright and Beautiful

Refrain

All things bright and beau-ti-ful, all crea-tures great and small,

all things wise and won-der-ful, the Lord God made them all.

Fine

1 Each lit-tle flower that o-pens, each lit-tle bird that sings,
2 The pur-ple-head-ed moun-tain, the riv-er run-ning by,
3 The cold wind in the win-ter, the pleas-ant sum-mer sun,
4 God gave us eyes to see them, and lips that we might tell

to Refrain

God made their glow-ing col-ors; God made their ti-ny wings.
the sun-set, and the morn-ing that bright-ens up the sky:
the ripe fruits in the gar-den, God made them ev-ery one.
how great is God Al-might-y, who has made all things well.

One of a series of hymns the author wrote for children on the Apostles' Creed, this text (originally in seven stanzas) expands "Maker of heaven and earth." The first stanza became the refrain when the text was later set to a popular tune from the age of King Charles II.

TEXT: Cecil Frances Alexander, 1848, alt.
MUSIC: English melody, 17th cent.; adapt. Martin Shaw, 1915; harm. *The Hymnbook*, 1955
Music Harm. © 1955, ren. 1983 John Ribble (admin. Westminster John Knox Press)

ROYAL OAK
7.6.7.6 with refrain

Many and Great, O God, Are Thy Works

21

1 Man - y and great, O God, are thy works,
2 Grant un - to us com - mu - nion with thee,

Mak - er of earth and sky. Thy hands have
thou star - a - bid - ing One. Come un - to

set the heav - ens with stars; thy fin - gers spread the
us and dwell with us. With thee are found the

moun - tains and plains. Lo, at thy word the
gifts of life. Bless us with life that

wa - ters were formed. Deep seas o - bey thy voice.
has no end, e - ter - nal life with thee.

First came the evocative Dakota chant, bearing a French name ("the lake that speaks") for the site of a Native American mission in western Minnesota. That was where the original seven-stanza text based on Jeremiah 10:12–13 was written in the Dakota language to fit the tune.

TEXT: Joseph R. Renville, 1842; trans. Philip Frazier, 1929, alt.
MUSIC: Dakota melody; harm. Emily R. Brink, 1995
Music Harm. © 1995 Faith Alive Christian Resources

LACQUIPARLE
Irregular

22 God of the Sparrow

1 God of the spar - row God of the whale God of the
2 God of the earth - quake God of the storm God of the
3 God of the rain - bow God of the cross God of the
4 God of the hun - gry God of the sick God of the
5 God of the neigh - bor God of the foe God of the
6 God of the a - ges God near at hand God of the

swirl - ing stars How does the crea - ture say Awe
trum - pet blast How does the crea - ture cry Woe
emp - ty grave How does the crea - ture say Grace
prod - i - gal How does the crea - ture say Care
prun - ing hook How does the crea - ture say Love
lov - ing heart How do your chil - dren say Joy

How does the crea - ture say Praise
How does the crea - ture cry Save
How does the crea - ture say Thanks
How does the crea - ture say Life
How does the crea - ture say Peace
How do your chil - dren say Home

Guitar chords do not correspond with keyboard harmony.

Though a lack of punctuation makes this text appear freeform and the flowing tune enhances a sense of movement, each stanza here is firmly anchored by a final weighty word (praise, save, thanks, life, peace, home), a sign of God's eternal presence in an ever-changing world.

TEXT: Jaroslav J. Vajda, 1983
MUSIC: Carl F. Schalk, 1983
Text © 1983 Concordia Publishing House
Music © 1983 GIA Publications, Inc.

ROEDER
9.6.7.7

God, You Spin the Whirling Planets 23

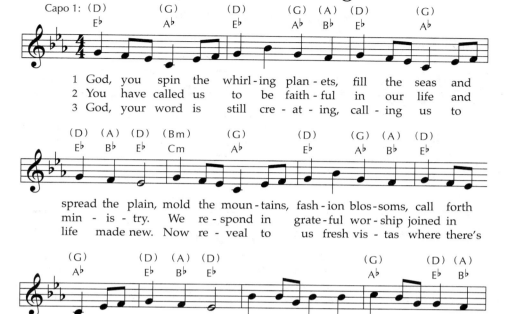

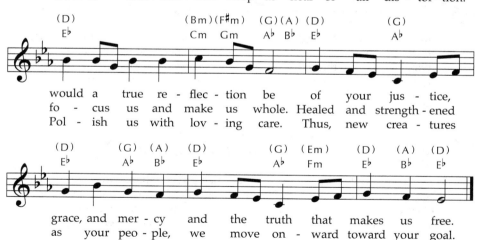

1 God, you spin the whirl-ing plan-ets, fill the seas and
2 You have called us to be faith-ful in our life and
3 God, your word is still cre-at-ing, call-ing us to

spread the plain, mold the moun-tains, fash-ion blos-soms, call forth
min-is-try. We re-spond in grate-ful wor-ship joined in
life made new. Now re-veal to us fresh vis-tas where there's

sun-shine, wind, and rain. We, cre-at-ed in your im-age,
one com-mu-ni-ty. When we blur your gra-cious im-age,
work to dare and do. Keep us clear of all dis-tor-tion.

would a true re-flec-tion be of your jus-tice,
fo-cus us and make us whole. Healed and strength-ened
Pol-ish us with lov-ing care. Thus, new crea-tures

grace, and mer-cy and the truth that makes us free.
as your peo-ple, we move on-ward toward your goal.
in your im-age, we'll pro-claim Christ ev-ery-where.

This text was written for the 1979 National Meeting of United Presbyterian Women, whose theme, "In the Image of God," is variously considered here as reflection, focus, distortion, and polishing for clarity. The words are well set to an anonymous 19th-century American tune.

TEXT: Jane Parker Huber, 1978
MUSIC: American melody, 1830; harm. Richard Proulx, 1986
Text © 1980 Jane Parker Huber (admin. Westminster John Knox Press)
Music Harm. © 1986 GIA Publications, Inc.

PLEADING SAVIOR
8.7.8.7.D
(alternate harmonization, 717)
(alternate tune: AUSTRIAN HYMN)

24 God, Who Stretched the Spangled Heavens

1 God, who stretched the span - gled heav - ens in - fi -
2 Proud - ly rise our mod - ern cit - ies, state - ly
3 We have ven - tured worlds un - dreamed of since the
4 As each far ho - ri - zon beck - ons, may it

nite in time and place, flung the suns in burn - ing
build - ings row on row. Yet their win - dows, blank, un -
child - hood of our race; known the ec - sta - sy of
chal - lenge us a - new, chil - dren of cre - a - tive

ra - diance through the si - lent fields of space,
feel - ing, stare on can - yoned streets be - low,
wing - ing through un - trav - eled realms of space;
pur - pose, serv - ing oth - ers, hon - oring you.

we, your chil - dren in your like - ness, share in - ven - tive
where the lone - ly drift un - no - ticed in the cit - y's
probed the se - crets of the at - om, yield - ing un - i -
May our dreams prove rich with prom - ise, each en - deav - or

The crux of this text comes in the second stanza: if we dare to claim God-given abilities, we need also to show God-like compassion for the human needs that confront us daily. The earthy shape note tune provides a further reminder that we must not lose our heads in the clouds.

TEXT: Catherine Cameron, 1967, alt.
MUSIC: Attr. William Moore, 1825; harm. Charles Anders, 1969
Text © 1967 Hope Publishing Company
Music Harm. © 1969 Contemporary Music I: Hymns (admin. Augsburg Fortress)

HOLY MANNA
8.7.8.7.D
(alternate harmonization, 396)

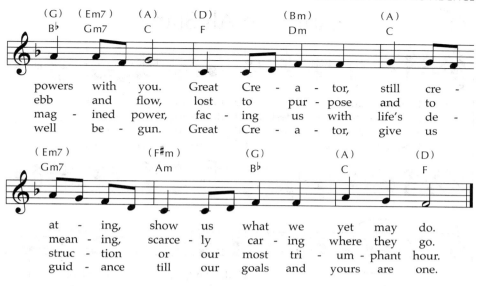

(G) (Em7) (A) (D) (Bm) (A)
B♭ Gm7 C F Dm C

powers with you. Great Cre - a - tor, still cre -
ebb and flow, lost to pur - pose and to
mag - ined power, fac - ing us with life's de -
well be - gun. Great Cre - a - tor, give us

(Em7) (F♯m) (G) (A) (D)
Gm7 Am B♭ C F

at - ing, show us what we yet may do.
mean - ing, scarce - ly car - ing where they go.
struc - tion or our most tri - um - phant hour.
guid - ance till our goals and yours are one.

O Lord, Our God, How Excellent 25
(Psalm 8)

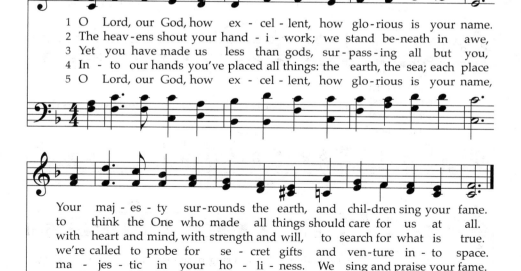

1 O Lord, our God, how ex - cel - lent, how glo - rious is your name.
2 The heav - ens shout your hand - i - work; we stand be - neath in awe,
3 Yet you have made us less than gods, sur - pass - ing all but you,
4 In - to our hands you've placed all things: the earth, the sea; each place
5 O Lord, our God, how ex - cel - lent, how glo - rious is your name,

Your maj - es - ty sur - rounds the earth, and chil - dren sing your fame.
to think the One who made all things should care for us at all.
with heart and mind, with strength and will, to search for what is true.
we're called to probe for se - cret gifts and ven - ture in - to space.
ma - jes - tic in your ho - li - ness. We sing and praise your fame.

The middle stanzas of this paraphrase of Psalm 8 probe the ancient but enduring paradox of declaring the grandeur of God's creation while realizing how small mortals are in the midst of it all. These words are set to one of the most durable 18th-century English psalm tunes.

TEXT: Fred R. Anderson, 1986
MUSIC: Este's *Psalmes*, 1592; harm. George Kirbye, 1592
Text © 1986 Fred R. Anderson

WINCHESTER OLD
CM

26 Earth and All Stars!

1 Earth and all stars! Loud rush-ing plan-ets!
2 Trum-pet and pipes! Loud clash-ing cym-bals! Sing to the
3 En - gines and steel! Loud pound-ing ham-mers!
4 Knowl-edge and truth! Loud sound-ing wis - dom!

Lord   a new song!
Hail, wind, and rain! Loud blow-ing
Harp, lute, and lyre! Loud hum-ming
Lime-stone and beams! Loud build-ing
Daugh-ter and son! Loud pray-ing

snow - storm!
cel - los! Sing to the Lord   a new song! God has done
work - ers!
mem - bers!

mar - vel-ous things. We too sing prais-es with a new song!

This lively text was written for the 90th anniversary of St. Olaf College in Northfield, Minnesota. Echoing
Psalm 98, it is a prime example of a 20th-century hymn style based on phrases rather than complete
sentences. The exuberant tune was created expressly for these words.

TEXT: Herbert Frederick Brokering, 1964
MUSIC: David N. Johnson, 1968
Text and Music © 1968 Augsburg Publishing House (admin. Augsburg Fortress)

EARTH AND ALL STARS
4.5.7.D with refrain

Sacred the Body

1 Sa - cred the bod - y God has cre - at - ed,
2 Bod - ies are var - ied, made in all siz - es,
3 Love re - spects per - sons, bod - ies and bound - aries.
4 Ho - ly of ho - lies, God ev - er lov - ing,

tem - ple of Spir - it that dwells deep in - side.
pale, full of col - or; both frag - ile and strong.
Love does not bat - ter, ne - glect, or a - buse.
make us your tem - ples; in - dwell all we do.

Cher - ish each per - son; nur - ture re - la - tion.
Ho - ly the dif - ference, gift of the Mak - er,
Love touch - es gent - ly, nev - er co - erc - ing.
May we be care - ful, ten - der and car - ing,

Treat flesh as ho - ly, that love may a - bide.
so let us hon - or each sto - ry and song.
Love leaves the oth - er with pow - er to choose.
so may our bod - ies give hon - or to you.

Despite biblical directives to "honor God with your body" (1 Corinthians 6:20) and "offer your bodies as living sacrifices, holy and pleasing to God" (Romans 12:1), Christians have often scorned the body, failing to see how the mystery of the Incarnation continues in each person.

TEXT: Ruth Duck, 1997
MUSIC: Colin Gibson, 1992
Text © 1997 The Pilgrim Press
Music © 1992 Hope Publishing Company

TENDERNESS
5.5.10.D

28 You Are Before Me, Lord
(Psalm 139)

1 You are be - fore me, Lord, you are be - hind,
2 Then from your Spir - it where, Lord, shall I go;
3 If I should take my flight in - to the dawn,
4 If I should say, "Let dark - ness cov - er me,
5 Search me, O God; search me and know my heart;

and o - ver me you have spread out your hand;
and from your pres - ence where, Lord, shall I fly?
if I should dwell on o - cean's far - thest shore,
and I shall hide with - in the veil of night,"
try me, O God; my mind and spir - it try;

such knowl - edge is too won - der - ful for me,
If I as - cend to heav - en you are there,
your might - y hand will rest up - on me still,
sure - ly the dark - ness is not dark to you:
keep me from an - y path that gives you pain,

too high to grasp, too great to un - der - stand.
and still are with me if in hell I lie.
and your right hand will guard me ev - er - more.
the night is as the day, the dark - ness light.
and lead me in the ev - er - last - ing way.

Guitar chords do not correspond with keyboard harmony.

The effectiveness of this paraphrase of Psalm 139:1–12, 23–24 partly derives from its imitation of the characteristic repetitions that give emotional intensity to Hebrew poetry. Such patterns of repetitiveness can also be seen in the last three notes of each phrase of the tune.

TEXT: Ian Pitt-Watson, 1973, 1989
MUSIC: Alfred Morton Smith, 1941
Text © 1973 Ian Pitt-Watson
Music used by permission of Estate of Doris Wright Smith

SURSUM CORDA (Smith)
10.10.10.10

O God, You Search Me

29

(Psalm 139)

1 O God, you search me and you know me. All my
2 You know my rest-ing and my ris-ing. You dis-
3 Be - fore a word is on my tongue, Lord, you have
4 Al - though your Spir - it is up - on me, still I
5 For you cre - at - ed me and shaped me, gave me

thoughts lie o - pen to your gaze. When I
cern my pur - pose from a - far, and with
known its mean - ing through and through. You are
search for shel - ter from your light. There is
life with - in my moth - er's womb. For the

walk or lie down you are be - fore me: ev - er the
love ev - er - last - ing you be - siege me: in ev - ery
with me be - yond my un - der - stand - ing: God of my
no - where on earth I can es - cape you: e - ven the
won - der of who I am, I praise you: safe in your

mak - er and keep - er of my days.
mo - ment of life or death, you are.
pres - ent, my past, and fu - ture, too.
dark - ness is ra - diant in your sight.
hands, all cre - a - tion is made new.

Psalm 139 is one of the most introspective and most intimate of all the psalms, showing an acute mindfulness of God's presence in all aspects of one's life. Sometimes resisted, this omnipresence ultimately becomes a ground of hope, a promise that we never stray beyond God's care.

TEXT and MUSIC: Bernadette Farrell, 1992
Text and Music © 1992 Bernadette Farrell (Published by OCP)

O GOD, YOU SEARCH ME
9.9.11.11

30   O God, in a Mysterious Way

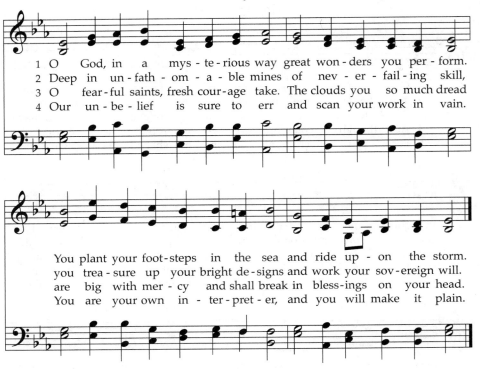

1 O God, in a mys-te-rious way great won-ders you per-form.
2 Deep in un-fath-om-a-ble mines of nev-er-fail-ing skill,
3 O fear-ful saints, fresh cour-age take. The clouds you so much dread
4 Our un-be-lief is sure to err and scan your work in vain.

You plant your foot-steps in the sea and ride up-on the storm.
you trea-sure up your bright de-signs and work your sov-ereign will.
are big with mer-cy and shall break in bless-ings on your head.
You are your own in-ter-pret-er, and you will make it plain.

This classic text gains renewed energy and focus from its recasting here: despite our fear and confusion, we can trust that God's providential purposes will eventually be revealed. In its original source the tune printed here is one of twelve not assigned to a specific hymn.

TEXT: William Cowper, 1773, alt.
MUSIC: Scottish Psalter, 1615

DUNDEE
CM
(alternate harmonization, 45)

Let Us with a Gladsome Mind 31

(Psalm 136)

1 Let us with a glad - some mind praise the
2 God, with all - com - mand - ing might, filled the
3 All things liv - ing God does feed; with full
4 Let us with a glad - some mind praise the

Lord who is so kind:
new - made world with light:
mea - sure, meets their need:
Lord who is so kind:

for God's mer - cies

shall en - dure, ev - er faith - ful, ev - er sure.

These few stanzas are among the least florid of the two dozen that make up the rather flamboyant paraphrase of Psalm 136 written by the fifteen-year-old who would become one of the greatest English poets. It is set here to a sprightly tune with Moravian connections.

TEXT: John Milton, 1624, alt.
MUSIC: Attr. John Antes, c. 1790; harm. John B. Wilkes, 1861

MONKLAND
7.7.7.7

32 I Sing the Mighty Power of God

1 I sing the might-y power of God that made the moun-tains rise,
2 I sing the good-ness of the Lord who filled the earth with food.
3 There's not a plant or flower be-low but makes thy glo-ries known.

that spread the flow-ing seas a-broad and built the loft-y
God formed the crea-tures through the Word, and then pro-nounced them
And clouds a-rise, and tem-pests blow, by or-der from thy

skies. I sing the wis-dom that or-dained the sun to rule the day.
good. Lord, how thy won-ders are dis-played, wher-e'er I turn my eye,
throne, while all that bor-rows life from thee is ev-er in thy care,

The moon shines full at God's com-mand, and all the stars o-bey.
if I sur-vey the ground I tread, or gaze up-on the sky!
and ev-ery-where that we can be, thou, God, art pres-ent there.

With minimal revision this text brings together six of the eight four-line stanzas in an 18th-century hymn written for children and originally headed "Praise for Creation and Providence." The anonymous German tune provides a fitting sense of breadth and wonder.

TEXT: Isaac Watts, 1715, alt.
MUSIC: *Gesangbuch der Herzogl. Wirtembergischen Katholischen Hofkapelle*, 1784; alt. 1868

ELLACOMBE
CMD

Praise the Lord! God's Glories Show 33
(Psalm 150)

1 Praise the Lord! God's glo - ries show,
2 Earth to heaven ex - alt the strain, Al - le - lu - ia!
3 Strings and voic - es, hands and hearts,

saints with - in God's courts be - low,
Send it, heaven, to earth a - gain, Al - le - lu - ia!
in the con - cert, bear your parts,

an - gels round the throne a - bove,
Age to age, God's mer - cies trace, Al - le - lu - ia!
All that breathes, your Lord a - dore,

all who see and share God's love.
Praise God's prov - i - dence and grace! Al - le - lu - ia!
sing - ing praise for - ev - er - more,

Originally cast as two eight-line stanzas, this 19th-century paraphrase of Psalm 150 was slightly shortened when it was set to the present tune with recurring Alleluias. The Welsh tune is actually older than the text and bears a name meaning "the church of St. Mary."

TEXT: Henry Francis Lyte, 1834; rev. 1836, alt.
MUSIC: Robert Williams, 1817; harm. David Evans, 1927
Music Harm. © 1927 Oxford University Press

LLANFAIR
7.7.7.7 with alleluias

34 Bless the Lord, My Soul and Being!

(Psalm 104)

1 Bless the Lord, my soul and be-ing! Lord my God, you
2 Lord, you laid the earth's foun-da-tion that it would be
3 Grass you cause to grow for cat-tle, plants for us to
4 Lord, how great are all your work-ings; wis-dom marks them
5 May your glo-ry reign for-ev-er. Lord, re-joice in

have such might. Cloaked with hon-or, grand and glo-rious,
al-ways sound. By the word of your com-mand-ing,
cul-ti-vate. Food you bring forth from our la-bor,
through and through. All the earth is your pos-ses-sion;
all you make! As you look on your cre-a-tion,

you are clothed with pur-est light. Stretch-ing out the
you set forth each o-cean's bound. Springs gush forth at
wine for joy and bread for plate. Trees you give the
great and small be-long to you. Food you give in
moun-tains smoke, foun-da-tions shake. May these words and

This 20th-century paraphrase of Psalm 104 is careful to include the details of creation that give this psalm its character. This comprehensive text is well served by its expansive Victorian tune, named for the town in Sussex where the composer lived in his later years.

TEXT: Fred R. Anderson, 1986
MUSIC: C. Hubert H. Parry, 1897
Text © 1986 Fred R. Anderson

RUSTINGTON
8.7.8.7.D

heavens like tent cloth, you are cham - bered on the deep. Rid - ing
your own bid - ding, giv - ing drink to ev - ery field. Bird and
birds for shel - ter, moun-tain rock and cave for beast. Sun and
each due sea - son; at your hand come all good things. By your
thoughts be pleas - ing, for in you my joy is found. Bless the

on the wings of wind-storm, flame and fire your bid - ding keep.
beast and all your crea-tures in that cool - ness find thirst healed.
moon both mark the sea - sons; in their light we work and feast.
Spir - it you cre - ate us; Lord, your breath re - new - al brings.
Lord, my soul and be - ing! With this song let praise a - bound.

35 Praise Ye the Lord, the Almighty

1 Praise ye the Lord, the Al-might-y, the King of cre-
2 Praise ye the Lord, who o'er all things so won-drous-ly
3 Praise ye the Lord! O let all that is in me a-

a-tion! O my soul, praise him, for he is thy
reign-eth, shel-ters thee un-der his wings, yea, so
dore him! All that hath life and breath, come now with

health and sal-va-tion! All ye who hear, now to his
gen-tly sus-tain-eth! Hast thou not seen how thy de-
prais-es be-fore him! Let the a-men sound from his

tem-ple draw near; join me in glad ad-o-ra-tion!
sires e'er have been grant-ed in what he or-dain-eth?
peo-ple a-gain; glad-ly for aye we a-dore him.

This very strong 17th-century German hymn employs many phrases from the psalms, especially Psalms 150 and 103:1–6. It did not receive an effective English translation until the mid-19th century, but has remained popular ever since, thanks in part to its stirring tune.

TEXT: Joachim Neander, 1680; trans. Catherine Winkworth, 1863, alt.
MUSIC: Stralsund *Ernewerten Gesangbuch*, 1665; harm. *The Chorale Book for England*, 1863

LOBE DEN HERREN
14.14.4.7.8

For the Fruit of All Creation

36

1 For the fruit of all cre-a-tion, thanks be to God.
2 In the just re-ward of la-bor, God's will be done.
3 For the har-vests of the Spir-it, thanks be to God.

For the gifts to ev-ery na-tion, thanks be to God.
In the help we give our neigh-bor, God's will be done.
For the good we all in-her-it, thanks be to God.

For the plow-ing, sow-ing, reap-ing, si-lent growth while we are
In our world-wide task of car-ing for the hun-gry and de-
For the won-ders that as-tound us, for the truths that still con-

sleep-ing, fu-ture needs in earth's safe-keep-ing, thanks be to God.
spair-ing, in the har-vests we are shar-ing, God's will be done.
found us, most of all that love has found us, thanks be to God.

Originally called "Harvest Hymn," this text is much more comprehensive than that title implies. It also deals with stewardship, thanksgiving, and God's endless gifts that continue to astound us. It is set to a familiar Welsh tune whose name means "throughout the night."

TEXT: Fred Pratt Green, 1970, alt.
MUSIC: Welsh melody, c. 1784
Text © 1970 Hope Publishing Company

AR HYD Y NOS
8.4.8.4.8.8.8.4

37 Let All Things Now Living

1 Let all things now liv-ing a song of thanks-giv-ing
2 By law God en-forc-es, the stars in their cours-es,

to God our Cre-a-tor tri-um-phant-ly raise;
the sun in its or-bit o-be-dient-ly shine;

who fash-ioned and made us, pro-tect-ed and stayed us,
the hills and the moun-tains, the riv-ers and foun-tains,

by guid-ing us on to the end of our days.
the depths of the o-cean pro-claim God di-vine.

Harmony

God's ban-ners are o'er us; pure light goes be-fore us,
We too should be voic-ing our love and re-joic-ing;

a pil-lar of fire shin-ing forth in the night:
with glad ad-o-ra-tion, a song let us raise,

Written for an easy-to-sing folk melody familiar in England as well as Wales, this 20th-century North American text bears many resemblances to both Psalm 148 and the traditional canticle *Benedicite, omnia opera Domini* (Bless the Lord, all you works of the Lord).

TEXT: Katherine K. Davis, 1939, alt.
MUSIC: Welsh folk melody; harm. Gerald H. Knight, 20th cent.
Text © 1939, 1966 E. C. Schirmer Music Company
Music Harm. © Royal School of Church Music

ASH GROVE
6.6.11.6.6.11.D

till shad-ows have van-ished, all fear-ful-ness ban-ished,
till all things now liv-ing u - nite in thanks-giv-ing:

as for - ward we trav - el from light in - to light.
to God in the high - est, ho - san - na and praise!

To Bless the Earth   38
(Psalm 65)

1 To bless the earth God sends us from
2 The seed by God pro - vid - ed is
3 God crowns the year with good - ness; the
4 With grain the fields are cov - ered; the

heaven's a - bun - dant store the wa - ters of the
sown o'er hill and plain, and then come gen - tle
earth God's mer - cy fills; the wil - der - ness is
flocks in pas - tures graze; all na - ture joins in

spring - time, en - rich - ing it once more.
show - ers to bless the spring - ing grain.
fruit - ful, and joy - ful are the hills.
sing - ing a joy - ful song of praise.

These four stanzas present a paraphrase of Psalm 65:9–13, a celebration of God's providential care, which in turn draws forth a song of praise from all creation. This text is set to an early 17th-century tune composed for an affirmative chorale text often used at funerals.

TEXT: *The New Metrical Version of the Psalms*, 1909, alt.
MUSIC: Melchior Vulpius, 1609

CHRISTUS, DER IST MEIN LEBEN
7.6.7.6

39 Great Is Thy Faithfulness

1 *Great is thy faith-ful-ness, O God my Fa-ther;
2 Sum-mer and win-ter, and spring-time and har-vest,
3 Par-don for sin and a peace that en-dur-eth,

there is no shad-ow of turn-ing with thee.
sun, moon, and stars in their cours-es a-bove
thine own dear pres-ence to cheer and to guide,

Thou chang-est not; thy com-pas-sions they fail not.
join with all na-ture in man-i-fold wit-ness
strength for to-day and bright hope for to-mor-row:

As thou hast been thou for-ev-er wilt be.
to thy great faith-ful-ness, mer-cy, and love.
bless-ings all mine, with ten thou-sand be-side!

*Or "Great is thy faithfulness, O God, Creator."

Written as a meditation on Lamentations 3:22–23, this text is one of the few hymns among the 1200 poems by this Methodist writer and pastor that has gained much currency. The tune that appears here was composed especially for these words, and the pairing has proved enduring.

TEXT: Thomas O. Chisholm, 1923
MUSIC: William Marion Runyan, 1923
Text and Music © 1923, ren. 1951 Hope Publishing Company

FAITHFULNESS
11.10.11.10 with refrain

Refrain

Great is thy faith - ful - ness! Great is thy faith - ful - ness!
오 신 실 하 신 주 오 신 실 하 신 주

Morn - ing by morn - ing, new mer - cies I see.
날 마 다 자 비 를 베 푸 시 며

All I have need - ed thy hand hath pro - vid - ed.
일 용 할 모 든 것 내 려 주 시 니

Great is thy faith - ful - ness, Lord un - to me!
오 신 실 하 신 주 나 의 구 주

40 God's Word Is Upright

La palabra del Señor
(Psalm 33)

In this paraphrase of Psalm 33, the refrain is drawn from verses 4–5, stanza one from verses 6–7, and stanza two from verses 8–11. The psalm itself is a condensed remembering of the creation story from Genesis 1:1–2:3 and the story of Israel's deliverance from Exodus 3:1–15:21.

TEXT: Juan Luis García, 1979; trans. Mary Louise Bringle, 2011
MUSIC: Juan Luis García, 1979
Text and Music © 1979 Juan Luis García

NELSON
LMD with refrain

41 O Worship the King, All Glorious Above!

1 O worship the King, all glorious above!
2 O tell of God's might; O sing of God's grace,
3 The earth with its store of wonders untold,
4 Your bountiful care what tongue can recite?
5 Frail children of dust, and feeble as frail,

O gratefully sing God's power and God's love:
whose robe is the light, whose canopy space,
Almighty, your power has founded of old;
It breathes in the air; it shines in the light;
in you do we trust, nor find you to fail;

our shield and defender, the Ancient of Days,
whose chariots of wrath the deep thunderclouds form;
established it fast by a changeless decree,
it streams from the hills; it descends to the plain,
your mercies, how tender, how firm to the end,

pavilioned in splendor and girded with praise.
and bright is God's path on the wings of the storm.
and round it has cast, like a mantle, the sea.
and sweetly distills in the dew and the rain.
our Maker, Defender, Redeemer, and Friend.

Addressing the first two stanzas to the singers of the hymn and the last three to God, this free paraphrase of Psalm 104 recasts the psalmist's imagery with baroque verve. Though it was first published in England, the tune has been more popular in North America than there.

TEXT: Robert Grant, 1833, alt.
MUSIC: Joseph Martin Kraus, 1784, alt.

LYONS
10.10.11.11

Your Faithfulness, O Lord, Is Sure 42

(Psalm 145)

1 Your faith - ful - ness, O Lord, is sure in
2 The eyes of all are fixed on you; by
3 Lord, you are just in all your ways, and
4 My mouth shall speak your praise, O Lord; my

all your words, your gra - cious deeds; you gen - tly lift all
you their wants are all sup - plied; your o - pen hand is
kind in ev - ery - thing you do; for - ev - er near you
soul shall bless your ho - ly name; let all things liv - ing

bur - dened souls and well pro - vide for all our needs.
boun - ti - ful and ev - ery soul is sat - is - fied.
stand to hear and help all those who call on you.
join the song of praise, from age to age the same.

This paraphrase of verses from the latter part of Psalm 145 celebrates God's providential care for all creation, especially for those in any need or trouble. This anonymous German tune was apparently introduced to English hymnody by John Wesley in a 1742 music collection.

TEXT: Joy F. Patterson, 1989
MUSIC: *Musikalisches Handbuch,* 1690; harm. William Henry Havergal, 1847, alt.
Text © 1990 Joy F. Patterson

WINCHESTER NEW
LM

43 You Who Dwell in the Shelter of the Lord

On Eagle's Wings (Psalm 91)

Leader or All

1 You who dwell in the shel-ter of the Lord, who a-
bide in his shad-ow for life, say to the Lord, "My
ref-uge, my rock in whom I trust!"

Refrain *All*

And he will raise you up on ea-gle's wings, bear you on the
breath of dawn, make you to shine like the sun,
and hold you in the palm of his hand. *Fine*

Leader or All

2 The snare of the fowl-er will nev-er cap-ture you, and
fam-ine will bring you no fear: un-der his wings, your

Although the body of this text is a paraphrase of Psalm 91, the refrain combines allusions to Exodus 19:4, Psalm 139:9, and Isaiah 40:31; 49:16. Written in response to the death of a friend's father, this piece has been a source of consolation to many people.

TEXT: Michael Joncas, 1978, alt.
MUSIC: Michael Joncas, 1978
Text and Music © 1979 Jan Michael Joncas (Published by OCP)

ON EAGLE'S WINGS
Irregular

44 Like a Mother Who Has Borne Us

1 Like a moth - er who has borne us, held us
2 Like a fa - ther who has taught us, grasped our
3 Though as chil - dren we have wan - dered, placed our
4 When we of - fer food and com - fort, grasp our

close in her de - light, fed us free - ly from her
hand and been our guide, lift - ed us and healed our
trust in power and might, left be - hind our broth - ers,
neigh - bor's hand in love, tread the path of peace and

bod - y, God has called us in - to life.
sor - rows, God has walked with us in life.
sis - ters, God still calls us in - to life.
jus - tice, God still walks with us in life.

This text was inspired by how the prophet Hosea describes the parental nature of God's relationship with
Israel (Hosea 11:1–19). The last stanza echoes Christ's teachings about love of neighbor (Matthew 22:37–40/
Mark 12:29–31) and care for "the least of these" (Matthew 25:31–46).

TEXT: Daniel Bechtel, 1986
MUSIC: William P. Rowan, 1992
Text © 1986 Daniel R. Bechtel
Music © 1993 Selah Publishing Co., Inc.

AUSTIN
8.7.8.7

I to the Hills Will Lift My Eyes 45
(Psalm 121)

1 I to the hills will lift my eyes; from
2 God will not let your foot be moved; your
3 Your faith - ful keep - er is the Lord, your
4 From e - vil God will keep you safe, pro -

whence shall come my aid? My help is from the
guard - ian nev - er sleeps; God's watch - ful and un -
shel - ter and your shade. 'Neath sun or moon, by
vide for all you need. Your go - ing out, your

Lord a - lone, who heaven and earth has made.
slum - bering care pro - tects and safe - ly keeps.
day or night, you shall not be a - fraid.
com - ing in, God will for - ev - er lead.

Although the first stanza of this paraphrase of Psalm 121 draws heavily on 17th-century Scottish psalters, most of this version dates from the early 20th century. In its original source the tune printed here is one of twelve not assigned for use with a specific psalm.

TEXT: *The New Metrical Version of the Psalms*, 1909, alt.
MUSIC: Scottish Psalter, 1615

DUNDEE
CM
(alternate harmonization, 30)

46 Unless the Lord the House Shall Build
(Psalm 127)

1 Un - less the Lord the house shall build, the
2 In vain you rise at morn - ing break, and
3 Like ar - rows in full quiv - ers stored are

wea - ry build - ers toil in vain; un - less the Lord the
late your night - ly vig - ils keep, and wea - ry days of
chil - dren given in days of youth; for chil - dren are a

cit - y shield, the guards a use - less watch main - tain.
toil par - take; for God's be - lov - ed there is sleep.
great re - ward, a gift from God in ver - y truth.

As this paraphrase of Psalm 127 makes clear, human beings need to recognize both that our efforts will be in vain without God's help and that our blessings come from God. These enduring truths are linked to each other by this shape note tune that ends as it begins.

TEXT: *The Psalter*, 1872, alt.
MUSIC: Attr. Freeman Lewis, 1814; harm. John Leon Hooker, 1984
Music Harm. © 1984 John Leon Hooker

BOURBON
LM

Bless All Who Trust in God
(Psalm 128)

47

1 Bless all who trust in God and walk with-in God's ways;
2 Let fam-i-lies be strong and spar-kle bright as wine;
3 And since we may not boast such joys are ours by right,

bless ev-ery soul whose hap-pi-ness springs from the Lord's own praise!
let part-ners and let chil-dren thrive and flour-ish like the vine!
teach us, good Lord, to take your gifts with thanks and with de-light.

This paraphrase of Psalm 128 effectively communicates the central theme of this short psalm that would have been sung by pilgrims while making their way to Jerusalem: trusting in God's sovereignty is the only true source of blessing, both for ourselves and for those we love.

TEXT: David Mowbray, 1989, alt.
MUSIC: Johann B. König, 1738; arr. William Henry Havergal, 1847
Text © 1990 The Jubilate Group (admin. Hope Publishing Company)

FRANCONIA
SM

Rain Down

48

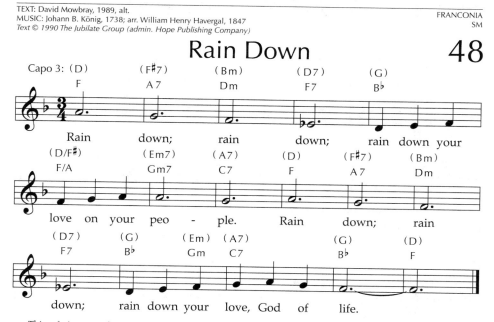

Capo 3: (D)   (F♯7)   (Bm)   (D7)   (G)
F   A7   Dm   F7   B♭

Rain   down;   rain   down;   rain down your

(D/F♯)   (Em7)   (A7)   (D)   (F♯7)   (Bm)
F/A   Gm7   C7   F   A7   Dm

love on your peo - ple.   Rain   down;   rain

(D7)   (G)   (Em) (A7)   (G)   (D)
F7   B♭   Gm   C7   B♭   F

down;   rain down your love, God of life.

This refrain comes from a longer song based on Psalm 33, but the striking image of God's love falling like rain is not actually present in that psalm. That image may be based on Ezekiel 34:26, where God promises to send showers of blessing upon the people of the covenant.

TEXT: Jaime Cortez, 1991
MUSIC: Jaime Cortez, 1991; arr. John Carter, 2001
Text and Music © 1992 Jaime Cortez (Published by OCP)

RAIN DOWN
Irregular

49 The God of Abraham Praise

1 The God of A-braham praise, who reigns en-throned a-bove,
2 Your spir-it still flows free, high surg-ing where it will.
3 Your good-ly land we seek, with peace and plen-ty blest,
4 You have e-ter-nal life im-plant-ed in the soul;

the An-cient of E-ter-nal Days, the God of love!
In proph-et's word you spoke of old and you speak still.
a land of sa-cred lib-er-ty and Sab-bath rest.
your love shall be our strength and stay, while a-ges roll.

The Lord, the great I AM, by earth and heaven con-fessed,
Es-tab-lished is your law, and change-less it shall stand,
There milk and hon-ey flow, and oil and wine a-bound,
We praise you, liv-ing God! We praise your ho-ly name:

we bow be-fore your ho-ly name, for-ev-er blest.
deep writ up-on the hu-man heart by your strong hand.
and trees of life for-ev-er grow with mer-cy crowned.
the first, the last, be-yond all thought, and still the same!

Shaped by its traditional Jewish tune, this selection of English stanzas conveys the essence of the *Yigdal,* a canticle based on a medieval Hebrew statement of faith about the nature of God and often used in synagogue worship, alternately chanted by cantor and congregation.

TEXT: Moses Maimonides, 12th cent.; vers. Daniel ben Judah Dayan, 1404; stanzas 1, 3, trans. Thomas Olivers, c.1770, alt.; stanzas 2, 4, trans. Max Landsberg, Newton M. Mann, and William C. Gannett, 1884, 1910, alt.
MUSIC: Jewish melody, 17th cent.; adapt. Meyer Lyon and Thomas Olivers, 1770

LEONI
6.6.8.4.D

Deep in the Shadows of the Past 50

1 Deep in the shad-ows of the past, far out from set - tled lands,
2 While oth-ers bowed to change-less gods, they met a mys - ter - y,
3 From Ex - o - dus to Pen - te - cost the prom-ise changed and grew,
4 For all the writ-ings that sur-vived, for lead-ers, long a - go,

some no - mads trav-eled with their God a-cross the des - ert sands.
in - vis - i - ble, with-out a name: "I AM WHAT I WILL BE";
while some, re - mem-ber-ing the past, re - cord-ed what they knew,
who sift - ed, cop - ied, and pre - served the Bi - ble that we know,

The dawn-ing hope of hu - man-kind by them was sensed and shown:
and by their tents, a-round their fires in sto - ry, song, and law,
or with their let-ters and la - ments, their proph-e - cy and praise,
give thanks, and find its sto - ry yet our prom-ise, strength, and call,

a prom-ise call - ing them a - head, a fu - ture yet un-known.
they praised, re-mem-bered, hand-ed on a past that prom-ised more.
re - cov-ered, kin-dled, and ex-pressed new hope for chang-ing days.
the mod - el of e - merg-ing faith, a - live with hope for all.

This vivid text reminds us of two truths we often forget: how deeply our faith is rooted in God's enduring covenant with the descendants of Abraham, Isaac, and Jacob, and how much we can learn from their story. The tune began life as the setting for a family Christmas card.

TEXT: Brian Wren, 1973; rev. 1994
MUSIC: Annabeth McClelland Gay, 1952
Text © 1975, rev. 1995 Hope Publishing Company
Music © 1958, ren. 1986 The Pilgrim Press

SHEPHERDS' PIPES
CMD

51 To Abraham and Sarah

I Will Be Your God

1 To A-bra-ham and Sa - rah the call of God was clear:
2 From A-bra-ham and Sa - rah a - rose a pil-grim race,
3 We of this gen-er-a - tion on whom God's hand is laid

"Go forth and I will show you a coun-try rich and fair.
de - pen-dent for their jour - ney on God's a - bun-dant grace;
can jour-ney to the fu - ture se - cure and un - a - fraid,

You need not fear the jour - ney, for I have pledged my word
and in their heart was writ - ten by God this sav - ing word,
re - joic-ing in God's good-ness and trust-ing in this word,

that you shall be my peo - ple and I will be your God."
"That you shall be my peo - ple and I will be your God."
"That you shall be my peo - ple and I will be your God."

This hymn condenses the narrative of Genesis 17:1–22 and grounds it in the recurring statement of the covenant relationship between God and the people God has chosen. This Welsh tune also occurs in a minor version called LLANGLOFFAN, used elsewhere in this hymnal (see no. 362).

TEXT: Judith A. Fetter, 1984
MUSIC: Welsh melody
Text © 1984 Judith A. Fetter

LLANFYLLIN
7.6.7.6.D

When Israel Was in Egypt's Land 52

1 When Is-rael was in E-gypt's land, let my peo-ple go;
2 "Thus saith the Lord," bold Mo-ses said, "Let my peo-ple go!
3 "No more shall they in bond-age toil: let my peo-ple go!
4 O let us all from bond-age flee; let my peo-ple go!

op-pressed so hard they could not stand, let my peo-ple go!
If not, I'll smite your first-born dead. Let my peo-ple go!"
Let them come out with E-gypt's spoil: let my peo-ple go!"
And let us all in Christ be free: let my peo-ple go!

Refrain

Go down, (go down,) Mo-ses, (Mo-ses,) way down in E-gypt's

land; tell old Pha-raoh: let my peo-ple go!

Nothing in Hebrew Scripture resonated more deeply with the experience of African Americans in North America than Israel's slavery in Egypt. In this spiritual's recurring line, "Let my people go," past and present became one, as they still do for all who are oppressed.

TEXT: African American spiritual
MUSIC: African American spiritual; arr. Melva Wilson Costen, 1989
Music Arr. © 1990 Melva Wilson Costen

GO DOWN MOSES
8.5.8.5 with refrain

53   O God, Who Gives Us Life

1 O God, who gives us life and breath, who shapes us in the womb,
2 O God, who calls your peo-ple out to ven-ture and to dare,
3 O God of cov-e-nant and law, re-vealed in cloud and flame,

who guards our lives from birth to death, then leads us from the tomb:
to plumb the bleak a-byss of doubt and find you e-ven there:
your might-y deeds e-voke our awe; we dare not speak your name.

de-liv-er us from fears that kill the life we have from you.
when we de-spair in wan-der-ing through wastes of emp-ty lies,
Yet we by faith are drawn to you and will your peo-ple prove,

Help us to know your Spir-it still is mak-ing all things new.
re-fresh us with the liv-ing spring of hope that nev-er dies.
as on our hearts you write a-new the cov-e-nant of love.

Christians often fail to appreciate how much we can learn about God from the Hebrew Scriptures. This text draws on a variety of passages that call attention to God's faithfulness toward the Chosen People and the promise of a new covenant written on the heart (Jeremiah 31:31–34).

TEXT: Carl P. Daw Jr., 1990
MUSIC: English melody; arr. Arthur S. Sullivan, 1874
Text © 1990 Hope Publishing Company

NOEL
CMD

Make a Joyful Noise to God! 54

(Psalm 66)

1 Make a joy-ful noise to God! All cre-a-tion sings your praise!
2 Come and see what God has done, great the bless-ings to the just:
3 Bless the Lord, our ref-uge sure; let our songs of praise be heard!

Great your won-ders here dis-played, un-ex-celled through-out our days.
walked the cho-sen through the sea, brought their en-e-mies to dust.
By whose jus-tice, we are tried; by whose grace, our guilt de-ferred.

Glo-rious is your sa-cred name, a-ges old, yet still the same.
Let us lift a thank-ful voice for God's mer-cies, and re-joice!
When our life's sure end shall come, bring us to your heaven-ly home.

This paraphrase of Psalm 66 maintains a corporate tone more suitable for congregational singing than does the original psalm, which moves to a personal narrative in its latter part. The reference to "all creation" is strengthened by the associations of the tune (see no. 14).

TEXT: Michael Morgan, 1995, alt.
MUSIC: Conrad Kocher, 1838; abr. William Henry Monk, 1861; harm. *The English Hymnal*, 1906
Text © 2010 Michael Morgan (admin. Congregational Ministries Publishing, Presbyterian Church (U.S.A.))

DIX
7.7.7.7.7.7

55 Come like Driving Wind, O God
(Psalm 68)

1 Come like driv - ing wind, O God, let your
2 Let your peo - ple shout for joy; let them
3 Or - phan's fa - ther, wid - ow's hope, grace from
4 When you led your peo - ple out, march - ing
5 Sing to God, all round the earth, God whose

en - e - mies be smoke. Come like sear - ing
cheer and chant your name, sing - ing of the
heav - en for the earth, you bring home the
through the wil - der - ness, earth was shak - ing
free - dom has no bound, God who speaks for

fire, O God, let your en - e - mies be wax.
path you take, rid - ing on the glo - ry clouds.
dis - pos - sessed; you set slaves and pris - oners free.
as you went, rain was pour - ing from the sky.
all to hear, God whose bless - ing is our life.

This unrhymed 21st-century paraphrase effectively communicates the urgency of Psalm 68 and its celebration of God's power, manifest both in destroying all that hinders God's purposes and in caring for those who have no other helper. Such a God deserves our thanks and praise.

TEXT: Richard Leach, 2007
MUSIC: Erfurt *Enchiridion*, 1524; harm. Sethus Calvisius, 1594
Text © 2007 Selah Publishing Co., Inc.

NUN KOMM, DER HEIDEN HEILAND
7.7.7.7

Sing Out with Joy to God Our Strength 56
(Psalm 81)

1 Sing out with joy to God our strength. The God of Ja-cob praise,
2 But we, your peo-ple, would not hear, nor lis-ten to your voice.
3 You plead for us to hear your voice, to heark-en and o-bey.

who brought us forth from E-gypt's grip: from slav-ery we were saved.
Our self-ish wills would not sub-mit, nor make your way our choice.
You prom-ise to sub-due our foes, and sweep them all a-way.

God prom-ised to pro-vide for us, to nur-ture and to feed,
You gave us to our stub-born hearts, their coun-sel to o-bey.
You pledge to give us all we need, with fin-est wheat sup-ply,

to fill our mouths with all good things, to give us all we need.
We turned from all your prom-is-es, to walk in our own way.
and give us hon-ey from the rock, rich food to sat-is-fy.

A key word running through this paraphrase of Psalm 81 is "promise." The first stanza recalls how God fulfilled the promise of deliverance from Egypt and protection in the wilderness. The final two stanzas admit that God's promises were ignored, but they continue to be offered.

TEXT: Fred R. Anderson, 2010
MUSIC: Annabeth McClelland Gay, 1952
Text © 2010 Fred R. Anderson
Music © 1958, ren. 1986 The Pilgrim Press

SHEPHERDS' PIPES
CMD

57 Tremble, O Tremble

(Psalm 99)

1 Trem - ble, O trem - ble! The God whose throne is
2 Trem - ble, O trem - ble! The jus - tice done by
3 Trem - ble, O trem - ble! When Mo - ses, Aar - on,
4 Trem - ble, O trem - ble! A tow - er made of
5 Trem - ble, O trem - ble! Our God for - gives, and

near to us is rul - er of the world. The Ho - ly One!
God for us will shake and mend the world. O Ho - ly One!
Sam - u - el cried out, our God re - plied. The Ho - ly One!
cloud, a voice that spoke a last - ing law. The Ho - ly One!
yet our sin must be set right at last. O Ho - ly One!

The German theologian Rudolph Otto described holiness as *mysterium tremendum et fascinans*, a terrifying and fascinating mystery. The awareness of such a divine encounter lies behind Psalm 99, and this 21st-century paraphrase conveys how God remains both personal and unfathomable.

TEXT: Richard Leach, 2007
MUSIC: Alfred V. Fedak, 2011
Text © 2007 Selah Publishing Co., Inc.
Music © 2011 Selah Publishing Co., Inc.

TROMBLEY
5.8.6.4

When Israel Was Going Forth 58

(Psalm 114)

1 When Is - ra - el was go - ing forth from
2 to be God's ho - ly dwell - ing place, God's
3 The sea be - held and fled a - way; the
4 O sea, why did you run a - way? O
5 O trem - ble, earth, be - fore the Lord; the

out of E - gypt's land, and Ja - cob's house from
choice on Ju - dah fell, and there as God's do -
Jor - dan stopped its flow. The moun - tains skipped like
Jor - dan, why turn tide? You mounts and hills, like
God of Ja - cob fear; God made the rock a

for - eign tongues they could not un - der - stand,
min - ion took God's cho - sen Is - ra - el.
rams; the hills like lambs skipped to and fro.
rams and lambs, why leap on ev - ery side?
wa - ter pool, the stone a foun - tain clear.

The events described in Psalm 114 form the essential elements of Israel's story: exodus, provision in the wilderness, entry into the promised land. These events were all the result of God's sovereignty, which not only amazes human beings but also evokes awe from creation.

TEXT: Anon.
MUSIC: *Kentucky Harmony*, 1816; arr. Alfred V. Fedak, 2012
Music Arr. © 2012 Alfred V. Fedak

PISGAH
CM

59 The Steadfast Love of the Lord
(Psalm 105)

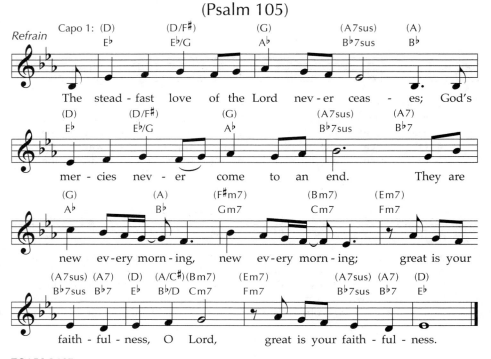

PSALM 105

Refrain

1 Give thanks to the LORD
      and call upon God's name;
   make known the deeds of the LORD
      among the peoples.

2 **Sing to the LORD, sing praises,**
      and speak of all God's
      marvelous works.

3 Glory in God's holy name;
      let the hearts of those
      who seek the LORD rejoice.

4 **Search for the LORD**
      and the strength of the LORD;
      continually seek the face of God.

5 Remember the marvels God has done,
      the wonders and the judgments
      of God's mouth,

6 **O offspring of Abraham, God's servant,**
      O children of Jacob, God's chosen.
                                    Refrain

7 The LORD is our God,
      whose judgments prevail
      in all the world.

8 **The LORD has always been mindful**
      of the covenant,
      the promise made
      for a thousand generations:

9 The covenant made with Abraham,
      the oath sworn to Isaac,

10 **which God established**
      as a statute for Jacob,
      an everlasting covenant for Israel.

42 For God remembered
      the holy promise
      and Abraham, chosen to serve.

43 **So God led forth the people**
      with gladness,
      the chosen ones with shouts of joy.
                                    Refrain

This psalm refrain quotes (with a few modifications) Lamentations 3:22–23, and the double singing of the final two phrases accentuates a sense of wonder. Finding ways to put Scripture, especially psalms, to music has long been a characteristic of the Reformed tradition.

TEXT and MUSIC (Refrain): Edith McNeill, 1974
Text and Music © 1974, 1975 Celebration
Responsive Reading © 1993 Order of St. Benedict (admin. The Liturgical Press)

THE STEADFAST LOVE OF THE LORD
Irregular

Your Endless Love, Your Mighty Acts 60
(Psalm 106)

1 Your end-less love, your might-y acts sur-
2 Our reb-el fore-bears rare-ly grasped your
3 Be-fore a gold-en calf they bowed— an
4 But when they spurned the prom-ised land, you
5 Yet those whom once you sold in wrath, in

pass what words can tell; Lord, may the joys your
mer-cy or your might; we need your mer-cy,
i-dol in your place!— un-til, by Mo-ses'
made your an-ger plain: they wan-dered long on
mer-cy you re-stored; may we, like them, be

peo-ple know be mine to share as well.
just like them: we, too, do wrong not right.
faith-ful prayer, you drew them back to grace.
des-ert paths, and served the Baals a-gain.
gath-ered in to thank and praise you, Lord.

The good news of this paraphrase of Psalm 106 is that God does not give up on us when we are disobedient. As the history of God's dealings with Israel demonstrates, divine mercy always outlasts human rebellion and waywardness. Though we rebel and stray, God's love is steadfast.

TEXT: Martin E. Leckebusch, 2006
MUSIC: Jeremiah Clarke, 1707
Text © 2006 Kevin Mayhew Ltd.

ST. MAGNUS
CM

61 Your Law, O Lord, Is Perfect
(Psalm 19)

1 Your law, O Lord, is per - fect, the sim - ple mak - ing wise;
2 More to be sought than rich - es, your words are my soul's wealth;
3 My strength and my re - deem - er, law - giv - er and true light,

how pure are your com - mand - ments, en - light - en - ing my eyes!
their taste is sweet like hon - ey, im - part - ing life and health.
my words and med - i - ta - tions make wor - thy in your sight.

Celebrating God's law in this paraphrase of the second half of Psalm 19 may seem odd if "law" is thought of simply as a list of things not to do. But in Jewish understanding, the law is seen as a gift, because it provides the signposts that show how to live as the people of God.

TEXT: Keith Landis, 1987
MUSIC: Melchior Vulpius, 1609
Text © 1994 Selah Publishing Co., Inc.

CHRISTUS, DER IST MEIN LEBEN
7.6.7.6

62 Love the Lord Your God

Capo 4: (C) (G) (F) (C)
E B A E

Love the Lord your God with all your heart.

(C) (G) (F) (C)
E B A E

Love the Lord your God with all your soul.

In the three synoptic gospels (Matthew 22:37 / Mark 12:30 / Luke 10:27–28), Jesus identifies the great commandment with these precepts drawn from Deuteronomy 6:5. In all three accounts, this commandment is followed by a second, to "love your neighbor as yourself" (Leviticus 19:18).

TEXT and MUSIC: Jean and Jim Strathdee, 1991
Text and Music © 1991 Desert Flower Music

GREAT COMMANDMENT
Irregular

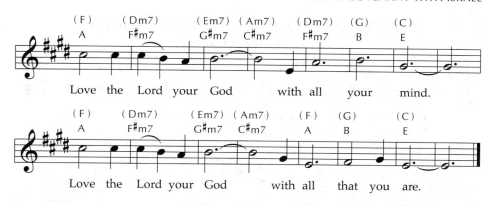

(F)   (Dm7)   (Em7) (Am7)   (Dm7)   (G)   (C)
A   F#m7   G#m7 C#m7   F#m7   B   E

Love the Lord your God   with all   your   mind.

(F)   (Dm7)   (Em7) (Am7)   (F)   (G)   (C)
A   F#m7   G#m7 C#m7   A   B   E

Love the Lord your God   with all   that you are.

The Lord Is God   63

1 The Lord is   God, the Lord a - lone! Give hon - or, thanks, and praise
2 With all your heart, with all your soul, with all your mind and might,
3 At night or   day, at home, a - way, to - geth - er   and   a - part,
4 The Lord is   God, the Lord a - lone! Give hon - or, thanks, and praise

to God, the mak - er   of   all things and giv - er of our days.
O peo - ple, love the Lord your God, the source of truth and light.
O chil - dren, take these ho - ly words and keep them in your heart.
to God, the mak - er   of   all things and giv - er of our days.

This hymn paraphrases the *Shema* (Deuteronomy 6:4–9), an ancient and central affirmation of Jewish monotheistic faith that observant Jews still recite twice a day. Jesus knew it well and called it the first and great commandment (Matthew 22:38 / Mark 12:28–29 / Luke 10:26–28).

TEXT: David Gambrell, 2011
MUSIC: Carl Gotthelf Gläser, 1828; arr. Lowell Mason, 1839
Text © 2011 David Gambrell (admin. Presbyterian Publishing Corp.)

AZMON
CM

64 I Long for Your Commandments
(Psalm 119)

1 I long for your com-mand-ments; your judg-ments all are
2 With-out your lamp to guide me I wan-der from the
3 O God, I love your knowl-edge, more pre-cious than pure

just. With-in your words is wis-dom, your teach-ings
way. With-out your laws and pre-cepts I stum-ble
gold. It sat-is-fies like hon-ey, a sweet-ness

un-der-stood are com-fort to my spir-it's need and
in the dark. Your un-der-stand-ings are my hope that
on my tongue. It leads me to sal-va-tion's door where

in the night my so-lace. Your stat-utes are my song.
I may run in free-dom. Your ways are my re-lease.
you have spread your ta-ble. O, lead me to your home.

Although this paraphrase is based on only a small part of Psalm 119, it incorporates many of the synonyms that weave through this extended acrostic psalm celebrating God's Law: commandments, judgments, words, teachings, wisdom, statutes, laws, precepts, understandings, ways.

TEXT: Jean Janzen, 1991, alt.
MUSIC: Heinrich Schütz, 1661
Text © 1991 Jean Janzen

WOHL DENEN, DIE DA WANDELN
7.6.7.6.8.7.6

Guide Me, O Thou Great Jehovah 65

1 Guide me, O thou great Je - ho - vah, pil - grim through this
2 O - pen now the crys - tal foun - tain, whence the heal - ing
3 When I tread the verge of Jor - dan, bid my anx - ious

bar - ren land. I am weak, but thou art might - y. Hold me
stream doth flow. Let the fire and cloud - y pil - lar lead me
fears sub - side. Death of death, and hell's de - struc - tion, land me

with thy power - ful hand. Bread of heav - en, bread of heav - en,
all my jour - ney through. Strong de - liv - erer, strong de - liv - erer,
safe on Ca - naan's side. Songs of prais - es, songs of prais - es

feed me till I want no more; feed me till I want no more.
be thou still my strength and shield; be thou still my strength and shield.
I will ev - er give to thee; I will ev - er give to thee.

Few Welsh hymns are as well known or loved as this 18th-century text that did not gain its popular tune until the early 20th century. In both its original text and in English translation, it is a stirring hymn of pilgrimage filled with vivid imagery from Hebrew Scripture.

TEXT: William Williams, 1762; stanza 1, trans. Peter Williams, 1771; stanzas 2–3, trans. William Williams, 1772
MUSIC: John Hughes, 1907

CWM RHONDDA
8.7.8.7.8.7.7

66 Every Time I Feel the Spirit

Refrain

Ev - ery time I feel the Spir - it mov - ing in my

heart I will pray. Yes, ev - ery time I feel the

Spir - it mov - ing in my heart I will pray.

Fine

1 Up - on the moun - tain, when my Lord spoke, out of God's
2 Jor - dan Riv - er, chil - ly and cold, it chills the

mouth came fire and smoke. Looked all a - round me, it looked so
bod - y but not the soul. There is but one train up - on this

to Refrain

fine, till I asked my Lord if all was mine.
track. It runs to heav - en and then right back.

Like many African American spirituals, this one mixes the language of biblical narrative with veiled but effective allusions to the hope of escape from slavery, either by crossing rivers into free states or by participating in organized efforts like the Underground Railroad.

TEXT: African American spiritual
MUSIC: African American spiritual; arr. Joseph T. Jones, 20th cent.; adapt. Melva Wilson Costen, 1989
Music Adapt. © 1990 Melva Wilson Costen

PENTECOST
Irregular

My Song Forever Shall Record 67
(Psalm 89)

1 My song for-ev-er shall re-cord the ten-der
2 I sing of mer-cies that en-dure, for-ev-er
3 Al-might-y God, your loft-y throne has jus-tice
4 With bless-ing is the na-tion crowned whose peo-ple

mer-cies of the Lord; your faith-ful love will
firm, for-ev-er sure, a strong sup-port that
for its cor-ner-stone, and shin-ing bright be-
know the joy-ful sound; they in the light, O

I pro-claim, and ev-ery age shall know your name.
nev-er dies, es-tab-lished change-less in the skies.
fore your face are truth and love and bound-less grace.
Lord, shall live, the light your face and fa-vor give.

This abbreviated paraphrase of Psalm 89 passes by the numerous theological and historical details of the
full psalm in order to focus on the sovereignty of God, made known through mercy and steadfast love. God's
people affirm this covenant relationship through joyful worship.

TEXT: *The New Metrical Version of the Psalms*, 1909, alt.
MUSIC: Trier ms., 15th cent.; adapt. Michael Praetorius, 1609; harm. George Ratcliffe Woodward, 1902

PUER NOBIS NASCITUR
LM
(alternate harmonization, 487)

68 Heaven Opened to Isaiah

Holy, Holy, You Are Holy

1 Heav-en o-pened to I-sa-iah, show-ing him God's glo-rious
2 Ser-a-phim con-ti-nue sing-ing; cher-u-bim still lift their
3 One day heav-en will be o-pened and be-fore the Sav-ior's

throne: Lord of might, high and ex-alt-ed, tem-ple flow-ing
praise. Earth and all its crea-tures wor-ship; moon and stars are
throne, saints from ev-ery time and na-tion will be-gin their

with his robe. Ser-a-phim flew all a-round him,
still a-mazed. Now a-bove cre-a-tion's cho-rus
end-less song: "To our God of all sal-va-tion,

hum-bled at the ho-ly sight. As they cir-cled they were
comes an-oth-er fer-vent cry: all of earth's re-deemed are
to the high and ho-ly Lamb, to the bless-ed Ho-ly

This hymn from Rwanda brings together the vision of Isaiah (Isaiah 6:1–3) and its recollection in John's apocalyptic vision of worship in the new Jerusalem (Revelation 4:8; 5:13). The last line of stanza two also suggests the *Gloria in excelsis* (expanded from Luke 2:14).

TEXT: Anon. Rwandan; para. Greg Scheer, 2008
MUSIC: Rwandan melody; arr. Greg Scheer, 2008
Text and Music Arr. © 2008 Greg Scheer

URI UWER' UWER' UWERA
8.7.8.7.D with refrain

sing - ing, call - ing out with all their might.
sing - ing, "Glo - ry to the Lord on high!"
Spir - it be for - ev - er praise. A - men!"

Refrain

"Ho - ly, ho - ly, you are ho - ly," ev - ery

an - gel voice pro - claims; "All the earth re - flects your

glo - ry; ev - ery tongue sings out your praise!"

69 I, the Lord of Sea and Sky

Here I Am, Lord

1 I, the Lord of sea and sky, I have heard my peo-ple cry.
2 I, the Lord of snow and rain, I have borne my peo-ple's pain.
3 I, the Lord of wind and flame, I will tend the poor and lame.

All who dwell in dark and sin my hand will save. I, who
I have wept for love of them. They turn a-way. I will
I will set a feast for them. My hand will save. Fin-est

made the stars of night, I will make their dark-ness bright.
break their hearts of stone, give them hearts for love a-lone.
bread I will pro-vide till their hearts be sat-is-fied.

Who will bear my light to them? Whom shall I send?
I will speak my word to them. Whom shall I send?
I will give my life to them. Whom shall I send?

Refrain

Here I am, Lord. Is it I, Lord? I have heard you

call-ing in the night. I will go, Lord, if you

lead me. I will hold your peo-ple in my heart.

The stanzas here need to be understood as representing the voice of God, while the refrain (based on Isaiah 6:8) is the faithful human response to God's call. This becomes clearer if a leader or small group sings the stanzas, with the congregation joining on the refrain.

TEXT: Daniel L. Schutte, 1981, alt.
MUSIC: Daniel L. Schutte, 1981; harm. Alfred V. Fedak, 2011
Text and Music © 1981, 2000 OCP

HERE I AM (Schutte)
7.7.7.4.D with refrain

What Does the Lord Require of You? 70

*The three melodic phrases may be sung consecutively, as a canon, or in any combination.

This text is a very slight paraphrase of the latter part of Micah 6:8. That verse sums up in a single sentence the legal, ethical, and covenantal requirements of religion. The intertwining of these commitments can be suggested by singing these phrases in an overlapping canon.

TEXT and MUSIC: Jim Strathdee, 1986
Text and Music © 1986 Desert Flower Music

MOON
Irregular

71 Surely, It Is God Who Saves Me

Refrain

Sure-ly, it is God who saves me; I will trust and not be a-fraid. For the Lord is my strong-hold and my sure de-fense, and God will be my Sav-ior.

1 There - fore you shall draw wa-ter with re-joic-ing from the springs of sal-va-tion and on that day you shall say, "Give thanks to the Lord and call up-on God's name."

2 Make God's deeds known a-mong the peo-ples; see that they re-mem-ber that the Lord is ex-alt-ed. Sing the prais-es of the Lord,

This text is a slightly altered form of an adaptation of Isaiah 12:2–6 that appears as a canticle for Morning Prayer in the 1979 Book of Common Prayer of the Episcopal Church. This selection is identified there as The First Song of Isaiah, a title that influenced the tune name.

TEXT: The Draft Proposed Book of Common Prayer, 1976, alt.
MUSIC: Jack Noble White, 1976
Music © 1977 Charles Mortimer Guilbert (admin. Church Publishing, Inc.)

FIRST SONG
Irregular

for God has done great things and this is known in all the world.

Leader or All

3 Cry a-loud, in-hab-i-tants of Zi-on; ring out your joy, for the

great one in the midst of you is the Ho-ly One of Is-rael.

By the Babylonian Rivers 72
(Psalm 137)

1 By the Bab-y-lo-nian riv-ers we sat
2 There our cap-tors in de-ri-sion did re-
3 How shall we sing the Lord's song in a

down in grief and wept, hung our harps up-on the
quire of us a song; so we sat with star-ing
strange and bit-ter land; can our voic-es veil the

wil-low, mourned for Zi-on when we slept.
vi-sion, and the days were hard and long.
sor-row? Lord God, hold your ho-ly band.

Babylon is both geographic and symbolic, the city where exiled Jews were taken and any place where people are forced to remain away from what is dear and holy to them. So we sing this paraphrase of Psalm 137 to its doleful minor tune in solidarity with all displaced people.

TEXT: Ewald Bash, 1964
MUSIC: Latvian melody; harm. Geoffrey Laycock, 1971
Text © 1964 American Lutheran Church (admin. Augsburg Fortress)

KAS DZIEDAJA
8.7.8.7

73 When God Delivered Israel

(Psalm 126)

1 When God de-liv-ered Is - rael from bond-age long a - go, they
2 The god-less na-tions round them could not de - ny that power; they
3 O God, re-store our na - tion; come, ir - ri-gate dry souls, that

thought that they were dream-ing, but soon they turned to laugh-ing
cried, "O see this mar - vel!" "God's work," re - plied the peo - ple,
those who sow in sad - ness may reap their sheaves with glad - ness

1, 2

and sang the song of joy, and sang the song of joy.
and so they sang for joy, and so they sang for joy.

3

and sing the song of joy, and sing the song of joy.

This condensed 20th-century paraphrase of Psalm 126 sketches Israel's central identifying narrative, the deliverance from bondage in Egypt, and uses it as a ground of hope for all who are now in distress. The modal tune created for these words gives them weight and urgency.

TEXT: Michael J. Saward, 1973, alt.
MUSIC: Norman L. Warren, 1973
Text and Music © 1973 The Jubilate Group (admin. Hope Publishing Company)

SHEAVES
7.6.7.7.6.6

When God Restored Our Common Life

(Psalm 126)

1 When God re-stored our com-mon life, our hope, our lib-er-
2 We went forth weep-ing, sow-ing seeds in hard, un-yield-ing
3 Great lib-er-at-ing God, we pray for all who are op-

ty, at first it seemed a pass-ing dream, a
soil; with laugh-ing hearts we car-ry home the
pressed. May those who long for what is right with

wak-ing fan-ta-sy; a shock of joy swept
fruit of all our toil. We praise the One who
jus-tice now be blest. We pray for those who

o-ver us, for we had wept so long; the
gave the growth, with voic-es full and strong. The
mourn this day, and all who suf-fer wrong; may

seeds we wa-tered once with tears sprang up in-to a song.
seeds we wa-tered once with tears sprang up in-to a song.
seeds they wa-ter now with tears spring up in-to a song.

Guitar chords do not correspond with keyboard harmony.

This paraphrase brings Psalm 126 to life in two ways: by turning the "they" of the final verses of the psalm to "we," and by adding a prayer for all who still wait for release from oppression. The shape note tune provides just the right balance of gratitude and urgency.

TEXT: Ruth Duck, 1981
MUSIC: U.S.A. folk melody, Lewis's *Beauties of Harmony*, 1828; harm. Erik Routley, 1976
Text © 1992 GIA Publications, Inc.
Music Harm. © 1976 Hinshaw Music, Inc.

RESIGNATION
CMD
(alternate harmonization, 803)
(alternate tune: NOEL)

75 We Give Thanks unto You
Your Love Is Never Ending (Psalm 136)

1 We give thanks un-to you, O God of might,
2 In your wis-dom and love you shaped the skies,
3 You have filled all the skies with glo-ry and light,
4 From of old you have led your peo-ple in faith,
5 You de-liv-ered the ones who called un-to you,
6 You have o-pened the sea and brought your peo-ple through,
7 You re-mem-ber your prom-ise age to age,
8 You give food and life to all liv-ing things,

for your love is nev-er end-ing;

we give thanks un-to you, the God of gods,
you spread out the earth up-on the sea,
the sun for the day and the moon for night,
you have shown your com-pas-sion, strength, and love,

from bond-age to free-dom, you brought them forth,
brought them in-to a land that flows with life,
you show mer-cy on those of low de-gree,
we give thanks un-to you, the God of all,

for your love is nev-er end-ing.

A recurring refrain ends each verse of Psalm 136, so the stanzas of this paraphrase follow that pattern. This feature strongly suggests that this psalm was used in worship, with the narrative of God's mighty deeds sung by a cantor and the congregation responding with the refrain.

TEXT: Marty Haugen, 1987, alt.
MUSIC: Marty Haugen, 1987
Text and Music © 1987 GIA Publications, Inc.

WE GIVE THANKS UNTO YOU
Irregular

Do Not Be Afraid

Refrain

Do not be a-fraid, for I am with you. Cho-sen and be-loved, you are my own. Do not be a-fraid, for I have re-deemed you: by your name I called you for my own.

Leader or All

1. Look up, a new thing I am do-ing;
2. I am God, who blots out your trans-gres-sions;
3. The Lord, the Ho-ly One of Is-rael

it springs forth; look and see it grow.
for my own sake I do not chide or blame.
has prom-ised to lead us on our way,

Through wil-der-ness I'll make a lev-el high-way;
On-ly this much I ask, that you love me
and we who love and wor-ship God our Mak-er

to Refrain

through des-erts, make streams and riv-ers flow.
and seek me and hon-or my name.
will lis-ten to hear the Spir-it say:

Several verses from Isaiah 43 are paraphrased here: 1b (refrain), 19 (stanza 1), 25 (stanza 2). That prophetic oracle of salvation is rooted in the assurance of God's presence with the People of the Covenant. They, in turn, are called to seek God's will and proclaim God's power.

TEXT: Joy F. Patterson, 2004
MUSIC: Sally Ann Morris, 2008
Text and Music © 2009 GIA Publications, Inc.

ISAIAH 43
Irregular

77 Isaiah the Prophet Has Written of Old

1 I - sa - iah the proph - et has writ - ten of old how
2 Yet na - tions still prey on the meek of the world, and

God's new cre - a - tion shall come. In - stead of the thorn tree, the
con - flict turns par - ent from child. Your peo - ple de - spoil all the

fir tree shall grow; the wolf shall lie down with the lamb. The
sweet - ness of earth; the briar and the thorn tree grow wild. God,

moun - tains and hills shall burst forth in - to song, the
bring to fru - i - tion your will for the earth, that

This 20th-century paraphrase of Isaiah 11:6–9 and 55:11–13 was created specifically for this anonymous shape note tune (whose name is Hebrew for "listener"). The movement from near rhymes in stanza one to exact rhymes in stanza two reinforces the theme of fulfilled prophecy.

TEXT: Joy F. Patterson, 1982
MUSIC: American folk melody; arr. Robert Shaw and Alice Parker, 1961
Text © 1982 The Hymn Society (admin. Hope Publishing Company)
Music Arr. © 1961, ren. Lawson-Gould Music Publishers, Inc. (admin. Alfred Music Publishing)

SAMANTHRA
11.8.11.8.D

peo-ples be led forth in peace, for the earth shall be filled
no one shall hurt or de-stroy, that wis-dom and jus-

with the knowl-edge of God as the wa-ters cov-er the sea.
tice shall reign in the land and your peo-ple shall go forth in joy.

You Thirsty Ones, Come 78

1 You thirst-y ones, come to the spring! Have you no mon-ey?
2 Why do you work and earn and spend on that which is not
3 This food de-lights and sat-is-fies, the food your God can
4 Re-turn while God may still be found, and call while God will
5 My word like heav-en's snow de-scends; it falls like heav-en's

Come, buy wine and milk; come, buy and eat with-out a
bread? O lis-ten now and come to me; eat what is
give; in-cline your ear and come to me; O hear that
hear; now let the wick-ed quit their ways while yet the
rain; it wa-ters all the thirst-y earth and shall not

price or sum, with-out a price or sum.
good in-stead; eat what is good in-stead.
you may live; O hear that you may live.
Lord is near, while yet the Lord is near.
go in vain, and shall not go in vain.

This text is a paraphrase of Isaiah 55:1–11 and was created by a co-editor of the 1997 Canadian Presbyterian hymnal, *The Book of Praise*. The tune composed for it includes an additional line of music, allowing the final line of text to be repeated, meditated on, and savored.

TEXT: Andrew Donaldson, 1996
MUSIC: James E. Clemens, 2008
Text © 1996 Andrew Donaldson
Music © 2008 James E. Clemens

HEAVEN'S RAIN
CM extended

79 Light Dawns on a Weary World

1 Light dawns on a wea - ry world when eyes be - gin to
2 Love grows in a wea - ry world when hun - gry hearts find
3 Hope blooms in a wea - ry world when crea - tures, once for -

see all peo - ple's dig - ni - ty. Light dawns on a
bread and chil - dren's dreams are fed. Love grows in a
lorn, find wil - der - ness re - born. Hope blooms in a

wea - ry world: the prom - ised day of jus - tice comes.
wea - ry world: the prom - ised feast of plen - ty comes.
wea - ry world: the prom - ised green of E - den comes.

Refrain

The trees shall clap their hands; the dry lands, gush with springs;

the hills and moun - tains shall break forth with sing - ing!

We shall go out in joy, and be led forth in peace,

as all the world in won - der ech - oes *sha - lom.*

This is a hymn whose tune came first. Upon hearing it, the author recalled the watered garden of Isaiah 58:11, which in turn led to Isaiah 55:12, paraphrased in the refrain. Then came the stanzas, organized around their first two words: Light dawns, Love grows, Hope blooms.

TEXT: Mary Louise Bringle, 2001
MUSIC: William P. Rowan, 2000
Text © 2002 GIA Publications, Inc.
Music © 2000 William P. Rowan (admin. GIA Publications, Inc.)

TEMPLE OF PEACE
7.6.6.7.8 with refrain

You Shall Go Out with Joy

80

The Trees of the Field

*Clap hands.

This text paraphrases Isaiah 55:12, which is generally understood to describe a "second exodus," this time from Babylon rather than from Egypt. This release of God's people and their return to their own land gives rise to a joyful celebration involving all creation.

TEXT: Steffi Geiser Rubin, 1975
MUSIC: Stuart Dauermann, 1975
Text and Music © 1975 Lillenas Publishing Co. (admin. Music Services)

THE TREES OF THE FIELD
Irregular

81 Glorious Things of Thee Are Spoken

1 Glo - rious things of thee are spo - ken, Zi - on, cit - y of our God.
2 Round each hab - i - ta - tion hov - ering, see the cloud and fire ap - pear
3 See, the streams of liv - ing wa - ters, spring-ing from e - ter - nal love,

God, whose word can - not be bro - ken, formed thee for a blest a - bode.
for a glo - ry and a cov - ering, show-ing that the Lord is near.
well sup - ply thy sons and daugh-ters and all fear of want re-move.

On the rock of a - ges found-ed, what can shake thy sure re - pose?
Thus de - riv - ing from their ban - ner light by night and shade by day,
Who can faint while such a riv - er ev - er flows, their thirst to as-suage?

With sal - va - tion's walls sur-round-ed, thou may'st smile at all thy foes.
safe they feed up - on the man - na which God gives them when they pray.
Grace, so like the Lord the giv - er, nev - er fails from age to age.

The Nazi appropriation of this tune for propaganda purposes has clouded a noble piece of music first associated with this text in 1889. In a 1779 collection, the author indicated that this hymn is primarily based on Isaiah 33:20–21 with allusions to several other passages.

TEXT: John Newton, 1775, alt.
MUSIC: Franz Joseph Haydn, 1797, alt.

AUSTRIAN HYMN
8.7.8.7.D

Come, Thou Long-Expected Jesus 82

1 Come, thou long - ex - pect-ed Je - sus, born to set thy peo-ple free;
2 Born thy peo - ple to de - liv - er, born a child and yet a king,

from our fears and sins re - lease us; let us find our rest in thee.
born to reign in us for - ev - er, now thy gra-cious king-dom bring.

Is-rael's strength and con - so - la - tion, hope of all the earth thou art;
By thine own e - ter - nal Spir - it rule in all our hearts a - lone;

dear de - sire of ev - ery na - tion, joy of ev - ery long-ing heart.
by thine all - suf - fi - cient mer - it raise us to thy glo-rious throne.

With its opening "Come," this hymn sounds the note of entreaty and invitation that characterizes the Advent season (from the Latin *adventus* = "coming"). Its blending of memory and hope helps us to give voice to our present faith as we stand between the past and the future.

TEXT: Charles Wesley, 1744
MUSIC: Rowland Hugh Prichard, 1830; harm. Ralph Vaughan Williams, 1906

HYFRYDOL
8.7.8.7.D
(alternate tune: STUTTGART, 83)

83 Come, Thou Long-Expected Jesus

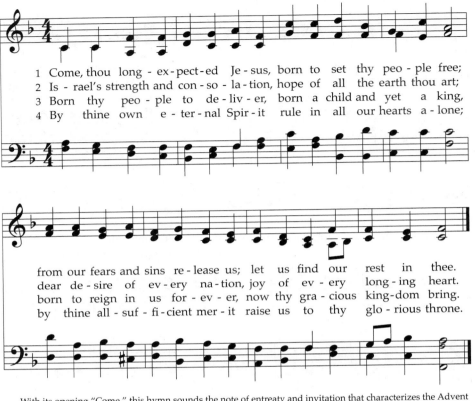

1 Come, thou long-ex-pect-ed Je-sus, born to set thy peo-ple free;
2 Is-rael's strength and con-so-la-tion, hope of all the earth thou art;
3 Born thy peo-ple to de-liv-er, born a child and yet a king,
4 By thine own e-ter-nal Spir-it rule in all our hearts a-lone;

from our fears and sins re-lease us; let us find our rest in thee.
dear de-sire of ev-ery na-tion, joy of ev-ery long-ing heart.
born to reign in us for-ev-er, now thy gra-cious king-dom bring.
by thine all-suf-fi-cient mer-it raise us to thy glo-rious throne.

With its opening "Come," this hymn sounds the note of entreaty and invitation that characterizes the Advent season (from the Latin *adventus* = "coming"). Its blending of memory and hope helps us to give voice to our present faith as we stand between the past and the future.

TEXT: Charles Wesley, 1744
MUSIC: Witt's *Psalmodia Sacra*, 1715, alt.

STUTTGART
8.7.8.7
(alternate tune: HYFRYDOL, 82)

84 Creator of the Stars of Night

1 Cre-a-tor of the stars of night, your peo-ple's ev-er-
2 When this old world drew on toward night, you came; but not in
3 At your great name, O Je-sus, now all knees must bend, all
4 To God the Fa-ther, God the Son, and God the Spir-it,

The Latin original of this text for Advent dates from at least the 9th century, and the English version was created a millennium later as part of the 19th-century recovery of early Christian hymns. It is provided here with its traditional plainchant setting.

TEXT: Latin hymn, 9th cent.; trans. John Mason Neale, 1851; as in *The Hymnal 1940*, alt.
MUSIC: Sarum plainsong, Mode IV, 9th cent.; harm. Alfred V. Fedak, 2011
Text Alt. © 1940 Church Pension Fund
Music Harm. © 2011 Alfred V. Fedak

CONDITOR ALME SIDERUM
LM
(alternate harmonization, 671)
(alternate tune: PUER NOBIS NASCITUR)

last - ing light, O Christ, re - deem - er of us all,
splen - dor bright, not as a mon - arch, but the child
hearts must bow: all things on earth with one ac - cord,
Three in One, praise, hon - or, might, and glo - ry be

we pray you, hear us when we call.
of Mar - y, blame - less moth - er mild.
like those in heaven, shall call you Lord.
from age to age e - ter - nal - ly. A - men.

Light One Candle to Watch for Messiah 85

1 Light one can - dle to watch for Mes - si - ah: let the
2 Light two can - dles to watch for Mes - si - ah: let the
3 Light three can - dles to watch for Mes - si - ah: let the
4 Light four can - dles to watch for Mes - si - ah: let the

light ban - ish dark - ness. He shall bring sal -
light ban - ish dark - ness. He shall feed the
light ban - ish dark - ness. Lift your heads and
light ban - ish dark - ness. He is com - ing;

va - tion to Is - rael, God ful - fills the prom - ise.
flock like a shep - herd, gent - ly lead them home - ward.
lift high the gate - way for the King of glo - ry.
tell the glad ti - dings. Let your lights be shin - ing.

This text works best when used incrementally during the four weeks of Advent. It underscores the "waiting" theme of the season and concludes appropriately with reference to Matthew 25:1–13. The tune name meaning "deep in the forest" comes from the opening of a Yiddish love song.

TEXT: Wayne L. Wold, 1984
MUSIC: Yiddish folk song; arr. Wayne L. Wold, 1984
Text and Music Arr. © 1984 Fortress Press (admin. Augsburg Fortress)

TIF IN VELDELE
10.7.9.6

86 The People Who Walked in Darkness

Capo 3: (Em) (C/E) (Em) (C/E) (Em)

1 The peo - ple who walked in dark - ness a - wak - en to
2 For God has en - larged the na - tion, and pros - pered the
3 The yoke of de - spair and bond - age, the chains of the
4 For us now a child is giv - en, for all the de -
5 How vast is our God's do - min - ion! How far truth and

see a great light. The peo - ple who dwelt in the
fruit of its land. God's peo - ple are blest with the
slave mas - ter's rod are shat - tered and scat - tered like
spised and for - lorn. The rule of com - pas - sion shall
mer - cy ex - tend. The zeal of the Lord will ac -

land of the shad - ow rise to a star shin - ing bright.
har - vest of vic - tory, gift from a boun - ti - ful hand.
dust in a wind-storm, loosed by the jus - tice of God.
rest on his shoul - der. God's own Mes - si - ah is born!
com - plish its pur - pose: jus - tice shall reign with - out end.

Refrain

His name is Won - der - ful, Coun - sel - or, Al - might - y God,

Fa - ther for - ev - er, Prince of Peace.

Peace. *(to stanzas)* Peace.

One of the great virtues of scriptural paraphrases is that they bring fresh understanding and appreciation to familiar passages. This adaptation of a customary Advent text, Isaiah 9:2–7, provides an effective example of how revisited verses can take on new life when recast.

TEXT: Mary Louise Bringle, 2008
MUSIC: Sally Ann Morris, 2008
Text and Music © 2009 GIA Publications, Inc.

ISAIAH 9
8.8.12.7 with refrain

Comfort, Comfort Now My People 87

1 "Com - fort, com - fort now my peo - ple; tell of peace!" So says our God.
2 For the her - ald's voice is cry - ing in the des - ert far and near,
3 Straight shall be what long was crook - ed, and the rough - er plac - es plain.

"Com - fort those who sit in dark - ness mourn - ing un - der sor - row's load.
call - ing us to true re - pen - tance, since the reign of God is here.
Let your hearts be true and hum - ble, as be - fits God's ho - ly reign.

To my peo - ple now pro - claim that my par - don waits for them!
O, that warn - ing cry o - bey! Now pre - pare for God a way.
For the glo - ry of the Lord now on earth is shed a - broad,

Tell them that their sins I cov - er, and their war - fare now is o - ver."
Let the val - leys rise in meet - ing and the hills bow down in greet - ing.
and all flesh shall see the to - ken that God's word is nev - er bro - ken.

This 17th-century German paraphrase of Isaiah 40:1–5 was one of the texts translated as part of the 19th-century British interest in German religious poetry. It is set here to one of the most popular Genevan Psalter tunes, probably derived from an earlier French folksong.

TEXT: Johannes Olearius, 1671; trans. Catherine Winkworth, 1863, alt.
MUSIC: Genevan Psalter, 1551

GENEVAN 42
8.7.8.7.7.7.8.8

88 O Come, O Come, Emmanuel

1 O come, O come, Em - man - u - el, and ran - som
2 O come, thou Wis - dom from on high, who or - derest
3 O come, O come, thou Lord of might, who to thy
4 O come, thou Root of Jes - se, free thine own from

cap - tive Is - ra - el, that mourns in lone - ly ex - ile
all things might - i - ly: to us the path of knowl - edge
tribes on Si - nai's height in an - cient times didst give the
Sa - tan's tyr - an - ny; from depths of hell thy peo - ple

here un - til the Son of God ap - pear.
show; and teach us in her ways to go.
law in cloud and maj - es - ty and awe.
save and give them vic - tory o'er the grave.

Re - joice! Re - joice!

Em - man - u - el shall come to thee, O Is - ra - el.

5 O come, thou Key of David, come,
and open wide our heavenly home;
make safe the way that leads on high,
and close the path to misery.
Rejoice! Rejoice! Emmanuel
shall come to thee, O Israel.

6 O come, thou Dayspring, come and cheer
our spirits by thine advent here;
disperse the gloomy clouds of night,
and death's dark shadows put to flight.
Rejoice! Rejoice! Emmanuel
shall come to thee, O Israel.

7 O come, Desire of nations, bind
all peoples in one heart and mind;
bid envy, strife, and discord cease;
fill the whole world with heaven's peace.
Rejoice! Rejoice! Emmanuel
shall come to thee, O Israel.

One stanza of this paraphrase of the great O Antiphons may be sung on each of the last days of Advent as follows:

Dec. 17: O Wisdom (2)   *Dec. 20: O Key of David (5)*   *Dec. 23: O Emmanuel (1)*
Dec. 18: O Lord of might (3)   *Dec. 21: O Dayspring (6)*
Dec. 19: O Root of Jesse (4)   *Dec. 22: O Desire of Nations (7)*

These titles of the coming Christ appeared in daily Vesper antiphons sung during the week before Christmas;
their roots date at least to the reign of Charlemagne. Both text and tune are the fruit of 19th-century efforts to
reclaim Christian treasures from pre-Reformation sources.

TEXT: Latin prose, pre-9th cent.; trans. composite
MUSIC: Plainsong; adapt. Thomas Helmore, 1852; arr. John Weaver, 1988
Music Arr. © 1990 John Weaver

VENI EMMANUEL
LM with refrain

For You, O Lord, My Soul in Stillness Waits

89

My Soul in Stillness Waits

For you, O Lord, my soul in still-ness waits; tru-ly my hope is in you.

1 O Lord of Light, our on-ly hope of glo - ry,
2 O Spring of Joy, rain down up-on our spir - its;
3 O Root of Life, im - plant your seed with - in us,
4 O Key of Knowl-edge, guide us in our pil - grim-age;
5 Come, let us bow be - fore the God who made us;
6 Here we shall meet the Mak-er of the heav - ens,

your ra-diance shines in all who look to you; come, light the
our thirst-y hearts are yearn - ing for your word; come, make us
and in your ad - vent, draw us all to you, our hope re -
we ev - er seek, yet un - ful-filled re - main; o - pen to
let ev - ery heart be o - pened to the Lord, for we are
Cre - a - tor of the moun-tains and the seas, Lord of the

hearts of all in dark and shad - ow.
whole, be com - fort to our hearts.
born in dy - ing and in ris - ing.

us the path-way of your peace.
all the peo - ple of God's hand.
stars, and pres - ent to us now.

With a paraphrase of Psalm 62:5 as a refrain, this Advent text adapts four of the "Great O" antiphons (all of which can be seen in no. 88), combining them with a paraphrase of Psalm 95:6–7 and an echo of a medieval hymn. This rich blend yields a wealth of imagery and meaning.

TEXT and MUSIC: Marty Haugen, 1982
Text and Music © 1982 GIA Publications, Inc.

MY SOUL IN STILLNESS WAITS
Irregular

90

Wait for the Lord
(Psalm 27)

Refrain

Wait for the Lord, whose day is near.

Wait for the Lord; be strong; take heart!

PSALM 27

Refrain

1 The LORD is my light and my salvation;
whom then shall I fear?
    the LORD is the strength of my life;
    of whom then shall I be afraid?

2 **When evildoers came upon me to eat up my flesh,**
    it was they, my foes and my adversaries, who stumbled and fell.

3 Though an army should encamp against me,
yet my heart shall not be afraid;

    and though war should rise up against me,
    yet will I put my trust in the LORD.

4 One thing have I asked of the LORD;
one thing I seek;
    that I may dwell in the house of the LORD all the days of my life;

    to behold the fair beauty of the LORD,
    to seek God in the temple. *Refrain*

5 For on the day of trouble the LORD shall shelter me in safety;
    the LORD shall hide me in the secrecy of the holy place
    and set me high upon a rock.

6 **Even now the LORD lifts up my head**
    above my enemies round about me.

    Therefore I will offer in the holy place an oblation
    with sounds of great gladness;
    I will sing and make music to the LORD. *Refrain*

The refrain for this psalm, drawn from Psalm 27:14, comes from the ecumenical Community of Taizé in France and is most effective when sung in parts. With repeated singing, it can also be used by itself as a contemplative prayer and is especially appropriate in Advent.

TEXT Ref. Taizé Community, 1984
MUSIC: Jacques Berthier, 1984
Text and Music © 1984 Les Presses de Taizé (admin. GIA Publications, Inc.)
Responsive Reading © 1993 the Order of St. Benedict (admin. The Liturgical Press)

WAIT FOR THE LORD
8.8

7 Hearken to my voice, O L<small>ORD</small>, when I call;
   have mercy on me and answer me.

8 **You speak in my heart and say, "Seek my face."**
   Your face, L<small>ORD</small>, will I seek.

9 Hide not your face from me,
   nor turn away your servant in displeasure.

   You have been my helper;
   cast me not away;
   do not forsake me, O God of my salvation.

10 Though my father and my mother forsake me,
   the L<small>ORD</small> will sustain me.   *Refrain*

11 Show me your way, O L<small>ORD</small>;
   lead me on a level path, because of my enemies.

12 **Deliver me not into the hand of my adversaries,**
   for false witnesses have risen up against me,
   and also those who speak malice.

13 What if I had not believed
   that I should see the goodness of the L<small>ORD</small>
   in the land of the living!

14 **O tarry and await the L<small>ORD</small>'s pleasure;**
   be strong, and the L<small>ORD</small> shall comfort your heart;
   wait patiently for the L<small>ORD</small>.   *Refrain*

Come, Come Emmanuel   91

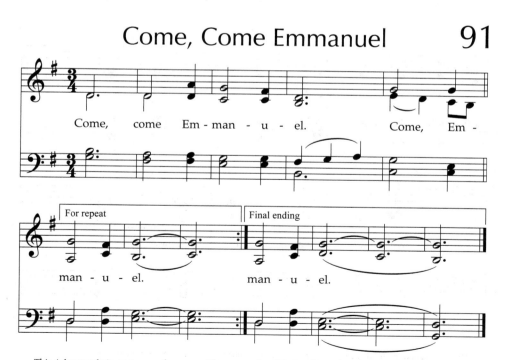

This Advent refrain centers on the name of Jesus meaning "God with us" (Matthew 1:23, quoting Isaiah 7:14). Intended for repeated congregational singing, it can be expanded by the addition of stanzas sung by a soloist or choir, or it can serve effectively as a prayer response.

TEXT and MUSIC: James J. Chepponis, 1995
Text and Music © 1995 GIA Publications, Inc.

COME, COME EMMANUEL
6.5

92 While We Are Waiting, Come

1 While we are wait - ing, come;
2 With power and glo - ry, come;
3 Come, Sav - ior, quick - ly come;

while we are wait - ing, come.
with power and glo - ry, come.
come, Sav - ior, quick - ly come.

Je - sus, our Lord, Em - man - u - el,

while we are wait - ing, come.

This simple and meditative Advent hymn is so uncomplicated in both text and tune that it can be learned quickly and sung without reference to a book, which might make it effective as a prayer response. It would also lend itself to improvised stanzas on appropriate occasions.

TEXT: Claire Cloninger, 1986
MUSIC: Don Cason, 1986
Text and Music © 1986 Word Music, LLC

WAITING (Cason)
SM

Lift Up Your Heads, Ye Mighty Gates 93

1 Lift up your heads, ye might-y gates; be-hold the
2 Fling wide the por-tals of your heart; make it a
3 Re-deem-er, come! I o-pen wide my heart to

King of glo-ry waits; the King of kings is
tem-ple, set a-part from earth-ly use for
thee; here, Lord, a-bide. Let me thy in-ner

draw-ing near; the Sav-ior of the world is here.
heaven's em-ploy, a-dorned with prayer and love and joy.
pres-ence feel; thy grace and love in me re-veal.

Beginning as a paraphrase of Psalm 24:7–10, this text then applies the door imagery to the singer's heart, and concludes with the individual's welcome of the approaching Savior. It is set to a very effective anonymous 18th-century English tune that has served many texts.

TEXT: Georg Weissel, 1642; trans. Catherine Winkworth, 1855, 1863
MUSIC: *Musica Sacra*, c. 1778

TRURO
LM

94 Now the Heavens Start to Whisper

1 Now the heav-ens start to whis-per, as the veil is
2 Heav-y clouds that block the moon-light now be-gin to
3 Christ, e-ter-nal Sun of jus-tice, Christ, the rose of

grow-ing thin. Earth from slum-ber wakes to lis-ten
drift a-way. Dia-mond bril-liance through the dark-ness
wis-dom's seed, come to bless with fire and fra-grance

to the stir-ring, faint with-in: seed of prom-ise, deep-ly
shines the hope of com-ing day. Christ, the morn-ing star of
hours of yearn-ing, hurt, and need. In the lone-ly, in the

This Advent text artfully interweaves what is hidden and what is revealed, primarily in the coming of the long-awaited Messiah. But Christ himself taught us about another hidden truth, his presence in the "least of these" (Matthew 25:40, 45), whom we are also called to welcome.

TEXT: Mary Louise Bringle, 2005
MUSIC: Alexander Johnson's *Tennessee Harmony*, 1818; harm. *Lutheran Book of Worship*, 1978
Text © 2006 GIA Publications, Inc.
Music Harm. © 1978 Lutheran Book of Worship (admin. Augsburg Fortress)

JEFFERSON
8.7.8.7.D

plant - ed, child   to spring from Jes - se's   stem! Like the   soil be -
splen - dor, gleams with - in   a   world grown dim. Heav - en's   em - ber
strang - er,   in   the out - cast, hid   from   view: child who comes to

neath the   frost - line,   hearts grow soft   to   wel - come him.
fans   to   full - ness;   hearts grow warm   to   wel - come him.
grace the   man - ger,   teach   our   hearts   to   wel - come you.

Prepare the Way of the Lord   95

Capo 1: (D)   (G)   (D)

Pre - pare   the way of the Lord.   Pre - pare   the way of the Lord,

and   all   peo - ple will see   the   sal - va - tion of   our   God.

May be sung as a canon.

All three synoptic gospels identify John the Baptist as the forerunner of the Messiah (Matthew 3:3 / Mark 1:2–3 / Luke 3:4) in accord with Isaiah's prophecy (Isaiah 40:3b). Because the latter part of the text (Isaiah 52:10b) has yet to be accomplished, this is still our mission today.

TEXT: Taizé Community, 1984
MUSIC: Jacques Berthier, 1984
Text and Music © 1984 Les Presses de Taizé (admin. GIA Publications, Inc.)

PREPARE THE WAY
7.7.6.7

96 On Jordan's Bank the Baptist's Cry

1 On Jor - dan's bank the Bap - tist's cry an -
2 Then cleansed be ev - ery life from sin; make
3 We hail you as our Sav - ior, Lord, our
4 Stretch forth your hand; our health re - store, and

nounc - es that the Lord is nigh; a - wake and heark - en,
straight the way for God with - in, and let us all our
ref - uge and our great re - ward; with - out your grace we
make us rise to fall no more. O let your face up -

for he brings glad ti - dings of the King of kings!
hearts pre - pare for Christ to come and en - ter there.
waste a - way like flowers that with - er and de - cay.
on us shine and fill the world with love di - vine.

This hymn shows how once-unconnected parts can work together. The text about John the Baptist was written in Latin in the 18th century and translated into English in the 19th century. Similarly, the 17th-century melody was adapted to its present form in the 19th century.

TEXT: Charles Coffin, 1736; trans. John Chandler, 1837, alt.
MUSIC: *Musikalisches Handbuch*, 1690; harm. William Henry Monk, 1847, alt.

WINCHESTER NEW
LM
(alternate tune: PUER NOBIS NASCITUR)

Watchman, Tell Us of the Night 97

1 Watch-man, tell us of the night, what its signs of prom-ise are.
2 Watch-man, tell us of the night; high-er yet that star as-cends.
3 Watch-man, tell us of the night, for the morn-ing seems to dawn.

Trav-eler, what a won-drous sight: see that glo-ry-beam-ing star.
Trav-eler, bless-ed-ness and light, peace and truth its course por-tends.
Trav-eler, shad-ows take their flight; doubt and ter-ror are with-drawn.

Watch-man, does its beau-teous ray news of joy or hope fore-tell?
Watch-man, will its beams a-lone gild the spot that gave them birth?
Watch-man, you may go your way; has-ten to your qui-et home.

Trav-eler, yes; it brings the day, prom-ised day of Is-ra-el.
Trav-eler, a-ges are its own; see, it bursts o'er all the earth.
Trav-eler, we re-joice to-day, for Em-man-u-el has come!

May be sung antiphonally.

This unusual dialogue hymn alternates between the voice of a traveler and that of a watchman, setting up an exchange that creates parallels between the coming of dawn and the birth of Christ. The tune is named for a Welsh town whose name means "mouth of the bending river."

TEXT: John Bowring, 1825, alt.
MUSIC: Joseph Parry, 1876

ABERYSTWYTH
7.7.7.7.D

98 To a Maid Whose Name Was Mary

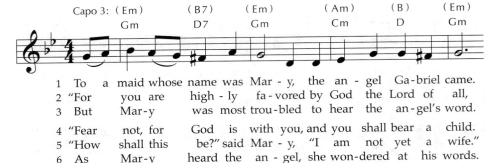

1 To a maid whose name was Mar - y, the an - gel Ga - briel came.
2 "For you are high - ly fa - vored by God the Lord of all,
3 But Mar - y was most trou - bled to hear the an - gel's word.

4 "Fear not, for God is with you, and you shall bear a child.
5 "How shall this be?" said Mar - y, "I am not yet a wife."
6 As Mar - y heard the an - gel, she won - dered at his words.

"Fear not," the an - gel told her, "I come to bring good news;
who e - ven now is with you. You are on earth most blest;
What was the an - gel say - ing? It trou - bled her to hear,

His name shall be called Je - sus, God's off - spring from on high.
The an - gel an - swered quick - ly, "The power of the Most High
"Be - hold, I am your hand - maid," she said un - to her God.

good news I come to tell you, good news, I say, good news."
you are most blest, most bless - ed; God chose you, you are blest!"
to hear the an - gel's mes - sage, it trou - bled her to hear.

And he shall reign for - ev - er, for - ev - er reign on high."
will come up - on you short - ly, your child shall be God's child."
"So be it; I am read - y ac - cord - ing to your word."

Guitar chords do not correspond with keyboard harmony.

This 20th-century ballad-like retelling of the Annunciation (Luke 1:26–38) displays many characteristics of a folksong style, especially repetition in both text and tune and short quotations included in the narrative. Such features help to make a song both memorable and singable.

TEXT: Gracia Grindal, 1982, alt.
MUSIC: Rusty Edwards, 1982
Text and Music © 1984 Hope Publishing Company

ANNUNCIATION
7.6.7.6.7.6

My Soul Gives Glory to My God 99
Song of Mary

1 My soul gives glo - ry to my God; my
2 My God has done great things for me: yes,
3 From age to age to all who fear, such
4 Love casts the might - y from their thrones, pro -
5 Praise God, whose lov - ing cov - e - nant sup -

heart pours out its praise. God lift - ed up my
ho - ly is God's name. All peo - ple will de -
mer - cy love im - parts, dis - pens - ing jus - tice
motes the in - se - cure, leaves hun - gry spir - its
ports those in dis - tress, re - mem - ber - ing past

low - li - ness in man - y mar - vel - ous ways.
clare me blessed, and bless - ings they shall claim.
far and near, dis - miss - ing self - ish hearts.
sat - is - fied; the rich seem sud - den - ly poor.
prom - is - es with pres - ent faith - ful - ness.

This 20th-century paraphrase is based on the Song of Mary (Luke 1:46–55), commonly known by its opening Latin word, *Magnificat*. This song of praise offers clear reminders that God's purposes often lead to the reversal of human values, exalting the poor and dethroning the mighty.

TEXT: Miriam Therese Winter, 1979; rev. 1987
MUSIC: Wyeth's *Repository of Sacred Music*, 1813; harm. C. Winfred Douglas, 1940
Text © 1978, 1987 Medical Mission Sisters
Music Harm. © 1943, 1961, 1985 Church Pension Fund

MORNING SONG
CM

100 My Soul Cries Out with a Joyful Shout

Canticle of the Turning

1 My soul cries out with a joy - ful shout that the
2 Though I am small, my God, my all, you
3 From the halls of power to the for - tress tower, not a
4 Though the na - tions rage from age to age, we re -

God of my heart is great, and my spir - it sings of the
work great things in me, and your mer - cy will last from the
stone will be left on stone. Let the king be - ware for your
mem - ber who holds us fast: God's mer - cy must de -

won - drous things that you bring to the ones who wait.
depths of the past to the end of the age to be.
jus - tice tears ev - ery ty - rant from his throne.
liv - er us from the con - quer-or's crush - ing grasp.

You fixed your sight on your ser - vant's plight, and my
Your ver - y name puts the proud to shame, and to
The hun - gry poor shall weep no more, for the
This sav - ing word that our fore - bears heard is the

weak - ness you did not spurn, so from east to west shall my
those who would for you yearn, you will show your might, put the
food they can nev - er earn; there are ta - bles spread; ev - ery
prom - ise which holds us bound, till the spear and rod can be

By employing an energetic Irish folk song for its melody, this ballad-like paraphrase of the *Magnificat*, Mary's song at her meeting with her relative Elizabeth (Luke 1:46–55), recaptures both the wonder and the faith of the young woman who first recognized what God was doing.

TEXT: Rory Cooney, 1990
MUSIC: Irish melody; arr. Rory Cooney, 1990
Text and Music Arr. © 1990 GIA Publications, Inc.

STAR OF THE COUNTY DOWN
Irregular

name   be   blest. Could the world be   a - bout   to   turn?
strong   to   flight, for the world   is   a - bout   to   turn.
mouth   be   fed,   for the world   is   a - bout   to   turn.
crushed   by   God,   who is   turn - ing the world   a - round.

Refrain

My   heart   shall   sing   of   the   day   you   bring. Let the

fires   of   your   jus - tice   burn.   Wipe a - way   all   tears,   for the

dawn   draws near,   and the world   is   a - bout   to   turn.

101 No Wind at the Window

1 No wind at the win-dow, no knock on the door;
2 "O Mar-y, O Mar-y, don't hide from my face.
3 "This child must be born that the king-dom might come:
4 No pay-ment was prom-ised, no prom-is-es made;

no light from the lamp-stand, no foot on the floor;
Be glad that you're fa-vored and filled with God's grace.
sal - va-tion for man-y, de - struc-tion for some;
no wed-ding was dat-ed, no blue-print dis-played.

no dream born of tired-ness, no ghost raised by fear:
The time for re - deem-ing the world has be - gun,
both end and be - gin-ning, both mes-sage and sign;
Yet Mar-y, con - sent-ing to what none could guess,

just an an - gel and a wom-an and a voice in her ear.
and you are re - quest-ed to moth - er God's Son."
both vic - tor and vic - tim, both yours and di - vine."
re - plied with con - vic - tion, "Tell God I say, Yes."

This 20th-century retelling of the Annunciation (Luke 1:26–38) effectively incorporates characteristic features of the folksong style its Irish tune requires, especially in the lists of "no" and "both." The tune is named for a many-talented Irish saint of the 6th century.

TEXT: John L. Bell, 1992
MUSIC: Irish melody; arr. John L. Bell, 1992
Text and Music © 1992 WGRG, Iona Community (admin. GIA Publications, Inc.)

COLUMCILLE
11.11.11.11

Savior of the Nations, Come   102

1 Savior of the nations, come; virgin's son, make here your home. Marvel now, O heaven and earth, that the Lord chose such a birth.

2 From God's heart the Savior speeds; back to God his pathway leads; out to vanquish death's command, back to reign at God's right hand.

3 Now your manger, shining bright, hallows night with newborn light. Night cannot this light subdue; let our faith shine ever new.

4 Praise we sing to Christ the Lord, virgin's son, incarnate Word! To the holy Trinity praise we sing eternally.

Though some hymns attributed to Ambrose are doubtful, this one seems rather surely to be by him. Luther's German version (commemorated in the tune name) dropped one syllable from each line of the Latin text, giving the hymn its characteristically declarative Lutheran form.

TEXT: Attr. Ambrose of Milan, 4th cent.; German para. Martin Luther, 1523;
English trans. stanza 1, William Morton Reynolds, 1850, alt.;
English trans. stanzas 2–4, *Evangelical Lutheran Worship*, 2006
MUSIC: Erfurt *Enchiridion*, 1524; harm. Sethus Calvisius, 1594
English Trans. Sts. 2-4 © 2006 Augsburg Fortress

NUN KOMM, DER HEIDEN HEILAND
7.7.7.7

103 Come Now, O Prince of Peace

오소서

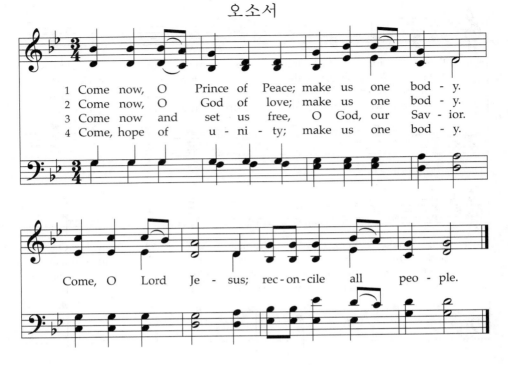

1 Come now, O Prince of Peace; make us one bod - y.
2 Come now, O God of love; make us one bod - y.
3 Come now and set us free, O God, our Sav - ior.
4 Come, hope of u - ni - ty; make us one bod - y.

Come, O Lord Je - sus; rec - on - cile all peo - ple.

KOREAN

1 오소서 오소서 평화의 임금
  우리가 한몸 이루게 하소서

2 오소서 오소서 사랑의 임금
  우리가 한몸 이루게 하소서

3 오소서 오소서 자유의 임금
  우리가 한몸 이루게 하소서

4 오소서 오소서 통일의 임금
  우리가 한몸 이루게 하소서

Originally created for a 1988 world conference for the peace and reunification of the Korean peninsula, these four stanzas centering on peace, love, freedom, and unity demonstrate how texts for particular situations can become hymns that speak deeply to shared human longings.

TEXT: Geonyong Lee, 1988; English trans. Marion Pope, c. 1990
MUSIC: Geonyong Lee, 1988
Text and Music © 1988 Geonyong Lee

O-SO-SO
6.5.5.6

O Lord, How Shall I Meet You 104

1 O Lord, how shall I meet you, how wel-come you a-right?
2 Love caused your in - car - na - tion; love brought you down to me;
3 You come, O Lord, with glad - ness, in mer - cy and good-will,

Your peo - ple long to greet you, my hope, my heart's de - light!
your thirst for my sal - va - tion pro-cured my lib - er - ty.
to bring an end to sad - ness and bid our fears be still.

O kin - dle, Lord most ho - ly, a lamp with - in my breast,
O love be-yond all tell - ing, that led you to em - brace
In pa - tient ex - pec - ta - tion we live for that great day

to do in spir - it low - ly all that may please you best.
in love, all loves ex - cel - ling, our lost and fal - len race.
when your re-newed cre - a - tion your glo - ry shall dis - play.

Though many Advent hymns address Christ with entreaty and invitation, this more contemplative text considers how an individual prepares for and responds to Christ's coming. It also brings together a recollection of the First Coming with an anticipation of the Second Coming.

TEXT: Paul Gerhardt, 1653; trans. Catherine Winkworth and others, 1863, alt.
MUSIC: Melchior Teschner, 1614; harm. William Henry Monk, 1861

VALET WILL ICH DIR GEBEN
7.6.7.6.D

105 People, Look East

1 Peo - ple, look east. The time is near of the
2 Fur - rows, be glad. Though earth is bare, one more
3 Birds, though you long have ceased to build, guard the
4 Stars, keep the watch. When night is dim one more
5 An - gels, an-nounce with shouts of mirth Christ who

crown - ing of the year. Make your house fair as you are
seed is plant - ed there. Give up your strength the seed to
nest that must be filled. E - ven the hour when wings are
light the bowl shall brim, shin - ing be - yond the frost - y
brings new life to earth. Set ev - ery peak and val - ley

Peo - ple, look

a - ble; trim the hearth and set the ta - ble.
nour - ish, that in course the flower may flour - ish.
fro - zen God for fledg - ing time has cho - sen.
weath - er, bright as sun and moon to - geth - er.
hum - ming with the word, the Lord is com - ing.

This text was written to provide a new Advent text for an existing carol tune, here named for the city in
eastern France where it originated. The author has imaginatively expressed the cosmic implications of
Christ's coming by addressing each stanza to a part of creation.

TEXT: Eleanor Farjeon, 1928, alt.
MUSIC: French folk melody; harm. Martin Shaw, 1928
Text © 1960 David Higham Associates, Ltd.
Music Harm. © 1928 Oxford University Press

BESANÇON
8.7.9.8.8.7

east   and sing   to - day:

Peo - ple, look   east:

Love, the Guest, is on the way.
Love, the Rose, is on the way.
Love, the Bird, is on the way.
Love, the Star, is on the way.
Love, the Lord, is on the way.

Peo - ple, look east: (Love is on the way.)

Prepare the Way, O Zion   106

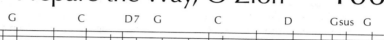

1 Pre - pare the way, O Zi - on, your Christ is draw-ing near!
2 He brings God's rule, O Zi - on; he comes from heaven a - bove.
3 Fling wide your gates, O Zi - on; your Sav - ior's rule em - brace,

Let ev - ery hill and val - ley a lev - el way ap - pear.
His rule is peace and free - dom, and jus - tice, truth, and love.
and ti - dings of sal - va - tion pro-claim in ev - ery place.

Greet One who comes in glo - ry, fore-told in sa - cred sto - ry.
Lift high your praise re-sound - ing, for grace and joy a - bound - ing.
All lands will bow re - joic - ing, their ad - o - ra - tion voic - ing.

Refrain

O blest is Christ who came in God's most ho - ly name.

Guitar chords do not correspond with keyboard harmony.

This engaging Advent text based on Isaiah 40:3–5 and Psalm 24:7–10 has been in use in the Church of Sweden for almost two hundred years. It is set to a version of an even older Swedish tune, which in turn seems to be derived from a German folktune that spread to Scandinavia.

TEXT: Frans Mikael Franzen, 1812; rev. 1819; trans. Augustus Nelson, 1958;
adapt. Charles P. Price, 1980, alt.
MUSIC: *Then Swenska Psalmboken,* 1697; arr. *American Lutheran Hymnal,* 1930
Text © 1982 Hope Publishing Company

BEREDEN VÄG FÖR HERRAN
7.6.7.6.7.7 with refrain

107 Awake! Awake, and Greet the New Morn

1 A - wake! A - wake, and greet the new morn, for an - gels
2 To us, to all in sor - row and fear, Em - man - u -
3 In dark - est night his com - ing shall be, when all the
4 Re - joice, re - joice, take heart in the night. Though dark the

her - ald its dawn - ing. Sing out your joy, for soon he is
el comes a - sing - ing; his hum - ble song is qui - et and
world is de - spair - ing, as morn - ing light so qui - et and
win - ter and cheer - less, the ris - ing sun shall crown you with

born, be - hold! the Child of our long - ing. Come as a ba - by
near, yet fills the earth with its ring - ing; mu - sic to heal the
free, so warm and gen - tle and car - ing. Then shall the mute break
light; be strong and lov - ing and fear - less. Love be our song and

weak and poor, to bring all hearts to - geth - er, he o - pens
bro - ken soul and hymns of lov - ing - kind - ness. The thun - der
forth in song, the lame shall leap in won - der, the weak be
love our prayer and love our end - less sto - ry; may God fill

wide the heaven - ly door and lives now in - side us for - ev - er.
of his an - thems rolls to shat - ter all ha - tred and vio - lence.
raised a - bove the strong, and weap-ons be bro - ken a - sun - der.
ev - ery day we share and bring us at last in - to glo - ry.

After attending a carol concert, the author and composer of this hymn was moved to create a contemporary, accessible carol that drew on the familiar images in a new way. There are echoes here of passages such as Isaiah 9:6, Isaiah 7:14/Matthew 1:23, Isaiah 35:5–6, Isaiah 2:4.

TEXT: Marty Haugen, 1983, alt.
MUSIC: Marty Haugen, 1983
Text and Music © 1983 GIA Publications, Inc.

REJOICE, REJOICE
9.8.9.8.8.7.8.9

Of the Father's Love Begotten 108

1 Of the Fa-ther's love be-got-ten, ere the worlds be-gan
2 By his Word was all cre-at-ed; he com-mand-ed; it
3 O, that birth for-ev-er bless-ed when the Vir-gin, full
4 This is he whom seers in old time chant-ed of with one
5 O ye heights of heaven, a-dore him. An-gel hosts, his prais-
6 Christ, to thee with God the Fa-ther, and, O Ho-ly Ghost,

to be, he is Al-pha and O-me-ga; he the
was done: heaven and earth and depths of o-cean, u-ni-
of grace, by the Ho-ly Ghost con-ceiv-ing, bore the
ac-cord, whom the voic-es of the proph-ets prom-ised
es sing. Powers, do-min-ions, bow be-fore him, and ex-
to thee, hymn and chant and high thanks-giv-ing and un-

source, the end-ing he, of the things that are, that
verse of three in one, all that sees the moon's soft
Sav-ior of our race, and the babe, the world's Re-
in their faith-ful word. Now he shines, the long-ex-
tol our God and King. Let no tongue on earth be
wea-ried prais-es be. Hon-or, glo-ry, and do-

have been, and that fu-ture years shall see,
shin- ing, all that breathes be-neath the sun,
deem- er, first re-vealed his sa-cred face,
pect- ed. Let cre-a-tion praise its Lord,
si- lent; ev-ery voice in con-cert ring,
min- ion, and e-ter-nal vic-to-ry,

(after stanza 6)

ev-er-more and ev-er-more! A-men.

Seldom has the wonder of the Incarnation been expressed so beautifully as in this text, created in the era when the Apostles' and Nicene Creeds were being codified and mindful of similar theological affirmations. It is set here to a plainchant melody from the late Middle Ages.

TEXT: Aurelius Clemens Prudentius, 5th cent.;
    trans. John Mason Neale, 1854, alt., and Henry Williams Baker, 1859, alt.
MUSIC: Plainsong, Mode V; harm. C. Winfred Douglas, 1940
Music Harm. © 1943, 1961, 1985 Church Pension Fund

DIVINUM MYSTERIUM
8.7.8.7.8.7.7

109 Blest Be the God of Israel
Song of Zechariah

1 Blest be the God of Is - rael, who comes to set us free;
2 God from the house of Da - vid a child of grace has given;
3 On those who sit in dark - ness the sun be - gins to rise,

who vis - its and re - deems us, who grants us lib - er - ty.
a Sav - ior comes a - mong us to raise us up to heaven.
the dawn - ing of for - give - ness up - on the sin - ner's eyes.

The proph - ets spoke of mer - cy, of free - dom and re - lease;
Be - fore him goes the her - ald, fore - run - ner in the way,
God guides the feet of pil - grims a - long the paths of peace.

God shall ful - fill that prom - ise and bring the peo - ple peace.
the proph - et of sal - va - tion, the har - bin - ger of day.
O bless our God and Sav - ior with songs that nev - er cease!

This 20th-century British paraphrase of the Song of Zechariah (Luke 1:68–79) broadens the implications of what John the Baptist's father says in order to affirm that God's work is ongoing. The tune is named for the composer's oldest sister, who was his first piano teacher.

TEXT: Michael Perry, 1973, alt.
MUSIC: Hal H. Hopson, 1983
Text © 1973 The Jubilate Group (admin. Hope Publishing Company)
Music © 1983 Hope Publishing Company

MERLE'S TUNE
7.6.7.6.D

Love Has Come

110

1 Love has come: a light in the dark - ness!
2 Love is born! Come, share in the won - der.
3 Love has come and nev - er will leave us!

Love shines forth in the Beth - le - hem skies. See, all
Love is God now a - sleep in the hay. See the
Love is life ev - er - last - ing and free. Love is

heav - en has come to pro - claim it; hear how their song of
glow in the eyes of his moth - er; what is the name her
Je - sus with - in and a - mong us. Love is the peace our

joy a - ris - es: Love! Love! Born un - to you, a
heart is say - ing? Love! Love! Love is the name she
hearts are seek - ing. Love! Love! Love is the gift of

Sav - ior! Love! Love! Glo - ry to God on high.
whis - pers. Love! Love! Je - sus, Em - man - u - el.
Christ-mas. Love! Love! Praise to you, God on high!

Here is a chance to sing a familiar French carol tune with new words, the most important clearly being
"Love." The senses "seen and heard" (as in Acts 4:20 and elsewhere) organize the first two stanzas, while
the third holds the summary statement: "Love is the gift of Christmas."

TEXT: Ken Bible, 1996
MUSIC: French melody; arr. Eric T. Myers, 2012
Text © 1996 LNWhymns.com (admin. Music Services)
Music Arr. © 2012 Eric T. Myers

BRING A TORCH
9.9.10.9.9.8

111 From Heaven Above

1 "From heaven a - bove to earth I come to bring good
2 "To you this night is born a child of Mar - y,
3 "This is the Christ, God's Son most high, who hears your
4 My heart for ver - y joy now leaps; my voice no
5 "Glo - ry to God in high - est heaven, who un - to

news to ev - ery - one! Glad ti - dings of great
cho - sen vir - gin mild; this new - born child of
sad and bit - ter cry; he will him - self your
lon - ger si - lence keeps; I too must sing with
us the Christ has given." With an - gels sing the

joy I bring to all the world, and glad - ly sing:
low - ly birth shall be the joy of all the earth.
Sav - ior be and from all sin will set you free."
joy - ful tongue the sweet - est an - cient cra - dle - song:
Sav - ior's birth, a glad new year to all the earth.

This Christmas hymn gives us a rare glimpse of Martin Luther as a father creating verses for his children to sing at home on Christmas Eve for a retelling of Luke 2:8–14. The first three stanzas paraphrase the angel's song, and the final two provide the human response.

TEXT: Martin Luther, 1535; trans. *Lutheran Book of Worship*, 1978, alt.
MUSIC: Schumann's *Geistliche Lieder*, 1539
Text © 1978 Lutheran Book of Worship (admin. Augsburg Fortress)

VOM HIMMEL HOCH
LM

On Christmas Night All Christians Sing 112

The words of this carol first appeared in 1684 in a collection by an Irish bishop, Luke Wadding. Whether they were his own work or something gleaned from popular use is not clear. The tune name recalls that the tune was collected in 1904 from Mrs. Verrall of Monk's Gate, Sussex.

TEXT: English carol
MUSIC: English carol; arr. Ralph Vaughan Williams, 1912

SUSSEX CAROL
8.8.8.8.8.8

113 Angels We Have Heard on High

1 An - gels we have heard on high, sweet-ly sing-ing o'er the plains,
2 Shep-herds, why this ju - bi - lee? Why your joy-ous strains pro-long?
3 Come to Beth - le - hem and see him whose birth the an - gels sing;

and the moun-tains in re - ply ech - o - ing their joy - ous strains.
What the glad-some ti - dings be which in-spire your heaven-ly song?
come, a - dore on bend - ed knee Christ, the Lord, the new - born King.

Refrain

Glo - - - ri - a

in ex - cel - sis De - o! Glo -

This French carol probably dates from the 1700s, though it was not printed until the following century. Because it uses a vernacular language for the narrative stanzas and Latin for the refrain, it belongs to a special category called "macaronic" or mixed-language texts.

TEXT: French carol; trans. James Chadwick, 1860, alt.
MUSIC: French carol; arr. Edward Shippen Barnes, 1937
Music © 1937, ren. 1965 H. Augustine Smith Jr.
    (admin. Fleming H. Revell Company, a div. of Baker Publishing Group)

GLORIA
7.7.7.7 with refrain

- ri - a in ex - cel - sis De - o!

Away in a Manger 114

Capo 5: (C) (Am) (C) (Dm)
F Dm F Gm

1 A - way in a man - ger, no crib for his bed,
2 The cat - tle are low - ing; the poor ba - by wakes,
3 Be near me, Lord Je - sus; I ask thee to stay

(F) (G) (C) (Dm) (F) (G)
Bb C F Gm Bb C

the lit - tle Lord Je - sus laid down his sweet head.
but lit - tle Lord Je - sus, no cry - ing he makes.
close by me for - ev - er and love me, I pray.

(C) (Dm)
F Gm

The stars in the bright sky looked down where he lay,
I love thee, Lord Je - sus; look down from the sky,
Bless all the dear chil - dren in thy ten - der care,

(G) (C) (Dm) (G) (C)
C F Gm C F

the lit - tle Lord Je - sus a - sleep on the hay.
and stay by my side un - til morn - ing is nigh.
and fit us for heav - en to live with thee there.

This anonymous carol probably originated among Pennsylvania Lutherans in the late 19th century, giving rise to a mistaken assertion that it had been written by Martin Luther. This tune is also by an American but has become the one usually used in Canada and Great Britain.

TEXT: Stanzas 1–2, *Little Children's Book for Schools and Families*, c. 1885;
stanza 3, Gabriel's *Vineyard Songs*, 1892
MUSIC: William James Kirkpatrick, 1895

CRADLE SONG
11.11.11.11
(alternate tune: MUELLER, 115)

115 Away in a Manger

Capo 3: (D)
F

(G)
B♭

(D)
F

1 A - way in a man - ger, no crib for his bed,
2 The cat - tle are low - ing; the poor ba - by wakes,
3 Be near me, Lord Je - sus; I ask thee to stay

(A7)
C7

(D)
F

the lit - tle Lord Je - sus laid down his sweet head.
but lit - tle Lord Je - sus, no cry - ing he makes.
close by me for - ev - er and love me, I pray.

(G)
B♭

(D)
F

The stars in the bright sky looked down where he lay,
I love thee, Lord Je - sus; look down from the sky,
Bless all the dear chil - dren in thy ten - der care,

(A7)
C7

(D)
F

(Em)
Gm

(A7)
C7

(D)
F

the lit - tle Lord Je - sus a - sleep on the hay.
and stay by my side un - til morn - ing is nigh.
and fit us for heav - en to live with thee there.

Though erroneously attributed to Martin Luther, this anonymous carol has North American roots, probably originating among Pennsylvania Lutherans. Although more than forty melodies have been connected with these words, this tune was among the earliest written for them.

TEXT: Stanzas 1–2, *Little Children's Book for Schools and Families*, c. 1885; stanza 3, Gabriel's *Vineyard Songs*, 1892
MUSIC: James R. Murray, 1887

MUELLER
11.11.11.11
(alternate tune: CRADLE SONG, 114)

The Snow Lay on the Ground 116

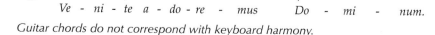

(Music notation, key of G, 6/8 time)

Chords: G — C G D

1 The snow lay on the ground; the stars shone bright,
2 'Twas gen - tle Mar - y maid, so young and strong,
3 Saint Jo - seph too was by to tend the child,
4 And thus that man - ger poor be - came a throne;

Chords: C — D7 — G D7 G

when Christ our Lord was born on Christ - mas night.
who wel - comed here the Christ - child with a song.
to guard him, and pro - tect his moth - er mild.
for he whom Mar - y bore was God the Son.

Chords: G — C G D

Ve - ni - te a - do - re - mus Do - mi - num.
She laid him in a stall at Beth - le - hem;
The an - gels hov - ered round and sang this song:
O come, then, let us join the heaven - ly host

Chords: C — D7 — G D7 G

Ve - ni - te a - do - re - mus Do - mi - num.
the ass and ox - en shared the roof with them.
Ve - ni - te a - do - re - mus Do - mi - num.
to praise the Fa - ther, Son, and Ho - ly Ghost.

Refrain

Chords: G — Am E Am

Ve - ni - te a - do - re - mus Do - mi - num.

Chords: D7 — G D7 G

Ve - ni - te a - do - re - mus Do - mi - num.

Guitar chords do not correspond with keyboard harmony.

This is one of the few instances where we can see how one Christmas carol has been built upon another. The refrain here quotes the original Latin refrain of "O Come, All Ye Faithful" (see no. 133), which means this text was created later than the first half of the 18th century.

TEXT: Anglo-Irish carol; *Catholic Hymns*, 1860, alt.
MUSIC: Italian folk melody; *Children's Praise*, 1871; harm. Leo Sowerby, 1941
Music Harm. © 1941 Leo Sowerby

VENITE ADOREMUS
10.10.10.10 with refrain

117 While Shepherds Watched Their Flocks

1 While shep - herds watched their flocks by night, all
2 "Fear not," said he, for might - y dread had
3 "To you, in Da - vid's town this day, is
4 "The heaven - ly babe you there shall find to

seat - ed on the ground, the an - gel of the
seized their trou - bled mind: "Glad ti - dings of great
born of Da - vid's line the Sav - ior, who is
hu - man view dis - played, all hum - bly wrapped in

Lord came down, and glo - ry shone a - round.
joy I bring to you and hu - man - kind.
Christ the Lord, and this shall be the sign:
swath - ing bands, and in a man - ger laid."

5 Thus spoke the seraph, and forthwith
   appeared a shining throng
   of angels praising God, who thus
   addressed their joyful song:

6 "All glory be to God on high,
   and to the earth be peace;
   good will to all from highest heaven
   begin and never cease!"

This was one of the first metrical texts to deal with a New Testament narrative rather than paraphrase one of the Psalms. It is set here to a psalm tune that is more than a century older than the words, though the two were not firmly joined until the mid-19th century.

TEXT: Nahum Tate, 1700, alt.
MUSIC: Este's *Psalmes*, 1592; harm. George Kirbye, 1592

WINCHESTER OLD
CM
(alternate tune: CHRISTMAS, 118)

While Shepherds Watched Their Flocks 118

1 While shep-herds watched their flocks by night, all seat-ed
2 "Fear not," said he, for might-y dread had seized their
3 "To you, in Da - vid's town this day, is born of
4 "The heaven-ly babe you there shall find to hu-man

on the ground, the an - gel of the Lord came down, and
trou - bled mind: "Glad ti - dings of great joy I bring to
Da - vid's line the Sav - ior, who is Christ the Lord, and
view dis - played, all hum-bly wrapped in swath-ing bands, and

glo - ry shone a - round, and glo - ry shone a - round.
you and hu - man - kind, to you and hu - man - kind.
this shall be the sign, and this shall be the sign:
in a man - ger laid, and in a man - ger laid."

5 Thus spoke the seraph, and forthwith
appeared a shining throng
of angels praising God, who thus
addressed their joyful song,
addressed their joyful song:

6 "All glory be to God on high,
and to the earth be peace;
good will to all from highest heaven
begin and never cease,
begin and never cease!"

The publication of this text in the late 17th century marked an important moment in the transition from the older practice of psalm-singing to the newer style of hymn-singing. This tune was not originally written for church use but was derived from an operatic aria.

TEXT: Nahum Tate, 1700, alt.
MUSIC: George Frederick Handel, 1728; arr. Lowell Mason, 1821

CHRISTMAS
CM with repeat
(alternate tune: WINCHESTER OLD, 117)

119 Hark! The Herald Angels Sing

1 Hark! The her - ald an-gels sing, "Glo - ry to the new-born king.
2 Christ, by high - est heaven a-dored, Christ, the ev - er - last - ing Lord,
3 Hail the heaven-born Prince of Peace! Hail the sun of right-teous-ness!

Peace on earth and mer - cy mild, God and sin - ners rec - on - ciled!"
late in time be-hold him come, off-spring of the vir-gin's womb.
Light and life to all he brings, risen with heal - ing in his wings.

Joy - ful, all ye na - tions, rise; join the tri - umph of the skies;
Veiled in flesh the God-head see; hail the in-car - nate de - i - ty,
Mild he lays his glo - ry by, born that we no more may die,

with the an-gel - ic host pro-claim, "Christ is born in Beth - le - hem!"
pleased in flesh with us to dwell, Je - sus, our Em-man - u - el.
born to raise us from the earth, born to give us sec - ond birth.

Brought together in the mid-19th century, the text and tune of this familiar carol began in quite different forms. The text had ten stanzas and began, "Hark, how all the welkin rings." The tune was created for a festival celebrating Gutenberg's introduction of moveable type.

TEXT: Charles Wesley, 1739, alt.
MUSIC: Felix Mendelssohn, 1840; arr. William Hayman Cummings, 1855

MENDELSSOHN
7.7.7.7.D with refrain

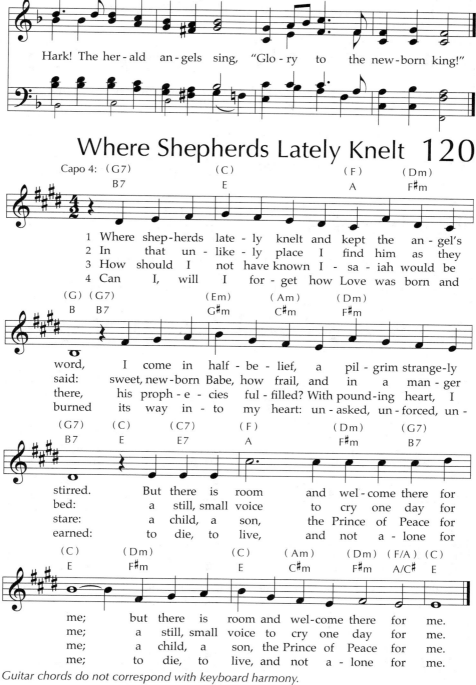

Hark! The her-ald an-gels sing, "Glo-ry to the new-born king!"

Where Shepherds Lately Knelt 120

Capo 4: (G7)   (C)   (F)   (Dm)
B7   E   A   F#m

1 Where shep-herds late-ly knelt and kept the an-gel's
2 In that un-like-ly place I find him as they
3 How should I not have known I-sa-iah would be
4 Can I, will I for-get how Love was born and

(G) (G7)   (Em)   (Am)   (Dm)
B B7   G#m   C#m   F#m

word, I come in half-be-lief, a pil-grim strange-ly
said: sweet, new-born Babe, how frail, and in a man-ger
there, his proph-e-cies ful-filled? With pound-ing heart, I
burned its way in-to my heart: un-asked, un-forced, un-

(G7) (C) (C7)   (F)   (Dm)   (G7)
B7 E E7   A   F#m   B7

stirred. But there is room and wel-come there for
bed: a still, small voice to cry one day for
stare: a child, a son, the Prince of Peace for
earned: to die, to live, and not a-lone for

(C) (Dm)   (C)   (Am)   (Dm) (F/A) (C)
E F#m   E   C#m   F#m A/C# E

me; but there is room and wel-come there for me.
me; a still, small voice to cry one day for me.
me; a child, a son, the Prince of Peace for me.
me; to die, to live, and not a-lone for me.

Guitar chords do not correspond with keyboard harmony.

Witnessing the beginning or the end of life evokes very personal responses (emphasized by the "for me" at the end of each stanza), especially when the scale is intimate, as in this imagined visit to Christ's manger. The prophecies recalled in stanza three come from Isaiah 9:6.

TEXT: Jaroslav J. Vajda, 1986
MUSIC: Carl F. Schalk, 1986
Text © 1987 Concordia Publishing House
Music © 1986 GIA Publications, Inc.

MANGER SONG
12.12.10.10

121 O Little Town of Bethlehem

1 O lit-tle town of Beth-le-hem, how still we see thee lie!
2 For Christ is born of Mar - y and, gath-ered all a-bove,
3 How si-lent-ly, how si-lent-ly, the won-drous gift is given!
4 O ho-ly child of Beth-le-hem, de-scend to us, we pray;

A - bove thy deep and dream-less sleep the si - lent stars go by.
while mor-tals sleep, the an - gels keep their watch of won-dering love.
So God im-parts to hu - man hearts the bless-ings of his heaven.
cast out our sin and en - ter in; be born in us to - day.

Yet in thy dark streets shin - eth the ev - er-last-ing light;
O morn-ing stars, to - geth - er pro - claim the ho - ly birth,
No ear may hear his com - ing, but in this world of sin,
We hear the Christ-mas an - gels the great glad ti-dings tell;

the hopes and fears of all the years are met in thee to-night.
and prais - es sing to God the king, and peace to all on earth.
where meek souls will re - ceive him, still the dear Christ en-ters in.
O come to us; a - bide with us, our Lord Em - man-u - el!

Though he was famed during his lifetime as a great preacher, no sermon Phillips Brooks ever preached has been heard or read by as many people as have sung this carol he wrote in December 1868 for the Sunday School children of Holy Trinity Episcopal Church in Philadelphia.

TEXT: Phillips Brooks, 1868
MUSIC: Lewis Henry Redner, 1868

ST. LOUIS
8.6.8.6.7.6.8.6
(alternate tune: FOREST GREEN)

Silent Night, Holy Night!

1 Si - lent night, ho - ly night! All is calm, all is bright
2 Si - lent night, ho - ly night! Shep - herds quake at the sight;
3 Si - lent night, ho - ly night! Son of God, love's pure light
4 Si - lent night, ho - ly night! Won - drous star, lend thy light;

'round yon vir - gin moth - er and child! Ho - ly In - fant, so ten - der and
glo - ries stream from heav - en a - far, heaven - ly hosts sing "Al - le - lu -
ra - diant beams from thy ho - ly face, with the dawn of re - deem - ing
with the an - gels let us sing Al - le - lu - ia to our

mild, sleep in heav - en - ly peace, sleep in heav - en - ly peace.
ia: Christ the Sav - ior is born; Christ the Sav - ior is born!"
grace, Je - sus, Lord, at thy birth, Je - sus, Lord, at thy birth.
King: Christ the Sav - ior is born; Christ the Sav - ior is born.

GERMAN

1 *Stille Nacht, heilige Nacht!*
   Alles schläft, einsam wacht
   nur das traute, hochheilige Paar.
   Holder Knabe im lockigen Haar,
   schlaf in himmlischer Ruh,
   schlaf in himmlischer Ruh!

SPANISH

1 *¡Noche de paz, noche de amor!*
   Todo duerme en derredor,
   entre los astros que esparcen su luz,
   bella, anunciando al niñito Jesús,
   brilla la estrella de paz,
   brilla la estrella de paz.

KOREAN

1 고요한밤 거룩한밤
   어둠에 묻힌밤
   주의부모 앉아서
   감사기도 드릴때
   아기잘도 잔다
   아기잘도 잔다

The tradition that this carol's tune was created for guitar accompaniment at its first singing on Christmas Eve 1818 seems reliable, though a recent find shows that the text was about two years old. But there is no question that this is now a favorite Christmas carol worldwide.

TEXT: Joseph Mohr, 1816; stanzas 1–3, English trans. John Freeman Young, 1863; stanza 4, English trans. Jane Montgomery Campbell, 1863, alt.
MUSIC: Franz Xaver Gruber, 1818
Korean Trans. © The Christian Literature Society of Korea

STILLE NACHT
Irregular

123 It Came Upon the Midnight Clear

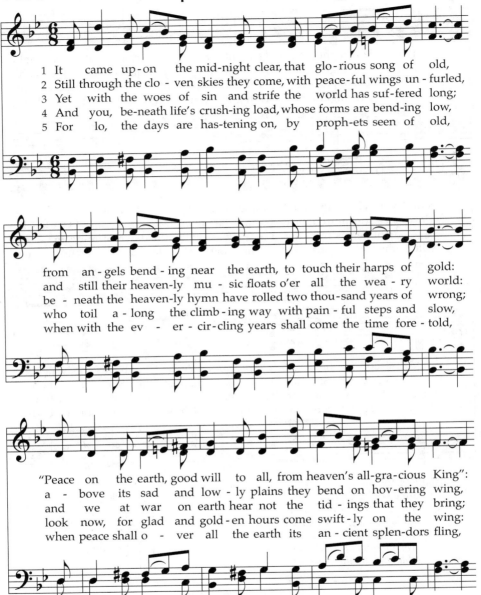

1 It came up-on the mid-night clear, that glo-rious song of old,
2 Still through the clo-ven skies they come, with peace-ful wings un-furled,
3 Yet with the woes of sin and strife the world has suf-fered long;
4 And you, be-neath life's crush-ing load, whose forms are bend-ing low,
5 For lo, the days are has-tening on, by proph-ets seen of old,

from an-gels bend-ing near the earth, to touch their harps of gold:
and still their heaven-ly mu-sic floats o'er all the wea-ry world:
be-neath the heaven-ly hymn have rolled two thou-sand years of wrong;
who toil a-long the climb-ing way with pain-ful steps and slow,
when with the ev - er-cir-cling years shall come the time fore-told,

"Peace on the earth, good will to all, from heaven's all-gra-cious King":
a - bove its sad and low-ly plains they bend on hov-ering wing,
and we at war on earth hear not the tid-ings that they bring;
look now, for glad and gold-en hours come swift-ly on the wing:
when peace shall o - ver all the earth its an-cient splen-dors fling,

The "it" of the first line of this text by a Unitarian minister does not refer to the birth of Jesus, but to "that glorious song of old," the angelic tidings of peace on earth. The restored third stanza laments how often the noise of human strife has obscured that message.

TEXT: Edmund Hamilton Sears, 1849, alt.
MUSIC: Richard Storrs Willis, 1850

CAROL
CMD
(alternate tune: NOEL)

the world in sol - emn still - ness lay, to hear the an - gels sing.
and ev - er o'er its Ba - bel sounds the bless - ed an - gels sing.
O, hush the noise and cease the strife to hear the an - gels sing!
O, rest be - side the wea - ry road, and hear the an - gels sing.
and the whole world give back the song which now the an - gels sing.

Still, Still, Still

124

1 Still, still, still, he sleeps this night so chill! The vir - gin's
2 Sleep, sleep, sleep, he lies in slum - ber deep while an - gel

ten - der arms en - fold - ing, warm and safe the child are hold - ing.
hosts from heaven come wing - ing, sweet - est songs of joy are sing - ing.

Still, still, still, he sleeps this night so chill.
Sleep, sleep, sleep, he lies in slum - ber deep.

The great virtue of this Austrian carol is its sheer simplicity, which is reinforced by the re-use of the first two lines as the last two. This narrow scope makes the text into the verbal equivalent of a close-up photograph or painting, so that the sleeping child seems very near.

TEXT: Austrian carol; trans. George K. Evans, 1963
MUSIC: Austrian carol; arr. Walter Ehret, 1963
Text and Music © 1963, 1980 Walter Ehret and George K. Evans (admin. Walton Music Corp.)

STILL, STILL, STILL
3.6.9.8.3.6

125 Before the Marvel of This Night

Capo 1:

1 Be - fore the mar - vel of this night, a - dor - ing,
2 A - wake the sleep - ing world with song: this is the
3 The love that we have al - ways known, our con - stant

fold your wings and bow; then tear the sky a - part with
day the Lord has made. As - sem - ble here, ce - les - tial
joy and end - less light, now to the love - less world be

light and with your news the world en - dow.
throng, in roy - al splen - dor come ar - rayed.
shown, now break up - on its death - ly night.

Pro - claim the birth of Christ and peace, that fear and
Give earth a glimpse of heav - en - ly bliss, a teas - ing
In - to one song com - press the love that rules our

death and sor - row cease: sing peace; sing peace; sing
taste of what they miss: sing bliss; sing bliss; sing
u - ni - verse a - bove: sing love; sing love; sing

gift of peace; sing peace; sing gift of peace!
end - less bliss; sing bliss; sing end - less bliss!
God is love; sing love; sing God is love!

Guitar chords do not correspond with keyboard harmony.

This text is unusual because it is addressed to angels ("fold your wings and bow") rather than to human beings. It achieves maximum effect when actually used on Christmas Eve, but the event it celebrates is so well known that it can be sung at many points throughout the season.

TEXT: Jaroslav J. Vajda, 1979
MUSIC: Carl F. Schalk, 1979
Text © 1981 Concordia Publishing House
Music © 1979 GIA Publications, Inc.

MARVEL
Irregular

Jesus, Jesus, O What a Wonderful Child 126

Je-sus, Je-sus, O what a won-der-ful child.

Je-sus, Je-sus, so ho-ly, meek and mild;

new life, new hope the child will bring.

Lis-ten to the an-gels sing: "Glo-ry,

glo-ry, glo-ry!" Let the heav-ens ring.

Specific sources for the words and the music of this piece from the African American heritage remain uncertain. The predictable rhymes suggest that, like "Jesus, the Light of the World" (see no. 127), it may have originated as a reflection on an existing Christmas carol.

TEXT: African American; alt.
MUSIC: African American; harm. Jeffrey Radford; arr. Horace Clarence Boyer, 2000
Music Harm. © 1992 The Pilgrim Press
Music Arr. © 2000 Horace Clarence Boyer

WONDERFUL CHILD
Irregular

127 Hark! The Herald Angels Sing
Jesus, the Light of the World

With a gospel feel

1 Hark! the her - ald an - gels sing.
2 Joy - ful all you na - tions, rise.
3 Christ by high - est heaven a - dored;
4 Hail, the heaven - born Prince of Peace!

Je - sus, the light of the world.

Glo - ry to the new - born King,
Join the tri - umph of the skies.
Christ, the ev - er - last - ing Lord;
Hail, the Sun of righ - teous - ness!

Je - sus, the light of the world.

This blues-tinged setting of a familiar Christmas carol participates in a longstanding African American practice of adapting Anglo-European texts, as is done here by incorporating a repeated internal line and by appending a refrain that expands that line's language and imagery.

TEXT: Stanzas, Charles Wesley, 1739; ref., George D. Elderkin, 1890
MUSIC: George D. Elderkin, 1890; arr. Evelyn Simpson-Curenton, 2000
Music Arr. © 2000 GIA Publications, Inc.

WE'LL WALK IN THE LIGHT
7.7.7.7 with refrain

Refrain

We'll walk in the light, beau - ti - ful light.

Come where the dew - drops of mer - cy shine bright.

O, shine all a - round us by day and by

night. Je - sus, the light of the world.

128 Infant Holy, Infant Lowly

1 In - fant ho - ly, in - fant low - ly, for his bed a cat-tle stall;
2 Flocks were sleep-ing; shep-herds keep-ing vig-il till the morn-ing new

ox - en low - ing, lit - tle know-ing Christ the babe is Lord of all.
saw the glo - ry, heard the sto - ry, ti - dings of the gos-pel true.

Swift are wing-ing an - gels sing - ing, no - els ring-ing, ti-dings bring-ing:
Thus re - joic - ing, free from sor - row, prais-es voic-ing greet the mor - row:

Christ the babe is Lord of all! Christ the babe is Lord of all!
Christ the babe was born for you! Christ the babe was born for you!

The English text of this 13th- or 14th-century Polish carol does not try to tell a story but to offer verbal
snapshots of the well-known Nativity narrative of Luke 2:6–20. The tune name quotes the opening of the
Polish text and means "He lies in a cradle" or "In manger lying."

TEXT: Polish carol; trans. Edith M. G. Reed, 1920; rev. 1921
MUSIC: Polish folk melody; harm. Arthur E. Rusbridge, 1962

W ŻŁOBIE LEŻY
8.7.8.7.8.8.7.7
(this tune in a lower key, 410)

Lo, How a Rose E'er Blooming 129

1 Lo, how a rose e'er bloom-ing from ten-der stem hath sprung,
2 I - sa - iah 'twas fore-told it, the rose I have in mind;
3 This flower, whose fra-grance ten - der with sweet-ness fills the air,

of Jes - se's lin-eage com - ing, by faith-ful proph - ets sung.
with Mar - y we be - hold it, the vir - gin moth - er kind.
dis - pels with glo-rious splen-dor the dark-ness ev - ery-where.

It came, a flower-et bright, a - mid the cold of
To show God's love a - right she bore for us a
En - fleshed, yet ver - y God, from sin and death he

win - ter, when half spent was the night.
Sav - ior, when half spent was the night.
saves us and light - ens ev - ery load.

Although the early copies of this 15th-century German text include many more stanzas than are printed here, this simpler, shorter form has much to commend it. This early 17th-century harmonization of the traditional chorale melody invites and rewards singing in parts.

TEXT: German carol; stanzas 1, 2 trans. Theodore Baker, 1894, alt.; stanza 3 trans. Harriet Knuth Spaeth, 1985, alt.
MUSIC: *Alte Catholische Geistliche Kirchengesäng*, 1599; arr. Michael Praetorius, 1609

ES IST EIN' ROS'
7.6.7.6.6.7.6

130 Break Forth, O Beauteous Heavenly Light

Break forth, O beau-teous heaven-ly light, and ush-er in the morn-ing. You shep-herds, shud-der not with fright, but hear the an-gel's warn-ing. This child, now weak in in-fan-cy, our con-fi-dence and joy shall be, the power of Sa-tan break-ing, our peace e-ter-nal mak-ing.

This exuberant text, based on Isaiah 9:2–7, was the ninth of twelve stanzas in its original German hymn. The chorale tune associated with this hymn went through many changes at the hands of later composers, reaching its present form in J. S. Bach's *Christmas Oratorio*.

TEXT: Johann Rist, 1641; trans. John Troutbeck, 1873
MUSIC: Johann Schop, 1641; harm. Johann Sebastian Bach, 1734

ERMUNTRE DICH
8.7.8.7.8.8.7.7

In the Heavens Shone a Star 131

1 In the heav-ens shone a star, van-quish-
2 From the an-gels shep-herds heard the good
3 Wise men saw the heaven-ly sign, jour-neyed
4 Filled with won-der and with awe, at his

ing the gloom of night, her-ald-ing a won-drous
ti-dings of his birth, and to Beth-le-hem they
far from O-rient land, him their Lord and King to
cra-dle low we bow to a-dore the ho-ly

birth; God's own Son now comes to earth.
sped to be-hold his man-ger bed.
greet, of-fering trea-sures at his feet.
child, Son of God, and yet so mild.

Refrain

Je-sus Christ is born to-day, Christ-mas Day!

The collaboration of a Philippine linguist and an American missionary, this text includes the usual harmonized Christmas and Epiphany elements, but they gain a distinctive flavor from the musical setting using the five-note scale of the Kalinga people who live in northern Luzon.

TEXT: Jonathan Malicsi and Ellsworth Chandlee, 20th cent.
MUSIC: Kalinga melody; arr. Joel Navarro, 2010
Text © 1990, 2000 Christian Conference of Asia (admin. GIA Publications, Inc.)
Music © 2010 Faith Alive Christian Resources

KALINGA
7.7.7.7 with refrain

132 Good Christian Friends, Rejoice

1 Good Chris-tian friends, re - joice with heart and soul and voice;
2 Good Chris-tian friends, re - joice with heart and soul and voice;
3 Good Chris-tian friends, re - joice with heart and soul and voice;

give ye heed to what we say: Je - sus Christ is born to - day;
now ye hear of end - less bliss: Je - sus Christ was born for this!
now ye need not fear the grave: Je - sus Christ was born to save!

ox and ass be - fore him bow, and he is in the man-ger now.
He has o-pened heav-en's door, and we are blest for - ev - er - more.
Calls you one and calls you all to gain the ev - er - last - ing hall.

Christ is born to - day! Christ is born to - day!
Christ was born for this! Christ was born for this!
Christ was born to save! Christ was born to save!

Carols using two languages, like this one dating from at least the 14th century, belong to a special group called "macaronic," the original languages here being German and Latin. Though the present version is only in English, it is sung to the traditional German folk melody.

IN DULCI JUBILO
6.6.7.7.7.8.5.5

TEXT: Medieval Latin; trans. and para. John Mason Neale, 1853, alt.
MUSIC: German folk melody, 14th cent.; harm. David Hugh Jones, 1953
Music Harm. © 1955, ren. 1983 John Ribble (admin. Westminster John Knox Press)

O Come, All Ye Faithful

1 O come, all ye faith-ful, joy-ful and tri-um-phant; O come
2 True God from true God, Light from light e-ter-nal,
3 Sing, choirs of an-gels; sing in ex-ul-ta-tion;
4 Yea, Lord, we greet thee, born this hap-py morn-ing;

ye; O come ye to Beth-le-hem! Come, and be-hold him,
of a vir-gin, a mor-tal he comes; ver-y God, beall ye cit-i-zens of heaven a-bove! Glo-ry to God, all
sus, to thee be all glo-ry given; Word of the Fa-ther,

born the King of an-gels!
got-ten, not cre-at-ed!
glo-ry in the high-est!
now in flesh ap-pear-ing!

Refrain

O come, let us a-dore him; O come, let

us a-dore him; O come, let us a-dore him, Christ, the Lord!

From its Roman Catholic origins, this 18th-century hymn has spread to worldwide use by many denominations in both Latin and vernacular versions. Once popular with a wide range of hymn texts, this tune is now firmly associated with this Christmas text from which it is named.

TEXT: John Francis Wade, c. 1743; trans. Frederick Oakeley, 1841, alt.
MUSIC: John Francis Wade, c. 1743; harm. *The English Hymnal*, 1906

ADESTE FIDELES
Irregular

134 Joy to the World

1 Joy to the world, the Lord is come! Let earth re- ceive
2 Joy to the earth, the Sav- ior reigns! Let all their songs
3 No more let sins and sor- rows grow, nor thorns in- fest
4 He rules the world with truth and grace, and makes the na -

her king; let ev - ery heart pre - pare him room,
em - ploy, while fields and floods, rocks, hills, and plains
the ground; he comes to make his bless - ings flow
tions prove the glo - ries of his righ - teous - ness

and heaven and na - ture sing, and heaven and na - ture
re - peat the sound-ing joy, re - peat the sound-ing
far as the curse is found, far as the curse is
and won - ders of his love, and won - ders of his
and heaven and na - ture sing,
and

sing, and heaven, and heaven and na - ture sing.
joy, re - peat, re - peat the sound - ing joy.
found, far as, far as the curse is found.
love, and won - ders, won - ders of his love.
heaven and na - ture sing,

While Isaac Watts did not write this text strictly for Christmas use, he did purposely cast his paraphrase of Psalm 98:4–9 in Christian terms, titling it "The Messiah's coming and kingdom." So "the Lord" here is Jesus Christ, rather than the God of Abraham, Isaac, and Jacob.

TEXT: Isaac Watts, 1719, alt.
MUSIC: Attr. George Frederick Handel, 1742; arr. Lowell Mason, 1836

ANTIOCH
CM with repeat
(alternate tune: RICHMOND, 266)

There's a Star in the East

Rise Up, Shepherd, and Follow

135

1 There's a star in the east on Christ-mas morn. Rise up, shep-herd, and
2 If you take good heed to the an - gel's words, rise up, shep-herd, and

fol - low. It will lead to the place where the Christ was born.
fol - low. You'll for - get your flocks; you'll for - get your herds.

Refrain

Rise up, shep-herd, and fol - low. Fol - low, fol - low;

rise up, shep-herd, and fol - low. Fol - low the star of

Beth - le - hem. Rise up, shep-herd, and fol - low.

This African American spiritual, cast in a characteristic call-and-response style, provides a reminder that the good news of the Incarnation should lead Christians not only to awe and adoration but also to living and acting in ways that make God's purposes known to others.

TEXT and MUSIC: African American spiritual

FOLLOW
Irregular

136 Go, Tell It on the Mountain

Go, tell it on the moun-tain, o-ver the hills and ev-ery-where;

go, tell it on the moun-tain that Je-sus Christ is born!

1 While shep-herds kept their watch-ing o'er si-lent flocks by night,
2 The shep-herds feared and trem-bled when lo! a-bove the earth
3 Down in a low-ly man-ger the hum-ble Christ was born,

be-hold, through-out the heav-ens there shone a ho-ly light.
rang out the an-gel cho-rus that hailed our Sav-ior's birth.
and God sent us sal-va-tion that bless-ed Christ-mas morn.

Like other material from oral traditions, 19th-century African American spirituals flourished without being written down. Their refrains were their most stable parts, and narrative stanzas were often improvised to fit. These Nativity stanzas attempt to recall that tradition.

TEXT: African American spiritual; stanzas, John W. Work II, 1940
MUSIC: African American spiritual; arr. John W. Work III, 1940; harm. Melva Wilson Costen, 1987
Music Harm. © 1989 Melva Wilson Costen

GO TELL IT
7.6.7.6 with refrain

He Came Down

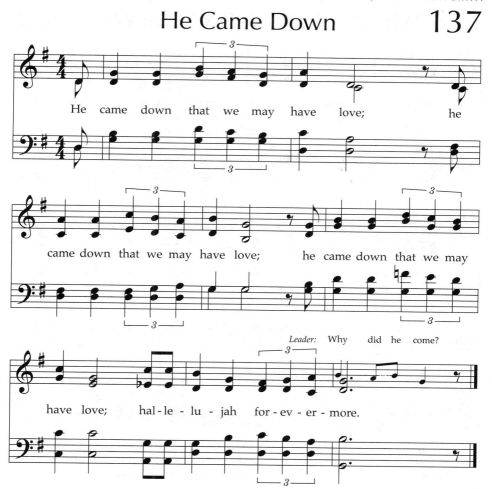

He came down that we may have love; he came down that we may have love; he came down that we may have love; hal-le-lu-jah for-ev-er-more.

Leader: Why did he come?

Additional stanzas:

… that we may have light

… that we may have peace

… that we may have joy

Because this traditional Cameroon piece begins with the refrain, it does not initially reveal that it is cast as a call-and-response song. Assigning the answers to the congregation rather than to the leader is a notable affirmation of the corporate wisdom of God's people.

TEXT: Cameroon song
MUSIC: Cameroon melody; transcr. and arr. John L. Bell, 1986
Music Arr. © 1986 WGRG, Iona Community (admin. GIA Publications, Inc.)

HE CAME DOWN
LM

138 Who Would Think That What Was Needed

1 Who would think that what was need-ed to trans-
2 Shep-herds watch and wise men won-der; mon-archs
3 Cen-tu-ries of skill and sci-ence span the

form and save the earth might not be a
scorn and an-gels sing; such a place as
past from which we move, yet ex-pe-rience

plan or ar-my, proud in pur-pose, proved in
none would reck-on hosts a ho-ly help-less
ques-tions wheth-er, with such prog-ress, we im-

worth? Who would think, de-spite de-ri-sion, that a
thing. Sta-ble beasts and by-passed strang-ers watch a
prove. While the hu-man lot we pon-der, lest our

Hindsight is nearly always clearer than foresight, and with gentle good humor this Christmas hymn points out how great was the gap between human expectation and God's actual way of providing a means of salvation for us. God's ways continually exceed our claims to comprehend them.

TEXT: John L. Bell and Graham Maule, 1987
MUSIC: John L. Bell, 2005
Text and Music © 1987, 2005 WGRG, Iona Community (admin. GIA Publications, Inc.)

WHITE ROSETTES
8.7.8.7.D

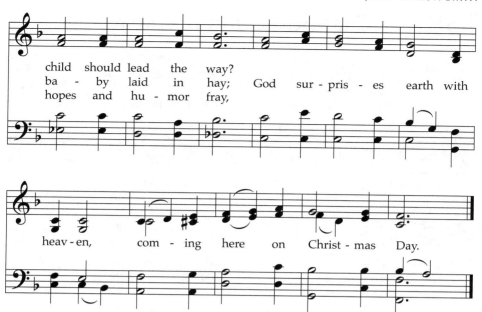

child should lead the way?
ba - by laid in hay; God sur - pris - es earth with
hopes and hu - mor fray,

heav - en, com - ing here on Christ - mas Day.

139 That Boy-Child of Mary

1 What shall we call him, child of the man - ger?
2 His name is Je - sus, God ev - er with us,
3 How can he save us; how can he help us,
4 Gift of the Fa - ther, to hu - man moth - er,
5 One with the Fa - ther, he is our Sav - ior,
6 Glad - ly we praise him, love and a - dore him,

What name is giv - en in Beth - le - hem?
God giv - en for us in Beth - le - hem.
born here a - mong us in Beth - le - hem?
makes him our broth - er of Beth - le - hem.
heav - en - sent help - er of Beth - le - hem.
give our - selves to him of Beth - le - hem.

Written by a Scottish missionary for use at St. Michael's Cathedral in Blantyre, Malawi, this hymn on the meaning of Christ's birth and name reflects an aspect of that African culture, where naming often expresses the conditions of a child's birth or hopes for his or her life.

TEXT: Tom Colvin, 1967
MUSIC: Malawi melody; adapt. Tom Colvin, 1967
Text and Music © 1969 Hope Publishing Company

BLANTYRE
Irregular

Once in Royal David's City 140

1 Once in roy - al Da - vid's cit - y stood a low - ly
2 He came down to earth from heav - en who is God and
3 Je - sus is our child - hood's pat - tern; day by day like
4 And our eyes at last shall see him, through his own re -

cat - tle shed, where a moth - er laid her ba - by in a
Lord of all, and his shel - ter was a sta - ble, and his
us he grew; he was lit - tle, weak and help - less; tears and
deem - ing love; for that child so dear and gen - tle is our

man - ger for his bed: Mar - y was that moth - er
cra - dle was a stall; with the poor and meek and
smiles like us he knew; and he feels for all our
Lord in heaven a - bove; and he leads his chil - dren

mild; Je - sus Christ, her lit - tle child.
low - ly, lived on earth our Sav - ior ho - ly.
sad - ness, and he shares in all our glad - ness.
on to the place where he is gone.

Like "All Things Bright and Beautiful" (see no. 20), this popular Christmas hymn was written by an Irish poet to illustrate for children the various articles of the Apostles' Creed. It is not known which of several English villages the composer had in mind when naming this tune.

TEXT: Cecil Frances Alexander, 1848, alt.
MUSIC: Henry John Gauntlett, 1849; harm. Arthur Henry Mann, 1919

IRBY
8.7.8.7.7.7

141 On This Day Earth Shall Ring

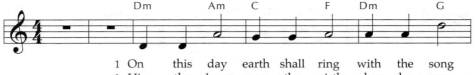

1 On this day earth shall ring with the song
2 His the doom, ours the mirth; when he came
3 God's bright star, o'er his head, wise men three
4 On this day an - gels sing; with their song

chil - dren sing to the Lord, Christ our King, born on earth to
down to earth Beth - le - hem saw his birth; ox and ass be -
to him led; kneel they low by his bed, lay their gifts be -
earth shall ring, prais - ing Christ, heav - en's King, born on earth to

Refrain

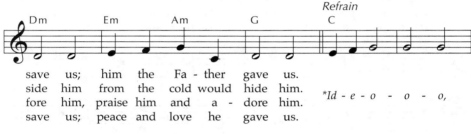

save us; him the Fa - ther gave us.
side him from the cold would hide him. *Id - e - o - o - o,
fore him, praise him and a - dore him.
save us; peace and love he gave us.

id - e - o - o - o, id - e - o glo - ri - a in ex - cel - sis De - o!

Therefore, glory to God in the highest.

Guitar chords do not correspond with keyboard harmony.

Although this Latin carol for Christmas may have roots several centuries older than its 16th-century emergence, the text was all in one language until its 20th-century translator chose to adopt the original last two lines of the fourth stanza as a unifying refrain in all stanzas.

TEXT: *Piae Cantiones*, 1582; trans. Jane Marion Joseph, c. 1917
MUSIC: *Piae Cantiones*, 1582; arr. Gustav Holst, c. 1917
Text and Music Arr. © 1924, ren. J. Curwen & Sons Ltd.

PERSONENT HODIE
6.6.6.6.6 with refrain

'Twas in the Moon of Wintertime 142

Capo 3: (Em)   (Am)   (Bm7) (Em)
Gm   Cm   Dm7 Gm

1 'Twas in the moon of win-ter-time, when all the birds had fled,
2 With-in a lodge of bro-ken bark the ten-der babe was found.
3 The ear-liest moon of win-ter-time is not so round and fair
4 O chil-dren of the for-est free, the an-gel song is true:

(Em)   (Am)   (Bm7) (Em)
Gm   Cm   Dm7 Gm

Great Spir-it, Lord of all the earth sent an-gel choirs in-stead.
A rag-ged robe of rab-bit skin en-wrapped his beau-ty round.
as was the ring of glo-ry on the help-less in-fant there.
the ho-ly child of earth and heaven is born to-day for you.

(Bm)   (Am)   (G)
Dm   Cm   B♭

Be-fore their light the stars grew dim and wan-dering
But as the hunt-ers brave drew nigh the an-gel
The chiefs from far be-fore him knelt with gifts of
Come kneel be-fore the ra-diant boy who brings you

Refrain

(C) (Am) (Bm7) (Em) (Bm)
E♭ Cm Dm7 Gm Dm

hunt-ers heard the hymn:
song rang loud and high: Je-sus, your king, is born;
fox and bea-ver pelt.
beau-ty, peace, and joy.

(C) (Bm) (Em) (Am) (Bm7) (Em)
E♭ Dm Gm Cm Dm7 Gm

Je-sus is born. *In ex-cel-sis glo-ri-a.*

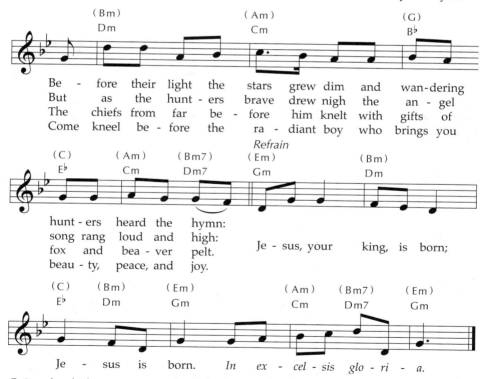

Guitar chords do not correspond with keyboard harmony.

This English text preserves the earliest known Canadian hymn, originally written in the Huron language by a missionary, later translated into French, and eventually paraphrased in English. It is set to a French noël tune old enough to have been used for the original version.

TEXT: Jean de Brébeuf, c. 1641; trans. Jesse Edgar Middleton, 1926, alt.
MUSIC: French folk melody; arr. H. Barrie Cabena, 1970
Music Arr. © 1971 H. Barrie Cabena

UNE JEUNE PUCELLE
8.6.8.6.8.8.8 with refrain

143 Angels, from the Realms of Glory

1 An - gels, from the realms of glo - ry, wing your flight o'er
2 Shep - herds, in the fields a - bid - ing, watch - ing o'er your
3 Sag - es, leave your con - tem - pla - tions; bright - er vi - sions
4 All cre - a - tion, join in prais - ing God the Fa - ther,

all the earth; you, who sang cre - a - tion's sto - ry,
flocks by night, God with us is now re - sid - ing;
beam a - far; seek the great de - sire of na - tions;
Spir - it, Son, ev - er - more your voic - es rais - ing

now pro - claim Mes - si - ah's birth:
yon - der shines the in - fant light: come and wor - ship,
you have seen his na - tal star:
to the e - ter - nal Three in One:

come and wor - ship, wor - ship Christ, the new - born king!

This familiar carol was first published as a poem in the Christmas Eve 1816 issue of a newspaper the author edited in Sheffield, England. The tune name celebrates the location of a prominent Presbyterian Church in London, sometimes called the "Presbyterian cathedral."

TEXT: Stanzas 1–3, James Montgomery, 1816, 1825; stanza 4, *Salisbury Hymn Book,* 1857
MUSIC: Henry Thomas Smart, 1867

REGENT SQUARE
8.7.8.7.8.7

In the Bleak Midwinter

144

1 In the bleak mid-win-ter, frost-y wind made moan;
2 Our God, heaven can-not hold him, nor earth sus-tain;
3 An-gels and arch-an-gels may have gath-ered there;
4 What can I give him, poor as I am?

earth stood hard as i-ron, wa-ter like a stone;
heaven and earth shall flee a-way when he comes to reign:
cher-u-bim and ser-a-phim thronged the air;
If I were a shep-herd, I would bring a lamb;

snow had fall-en, snow on snow, snow on snow,
in the bleak mid-win-ter a sta-ble place suf-ficed
but his moth-er on-ly, in her maid-en bliss,
if I were a wise man, I would do my part;

in the bleak mid-win-ter, long a-go.
the Lord God in-car-nate, Je-sus Christ.
wor-shiped the be-lov-ed with a kiss.
yet what I can I give him: give my heart.

Though this text describes winter weather in England rather than in Palestine, the poet is using familiar surroundings as a means of making the Nativity more immediate and personal. The tune name honors a Gloucestershire village near the composer's birthplace in Cheltenham.

TEXT: Christina Rossetti, c. 1872, alt.
MUSIC: Gustav Holst, 1906

CRANHAM
Irregular

145 What Child Is This

1 What child is this, who, laid to rest, on Mar-y's lap is sleep-ing?
2 Why lies he in such mean es-tate where ox and ass are feed-ing?
3 So bring him in-cense, gold, and myrrh; come, one and all, to own him.

Whom an-gels greet with an-thems sweet while shep-herds watch are keep-ing?
Good Chris-tian, fear; for sin-ners here the si - lent Word is plead-ing.
The King of kings sal-va-tion brings; let lov - ing hearts en-throne him.

This, this is Christ the King, whom shep-herds guard and an-gels sing;
Nails, spear, shall pierce him through; the cross be borne for me, for you.
Raise, raise the song on high. The vir - gin sings her lul - la - by.

haste, haste to bring him laud, the babe, the son of Mar - y!
Hail, hail, the Word made flesh, the babe, the son of Mar - y!
Joy, joy, for Christ is born, the babe, the son of Mar - y!

This Victorian text gains scope and power by having the original second halves of stanzas two and three restored. They give a stark forward glimpse of what lies ahead for this "babe, the son of Mary!" The tune is much older, dating from Tudor England.

TEXT: William Chatterton Dix, 1871
MUSIC: English ballad, 16th cent.; arr. *Christmas Carols New and Old,* 1871

GREENSLEEVES
8.7.8.7.6.8.6.7

Gentle Mary Laid Her Child 146

1 Gen-tle Mar-y laid her child low-ly in a man-ger;
2 An-gels sang a-bout his birth; wise men sought and found him;
3 Gen-tle Mar-y laid her child low-ly in a man-ger;

there he lay, the un-de-filed, to the world a strang-er.
heav-en's star shone bright-ly forth, glo-ry all a-round him.
he is still the un-de-filed, but no more a strang-er.

Such a babe in such a place, can he be the Sav-ior?
Shep-herds saw the won-drous sight, heard the an-gels sing-ing;
Son of God, of hum-ble birth, beau-ti-ful the sto-ry;

Ask the saved of all the race who have found his fa - vor.
all the plains were lit that night; all the hills were ring - ing.
praise his name in all the earth; hail the King of glo - ry!

This 20th-century Christmas text by an English-born Canadian clergyman was originally a poem called "The Manger Prince." It gains a certain antique flavor by being set to a late medieval song associated with springtime. (The tune name means "The flowering time is near.")

TEXT: Joseph Simpson Cook, 1919; rev. 1930
MUSIC: *Piae Cantiones*, 1582; arr. Ernest C. MacMillan, 1930

TEMPUS ADEST FLORIDUM
7.6.7.6.D

147 The First Nowell

1 The first Now-ell the an-gel did say was to cer-tain poor
2 They look-ed up and saw a star shin-ing in the
3 And by the light of that same star three wise men
4 This star drew nigh to the north-west; o'er Beth - le -

shep-herds in fields as they lay, in fields where they lay keep-ing
east be-yond them far; and to the earth it gave
came from coun - try far; to seek for a king was their
hem it took its rest, and there it did both stop

their sheep, on a cold win-ter's night that was so deep.
great light, and so it con - tin-ued both day and night.
in - tent, and to fol-low the star wher-ev - er it went.
and stay, right o - ver the place where Je - sus lay.

Refrain

Now - ell, Now - ell, Now - ell, Now - ell,

"Nowell" is the English form of the French "noel," a shout of joy formerly used at Christmas (as in Chaucer's "Franklin's Tale"), a clue that the word is older than its first printing. It may have Latin and French roots related to "born" (*natus / né*) as well to "news" (*nova / nouvelle*).

TEXT: English carol; *Some Ancient Christmas Carols*, 2nd ed., 1823, alt.
MUSIC: English carol; Sandys' *Christmas Carols*, 1833

THE FIRST NOWELL
Irregular

born is the King of Is - ra - el.

5 Then entered in those wise men three,
full reverently upon their knee,
and offered there in his presence
their gold, and myrrh, and
   frankincense.
Refrain

6 Then let us all with one accord
sing praises to our heavenly Lord,
that hath made heaven and earth of nought,
and with his blood our life hath bought.
Refrain

Mary and Joseph Came to the Temple 148

1 Mar-y and Jo - seph came to the tem - ple brought the boy
2 An - na had prayed there, wid - owed, long wait - ing, wor - ship - ing
3 Sim - e - on sings now: God prof - fers bless - ing, bril - liant - ly

Je - sus, of - fered him there. Peo - ple were wait - ing
God by day and by night. Now she is prais - ing,
gild - ing dawn of his day. Light in the dark - ness,

want - ing to greet him; long had they sought him, so - lace for care.
filled with e - la - tion: here is God's prom - ise, Christ is her light.
nev - er ex - tin-guished, Light of all na - tions, light up our way.

This text retells the story in Luke 2:22–39, usually called the Presentation of Christ in the Temple, which took place forty days after his birth. Mary, Joseph, and the Christ-child encounter there two devout people, Anna and Simeon, who identify this baby as the promised Messiah.

TEXT: Andrew Pratt, 1994
MUSIC: David Haas, 1985
Text © 1997 Stainer & Bell, Ltd. (admin. Hope Publishing Company)
Music © 1985 GIA Publications, Inc.

EVENING HYMN
5.5.5.4.D

149 All Hail to God's Anointed
(Psalm 72)

1 All hail to God's a - noint-ed, great Da - vid's great-er Son!
2 You come with res - cue speed - y to those who suf - fer wrong,
3 You shall come down like show - ers up - on the fruit - ful earth;
4 All rul - ers bow be - fore you, and gold and in - cense bring.

All hail, in time ap - point - ed, your reign on earth be - gun!
to help the poor and need - y and bid the weak be strong;
love, joy, and hope, like flow - ers, spring in your path to birth.
All na - tions shall a - dore you; your praise all peo - ple sing.

You come to break op - pres - sion, to set the cap - tive free,
to give them songs for sigh - ing, their dark-ness turn to light,
Be - fore you on the moun-tains shall peace, the her - ald, go,
To you shall prayer un - ceas - ing and dai - ly vows as - cend.

to take a - way trans - gres - sion and rule in eq - ui - ty.
whose souls, con-demned and dy - ing, are pre-cious in your sight.
and righ-teous-ness in foun - tains from hill to val - ley flow.
Your rule is still in - creas - ing; your rule is with-out end.

Originally a celebration of God's sovereignty, Psalm 72 has often been given a Christological interpretation, notably in Isaac Watts's "Jesus Shall Reign" (see no. 265). The references to rulers here probably influenced the view that the Magi of Matthew 2 were kings (see no. 151).

TEXT: James Montgomery, 1821, alt.
MUSIC: Thomas Tertuis Noble, 1938
Music © 1941 United Church Press (admin. The Pilgrim Press)

ROCKPORT
7.6.7.6.D

As with Gladness Men of Old 150

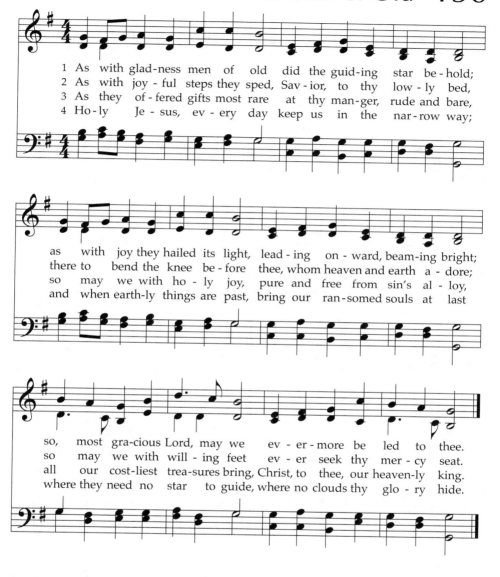

1 As with glad-ness men of old did the guid-ing star be-hold;
2 As with joy-ful steps they sped, Sav-ior, to thy low-ly bed,
3 As they of-fered gifts most rare at thy man-ger, rude and bare,
4 Ho-ly Je-sus, ev-ery day keep us in the nar-row way;

as with joy they hailed its light, lead-ing on-ward, beam-ing bright;
there to bend the knee be-fore thee, whom heaven and earth a-dore;
so may we with ho-ly joy, pure and free from sin's al-loy,
and when earth-ly things are past, bring our ran-somed souls at last

so, most gra-cious Lord, may we ev-er-more be led to thee.
so may we with will-ing feet ev-er seek thy mer-cy seat.
all our cost-liest trea-sures bring, Christ, to thee, our heaven-ly king.
where they need no star to guide, where no clouds thy glo-ry hide.

The first three stanzas here use an as/so structure to draw parallels between the coming of the Magi and the spiritual lives of the singers, summed up in the prayer of the fourth stanza. Even though this adapted German tune was named for him, the author did not care for it.

TEXT: William Chatterton Dix, c. 1858
MUSIC: Conrad Kocher, 1838; abr. William Henry Monk, 1861; harm. The English Hymnal, 1906

DIX
7.7.7.7.7.7

151 We Three Kings of Orient Are

1 We three kings of O-ri-ent are; bear-ing gifts we tra-verse a-far,
2 Born a King on Beth-le-hem's plain, gold I bring to crown him a-gain,
3 Frank-in-cense to of-fer have I; in-cense owns a de-i-ty nigh;
4 Myrrh is mine; its bit-ter per-fume breathes a life of gath-er-ing gloom;
5 Glo-rious now be-hold him a-rise, King and God and Sac - ri-fice:

field and foun-tain, moor and moun-tain, fol - low - ing yon-der star.
King for - ev - er, ceas-ing nev - er o - ver us all to reign.
prayer and prais-ing glad - ly rais - ing, wor - ship - ing God Most High.
sor-rowing, sigh-ing, bleed-ing, dy - ing, sealed in the stone-cold tomb.
Al - le - lu - ia! Al - le-lu - ia! sounds through the earth and skies.

Refrain

O star of won - der, star of night, star with roy - al beau-ty bright,

west-ward lead-ing, still pro-ceed-ing, guide us to thy per-fect light!

Although Christians had begun by the 2nd century to speak of these visitors from eastern countries (Matthew 2:1–12) as "kings," perhaps because of passages like Psalm 72:10 and Isaiah 60:3, it is more accurate to think of them as magi or astrologers, the scholars of their day.

TEXT and MUSIC: John Henry Hopkins Jr., 1857, alt.

KINGS OF ORIENT
8.8.8.6 with refrain

What Star Is This, with Beams So Bright 152

Capo 2: (C) (Am) (G) (C) (F) (C) (G) (C) (F)
D Bm A D G D A D G

1 What star is this, with beams so bright, more
2 'Tis now ful - filled what God de - creed, "From
3 While out - ward signs the star dis - plays, an
4 O Je - sus, while the star of grace im -

(C) (G) (C) (F) (C) (G)
D A D G D A

love - ly than the noon - day light? 'Tis
Ja - cob shall a star pro - ceed"; and
in - ward light the Lord con - veys and
pels us on to seek your face, let

(Am) (D7) (G) (C) (F) (C) (Dm)
Bm E7 A D G D Em

sent to an - nounce a new - born king, glad
lo! the east - ern sa - ges stand to
urg - es them, with ten - der might, to
not our sloth - ful hearts re - fuse the

(G) (C) (G) (C) (F) (G) (C)
A D A D G A D

ti - dings of our God to bring.
read in heaven the Lord's com - mand.
seek the giv - er of the light.
guid - ance of your light to use.

This 18th-century Latin text calls attention to three kinds of light: the light of the star leading the Magi to the Christ-child, the inward light inspiring their journey, and Christ who is the Light of the world. The simple unison melody unites everything in a gentle arc.

TEXT: Charles Coffin, 1736; trans. John Chandler, 1837, alt.
MUSIC: Trier ms.; 15th cent.; adapt. Michael Praetorius, 1609; harm. George Ratcliffe Woodward, 1910

PUER NOBIS NASCITUR
LM
(alternate harmonization, 254)

153 In Bethlehem a Newborn Boy

1 In Beth-le-hem a new-born boy was hailed with
2 The sol-diers sought the child in vain: not yet was
3 Still rage the fires of hate to-day, and in-no-
4 Lord Je-sus, through our night of loss shines out the
5 May that great love our lives con-trol and con-quer

songs of praise and joy. Then warn-ing came of
he to share our pain; but down the a-ges
cents the price must pay, while ach-ing hearts in
won-der of your cross, the love that can-not
hate in ev-ery soul, till, pledged to build and

dan-ger near: King Her-od's troops would soon ap-pear.
rings the cry of those who saw their chil-dren die.
ev-ery land cry out, "We can-not un-der-stand!"
cease to bear our hu-man an-guish ev-ery-where.
not de-stroy, we share your pain and find your joy.

Guitar chords do not correspond with keyboard harmony.

The Slaughter of the Innocents (Matthew 2:16–18) is not an event we like to think about, but this text shows how it connects to the ongoing suffering of parents and children in our world today. Only the love that led Christ to the cross can bear the weight of such human anguish.

TEXT: Rosamond E. Herklots, 1969, alt.   IN BETHLEHEM
MUSIC: Wilbur Held, 1983   LM
Text © 1981 Oxford University Press
Music © 1983 Wilbur Held

Jesus Entered Egypt

154

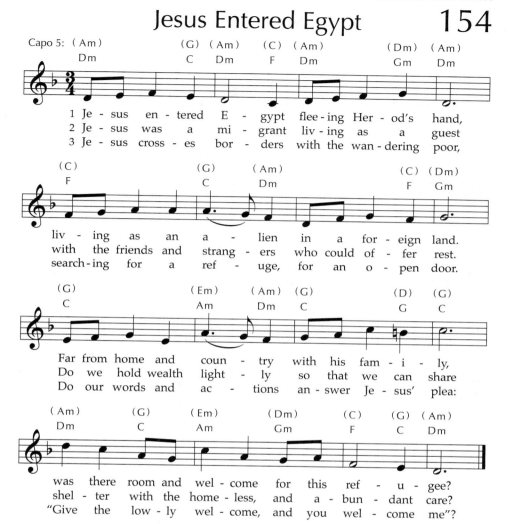

1 Je - sus en - tered E - gypt flee - ing Her - od's hand,
2 Je - sus was a mi - grant liv - ing as a guest
3 Je - sus cross - es bor - ders with the wan - dering poor,

liv - ing as an a - lien in a for - eign land.
with the friends and strang - ers who could of - fer rest.
search - ing for a ref - uge, for an o - pen door.

Far from home and coun - try with his fam - i - ly,
Do we hold wealth light - ly so that we can share
Do our words and ac - tions an - swer Je - sus' plea:

was there room and wel - come for this ref - u - gee?
shel - ter with the home - less, and a - bun - dant care?
"Give the low - ly wel - come, and you wel - come me"?

Guitar chords do not correspond with keyboard harmony.

Human beings create divisions for many political, social, economic, and military reasons, but God is no respecter of the boundaries we erect. Jesus taught us to look for and respect the image of God that can be found in every human being, and to care for "the least of these."

TEXT: Adam M. L. Tice, 2007
MUSIC: Ralph Vaughan Williams, 1925
Text © 2009 GIA Publications, Inc.
Music © 1925 Oxford University Press

KING'S WESTON
6.5.6.5.D

155 Raise a Song of Gladness

Jubilate Deo

Raise a song of glad-ness, peo-ples of the earth.
Ju - bi - la - te De - o om - nis ter - ra.

Christ has come, bring-ing peace, joy to ev-ery heart.
Ser - vi - te Do - mi - no in lae - ti - ti - a.

Al - le - lu - ia, al - le - lu - ia, joy to ev-ery heart!
Al - le - lu - ia, al - le - lu - ia, in lae - ti - ti - a!

Al - le - lu - ia, al - le - lu - ia, joy to ev-ery heart!
Al - le - lu - ia, al - le - lu - ia, in lae - ti - ti - a!

May be sung as a canon.

The Latin text here, for which the musical setting was originally composed, is from Psalm 100:1. The English paraphrase gives this verse a Christian interpretation, much as Isaac Watts did when he paraphrased Psalm 98 to produce "Joy to the World! The Lord Is Come" (see no. 134).

TEXT: Taizé Community, 1978
MUSIC: Jacques Berthier, 1978
Text and Music © 1979 Les Presses de Taizé (admin. GIA Publications, Inc.)

JUBILATE DEO
Irregular

Sing of God Made Manifest

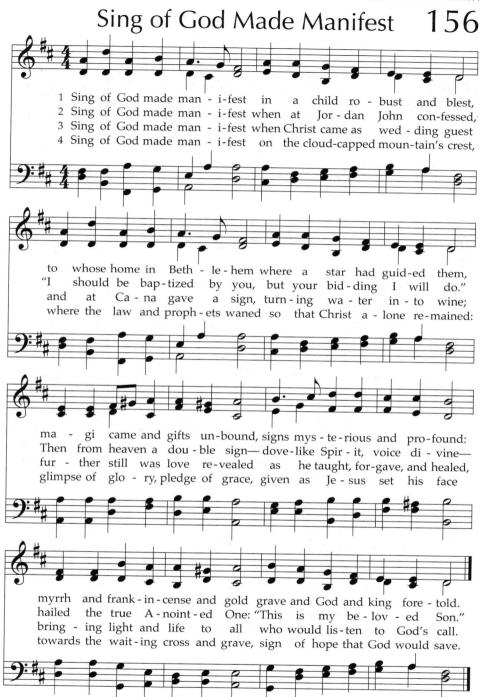

1 Sing of God made man-i-fest in a child ro-bust and blest,
2 Sing of God made man-i-fest when at Jor-dan John con-fessed,
3 Sing of God made man-i-fest when Christ came as wed-ding guest
4 Sing of God made man-i-fest on the cloud-capped moun-tain's crest,

to whose home in Beth-le-hem where a star had guid-ed them,
"I should be bap-tized by you, but your bid-ding I will do."
and at Ca-na gave a sign, turn-ing wa-ter in-to wine;
where the law and proph-ets waned so that Christ a-lone re-mained:

ma-gi came and gifts un-bound, signs mys-te-rious and pro-found:
Then from heaven a dou-ble sign—dove-like Spir-it, voice di-vine—
fur-ther still was love re-vealed as he taught, for-gave, and healed,
glimpse of glo-ry, pledge of grace, given as Je-sus set his face

myrrh and frank-in-cense and gold grave and God and king fore-told.
hailed the true A-noint-ed One: "This is my be-lov-ed Son."
bring-ing light and life to all who would lis-ten to God's call.
towards the wait-ing cross and grave, sign of hope that God would save.

"Epiphany" means "manifestation" or "showing forth," and this text cites key disclosures of Jesus as Messiah: the coming of the Magi, his baptism by John the Baptist, the wedding at Cana. All are summed up in the Transfiguration, recalled on the Last Sunday after the Epiphany.

TEXT: Carl P. Daw Jr., 1990
MUSIC: Jakob Hintze, 1678; arr. Johann Sebastian Bach
Text © 1990 Hope Publishing Company

SALZBURG
7.7.7.7.D

157 I Danced in the Morning

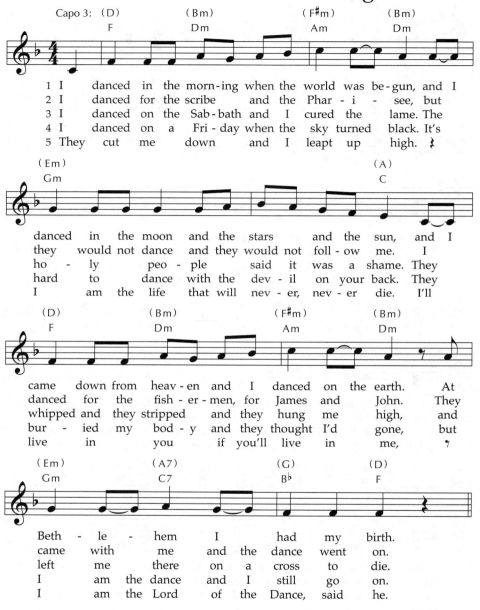

Capo 3: (D)   (Bm)   (F#m)   (Bm)
F   Dm   Am   Dm

1 I danced in the morn-ing when the world was be-gun, and I
2 I danced for the scribe and the Phar-i-see, but
3 I danced on the Sab-bath and I cured the lame. The
4 I danced on a Fri-day when the sky turned black. It's
5 They cut me down and I leapt up high. ⸭

(Em)   (A)
Gm   C

danced in the moon and the stars and the sun, and I
they would not dance and they would not foll-ow me. I
ho-ly peo-ple said it was a shame. They
hard to dance with the dev-il on your back. They
I am the life that will nev-er, nev-er die. I'll

(D)   (Bm)   (F#m)   (Bm)
F   Dm   Am   Dm

came down from heav-en and I danced on the earth. At
danced for the fish-er-men, for James and John. They
whipped and they stripped and they hung me high, and
bur-ied my bod-y and they thought I'd gone, but
live in you if you'll live in me, ⸭

(Em)   (A7)   (G)   (D)
Gm   C7   Bb   F

Beth-le-hem I had my birth.
came with me and the dance went on.
left me there on a cross to die.
I am the dance and I still go on.
I am the Lord of the Dance, said he.

This 20th-century ballad-like retelling of the life of Christ, though written for this Shaker tune, has many similarities with the pre-Reformation carol "Tomorrow shall be my dancing day." Such narrative carols were common both at Christmas and as part of medieval mystery plays.

TEXT: Sydney Carter, 1963
MUSIC: American Shaker melody; adapt. Sydney Carter, 1963
Text and Music © 1963 Stainer & Bell, Ltd. (admin. Hope Publishing Company)

LORD OF THE DANCE
Irregular

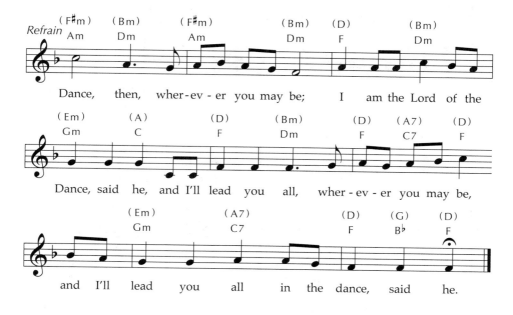

Refrain

Dance, then, wher-ev-er you may be; I am the Lord of the
Dance, said he, and I'll lead you all, wher-ev-er you may be,
and I'll lead you all in the dance, said he.

Born in the Night, Mary's Child 158

1 Born in the night, Mar-y's Child, a long way from your home;
2 Clear shin-ing light, Mar-y's Child, your face lights up our way;
3 Truth of our life, Mar-y's Child, you tell us God is good;
4 Hope of the world, Mar-y's Child, you're com-ing soon to reign;

com - ing in need, Mar-y's Child, born in a bor-rowed room.
Light of the world, Mar-y's Child, dawn on our dark-ened day.
yes, it is true, Mar-y's Child, shown on your cross of wood.
King of the earth, Mar-y's Child, walk in our streets a - gain.

Guitar chords do not correspond with keyboard harmony.

Carried by a blues-like tune, this text of clustered phrases centers on the core words "Mary's Child,"
initially linking images that suggest a Nativity hymn, but by the third stanza widening to the full arc
of the Incarnation: birth, life, death, resurrection, ascension, return.

TEXT: Geoffrey Ainger, 1964, alt.
MUSIC: Geoffrey Ainger, 1964; harm. Richard D. Wetzel, 1972
Text and Music © 1964 Stainer & Bell, Ltd. (admin. Hope Publishing Company)

MARY'S CHILD
7.6.7.6

159 O Sing a Song of Bethlehem

1 O sing a song of Beth-le-hem, of shep-herds watch-ing there,
2 O sing a song of Naz-a-reth, of sun-ny days of joy;
3 O sing a song of Gal-i-lee, of lake and woods and hill,
4 O sing a song of Cal-va-ry, its glo-ry and dis-may,

and of the news that came to them from an-gels in the air.
O sing of fra-grant flow-ers' breath, and of the sin - less boy.
of him who walked up-on the sea and bade its waves be still.
of him who hung up-on the tree, and took our sins a - way.

The light that shone on Beth-le-hem fills all the world to - day.
For now the flowers of Naz-a-reth in ev - ery heart may grow.
For though, like waves on Gal-i-lee, dark seas of trou-ble roll,
For he who died on Cal-va-ry is ris-en from the grave,

Of Je - sus' birth and peace on earth the an-gels sing al - way.
Now spreads the fame of his dear name on all the winds that blow.
when faith has heard the Mas-ter's word, falls peace up-on the soul.
and Christ, our Lord, by heaven a-dored, is might-y now to save.

This hymn created by a noted Presbyterian hymnal editor and scholar employs place names and sensory images (light, fragrance, wind) to sketch the events of Christ's life. The tune name commemorates the village in Sussex where the arranger first heard the traditional melody.

TEXT: Louis FitzGerald Benson, 1899
MUSIC: *English County Songs*, 1893; harm. Ralph Vaughan Williams, 1906

KINGSFOLD
CMD

A Stable Lamp Is Lighted

160

Guitar chords do not correspond with keyboard harmony.

The doubled lines in each stanza of this reflection on Christ's birth and death echo his saying (Luke 19:40) that creation will praise him if people are silent. This text by a former Poet Laureate of the United States is set to a lullaby-like tune specially composed for it.

TEXT: Richard Wilbur, 1959
MUSIC: David Hurd, 1984
Text © 1961, ren. 1989 Richard Wilbur (admin. Houghton Mifflin Harcourt Publishing Co.)
Music © 1984 GIA Publications, Inc.

ANDUJAR
7.6.7.6.6.6.7.6

161 Woman in the Night

1 Wom-an in the night, spent from giv-ing birth,
2 Wom-an at the well, ques-tion the Mes-siah;
3 Wom-an in the house, nur-tured to be meek,
4 Wom-en on the hill, stand when men have fled;

guard our pre-cious light; peace is on the earth.
find your friends and tell: drink your heart's de-sire!
leave your sec-ond place, lis-ten, think, and speak!
Christ needs lov-ing still, though your hope is dead.

Wom-an in the crowd, creep-ing up be-hind,
Wom-an at the feast, let the righ-teous stare;
Wom-en on the road, from your sick-ness freed,
Wom-en in the dawn, care and spic-es bring,

touch-ing is al-lowed: seek and you will find!
come and go in peace; love him with your hair!
wit-ness and pro-vide, join-ing word and deed:
ear-li-est to mourn, ear-li-est to sing!

Refrain

Come and join the song, wom-en, chil-dren, men.

Je-sus makes us free to live a-gain!

Guitar chords do not correspond with keyboard harmony.

Beginning with a reference to Mary giving birth to Jesus, this text describes a series of women who had important encounters with his life, ministry, death, and resurrection. The dancelike refrain celebrates how their experiences reveal that the Good News is for all people.

TEXT: Brian Wren, 1982; rev. 1995
MUSIC: Alfred V. Fedak, 1989
Text © 1983, rev. 1995 Hope Publishing Company
Music © 1990 Selah Publishing Co., Inc.

NEW DISCIPLES (Fedak)
5.5.5.5.D with refrain

O Carpenter, Why Leave the Bench 162

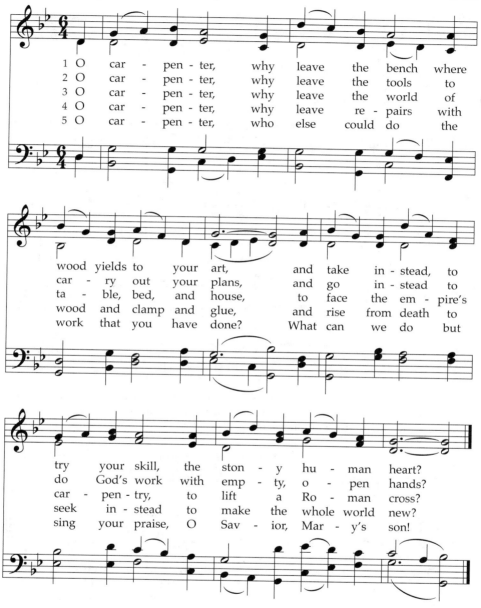

1 O car - pen - ter, why leave the bench where
2 O car - pen - ter, why leave the tools to
3 O car - pen - ter, why leave the world of
4 O car - pen - ter, why leave re - pairs with
5 O car - pen - ter, who else could do the

wood yields to your art, and take in - stead, to
car - ry out your plans, and go in - stead to
ta - ble, bed, and house, to face the em - pire's
wood and clamp and glue, and rise from death to
work that you have done? What can we do but

try your skill, the ston - y hu - man heart?
do God's work with emp - ty, o - pen hands?
car - pen - try, to lift a Ro - man cross?
seek in - stead to make the whole world new?
sing your praise, O Sav - ior, Mar - y's son!

By dismissing Jesus as "the carpenter" (Mark 6:3) or "the carpenter's son" (Matthew 13:55), his neighbors convinced themselves that they could ignore his teaching. This reflective text explores the distance between that humble craft and the great importance of Christ's true work.

TEXT: Richard Leach, 1989
MUSIC: William Billings, 1794
Text © 1994 Selah Publishing Co., Inc.
Music Harm. © 1978 Lutheran Book of Worship (admin. Augsburg Fortress)

LEWIS-TOWN
CM

163 Wild and Lone the Prophet's Voice

1 Wild and lone the proph-et's voice ech-oes through the des - ert still,
2 "Bear the fruit re - pen-tance sows: lives of jus - tice, truth, and love.
3 With such preach-ing, stark and bold, John pro-claimed sal - va - tion near,

call - ing us to make a choice, bid - ding us to do God's will:
Trust no oth - er claim than those; set your heart on things a - bove.
and his time-less warn-ings hold words of hope to all who hear.

"Turn from sin and be bap-tized; cleanse your heart and mind and soul.
Soon the Lord will come in power, burn-ing clean the thresh-ing floor:
So we dare to jour - ney on, led by faith through ways un - trod,

Quit-ting all the sins you prized, yield your life to God's con - trol.
then will flames the chaff de - vour; wheat a - lone shall fill God's store."
till we come at last like John to be - hold the Lamb of God.

While all four gospels identify John the Baptist with the prophecy of Isaiah 40:3, this text (well set to a vigorous Welsh tune) draws on the report of his preaching in Matthew 3:1–12. The final lines recall that he was the first to name Jesus "the Lamb of God" (John 1:29, 36).

TEXT: Carl P. Daw Jr., 1985
MUSIC: Joseph Parry, 1876
Text © 1989 Hope Publishing Company

ABERYSTWYTH
7.7.7.7.D

Down Galilee's Slow Roadways 164

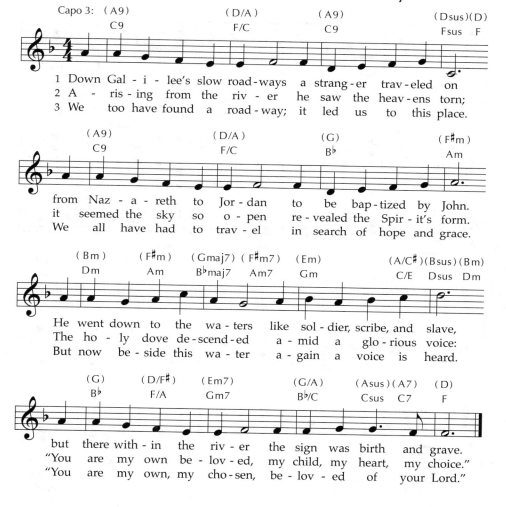

1 Down Gal - i - lee's slow road - ways a strang - er trav - eled on
2 A - ris - ing from the riv - er he saw the heav - ens torn;
3 We too have found a road - way; it led us to this place.

from Naz - a - reth to Jor - dan to be bap - tized by John.
it seemed the sky so o - pen re - vealed the Spir - it's form.
We all have had to trav - el in search of hope and grace.

He went down to the wa - ters like sol - dier, scribe, and slave,
The ho - ly dove de - scend - ed a - mid a glo - rious voice:
But now be - side this wa - ter a - gain a voice is heard.

but there with - in the riv - er the sign was birth and grave.
"You are my own be - lov - ed, my child, my heart, my choice."
"You are my own, my cho - sen, be - lov - ed of your Lord."

When reviewing baptismal resources with other members of the United Church of Canada's Working Unit on Worship, the author was struck by how few hymns had been written for adult baptism. This meditative text on the Baptism of Jesus is an effort to remedy that situation.

TEXT: Sylvia G. Dunstan, 1991
MUSIC: John D. Horman, 1998
Text © 1991 GIA Publications, Inc.
Music © 1998 Abingdon Press (admin. The Copyright Company)

WEST MAIN
7.6.7.6.D
(alternate tune: WIE LIEBLICH IST DER MAIEN)

165 The Glory of These Forty Days

1 The glory of these forty days we
2 A - lone and fast - ing Mo - ses saw the
3 So Dan - iel trained his mys - tic sight, de -
4 Then grant that we like them be true, con -

cel - e - brate with songs of praise; for Christ, by whom all
lov - ing God who gave the law; and to E - li - jah,
liv - ered from the li - ons' might; and John, the Bride-groom's
sumed in fast and prayer with you; our spir - its strength-en

things were made, him - self has fast - ed and has prayed.
fast - ing, came the steeds and char - i - ots of flame.
friend, be - came the her - ald of Mes - si - ah's name.
with your grace, and give us joy to see your face.

Appropriate for singing at any time during Lent, this stately text connects Jesus' wilderness fast with the solitary testing of other prophetic souls: Moses, Elijah, Daniel, and John the Baptist. This sturdy 16th-century chorale melody formed the basis of Bach's *Cantata 126*.

TEXT: Gregory the Great, 6th cent.; trans. Maurice F. Bell, 1906, alt.
MUSIC: Klug's *Geistliche Lieder,* 1543; harm. Johann Sebastian Bach, 1725

ERHALT UNS, HERR
LM

Lord, Who throughout These Forty Days

166

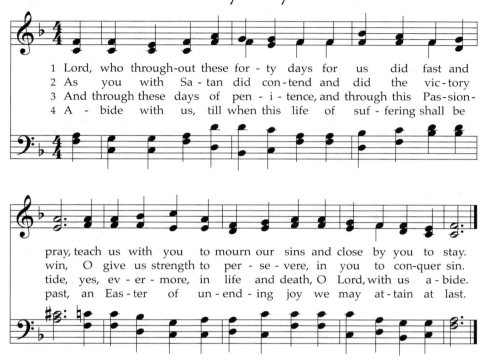

1 Lord, who through-out these for - ty days for us did fast and
2 As you with Sa - tan did con-tend and did the vic - tory
3 And through these days of pen - i - tence, and through this Pas-sion-
4 A - bide with us, till when this life of suf - fering shall be

pray, teach us with you to mourn our sins and close by you to stay.
win, O give us strength to per - se - vere, in you to con-quer sin.
tide, yes, ev - er - more, in life and death, O Lord, with us a - bide.
past, an Eas - ter of un - end - ing joy we may at-tain at last.

Like many of this author's hymns, this text was written primarily for children but works equally well in reminding adults how Lent connects us with Christ's temptation in the wilderness and prepares us for Easter. The 16th-century English psalm tune provides sturdy support.

TEXT: Claudia F. I. Hernaman, 1873, alt.
MUSIC: Day's *Psalter*, 1562

ST. FLAVIAN
CM

167 Forty Days and Forty Nights

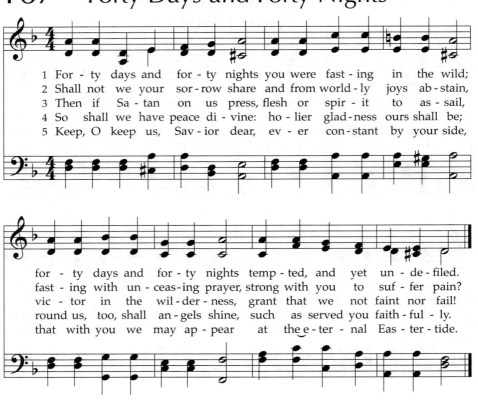

1 For-ty days and for-ty nights you were fast-ing in the wild;
2 Shall not we your sor-row share and from world-ly joys ab-stain,
3 Then if Sa-tan on us press, flesh or spir-it to as-sail,
4 So shall we have peace di-vine: ho-lier glad-ness ours shall be;
5 Keep, O keep us, Sav-ior dear, ev-er con-stant by your side,

for-ty days and for-ty nights temp-ted, and yet un-de-filed.
fast-ing with un-ceas-ing prayer, strong with you to suf-fer pain?
vic-tor in the wil-der-ness, grant that we not faint nor fail!
round us, too, shall an-gels shine, such as served you faith-ful-ly.
that with you we may ap-pear at the e-ter-nal Eas-ter-tide.

This text, given sharper focus by being reduced from nine stanzas to five, reflects both on Christ's temptation in the wilderness and on the purpose and goal of Lent as preparation for Easter. It pairs well with a 17th-century German chorale setting for Psalm 130.

TEXT: George Hunt Smyttan, 1856, alt.
MUSIC: Attr. Martin Herbst, 1676

AUS DER TIEFE RUFE ICH
7.7.7.7

Within Your Shelter, Loving God 168
(Psalm 91)

1 With-in your shel-ter, lov-ing God, my ref-uge and my tower,
2 Be-cause I trust in you a-lone, no e-vil shall come near.
3 Your ho-ly an-gels bear me up and keep my feet se-cure.
4 As of-ten as I call to you, you kind-ly hear my prayer.
5 All those who know your name on earth shall life a-bun-dant know.

I safe-ly walk by day and night be-neath your guid-ing power.
The strong de-fend-er of my home, with you I have no fear.
Though fierce and an-gry foes as-sail, in you my way is sure.
In times of trou-ble and dis-tress I rest in your own care.
On all a-bid-ing in your love your sav-ing grace be-stow.

The most familiar part of this paraphrase of Psalm 91 may be the third stanza, based on verses Satan quotes when tempting Jesus to throw himself off a pinnacle of the Temple (Matthew 4:5–6 / Luke 4:9–11). Citing Scripture outside the context of faith undercuts its true power.

TEXT: John G. Dunn, 1982
MUSIC: Scottish Psalter, 1615
Text © 1983, rev. 1985 John G. Dunn

ABBEY
CM

169 Dear Lord and Father of Mankind

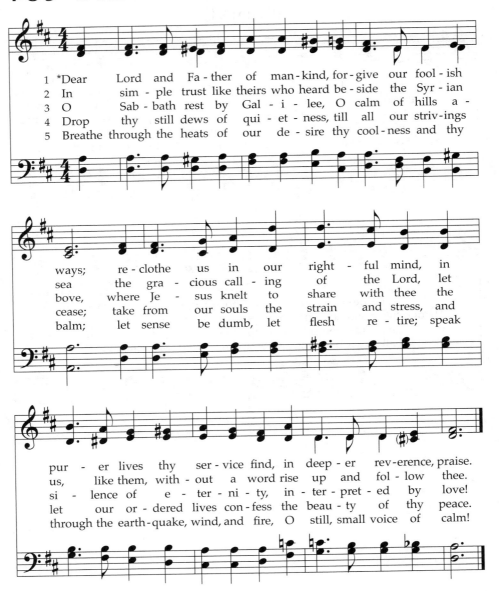

1 *Dear Lord and Father of mankind, forgive our foolish
2 In simple trust like theirs who heard beside the Syrian
3 O Sabbath rest by Galilee, O calm of hills a-
4 Drop thy still dews of quietness, till all our strivings
5 Breathe through the heats of our desire thy coolness and thy

ways; reclothe us in our rightful mind, in
sea the gracious calling of the Lord, let
bove, where Jesus knelt to share with thee the
cease; take from our souls the strain and stress, and
balm; let sense be dumb, let flesh retire; speak

purer lives thy service find, in deeper reverence, praise.
us, like them, without a word rise up and follow thee.
silence of eternity, interpreted by love!
let our ordered lives confess the beauty of thy peace.
through the earthquake, wind, and fire, O still, small voice of calm!

*Or "Dear Lord, Creator good and kind"

These stanzas were carved into a hymn from a much longer poem describing a frenzied ritual by an obscure
sect in India, but they culminate in a reference to 1 Kings 19:11–12 that celebrates silence (as befits a Quaker
poet). This tune was created especially for these words.

TEXT: John Greenleaf Whittier, 1872
MUSIC: Frederick Charles Maker, 1887

REST
8.6.8.8.6
(alternate tune: REPTON)

You Walk along Our Shoreline 170

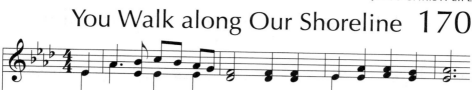

1 You walk a-long our shore-line where land meets un-known sea.
2 You call us, Christ, to gath-er the peo-ple of the earth.
3 We cast our net, O Je-sus; we cry the king-dom's name;

We hear your voice of pow-er, "Now come and fol-low me.
We can-not fish for on-ly those lives we think have worth.
we work for love and jus-tice; we learn to hope through pain.

And if you still will fol-low through storm and wave and shoal,
We spread your net of gos-pel a-cross the wa-ter's face,
You call us, Lord, to gath-er God's daugh-ters and God's sons,

then I will make you fish-ers but of the hu-man soul."
our boat a com-mon shel-ter for all found by your grace.
to let your judg-ment heal us so that all may be one.

Based on Jesus' calling of the disciples (Matthew 4:18–22 / Mark 1:16–20 / Luke 5:4–11), this hymn notes that their mode of fishing involved nets requiring the participation of more than one person. Likewise, in our work of love and justice we are called to bear witness in community.

TEXT: Sylvia G. Dunstan, 1984
MUSIC: Johann Steurlein, 1575
Text © 1991 GIA Publications, Inc.

WIE LIEBLICH IST DER MAIEN
7.6.7.6.D

171 A Sower Came from Ancient Hills

1 A Sow-er came from an-cient hills and cast good
2 A Sow-er walked through-out the land and, ev-ery-
3 The Seed was bur-ied deep in death be-neath a
4 O Christ, you come a-mong us still, the Sow-er

seed a-broad: his field, ten thou-sand hu-man hearts; his
where he trod, he sowed his life be-cause he was him-
blood-red sky, and deep-er still was bur-ied hope for
and the Seed. As once you sowed the truth of God in

seed, the word of God. And some who lis-tened would not
self the Seed of God. But then, a-top a bar-ren
those who watched him die. But then, in Jo-seph's gar-den
glow-ing word and deed, im-plant your Word in wait-ing

hear, and some who heard for-got. But some re-ceived in
hill, be-neath a dark-ening sky, they threw God's Seed on
fair, as dawn broke o'er the land, the Seed, from three days'
hearts, and let it there take hold, un-til it bears in

fer-tile soil the truth the Sow-er taught.
ston-y ground and left it there to die.
si-lent sleep, a-woke at God's com-mand!
fruit-ful lives a har-vest hun-dred-fold.

Guitar chords do not correspond with keyboard harmony.

All three synoptic gospels record both the telling and the explanation of Jesus' parable of the Sower (Matthew 13:3–8, 18–23/Mark 4:3–8, 14–20/Luke 8:5–8, 11–15). Because the seed equals "the word," Jesus (as the Word made flesh) becomes the Seed in this expansion of the parable.

TEXT: Herman G. Stuempfle Jr., 1998
MUSIC: John D. Horman, 2003
Text © 2006 GIA Publications, Inc.
Music © 2003 Zimbel Press

SEACHRIST
CMD

Blest Are They

1 Blest are they, the poor in spir - it; theirs is the king - dom of God. Blest are they,
2 Blest are they, the low - ly ones; they shall in - her - it the earth. Blest are they who
3 Blest are they who show mer - cy; mer - cy shall be theirs. Blest are they, the
4 Blest are they who seek peace; they are the chil - dren of God. Blest are they who
5 Blest are you who suf - fer hate, all be - cause of me. Re - joice, be glad;

full of sor - row; they shall be con - soled.
hun - ger and thirst; they shall have their fill.
pure of heart; they shall see God.
suf - fer in faith; the glo - ry of God is theirs.
yours is the king - dom; shine for all to see.

Refrain

Re - joice and be glad! Bless - ed are you;
ho - ly are you! Re - joice and be glad!
Yours is the king - dom of God!

This hymn paraphrases the Beatitudes (Matthew 5:1–12), the opening portion of Christ's Sermon on the Mount. Similar words of blessing also occur in the Sermon on the Plain (Luke 6:20–23). Both sets of sayings reverse worldly values and offer a new understanding of God's ways.

TEXT: David Haas, 1985
MUSIC: David Haas, 1985; arr. David Haas and Michael Joncas, 1985
Text and Music © 1985 GIA Publications, Inc.

BLEST ARE THEY
Irregular

173 A Woman and a Coin

1 A wom-an and a coin: the coin is lost!
2 A shep-herd and a sheep: the sheep is lost!
3 A par-ent and a child: the child is lost!
4 Dear God, you sought us when the world was lost;

How much it means to her, what time and toil,
Far from the flock, the one in hun-dred cries,
The par-ent feeds on mem-o-ries and hope,
you gave your on-ly son at what a cost;

what part it was to play in her bright dreams!
then, risk-ing life, the shep-herd's voice and staff!
the prod-i-gal on husks and one last chance.
your Spir-it wel-comes home the tem-pest-tossed:

Am I that trea-sured coin worth search-ing for?
Am I that trea-sured sheep worth dy-ing for?
Am I that trea-sured child worth wait-ing for?
now we can be all you were dream-ing of.

I'm found, and you re-joice! What love! What love!
I live, and you re-joice! What love! What love!
I'm home, and you re-joice! What love! What love!
We're safe, and you re-joice! What love! What love!

This text is a summary and interpretation of the three parables of Jesus recorded in Luke 15:3–32. The order has been partly rearranged (the second and first are interchanged) to create an ascending order of significance and to provide a context for the well-known third parable.

TEXT: Jaroslav J. Vajda, 1990
MUSIC: Fred Kimball Graham, 1995
Text © 1990 Concordia Publishing House
Music © 1995 Fred Kimball Graham

LIFE RESTORED
Irregular

Come and Seek the Ways of Wisdom

174

1 Come and seek the ways of Wis-dom, she who danced when
2 Lis - ten to the voice of Wis-dom, cry - ing in the
3 Sis - ter Wis-dom, come, as - sist us; nur - ture all who

earth was new. Fol - low close - ly what she teach - es,
mar - ket - place. Hear the Word made flesh a - mong us,
seek re - birth. Spir - it - guide and close com - pan - ion,

for her words are right and true. Wis - dom clears the
full of glo - ry, truth, and grace. When the word takes
bring to light our sa - cred worth. Free us to be -

path to jus - tice, show - ing us what love must do.
root and rip - ens, peace and righ - teous - ness em - brace.
come your peo - ple, ho - ly friends of God and earth.

Drawing on numerous scriptural images of Wisdom (Greek: *Sophia*), especially in Proverbs, this text offers an alternative perspective on Trinitarian theology. The Wisdom tradition has played a role in Christian mysticism for centuries, as witnessed by the Hagia Sophia in Istanbul.

TEXT: Ruth Duck, 1993
MUSIC: Donna Kasbohm, 1995
Text © 1996 The Pilgrim Press
Music © 1997 The Pilgrim Press

MADELEINE
8.7.8.7.8.7

175

Seek Ye First

Descant

Al - le - lu - ia,

1 Seek ye first the king - dom of God
2 Ask, and it shall be giv - en un - to you;
3 You shall not live by bread a - lone,

al - le - lu - ia,

and its righ - teous - ness,
seek, and you shall find;
but by ev - ery word

The author and composer wrote the first stanza and folk-style tune after attending a Bible study on Matthew 6:33. The later stanzas, based respectively on Matthew 7:7 and Matthew 4:4, emerged anonymously. Such meditative singing of scripture is an important form of sung prayer.

TEXT: Stanza 1, Karen Lafferty, 1971, alt.; stanzas 2–3, anon.; Spanish trans. anon.;
    Korean trans. The United Methodist Korean Hymnal Committee
MUSIC: Karen Lafferty, 1971
*Text and Music © 1972 Universal Music – Brentwood Publishing/Calvary Chapel Costa Mesa dba CCCM Music
    (admin. Universal Music – Brentwood Benson Publishing)*

LAFFERTY
Irregular

al - le - lu - ia,

and all these things shall be add-ed un-to you.
knock, and the door shall be o-pened un-to you.
that pro - ceeds from the mouth of God.

al - le - lu - ia!

Al - le - lu, al-le-lu - ia!

SPANISH

1 Busca primero el reino de Dios
   y su perfecta justicia,
   que lo demás lo añadirá el Señor.
   Alelu, aleluya.

KOREAN

1 너희는 먼저- 주의 나라와
   그의를 구하-면
   이모든것 네게 더하시리라
   알렐-루 알렐루야

176 If You Only Had Faith
Si tuvieras fe

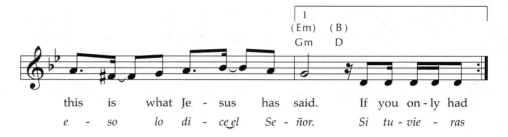

If you on-ly had faith, just like a lit-tle seed of mus-tard:
Si tu-vie-ras fe co-mo un gra-ni-to de mos-ta-za:

this is what Je - sus has said. If you on-ly had
e - so lo di - ce el Se - ñor. Si tu-vie - ras

said. You would be a - ble to tell this moun-tain: Move a -
ñor. Tú le di - rí - as a e-sa mon - ta - ña: ¡mué-ve-

way! Move a - way! You would be way! Move a -
te, mué - ve - te! Tú le di te, mué-ve-

This very singable musical version of Matthew 17:20/Luke 17:6 provides a memorable paraphrase of Jesus' arresting saying intended to assure his disciples that nothing will be impossible for those who have faith. Similar sayings appear in Matthew 21:21 and Mark 11:22–23.

TEXT: Caribbean Pentecostal chorus; English trans. Pablo Sosa, 2006
MUSIC: Caribbean Pentecostal chorus; transcr. and harm. Jorge Lockward, 2008
English Trans. © 2006 GIA Publications, Inc.
Music Transcr. and Harm. © 2008 General Board of Global Ministries t/a GBGMusik

SI TUVIERAS FE
Irregular

way! And then the moun-tain will move a - way, will move a-way,

te! Y la mon-ta - ña se mo - ve - rá, se mo-ve-rá,

Repeat ad lib Last time

will move a - way. And then the moun-tain will move a - way.

se mo-ve - rá. Y la mon-ta - ña se mo - ve - rá.

177 I Will Come to You

You Are Mine

1 "I will come to you in the si - lence;
2 "I am hope for all who are hope - less;
3 "I am strength for all the de - spair - ing,
(4) am the Word that leads all to free - dom; I

I will lift you from all your fear.
I am eyes for all who long to see. (2) In the
heal - ing for the ones who dwell in shame.
am the peace the world can - not give.

You will hear my voice; I claim you as my choice. Be
shad - ows of the night, I will be your light.
All the blind will see; the lame will all run free, and
I will call your name, em - brac - ing all your pain. Stand

still and know I am here. *(to stanza 2)*
Come and rest in me. *(to Refrain)*
all will know my name. *(to Refrain)*
up, now walk and live! *(to Refrain)*

Refrain *All*

Do not be a - fraid, I am with you. I have called you each by

name. Come and fol - low me, I will bring you home; I

love you and you are mine." 4 "I

Presuming to speak in the voice of God, as this song does, can only be done with integrity if the singers understand their words as an expression of what they believe about God's nature and God's intentions. It is an occasion for affirming faith, not for wishful thinking.

TEXT and MUSIC: David Haas, 1991
Text and Music © 1991 GIA Publications, Inc.

YOU ARE MINE
Irregular

The Woman Hiding in the Crowd 178

1 The wom - an hid - ing in the crowd reached
2 From Christ went forth the heal - ing grace, her
3 The wom - an knelt be - fore him then with
4 The bur - dens now that weigh us down, the
5 So touch us, Lord, with heal - ing grace and

for Christ's gar - ment hem that sim - ply by the
health and life re - stored. "Who touched my clothes?" the
joy and anx - ious fear, and Je - sus blessed her
sins we fear to speak, the ache of heart and
make us whole a - gain that we may al - ways

touch of it she might be healed with - in.
Sav - ior asked, but no one said a word.
lov - ing - ly: "In peace go forth from here."
emp - ty soul we lay be - fore your feet.
live in you and know your peace with - in.

The first three stanzas are based on the story of Christ's healing of a woman with an internal hemorrhage (Mark 5:24b–34/Luke 8:42b–48). By expanding and applying this event, the final two stanzas provide a helpful model of how scripture can be related to our own lives.

TEXT: J. Dudley Weaver Jr., 2008
MUSIC: William P. Rowan, 1992
Text © 2008 J. Dudley Weaver Jr.
Music © 1993 Selah Publishing Co., Inc.

SIMMONS
CM

179 Ten Lepers Facing Constant Scorn

1 Ten lep-ers fac-ing con-stant scorn, em-bold-ened by their
2 A name-less junc-tion in the road be-came a ho-ly
3 Would we have stopped, re-traced our steps, and then em-braced the

dai-ly plight, en-coun-tered One whose heal-ing touch was
turn-a-bout. One awe-struck con-vert spun a-round and,
liv-ing Lord whose word had ban-ished all our sores? What

known to put dis-ease to flight. The ten out-sid-ers sought re-
prais-ing God, be-gan to shout. God gave the space to turn a-
kind of thanks would we af-ford? God, make of us your liv-ing

lief: "Have mer-cy, Mas-ter, hear our plea." "Seek out the priests," the
round to all the oth-ers on the way, but on-ly one re-
tithes; the first fruits, fit to work for you. Let each be like that

Heal-er said. He knew the walk could set them free.
solved to seize the mir-a-cle of grace that day.
one in ten: trans-formed and cleansed, re-stored, made new.

Guitar chords do not correspond with keyboard harmony.

Each successive stanza of this text serves to retell, interpret, or apply Jesus' encounter with ten lepers outside an unnamed village on the border of Samaria and Galilee. This event, mentioned only in Luke 17:11–19, is characteristic of that gospel's emphasis on forgiveness.

TEXT: John Thornburg, 1995
MUSIC: Thomas Pavlechko, 1993
Text © 2003 John Thornburg (admin. Wayne Leupold Editions)
Music © 1994 Hope Publishing Company

RADIANT CITY
LMD

Silence! Frenzied, Unclean Spirit 180

1 "Si - lence! Fren - zied, un - clean spir - it," cried God's heal - ing,
2 Lord, the de - mons still are thriv - ing in the gray cells
3 Si - lence, Lord, the un - clean spir - it, in our mind and

Ho - ly One. "Cease your rant - ing! Flesh can't bear it.
of the mind: ty - rant voic - es, shrill and driv - ing,
in our heart. Speak your word that when we hear it

Flee as night be - fore the sun." At Christ's voice the de - mon
twist - ed thoughts that grip and bind, doubts that stir the heart to
all our de - mons shall de - part. Clear our thought and calm our

trem - bled, from its vic - tim mad - ly rushed, while the crowd that
pan - ic, fears dis - tort - ing rea - son's sight, guilt that makes our
feel - ing; still the frac - tured, war - ring soul. By the pow - er

was as - sem - bled stood in won - der, stunned, and hushed.
lov - ing fran - tic, dreams that cloud the soul with fright.
of your heal - ing make us faith - ful, true, and whole.

Based on Mark 1:21–28/Luke 4:31–37, this text recalls how Jesus exorcized a demon, ponders what demons mean today, and concludes with a prayer for wholeness. From percussive opening to melodic close, the collaboratively created tune suggests the movement from distress to healing.

TEXT: Thomas H. Troeger, 1984
MUSIC: Carol Doran, 1984
Text and Music © 1986 Oxford University Press

AUTHORITY
8.7.8.7.D
(alternate tune: EBENEZER, 181)

181 Silence! Frenzied, Unclean Spirit

1 "Si - lence! Fren - zied, un - clean spir - it," cried God's
2 Lord, the de - mons still are thriv - ing in the
3 Si - lence, Lord, the un - clean spir - it, in our

heal - ing, Ho - ly One. "Cease your rant - ing! Flesh can't
gray cells of the mind: ty - rant voic - es, shrill and
mind and in our heart. Speak your word that when we

bear it. Flee as night be - fore the sun."
driv - ing, twist - ed thoughts that grip and bind,
hear it all our de - mons shall de - part.

Based on Mark 1:21–28/Luke 4:31–37, this text recalls how Jesus exorcized a demon, ponders what demons mean today, and concludes with a prayer for wholeness. It is set here to a familiar Welsh tune whose recurring three-note figures help to convey a sense of internal turmoil.

TEXT: Thomas H. Troeger, 1984
MUSIC: Thomas John Williams, 1890
Text © 1986 Oxford University Press

EBENEZER
8.7.8.7.D
(alternate tune: AUTHORITY, 180)

At Christ's voice the de - mon trem-bled, from its vic - tim
doubts that stir the heart to pan - ic, fears dis - tort - ing
Clear our thought and calm our feel - ing; still the frac - tured,

mad - ly rushed, while the crowd that was as -
rea - son's sight, guilt that makes our lov - ing
war - ring soul. By the pow - er of your

sem - bled stood in won - der, stunned, and hushed.
fran - tic, dreams that cloud the soul with fright.
heal - ing make us faith - ful, true, and whole.

182 I Heard the Voice of Jesus Say

1 I heard the voice of Je-sus say, "Come un-to me and rest;
2 I heard the voice of Je-sus say, "Be-hold, I free-ly give
3 I heard the voice of Je-sus say, "I am this dark world's light;

lay down, O wea-ry one, lay down your head up-on my breast."
the liv-ing wa-ter, thirst-y one; stoop down and drink and live."
look un-to me, your morn shall rise, and all your day be bright."

I came to Je-sus as I was, so wea-ry, worn, and sad; I
I came to Je-sus, and I drank of that life-giv-ing stream; my
I looked to Je-sus, and I found in him my star, my sun; and

found in him a rest-ing place, and he has made me glad.
thirst was quenched, my soul re-vived, and now I live in him.
in that light of life I'll walk till trav-eling days are done.

Each stanza here pairs an invitation from Jesus with a response from the narrator. These three invitations recall how Jesus welcomed those who were heavy laden (Matthew 11:28), offered living water (John 4:10–14), and identified himself as the light of the world (John 8:12, 9:5).

TEXT: Horatius Bonar, 1846, alt.
MUSIC: *English County Songs*, 1893; harm. Ralph Vaughan Williams, 1906

KINGSFOLD
CMD

Come to Me, O Weary Traveler 183

1 "Come to me, O wea-ry trav-eler; come to me with your dis-tress;
2 "Do not fear, my yoke is eas-y; do not fear, my bur-den's light;
3 "Take my yoke and leave your trou-bles; take my yoke and come with me.
4 "Rest in me, O wea-ry trav-eler; rest in me and do not fear.

come to me, you heav-y bur-dened; come to me and find your rest."
do not fear the path be-fore you; do not run from me in fright."
Take my yoke, I am be-side you; take and learn hu-mil-i-ty."
Rest in me, my heart is gen-tle; rest and cast a-way your care."

This paraphrase and expansion of Matthew 11:28–30 by a Canadian minister is structured so that the first three syllables of each stanza provide the hymn's skeleton and summary. The immediacy of the text is enhanced by the folksong-like setting later composed for it.

TEXT: Sylvia G. Dunstan, 1991
MUSIC: William P. Rowan, 1992
Text © 1991 GIA Publications, Inc.
Music © 1993 Selah Publishing Co., Inc.

AUSTIN
8.7.8.7

Calm to the Waves 184

Calm to the waves. Calm to the wind. Je - sus whis-pers, "Peace, be

still." Balm to our hearts. Fears at an end. In still-ness, hear his voice.

The first half of this refrain text deals with the external environment, while the second half concerns our interior response. Similarly, the first half of the music gradually moves upward, while the direction of the second half is downward, enhancing a sense of centeredness.

TEXT: Mary Louise Bringle, 2002
MUSIC: Thomas Pavlechko, 2002
Text © 2002 GIA Publications, Inc.
Music © 2002 Selah Publishing Co., Inc.

CALM SEAS
4.4.7.4.4.6

185

Lonely the Boat

캄캄한 밤

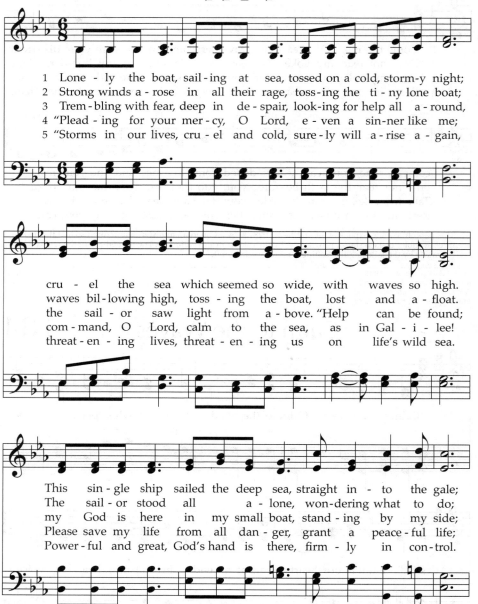

1 Lone - ly the boat, sail - ing at sea, tossed on a cold, storm - y night;
2 Strong winds a - rose in all their rage, toss - ing the ti - ny lone boat;
3 Trem - bling with fear, deep in de - spair, look - ing for help all a - round,
4 "Plead - ing for your mer - cy, O Lord, e - ven a sin - ner like me;
5 "Storms in our lives, cru - el and cold, sure - ly will a - rise a - gain,

cru - el the sea which seemed so wide, with waves so high.
waves bil - low - ing high, toss - ing the boat, lost and a - float.
the sail - or saw light from a - bove. "Help can be found;
com - mand, O Lord, calm to the sea, as in Gal - i - lee!
threat - en - ing lives, threat - en - ing us on life's wild sea.

This sin - gle ship sailed the deep sea, straight in - to the gale;
The sail - or stood all a - lone, won - der - ing what to do;
my God is here in my small boat, stand - ing by my side;
Please save my life from all dan - ger, grant a peace - ful life;
Power - ful and great, God's hand is there, firm - ly in con - trol.

This Korean hymn effectively uses the story of Jesus' calming of the storm (Matthew 8:23–27 / Mark 4:35–41 / Luke 8:22–25) as a parallel for the strength and comfort available to individuals on "life's wild sea." The universal immediacy of this image transcends cultural barriers.

TEXT: Helen Kim, 1921; English trans. Hae Jong Kim, 1980; vers. Hope C. Kawashima, 1987
MUSIC: Dong Hoon Lee, 1967
English Trans. © 1980 The Hymnal Society of Korea
English Vers. and Music © 1967, 1989 The United Methodist Publishing House (admin. The Copyright Company)

BAI
Irregular

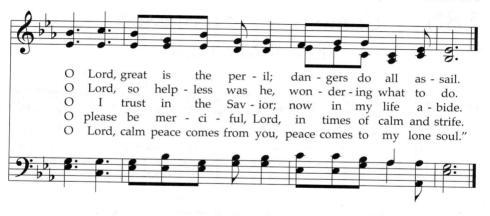

O Lord, great is the per - il; dan - gers do all as - sail.
O Lord, so help - less was he, won - der - ing what to do.
O I trust in the Sav - ior; now in my life a - bide.
O please be mer - ci - ful, Lord, in times of calm and strife.
O Lord, calm peace comes from you, peace comes to my lone soul."

KOREAN

1 캄캄한 밤 사-나운 바-람 불--때
만경창파 망-망한 바-다에
외로운배 한-척이 떠-나가니
아- 위태하구나 위-태하구나

2 비바람이 무-섭게 몰-아치--고
그 놀란물 큰- 파도 일-때에
저뱃사공 어-쩔줄 몰-라하니
아- 가련하구나 가-련하구나

3 절망중에 그- 사공 떨-면서--도
한 줄기의 밝-은빛 보-고서
배안에도 하-나님 계-심믿고
오- 기도올린다 기-도올린다

4 아버지여 이- 죄인 굽-어보--사
성난풍랑 잔-잔케 하-시고
이불쌍한 인-생을 살-리소서
오- 우리 하나님 우-리 하나님

5 모진바람 또- 험한 큰- 물결--이
제아무리 성-내어 덮-쳐도
권능의 손 그- 노를 저-으시니
오- 맑은 바다라 맑-은 바다라

186 Come Now, You Blessed, Eat at My Table

1 "Come now, you bless - ed, eat at my ta - ble," said Je - sus
2 When did we see you hun - gry or thirst - y? When were you
3 "When you gave bread to earth's hun - gry chil - dren, when you gave
4 Christ, when we see you out on life's road - ways, look - ing to

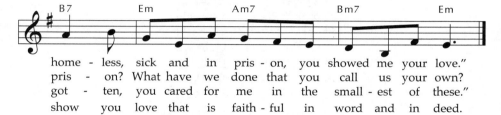

Christ to the right-teous a - bove. "When I was hun - gry, thirst - y, and
home - less, a strang - er a - lone? When did we see you sick or in
shel - ter to war's ref - u - gees, when you re - mem - bered those most for -
us in the fac - es of need, then may we know you, wel - come, and

home - less, sick and in pris - on, you showed me your love."
pris - on? What have we done that you call us your own?
got - ten, you cared for me in the small - est of these."
show you love that is faith - ful in word and in deed.

This text reproduces Matthew 25:34–39 so faithfully that it can appropriately be regarded as a paraphrase of that passage; but like all effective paraphrases, it adds just enough detail to give the familiar language a sense of freshness and immediacy that helps us hear it anew.

TEXT: Ruth Duck, 1979
MUSIC: Jeeva Sam, 1994; arr. Ron Klusmeier, 1995
Text © 1992 GIA Publications, Inc.
Music © 1995 Jeeva Sam
Music Arr. © 1995 Ron Klusmeier (admin. Musiklus)

COME NOW, YOU BLESSED
10.10.10.10

Savior, like a Shepherd Lead Us 187

1 Sav - ior, like a shep-herd lead us; much we need your ten-der care.
2 We are yours: in love be - friend us; be the guard-ian of our way.
3 You have prom-ised to re - ceive us, poor and sin-ful though we be;
4 Ear - ly let us seek your fa - vor; ear - ly let us do your will.

In your pleas-ant pas-tures feed us; for our use your fold pre-pare.
Keep your flock: from sin de - fend us; seek us when we go a-stray.
you have mer - cy to re - lieve us, grace to cleanse, and power to free.
Bless - ed Lord and on - ly Sav - ior, with your love our spir - its fill.

Bless-ed Je - sus, bless-ed Je - sus, you have bought us: we are yours.
Bless-ed Je - sus, bless-ed Je - sus, hear your chil - dren when we pray.
Bless-ed Je - sus, bless-ed Je - sus, ear - ly let us turn to you.
Bless-ed Je - sus, bless-ed Je - sus, you have loved us; love us still.

Bless-ed Je - sus, bless-ed Je - sus, you have bought us: we are yours.
Bless-ed Je - sus, bless-ed Je - sus, hear your chil - dren when we pray.
Bless-ed Je - sus, bless-ed Je - sus, ear - ly let us turn to you.
Bless-ed Je - sus, bless-ed Je - sus, you have loved us; love us still.

This unattributed hymn, like many that are now meaningful to adults, was written for children and develops shepherd imagery from Psalm 23 and John 10:1–18. The tune, composed for these words, was originally named for the text but has come to be known by the composer's name.

TEXT: Thrupp's *Hymns for the Young*, 1836, alt.
MUSIC: William Batchelder Bradbury, 1859, alt.

BRADBURY
8.7.8.7.D

188 Jesus Loves Me!

1 Je - sus loves me! This I know, for the Bi - ble tells me so.
2 Je - sus loves me! This I know, as he loved so long a - go,

Lit - tle ones to him be - long. They are weak, but he is strong.
tak - ing chil - dren on his knee, say - ing, "Let them come to me."

Refrain

Yes, Je - sus loves me! Yes, Je - sus loves me!

Yes, Je - sus loves me! The Bi - ble tells me so.

Few songs of faith have supported people from cradle to grave like this one. The great theologian Karl Barth said that its opening two lines were a summary of all that he had learned. The composer formed the refrain from those lines when creating this universally used tune.

TEXT: Stanza 1, Anna Bartlett Warner, 1859; stanza 2, David Rutherford McGuire, 1971
MUSIC: William Batchelder Bradbury, 1862, alt.

JESUS LOVES ME
7.7.7.7 with refrain

O Wondrous Sight, O Vision Fair 189

1 O won - drous sight, O vi - sion fair
2 From age to age the tale de - clare,
3 The law and proph - ets there have place,
4 With shin - ing face and bright ar - ray
5 And faith - ful hearts are raised on high

of glo - ry that the church shall share,
how with the three dis - ci - ples there,
two cho - sen wit - ness - es of grace;
Christ deigns to man - i - fest to - day
by this great vi - sion's mys - ter - y,

which Christ up - on the moun - tain shows,
where Mo - ses and E - li - jah meet,
the Fa - ther's voice from out the cloud
what glo - ry shall be theirs a - bove
for which in joy - ful strains we raise

where bright - er than the sun he glows!
the Lord holds con - verse high and sweet.
pro - claims his on - ly Son a - loud.
who joy in God with per - fect love.
the voice of prayer, the hymn of praise.

Guitar chords do not correspond with keyboard harmony.

This translation of a 15th-century Latin devotional text is set here to a majestic 15th-century tune celebrating
the victory of an English king; they combine to evoke the awe and wonder of that moment of revelation the
three disciples experienced in Christ's Transfiguration.

TEXT: Latin, 15th cent.; trans. John Mason Neale, 1851, alt.
MUSIC: "The Agincourt Song," c. 1415; harm. *The Hymnal*, 1933

DEO GRACIAS
LM
(alternate harmonization, 258)

190 Swiftly Pass the Clouds of Glory

1 Swift - ly pass the clouds of glo - ry, heav - en's voice, the
2 Glimpsed and gone the rev - e - la - tion, they shall gain and
3 Lord, trans - fig - ure our per - cep - tion with the pur - est

daz - zling light; Mo - ses and E - li - jah van - ish;
keep its truth, not by build - ing on the moun - tain
light that shines, and re - cast our life's in - ten - tions

Christ a - lone com - mands the height! Pe - ter, James, and
an - y shrine or sa - cred booth, but by fol - low -
to the shape of your de - signs, till we seek no

John fall si - lent, turn - ing from the sum - mit's rise down - ward
ing the Sav - ior through the val - ley to the cross and by
oth - er glo - ry than what lies past Cal - vary's hill and our

toward the shad - owed val - ley where their Lord has fixed his eyes.
test - ing faith's re - sil - ience through be - tray - al, pain, and loss.
liv - ing and our dy - ing and our ris - ing by your will.

The first two stanzas of this 20th-century Transfiguration hymn guide singers through a contemplation of the disciples' experience of that event. The final stanza becomes a corporate prayer for enlightenment and for a renewed sense of commitment to doing God's will.

TEXT: Thomas H. Troeger, 1985
MUSIC: George Henry Day, 1940
Text © 1985 Oxford University Press
Music © 1943, 1961, 1985 Church Pension Fund

GENEVA
8.7.8.7.D
(alternate tune: EBENEZER)

We Have Come at Christ's Own Bidding

1 We have come at Christ's own bid - ding to this high and
2 Light breaks through our clouds and shad - ows; splen - dor bathes the
3 Strength - ened by this glimpse of glo - ry, fear - ful lest our

ho - ly place, where we wait with hope and long - ing
flesh - joined Word; Mo - ses and E - li - jah mar - vel
faith de - cline, we like Pe - ter find it tempt - ing

for some to - ken of God's grace. Here we pray for new as -
as the heaven - ly voice is heard. Eyes and hearts be - hold with
to re - main and build a shrine. But true wor - ship gives us

sur - ance that our faith is not in vain, search - ing like those
won - der how the law and proph - ets meet: Christ, with gar - ments
cour - age to pro - claim what we pro - fess, that our dai - ly

first dis - ci - ples for a sign both clear and plain.
drenched in bright - ness, stands trans - fig - ured and com - plete.
lives may prove us peo - ple of the God we bless.

Guitar chords do not correspond with keyboard harmony.

Through this Transfiguration hymn runs an implicit comparison between the attitudes and assumptions of the three disciples on that mountain and the expectations of present-day Christians as they gather for worship. This event is reported in Matthew 17:1–9/Mark 9:2–9/Luke 9:28–36.

TEXT: Carl P. Daw Jr., 1988, alt.
MUSIC: David Ashley White, 1991
Text © 1988 Hope Publishing Company
Music © 1991 Selah Publishing Co., Inc.

BREWER
8.7.8.7.D

192 Lord, the Light of Your Love Is Shining

Shine, Jesus, Shine

1 Lord, the light of your love is shin-ing, in the midst of the dark-ness, shin-ing; Je-sus, Light of the World, shine up-on us; set us free by the truth you now bring us. Shine on me; shine on me.

2 Lord, I come to your awe-some pres-ence, from the shad-ows in-to your ra-diance; by the blood I may en-ter your bright-ness. Search me; try me; con-sume all my dark-ness. Shine on me; shine on me.

3 As we gaze on your king-ly bright-ness, so our fac-es dis-play your like-ness; ev-er chang-ing from glo-ry to glo-ry, mir-rored here may our lives tell your sto-ry. Shine on me; shine on me.

Refrain
Shine, Je-sus, shine; fill this land with the Fa-ther's glo-ry.

While the reference to Jesus as the Light of the world (John 8:12, 9:5) can be understood generally, this hymn is perhaps best understood as a response to the Transfiguration (Matthew 17:1–8/Mark 9:2–8/Luke 9:28–36). This is the most popular of the author/composer's many songs.

TEXT and MUSIC: Graham Kendrick, 1987
Text and Music © 1987 Make Way Music (admin. Music Services)

SHINE, JESUS, SHINE
Irregular

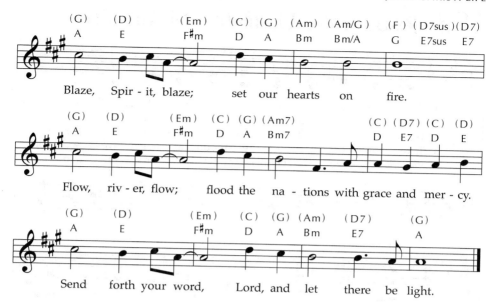

Blaze, Spir - it, blaze; set our hearts on fire.

Flow, riv - er, flow; flood the na - tions with grace and mer - cy.

Send forth your word, Lord, and let there be light.

193 Jesus, Take Us to the Mountain

1 Je - sus, take us to the moun - tain, where, with Pe - ter,
2 What do you want us to see there, that your close com -
3 What do you want us to hear there, that your dear dis -
4 Take us to that oth - er moun - tain where we see you
5 We who have be - held your glo - ry, ris - en and as -

James, and John, we are daz - zled by your glo - ry,
pan - ions saw? Your di - vin - i - ty re - vealed there
ci - ples heard? Once a - gain the voice from heav - en
glo - ri - fied, where you shout - ed "It is fin - ished!"
cend - ed Lord, can - not help but tell the sto - ry,

light as blind - ing as the sun. There pre - pare us
fills us with the self - same awe. Clothed in flesh like
says of the In - car - nate Word, "Lis - ten, lis - ten,
where for all the world you died. Hear the stunned cen -
all that we have seen and heard; say with Pe - ter,

Some version of the Transfiguration (Matthew 17:1–9 / Mark 9:2–9 / Luke 9:28–36) is always read on the last
Sunday after the Epiphany. In this text that foretaste of Christ's glorification helps to prepare Peter, James,
and John for their roles as proclaimers of "God's beloved Son."

TEXT: Jaroslav J. Vajda, 1991
MUSIC: Joachim Neander, 1680; harm. *The Chorale Book for England*, 1863, alt.
Text © 1991 Concordia Publishing House

UNSER HERRSCHER
8.7.8.7.7.7

for   the   night   by   the   vi - sion   of   that   sight.
ours   you   go,   matched to   meet   our   dead - liest foe.
ev - ery - one: this   is   my   be - lov - ed   Son."
tur - i - on: "Tru - ly   this   was   God's own   Son!"
James, and   John: "You   are   God's be - lov - ed   Son!"

When Jesus Wept   194

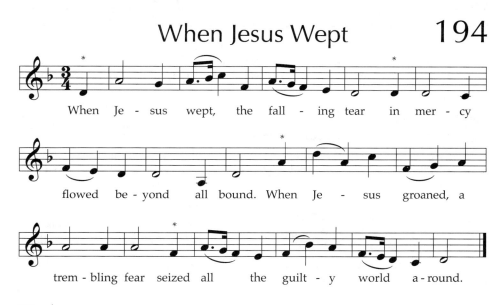

When Je - sus wept, the fall - ing tear in mer - cy

flowed be - yond all bound. When Je - sus groaned, a

trem - bling fear seized all the guilt - y world a - round.

May be sung as a canon.

Like Paul Revere's engraving of people singing around a table that formed the frontispiece of the volume where this canon appeared, its music and words (based on John 11:35, 38) were the fruits of the lively cultural scene in Boston during an era of growing colonial unrest.

TEXT: Perez Morton, 1770
MUSIC: William Billings, 1770

WHEN JESUS WEPT
LM

195   When Twilight Comes

Em   *Am*

1 When twi - light comes and the sun sets, moth - er
2 One day the Rab - bi, Lord Je - sus, called the
3 So gath - er round once a - gain, friends, touched by

B7   *Em*   *C*

hen pre - pares for night's rest. As her brood shel - ters
twelve to share his last meal. As the hen tends her
fad - ing glow of sun's gold, and re - count all our

Em   *Am6*   *Em*   *Am*

un - der her wings she gives the love of God to her
young, so for them he spent him - self to seek and to
frail hu - man hopes, the dreams of young and sto - ries of

B7   *G*   *Em*   *Am*

nest. O! what joy to feel her warm heart beat
heal. O! what joy to be with Christ Je - sus,
old. O! what joy to pray close to - geth - er,

B   *Em*

and be near her all night long; so the
hear his voice, O! sheer de - light, and re -
kneel - ing as one fam - i - ly, by a

Am6   *B*   *Em*

young can find re - pose, then re - new to - mor - row's song.
ceive his ser - vant care, all be - fore the com - ing night.
moth - er's love em - braced in the bless - ed Trin - i - ty.

In the image of a mother hen taking her brood under her wings, this evening hymn from the Philippines connects farmyard experience and Jesus' lament over Jerusalem (Matthew 23:37 / Luke 13:34). The composer has described the tune as being like a bird jumping from branch to branch.

TEXT: Moises B. Andrade, 1990; English trans. James Minchin, 1990   DAPIT HAPON
MUSIC: Francisco F. Feliciano, 1990; arr. *Evangelical Lutheran Worship*, 2006   8.8.9.9.9.7.7.7
English Trans. © 1990 James Minchin (admin. Asian Institute for Liturgy and Music)
Music © 1990 Francisco F. Feliciano (admin. Asian Institute for Liturgy and Music)
   Music Arr. © 2006 Augsburg Fortress

All Glory, Laud, and Honor

196

Refrain

All glo-ry, laud, and hon - or to thee, Re-deem-er, King,

Fine

to whom the lips of chil - dren made sweet ho-san-nas ring!

1 Thou art the King of Is - ra - el, thou Da - vid's roy - al Son,
2 The peo - ple of the He - brews with palms be - fore thee went;
3 To thee, be - fore thy pas - sion, they sang their hymns of praise;
4 Thou didst ac - cept their prais - es; ac - cept the prayers we bring,

to Refrain

who in the Lord's name com - est, the King and bless - ed One.
our praise and prayers and an - thems be - fore thee we pre - sent.
to thee, now high ex - alt - ed, our mel - o - dy we raise.
who in all good de - light - est, thou good and gra - cious King!

These stanzas for Palm Sunday have been selected and translated from a much longer Latin poem written by a bishop who was the leading theologian in Charlemagne's court. They are sung to a 17th-century German chorale, as adapted for these words in the mid-19th century.

TEXT: Theodulph of Orleans, c. 820; trans. John Mason Neale, 1851, alt.
MUSIC: Melchior Teschner, 1614; arr. William Henry Monk, 1861

VALET WILL ICH DIR GEBEN
7.6.7.6.D

197 Hosanna, Loud Hosanna

1 Ho - san - na, loud ho - san - na, the lit - tle chil - dren sang;
2 From Ol - i - vet they fol - lowed 'mid an ex - ult - ant crowd,
3 "Ho - san - na in the high - est!" That an - cient song we sing,

through pil - lared court and tem - ple the joy - ful an - them rang.
the vic - tor palm branch wav - ing, and chant-ing clear and loud;
for Christ is our Re - deem - er; the Lord of heaven, our King.

To Je - sus, who had blessed them, close fold - ed to his breast,
the Lord of earth and heav - en rode on in low - ly state,
O may we ev - er praise him with heart and life and voice,

the chil - dren sang their prais - es, the sim - plest and the best.
nor scorned that lit - tle chil - dren should on his bid - ding wait.
and in his bliss - ful pres - ence e - ter - nal - ly re - joice.

The opening two stanzas narrate the first Palm Sunday in the past tense, but the third stanza shifts to the present tense to emphasize what current singers do and believe. The repeated elements in this anonymous German tune suggest the repetitive patterns in a crowd's chant.

TEXT: Jennette Threlfall, 1873, alt.
MUSIC: *Gesangbuch der Herzogl. Wirtembergischen Katholischen Hofkapelle*, 1784; alt.

ELLACOMBE
7.6.7.6.D

Ride On! Ride On in Majesty! 198

1 Ride on! ride on in maj - es - ty! Hark! all the
2 Ride on! ride on in maj - es - ty! In low - ly
3 Ride on! ride on in maj - es - ty! The hosts of
4 Ride on! ride on in maj - es - ty! In low - ly

tribes ho - san - na cry; thy hum - ble beast pur -
pomp ride on to die; O Christ, thy tri - umphs
an - gels in the sky look down with sad and
pomp ride on to die; bow thy meek head to

sues its road with palms and scat - tered gar - ments strowed.
now be - gin o'er cap - tive death and con - quered sin.
won-dering eyes to see the ap-proach-ing sac - ri - fice.
mor - tal pain; then take, O God, thy power, and reign.

This 19th-century Palm Sunday text is better understood as the reflections of someone standing outside the event rather than as coming from those participating in the actual procession. This poignant text is set to a tune written especially for it later in the same century.

TEXT: Henry Hart Milman, 1827, alt.
MUSIC: John Bacchus Dykes, 1862

ST. DROSTANE
LM

199 Filled with Excitement
Mantos y palmas

1 Filled with ex-cite-ment, all the hap-py throng spread cloaks and
2 As in that en-trance to Je-ru-sa-lem, ho-san-nas
1 *Man-tos y pal-mas es-par-cien-do va el pue-blo a-*
2 *Co-mo en la en-tra-da de Je-ru-sa-lén, to-dos can-*

branch-es on the cit-y streets. There in the dis-tance they be-
we will sing to Je-sus Christ, to our Re-deem-er who still
le-gre de Je-ru-sa-lén. A-llá a lo le-jos se vis-
ta-mos a Je-sús el rey, al Cris-to vi-vo que nos

gin to see, there on a don-key comes the Sav-ior Christ.
calls to-day, asks us to fol-low with our love and faith.
lum-bra ya en un po-lli-no al Sal-va-dor Je-sús.
lla-ma hoy pa-ra se-guir-le con a-mor y fe.

Refrain / Estribillo

From ev-ery cor-ner a thou-sand voic-es sing praise to the One who comes
Mien-tras mil vo-ces re-sue-nan por do-quier; ho-sa-na al que vie-ne en el

in the name of God. Our ac-cla-ma-tion breaks forth in shouts of
nom-bre de Dios. Con un a-lien-to de gran ex-cla-ma-

Though they have different perspectives, all four gospels give an account of Christ's entry to Jerusalem (Matthew 21:7–9 / Mark 11:7–10 / Luke 19:35–38 / John 12:12–15). This Mexican hymn, appropriate for the beginning of worship on Passion / Palm Sunday, captures the crowd's enthusiasm.

TEXT: Rubén Ruíz Ávila, 1972; English trans. Gertrude Suppe, 1979, alt.
MUSIC: Rubén Ruíz Ávila, 1972; arr. Alvin Schutmaat, 1979
Text and Music © 1972 The United Methodist Publishing House (admin. The Copyright Company)
English Trans. © 1979 The United Methodist Publishing House (admin. The Copyright Company)

HOSANNA
10.10.10.10 with refrain

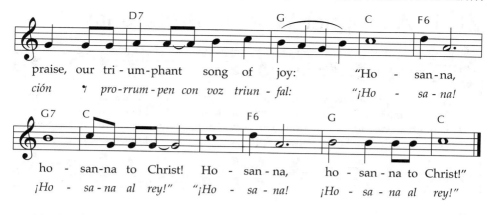

praise, our tri-um-phant song of joy: "Ho - san-na,
ción ╕ pro-rrum-pen con voz triun - fal: "¡Ho - sa - na!

ho - san-na to Christ! Ho - san - na, ho - san - na to Christ!"
¡Ho - sa - na al rey!" "¡Ho - sa - na! ¡Ho - sa - na al rey!"

A Cheering, Chanting, Dizzy Crowd 200

1 A cheer - ing, chant - ing, diz - zy crowd had
2 They laid their gar - ments in the road and
3 When day dimmed down to deep - ening dark the
4 Lest we be fooled be - cause our hearts have
5 In - stead of palms, a wind - ing sheet will

stripped the green trees bare, and hail - ing Christ as
spread his path with palms and vows of last - ing
crowd be - gan to fade till on - ly tram - pled
surged with pass - ing praise, re - mind us, God, as
have to be un - rolled, a car - pet much more

king a - loud, waved branch - es in the air.
love be - stowed with roy - al hymns and psalms.
leaves and bark were left from the pa - rade.
this week starts where Christ has fixed his gaze.
fit to greet the king a cross will hold.

This Palm Sunday hymn recreates the contrasting sounds of Holy Week, moving from the noisy public acclaim of Jesus' entry into Jerusalem to the solitary silence of his body being prepared for burial. It gently reminds us that self-giving is the mark of Christ's true sovereignty.

TEXT: Thomas H. Troeger, 1985
MUSIC: Paul Benoit, OSB, 1959, alt.
Text © 1985 Oxford University Press
Music © 1960 World Library Publications

CHRISTIAN LOVE
CM

201 A Prophet-Woman Broke a Jar

1 A proph-et-wom-an broke a jar, by Love's di-vine ap-
2 A faith-ful wom-an left a tomb by Love's di-vine com-
3 Though wom-an-wis-dom, wom-an-truth, for cen-tu-ries were
4 The Spir-it knows; the Spir-it calls, by Love's di-vine or-

point-ing. With rare per-fume she filled the room, pre-
mis-sion. She saw; she heard; she preached the Word, a-
hid-den, un-sung, un-writ-ten, and un-heard, de-
dain-ing, the friends we need, to serve and lead, their

sid-ing and a-noint-ing. A proph-et-wom-an broke a jar,
ris-ing from sub-mis-sion. A faith-ful wom-an left a tomb,
rid-ed and for-bid-den, the Spir-it's breath, the Spir-it's fire,
powers and gifts un-chain-ing. The Spir-it knows; the Spir-it calls,

the sneers of scorn de-fy-ing. With rare per-fume she
with res-ur-rec-tion gos-pel. She saw; she heard; she
on free and slave de-scend-ing, can tum-ble our di-
from wom-en, men, and chil-dren, the friends we need, to

This text seeks to reverse the neglected witness of biblical women by celebrating the woman who washed
Jesus' feet (unnamed in Matthew 26:6–13/Mark 14:3–9/Luke 7:36–50; Mary of Bethany in John 12:1–8) and
Mary Magdalene (John 20:1–18; Matthew 28:1–10/Mark 16:1–7/Luke 24:10).

TEXT: Brian Wren, 1991
MUSIC: Robert Lowry, 1869, alt.
Text © 1993 Hope Publishing Company

HOW CAN I KEEP FROM SINGING
8.7.8.7.D

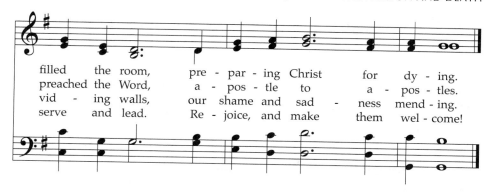

filled the room, pre - par - ing Christ for dy - ing.
preached the Word, a - pos - tle to a - pos - tles.
vid - ing walls, our shame and sad - ness mend - ing.
serve and lead. Re - joice, and make them wel - come!

An Upper Room Did Our Lord Prepare 202

1 An up - per room did our Lord pre - pare for those he
2 A last - ing gift Je - sus gave his own: to share his
3 And af - ter sup - per he washed their feet, for ser - vice,
4 No end there is! We de - part in peace. He loves be -

loved un - til the end: and his dis - ci - ples still
bread, his lov - ing cup. What - ev - er bur - dens may
too, is sac - ra - ment. In Christ our joy shall be
yond our ut - ter - most: in ev - ery room in our

gath - er there to cel - e - brate their ris - en friend.
bow us down, he by his cross shall lift us up.
made com - plete: sent out to serve, as he was sent.
Fa - ther's house Christ will be there, as Lord and Host.

Guitar chords do not correspond with keyboard harmony.

This text brings together the two New Testament traditions regarding Jesus' final evening with his disciples: the Synoptic account of the Last Supper (Matthew 26:26–29 / Mark 14:22–25 / Luke 22:14–20) and the Fourth Gospel's report of his washing the disciples' feet (John 13:3–17).

TEXT: Fred Pratt Green, 1973, alt.
MUSIC: English folk melody; harm. John Weaver, 1988
Text © 1974 Hope Publishing Company
Music Harm. © 1990 Hope Publishing Company

O WALY WALY
9.8.9.8

203 Jesu, Jesu, Fill Us with Your Love

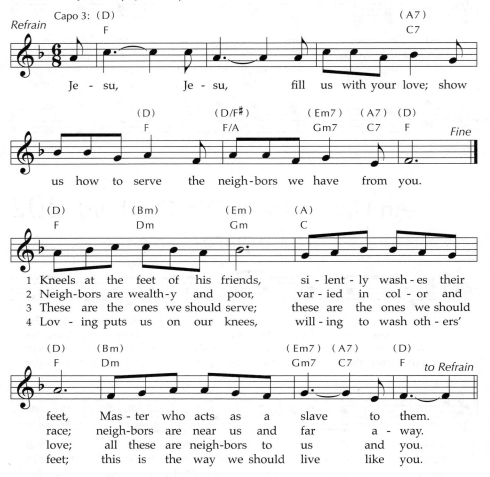

Considering that this text comes from a part of the world where Christianity is not the primary religion gives these simple but powerful words even more depth and meaning. The tune name recalls the district in the Northern Region of Ghana where this tune was collected.

TEXT: Tom Colvin, 1969; rev. 1997, alt.
MUSIC: Ghanaian folk melody; adapt. Tom Colvin, 1963; arr. Jane Marshall, 1982
Text and Music © 1969 Hope Publishing Company
Music Arr. © 1982 Hope Publishing Company

CHEREPONI
7.7.9 with refrain

Stay with Me

Stay with me; re- main here with me; watch and
pray. Watch and pray.

This chant from Taizé intended for repeated singing is based on Jesus' request to the disciples in the Garden of Gethsemane (Matthew 26:38 / Mark 14:34), a simple request they did not fulfill. When singing these words we need to hear in them an ongoing call to be alert and faithful.

TEXT: Taizé Community, 1982
MUSIC: Jacques Berthier, 1982
Text and Music © 1984 Les Presses de Taizé (admin. GIA Publications, Inc.)

STAY WITH ME
Irregular

Live in Charity
Ubi caritas

Live in char- i- ty and stead- fast love.
U- bi ca- ri- tas et a- mor,

Live in char- i- ty; God will dwell with you.
u- bi ca- ri- tas De- us i- bi est.

This refrain comes from a Latin hymn associated with the washing of feet on Maundy Thursday. Whether in English or Latin, it is most effective when sung unaccompanied and in parts. In many ways it is a miniature equivalent of "Will You Let Me Be Your Servant" (see no. 727).

TEXT: Latin, 8th cent.; English trans. Taizé Community, 1991
MUSIC: Jacques Berthier, 1979
Text and Music © 1979 Les Presses de Taizé (admin. GIA Publications, Inc.)

UBI CARITAS (Taizé)
Irregular

206 This Is the Night

Capo 1: (Em) (D) (Em) (D)

1 This is the night, dear friends, the night for weep - ing,
2 This night the trai - tor, wolf with - in the sheep - fold,
3 This night Christ in - sti - tutes his ho - ly sup - per,
4 This night the Lord by slaves shall be ar - rest - ed,
5 O make us shar - ers, Sav - ior, of your Pas - sion,

when powers of dark - ness o - ver - come the day,
be - trays him - self in - to his vic - tim's will,
blest food and drink for heart and soul and mind;
he who de - stroys our slav - er - y to sin;
that we may share your glo - ry that shall be;

the night the faith - ful mourn the weight of e - vil
the Lamb of God for sac - ri - fice pre - par - ing:
this night in - jus - tice joins its hand to trea - son's,
ac - cused of crime, to crim - i - nals be giv - en,
let us pass through these three dark nights of sor - row

where - by our sins the Son of Man be - tray.
sin brings a - bout the cure for sin's own ill.
and buys the ran - som - price of hu - man - kind.
that judg - ment on the righ - teous Judge be - gin.
to Eas - ter's laugh - ter and its lib - er - ty.

This text conveys well the paradox of despair and expectancy felt on Maundy Thursday. The somber repetition of "this night" here contrasts with and prepares for the joyful "this is the night" repeated in the *Exsultet*, the ancient Easter hymn at the lighting of the paschal candle.

TEXT: Peter Abélard, 12th cent.; trans. Richard Lyman Sturch, 1990
MUSIC: Margaret R. Tucker, 1991
Text © 1990 Stainer & Bell, Ltd. (admin. Hope Publishing Company)
Music © 1998 Hope Publishing Company

MY NEIGHBOR
11.10.11.10

Sharing Paschal Bread and Wine 207
Shadows Lengthen into Night

1 Shar - ing Pas-chal bread and wine as the day-light ebbs a - way,
2 In a grove of ol - ive trees un - der-neath a dark-ening sky,
3 In the gar-den, still and deep, those he asked to watch and pray,
4 Deep - er in the gar-den's chill, Je - sus kneels to pray a - lone,
5 All too soon, the si - lence rends, with a crash of club and sword.
6 Christ's dis - ci - ples, weak with fear, fail one fur - ther, strin-gent test—
7 While the web of dark-ness grows, Je - sus suf - fers through his trial.
8 Lift - ed high up - on a cross, per-fect love hangs pierced with nails.

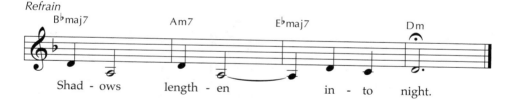

friends at ta - ble join to dine. One of them will soon be - tray.
Je - sus warns as he fore - sees: Pe - ter al - so will de - ny.
heav - y - lid - ded, fall a - sleep, wea - ry from the anx - ious day.
wrest - ling with God's ho - ly will, cry - ing out, "Let it be done!"

Ju - das, still re - ceived as "Friend," with a kiss be - trays his Lord.
so like us, with trou - ble near—flee - ing far at his ar - rest.
As the her - ald roost - er crows, Pe - ter speaks his third de - nial.
All cre - a - tion grieves its loss, as the ver - y sun-light fails.

Refrain

Shad - ows length - en in - to night.

This text is unusual among Passion hymns because it bridges a longer narrative than most, including the events from the Last Supper through the Crucifixion that are often treated separately. As the tune name suggests, this hymn could be used effectively in a Tenebrae service.

TEXT: Mary Louise Bringle, 2006
MUSIC: Sally Ann Morris, 2006
Text and Music © 2006 GIA Publications, Inc.

TENEBRAE
7.7.7.7 with refrain

208 O Blest Are They Who in Their Love

(Psalm 41)

1 O blest are they who in their love com - pas - sion
2 When all the e - vils earth can dream are cast on
3 The hands which shared my bro - ken bread, my love with
4 To me, O Lord, in mer - cy turn; your fa - vor,

hold for those in need; for they shall find, when
me, my faith to break, their rage I tem - per
their de - ceit re - paid; and friends whose trust I
my most trea - sured prize; my mouth shall sing re -

faced by foes, the Lord is their de - fense in - deed.
through God's grace, and bear them bold - ly for God's sake.
count - ed mine have left me wound-ed and be - trayed.
demp - tion's song, and tears of love wash clean my eyes.

This 20th-century paraphrase follows the structure of Psalm 41 by devoting the first stanza to a general statement about God's favor bestowed on those who are merciful to the poor. The remaining stanzas provide the details of a first-person testimony to this general principle.

TEXT: Michael Morgan, 1995
MUSIC: Thurlow Weed, 2009
Text © 2010 Michael Morgan (admin. Congregational Ministries Publishing, Presbyterian Church (U.S.A.))
Music © 2009 Thurlow Weed

GUILSBOROUGH
LM

My Song Is Love Unknown 209

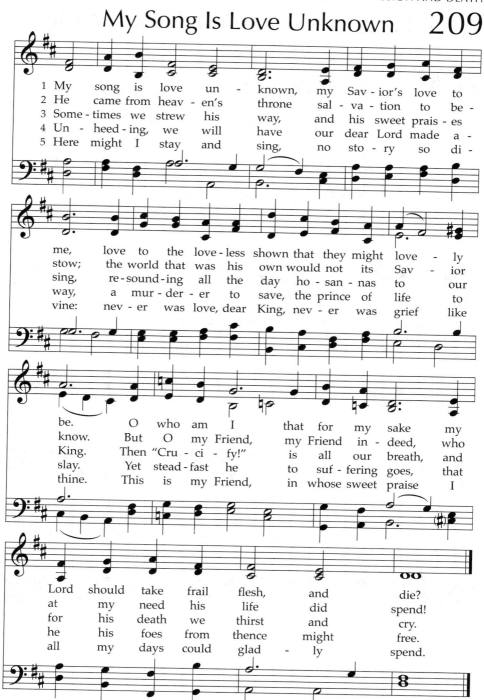

1 My song is love un-known, my Sav-ior's love to
2 He came from heav-en's throne, sal-va-tion to be-
3 Some-times we strew his way, and his sweet prais-es
4 Un-heed-ing, we will have our dear Lord made a-
5 Here might I stay and sing, no sto-ry so di-

me, love to the love-less shown that they might love- ly
stow; the world that was his own would not its Sav- ior
sing, re-sound-ing all the day ho-san-nas to our
way, a mur-der-er to save, the prince of life to
vine: nev-er was love, dear King, nev-er was grief like

be. O who am I that for my sake my
know. But O my Friend, my Friend in-deed, who
King. Then "Cru-ci-fy!" is all our breath, and
slay. Yet stead-fast he to suf-fering goes, that
thine. This is my Friend, in whose sweet praise I

Lord should take frail flesh, and die?
at my need his life did spend!
for his death we thirst and cry.
he his foes from thence might free.
all my days could glad- ly spend.

The opening line here could equally well have been a courtier's lament for a secret affair, but it soon becomes a path into a vivid and poignant reflection on Christ's Passion. This 17th-century text is beautifully embraced by its sensitive and lyrical 20th-century tune.

TEXT: Samuel Crossman, 1664, alt.
MUSIC: John Ireland, 1918
Music © 1924 Trustees of the John Ireland Charitable Trust

LOVE UNKNOWN
6.6.6.6.4.4.4.4

210 Lord, Why Have You Forsaken Me
(Psalm 22)

1 Lord, why have you for - sak - en me, and
2 Yet you are ho - ly, and the songs of
3 But I am mocked and put to scorn. All
4 Yet you, O Lord, have been my God and

why are you so far a - way from my com - plaint and
praise of Is - rael are your throne; when our an - ces - tors
those who see me laugh and say, "You trust in God, so
on - ly hope since I was born. With trou - ble near me,

my dis - tress poured out be - fore you night and day?
called on you, you saved them, res - cued all your own.
let us see the help of God to whom you pray."
none can help. My Sav - ior, leave me not for - lorn.

Although Psalm 22 paraphrased here begins in despair keen enough to be repeated on the lips of a dying
Jesus (Matthew 27:46/Mark 15:34), it is replete with a faith that withstands even the mockery of disbelievers.
The spareness of the shape note tune fits the text well.

TEXT: Christopher L. Webber, 1986, alt.   DISTRESS
MUSIC: Walker's *Southern Harmony*, 1835   LM
Text © 1986 Christopher L. Webber   (alternate harmonization, 780)

Hear, O Lord, My Plea for Justice 211
(Psalm 17)

1 Hear, O Lord, my plea for jus - tice; lis - ten
2 Test my heart for its af - flic - tion; pu - ri -
3 Keep me, Lord, in sure pro - tec - tion, as the
4 In its wake, send vin - di - ca - tion; to its

to my heart - felt prayer. In your just de -
fy my soul with fire; let my mor - tal
ap - ple of your eye. Shel - ter me be -
dark - ness, show your face. Bring me to my

lib - er - a - tion may I find re - demp - tion there.
tongue speak wis-dom, righ - teous - ness be my de - sire.
neath your shad-ow when my hour of death draws nigh.
res - ur - rec - tion clothed in gar - ments of your grace.

Guitar chords do not correspond with keyboard harmony.

This paraphrase emphasizes the prayerful qualities of Psalm 17 by keeping the focus on the relationship between the psalmist and God, rather than denouncing the faults of the enemy. This is a helpful reminder that our prayers need to be grounded in honest and unpretentious faith.

TEXT: Michael Morgan, 1995; rev. 2010
MUSIC: *The United States Sacred Harmony*, 1799; harm. Carlton R. Young, 1964
Text © 2010 Michael Morgan (admin. Congregational Ministries Publishing, Presbyterian Church (U.S.A.))
Music Harm. © 1965 Abingdon Press (admin. The Copyright Company)

CHARLESTOWN
8.7.8.7

212 Alas! And Did My Savior Bleed

1 Alas! And did my Savior bleed, and did my Sovereign die! Would he devote that sacred head for sinners such as I!

2 Was it for sins that I have done he suffered on the tree? Amazing pity! Grace unknown! And love beyond degree!

3 Well might the sun in darkness hide and shut its glories in, when Christ, the great Redeemer, died for human creatures' sin.

4 But drops of grief can ne'er repay the debt of love I owe; here, Lord, I give myself away; 'tis all that I can do.

Much like this author's "When I Survey the Wondrous Cross" (nos. 223, 224), this more introspective treatment of Christ's crucifixion calls forth self-sacrifice from the beholder. It is set here to a tune that may well have originated as an 18th-century Scottish folk song.

MARTYRDOM
CM

TEXT: Isaac Watts, 1707
MUSIC: Hugh Wilson, c. 1800; adapt. and harm. Robert Smith, 1825

In the Cross of Christ I Glory 213

1 In the cross of Christ I glo - ry, tower - ing
2 When the woes of life o'er - take me, hopes de -
3 When the sun of bliss is beam - ing light and
4 Bane and bless - ing, pain and plea - sure, by the
5 In the cross of Christ I glo - ry, tower - ing

o'er the wrecks of time; all the light of sa - cred
ceive, and fears an - noy, nev - er shall the cross for -
love up - on my way, from the cross the ra - diance
cross are sanc - ti - fied; peace is there that knows no
o'er the wrecks of time; all the light of sa - cred

sto - ry gath - ers round its head sub - lime.
sake me; lo, it glows with peace and joy.
stream - ing adds more lus - ter to the day.
mea - sure, joys that through all time a - bide.
sto - ry gath - ers round its head sub - lime.

Like Isaac Watts's "When I Survey the Wondrous Cross" (nos. 223, 224), this hymn is a reflection on Galatians 6:14, but this text is more abstract and devotes no attention to the person hanging on the cross. The tune is named for a soloist in the composer's Connecticut choir.

TEXT: John Bowring, 1825
MUSIC: Ithamar Conkey, 1849

RATHBUN
8.7.8.7

214 You Are My Refuge, Faithful God

(Psalm 31)

1 You are my ref - uge, faith - ful God; you
2 De - liv - er me from hid - den snares, from
3 Be gra - cious, God, in my dis - tress, and
4 I am a wretch - ed sight to see: a
5 And yet I trust in you, O God; your

shel - ter me from shame. I put my spir - it
sor - row, pain, and strife. When trou - bles seem to
dry my bit - ter tears. My life is spent in
bro - ken, emp - ty thing, with on - ly ter - ror
cov - e - nant still stands. Re - deem me, in your

in your hands and call up - on your name.
smoth - er me, take heed, and save my life!
mis - er - y; I sigh a - way my years.
all a - round, and death - ly whis - per - ing.
faith - ful love: my life is in your hands.

What John Calvin said about Psalm 31:5 can be applied to this paraphrase of the psalm as a whole: it is one of the places in scripture "most suitable for correcting distrust." That verse was on Jesus' dying lips (Luke 23:46), and this psalm is appointed for Passion/Palm Sunday.

TEXT: David Gambrell, 2009
MUSIC: Wyeth's *Repository of Sacred Music, Part Second*, 1813; harm. C. Winfred Douglas, 1940
Text © 2011 David Gambrell (admin. Presbyterian Publishing Corp.)
Music Harm. © 1943, 1961, 1985 Church Pension Fund

MORNING SONG
CM

What Wondrous Love Is This 215

1 What won-drous love is this, O my soul, O my
2 When I was sink-ing down, sink-ing down, sink-ing
3 To God and to the Lamb, I will sing, I will
4 And when from death I'm free, I'll sing on, I'll sing

soul, what won-drous love is this, O my soul! What
down, when I was sink-ing down, sink-ing down, when
sing, to God and to the Lamb, I will sing; to
on; and when from death I'm free, I'll sing on; and

won-drous love is this that caused the Lord of
I was sink-ing down be - neath God's righ-teous
God and to the Lamb who is the great I
when from death I'm free, I'll sing and joy-ful

bliss to bear the dread-ful curse for my soul, for my
frown, Christ laid a - side his crown for my soul, for my
AM, while mil - lions join the theme, I will sing, I will
be, and through e - ter - ni - ty, I'll sing on, I'll sing

soul, to bear the dread-ful curse for my soul!
soul, Christ laid a - side his crown for my soul!
sing; while mil - lions join the theme, I will sing!
on; and through e - ter - ni - ty I'll sing on.

With its ballad-like repetitions before and after each stanza's central narrative lines, this meditative text needs performance in order to be effective. Its haunting melody proves the means of convincing us that the only adequate response to "wondrous love" is to "sing on."

TEXT: American folk hymn, c. 1811
MUSIC: Walker's *Southern Harmony*, 1835; harm. Carlton R. Young, 1965
Music Harm. © 1965 Abingdon Press (admin. The Copyright Company)

WONDROUS LOVE
12.9.12.12.9

216 Beneath the Cross of Jesus

1 Be-neath the cross of Je-sus I fain would take my stand,
2 Up-on the cross of Je-sus mine eye at times can see
3 I take, O cross, thy shad-ow for my a-bid-ing place;

the shad-ow of a might-y rock with-in a wea-ry land;
the ver-y dy-ing form of One who suf-fered there for me;
I ask no oth-er sun-shine than the sun-shine of his face;

a home with-in the wil-der-ness, a rest up-on the way,
and from my strick-en heart with tears two won-ders I con-fess:
con-tent to let the world go by, to know no gain or loss,

from the burn-ing of the noon-tide heat, and the bur-den of the day.
the won-ders of re-deem-ing love and my un-wor-thi-ness.
my sin-ful self my on-ly shame, my glo-ry all the cross.

For sheer intensity of feeling few hymns can match this meditation on the cross; impressive images and
strong contrasts combine to give the text its ardor. The passionate language is augmented by the highly
chromatic tune later composed for these words.

TEXT: Elizabeth Cecilia Douglas Clephane, 1868, alt.
MUSIC: Frederick Charles Maker, 1881

ST. CHRISTOPHER
7.6.8.6.8.6.8.6

On a Barren Hilltop

Come Boldly

217

1 On a bar-ren hill - top just out-side the walls
2 Test-ed just as we are, in a world of strife,
3 Let us then come bold - ly to the heaven - ly throne,

of an an - cient cit - y as the eve - ning falls,
through the pain and con - flict of a hu - man life,
where our hu - man weak - ness is so ful - ly known,

speaks a dy - ing fig - ure hang - ing on a tree,
here at last com - plet - ed with his fi - nal breath
and the mer - cy giv - en by which we are freed,

say - ing "It is fin - ished," words of vic - to - ry.
is a life tri - um - phant o - ver sin and death.
and the grace pro - vid - ed for our time of need.

Guitar chords do not correspond with keyboard harmony.

The first stanza of this text is based on John 19:17, 30 and the second and third stanzas on Hebrews 4:14–16. These passages and others provide the basis for the classic understanding of the atonement that sees Christ's redeeming work as a victory over all the powers of evil.

TEXT: Christopher L. Webber, 2008
MUSIC: Ralph Vaughan Williams, 1925
Text © 2008 Faith Alive Christian Resources
Music © 1925 Oxford University Press

KING'S WESTON
6.5.6.5.D

218 Ah, Holy Jesus

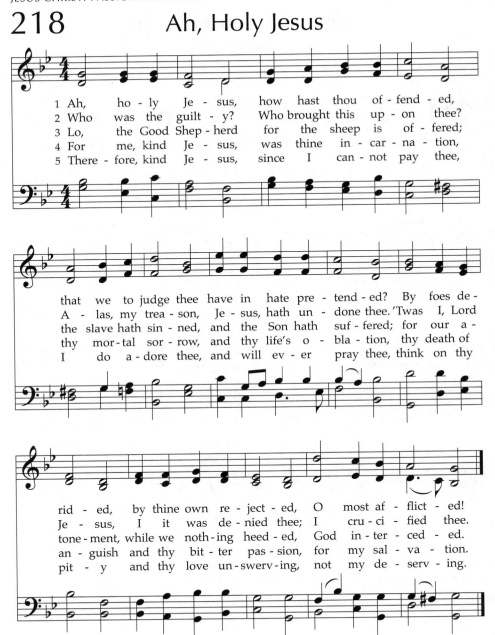

1 Ah, ho-ly Je-sus, how hast thou of-fend-ed, that we to judge thee have in hate pre-tend-ed? By foes de-rid-ed, by thine own re-ject-ed, O most af-flict-ed!

2 Who was the guilt-y? Who brought this up-on thee? A-las, my trea-son, Je-sus, hath un-done thee. 'Twas I, Lord Je-sus, I it was de-nied thee; I cru-ci-fied thee.

3 Lo, the Good Shep-herd for the sheep is of-fered; the slave hath sin-ned, and the Son hath suf-fered; for our a-tone-ment, while we noth-ing heed-ed, God in-ter-ced-ed.

4 For me, kind Je-sus, was thine in-car-na-tion, thy mor-tal sor-row, and thy life's o-bla-tion, thy death of an-guish and thy bit-ter pas-sion, for my sal-va-tion.

5 There-fore, kind Je-sus, since I can-not pay thee, I do a-dore thee, and will ev-er pray thee, think on thy pit-y and thy love un-swerv-ing, not my de-serv-ing.

This beautiful English paraphrase of a German meditation on Christ's Passion bears testimony to the unobtrusive poetic skill and musical sensitivity of a future Poet Laureate of England. The associated chorale is no less carefully crafted and rewards singing in parts.

TEXT: Johann Heermann, 1630; trans. Robert Seymour Bridges, 1899, alt.
MUSIC: Johann Crüger, 1640

HERZLIEBSTER JESU
11.11.11.5

They Crucified My Lord

219

He Never Said a Mumbalin' Word

1 They cru-ci-fied my Lord,
2 They nailed him to a tree,
3 They pierced him in the side, and he nev-er said a
4 The blood came trick-a-lin' down,
5 He bowed his head and died,

mum-ba-lin' word; they cru-ci-fied my Lord,
they nailed him to a tree,
they pierced him in the side,
the blood came trick-a-lin' down,
he bowed his head and died,

and he nev-er said a mum-ba-lin' word.

Not a word, not a word, not a word.

The African American spirituals recalling Christ's Passion provide poignant evidence of the eloquence and empathy born of shared suffering. The call-and-response singing style also provides a means of affirming the communal wisdom expressed in recurring phrases and refrains.

TEXT and MUSIC: African American spiritual

CRUCIFIXION
Irregular

220 Go to Dark Gethsemane

1 Go to dark Geth-sem-a-ne, all who feel the
2 Fol-low to the judg-ment hall; view the Lord of
3 Cal-vary's mourn-ful moun-tain climb; there, a-dor-ing
4 Ear-ly has-ten to the tomb where they laid his

tempt-er's power; your Re-deem-er's con-flict see;
life ar-raigned; O the worm-wood and the gall!
at his feet, mark that mir-a-cle of time,
breath-less clay: all is sol-i-tude and gloom.

watch with him one bit-ter hour; turn not from his
O the pangs his soul sus-tained! Shun not suf-fering,
God's own sac-ri-fice com-plete; "It is fin-ished!"
Who has tak-en him a-way? Christ is risen! He

griefs a-way; learn from Je-sus Christ to pray.
shame, or loss; learn from him to bear the cross.
hear him cry; learn from Je-sus Christ to die.
meets our eyes. Sav-ior, teach us so to rise.

The composer intended this tune for "Rock of Ages, Cleft for Me" (no. 438), but its solemn tone and small range make it an effective setting for this series of somber vignettes portraying what Christians can learn from Christ: to pray, to bear the cross, to die, and to rise.

TEXT: James Montgomery, 1820, 1825, alt.
MUSIC: Richard Redhead, 1853

REDHEAD 76
7.7.7.7.7.7

O Sacred Head, Now Wounded 221

1 O sa - cred head, now wound-ed, with grief and shame weighed down;
2 What thou, my Lord, hast suf - fered was all for sin - ners' gain:
3 What lan-guage shall I bor - row to thank thee, dear-est friend,

now scorn-ful-ly sur - round - ed with thorns, thine on - ly crown;
mine, mine was the trans - gres - sion, but thine the dead-ly pain.
for this thy dy - ing sor - row, thy pit - y with-out end?

O sa - cred head, what glo - ry, what bliss till now was thine!
Lo, here I fall, my Sav - ior! 'Tis I de - serve thy place;
O make me thine for - ev - er; and should I faint-ing be,

Yet, though de - spised and gor - y, I joy to call thee mine.
look on me with thy fa - vor, and grant to me thy grace.
Lord, let me nev - er, nev - er out - live my love to thee.

This poignant hymn originated in a series of Holy Week meditations focused on the parts of Christ's crucified body: feet, knees, hands, side, breast, heart, face. First joined to secular words, this chorale melody has appeared with this text since the mid-17th century.

TEXT: Latin, 12th or 13th cent.; trans. James Waddell Alexander, 1830, alt.
MUSIC: Hans Leo Hassler, 1601; harm. Johann Sebastian Bach, 1729

PASSION CHORALE
7.6.7.6.D

222 Rejected and Despised

1 Re - ject - ed and de - spised by men and wom - en of our
2 In all the vic - tims of our age, the bat - tered and the
3 For - give us, Lord, as you for - gave with your ex - pir - ing

race, he bears trans - gres - sion's wound - ing weight and an - guish
bruised, Christ lives a - gain, a - like with them by hu - man
breath the ones whose guilt - y hands, like ours, re - quired a

mars his face. This Man of Sor - rows, born to loss, ac -
sin a - bused: as - cend - ing on a cross to die, de -
guilt - less death. O mys - tery of such cost - ly love, O

quaint - ed with our grief: this Christ of God now
scend - ing in - to hell; in tor - ment, suf - fering,
depth of grace re - vealed: in scourge - marked flesh, we

cru - ci - fied as - ton - ish - es be - lief.
scorn, and pain, we meet our God as well.
find our Christ, and by his stripes are healed.

Guitar chords do not correspond with keyboard harmony.

Since apostolic times (see Acts 8:26–39), Christians have seen parallels between the Fourth Servant Song (Isaiah 52:13–53:12) and Christ's Passion. This reflection on that passage reminds us how the suffering Christ continues to be present in the victimized people of our own day.

TEXT: Mary Louise Bringle, 2000
MUSIC: William P. Rowan, 1990
Text © 2002 GIA Publications, Inc.
Music © 1993 Selah Publishing Co., Inc.

CARDINAL
CMD

When I Survey the Wondrous Cross 223

1 When I sur-vey the won-drous cross on which the
2 For-bid it, Lord, that I should boast, save in the
3 See, from his head, his hands, his feet, sor-row and
4 Were the whole realm of na-ture mine, that were a

Prince of glo-ry died, my rich-est gain I
death of Christ my God; all the vain things that
love flow min-gled down; did e'er such love and
pres-ent far too small; love so a-maz-ing,

count but loss, and pour con-tempt on all my pride.
charm me most, I sac-ri-fice them to his blood.
sor-row meet, or thorns com-pose so rich a crown?
so di-vine, de-mands my soul, my life, my all.

This familiar text from the beginning of the 18th century grew out of Isaac Watts's desire to give Christians the ability to sing about gospel events. It is set here to a very restrained tune from the early 19th century inspired by the patterns of Gregorian chant.

TEXT: Isaac Watts, 1707
MUSIC: Lowell Mason, 1824

HAMBURG
LM
(alternate tune: ROCKINGHAM, 224)

224 When I Survey the Wondrous Cross

1 When I sur - vey the won - drous cross on which the
2 For - bid it, Lord, that I should boast, save in the
3 See, from his head, his hands, his feet, sor - row and
4 Were the whole realm of na - ture mine, that were a

Prince of glo - ry died, my rich - est gain I
death of Christ my God; all the vain things that
love flow min - gled down; did e'er such love and
pres - ent far too small; love so a - maz - ing,

count but loss, and pour con - tempt on all my pride.
charm me most, I sac - ri - fice them to his blood.
sor - row meet, or thorns com - pose so rich a crown?
so di - vine, de - mands my soul, my life, my all.

This carefully crafted text from the beginning of the 18th century conveys much the same intensity and vividness as a miniature painting of Christ's crucifixion, and this lyrical and dignified tune reinforces the sense that time stands still while we share such meditation.

TEXT: Isaac Watts, 1707
MUSIC: *Second Supplement to Psalmody in Miniature*, 1783; harm. Edward Miller, 1790

ROCKINGHAM
LM
(alternate tune: HAMBURG, 223)

Sing, My Tongue, the Glorious Battle 225

Capo 5: (Am)(Em) (Am) (Dm) (Am) (C) (Am)

1 Sing, my tongue, the glo - rious bat - tle; tell the tri - umph
2 God in mer - cy saw us fall - en, sunk in shame and
3 Tell how, when at length the full - ness of the ap - point - ed
4 Thir - ty years a - mong us dwell - ing, Je - sus went from
5 Faith - ful cross, true sign of tri - umph, be for all the

far and wide; tell a - loud the won - drous sto - ry
mis - er - y, felled to death in E - den's gar - den,
time was come, Christ, the Word, was born of wom - an,
Naz - a - reth, des - tined, ded - i - cat - ed, will - ing,
no - blest tree; none in fo - liage, none in blos - som,

of the cross, the Cru - ci - fied; tell how Christ, the
where in pride we claimed the tree; then an - oth - er
left for us the heaven - ly home, blazed the path of
did his work and met his death; like a lamb he
none in fruit your e - qual be; sym - bol of the

world's re - deem - er, van - quished death the day he died.
tree was cho - sen, which the world from death would free.
true o - be - dience, shone as light a - midst the gloom.
hum - bly yield - ed on the cross his dy - ing breath.
world's re - demp - tion, for your bur - den makes us free.

Guitar chords do not correspond with keyboard harmony.

This enduring and profound meditation on the mystery of the cross was written in Latin in the 6th century, translated into English in the 19th century, and revised in the 21st century. It is set here to a simple, dignified, and sturdy melody created for it in the 20th century.

TEXT: Venantius Honorius Fortunatus, 6th cent.; trans. John Mason Neale, 1851, alt.
MUSIC: Carl F. Schalk, 1967
Music © 1967 Concordia Publishing House

FORTUNATUS NEW
8.7.8.7.8.7

226 There in God's Garden

1 There in God's gar - den stands the tree of Wis - dom,
2 Its name is Je - sus, name that says, "Our Sav - ior!"
3 Thorns not its own are tan - gled in its fo - liage;
4 See how its branch - es reach to us in wel - come;

whose leaves hold forth the heal - ing of the na - tions:
There on its branch - es see the scars of suf - fering;
our greed has starved it; our de - spite has choked it.
hear what the Voice says, "Come to me, ye wea - ry!

tree of all knowl - edge, tree of all com -
see there the ten - drils of our hu - man
Yet, look! it lives! its grief has not de -
Give me your sick - ness; give me all your

These evocative stanzas on Christ's Passion come from a twelve-stanza hymn by a 17th-century Hungarian pastor, as translated by the preeminent 20th-century hymnologist of the English-speaking world. The tune name honors the composer's home in the foothills of the Appalachians.

TEXT: Pécselyi Király Imre, c. 1641; trans. Erik Routley, 1974
MUSIC: K. Lee Scott, 1976
Text © 1976 Hinshaw Music, Inc.
Music © 1987 Birnamwood Publications (a div. of MorningStar Music Publishers, Inc.)

SHADES MOUNTAIN
11.11.11.5

pas - sion, tree of all beau - ty.
self - hood feed on its life - blood.
stroyed it nor fire con - sumed it.
sor - row; I will give bless - ing."

5 This is my ending;
  this, my resurrection;
  into your hands,
  Lord, I commit my spirit.
  This have I searched for;
  now I can possess it.
  This ground is holy.

6 All heaven is singing,
  "Thanks to Christ whose passion
  offers in mercy
  healing, strength, and pardon.
  Peoples and nations,
  take it; take it freely!"
  Amen! My Master!

Jesus, Remember Me 227

Je - sus, re - mem - ber me when you come in - to your king - dom.

Je - sus, re - mem - ber me when you come in - to your king - dom.

This chant-like setting, intended for repeated singing, comes from the ecumenical monastic community in Taizé, France. Based on the prayer of the penitent thief crucified with Jesus (Luke 23:42), this text is a poignant expression of the desire to be present with Christ in glory.

TEXT: Taizé Community, 1981
MUSIC: Jacques Berthier, 1981
Text and Music © 1981 Les Presses de Taizé (admin. GIA Publications, Inc.)

REMEMBER ME
Irregular

228 Were You There

1 Were you there when they cru-ci-fied my Lord? (Were you
2 Were you there when they nailed him to the tree? (Were you
3 Were you there when they pierced him in the side? (Were you
4 Were you there when the sun re-fused to shine? (Were you
5 Were you there when they laid him in the tomb? (Were you

there?) Were you there when they cru-ci-fied my Lord?
there?) Were you there when they nailed him to the tree?
there?) Were you there when they pierced him in the side?
there?) Were you there when the sun re-fused to shine?
there?) Were you there when they laid him in the tomb?

O!   Some-times it caus-es me to

trem-ble,   trem-ble,   trem-ble. Were you

Few hymns from any culture have captured the pathos of Jesus' crucifixion as movingly as this African American spiritual. Its emotional climax (and highest pitch) comes in the great "O!" at the center of each stanza, a moment that moves beyond anything words can convey.

TEXT: African American spiritual
MUSIC: African American spiritual; arr. Melva Wilson Costen, 1987
Music Arr. © 1990 Melva Wilson Costen

WERE YOU THERE
Irregular

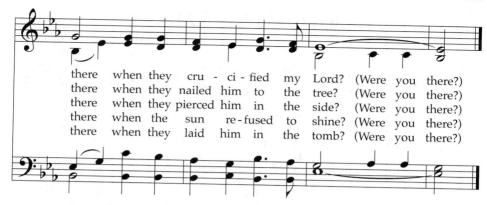

there | when they | cru - ci - fied | my | Lord? (Were you there?)
there | when they | nailed him | to | the | tree? (Were you there?)
there | when they | pierced him | in | the | side? (Were you there?)
there | when the | sun | re - fused | to | shine? (Were you there?)
there | when they | laid | him | in | the | tomb? (Were you there?)

Opt. 6   Were you there when he rose up from the dead?

In the Darkness of the Morning 229

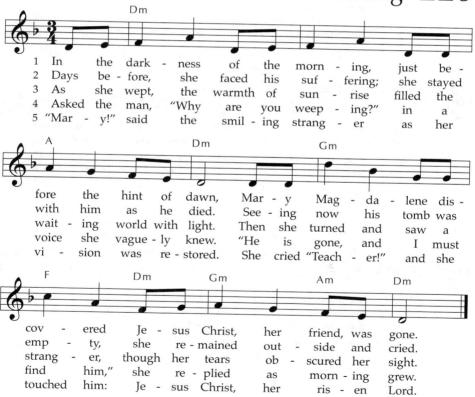

1 In the dark - ness of the morn - ing, just be -
2 Days be - fore, she faced his suf - fering; she stayed
3 As she wept, the warmth of sun - rise filled the
4 Asked the man, "Why are you weep - ing?" in a
5 "Mar - y!" said the smil - ing strang - er as her

fore the hint of dawn, Mar - y Mag - da - lene dis -
with him as he died. See - ing now his tomb was
wait - ing world with light. Then she turned and saw a
voice she vague - ly knew. "He is gone, and I must
vi - sion was re - stored. She cried "Teach - er!" and she

cov - ered Je - sus Christ, her friend, was gone.
emp - ty, she re - mained out - side and cried.
strang - er, though her tears ob - scured her sight.
find him," she re - plied as morn - ing grew.
touched him: Je - sus Christ, her ris - en Lord.

The moving Easter morning encounter between Mary Magdalene and the risen Christ, described in John 20:1–18, gives evidence of the importance of women in Jesus' life and ministry. As the first witness to his resurrection, Mary Magdalene became "the apostle to the apostles."

TEXT: Adam M. L. Tice, 2004
MUSIC: Latvian melody; harm. Geoffrey Laycock, 1971
Text © 2009 GIA Publications, Inc.
Music Harm. © 1995 GIA Publications, Inc.

KAS DZIEDAJA
8.7.8.7

230 Joyful Is the Dark

1 Joy - ful is the dark, ho - ly, hid - den God,
2 Joy - ful is the dark Spir - it of the deep,
3 Joy - ful is the dark, shad - owed sta - ble floor;
4 Joy - ful is the dark cool - ness of the tomb,
5 Joy - ful is the dark depth of love di - vine,

roll - ing cloud of night be - yond all nam - ing:
wing - ing wild - ly o'er the world's cre - a - tion,
an - gels flick - er, God on earth con - fess - ing,
wait - ing for the won - der of the morn - ing;
roar - ing, loom - ing thun - der-cloud of glo - ry,

maj - es - ty in dark - ness, en - er - gy of love,
silk - en sheen of mid - night plum - age black and bright,
as with ex - ul - ta - tion, Mar - y, giv - ing birth,
nev - er was that mid - night touched by dread and gloom:
ho - ly, haunt - ing beau - ty, liv - ing, lov - ing God.

Word - in - flesh, the mys - ter - y pro - claim - ing.
swoop - ing with the beau - ty of a ra - ven.
hails the in - fant cry of need and bless - ing.
dark - ness was the cra - dle of the dawn - ing.
Hal - le - lu - jah! Sing and tell the sto - ry!

Guitar chords do not correspond with keyboard harmony.

This text opens each stanza with a line inspired by the phrase "joyful darkness far beyond our seeing," which the author used in another text about the same time (see no. 760). Its numerous biblical images include Genesis 1:2, Exodus 20:18–21, 1 Kings 8:10–13, and Psalm 18:8–12.

TEXT: Brian Wren, 1986
MUSIC: Carlton R. Young, 1990
Text © 1989 Hope Publishing Company
Music © 1990 Hope Publishing Company

LINDNER
5.5.10.6.5.10

Christ Has Risen While Earth Slumbers 231

1 Christ has ris-en while earth slum-bers; Christ has ris-en where hope died,
2 Christ has ris-en for the peo-ple whom he died to love and save;
3 Christ has ris-en and for ev-er lives to chal-lenge and to change

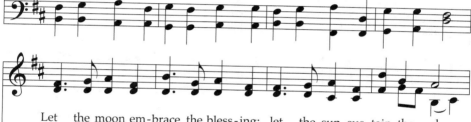

as he said and as he prom-ised, as we doubt-ed and de-nied.
Christ has ris-en for the wom-en bring-ing flowers to grace his grave.
all whose lives are messed or man-gled, all who find re-li-gion strange.

Let the moon em-brace the bless-ing; let the sun sus-tain the cheer;
Christ has ris-en for dis-ci-ples hud-dled in an up-stairs room.
Christ is ris-en, Christ is pres-ent mak-ing us what he has been:

let the world con-firm the ru-mor: Christ is ris-en, God is here!
He whose word in-spired cre-a-tion can't be si-lenced by the tomb.
ev-i-dence of trans-for-ma-tion in which God is known and seen.

Beginning with rather conventional Easter imagery, this text moves into unexpected territory by declaring that Christ's Resurrection is for "all whose lives are messed or mangled, all who find religion strange." The name of this traditional Welsh melody simply means "lullaby."

TEXT: John L. Bell and Graham Maule, 1988
MUSIC: Welsh melody; arr. Alfred V. Fedak, 2011
Text © 1988 WGRG, Iona Community (admin. GIA Publications, Inc.)
Music Arr. © 2011 Alfred V. Fedak

SUO GAN
8.7.8.7.D

232 Jesus Christ Is Risen Today

1 Je - sus Christ is risen to - day,
2 Hymns of praise then let us sing,
3 But the pains which he en - dured,
4 Sing we to our God a - bove,

Al - le - lu - ia!

our tri - um - phant ho - ly day,
un - to Christ, our heaven-ly King,
our sal - va - tion have pro - cured.
praise e - ter - nal as God's love.

Al - le - lu - ia!

who did once up - on the cross,
who en - dured the cross and grave,
Now a - bove the sky he's King,
Praise our God, ye heaven-ly host,

Al - le - lu - ia!

It seems likely that this beloved Easter text began in Latin and moved through German before reaching English, where it combined with the present tune in the emerging English evangelical style, a reaction to the restrained one-note-per-syllable psalmody that preceded it.

TEXT: Stanzas 1–3, *Lyra Davidica*, 1708; stanza 4, Charles Wesley, 1740
    Spanish trans. Juan Bautista Cabrera, alt.; Korean trans. The Christian Literature Society of Korea
MUSIC: *Lyra Davidica*, 1708; adapt. from *The Compleat Psalmodist*, 1749
Korean Trans. © The Christian Literature Society of Korea

EASTER HYMN
7.7.7.7 with alleluias

suf - fer   to   re - deem our   loss.
sin - ners   to   re - deem and   save.
where the   an - gels ev - er   sing.   Al -   le - lu - ia!
Fa - ther, Son, and Ho - ly   Ghost.

SPANISH

1 *El Señor resucitó, ¡Aleluya!*
   muerte y tumba ya venció. ¡Aleluya!
   Con su fuerza y su virtud ¡Aleluya!
   cautivó la esclavitud. ¡Aleluya!

2 *El que al polvo se humilló, ¡Aleluya!*
   vencedor se levantó. ¡Aleluya!
   Cante hoy la cristiandad ¡Aleluya!
   su gloriosa majestad. ¡Aleluya!

3 *Cristo, que la cruz sufrió, ¡Aleluya!*
   y en desolación se vio, ¡Aleluya!
   hoy en gloria celestial ¡Aleluya!
   reina vivo e inmortal. ¡Aleluya!

4 *Cristo, nuestro Salvador, ¡Aleluya!*
   de la muerte es triunfador. ¡Aleluya!
   En El hemos de confiar. ¡Aleluya!
   Cantaremos sin cesar. ¡Aleluya!

KOREAN

1 예수부활 했으니   할렐루야
   만민찬송 하여라
   천사들이 즐거워
   기쁜찬송 부르네

2 대속하신 주예수   할렐루야
   선한싸움 이겼네
   사망권세 이기고
   하늘문을 여셨네

3 마귀권세 이긴주   할렐루야
   왕의왕이 되셨네
   높은이름 세상에
   널리반포 하여라

4 길과진리 되신주   할렐루야
   우리부활 하겠네
   부활생명 되시니
   우리부활 하겠네

233 The Day of Resurrection!

1 The day of res-ur-rec-tion! Earth, tell it out a-broad,
2 Let hearts be purged of e-vil that we may see a-right
3 Now let the heavens be joy-ful; let earth its song be-gin;

the Pass-o-ver of glad-ness, the Pass-o-ver of God.
the Lord in rays e-ter-nal of res-ur-rec-tion light,
the round world keep high tri-umph and all that is there-in.

From death to life e-ter-nal, from sin's do-min-ion free,
and lis-tening to his ac-cents, may hear, so calm and plain,
Let all things seen and un-seen their notes of glad-ness blend,

our Christ has brought us o-ver with hymns of vic-to-ry.
his own "All hail!" and hear-ing, may raise the vic-tor strain.
for Christ the Lord has ris-en, our joy that has no end.

The roots of this English text come from a mid-8th century Greek hymn that continues to be used in
Orthodox churches at the midnight Eucharist marking the beginning of Easter. The tune is named for the
county in northwestern England where the composer was then an organist.

TEXT: John of Damascus, 8th cent.; trans. John Mason Neale, 1862, alt.
MUSIC: Henry Thomas Smart, c. 1835

LANCASHIRE
7.6.7.6.D
(this tune in a lower key, 269)

Come, You Faithful, Raise the Strain 234

1 Come, you faith - ful, raise the strain of tri - um - phant glad - ness!
2 'Tis the spring of souls to - day: Christ has burst his pris - on,
3 Now the queen of sea - sons, bright with the day of splen - dor,
4 Nei - ther could the gates of death, nor the tomb's dark por - tal,

God has brought forth Is - ra - el in - to joy from sad - ness,
and from three days' sleep in death as a sun has ris - en.
with the roy - al feast of feasts comes its joy to ren - der;
nor the watch - ers, nor the seal hold you as a mor - tal:

loosed from Pha - raoh's bit - ter yoke Ja - cob's sons and daugh - ters;
All the win - ter of our sins, long and dark, is fly - ing
comes to glad Je - ru - sa - lem, who with true af - fec - tion
but to - day, a - mong your own, you ap - pear, be - stow - ing

led them with un - moist - ened foot through the Red Sea wa - ters.
from the Light, to whom we give laud and praise un - dy - ing.
wel - comes in un - wea - ried strains Je - sus' res - ur - rec - tion!
your deep peace, which ev - er - more pass - es hu - man know - ing.

One of the many ancient hymns translated into English in the 19th century, this 8th-century Eastertide hymn was originally part of a longer Greek liturgical text. This tune was created for this text by a church organist who later rose to fame as a composer of operettas.

TEXT: John of Damascus, 8th cent.; trans. John Mason Neale, 1859, alt.
MUSIC: Arthur S. Sullivan, 1872, alt.

ST. KEVIN
7.6.7.6.D

235 O Sons and Daughters, Let Us Sing

Alleluia! Alleluia! Alleluia! Alleluia!

1 O sons and daugh-ters, let us sing with
2 That Eas-ter morn, at break of day, the
3 An an-gel clad in white they see, who
4 That night the a-pos-tles met in fear; a-
5 On this most ho-ly day of days, to

heaven-ly hosts to Christ our King; to-day the grave has
faith-ful wom-en went their way to seek the tomb where
sits, and speaks un-to the three, "Your Lord will go to
mong them came their Lord most dear, and said, "My peace be
God your hearts and voic-es raise, in laud and ju-bi-

Fine

lost its sting!
Je - sus lay.
Gal - i - lee." Alleluia! Alleluia!
with you here."
lee and praise.

These stanzas from a 19th-century translation of a 15th-century Latin text make up the Easter Sunday portion of a longer hymn. They are sung to a 15th-century French tune that probably originated outside the church but was adapted for religious texts.

TEXT: Attr. Jean Tisserand, 15th cent.; trans. John Mason Neale, 1852
MUSIC: French melody, 15th cent.; arr. *Airs sur les hymnes sacrez, odes et nöels*, 1623

O FILII ET FILIAE
8.8.8 with alleluias

The Strife Is O'er

236

Refrain (before stanza 1 and after stanza 4)

Al - le - lu - ia, al - le - lu - ia, al - le - lu - ia!

1 The strife is o'er, the bat - tle done; the vic - to -
2 The powers of death have done their worst, but Christ their
3 The three sad days are quick - ly sped; Christ ris - es
4 Lord, by the stripes which wound - ed thee, from death's dread

ry of life is won; the song of tri - umph
le - gions hath dis - persed: let shouts of ho - ly
glo - rious from the dead: all glo - ry to our
sting thy ser - vants free, that we may live, and

has be - gun.
joy out - burst.
ris - en Head!   Al - le - lu - ia!
sing to thee:

The Latin text from which this hymn has been translated may well be older than its earliest printing in a 17th-century collection published in Cologne. It is set to an adaptation of a portion of the Gloria Patri section from a 16th-century choral version of the Magnificat.

TEXT: Latin hymn, c. 1695; trans. Francis Pott, 1861
MUSIC: Giovanni Pierluigi da Palestrina, 1591; adapt. William Henry Monk, 1861

VICTORY
8.8.8 with alleluias

237 Christ Jesus Lay in Death's Strong Bands

1 Christ Jesus lay in death's strong bands for our of-fens-es
2 Our Sav-ior Je-sus, God's own Son, here in our stead de-
3 Here the true Pas-chal Lamb we see, whom God so free-ly
4 So let us keep the fes-ti - val where-to the Lord in-

giv - en; but now at God's right hand Christ stands and
scend - ed; the knot of sin has been un - done; the
gave us. He died on the ac-curs-ed tree so
vites us; Christ is the ver - y joy of all, the

brings us light from heav - en; there-fore let us
reign of death is end - ed. Christ has crushed the
strong his love to save us. See, his blood now
sun that warms and lights us. Now his grace to

The parallel transformations in this classic Lutheran hymn move from bondage ("death's strong bands"; "knot of sin") to freedom, from darkness to light, from death to life. This harmonization of the sturdy chorale tune uses moving inner parts and chromaticism to convey life.

TEXT: Martin Luther, 1524; trans. composite
MUSIC: *Geystliche gesangk Buchleyn,* 1524; adapt. and harm. Johann Sebastian Bach, c. 1707
Text St. 2 © 1999 Augsburg Fortress

CHRIST LAG IN TODESBANDEN
8.7.8.7.7.8.7.4

joy - ful be and sing to God right thank - ful - ly loud
power of hell; now death is but an emp - ty shell. Its
marks our door: faith points to it; death pass - es o'er, and
us im - parts e - ter - nal sun - shine to our hearts; the

songs of hal - le - lu - jah! Hal - le - lu - jah!
sting is lost for - ev - er! Hal - le - lu - jah!
Sa - tan can - not harm us. Hal - le - lu - jah!
night of sin is end - ed! Hal - le - lu - jah!

238 Thine Is the Glory

1 Thine is the glo - ry, ris - en, con-quering Son; end - less is
2 Lo! Je - sus meets us, ris - en from the tomb; lov - ing - ly
3 No more we doubt thee, glo - rious Prince of life! Life is naught

the vic - tory thou o'er death hast won. An - gels in bright rai - ment
he greets us, scat - ters fear and gloom. Let the church with glad-ness
with-out thee; aid us in our strife. Make us more than con-querors

rolled the stone a - way, kept the fold - ed grave-clothes
hymns of tri - umph sing, for the Lord now liv - eth;
through thy death - less love; bring us safe through Jor - dan

Refrain

where thy bod - y lay.
death hath lost its sting. Thine is the glo - ry, ris - en, con-quering
to thy home a - bove.

This Easter text, first in French and later in English, was written to fit the music, a chorus created for Handel's oratorio *Joshua* and moved to *Judas Maccabeus* in 1751. It grew widely popular following its use at the First Assembly of the World Council of Churches in 1948.

TEXT: Edmond Louis Budry, 1884; trans. R. Birch Hoyle, 1923, alt.
MUSIC: George Frederick Handel, 1748

JUDAS MACCABEUS
5.5.6.5.6.5.6.5 with refrain

Son; end - less is the vic - tory thou o'er death hast won.

Good Christians All, Rejoice and Sing! 239

1 Good Chris-tians all, re - joice and sing! Now is the tri - umph
2 The Lord of life is risen to - day! Death's might - y stone is
3 Praise we in songs of vic - to - ry that love, that life which
4 Your name we bless, O ris - en Lord, and sing to - day with

of our King! To all the world glad news we bring:
rolled a - way. Let all the earth re - joice and say:
can - not die, and sing with hearts up - lift - ed high:
one ac - cord the life laid down, the life re - stored:

Al - le - lu - ia! Al - le - lu - ia! Al - le - lu - ia!

This 20th-century Easter text is both a song of encouragement (stanzas 1–3 directed to the congregation) and a song of praise (stanza 4 addressed to the risen Christ), all ending with joyous alleluias. It was written specifically for the dancelike 17th-century tune found here.

TEXT: Cyril A. Alington, 1931, alt.
MUSIC: Melchior Vulpius, 1609; harm. *Pilgrim Hymnal*, 1958
Text © 1958, ren. 1986 Hymns Ancient & Modern (admin. Hope Publishing Company)

GELOBT SEI GOTT
8.8.8 with alleluias

240 Alleluia, Alleluia! Give Thanks

This text and tune were created together in the context of an ecumenical, charismatic, missionary Christian community in Ann Arbor, Michigan. Their energy and emphasis center in the opening and closing refrain's "Alleluia"—the essential Easter word of proclamation.

TEXT: Donald Fishel, 1971
MUSIC: Donald Fishel, 1971; arr. Betty Pulkingham and Donald Fishel, 1979
Text and Music © 1973 International Liturgy Publications

ALLELUIA NO. 1
8.8 with refrain

Woman, Weeping in the Garden 241

1 Wom-an, weep-ing in the gar - den, who has
2 Wom-an, wait-ing in the gar - den, af - ter
3 Wom-an, walk-ing in the gar - den, Je - sus
4 Wom-an, weep-ing in the gar - den, weep for
5 Wom-an, danc-ing from the gar - den, find the

pushed the stone a - side? Who has tak - en Je - sus'
men have come and gone, af - ter an - gels give their
takes you by sur - prise; when the gar - dener calls you,
joy, for you have seen Je - sus, the Mes - si - ah,
oth - ers and pro - claim Christ is ris - en as he

bod - y, Je - sus Christ the cru - ci - fied?
wit - ness, si - lent - ly you watch the dawn.
"Mar - y!" faith and joy meet in your eyes.
ris - en; Christ, of whom the proph - ets dream.
prom - ised; tell the world he knew your name!

This hymn focuses on Mary Magdalene, the first witness to Christ's Resurrection (John 20:1–18). Her frame of mind turns from sorrow and apprehension to joy and proclamation in the middle stanza when the supposed gardener calls her by name, and she recognizes the risen Christ.

TEXT: Daniel Charles Damon, 1991
MUSIC: V. Earle Copes, 1959
Text © 1992 Hope Publishing Company

KINGDOM
8.7.8.7

242 Day of Delight and Beauty Unbounded

Day of de-light and beau-ty un-bound-ed, tell the news, the
gos-pel spread! Day of all won-der, day of all splen-dor, praise Christ
ris - en from the dead!

1 Sing of the sun from dark-ness ap-
2 Sing now of mourn-ing turned in - to

pear - ing; sing of the seed from bar-ren earth green - ing;
danc - ing; sing now the mys - tery, hope of our glo - ry;

sing of cre - a - tion, al - le - lu - ia! Sing of the
sing with thanks-giv - ing, al - le - lu - ia! Sing now of

This joyful Easter hymn brings together many images and responses evoked by Christ's Resurrection. As the second stanza affirms, it does turn mourning into dancing (Psalm 30:11), for this 20th-century text was written to fit the rhythms of this 16th-century Italian dance-song.

TEXT: Delores Dufner, OSB, 1996
MUSIC: Giovanni Giacomo Gastoldi, 1591
Text © 2011 GIA Publications, Inc.

IN DIR IST FREUDE
Irregular

stream from Je - sus' side flow - ing; sing of the saints in
fast - ing turned in - to feast - ing; sing the Lord's fa - vor

wa - ter made ho - ly; sing of sal - va - tion, al - le - lu - ia!
last - ing for - ev - er; sing, all things liv - ing, al - le - lu - ia!

Be Not Afraid 243

Be not a - fraid; sing out for joy! Christ is ris-en, al - le - lu - ia!

Be not a - fraid; sing out for joy! Christ is ris-en, al - le - lu - ia!

Intended for repeated singing like other chants from the Taizé Community, this text began in Czech as "Nebojte se." The English version uses the language of the angel's greeting to Mary Magdalene and "the other Mary," who went to Jesus' tomb on Easter morning (Matthew 28:5–6).

TEXT: Taizé Community, 1998
MUSIC: Jacques Berthier, 1998
Text and Music © 1998 Les Presses de Taizé (admin. GIA Publications, Inc.)

BE NOT AFRAID
4.4.8.D

244 This Joyful Eastertide

1 This joy-ful Eas-ter-tide, a-way with sin and
2 My flesh in hope shall rest and for a sea-son
3 Death's flood has lost its chill since Je-sus crossed the

sor - row! My love, the Cru-ci-fied, has
slum - ber till trump from east to west shall
riv - er. Lov-er of souls, from ill my

Refrain

sprung to life this mor - row. Had Christ, who once was
wake the dead in num - ber.
pass-ing soul de-liv - er.

The verbal and musical elements of this hymn mesh so well because the words were written to fit this Dutch tune (whose name means "fruits"). The news of Christ's resurrection is joyfully conveyed by the ever-higher phrases and final cascade of notes at the end of the refrain.

TEXT: George Ratcliffe Woodward, 1894, alt.
MUSIC: *David's Psalmen*, 1685; harm. Charles Wood, 1902

VRUECHTEN
6.7.6.7 with refrain
(alternate harmonization, 249)

slain, not burst his three-day pris - on, our faith had been in

vain. But now has Christ a - ris - en, a - ris - en, a -

ris - en, a - ris - - - en.

245 Christ the Lord Is Risen Today!

1 "Christ the Lord is risen to - day!"
2 Love's re - deem - ing work is done,
3 Lives a - gain our glo - rious King,
4 Hail the Lord of earth and heaven!

Al - le - lu - ia!

All cre - a - tion, join to say:
Fought the fight, the bat - tle won,
Where, O death, is now your sting?
Praise to you by both be given,

Al - le - lu - ia!

Raise your joys and tri - umphs high,
Death in vain for - bids him rise,
Je - sus died, our souls to save,
Ev - ery knee to you shall bow,

Al - le - lu - ia!

Sing, O heavens, and earth re - ply,
Christ has o - pened par - a - dise.
Where your vic - to - ry, O grave?
Ris - en Christ, tri - um - phant now.

Al - le - lu - ia!

Originally printed as eleven four-line stanzas without alleluias, this Easter text was written during the first year following the author's life-changing conversion experience, yet it already shows his enduring emphasis on the theme of love. This lively Welsh tune sets it well.

TEXT: Charles Wesley, 1739, alt.
MUSIC: Robert Williams, 1817; harm. David Evans, 1927
Music Harm. © 1927 Oxford University Press

LLANFAIR
7.7.7.7 with alleluias

Christ Is Alive!

1 Christ is a - live! Let Chris - tians sing. The cross stands
2 Christ is a - live! No lon - ger bound to dis - tant
3 In ev - ery in - sult, rift, and war where col - or,
4 Wom - en and men, in age and youth, can feel the
5 Christ is a - live, and comes to bring good news to

emp - ty to the sky. Let streets and homes with
years in Pal - es - tine, but sav - ing, heal - ing,
scorn, or wealth di - vide, Christ suf - fers still, yet
Spir - it, hear the call, and find the way, the
this and ev - ery age, till earth and sky and

prais - es ring. Love, drowned in death, shall nev - er die.
here and now, and touch - ing ev - ery place and time.
loves the more, and lives, where e - ven hope has died.
life, the truth, re - vealed in Je - sus, freed for all.
o - cean ring with joy, with jus - tice, love, and praise.

In 1968 Easter fell ten days after the assassination of Martin Luther King Jr., and this text was written to express an Easter hope while mindful of that terrible event. Buoyed by a triple-arched tune, it affirms the presence of a wounded, risen Christ with all who suffer.

TEXT: Brian Wren, 1968; rev. 1995
MUSIC: *Musica Sacra*, c. 1778
Text © 1975, rev. 1995 Hope Publishing Company

TRURO
LM

247 Now the Green Blade Rises

1 Now the green blade ris - es from the bur - ied grain,
2 In the grave they laid him, love by ha - tred slain,
3 Forth he came at Eas - ter like the ris - en grain,
4 When our hearts are win - try, griev - ing, or in pain,

wheat that in dark earth man - y days has lain;
think - ing that he would nev - er wake a - gain,
he that for three days in the grave had lain;
your touch can call us back to life a - gain;

love lives a - gain, that with the dead has been;
laid in the earth like grain that sleeps un - seen;
raised from the dead, my liv - ing Lord is seen;
fields of our hearts that dead and bare have been:

love is come a - gain like wheat a - ris - ing green.

Although there were some traditional Easter carols, this hybrid one has been created by grafting a 20th-century English text onto a late 15th-century French tune. The allegory of the dying and rising grain as a parallel for Christ's Resurrection is probably based on John 12:24.

TEXT: John M. C. Crum, 1928, alt.
MUSIC: French carol, 15th cent.; harm. Martin Shaw, 1928
Text and Music Harm. © 1928 Oxford University Press

NOËL NOUVELET
11.10.10.11

Christ Is Risen! Shout Hosanna! 248

1 Christ is ris - en! Shout Ho - san - na! Cel - e - brate this day of days!
2 Christ is ris - en! Raise your spir - its from the cav - erns of de - spair.
3 Christ is ris - en! Earth and heav - en nev - er - more shall be the same.

Christ is ris - en! Hush in won - der: all cre - a - tion is a - mazed.
Walk with glad - ness in the morn - ing. See what love can do and dare.
Break the bread of new cre - a - tion where the world is still in pain.

In the des - ert all - sur - round - ing, see, a spread - ing tree has grown.
Drink the wine of res - ur - rec - tion, not a ser - vant, but a friend.
Tell its grim, de - mon - ic cho - rus: "Christ is ris - en! Get you gone!"

Heal - ing leaves of grace a - bound - ing bring a taste of love un - known.
Je - sus is our strong com - pan - ion. Joy and peace shall nev - er end.
God the First and Last is with us. Sing Ho - san - na ev - ery - one!

In commenting on this late 20th-century text, the author has stressed his intention to affirm the social implications of an Easter faith: "Christian peace and justice action finds its wellspring, not in moral zeal or guilty conscience, but in the resurrection."

TEXT: Brian Wren, 1984
MUSIC: Ludwig van Beethoven, 1824; adapt. Edward Hodges, 1842, alt.
Text © 1986 Hope Publishing Company

HYMN TO JOY
8.7.8.7.D

249 Because You Live, O Christ

1 Be-cause you live, O Christ, the gar-den of the world has come to
2 Be-cause you live, O Christ, the spir-it bird of hope is freed for
3 Be-cause you live, O Christ, the rain-bow of your peace will span cre -

flow - er; the dark-ness of the tomb is flood-ed with your
fly - ing; our ca-ges of de-spair no lon-ger keep us
a - tion; the col-ors of your love will draw all hu-man -

Refrain

res - ur - rec - tion pow - er.
closed and life-de - ny - ing. The stone has rolled a-way and death can-
kind to ad-o - ra - tion.

not im-pris - on! O sing this Eas-ter day, for Je-sus Christ has

This New Zealand author's text contains no familiar images of springtime to bolster its message, because Easter in the Southern Hemisphere comes in autumn. This hymn resulted both from her dissatisfaction with existing hymns and from her love of this exuberant Dutch tune.

TEXT: Shirley Erena Murray, 1987
MUSIC: Dutch melody, 17th cent.; harm. Alice Parker, 1966
Text © 1987 Hope Publishing Company
Music Harm. © 1969 Hope Publishing Company

VRUECHTEN
6.11.6.11 with refrain
(alternate harmonization, 244)

ris - en, has ris - en, has ris - en, has ris - en!

In the Bulb There Is a Flower 250
Hymn of Promise

Capo 3: (D)

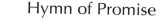

1 In the bulb there is a flow - er; in the seed, an ap - ple tree;
2 There's a song in ev-ery si - lence, seek-ing word and mel - o - dy;
3 In our end is our be - gin - ning; in our time, in - fin - i - ty;

in co - coons, a hid-den prom - ise: but - ter - flies will soon be free!
there's a dawn in ev-ery dark - ness, bring-ing hope to you and me.
in our doubt there is be - liev - ing; in our life, e - ter - ni - ty.

In the cold and snow of win - ter there's a spring that waits to be,
From the past will come the fu - ture; what it holds, a mys - ter - y,
In our death, a res - ur - rec - tion; at the last, a vic - to - ry,

un - re-vealed un - til its sea - son, some-thing God a - lone can see.

The writing of this hymn was spurred by a line from the poet T. S. Eliot: "In my end is my beginning." Shortly after this piece was completed, the author/composer's husband was diagnosed with what proved to be a terminal malignancy, and the original anthem version of this hymn was sung at his funeral.

TEXT and MUSIC: Natalie Sleeth, 1986
Text and Music © 1986 Hope Publishing Company

PROMISE
8.7.8.7.D

251 Christ Has Arisen, Alleluia

1 Christ has a-ris-en, al-le-lu-ia. Re-joice and
2 For three long days the grave did its worst un-til its
3 The an-gel said to them, "Do not fear. You look for
4 "Go spread the news: he's not in the grave. He has a-
5 Christ has a-ris-en to set us free. Al-le-lu-

praise him, al-le-lu-ia. For our re-deem-er
strength by God was dis-persed. He who gives life did
Je-sus who is not here. See for your-selves the
ris-en this world to save. Je-sus' re-deem-ing
ia, to him prais-es be. Je-sus is liv-ing!

burst from the tomb, e-ven from death, dis-pel-ling its gloom.
death un-der-go, and in its con-quest his might did show.
tomb is all bare. On-ly the grave clothes are ly-ing there."
la-bors are done. E-ven the bat-tle with sin is won."
Let us all sing; he reigns tri-um-phant, heav-en-ly King.

The good news of the Resurrection is retold in this lively hymn from Tanzania, blending 20th-century words with a traditional melody. In African call-and-response practice, the stanzas would ordinarily be sung by a soloist or small group and the refrain by the whole congregation.

TEXT: Bernard Kyamanywa, 1966; trans. Howard S. Olson, 1969
MUSIC: Tanzanian melody
Text © 1977 Howard S. Olson (admin. Augsburg Fortress)

MFURAHINI, HALELUYA
9.9.9.9 with refrain

Refrain

Let us sing praise to him with end-less joy. Death's fear-ful sting he has come to de-stroy. Our sin for-giv-ing, al-le-lu-ia! Je-sus is liv-ing, al-le-lu-ia!

252
Day of Arising

Capo 1: (Esus) (E) (B) (E)
Fsus F C F

1 Day of a - ris - ing, Christ on the road - way, un - known com -
2 When we are walk - ing, doubt - ful and dread - ing, blind - ed by
3 Lo, I am with you, Je - sus has spo - ken. This is Christ's
4 Christ, our com - pan - ion, hope for the jour - ney, bread of com -

(Amaj7) (F#m7) (B7) (Esus) (E)
Bbmaj7 Gm7 C7 Fsus F

pan - ion walks with his own. When they in - vite him,
sad - ness, slow - ness of heart, yet Christ walks with us,
prom - ise, this is Christ's sign: when the church gath - ers,
pas - sion, o - pen our eyes. Grant us your vi - sion,

(B) (E) (Amaj7) (B7) (E)
C F Bbmaj7 C7 F

as fades the first day, and bread is bro - ken, Christ is made known.
ev - er a - wait-ing our in - vi - ta - tion: Stay, do not part.
when bread is bro - ken, there Christ is with us, in bread and wine.
set all hearts burn-ing that all cre - a - tion with you may rise.

Guitar chords do not correspond with keyboard harmony.

Based on Luke 24:13–35, this text tells how Christ walked with two dejected believers on the way to Emmaus. This journey reminds us of our own spiritual wanderings, and the revelation of the risen Christ in the breaking of the bread gives us hope for such an encounter in worship.

TEXT: Susan Palo Cherwien, 1996   RAABE
MUSIC: Carl F. Schalk, 1999   5.5.5.4.D
Text © 1996 Susan Palo Cherwien (admin. Augsburg Fortress)
Music © 1999 Augsburg Fortress

253
Alleluia! Christ Is Arisen
¡Aleluya! Cristo resucitó

Refrain / Estribillo

Capo 2: (Am) (E7)
Bm F#7

Al - le - lu - ia! Christ is a - ris - en.
¡A - le - lu - ya! Cris - to re - su - ci - tó

With great artistry, this Latin American hymn condenses the Resurrection story into four stanzas. The first and third stanzas deal with groups (the women, the disciples), while the second and fourth focus on individuals (Mary Magdalene, Thomas). The refrain is Good News for all.

TEXT: Luis Bojos, 1974; English trans. Martin A. Seltz, 2000   SANTO DOMINGO
MUSIC: Luis Bojos, 1974   9.8.9.8 with refrain
Text and Music © 2001 Luis Bojos (Published by OCP)

Bright is the dawn-ing of the Lord's day.
la ma - dru - ga - da del do - min - go.

1 Run, faith - ful wom - en, to the grave - side.
2 Rise, Mag - da - le - na, from your weep - ing;
3 Gath - er, dis - ci - ples, in the eve - ning:
4 Thom - as, where were you on that eve - ning?

Mar - vel, the stone is rolled a - way!
Christ stands be - fore your ver - y eyes.
sud - den - ly Christ your Lord ap - pears.
"I'll not be - lieve un - less I see."

Hear from the an - gel, "He is ris - en."
Quick - ly re - turn to the dis - ci - ples;
"Look, it is I, your wound - ed Sav - ior.
Christ comes a - gain, and ev - ery Lord's day:

to Refrain / al Estribillo

Christ goes be - fore you all the way.
bear the good news: "He is a - live."
Peace be with you, and do not fear."
"Touch me and see; have faith in me."

SPANISH

1 *Fueron mujeres al sepulcro.*
La piedra un ángel removió;
les dijo: "Ha resucitado".
Y al irse, les salió el Señor.

2 *La Magdalena fue a llorarlo*
y Cristo se le apareció;
le pidió ir a sus hermanos
con un encargo que le dio.

3 *A los discípulos, de tarde,*
Cristo también se presentó.
Les enseñó las cinco heridas;
dando la paz los saludó.

4 *Tomás no estaba en ese encuentro;*
y ver, pidió, para creer.
Cristo volvió, le dijo: "Mira,
palpa mi herida y ten fe".

254 That Easter Day with Joy Was Bright

1 That Eas - ter day with joy was bright; the sun shone
2 He bade them see his hands, his side, where yet the
3 From ev - ery weap - on death can wield, your own re -

out with fair - er light when, to their long - ing
glo - rious wounds a - bide, the to - kens true which
deemed for - ev - er shield; O Lord of all, with

eyes re - stored, the a - pos - tles saw their ris - en Lord.
made it plain their Lord in - deed was risen a - gain.
us a - bide in this our joy - ful Eas - ter - tide.

These Eastertide stanzas are derived from a longer Latin text that was one of the earliest hymns written especially for a season of the church year. They are set here to a tune with Christmas associations, a means of linking the two great festivals of the Christian year.

TEXT: Latin hymn, 5th cent.; trans. John Mason Neale, 1852, alt.
MUSIC: Trier ms., 15th cent.; adapt. Michael Praetorius, 1609

PUER NOBIS NASCITUR
LM
(alternate harmonization, 67)

O Sons and Daughters, Let Us Sing 255

Al - le - lu - ia! Al - le - lu - ia! Al - le-lu - ia! Alle - lu - ia!

1 O sons and daugh - ters, let us sing with
2 That night the a - pos - tles met in fear; a -
3 When Thom - as first the ti - dings heard, how
4 "My pierc - ed side, O Thom - as, see; and

heaven-ly hosts to Christ our King; to - day the grave has
mong them came their Lord most dear, and said, "My peace be
they had seen the ris - en Lord, he doubt - ed the dis -
look up - on my hands, my feet; not faith - less, but be -

lost its sting!
with you here."
ci - ples' word.
liev - ing be."

Al - le - lu - ia! Al - le - lu - ia!

5 No longer Thomas then denied;
he saw the feet, the hands, the side;
"You are my Lord and God!" he cried.
Alleluia! Alleluia!

6 How blest are they who have not seen,
and yet whose faith has constant been,
for they eternal life shall win.
Alleluia! Alleluia!

These stanzas from a 19th-century translation of a longer 15th-century Latin text are the continuation of hymn no. 235 and are based on the traditional gospel reading for the Second Sunday of Easter. They are sung to a 15th-century French tune adapted for church use.

TEXT: Attr. Jean Tisserand, 15th cent.; trans. John Mason Neale, 1852
MUSIC: French melody, 15th cent.; arr. *Airs sur les hymnes sacrez, odes et nöels*, 1623

O FILII ET FILIAE
8.8.8 with alleluias

256 These Things Did Thomas Count as Real

1 These things did Thom-as count as real: the warmth of
2 The vi-sion of his skep-tic mind was keen e-
3 His rea-soned cer-tain-ties de-nied that one could
4 May we, O God, by grace be-lieve and thus the

blood, the chill of steel, the grain of wood, the heft of
nough to make him blind to an-y un-ex-pect-ed
live when one had died, un-til his fin-gers read like
ris-en Christ re-ceive, whose raw im-print-ed hands reached

stone, the last frail twitch of blood and bone.
act too large for his small world of fact.
Braille the mark-ings of the spear and nail.
out and beck-oned Thom-as from his doubt.

This 20th-century text provides a helpful corrective to a long history of negative attitudes toward Thomas for failing to believe the other disciples' report that Christ had risen. His fact-seeking "skeptic mind" sounds remarkably modern and makes him a more sympathetic figure.

TEXT: Thomas H. Troeger, 1984
MUSIC: Attr. Elkanah Kelsay Dare; harm. Pilsbury's *United States Harmony*, 1799, alt.
Text © 1986 Oxford University Press

KEDRON
LM

The Risen Christ

257

1 The ris - en Christ, who walks on wound - ed
2 The ris - en Christ, who stands with wound - ed
3 The ris - en Christ, who breaks with wound - ed
4 May we, Christ's bod - y, walk and serve and

feet from gar - den tomb through dark - ened cit - y
side, breathes out his Spir - it on them to a -
hand the bread for those who fail to un - der -
stand with the op - pressed in this and ev - ery

street, un - locks the door of grief, de - spair, and fear, and
bide whose faith still wa - vers, who dare not be - lieve; new
stand, re - veals him - self, de - spite their lin - gering tears, en -
land, till all are blessed and can a bless - ing be, re -

speaks a word of peace to all who hear.
grace, new strength, new pur - pose they re - ceive.
flames their hearts, then quick - ly dis - ap - pears.
stored in Christ to true hu - man - i - ty.

Guitar chords do not correspond with keyboard harmony.

This perceptive hymn centers on Christ's post-Resurrection appearances described in John 20:19–29 and Luke 24:13–48. The first three stanzas are shaped by the wounded body parts: feet, side, hand; the fourth prays for such woundedness in the witness of Christ's body, the Church.

TEXT: Nigel Weaver, 1993
MUSIC: Walter Greatorex, 1916
Text © 1993 Nigel Weaver

WOODLANDS
10.10.10.10

258 A Hymn of Glory Let Us Sing!

1 A hymn of glo-ry let us sing! New songs through-
2 The ho-ly ap-os-tol-ic band up-on the
3 To all, the shin-ing an-gels cry, "Why stand and
4 "You see him now, as-cend-ing high up to the
5 O ris-en Christ, as-cend-ed Lord, all praise to

out the world shall ring: Christ, by a road be-
Mount of Ol-ives stand, and with his fol-low-
gaze up-on the sky? This is the Sav-ior!"
por-tals of the sky. Here-af-ter you shall
you let earth ac-cord. You are, while end-less

fore un-trod, as-cends un-to the throne of God.
ers they see their Lord as-cend in maj-es-ty.
thus they say; "This is his glo-rious tri-umph-day."
Je-sus see re-turn-ing in great maj-es-ty."
a-ges run, with Fa-ther and with Spir-it one.

These stanzas have been crafted from various English translations of a much longer Latin hymn preserved in an 11th-century manuscript in the British Museum. This text celebrating Christ's majesty is well set to a 15th-century English tune commemorating a military victory.

TEXT: The Venerable Bede, 7th–8th cent.; trans. *Lutheran Book of Worship*, 1978, alt.
MUSIC: "The Agincourt Song," c. 1415; harm. Alfred V. Fedak, 2012
Text © 1978 Lutheran Book of Worship (admin. Augsburg Fortress)
Music Harm. © 2012 Alfred V. Fedak

DEO GRACIAS
LM
(alternate tune: LASST UNS ERFREUEN with "Alleluias," 15)
(alternate harmonization, 189)

The God of Heaven

259

(Psalm 29)

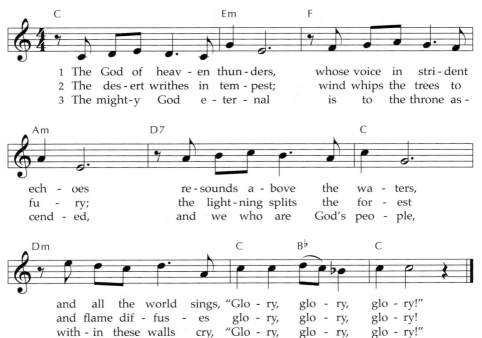

1 The God of heav - en thun - ders, whose voice in stri - dent
2 The des - ert writhes in tem - pest; wind whips the trees to
3 The might - y God e - ter - nal is to the throne as -

ech - oes re - sounds a - bove the wa - ters,
fu - ry; the light - ning splits the for - est
cend - ed, and we who are God's peo - ple,

and all the world sings, "Glo - ry, glo - ry, glo - ry!"
and flame dif - fus - es glo - ry, glo - ry, glo - ry!
with - in these walls cry, "Glo - ry, glo - ry, glo - ry!"

This rather telegraphic paraphrase of Psalm 29 effectively conveys the psalm's recurring contrast between the mighty voice of God heard in thunder and tempest and the awestruck response of creation. Above this tumult, God reigns in peace, and the people of God sing praise.

TEXT: Michael Perry, 1973, alt.
MUSIC: Norman L. Warren, 1973
Text and Music © 1973 The Jubilate Group (admin. Hope Publishing Company)

GLORY
Irregular

260 Alleluia! Sing to Jesus

1 Al - le - lu - ia! Sing to Je - sus; his the scep - ter, his the
2 Al - le - lu - ia! Not as or - phans are we left in sor - row
3 Al - le - lu - ia! Bread of an - gels, here on earth our food, our
4 Al - le - lu - ia! King e - ter - nal, Lord om - nip - o - tent we

throne; Al - le - lu - ia! his the tri - umph, his the vic - to -
now; Al - le - lu - ia! he is near us; faith be - lieves nor
stay; Al - le - lu - ia! here the sin - ful flee to you from
own; Al - le - lu - ia! born of Mar - y, earth your foot - stool,

ry a - lone! Hark! The songs of peace - ful Zi - on
ques - tions how. Though the cloud from sight re - ceived him,
day to day. In - ter - ces - sor, friend of sin - ners,
heaven your throne. As with - in the veil you en - tered,

The author regarded this text as a communion hymn, a theme that seems eclipsed by the attention to
Christ's exaltation, but a helpful reminder that such hymns are not always quiet and meek. This text is sung
to various tunes, but this rousing Welsh one is a favorite choice.

TEXT: William Chatterton Dix, 1866, alt.
MUSIC: Rowland Hugh Prichard, 1831, alt.

HYFRYDOL
8.7.8.7.D

thun - der like a might - y flood: "Je - sus out of
when the for - ty days were o'er, shall our hearts for -
earth's re - deem - er, hear our plea where the songs of
robed in flesh, our great high priest; here on earth both

ev - ery na - tion has re - deemed us by his blood."
get his prom - ise: "I am with you ev - er - more"?
all the sin - less sweep a - cross the crys - tal sea.
priest and vic - tim in the eu - cha - ris - tic feast.

261 Peoples, Clap Your Hands!

(Psalm 47)

1 Peo - ples, clap your hands! Shout to God with joy! King of all the earth
2 God as - cends the throne with a joy - ful cry, and with trum - pet sound

is the Lord Most High; all hu - man - i - ty stands in awe of God.
has gone up on high; sing your praise to God, sing with joy - ful voice!

With a might - y hand God brings na - tions low, and be - neath our feet
Rul - ers, peo - ples, now join to serve the Lord; for earth's might - y ones

casts down ev - ery foe; our in - her - i - tance comes from God the Lord.
all be - long to God, who ex - alt - ed reigns: now with psalms re - joice!

In joining this 20th-century English paraphrase of Psalm 47—a psalm long associated with Christ's Ascension—with the 16th-century Genevan psalm tune written for a French metrical version, an important affirmation of the continuity of Reformed tradition is being made.

TEXT: Joy F. Patterson, 1989
MUSIC: Genevan Psalter, 1551; harm. Claude Goudimel, 1564
Text © 1990 Joy F. Patterson

GENEVAN 47
10.10.10.10.10.10

Since Our Great High Priest, Christ Jesus 262

1 Since our great high priest, Christ Je - sus, bears the name a -
bove all names, reign - ing Son of God, sur - pass - ing
oth - er ti - tles, powers, and claims; since to heaven our
Lord has passed, let us hold our wit - ness fast!

2 Since we have a priest who suf - fered, know - ing weak - ness,
tears, and pain, who, like us, was tried and tempt - ed,
un - like us, with - out a stain; since he shared our
low - ly place, let us bold - ly seek his grace.

3 Sac - ri - fice and suf - fering o - ver, now he sits at
God's right hand, crowned with praise, no more an out - cast,
his pre - em - i - nence long planned; such a great high
priest we have, strong to help, su - preme to save.

4 Love's ex - am - ple, hope's at - trac - tion, faith's be - gin - ning
and its end, pi - o - neer of our sal - va - tion,
might - y ad - vo - cate and friend: Je - sus, high in
glo - ry raised, our as - cend - ed Lord, be praised!

Drawing on several passages in Hebrews (especially 4:14–16), this hymn celebrates the culmination of the Incarnation in Christ's exaltation, a source of encouragement to all who trust in this "pioneer of our salvation" (Hebrews 2:10, 12:2) who continues to intercede for us.

TEXT: Christopher M. Idle, 1973
MUSIC: *Geistreiches Gesangbuch*, 1698; harm. William Henry Monk, 1861, alt.
Text © 1973 The Jubilate Group (admin. Hope Publishing Company)

ALL SAINTS
8.7.8.7.7.7

263 All Hail the Power of Jesus' Name!

Descant

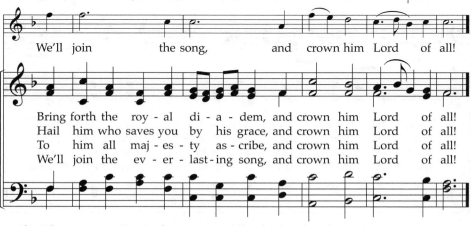

4 O that with yon-der sa-cred throng we at his feet may fall!

1 All hail the power of Je - sus' name! Let an - gels pros-trate fall;
2 Ye cho - sen seed of Is-rael's race, ye ran-somed from the fall,
3 Let ev - ery kin-dred, ev - ery tribe on this ter - res-trial ball
4 O that with yon - der sa-cred throng we at his feet may fall!

We'll join the song, and crown him Lord of all!

bring forth the roy - al di - a - dem, and crown him Lord of all!
hail him who saves you by his grace, and crown him Lord of all!
to him all maj - es - ty as-cribe, and crown him Lord of all!
We'll join the ev - er - last-ing song, and crown him Lord of all!

We'll join the song, and crown him Lord of all!

Bring forth the roy - al di - a - dem, and crown him Lord of all!
Hail him who saves you by his grace, and crown him Lord of all!
To him all maj - es - ty as-cribe, and crown him Lord of all!
We'll join the ev - er - last-ing song, and crown him Lord of all!

This 18th-century text celebrating the sovereignty of Christ has been through several expansions and contractions before reaching its present form. It is set here to the oldest American hymn tune in continuous use since first published in 1793, which was written for it.

TEXT: Stanzas 1–3, Edward Perronet, 1779, 1780; stanzas 2–3, alt. John Rippon, 1787; stanza 4, John Rippon, 1787   CORONATION
MUSIC: Oliver Holden, 1793; desc. Michael E. Young, 1979   8.6.8.6.8.6
Music Desc. © 1979 GIA Publications, Inc.

At the Name of Jesus

1 At the name of Je - sus ev - ery knee shall bow,
2 Hum - bled for a sea - son to re - ceive a name
3 Bore it up tri - um - phant, with its hu - man light,
4 Chris - tians, this Lord Je - sus shall re - turn a - gain,

ev - ery tongue con - fess him King of glo - ry now;
from the lips of sin - ners un - to whom he came,
through all ranks of crea - tures, to the cen - tral height,
with his Fa - ther's glo - ry o'er the earth to reign;

'tis the Fa - ther's plea - sure we should call him Lord,
faith - ful - ly he bore it spot - less to the last,
to the throne of God - head, to the Fa - ther's breast,
for all wreaths of em - pire meet up - on his brow,

who from the be - gin - ning was the might - y Word.
brought it back vic - to - rious, when from death he passed;
filled it with the glo - ry of that per - fect rest.
and our hearts con - fess him King of glo - ry now.

Guitar chords do not correspond with keyboard harmony.

This may well be a hymn based on a hymn, for scholars say that the passage behind it (Philippians 2:5–11), though not in the style of Greek poetry, shows traits of a communal creedal statement capable of being sung. It is set here to one of the composer's most sonorous tunes.

TEXT: Caroline Maria Noel, 1870, alt.
MUSIC: Ralph Vaughan Williams, 1925
Music © 1925 Oxford University Press

KING'S WESTON
6.5.6.5.D

265 Jesus Shall Reign Where'er the Sun

1 Je - sus shall reign wher - e'er the sun does its suc -
2 To him shall end - less prayer be made, and prais - es
3 Peo - ple and realms of ev - ery tongue dwell on his
4 Bless - ings a - bound wher - e'er he reigns: the pris - oners
5 Let ev - ery crea - ture rise and bring hon - ors pe -

ces - sive jour - neys run; his king-dom stretch from
throng to crown his head; his name, like sweet per -
love with sweet - est song, and in - fant voic - es
leap to loose their chains; the wea - ry find e -
cu - liar to our King; an - gels de - scend with

shore to shore, till moons shall wax and wane no more.
fume, shall rise with ev - ery morn - ing sac - ri - fice.
shall pro - claim their ear - ly bless - ings on his name.
ter - nal rest, and all who suf - fer want are blest.
songs a - gain, and earth re - peat the loud A - men!

This hymn is a classic example of how Isaac Watts Christianized the Psalms, in this case Psalm 72:5–19, by turning their messianic language to New Testament equivalents. The tune was at first nameless and anonymous, but is now called by the address of the supposed composer.

TEXT: Isaac Watts, 1719, alt.
MUSIC: Attr. John Hatton, c. 1793

DUKE STREET
LM

Joy to the World

1 Joy to the world, the Lord is come! Let
2 Joy to the earth, the Savior reigns! Let
3 No more let sins and sorrows grow, nor
4 He rules the world with truth and grace, and

earth receive her king; let every heart pre-
all their songs employ, while fields and floods, rocks,
thorns infest the ground; he comes to make his
makes the nations prove the glories of his

pare him room, and heaven and nature sing.
hills, and plains repeat the sounding joy.
bless-ings flow far as the curse is found.
righ-teous-ness and won-ders of his love.

While Isaac Watts did not write this text strictly for Christmas use, he did purposely cast his paraphrase of Psalm 98:4–9 in Christian terms, titling it "The Messiah's coming and kingdom." So "the Lord" here is Jesus Christ, rather than the God of Abraham, Isaac, and Jacob.

TEXT: Isaac Watts, 1719, alt.
MUSIC: Thomas Haweis, c. 1792; adapt. Samuel Webbe Jr., 1808

RICHMOND
CM
(alternate tune: ANTIOCH, 134)

267 Come, Christians, Join to Sing

1 Come, Chris-tians, join to sing: Al-le-lu-ia! A - men!
2 Come, lift your hearts on high: Al-le-lu-ia! A - men!
3 Praise yet our Christ a-gain: Al-le-lu-ia! A - men!

Loud praise to Christ our King: Al-le-lu-ia! A - men!
Let prais-es fill the sky: Al-le-lu-ia! A - men!
Life shall not end the strain: Al-le-lu-ia! A - men!

Let all, with heart and voice, be - fore his throne re-joice;
He is our guide and friend; to us he'll con-de-scend;
On heav-en's bliss-ful shore his good-ness we'll a-dore,

praise is his gra-cious choice: Al-le-lu-ia! A - men!
his love shall nev-er end: Al-le-lu-ia! A - men!
sing-ing for-ev-er-more: Al-le-lu-ia! A - men!

Like many other hymns of praise, this text was originally addressed to children but has been embraced by adults as well. Although the tune's repetitive elements suggest folk origins (possibly with alternating groups of singers), no specific source has been identified.

TEXT: Christian Henry Bateman, 1843
MUSIC: Spanish folk melody; arr. Benjamin Carr, 1824; harm. David Evans, 1927
Music Harm. © 1927 Oxford University Press

MADRID
6.6.6.6.D

Crown Him with Many Crowns 268

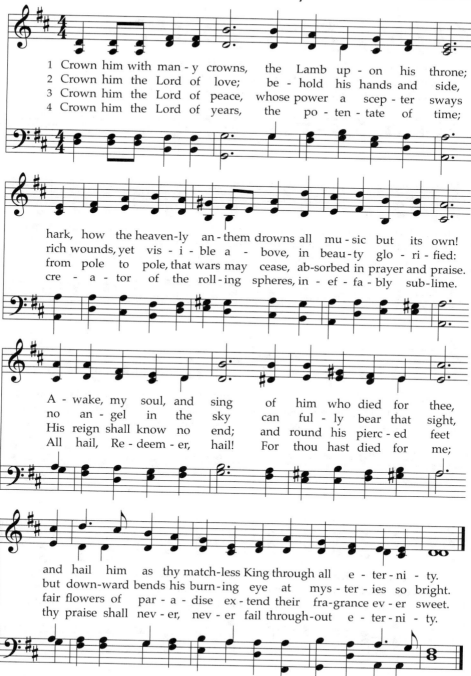

1 Crown him with man-y crowns, the Lamb up-on his throne;
2 Crown him the Lord of love; be-hold his hands and side,
3 Crown him the Lord of peace, whose power a scep-ter sways
4 Crown him the Lord of years, the po-ten-tate of time;

hark, how the heaven-ly an-them drowns all mu-sic but its own!
rich wounds, yet vis-i-ble a-bove, in beau-ty glo-ri-fied:
from pole to pole, that wars may cease, ab-sorbed in prayer and praise.
cre-a-tor of the roll-ing spheres, in-ef-fa-bly sub-lime.

A-wake, my soul, and sing of him who died for thee,
no an-gel in the sky can ful-ly bear that sight,
His reign shall know no end; and round his pierc-ed feet
All hail, Re-deem-er, hail! For thou hast died for me;

and hail him as thy match-less King through all e-ter-ni-ty.
but down-ward bends his burn-ing eye at mys-ter-ies so bright.
fair flowers of par-a-dise ex-tend their fra-grance ev-er sweet.
thy praise shall nev-er, nev-er fail through-out e-ter-ni-ty.

This text is so familiar that it is easy to miss all its paradox, mystery, suffering, and beauty; it rewards careful reading and meditation outside corporate worship. The tune's composer, chapel organist at Windsor Castle, had much experience in creating a royal sound.

TEXT: Matthew Bridges, 1851
MUSIC: George Job Elvey, 1868

DIADEMATA
SMD

269   Lead On, O King Eternal!

1 Lead on, O King e - ter - nal! The day of march has come;
2 Lead on, O King e - ter - nal, till sin's fierce war shall cease,
3 Lead on, O King e - ter - nal: we fol - low, not with fears,

hence-forth in fields of con - quest your tents shall be our home.
and ho - li - ness shall whis - per the sweet a - men of peace;
for glad-ness breaks like morn - ing wher - e'er your face ap - pears;

Through days of prep - a - ra - tion your grace has made us strong,
for not with swords' loud clash - ing, nor roll of stir - ring drums;
your cross is lift - ed o'er us; we jour - ney in its light.

and now, O King e - ter - nal, we lift our bat - tle song.
with deeds of love and mer - cy the heaven-ly king-dom comes.
The crown a - waits the con - quest; lead on, O God of might!

Not everything that looks like a battle ends up being one. This text, written for a seminary graduation, works well with its martial tune in the first stanza; but later stanzas turn from such imagery and focus on "deeds of love and mercy" and courage for life's journey.

TEXT: Ernest W. Shurtleff, 1888, alt.
MUSIC: Henry Thomas Smart, c. 1835

LANCASHIRE
7.6.7.6.D
(this tune in a higher key, 233)

O Lord, You Are My God and King 270
(Psalm 145)

1 O Lord, you are my God and King, and I will
2 How rich in grace are you, O Lord, full of com -
3 Your works will give you thanks, O Lord; your saints your

ev - er bless your name; I will ex - tol you ev - ery day, and
pas - sion, mer - ci - ful, your an - ger al - ways slow to rise; your
might - y acts will show, till all the peo - ples of the earth your

ev - er - more your praise pro - claim. You, Lord, are great - ly
stead - fast love you show to all, for you are good in
king - dom, pow - er, glo - ry know. E - ter - nal is your

to be praised; your great-ness is be - yond our thought; all
all your ways; your crea - tures know your con - stant care. To
king - dom, Lord, for - ev - er strong, for - ev - er sure; while

gen - er - a - tions shall tell forth the might - y won-ders you have wrought.
all your works your love ex-tends; all souls your ten-der mer-cies share.
gen - er - a - tions rise and die, your high do-min-ion will en - dure.

Guitar chords do not correspond with keyboard harmony.

Although this paraphrase of Psalm 145 is abbreviated (the original psalm has a verse for each letter of the Hebrew alphabet), it maintains the tone of praise that characterizes the final six psalms. In fact, the whole book takes its Hebrew name, *Tehillim* (praises), from them.

TEXT: *The New Metrical Version of the Psalms,* 1909, alt.
MUSIC: C. Hubert H. Parry, 1916; harm. Charles H. Webb, 1987
Music Harm. © 1989 The United Methodist Publishing House (admin. The Copyright Company)

JERUSALEM
LMD

271 The Lord Almighty Reigns
(Psalm 93)

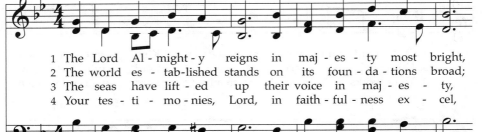

1 The Lord Al - might-y reigns in maj - es - ty most bright,
2 The world es - tab-lished stands on its foun - da - tions broad,
3 The seas have lift - ed up their voice in maj - es - ty,
4 Your tes - ti - mo - nies, Lord, in faith - ful - ness ex - cel,

ap - par-eled in om - nip - o - tence, and gird-ed round with might.
your throne is fixed, you reign su - preme, the ev - er - last - ing God.
but God on high, su - preme in might, is great-er than the sea.
and ho - ly must your ser - vants be who in your tem - ple dwell.

In Jewish practice Psalm 93, and other psalms sharing the same theme, acknowledged God's sovereignty over all creation, especially over chaotic powers such as those of the raging sea. In Christian use this psalm and its paraphrases have been sung to celebrate the reign of Christ.

TEXT: *The New Metrical Version of the Psalms*, 1909, alt.
MUSIC: Samuel Howard, 1762

ST. BRIDE
SM

272 God, You Rule with Royal Bearing
(Psalm 93)

1 God, you rule with roy - al bear - ing, clothed in glo - ry,
2 In its ev - er - last - ing sta - tion earth is fixed to
3 With all tones of wa - ter blend - ing, glo - rious is the
4 God, the words your lips are tell - ing are the per - fect

Like other psalms celebrating God's sovereignty, Psalm 93 has been applied in Christian practice to Christ's ascension and reign. That connection is reinforced by setting this paraphrase to a Welsh tune linked with a text on the Crucifixion (the tune name means "Mount Calvary").

TEXT: John Keble, 1839, alt.
MUSIC: William Owen, 1852

BRYN CALFARIA
8.7.8.7.4.4.4.7.7

love, and light: you have robed your - self ma - jes - tic,
quake no more;   you have laid your throne's foun - da - tion;
break - ing deep;   glo - rious, beau - teous, with - out end - ing,
and the true.   In your high e - ter - nal dwell - ing,

robed your - self with power and might. Hal - le - lu - jah!
you your - self are ev - er - more. Hal - le - lu - jah!
God, who reigns on heaven's high steep. Hal - le - lu - jah!
ho - li - ness shall live with you. Hal - le - lu - jah!

Hal - le - lu - jah! Hal - le - lu - jah! God who rules in
Hal - le - lu - jah! Hal - le - lu - jah! God, you are for -
Hal - le - lu - jah! Hal - le - lu - jah! Songs of o - cean
Hal - le - lu - jah! Hal - le - lu - jah! God, your word is

depth and height! God who rules in depth and height!
ev - er - more! God, you are for - ev - er - more!
nev - er sleep. Songs of o - cean nev - er sleep.
ev - er true. God, your word is ev - er true.

273 He Is King of Kings

Refrain

He is King of kings; he is Lord of lords, Je-sus Christ, the

first and last, no one works like him. O he is no one works like him.

1 He built his throne up in the air; and
2 He pitched his tents on Ca-naan ground; no one works like him; and
3 I know that my Re-deem-er lives; and

called his saints from ev-ery-where;
broke op-pres-sive king-doms down; no one works like him. O he is
by his love sweet bless-ing gives;

This African American spiritual is a classic example of how praise of God rises out of human experience. The repeated response "no one works like him" shows confidence that the sovereign, liberating Christ abounds with the very attribute the singers need in order to survive.

TEXT: African American spiritual
MUSIC: African American spiritual; arr. Joseph T. Jones, 1961; adapt. Melva Wilson Costen, 1989
Music Adapt. © 1990 Melva Wilson Costen

HE IS KING
8.5.8.5 with refrain

You, Lord, Are Both Lamb and Shepherd

274

Capo 5: (Am)

1 You, Lord, are both Lamb and Shep-herd. You, Lord, are both
2 Clothed in light up - on the moun-tain, stripped of might up -
3 You, who walk each day be - side us, sit in pow - er
4 Wor - thy is our earth - ly Je - sus! Wor - thy is our

prince and slave. You, peace-mak - er and sword-bring - er
on the cross, shin - ing in e - ter - nal glo - ry,
at God's side. You, who preach a way that's nar - row,
cos - mic Christ! Wor - thy your de - feat and vic - tory;

of the way you took and gave. You, the ev - er - last - ing
beg-gared by a sol - dier's toss, you, the ev - er - last - ing
have a love that reach - es wide. You, the ev - er - last - ing
wor - thy still your peace and strife. You, the ev - er - last - ing

in - stant; you, whom we both scorn and crave.
in - stant; you who are both gift and cost.
in - stant; you, who are our pil - grim guide.
in - stant; you, who are our death and life.

When it was first published, the author called this text "Christus Paradox," because so many attributes of Christ stand in tension with each other. Mindful of the works of Søren Kierkegaard, she drafted it on a commuter bus after "a particularly bad day" of prison ministry.

TEXT: Sylvia G. Dunstan, 1984
MUSIC: French melody, 17th cent.
Text © 1991 GIA Publications, Inc.

PICARDY
8.7.8.7.8.7
(alternate harmonization, 347)

275 A Mighty Fortress Is Our God

1 A might-y for - tress is our God, a bul-wark nev - er
2 Did we in our own strength con-fide, our striv-ing would be
3 And though this world, with dev - ils filled, should threat-en to un-
4 That word a - bove all earth-ly powers, no thanks to them, a -

fail - ing. Our help - er he, a - mid the flood of
los - ing, were not the right man on our side, the
do us, we will not fear, for God hath willed his
bid - eth. The Spir - it and the gifts are ours through

mor - tal ills pre - vail - ing. For still our an - cient foe doth
man of God's own choos - ing. Dost ask who that may be? Christ
truth to tri - umph through us. The Prince of Dark-ness grim, we
him who with us sid - eth. Let goods and kin - dred go, this

seek to work us woe. His craft and power are great, and
Je - sus, it is he. Lord Sab - a - oth his name, from
trem - ble not for him. His rage we can en - dure, for
mor - tal life al - so. The bod - y they may kill; God's

Long before Isaac Watts began to Christianize the Psalms, Martin Luther had already done so when he created the text and tune for this, his most famous hymn, which is based on Psalm 46. Luther encouraged metrical versions of psalms as well as chanted psalms and new hymns.

TEXT: Martin Luther, 1529; trans. Frederick Henry Hedge, 1852
MUSIC: Martin Luther, 1529, alt.

EIN' FESTE BURG
8.7.8.7.6.6.6.6.7

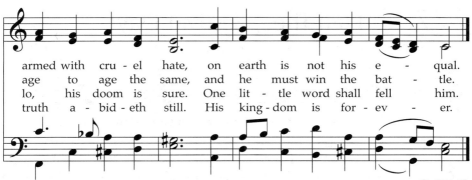

armed with cru-el hate, on earth is not his e - qual.
age to age the same, and he must win the bat - tle.
lo, his doom is sure. One lit - tle word shall fell him.
truth a - bid - eth still. His king-dom is for - ev - er.

Sing a New Song unto the Lord 276
(Psalm 98)

Refrain

Sing a new song un - to the Lord; let your song be
sung from moun - tains high. Sing a new song
un - to the Lord, sing-ing hal - le - lu - jah!

1 Shout with glad - ness! Dance for joy! O come be -
2 Rise, O chil - dren, from your sleep; your Sav - ior
3 Glad my soul for I have seen the glo - ry

fore the Lord. And play for God on
now has come. He has turned your
of the Lord. The trum - pet sounds; the

glad tam - bou - rines, and let your trum - pet sound.
sor - row to joy, and filled your soul with song.
dead shall be raised. I know my Sav - ior lives.

This loose paraphrase effectively conveys the joyful tone of Psalm 98, largely by incorporating allusions to many other Scriptures, such as Psalm 149:3, Romans 13:11, Psalm 16:9, 1 Corinthians 15:52, and Job 19:25. These familiar echoes help to give the text depth and breadth.

TEXT and MUSIC: Daniel L. Schutte, 1972, alt.
Text and Music © 1972, 2008 Daniel L. Schutte (Published by OCP)

SING A NEW SONG
Irregular

277 Hail Thee, Festival Day!

Guitar chords do not correspond with keyboard harmony.

This three-occasion hymn has been extracted from a much longer Latin original of fifty-five two-line stanzas. Though it is doubtful that the entire text was used much, selections from it have flourished for centuries. This celebratory tune is one of the composer's most effective.

TEXT: Venantius Honorius Fortunatus, c. 567–576; trans. *Lutheran Book of Worship*, 1978, alt.
MUSIC: Ralph Vaughan Williams, 1906
Text © 1978 Lutheran Book of Worship (admin. Augsburg Fortress)

SALVE FESTA DIES
Irregular

Easter 2 Rise from the grave now, O Lord, the au - thor of
Ascension 2 Dai - ly the love - li - ness grows a - dorned with the
Pentecost 2 Dai - ly the love - li - ness grows, a - dorned with the
4 Je - sus, the health of the world, en - light - en our
6 Praise to the giv - er of good! O Lov - er and

life and cre - a - tion. Tread - ing the path - way of
glo - ry of blos - som; heav - en its gates now un -
glo - ry of blos - som; heav - en its gates now un -
minds, great Re - deem - er, Son of the Fa - ther su -
Au - thor of con - cord, pour out your balm on our

death, new life you give to us all:
bars, fling - ing its in - crease of light:
bars, fling - ing its in - crease of light:
preme, on - ly be - got - ten of God:
days; or - der our ways in your peace:

278 Come, Holy Ghost, Our Souls Inspire

1 Come, Ho - ly Ghost, our souls in - spire, and light - en
2 Thy bless - ed unc - tion from a - bove is com - fort,
3 Teach us to know the Fa - ther, Son, and thee, of

with ce - les - tial fire; thou the a - noint - ing
life, and fire of love; en - a - ble with per -
both, to be but one, that through the a - ges

Spir - it art, who dost thy seven - fold gifts im - part.
pet - ual light the dull - ness of our mor - tal sight.
all a - long this may be our end - less song:

4 Praise to thine e - ter - nal mer - it, Fa - ther,

Son, and Ho - ly Spir - it. A - men.

This text, originally written in Latin in the 9th century, has had long and active use, both for Pentecost and for ordinations (where it has appeared in Anglican prayer books since 1662). Though created for an older hymn, this plainchant tune has set this text from earliest days.

TEXT: Attr. Rabanus Maurus, 9th cent.; trans. John Cosin, 1627, alt.
MUSIC: Plainsong, Mode VIII; arr. Healey Willan, 20th cent.
Music Arr. Reprinted with the permission of the executor of the Estate of Healey Willan

VENI CREATOR SPIRITUS
LM

Come, Holy Spirit, Heavenly Dove 279

1 Come, Ho - ly Spir - it, heaven - ly Dove,
2 In vain we tune our for - mal songs;
3 Dear Lord, and shall we ev - er live
4 Come, Ho - ly Spir - it, heaven - ly Dove,

with all thy quick - ening powers; kin - dle a flame of
in vain we strive to rise; ho - san - nas lan - guish
at this poor dy - ing rate? Our love so faint, so
with all thy quick - ening powers; come, shed a - broad a

sa - cred love in these cold hearts of ours.
on our tongues, and our de - vo - tion dies.
cold to thee, and thine to us so great!
Sav - ior's love, and that shall kin - dle ours.

In contrast with many hymns to the Holy Spirit, this one is notable for being in the plural, a valuable reminder that the Holy Spirit has been bestowed on the whole Church, not just on a few individuals. The tune was composed for "Jesus, the Very Thought of Thee" (no. 629).

TEXT: Isaac Watts, 1707, alt.
MUSIC: John Bacchus Dykes, 1866, alt.

ST. AGNES
CM

280 Come, O Spirit, Dwell Among Us

1 Come, O Spir-it, dwell a-mong us; come with
2 We would raise our al-le-lu-ias for the
3 Come, O Spir-it, dwell a-mong us; give us

Pen-te-cos-tal power; give the church a
grace of yes-ter-years; for to-mor-row's
words of fire and flame. Help our fee-ble

strong-er vi-sion; help us face each cru-cial hour.
un-known path-way, hear, O Lord, our hum-ble prayers.
lips to praise you, glo-ri-fy your ho-ly name.

Built up-on a firm foun-da-tion, Je-sus Christ, the
In the church's pil-grim jour-ney you have led us
Fa-ther, Son, and Ho-ly Spir-it, Three in One: what

This 20th-century text was written by a Presbyterian layperson and poet, who in her later years became
interested in writing hymns for the seasons of the church year and prepared a collection of them for her
congregation. It pairs effectively with this sturdy Welsh tune.

EBENEZER
8.7.8.7.D

TEXT: Janie Alford, 1979
MUSIC: Thomas John Williams, 1890
Text © 1979 Hope Publishing Company

Cor - ner - stone, still the church is called to
all the way; still in pres - ence move be -
mys - ter - y! We would sing our loud ho -

mis - sion that God's love shall be made known.
fore us, fire by night and cloud by day.
san - nas now and through e - ter - ni - ty.

Holy Spirit, Come to Us   281
Veni Sancte Spiritus

Ostinato (repeated continuously)

Ho - ly Spir - it, come to us.
Ve - ni San - cte Spi - ri - tus.

Like many other chants from the ecumenical monastic community at Taizé, France, this brief text is intended for repeated singing by the congregation while a soloist or choir sings a longer related text. These refrains often use Latin to avoid connection with any current nation.

TEXT: Taizé Community, 1979
MUSIC: Jacques Berthier, 1979
Text and Music © 1979 Les Presses de Taizé (admin. GIA Publications, Inc.)

VENI SANCTE SPIRITUS
Irregular

282 Come Down, O Love Divine

1 Come down, O Love Divine; seek out this soul of mine,
2 O let it freely burn, till earthly passions turn
3 And so the yearning strong, with which the soul will long,

and visit it with your own ardor glowing.
to dust and ashes in its heat consuming.
shall far outpass the power of human telling.

O Comforter, draw near; within my heart appear,
And let your glorious light shine ever on my sight,
For none can guess God's grace, till Love creates a place

and kindle it, your holy flame bestowing.
and clothe me round, the while my path illuming.
wherein the Holy Spirit makes a dwelling.

This *lauda spirituale,* a kind of vernacular Italian sacred song from the late Middle Ages and Renaissance, was translated into English in the 19th century but received little notice until this tune (named for the composer's birthplace) was created for *The English Hymnal.*

TEXT: Bianco da Siena, c. 1367; trans. Richard Frederick Littledale, 1867, alt.
MUSIC: Ralph Vaughan Williams, 1906

DOWN AMPNEY
6.6.11.D

Come, O Holy Spirit, Come   283

Wa wa wa Emimimo

This short gathering song from Nigeria was originally created in Yoruba, one of that country's three primary trade languages. Although it has a very different rhythm and feel, this is essentially the same sung prayer as the Taizé chant, "Veni Sancte Spiritus" (no. 281).

TEXT: Nigerian song; English trans. I-to Loh, 1986
MUSIC: Nigerian melody, taught by Samuel Solanke; transcr. I-to Loh, 1986
English Trans. and Music Transcr. © 1995 General Board of Global Ministries t/a GBGMusik

WA EMIMIMO
Irregular

284 Holy Spirit, Come to Us
Tui amoris ignem

Ho - ly Spir - it, come to us; kin-dle in us the fire of your love.
Ve - ni San - cte Spi - ri - tus, tu - i a - mo - ris i - gnem ac - cen - de.

Ho - ly Spir - it, come to us. Ho - ly Spir - it, come to us.
Ve - ni San - cte Spi - ri - tus. Ve - ni San - cte Spi - ri - tus.

The original text of this chant from Taizé is a shortened version of a text sung in the Latin mass after the reading of the gospel on Pentecost. The full text can be translated: "Come, Holy Spirit, fill the hearts of your faithful; and ignite the fire of your love within them."

TEXT: Taizé Community, 1998
MUSIC: Jacques Berthier, 1998
Text and Music © 1998 Les Presses de Taizé (admin. GIA Publications, Inc.)

TUI AMORIS IGNEM
Irregular

285 Like the Murmur of the Dove's Song

Capo 3: (G/A)   (D)   (A)   (D/F#)   (E7)
        B♭/C   F   C   F/A   G7

1 Like the mur - mur of the dove's song, like the chal-lenge of her
2 To the mem - bers of Christ's bod - y, to the branch - es of the
3 With the heal - ing of di - vi - sion, with the cease-less voice of

Guitar chords do not correspond with keyboard harmony.

This text on the Holy Spirit was written to fit the pre-existing tune. The three stanzas cluster around various themes developed through a series of images and grounded in the refrain: how the Spirit comes, to whom the Spirit comes, and for what purposes the Spirit comes.

TEXT: Carl P. Daw Jr., 1982, alt.
MUSIC: Peter Cutts, 1969
Text © 1982 Hope Publishing Company
Music © 1969 Hope Publishing Company

BRIDEGROOM
8.7.8.7.6

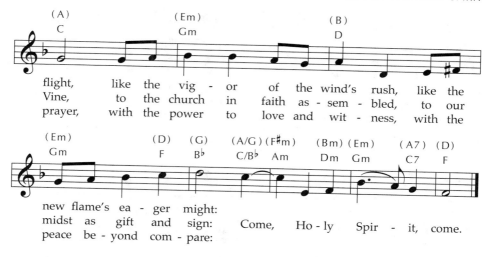

flight,   like   the   vig - or   of   the   wind's   rush,   like   the
Vine,   to   the   church   in   faith   as - sem - bled,   to   our
prayer,   with   the   power   to   love   and   wit - ness,   with   the

new flame's ea - ger might: Come,   Ho - ly   Spir - it,   come.
midst as gift and sign:
peace be - yond com - pare:

Breathe on Me, Breath of God 286

1 Breathe on me, Breath of God; fill me with life a - new,
2 Breathe on me, Breath of God, un - til my heart is pure,
3 Breathe on me, Breath of God, till I am whol - ly thine,
4 Breathe on me, Breath of God, so shall I nev - er die,

that I may love what thou dost love, and do what thou wouldst do.
un - til with thee I will one will, to do and to en - dure.
un - til this earth - ly part of me glows with thy fire di - vine.
but live with thee the per - fect life of thine e - ter - ni - ty.

In both Hebrew and Greek, the words for "spirit" can equally well be translated as "breath" or "wind," so it is very appropriate to address the Holy Spirit as the "Breath of God." This tune by an English organist has become the customary one in North American hymnals.

TEXT: Edwin Hatch, 1878
MUSIC: Robert Jackson, 1888

TRENTHAM
SM

287 Gracious Spirit, Heed Our Pleading

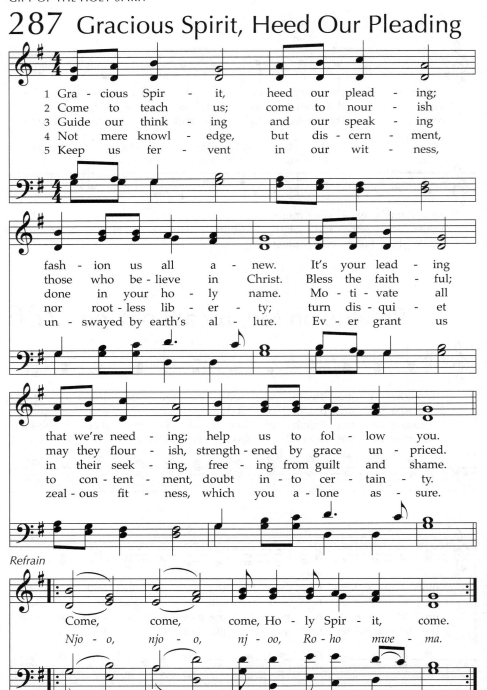

1 Gracious Spirit, heed our pleading;
2 Come to teach us; come to nourish
3 Guide our thinking and our speaking
4 Not mere knowledge, but discernment,
5 Keep us fervent in our witness,

fashion us all anew. It's your leading
those who believe in Christ. Bless the faithful;
done in your holy name. Motivate all
nor rootless liberty; turn disquiet
unswayed by earth's allure. Ever grant us

that we're needing; help us to follow you.
may they flourish, strengthened by grace unpriced.
in their seeking, freeing from guilt and shame.
to contentment, doubt into certainty.
zealous fitness, which you alone assure.

Refrain

Come, come, come, Holy Spirit, come.
Njo-o, njo-o, nj-oo, Ro-ho mwe-ma.

Originally written for the uniting of the Lutheran churches in Tanzania, this prayerful hymn touches on the need of the whole church at all times for the Holy Spirit's guidance and blessing. When appropriate, the refrain can effectively be used alone as a prayer response.

TEXT: Wilson Niwagila, 1965; trans. Howard S. Olson, 1968
MUSIC: Wilson Niwagila, 1965; arr. Egil Hovland, 1993
Text and Music © Lutheran Theological College, Makumira (admin. Augsburg Fortress)
Music Arr. © Egil Hovland

NJOO KWETU, ROHO MWEMA
CM with refrain

Spirit of the Living God

Spir - it of the liv - ing God, fall a-fresh on me.

Spir - it of the liv - ing God, fall a-fresh on me.

Melt me; mold me; fill me; use me.

Spir - it of the liv - ing God, fall a-fresh on me.

KOREAN

살아계신 주 성령 내게 오소서
살아계신 주 성령 내게 오소서
빚으시고 채우소서
살아계신 주 성령 내게 오소서

SPANISH

Santo Espíritu de Dios, ven sobre mí.
Santo Espíritu de Dios, ven sobre mí.
Tómame, cámbiame, lléname, úsame.
Santo Espíritu de Dios, ven sobre mí.

Both the words and the music of this prayer-song were written by a Presbyterian minister from Tarboro, North Carolina. The words were initially inspired by Jeremiah 18:1–6; a friend helped him set them to music during an evangelistic meeting in Orlando, Florida, where the song was first sung.

TEXT: Daniel Iverson, 1926; Korean trans. The United Methodist Korean Hymnal Committee; Spanish trans. anon.
MUSIC: Daniel Iverson, 1926
Text and Music © 1935 Birdwing Music (admin. EMICMGPublishing.com)
Korean Trans. © 2001 Birdwing Music (admin. EMICMGPublishing.com)

LIVING GOD
Irregular

289 On Pentecost They Gathered

1 On Pen-te-cost they gath-ered quite ear-ly in the day,
2 The peo-ple all a-round them were star-tled and a-mazed
3 God pours the Ho-ly Spir-it on all who would be-lieve,
4 O Spir-it, sent from heav-en on that day long a-go,

a band of Christ's dis-ci-ples, to wor-ship, sing, and pray.
to un-der-stand their lan-guage, as Christ the Lord they praised.
on wom-en, men, and chil-dren who would God's grace re-ceive.
re-kin-dle faith a-mong us in all life's ebb and flow.

A might-y wind came blow-ing, filled all the swirl-ing air,
What u-ni-ver-sal mes-sage, what great good news was here?
That Spir-it knows no lim-it, be-stow-ing life and power.
O give us ears to lis-ten and tongues a-flame with praise,

and tongues of fire a-glow-ing in-spired each per-son there.
That Christ, once dead, is ris-en to van-quish all our fear.
The church, formed and re-form-ing, re-sponds in ev-ery hour.
so folk of ev-ery na-tion glad songs of joy shall raise.

This narrative and interpretive text was written to fill what the author perceived as an unfortunate gap in available hymns concerning the Holy Spirit in general and Pentecost in particular. The setting of a 17th-century German tune is from Mendelssohn's oratorio *Elijah*.

TEXT: Jane Parker Huber, 1981
MUSIC: *Neuvermehrtes Meiningisches Gesangbuch*, 1693; adapt. Felix Mendelssohn, 1847
Text © 1981 Jane Parker Huber (admin. Westminster John Knox Press)

MUNICH
7.6.7.6.D

O Day of Joy and Wonder! 290

1 O day of joy and won - der! Christ's prom - ise
2 The world, in sheer a - maze - ment, the truth must
3 We too may know your pow - er; your cour - age

now ful - filled: the com - ing of the Spir - it that
now de - clare: that those who once were cow - ards are
makes us strong. Your love, your joy, your pa - tience can

ho - ly love has willed. Our Lord in hu - man
brave be - yond com - pare; and tongues, which could not
all to us be - long. Come now and dwell with -

bod - y to mor - tal eye is lost, yet comes in
ut - ter their faith in Je - sus' name, de - fy all
in us, O Com - fort - er di - vine. Come to our

flame up - on us at bless - ed Pen - te - cost.
per - se - cu - tion God's glo - ry to pro - claim!
hearts, and keep them; there let your bright - ness shine.

In a pattern common to many hymns, the first two stanzas here declare how the coming of the Holy Spirit
gave strength and courage to the early church, and the final stanza becomes a corporate prayer for a sense
of the presence of the Spirit, addressed as "Comforter divine."

TEXT: Violet Nita Buchanan, 1957, alt.
MUSIC: Hal H. Hopson, 1996
Text © Oxford University Press
Music © 1996 Hope Publishing Company

JONATHAN'S TUNE
7.6.7.6.D

291 Spirit, Spirit of Gentleness
Spirit

Refrain

Spir - it, spir - it of gen - tle - ness, blow through the
wil - der - ness, call - ing and free. Spir - it,
spir - it of rest - less - ness, stir me from plac - id - ness,
wind, wind on the sea. *Fine*

1 You moved on the wa - ters; you called to the
2 You swept through the des - ert; you stung with the
3 You sang in a sta - ble; you cried from a
4 You call from to - mor - row; you break an - cient

deep; then you coaxed up the moun - tains from the
sand; and you goad - ed your peo - ple with a
hill; then you whis - pered in si - lence when the
schemes; from the bond - age of sor - row the

As the author/composer reminds us in the refrain, the Spirit is both gentle and restless. The stanzas reinforce a sense of the Spirit's activity through a wide range of verbs, initially in the past tense; but they become more urgent in the present tense of the fourth stanza.

TEXT: James K. Manley, 1975, alt.
MUSIC: James K. Manley, 1976
Text and Music © 1978 James K. Manley

SPIRIT
Irregular

292

As the Wind Song

風之頌

1 As the wind song through the trees, as the
2 As the rain-bow af-ter rain, as the

1 風 之 頌, 林 中 吹 送, 輕 風
2 彩 之 虹, 雨 後 高 懸, 生 之

stir-ring of the breeze, so it is with the Spir-it of
hope that's born a-gain, so it is with the Spir-it of

送, 心 中 振 動, 上 主 的 靈 如 風 吹
盼, 人 間 再 現, 上 主 的 靈 如 風 吹

God, as the heart made strange-ly warm, as the
God, as the green in the spring, as a

送; 心 溫 暖, 奇 異 難 明, 風 浪
送; 春 天 裡, 青 山 綠 水, 線 上

voice with-in the storm, so it is with the Spir-it of
kite on a string, so it is with the Spir-it of

中, 靜 聽 主 聲, 上 主 的 靈 如 風 吹
繫 飛 揚 風 箏, 上 主 的 靈 如 風 吹

God. Nev-er seen, ev-er known where this wind has
God, mak-ing worlds that are new, mak-ing peace come

送; 眼 不 見, 心 未 明, 風 來 去 何
送; 大 地 萬 象 更 新, 和 平 終 實

Reversing the usual order, this hymn began with the music rather than the words. The composer (from Singapore) sent this tune to the author (in New Zealand) to see what text it might inspire from her. She also suggested the tune name, a Maori phrase meaning "Holy Spirit."

TEXT: Shirley Erena Murray, 2004; Chinese trans. Ee Suen Wong, 2005
MUSIC: Swee Hong Lim, 2004
Text and Music © 2005 Hope Publishing Company

WAIRUA TAPU
Irregular

blown bring-ing life, bring-ing power to the world,
true, bring-ing gifts, bring-ing love to the world,
蹤, 給 世 人 賜 生 命 加 力 量;
現, 給 世 人 帶 來 愛 和 禮 物;

as the danc - ing tongues of fire, as the soul's most deep de -
as the ris - ing of the yeast, as the wine at the
火 之 舌, 跳 動 飛 舞, 心 深 處, 朝 思 暮
麵 之 酵, 悄 然 膨 升, 盛 宴 上, 醇 香 美

sire, so it is with the Spir - it of God.
feast, so it is with the Spir - it of God.
想, 上 主 的 靈 如 風 吹 送。
酒, 上 主 的 靈 如 風 吹 送。

293 Loving Spirit

1 Lov - ing Spir - it, lov - ing Spir - it, you have cho - sen me to be,
2 Like a moth - er you en - fold me, hold my life with - in your own,
3 Like a fa - ther you pro - tect me, teach me the dis - cern - ing eye,
4 Friend and lov - er, in your close - ness I am known and held and blessed:
5 Lov - ing Spir - it, lov - ing Spir - it, you have cho - sen me to be,

you have drawn me to your won - der, you have set your sign on me.
feed me with your ver - y bod - y, form me of your flesh and bone.
hoist me up up - on your shoul - der, let me see the world from high.
in your prom - ise is my com - fort, in your pres - ence I may rest.
you have drawn me to your won - der, you have set your sign on me.

A gift to the whole church, the Holy Spirit is also experienced by individuals in meaningful ways such as those described in this reflective (and structurally circular) consideration of the relational aspects of the Spirit. The tune may have originated in a folk melody.

TEXT: Shirley Erena Murray, 1986
MUSIC: Corner's *Gross Catholisch Gesangbuch*, 1631; arr. William Smith Rockstro, 19th cent.
Text © 1987 The Hymn Society (admin. Hope Publishing Company)

OMNI DIE (Corner)
8.7.8.7

294 Within Our Darkest Night
Dans nos obscurités

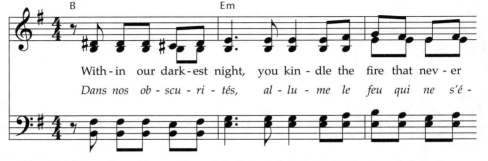

With - in our dark - est night, you kin - dle the fire that nev - er
Dans nos ob - scu - ri - tés, al - lu - me le feu qui ne s'é -

This Taizé chant can be used in several ways. Its inclusion in the Holy Spirit section connects the fire it celebrates with the gift of the Spirit at Pentecost. It might also be appropriate at evening services or as part of the Easter Vigil found in the *Book of Common Worship*.

TEXT: Taizé Community, 1991
MUSIC: Jacques Berthier, 1991
Text and Music © 1991 Les Presses de Taizé (admin. GIA Publications, Inc.)

DANS NOS OBSCURITÉS
Irregular

THE CHURCH

Go to the World!

295

1 Go to the world! Go in - to all the earth.
2 Go to the world! Go in - to ev - ery place.
3 Go to the world! Go strug - gle, bless, and pray;
4 Go to the world! Go as the ones I send,

Go preach the cross where Christ re - news life's worth,
Go live the word of God's re - deem - ing grace.
the nights of tears give way to joy - ous day.
for I am with you till the age shall end,

bap - tiz - ing as the sign of our re - birth.
Go seek God's pres - ence in each time and space.
As ser - vant church, you fol - low Christ's own way.
when all the hosts of glo - ry cry "A - men!"

Al - le - lu - ia. Al - le - lu - ia.

Based on Christ's great commission (Matthew 28:19–20), this text was written for a Convocation of Emmanuel College in Toronto, the largest theological school of the United Church of Canada, a denomination formed by the union of Methodists, Congregationalists, and Presbyterians.

TEXT: Sylvia G. Dunstan, 1985
MUSIC: Ralph Vaughan Williams, 1906
Text © 1991 GIA Publications, Inc.

SINE NOMINE
10.10.10 with alleluias

296 Go in Grace and Make Disciples

1 Go in grace and make dis-ci-ples. Bap-tize in God's
2 Go and fol-low Christ's ex-am-ple, not to van-quish,
3 Go in Pen-te-cos-tal spir-it, man-y tongues and

ho-ly name. Tell of death and res-ur-rec-tion; Eas-ter's
but to heal. Mend the wounds of sin's di-vi-sions. Ser-vant
man-y gifts. Feed the hearts of hun-gry peo-ple. Spread the

vic-tory now pro-claim. Christ's com-mis-sion sends us forth
love to all re-veal. Roles and ranks shall be re-versed;
gos-pel that up-lifts. Till the day of Christ's re-turn,

to the na-tions of the earth. Go in grace and
jus-tice flow for all who thirst. Go and fol-low
as dis-ci-ples, teach and learn. Go in Pen-te-

make dis-ci-ples, mid-wives for the world's re-birth.
Christ's ex-am-ple. Forge a world of last made first.
cos-tal spir-it: let God's flame of wit-ness burn.

Guitar chords do not correspond with keyboard harmony.

This text based on Jesus' Great Commission (Matthew 28:19–20) emphasizes that engaging in mission according to the model of Christ's life and ministry inspires service rather than conquest. The gospel message is a gift of life and hope made known in healing, justice, and peace.

TEXT: Mary Louise Bringle, 2001
MUSIC: William P. Rowan, 1999
Text © 2002 GIA Publications, Inc.
Music © 1999 William P. Rowan (admin. GIA Publications, Inc.)

WONDROUS LIGHT
8.7.8.7.7.7.8.7

In Christ Called to Baptize

1 In Christ called to bap - tize, we wit - ness to grace
2 In Christ called to ban - quet, one ta - ble we share,
3 In Christ called to wit - ness, by grace we will preach
4 U - nite us, a - noint us, O Spir - it of love,

and gath - er a peo - ple from each land and race.
a ha - ven of wel - come, a cir - cle of care.
the life - giv - ing gos - pel; God's love we will teach.
for you are with - in us, a - round us, a - bove.

In deep, flow - ing wa - ters, we share in Christ's death,
Al - though we are man - y, we share in one bread.
By grace may our liv - ing give proof to our praise
E - quip us for ser - vice with gifts you be - stow.

then, ris - ing to new life, give thanks with each breath.
One cup of thanks - giv - ing pro - claims Christ, our head.
in cost - ly com - pas - sion re - flect - ing Christ's ways.
In Christ is our call - ing. In Christ may we grow.

Written for use at the 1997 meeting of the Lutheran World Federation, this text about Christian vocation and ministry organizes the first three stanzas around verbs: baptize, banquet, witness. The final stanza is a prayer for the Spirit's gifts to empower all these callings.

TEXT: Ruth Duck, 1995
MUSIC: Welsh folk melody; adapt. in *Caniadau y Cyssegr,* 1839
Text © 1995 The Pilgrim Press

ST. DENIO
11.11.11.11

298 Lord, You Give the Great Commission

1 Lord, you give the great com-mis-sion: "Heal the sick and
2 Lord, you call us to your ser-vice: "In my name bap-
3 Lord, you make the com-mon ho-ly: "This, my bod-y;
4 Lord, you show us love's true mea-sure: "Fa-ther, what they
5 Lord, you bless with words as-sur-ing: "I am with you

preach the word." Lest the church ne-glect its mis-sion, and the
tize and teach." That the world may trust your prom-ise, life a-
this, my blood." Let us all, for earth's true glo-ry, dai-ly
do, for-give." Yet we hoard as pri-vate trea-sure all that
to the end." Faith and hope and love re-stor-ing, may we

gos-pel go un-heard, help us wit-ness to your
bun-dant meant for each, give us all new fer-vor,
lift life heav-en-ward, ask-ing that the world a-
you so free-ly give. May your care and mer-cy
serve as you in-tend, and, a-mid the cares that

United by the refrain after each stanza, this text relies on passages from Matthew and Luke to highlight
various dimensions of the church's mission and ministry in the world. It was written for use with this tune,
composed in the village near Bristol, England, for which it is named.

TEXT: Jeffery W. Rowthorn, 1978
MUSIC: Cyril Vincent Taylor, 1941
Text © 1978 Hope Publishing Company
Music © 1942, ren. 1970 Hope Publishing Company

ABBOT'S LEIGH
8.7.8.7.D

pur - pose with re - newed in - teg - ri - ty:
draw us clos - er in com - mu - ni - ty:
round us share your chil - dren's lib - er - ty:
lead us to a just so - ci - e - ty:
claim us, hold in mind e - ter - ni - ty:

with the Spir - it's

gifts em - power us for the work of min - is - try.

299 You Servants of God, Your Master Proclaim

1 You servants of God, your Master proclaim,
2 Ascended on high, almighty to save,
3 "Salvation to God, who sits on the throne!"
4 Then let us adore and give him his right:

and publish abroad Christ's wonderful name.
he still remains nigh; his presence we have.
Let all cry aloud and honor the Son.
all glory and power, all wisdom and might,

The name all victorious of Jesus extol,
The great congregation his triumph shall sing,
The praises of Jesus the angels proclaim,
all honor and blessing, with angels above,

whose kingdom is glorious, who rules over all.
ascribing salvation to Jesus our King.
fall down on their faces, and worship the Lamb.
and thanks never ceasing, and infinite love!

This hymn resembles many 18th-century drawings that show parallels between worship on earth and worship in heaven, especially as described in Revelation 7:9–11. This 18th-century tune has had many names; the one used here honors the dynasty of British monarchs, 1714–1901.

TEXT: Charles Wesley, 1744, alt.
MUSIC: Anon.; *A Supplement to the New Version of the Psalms*, 1708

HANOVER
10.10.11.11

We Are One in the Spirit

They'll Know We Are Christians by Our Love

A parish priest at St. Brendan's on the South Side of Chicago in the 1960s was very involved in the local Civil Rights movement and needed something for his youth choir to sing at ecumenical, interracial events. Finding nothing, he wrote this song in a single day.

TEXT and MUSIC: Peter Scholtes, 1966
Text and Music © 1966 F.E.L. Publications, assigned 1991 to The Lorenz Corp.

THEY'LL KNOW WE ARE CHRISTIANS
7.6.7.6.8.6 with refrain

301 Let Us Build a House

All Are Welcome

1 Let us build a house where love can dwell and all can
2 Let us build a house where proph-ets speak, and words are
3 Let us build a house where love is found in wa-ter,
4 Let us build a house where hands will reach be-yond the
5 Let us build a house where all are named, their songs and

safe-ly live, a place where saints and chil-dren tell
strong and true, where all God's chil-dren dare to seek
wine, and wheat; a ban-quet hall on ho-ly ground
wood and stone to heal and strength-en, serve and teach,
vi - sions heard and loved and trea-sured, taught and claimed

how hearts learn to for - give. Built of hopes and dreams and
to dream God's reign a - new. Here the cross shall stand as
where peace and jus - tice meet. Here the love of God, through
and live the Word they've known. Here the out - cast and the
as words with - in the Word. Built of tears and cries and

vi - sions, rock of faith and vault of grace; here the
wit - ness and as sym - bol of God's grace; here as
Je - sus, is re - vealed in time and space; as we
strang - er bear the im - age of God's face; let us
laugh - ter, prayers of faith and songs of grace; let this

Although it was written for a church dedication, this text is not about a physical structure but a spiritual one. The building is at best only a vessel for the essential love and hope, life and faith, peace and justice, hospitality and nurture that form the worshiping community.

TEXT and MUSIC: Marty Haugen, 1994
Text and Music © 1994 GIA Publications, Inc.

TWO OAKS
9.6.8.6.8.7.10 with refrain

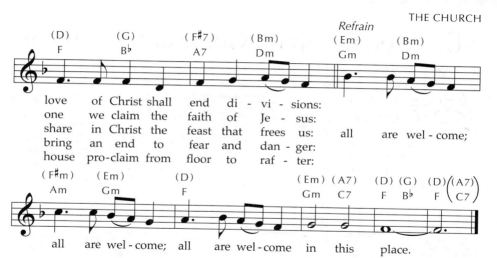

```
(D)      (G)      (F#7)     (Bm)              Refrain (Em)    (Bm)
 F        B♭      A7        Dm                        Gm       Dm
```

love   of Christ shall end   di - vi - sions:
one   we claim the   faith of Je - sus:
share   in Christ the   feast that frees us: all   are wel - come;
bring   an end to   fear and dan - ger:
house   pro-claim from   floor to raf - ter:

```
(F#m)    (Em)      (D)                  (Em) (A7)  (D) (G) (D)(A7)
 Am       Gm        F                    Gm   C7   F   B♭  F ( C7)
```

all   are wel - come; all   are wel-come in this place.

When Hands Reach Out and Fingers Trace   302

```
     D7              G            C            G
 #3/4
```

1 When hands reach out   and   fin - gers trace the beau - ty
2 When fin - gers spell and   signs ex - press our prayer and
3 When bro - ken bod - ies will not mend, we thank you,
4 And when the ways we   learn and grow are not the
5 Your Spir - it gives us   dif - fering ways to serve you

```
 Em           Am7          D            D7           G
```

of   a   loved one's face,   we thank you, God,   that
praise   and thank - ful - ness,   we thank you, God,   that
God,   for Christ our friend.   In him, our heal - ing
ways   that oth - ers know,   we thank you, God,   that
well   and of - fer praise.   When all are joined as

```
 D7           Em           C           D           D7           G
```

love   re - lies   on   gifts of grace not seen with eyes.
hands can sing; you bless the si - lent songs we bring.
can   be - gin;   he   wel-comes all   the wound - ed in.
we   have learned your love's a   gift, and nev - er earned.
one,   we'll be   your a - ble, strong com - mu - ni - ty.

Guitar chords do not correspond with keyboard harmony.

This hymn celebrates the breadth of human diversity and the variety of gifts and abilities through which
God's people serve the church and world. Incorporating such diversity provides a vital witness to the
hospitality of Christian community and to the inclusive nature of love.

TEXT: Carolyn Winfrey Gillette, 2001
MUSIC: English folk melody; harm. John Weaver, 1988
Text © 2001 Carolyn Winfrey Gillette
Music Harm. © 1990 Hope Publishing Company

O WALY WALY
LM

303 God the Spirit, Guide and Guardian

Capo 1: (Em) (Bm) (Em) (D) (G)

1 God the Spir-it, guide and guard-ian, wind-sped
2 Christ our Sav-ior, sov-ereign, shep-herd, Word made
3 Great Cre-a-tor, life-be-stow-er, truth be-
4 Tri-une God, mys-ter-ious be-ing, un-di-

flame and hov-ering dove, breath of life and
flesh, Love cru-ci-fied, teach-er, heal-er,
yond all thought's re-call, fount of wis-dom,
vid-ed and di-verse, deep-er than our

voice of proph-ets, sign of bless-ing, power of love:
suf-fering ser-vant, friend of sin-ners, foe of pride:
womb of mer-cy, giv-ing and for-giv-ing all:
minds can fath-om, great-er than our creeds re-hearse:

give to those who lead your peo-ple fresh a-
in your tend-ing may all *pas-tors learn and
as you know our strength and weak-ness, so may
help us in our var-ied call-ings your full

*Or "elders" or "deacons"

Guitar chords do not correspond with keyboard harmony.

This text affirms that the church's ministry is the combined witness of all its members. The first half of each stanza addresses either one of the divine Persons or the full Triune God, and the second half forms a prayer drawing on the attributes recalled in the first half.

TEXT: Carl P. Daw Jr., 1987, alt.
MUSIC: Alfred V. Fedak, 1988
Text © 1989 Hope Publishing Company
Music © 1989 Selah Publishing Co., Inc.

CHURCH UNITED
8.7.8.7.D

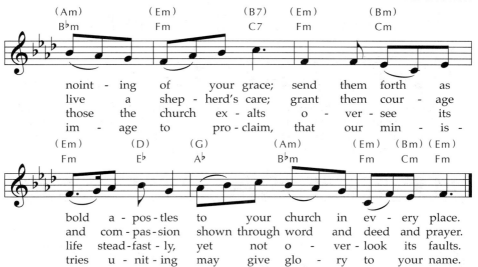

(Am)   (Em)   (B7) (Em)   (Bm)
B♭m   Fm   C7   Fm   Cm

noint - ing of   your grace; send them forth as
live   a   shep - herd's care; grant them cour - age
those the church ex - alts o - ver - see its
im - age to   pro - claim, that our min - is -

(Em)   (D)   (G)   (Am)   (Em) (Bm) (Em)
Fm   E♭   A♭   B♭m   Fm   Cm Fm

bold a - pos - tles to   your church in ev - ery place.
and com - pas - sion shown through word and deed and prayer.
life stead - fast - ly, yet   not o - ver - look its faults.
tries u - nit - ing may give glo - ry to your name.

O Sing a New Song to the Lord 304

(Psalm 96)

G   C   D7   G   C   Am   D

1 O   sing a new song to the Lord; sing, all the
2 Tell all the world God's won - drous ways; tell all the
3 The na - tions' gods are i - dols vain; the shin - ing
4 Let ev - ery tongue and ev - ery tribe give to the
5 Let heaven be glad, let earth re - joice; the teem - ing

G   Em   D Dm G7   C   Am   B

earth and bless that Name; from day to day God's praise re - cord;
na - tions far and near: great is the Lord, and great God's praise;
heavens the Lord sup - ports; both light and hon - or lead the train,
Lord due praise and sing; all glo - ry un - to God as - cribe;
sea re - sound with praise; let wav - ing fields lift high their voice,

Em   Am   C   D G   Em D7 G

the Lord's re - deem - ing grace pro - claim.
the Lord a - lone, let na - tions fear.
while strength and beau - ty fill the courts.
come, throng God's courts, and of - ferings bring.
and all the trees their an - them raise. Al - le - lu - ia!

Guitar chords do not correspond with keyboard harmony.

When this text appeared in *The Psalter,* 1912, it was titled "The Message of Redemption," a helpful reminder that the sung praise of God is a proclamation of "redeeming grace." The tune, created slightly later, is named with a French-derived word "gonfalon," meaning "banner."

TEXT: *The New Metrical Version of the Psalms,* 1909, alt.   GONFALON ROYAL
MUSIC: Percy C. Buck, 1918   LM

305 Come Sing, O Church, in Joy!

1 Come sing, O church, in joy! Come join, O church, in song!
2 Long years have come and gone, and still God reigns su-preme,
3 Let cour-age be our friend; let wis-dom be our guide,
4 Come sing, O church, in joy! Come join, O church, in song!

For Christ the Lord has led us through the a-ges long!
em-power-ing us to catch the vi-sion, dream the dream!
as we in mis-sion mag-ni-fy the Cru-ci-fied!
For Christ the Lord has tri-umphed o'er the a-ges long!

In bold ac-cord, come cel-e-brate the jour-ney now and praise the Lord!

This text was the winner in a hymn competition sponsored by the Presbyterian Church (U.S.A.) Bicentennial Committee for the 1988–1989 observance, which had the theme "Celebrate the Journey." The late 18th-century tune (first used with Psalm 148) is appropriately celebratory.

TEXT: Brian Dill, 1988
MUSIC: John Darwall, 1770
Text © 1989 Brian Dill

DARWALL'S 148TH
6.6.6.6.8.8

Blest Be the Tie That Binds

1 Blest be the tie that binds our hearts in
2 Be - fore our *Fa - ther's throne we pour our
3 We share our mu - tual woes; our mu - tual
4 When we are called to part, it gives us
5 From sor - row, toil, and pain, and sin we

Chris - tian love. The fel - low - ship of
ar - dent prayers. Our fears, our hopes, our
bur - dens bear. And of - ten for each
in - ward pain; but we shall still be
shall be free; and per - fect love and

kin - dred minds is like to that a - bove.
aims are one, our com - forts and our cares.
oth - er flows the sym - pa - thiz - ing tear.
joined in heart, and hope to meet a - gain.
friend - ship reign through all e - ter - ni - ty.

*Or "Maker's"

Written to express a pastor's unwillingness to leave a beloved congregation, this hymn is frequently used as an expression of Christian fellowship, especially at the conclusion of the Lord's Supper. The tune is attributed to an influential Swiss musician and publisher.

TEXT: John Fawcett, 1782
MUSIC: Johann Georg Nägeli, 1828; arr. Lowell Mason, 1845

DENNIS
SM

307 God of Grace and God of Glory

1 God of grace and God of glo - ry, on thy peo - ple
2 Lo! the hosts of e - vil round us scorn thy Christ, as -
3 Cure thy chil - dren's war - ring mad - ness; bend our pride to
4 Save us from weak res - ig - na - tion to the e - vils

pour thy power; crown thine an - cient chur - ch's sto - ry; bring its
sail his ways! From the fears that long have bound us free our
thy con - trol; shame our wan - ton, self - ish glad - ness, rich in
we de - plore. Let the gift of thy sal - va - tion be our

bud to glo - rious flower. Grant us wis - dom, grant us cour - age,
hearts to faith and praise. Grant us wis - dom, grant us cour - age,
things and poor in soul. Grant us wis - dom, grant us cour - age,
glo - ry ev - er - more. Grant us wis - dom, grant us cour - age,

for the fac - ing of this hour, for the fac - ing of this hour.
for the liv - ing of these days, for the liv - ing of these days.
lest we miss thy king-dom's goal, lest we miss thy king-dom's goal.
serv - ing thee whom we a - dore, serv - ing thee whom we a - dore.

This stirring hymn used at the opening of Riverside Church in New York in 1930 was penned by its widely-known and influential pastor, and it has gained a firm place in English-language hymnals around the world. The Welsh tune name honors the Rhondda Valley in Glamorganshire.

TEXT: Harry Emerson Fosdick, 1930, alt.
MUSIC: John Hughes, 1907

CWM RHONDDA
8.7.8.7.8.7.7

O God in Whom All Life Begins 308

1 O God in whom all life be-gins, who births the seed to fruit,
2 U - nite in mu - tual min - is - try our minds and hands and hearts
3 Through tears and laugh-ter, grief and joy, en - large our trust and care;

be - stow your bless - ing on our lives; here let your love find root.
that we may have the grace to seek the power your peace im - parts.
so bind us in com-mu - ni - ty that we may risk and dare.

Bring forth in us the Spir - it's gifts of pa - tience, joy, and peace;
So let our var - ied gifts com - bine to glo - ri - fy your Name
Be with us when we gath - er here to wor - ship, sing, and pray;

de - liv - er us from numb - ing fear, and grant our faith in-crease.
that in all things by word and deed we may your love pro-claim.
then send us forth in power and faith to live the words we say.

Although it was written for the installation of a pastor, this text is really about the mutual ministry shared by all members of a worshiping community, both when they are gathered and when they go forth into the world. The tune used here may have Christmas associations for some.

TEXT: Carl P. Daw Jr., 1990
MUSIC: English melody; arr. Arthur S. Sullivan, 1874
Text © 1990 Hope Publishing Company

NOEL
CMD

309 Come, Great God of All the Ages

1 Come, great God of all the a-ges; make your earth-ly
2 Come, Christ Je-sus, flesh and spir-it, sure foun-da-tion,
3 Come, great Spir-it, in and with us, tune our ears to
4 Come, O come, in cel-e-bra-tion, house-hold of the

mis-sion known; speak through ev-ery deed and per-son;
cor-ner-stone; help us form the church e-ter-nal;
hear your call; through the mov-ing of your pres-ence,
one true God; in com-mit-ment and re-joic-ing

let your way and will be shown. Guide the church to true com-
may your vi-sion be our own. Send a mes-sage to each
let re-deem-ing love re-call min-is-try in ded-i-
let us go where Christ has trod; as we act in faith and

mit-ment; give di-rec-tion now, we ask; fit us for the
fol-lower; lead all peo-ple to your way; urge us to strong
ca-tion, love em-bod-ied in our deeds; chal-lenge us to
rev-erence, let us, Lord, the fu-ture see; place us in the

This text was written in 1987 for the capital cornerstone campaign of the National Presbyterian Church in Washington, DC. It is set here to a mid-20th-century tune created in wartime England to replace a Haydn tune tainted by Nazi associations.

TEXT: Mary Jackson Cathey, 1987
MUSIC: Cyril Vincent Taylor, 1941
Text © 1990 Hope Publishing Company
Music © 1942, ren. 1970 Hope Publishing Company

ABBOT'S LEIGH
8.7.8.7.D

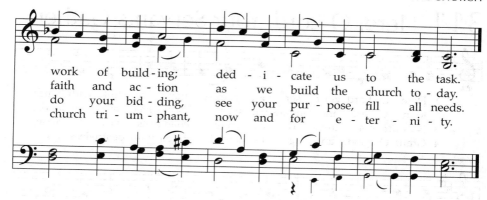

work of build-ing; ded - i - cate us to the task.
faith and ac - tion as we build the church to - day.
do your bid - ding, see your pur - pose, fill all needs.
church tri - um - phant, now and for e - ter - ni - ty.

I Love Thy Kingdom, Lord 310

1 I love thy king - dom, Lord, the house of thine a - bode,
2 I love thy church, O God. Her walls be - fore thee stand,
3 For her my tears shall fall; for her my prayers as - cend;
4 Be - yond my high - est joy I prize her heaven - ly ways:
5 Sure as thy truth shall last, to Zi - on shall be given

the church our blest Re - deem - er saved with his own pre - cious blood.
dear as the ap - ple of thine eye, and grav - en on thy hand.
to her my cares and toils be given, till toils and cares shall end.
her sweet com - mu - nion, sol - emn vows, her hymns of love and praise.
the bright - est glo - ries earth can yield, and bright - er bliss of heaven.

One of the oldest American hymn texts in continuous use, this paraphrase of Psalm 137 was created by a
president of Yale University while compiling a popular revision of Watts's *Psalms of David*. The arranger of
the tune was the clerk of a Presbyterian church in London.

TEXT: Timothy Dwight, 1800
MUSIC: *The Universal Psalmodist*, 1763; adapt. Aaron Williams, 1770

ST. THOMAS
SM

311 Here, O Lord, Your Servants Gather

1 Here, O Lord, your ser-vants gath-er, hand we link with hand;
2 Man-y are the tongues we speak, scat-tered are the lands;
3 Na-ture's se-crets o-pen wide, chang-es nev-er cease;
4 Grant, O God, an age re-newed, filled with death-less love;

look-ing toward our Sav-ior's cross, joined in love we stand.
yet our hearts are one in God, one in love's de-mands.
where, O where, can wea-ry souls find the source of peace?
help us as we work and pray; send us from a-bove

As we seek the realm of God, we u-nite to pray:
While in dark-ness hope ap-pears, call-ing age and youth:
Un-to all those sore dis-tressed, torn by end-less strife:
truth and cour-age, faith and power need-ed in our strife:

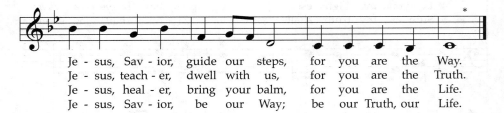

Je-sus, Sav-ior, guide our steps, for you are the Way.
Je-sus, teach-er, dwell with us, for you are the Truth.
Je-sus, heal-er, bring your balm, for you are the Life.
Je-sus, Sav-ior, be our Way; be our Truth, our Life.

*Optional finger cymbals

This gentle hymn was created for a 1958 international convention of Christian educators in Japan. The tune's use of the *gagaku* mode, originally from China but later limited to use in the Japanese court, serves as a subtle but significant affirmation of Christ's sovereignty.

TEXT: Tokuo Yamaguchi, 1958; trans. Everett M. Stowe, 1958, alt.
MUSIC: Japanese *gagaku* mode, Isao Koizumi, 1958
Text © 1958 The United Methodist Publishing House (admin. The Copyright Company)
Music Used by permission of Hiroshi Koizumi

TOKYO
7.5.7.5.D

Take Us As We Are, O God

1 Take us as we are, O God, and claim us as your own. As
2 Bless us for your ser - vice, Lord; no pow - er we de - vise will
3 Break us o - pen to dis - close how bro - ken - ness can heal, wher -
4 Give us to the world you love as light and salt and yeast, that

once you chose to tell your love in hu - man flesh and bone, so
ev - er give us strength e - nough or make us tru - ly wise, yet
ev - er bro - ken loaves suf - fice to give a crowd a meal and
we may nour - ish in your name the last, the lost, the least, un -

let our lives be used to make your sav - ing pur - pose known.
by your prom - ise we can know the peace your grace sup - plies.
graves break o - pen to re - lease new life from death's dread seal.
til at length you call us all to your un - end - ing feast.

Guitar chords do not correspond with keyboard harmony.

This Lord's Supper text is organized around the fourfold liturgical shape traced by Dom Gregory Dix in *The Shape of the Liturgy:* take, bless, break, give. It considers how the phrase "Body of Christ," used for sacramental bread, can also be applied to the baptized people of God.

TEXT: Carl P. Daw Jr., 1995
MUSIC: Alfred V. Fedak, 1995
Text © 1995 Hope Publishing Company
Music © 1995 Selah Publishing Co., Inc.

ENDLESS FEAST
7.6.8.6.8.6

313　Lord, Make Us More Holy

1 Lord, make us more ho - ly; Lord, make us more ho - ly;
2 Lord, make us more lov - ing; Lord, make us more lov - ing;
3 Lord, make us more pa - tient; Lord, make us more pa - tient;
4 Lord, make us more faith - ful; Lord, make us more faith - ful;

Lord, make us more ho - ly, un - til we meet a - gain:
Lord, make us more lov - ing, un - til we meet a - gain:
Lord, make us more pa - tient, un - til we meet a - gain:
Lord, make us more faith - ful, un - til we meet a - gain:

ho - ly, ho - ly, ho - ly, un - til we meet a - gain.
lov - ing, lov - ing, lov - ing, un - til we meet a - gain.
pa - tient, pa - tient, pa - tient, un - til we meet a - gain.
faith - ful, faith - ful, faith - ful, un - til we meet a - gain.

Like many African American spirituals, this one creates a framework for almost endless expansion beyond the four stanzas given here. This sung prayer is notable as an affirmation of God's active care for the once-gathered community while dispersed and of hope to be reunited.

TEXT and MUSIC: African American spiritual

LORD, MAKE US MORE HOLY
6.6.6.6.6.6

Longing for Light, We Wait in Darkness 314
Christ, Be Our Light

1 Long-ing for light, we wait in dark-ness. Long-ing for
2 Long-ing for peace, our world is trou-bled. Long-ing for
3 Long-ing for food, man - y are hun-gry. Long-ing for
4 Long-ing for shel - ter, man - y are home-less. Long-ing for
5 Man - y the gifts, man - y the peo - ple, man - y the

truth, we turn to you. Make us your own,
hope, man - y de - spair. Your word a - lone
wa - ter, man - y still thirst. Make us your bread,
warmth, man - y are cold. Make us your build - ing,
hearts that yearn to be - long. Let us be ser - vants

your ho - ly peo-ple, light for the world to see.
has power to save us. Make us your liv - ing voice.
bro - ken for oth - ers, shared un - til all are fed.
shel - ter - ing oth - ers, walls made of liv - ing stone.
to one an - oth - er, mak - ing your king - dom come.

Refrain

Christ, be our light! Shine in our hearts. Shine through the
dark - ness. Christ, be our light! Shine in your
church gath - ered to - day.

By blending biblical images and current vignettes in the present tense, this hymn connects Christ's promise that he is the Light of the world (John 8:12, 9:5) and his charge to his followers to be the light of the world (Matthew 5:14). This is part of the church's servant calling.

TEXT and MUSIC: Bernadette Farrell, 1993
Text and Music © 1993 Bernadette Farrell (Published by OCP)

CHRIST, BE OUR LIGHT
9.8.9.6 with refrain

315 In the Midst of New Dimensions

1 In the midst of new di-men-sions, in the face of
2 Through the flood of starv-ing peo-ple, war-ring fac-tions,
3 As we stand, a world di-vid-ed by our own self-
4 We are man and we are wom-an, all per-sua-sions,
5 Should the threats of dire pre-dic-tions cause us to with-

chang-ing ways, who will lead the pil-grim peo-ples
and de-spair, who will lift the ol-ive branch-es?
seek-ing schemes, grant that we, your glob-al vil-lage,
old and young, each a gift in your cre-a-tion,
draw in pain, may your blaz-ing phoe-nix spir-it

Refrain

wan-dering in their sep-arate ways?
Who will light the flame of care?
might en-vi-sion wid-er dreams. God of rain-bow, fi-ery pil-lar,
each a love song to be sung.
res-ur-rect the church a-gain.

lead-ing where the ea-gles soar, we your peo-ple, ours the jour-ney

In this simultaneously created text and tune, the author/composer was seeking to incorporate imagery from both Native American and Hebrew spiritual traditions. Also included is the mythological phoenix, which had received a Christian interpretation as early as the first century.

TEXT and MUSIC: Julian B. Rush, 1979; rev. 1985
Text and Music © 1994 Julian B. Rush

NEW DIMENSIONS
8.7.8.7 with refrain

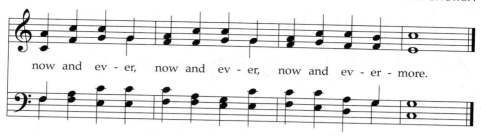

now and ev - er, now and ev - er, now and ev - er - more.

Where Charity and Love Prevail 316

1 Where char - i - ty and love pre - vail, there God is ev - er found;
2 Let us re - call that in our midst dwells Christ, God's ho - ly Son.
3 Let strife a - mong us be un - known; let all con - ten - tions cease.
4 Let us for - give each oth - er's faults as we our own con - fess,
5 Love can ex - clude no race or creed if hon - ored be God's name;

brought here to - geth - er by Christ's love, by love we thus are bound.
As mem - bers of each bod - y joined, in him we are made one.
Be God's the glo - ry that we seek; be his our on - ly peace.
that we may love each oth - er well in Chris - tian gen - tle - ness.
our com - mon life em - brac - es all whose Mak - er is the same.

This English paraphrase is based on a longer Latin hymn traditionally associated with the footwashing ritual on Maundy Thursday, an enactment of Christ's "new commandment" that we should love one another (John 13:34). For a chant setting of the first line of the hymn see no. 205.

TEXT: Latin, 8th cent.; trans. Omer Westendorf, 1960, alt.
MUSIC: Lucius Chapin, 1812
Text © 1960, ren. 1988 World Library Publications

TWENTY-FOURTH
CM

317 In Christ There Is No East or West

1 In Christ there is no east or west, in him no
2 In Christ shall true hearts ev - ery - where their high com -
3 Join hands, dis - ci - ples of the faith, what - e'er your
4 In Christ now meet both east and west; in him meet

south or north, but one great fel - low -
mu - nion find; his ser - vice is the
race may be. All chil - dren of the
south and north. All Christ - ly souls are

ship of love through - out the whole wide earth.
gold - en cord close - bind - ing hu - man - kind.
liv - ing God are sure - ly kin to me.
one in him through - out the whole wide earth.

This setting expands and enhances the thematic inclusiveness of an early 20th-century text by adapting the melody of a traditional spiritual to carry these words. This 1940 pairing marked the first use of African American musical material in a mainline North American hymnal.

TEXT: John Oxenham, 1908, alt.
MUSIC: African American spiritual; *Jubilee Songs,* 1884; adapt. Harry T. Burleigh, 1940

MC KEE
CM
(alternate tune: ST. PETER, 318)

In Christ There Is No East or West 318

1 In Christ there is no east or west, in
2 In Christ shall true hearts ev - ery - where their
3 Join hands, dis - ci - ples of the faith, what -
4 In Christ now meet both east and west; in

him no south or north, but one great fel - low -
high com - mu - nion find; his ser - vice is the
e'er your race may be. All chil - dren of the
him meet south and north. All Christ - ly souls are

ship of love through - out the whole wide earth.
gold - en cord close - bind - ing hu - man - kind.
liv - ing God are sure - ly kin to me.
one in him through - out the whole wide earth.

This text formed a very small part of an elaborate Christian missionary pageant in the early 20th century, yet it has endured while the grander aspects of that production have faded away. It is set to a simple 19th-century tune that does not get in the way of its message.

TEXT: John Oxenham, 1908, alt.
MUSIC: Alexander Robert Reinagle, 1836

ST. PETER
CM
(alternate tune: MC KEE, 317)

319 Men of Faith, Rise Up and Sing

Shout to the North

This praise and worship song comes from Delirious?, an English Christian rock and worship band. Although the style is new, the message is an enduring one: God will provide the strength we need to proclaim the good news of salvation to all parts of the world.

TEXT and MUSIC: Martin Smith, 1995
Text and Music © 1995 Curious? Music UK (admin. EMICMGPublishing.com)

SMITH
7.7.7.7 with chorus and bridge

Bridge

We've been through fire; we've been through rain;

we've been re-fined by the power of your name.

We've fall-en deep-er in love with you.

You've burned this truth on our lips. *to Chorus*

Coda *Repeat as desired*

earth. He is Lord of heav-en and earth.

320 The Church of Christ in Every Age

1 The church of Christ in ev - ery age, be - set by
2 A - cross the world, a - cross the street, the vic - tims
3 Then let the ser - vant church a - rise, a car - ing
4 For Christ a - lone, whose blood was shed, can cure the
5 We have no mis - sion but to serve in full o -

change but Spir - it - led, must claim and test its
of in - jus - tice cry for shel - ter and for
church that longs to be a part - ner in Christ's
fe - ver in our blood, and teach us how to
be - dience to our Lord: to care for all, with -

her - i - tage and keep on ris - ing from the dead.
bread to eat, and nev - er live be - fore they die.
sac - ri - fice, and clothed in Christ's hu - man - i - ty.
share our bread and feed the starv - ing mul - ti - tude.
out re - serve, and spread Christ's lib - er - at - ing word.

In this challenging text by a British Methodist minister, the odd-numbered stanzas develop the image of "the servant church," while the second surveys the many needs and the fourth describes the true source of strength for the task.

TEXT: Fred Pratt Green, 1969
MUSIC: William Knapp, 1738
Text © 1971 Hope Publishing Company

WAREHAM
LM
(alternate harmonization, 665)

The Church's One Foundation 321

1 The chur-ch's one foun-da - tion is Je - sus Christ her Lord.
2 E - lect from ev - ery na - tion, yet one o'er all the earth,
3 Though with a scorn - ful won - der this world sees her op-pressed,
4 Mid toil and trib - u - la - tion, and tu - mult of her war,
5 Yet she on earth has un - ion with God, the Three in One,

She is his new cre - a - tion by wa - ter and the word.
her char - ter of sal - va - tion: one Lord, one faith, one birth.
by schis-ms rent a - sun - der, by her - e - sies dis-tressed,
she waits the con-sum - ma - tion of peace for - ev - er-more:
and mys - tic sweet com - mu - nion with those whose rest is won:

From heaven he came and sought her to be his ho - ly bride.
One ho - ly name she bless - es, par-takes one ho - ly food,
yet saints their watch are keep - ing; their cry goes up: "How long?"
till with the vi - sion glo - rious her long-ing eyes are blest,
O hap - py ones and ho - ly! Lord, give us grace that we,

With his own blood he bought her, and for her life he died.
and to one hope she press - es, with ev - ery grace en-dued.
And soon the night of weep - ing shall be the morn of song.
and the great church vic - to - rious shall be the church at rest.
like them, the meek and low - ly, may live e - ter-nal - ly.

This hymn was one of twelve written by an English curate to affirm the articles of the Apostles' Creed with biblical allusions such as 1 Corinthians 3:11 here. Though not created for this text, the tune was joined to it in 1868, and the two have been inseparable ever since.

TEXT: Samuel John Stone, 1866, alt.
MUSIC: Samuel Sebastian Wesley, 1864

AURELIA
7.6.7.6.D

322 We Are One in Christ Jesus
Somos uno en Cristo

From Latin America comes this *corito*—a short, lively folk song based on scripture. This one draws on Ephesians 4:4–6 and manages to reproduce faithfully the repeated emphasis on the unity of revelation continued by the unity of discipleship under the care of the Holy Spirit.

TEXT: Anon.; English trans. Alice Parker, 1996
MUSIC: Anon.; arr. Philip W. Blycker, 1992
English Trans. © 1996 Abingdon Press (admin. The Copyright Company)
Music Arr. © 1992 Celebremos/Libros Alianza

SOMOS UNO
Irregular

the Ho - ly Spir - it, u - nit - ing all.
y é - se es el Con - so - la - dor.

Sound a Mystic Bamboo Song 323

Part 1

1 Sound a mys - tic bam - boo song; raise a
2 See the Christ in trib - al cloth, liv - ing
3 Free the Christ with - in the poor; break the
4 May your live - ly Spir - it, God, blow through -

Part 2

chant - ing lyr - ic voice; beat the drum and
in a squat - ter's shed, bend - ing as she
chains of wealth and power. Let the age of
out this rav - ished earth, giv - ing cul - tures,

play the flute; let the church of God re - joice.
plants the rice, sleep - ing on a pave - ment bed.
shar - ing dawn; sing the prom - ised gos - pel hour.
crea - tures, plants, whole - ness, still - ness, growth, and worth.

Optional finger cymbals

This text provides a meaningful way of affirming the worldwide nature of the church and of honoring the diversity of indigenous expressions of faith, unencumbered by Western expectations and practices. The final stanza is based on Psalm 104:30, a verse associated with Pentecost.

TEXT: Bill Wallace, 2000
MUSIC: I-to Loh, 2000
Text © 2000 Bill Wallace (admin. General Board of Global Ministries t/a GBGMusik)
Music © 2000 I-to Loh (admin. General Board of Global Ministries t/a GBGMusik)

MYSTIC BAMBOO SONG
7.7.7.7

324 For All the Faithful Women

Guitar chords do not correspond with keyboard harmony.

Created to honor the tenth anniversary of the first ordination of a woman in the Lutheran Church in America, this text celebrates representative women of the Bible: Miriam and Ruth from Hebrew Scripture, Mary, Martha, and Mary Magdalene from the gospels, and Dorcas from Acts.

TEXT: Herman G. Stuempfle Jr., 1975, alt.
MUSIC: Finnish folk melody; adapt. and harm. David Evans, 1927
Text © 1993 GIA Publications, Inc.
Music Harm. © 1927 Oxford University Press

NYLAND
7.6.7.6.D

By All Your Saints Still Striving 325

Capo 5: (Dm) (F) (Am) (G) (Dm)

Gm Bb Dm C Gm

1 By all your saints still striv - ing, for all your
2 We praise you for the Bap - tist, fore - run - ner
3 All praise, O Lord, for An - drew, the first to
4 For Mag - da - lene we praise you, stead - fast at
5 We pray for saints we know not, for saints still

(F) (Am) (C) (Am)
Bb Dm F Dm

saints at rest, your ho - ly name, O Je - sus, for -
of the Word, our true E - li - jah, mak - ing a
wel - come you, whose wit - ness to his broth - er named
cross and tomb. Your "Mar - y!" in the gar - den dis -
yet to be, for grace to bear true wit - ness and

(C) (F) (G) (C) (Am)
F Bb C F Dm

ev - er - more be blessed! For those passed on be -
high - way for the Lord. The last and great - est
you Mes - si - ah true. May we, with hearts kept
pelled her tears and gloom. A - pos - tle to the a -
serve you faith - ful - ly, till all the ran - somed

(F) (Em) (C) (G) (Em) (Bm)
Bb Am F C Am Em

fore us, we sing our praise a - new and, walk - ing
proph - et, he saw the dawn - ing ray of light that
o - pen to you through - out the year pro - claim to
pos - tles, she ran to spread the word. Send us to
num - ber who stand be - fore the throne as - cribe all

(Dm) (Am) (Em) (Dm) (Em) (Am)
Gm Dm Am Gm Am Dm

in their foot - steps, would live our lives for you.
grows in splen - dor un - til the per - fect day.
friend and neigh - bor your ad - vent ev - er near.
shout the good news that we have seen the Lord!
power and glo - ry and praise to God a - lone.

Guitar chords do not correspond with keyboard harmony.

These stanzas are selected and adapted from a much longer hymn by the nephew of the famous naval hero whose name he shares; it was intended for use on saints' days observed by the Church of England. The tune name honors the Norfolk seaport town where the tune was collected.

TEXT: Horatio Bolton Nelson, 1864, alt.
MUSIC: English melody; adapt. and harm. Ralph Vaughan Williams, 1906

KING'S LYNN
7.6.7.6.D

326 For All the Saints

1 For all the saints who from their la - bors rest, who
2 Thou wast their rock, their for - tress, and their might;
3 O blest com - mu - nion, fel - low - ship di - vine!
4 And when the strife is fierce, the war - fare long,
5 From earth's wide bounds, from o - cean's far - thest coast, through

thee by faith be - fore the world con - fessed, thy
thou, Lord, their cap - tain in the well - fought fight;
We fee - bly strug - gle; they in glo - ry shine; yet
steals on the ear the dis - tant tri - umph song, and
gates of pearl streams in the count - less host,

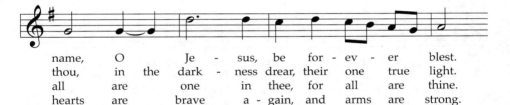

name, O Je - sus, be for - ev - er blest.
thou, in the dark - ness drear, their one true light.
all are one in thee, for all are thine.
hearts are brave a - gain, and arms are strong.
sing - ing to Fa - ther, Son, and Ho - ly Ghost,

Al - le - lu - ia! Al - le - lu - ia!

The broad and sweeping tune with which this hymn is so closely identified was created to be sung during a reverent but dramatic procession at the beginning of an All Saints' Day service, an enacted representation of the enduring "fellowship divine" celebrated by this text.

TEXT: William Walsham How, 1864
MUSIC: Ralph Vaughan Williams, 1906

SINE NOMINE
10.10.10 with alleluias

Harmony, stanza 3

3 O blest com - mu - nion, fel - low - ship di - vine!

We fee - bly strug - gle; they in glo - ry shine; yet

all are one in thee, for all are thine.

to stanza 4

Al - le - lu - ia!

Al - le - lu - ia! Al - le - lu - ia!

327 From All That Dwell Below the Skies

(Psalm 117)

1 From all that dwell be-low the skies let the Cre-a-tor's praise a-
2 In ev-ery land be-gin the song; to ev-ery land the strains be-
3 E-ter-nal are thy mer-cies, Lord; e-ter-nal truth at-tends thy

rise: Let the Re-deem-er's
long: Al-le-lu-ia! Al-le-lu-ia! In cheer-ful sound all
word: Thy praise shall sound from

name be sung through ev-ery land, in ev-ery tongue.
voic-es raise and fill the world with joy-ful praise.
shore to shore, till suns shall rise and set no more.

Al-le-lu-ia! Al-le-lu-ia! Al-le-lu-ia!

Because Psalm 117 contains only two verses, Watts's paraphrase had only two stanzas. Most later hymnals have created or borrowed additional stanzas, like the one included here, to enlarge the hymn. Perhaps the best solution is found by adding Alleluias, as this tune invites.

TEXT: Stanzas 1, 3, Isaac Watts, 1719; stanza 2, *A Pocket Hymn Book*, 1781
MUSIC: *Geistliche Kirchengesäng*, 1623, alt.; harm. Ralph Vaughan Williams, 1906

LASST UNS ERFREUEN
LM with alleluias
(this tune in a lower key, 10)

Unison

Al - le - lu - ia! Al - le - lu - ia!

Praise God, All You Nations 328
Da n'ase
(Psalm 117)

Praise God, all you na - tions. Peo - ple of God, sing praise!
Da n'a - se! Da n'a - se! Da On-ya-me a - se!

Praise God, all you na - tions. Peo - ple of God, sing praise:
Da n'a - se! Da n'a - se! Da On-ya-me a - se!

God's love is great and en - dures for - ev - er.
Ef - ia - se o - ye n'a n'a-do - e do-e so.

Praise God, all you na - tions. Peo - ple of God, sing praise!
Da n'a - se! Da n'a - se! Da On-ya-me a - se!

This paraphrase of Psalm 117 comes from Ghana and was originally created in the Twi language. Paradoxically, this shortest of all psalms is universal in scope, which makes it especially appropriate to sing in the words and music of people from another part of the world.

TEXT: Psalm 117; para. Presbyterian Committee on Congregational Song, 2011
MUSIC: Ghanaian melody; arr. Alfred V. Fedak, 2011
Music Arr. © 2011 Alfred V. Fedak

DA N'ASE
6.6.6.6.10.6.6

329 God Is Our Refuge and Our Strength
(Psalm 46)

1 God is our ref - uge and our strength, our
2 Though hills a - mid the seas be cast, though
3 Where God a - bides a riv - er flows; that
4 Since God is in the midst of it, the

ev - er - pres - ent aid, and there - fore, though the
foam - ing wa - ters roar, yea, though the might - y
cit - y will re - joice. But na - tions fear and
cit - y walls shall stand, se - cure and safe with

earth be moved, we will not be a - fraid;
bil - lows shake the moun - tains on the shore.
king - doms shake be - fore God's thun - dering voice.
God's sure help, when trou - ble is at hand.

The first two stanzas of this very condensed paraphrase of Psalm 46 were created early in the 20th century, and the last two stanzas were prepared near its end. The text is set to a late 16th-century psalm tune that comes from the first such collection to give tunes names.

TEXT: Stanzas 1–2, *The New Metrical Version of the Psalms,* 1909
MUSIC: Este's *Psalmes,* 1592; harm. George Kirbye, 1592

WINCHESTER OLD
CM

Our Help Is in the Name of God 330
(Psalm 124)

1 Our help is in the name of God the Lord, the One who
2 When e-vil seems to have the up-per hand, call on God's
3 Praise God the Lord who hears the cap-tives' prayer. Like birds es-

made the heav-ens with a word, cre-a-tor of the
name: the Lord, the great "I AM." When trou-bles rise and
cap-ing from the fowl-er's snare we are set free; our

world, each liv-ing thing. Come, bless the Lord, lift up your
all a-round gives way, re-mem-ber God stays with us
prais-es now as-cend: "Blessed be the Lord: Cre-a-tor,

hearts and sing: "Our help is in the name of God the Lord."
night and day. Our help is in the name of God the Lord.
Sav-ior, Friend. Our help is in the name of God the Lord."

As a means of fostering the continuity of Reformed tradition, this paraphrase of Psalm 124 has been created to fit the tune that was used for the French paraphrase of Psalm 124 in the 1551 Genevan Psalter. The early psalters in English generally avoided such longer poetic forms.

TEXT: Martin Tel, 2011
MUSIC: Genevan Psalter, 1551
Text © 2011 Martin Tel (admin. Faith Alive Christian Resources)

OLD 124TH
10.10.10.10.10

331 God of the Ages, Whose Almighty Hand

1 God of the a - ges, whose al-might-y
2 Thy love di - vine hath led us in the
3 From war's a - larms, from dead - ly pes - ti -
4 Re - fresh thy peo - ple on their toil-some

hand   leads forth in beau - ty all the star - ry band
past.   In this free land by thee our lot is cast.
lence,   be thy strong arm our ev - er sure de-fense.
way.   Lead us from night to nev - er-end-ing day.

of shin - ing worlds in splen - dor through the skies,
Be thou our rul - er, guard - ian, guide, and stay:
Thy true re - li - gion in our hearts in - crease.
Fill all our lives with love and grace di - vine,

our grate - ful songs be - fore thy throne a - rise.
thy word our law, thy paths our cho - sen way.
Thy boun - teous good - ness nour - ish us in peace.
and glo - ry, laud, and praise be ev - er thine.

This hymn was generated by 19th-century centennial celebrations: the words by the Declaration of Independence and the music by the adoption of the United States Constitution. Despite these origins, no specific nation is mentioned in this hymn of praise and prayer for peace.

NATIONAL HYMN
10.10.10.10

TEXT: Daniel Crane Roberts, 1876, alt.
MUSIC: George William Warren, 1892

The Right Hand of God 332

1 The right hand of God is writ-ing in our land, writ - ing with
2 The right hand of God is point-ing in our land, point - ing the
3 The right hand of God is strik-ing in our land, strik-ing out at
4 The right hand of God is heal-ing in our land, heal-ing bro - ken

pow - er and with love; our con - flicts and our fears, our
way we must go; so cloud - ed is the way, so
en - vy, hate, and greed. Our self - ish - ness and lust, our
bod - ies, minds, and souls; so won-drous is its touch with

tri-umphs and our tears, are re - cord-ed by the right hand of God.
eas - i - ly we stray, but we're guid-ed by the right hand of God.
pride and deeds un-just, are de - stroyed by the right hand of God.
love that means so much, when we're healed by the right hand of God.

OPTIONAL STANZA

5 The right hand of God
is planting in our land,
planting seeds of freedom, hope, and love;
in these Caribbean lands,
let people all join hands,
and be one with the right hand of God.

In biblical imagery, references to "the right hand of God" imply God's power and God's favor. Beginning with an allusion to the handwriting on the wall at Belshazzar's feast (Daniel 5:5), this vigorous Caribbean hymn proceeds to identify ways God continues to act in our own day.

TEXT: Patrick Prescod, 1980
MUSIC: Noel Dexter, 1980
Text and Music © 1981 Caribbean Conference of Churches

LA MANO DE DIOS
5.6.8.6.6.10

333 How Our Hearts with Joy Abound
(Psalm 45)

1 How our hearts with joy a-bound, with your beau-ty all a-round;
2 Fair - er still than hu - man frame, ev - er to our eyes the same,
3 Yours the scep - ter, yours the throne; you to us are God a - lone.

words are fee - ble to ex - press your great love and righ - teous-ness.
stead - fast love shines from your face; from your lips flow words of grace.
Vast the mer - cies to us given: wealth of earth, and joy of heaven.

Though it may have originated as a royal marriage ode, Psalm 45 has come to be understood in both Jewish and Christian traditions as having messianic overtones, and it is quoted that way in Hebrews 1:8–9. This 20th-century paraphrase skillfully maintains that double application.

TEXT: Michael Morgan, 1995
MUSIC: Freylinghausen's *Geistreiches Gesangbuch*, 1704, alt.
Text © 2010 Michael Morgan (admin. Congregational Ministries Publishing, Presbyterian Church (U.S.A.))

GOTT SEI DANK DURCH ALLE WELT
7.7.7.7

334 With Grateful Heart My Thanks I Bring
(Psalm 138)

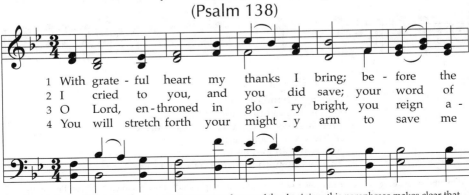

1 With grate - ful heart my thanks I bring; be - fore the
2 I cried to you, and you did save; your word of
3 O Lord, en - throned in glo - ry bright, you reign a -
4 You will stretch forth your might - y arm to save me

Though Psalm 138 is usually regarded as a personal song of thanksgiving, this paraphrase makes clear that it also deals with the theme of God's sovereignty over would-be deities and over all human rulers. The fourth stanza shows that the psalm looks forward as well as backward.

TEXT: *The New Metrical Version of the Psalms*, 1909, alt.
MUSIC: Dimitri S. Bortniansky, 1825, alt.

ST. PETERSBURG
8.8.8.8.8.8

"gods" your praise I sing. I wor - ship in your ho - ly
grace new cour - age gave. The kings of earth shall thank you,
lone in heaven-ly height; the proud in vain your fa - vor
when my foes a - larm. The work you have for me be -

place and praise you for your truth and grace; for truth and
Lord, for they have heard your won - drous word; yes, they shall
seek, but you have mer - cy for the meek. Through trou-ble
gun shall by your grace be ful - ly done. Your love for-

grace to - geth - er shine in your most ho - ly Word di - vine.
come with songs of praise for great and glo-rious are your ways.
though my path - way be, you will re - vive and strength-en me.
ev - er will en - dure: your mer - cy, Lord, is ev - er sure.

335 The Foolish in Their Hearts Deny

(Psalm 14)

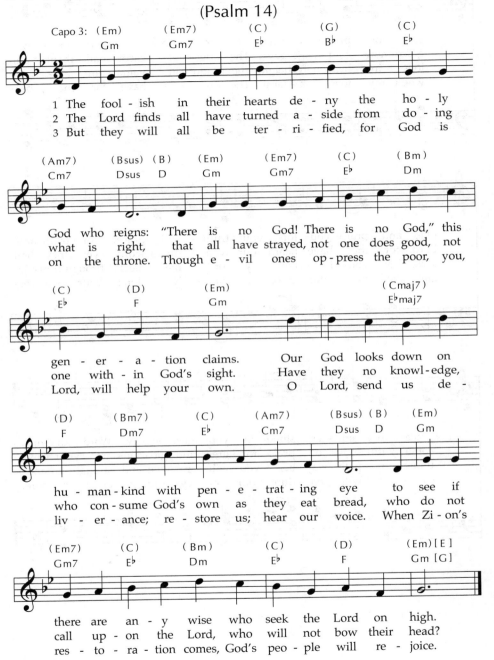

1 The fool-ish in their hearts de-ny the ho-ly
2 The Lord finds all have turned a-side from do-ing
3 But they will all be ter-ri-fied, for God is

God who reigns: "There is no God! There is no God," this
what is right, that all have strayed, not one does good, not
on the throne. Though e-vil ones op-press the poor, you,

gen-er-a-tion claims. Our God looks down on
one with-in God's sight. Have they no knowl-edge,
Lord, will help your own. O Lord, send us de-

hu-man-kind with pen-e-trat-ing eye to see if
who con-sume God's own as they eat bread, who do not
liv-er-ance; re-store us; hear our voice. When Zi-on's

there are an-y wise who seek the Lord on high.
call up-on the Lord, who will not bow their head?
res-to-ra-tion comes, God's peo-ple will re-joice.

This text paraphrases Psalm 14 (later repeated as Psalm 53), an unusual psalm because it deals with a general social evil rather than recounting the psalmist's own slight or affliction. Yet it ends on a note of confidence that God will vindicate the People of the Covenant.

MAPLE AVENUE
CMD

TEXT: Marie J. Post, 1983
MUSIC: Richard L. Van Oss, 1984
Text and Music © 1987 Faith Alive Christian Resources

We Gather Together

1 We gath - er to - geth - er to ask the Lord's bless - ing;
2 Be - side us to guide us, our God with us join - ing,
3 We all do ex - tol thee, thou lead - er tri - um - phant,

he chas - tens and has - tens his will to make known;
or - dain - ing, main - tain - ing his king - dom di - vine;
and pray that thou still our de - fend - er wilt be.

the wick - ed op - press - ing now cease from dis - tress - ing.
so from the be - gin - ning the fight we were win - ning;
Let thy con - gre - ga - tion es - cape trib - u - la - tion;

Sing prais - es to his name; he for - gets not his own.
thou, Lord, wast at our side; all glo - ry be thine!
thy name be ev - er praised! O Lord, make us free!

First published among songs celebrating the end of Spanish control of the Netherlands, this text's blend of patriotism and piety has made it popular at (often ecumenical) Thanksgiving Day services. The tune is named for the Viennese arranger whose male chorus popularized it.

TEXT: Attr. Adrianus Valerius, c. 1626; trans. Theodore Baker, 1894
MUSIC: Neder-landtsch Gedenck-Clanck, 1626; harm. Eduard Kremser, 1877

KREMSER
12.11.12.11
(this tune in a higher key, 612)

337 My Country, 'Tis of Thee

1 My coun-try, 'tis of thee, sweet land of
2 My na-tive coun-try, thee, land of the
3 Let mu-sic swell the breeze, and ring from
4 Our *fa-thers' God, to thee, au-thor of

lib-er-ty, of thee I sing: land where my
no-ble free, thy name I love; I love thy
all the trees sweet free-dom's song. Let mor-tal
lib-er-ty, to thee we sing. Long may our

*fa-thers died, land of the pil-grims' pride,
rocks and rills, thy woods and tem-pled hills;
tongues a-wake; let all that breathe par-take;
land be bright with free-dom's ho-ly light;

from ev-ery moun-tain-side let free-dom ring.
my heart with rap-ture thrills like that a-bove.
let rocks their si-lence break, the sound pro-long.
pro-tect us by thy might, great God, our King.

*Or "parents"

This now-familiar patriotic song was written by a Baptist minister and received its first public performance at an Independence Day celebration by the Boston Sabbath School Union in 1831. It was written to replace a German patriotic text sung to the same tune.

TEXT: Samuel Francis Smith, 1831
MUSIC: *Harmonia Anglicana,* c. 1744

AMERICA
6.6.4.6.6.6.4

O Beautiful for Spacious Skies 338

1 O beau-ti-ful for spa-cious skies, for am-ber waves of grain,
2 O beau-ti-ful for he-roes proved in lib-er-at-ing strife,
3 O beau-ti-ful for pa-triot dream that sees be-yond the years

for pur-ple moun-tain maj-es-ties a-bove the fruit-ed plain!
who more than self their coun-try loved, and mer-cy more than life!
thine al-a-bas-ter cit-ies gleam, un-dimmed by hu-man tears!

A-mer-i-ca! A-mer-i-ca! God shed his grace on thee,
A-mer-i-ca! A-mer-i-ca! God mend thine ev-ery flaw;
A-mer-i-ca! A-mer-i-ca! May God thy gold re-fine

and crown thy good with *broth-er-hood from sea to shin-ing sea!
con-firm thy soul in self-con-trol, thy lib-er-ty in law!
till all suc-cess be no-ble-ness and ev-ery gain di-vine!

*Or "servanthood"

This text (inspired by the vista from Pike's Peak and by a visit to Chicago's Columbian World Exposition) and tune (named MATERNA because it was composed for "O Mother, Dear Jerusalem") were joined in 1912. The combination proved immensely popular during World War I and afterwards.

TEXT: Katharine Lee Bates, 1893, alt.
MUSIC: Samuel Augustus Ward, 1882

MATERNA
CMD

339 Lift Every Voice and Sing

1 Lift ev-ery voice and sing till earth and heav - en
2 Ston - y the road we trod, bit - ter the chas - tening
3 God of our wea - ry years, God of our si - lent

ring, ring with the har - mo - nies of lib - er -
rod, felt in the days when hope un - born had
tears, thou who hast brought us thus far on the

ty. Let our re - joic - ing rise high as the lis - tening
died. Yet, with a stead - y beat, have not our wea - ry
way; thou who hast by thy might led us in - to the

skies; let it re - sound loud as the roll - ing sea.
feet come to the place for which our par - ents sighed?
light, keep us for - ev - er in the path, we pray.

Initially a poem for a school assembly at which Booker T. Washington spoke on Lincoln's birthday in 1900, this text and tune have gained national recognition and devotion, not only within the African American community, but also among all who seek liberation from oppression.

TEXT: James Weldon Johnson, 1900
MUSIC: J. Rosamond Johnson, 1905

LIFT EVERY VOICE
Irregular

Sing a song full of the faith that the dark past has taught us;
We have come o - ver a way that with tears has been wa - tered;
Lest our feet stray from the plac - es, our God, where we met thee;

sing a song full of the hope that the pres - ent has brought
we have come, tread - ing our path through the blood of the slaugh -
lest, our hearts drunk with the wine of the world, we for - get

us. Fac - ing the ris - ing sun of our new day be -
tered, out from the gloom - y past, till now we stand at
thee; shad - owed be - neath thy hand may we for - ev - er

gun, let us march on, till vic - to - ry is won.
last where the white gleam of our bright star is cast.
stand, true to our God, true to our na - tive land.

340 This Is My Song

1 This is my song, O God of all the na-tions,
2 My coun-try's skies are blu-er than the o-cean,
3 This is my prayer, O Lord of all earth's king-doms:

a song of peace for lands a-far and mine.
and sun-light beams on clo-ver-leaf and pine.
thy king-dom come; on earth thy will be done.

This is my home, the coun-try where my heart is;
But oth-er lands have sun-light too, and clo-ver,
Let Christ be lift-ed up till all shall serve him,

here are my hopes, my dreams, my ho-ly shrine;
and skies are ev-ery-where as blue as mine.
and hearts u-nit-ed learn to live as one.

The first two stanzas of this hymn were written between the 20th century's two world wars and focus on the theme of international peace. The third stanza, by another author and added later, uses the language of the Lord's Prayer to voice a distinctly Christian perspective.

TEXT: Stanzas 1–2, Lloyd Stone; stanza 3, Georgia Harkness, alt.
MUSIC: Jean Sibelius, 1899; arr. *The Hymnal*, 1933, alt.
Text Sts. 1–2 © 1934, ren. 1962 The Lorenz Corp.; St. 3 © 1964 The Lorenz Corp.
Music Arr. © 1933, ren. 1961 The Presbyterian Board of Christian Education (admin. Westminster John Knox Press)

FINLANDIA
11.10.11.10.11.10

but oth - er hearts in oth - er lands are beat - ing
So hear my song, O God of all the na - tions,
So hear my prayer, O God of all the na - tions:

with hopes and dreams as true and high as mine.
a song of peace for their land and for mine.
my - self I give thee; let thy will be done.

341 O God, Show Mercy to Us

(Psalm 67)

1 O God, show mer-cy to us, and bless us with your
2 For you will judge the peo-ples in truth and righ-teous-

grace; and cause to shine up-on us the bright-ness of your
ness, and on the earth all na-tions will your just rule con-

face, so that your way most ho-ly on earth may soon be
fess. Let all the peo-ples praise you; let all the na-tions

known, and un-to ev-ery peo-ple your sav-ing grace be
sing. Then earth in rich a-bun-dance to us its fruit will

As this paraphrase shows, Psalm 67 combines many themes: a communal prayer for blessing, a prayer for all people to acknowledge God, and thanksgiving for a bountiful harvest. In Jewish practice it was recited at the end of every Sabbath, a reminder of God's universal sovereignty.

TEXT: *The New Metrical Version of the Psalms,* 1909, alt.
MUSIC: Gustav Holst, 1918; harm. composite

THAXTED
13.13.13.13.13.13

shown. Let all the peo-ples praise you; let all the na-tions
bring. The Lord our God will bless us; our God will bless-ing

sing; in ev-ery land let prais-es and songs of glad-ness ring.
send, and all the earth will wor-ship to its re-mot-est end.

342 Judge Eternal, Throned in Splendor

1 Judge E-ter-nal, throned in splen-dor, Lord of lords and
2 Still the wea-ry folk are pin-ing for the hour that
3 Crown, O God, your own en-deav-or; cleave our dark-ness

King of kings, with your liv-ing fire of judg-ment
brings re-lease, and the cit-y's crowd-ed clang-or
with your sword; feed the faith-less and the hun-gry

purge this land of bit-ter things; so-lace all its
cries a-loud for sin to cease, and the home-steads
with the rich-ness of your word; cleanse the bod-y

wide do-min-ion with the heal-ing of your wings.
and the wood-lands plead in si-lence for their peace.
of this na-tion through the glo-ry of the Lord.

More than a century after it was written, this plea for national purification has lost none of its power, nor has the need for social justice grown less acute. It is set to a traditional Welsh tune named for a long-inhabited town in north Wales overlooking the River Clywd.

TEXT: Henry Scott Holland, 1902, alt.
MUSIC: Welsh melody; harm. *The English Hymnal*, 1906

RHUDDLAN
8.7.8.7.8.7

Where Cross the Crowded Ways of Life 343

1 Where cross the crowd - ed ways of life, where sound the
2 In haunts of wretch - ed - ness and need, on shad - owed
3 From ten - der child - hood's help - less - ness, from hu - man
4 The cup of wa - ter given for you still holds the

cries of race and clan, a - bove the noise of
thresh - olds fraught with fears, from paths where hide the
grief and bur - dened toil, from fam - ished souls, from
fresh - ness of your grace; yet long these mul - ti -

self - ish strife, we hear your voice, O Son of Man.
lures of greed, we catch the vi - sion of your tears.
sor - row's stress, your heart has nev - er known re - coil.
tudes to view the sweet com - pas - sion of your face.

5 O Master, from the mountainside,
make haste to heal these hearts of pain;
among these restless throngs abide;
O tread the city's streets again;

6 Till all the world shall learn your love,
and follow where your feet have trod;
till glorious from your heaven above
shall come the city of our God.

Because dense populations always result in concentrated hardships, this vivid yet timeless evocation of urban need connects to our own day as well as to Jesus' lament over Jerusalem (Matthew 23:37/Luke 13:34). This tune was the first used with this text and is now customary.

TEXT: Frank Mason North, 1903, alt.
MUSIC: Gardiner's *Sacred Melodies*, 1815

GERMANY
LM

344 Where Armies Scourge the Countryside
Bring Peace to Earth Again

1 Where ar - mies scourge the coun - try - side, and
2 Where an - ger fes - ters in the heart, and
3 Where homes are torn by bit - ter strife, and
4 O God, whose heart com - pas - sion - ate bears

peo - ple flee in fear, where si - rens scream through
strikes with cru - el hand; where vio - lence stalks the
love dis - solves in blame; where walls you meant for
ev - ery hu - man pain, re - deem this vio - lent,

flam - ing nights, and death is ev - er near:
trou - bled streets, and ter - ror haunts the land:
shel - tering care hide deeds of hurt and shame:
wound - ing world till gen - tle - ness shall reign.

Refrain

O God of mer - cy, hear our prayer. Bring peace to earth a - gain!

Guitar chords do not correspond with keyboard harmony.

This text was a response to several events: ethnic cleansing in the Balkans, the aftermath of the Oklahoma City bombing, revelations of child abuse, the general state of the world. For all such horrors, the only hope is the peace God offers. The tune name means "Peace, my God."

TEXT: Herman G. Stuempfle Jr., 1995
MUSIC: Perry Nelson, 1996
Text and Music © 1996 World Library Publications

PACE MIO DIO
8.6.8.6.8.6

In an Age of Twisted Values 345

1 In an age of twist-ed val-ues we have lost the
2 We have built dis-crim-i-na-tion on our prej-u-
3 When our fam-i-lies are bro-ken, when our homes are
4 We who hear your word so of-ten choose so rare-ly

truth we need. In so-phis-ti-cat-ed lan-guage we have
dice and fear. Ha-tred swift-ly turns to cruel-ty if we
full of strife, when our chil-dren are be-wil-dered, when they
to o-bey. Turn us from our will-ful wan-dering; give us

jus-ti-fied our greed. By our strug-gle for pos-ses-sions
hold re-sent-ments dear. For com-mu-ni-ties di-vid-ed
lose their way in life, when we fail to give the a-ged
truth to light our way. In the pow-er of your Spir-it

we have robbed the poor and weak. Hear our cry and
by the walls of class and race, hear our cry and
all the care we know they need, hear our cry and
come to cleanse us, make us new; hear our cry and

heal our na-tion; your for-give-ness, Lord, we seek.
heal our na-tion; show us, Lord, your love and grace.
heal our na-tion; help us show more love, we plead.
heal our na-tion till our na-tion hon-ors you.

Guitar chords do not correspond with keyboard harmony.

One of the ways Christians can show firm allegiance to the country where they live and express care for its well-being is to ensure that they are mindful of the broad range of human needs within that society. This hymn is a strong reminder of the values that need such attention.

TEXT: Martin E. Leckebusch, 1995
MUSIC: Alfred V. Fedak, 1988
Text © 1995 Kevin Mayhew Ltd.
Music © 1989 Selah Publishing Co., Inc.

CHURCH UNITED
8.7.8.7.D

346 For the Healing of the Nations

1 For the heal-ing of the na-tions, Lord, we pray with
2 Lead us for-ward in-to free-dom; from de-spair your
3 All that kills a-bun-dant liv-ing, let it from the
4 You, Cre-a-tor God, have writ-ten your great name on

one ac-cord; for a just and e-qual shar-ing
world re-lease, that, re-deemed from war and ha-tred,
earth be banned: pride of sta-tus, race, or school-ing,
hu-man-kind; for our grow-ing in your like-ness,

of the things that earth af-fords; to a life of
all may come and go in peace. Show us how through
dog-mas that ob-scure your plan. In our com-mon
bring the life of Christ to mind, that by our re-

love in ac-tion help us rise and pledge our word.
care and good-ness fear will die and hope in-crease.
quest for jus-tice may we hal-low life's brief span.
sponse and ser-vice earth its des-ti-ny may find.

The first line of this text quotes the declared purpose of the leaves of the tree of life growing beside the river of life in the heavenly Jerusalem (Revelation 22:2). The hymn continues by identifying some of the many ways we are called to share with God in this healing work.

TEXT: Fred Kaan, 1965
MUSIC: John Francis Wade, c. 1750; harm. *Hymns Ancient & Modern*, 1861
Text © 1968 Hope Publishing Company

ST. THOMAS (Wade)
8.7.8.7

Let All Mortal Flesh Keep Silence 347

1 Let all mor-tal flesh keep si-lence, and with fear and
2 King of kings, yet born of Mar - y, as of old on
3 Rank on rank the host of heav - en spreads its van-guard
4 At his feet the six - winged ser - aph, cher - u - bim, with

trem - bling stand; pon - der noth - ing earth - ly
earth he stood, Lord of lords, in hu - man
on the way, as the Light of light de -
sleep - less eye, veil their fac - es to the

mind - ed, for with bless - ing in his hand
ves - ture, in the bod - y and the blood,
scend - eth from the realms of end - less day,
pres - ence, as with cease - less voice they cry,

Christ our God to earth de - scend - eth,
he will give to all the faith - ful
that the powers of hell may van - ish
"Al - le - lu - ia, al - le - lu - ia,

our full hom - age to de - mand.
his own self for heaven - ly food.
as the shad - ows clear a - way.
al - le - lu - ia, Lord most high!"

The flowering of English hymnody in the 19th century included the rediscovery, translation, and versification of ancient Christian hymns, such as this text from one of the earliest existing Christian liturgies. It is set here to an adaptation of a 17th-century French melody.

TEXT: From Liturgy of St. James, 4th cent.; trans. Gerard Moultrie, 1864, alt.
MUSIC: French melody; arr. Ralph Vaughan Williams, 1906

PICARDY
8.7.8.7.8.7
(alternate harmonization, 274)

348 Lo, He Comes with Clouds Descending

1 Lo, he comes with clouds de-scend-ing,
2 Now re-demp-tion, long ex-pect-ed,
3 Yea, a-men, let all a-dore thee,

once for our sal-va-tion slain; thou-sand,
comes in sol-emn splen-dor near; all the
high on thine e-ter-nal throne; Sav-ior,

thou-sand saints at-tend-ing join to
saints this world re-ject-ed thrill the
take the power and glo-ry; claim the

Despite unclear musical origins, the result here is a characteristic early Methodist hymn tune, notable for its breadth and range. It effectively sets a text of similarly mixed sources, one that Charles Wesley regarded as related to "Thy kingdom come" in the Lord's Prayer.

TEXT: Stanzas 1, 3, Charles Wesley, 1758, alt.; stanza 2, John Cennick, 1752, alt.
MUSIC: Thomas Olivers, 1763; harm. Ralph Vaughan Williams, 1906

HELMSLEY
8.7.8.7.4.4.4.7

sing the glad re - frain: Al - le -
trum - pet sound to hear: Al - le -
king - dom as thine own. Come, Lord

lu - ia, al - le - lu - ia, al - le -
lu - ia, al - le - lu - ia, al - le -
Je - sus; come, Lord Je - sus; come, Lord

lu - ia! Christ the Lord re - turns to reign.
lu - ia! See the day of God ap - pear!
Je - sus. Thou shalt reign, and thou a - lone!

349   "Sleepers, Wake!" A Voice Astounds Us

1 "Sleep-ers, wake!" A voice as - tounds us; the shout of ram-part
2 Zi - on hears the watch - men sing - ing; her heart with joy - ful
3 Lamb of God, the heavens a - dore you; let saints and an - gels

guards sur - rounds us: "A - wake, Je - ru - sa - lem, a - rise!"
hope is spring - ing; she wakes and hur - ries through the night.
sing be - fore you, as harps and cym-bals swell the sound.

Mid - night's peace their cry has bro - ken, their ur - gent sum-mons
Forth he comes, her Bride-groom glo - rious in strength of grace, in
Twelve great pearls, the cit - y's por - tals: through them we stream to

This text is based on the parable of the wise and foolish bridesmaids (Matthew 25:1–13), but contains allusions to many other New Testament passages. Because one person created both text and tune, they combine majestically to form what is often called "the king of chorales."

TEXT: Philipp Nicolai, 1599; trans. Carl P. Daw Jr., 1982
MUSIC: Attr. Philipp Nicolai, 1599; harm. Johann Sebastian Bach, 1731
Text © 1982 Hope Publishing Company

WACHET AUF
Irregular

clear-ly spo - ken: "The time has come, O maid-ens wise!
truth vic - to - rious: her star is risen, her light grows bright.
join the im-mor - tals as we with joy your throne sur - round.

Rise up, and give us light; the Bride-groom is in
Now come, most wor - thy Lord, God's Son, in - car - nate
No eye has known the sight, no ear heard such de -

sight. Al - le - lu - ia! Your lamps pre - pare and has - ten there,
Word, Al - le - lu - ia! We fol - low all and heed your call
light: Al - le - lu - ia! There - fore we sing to greet our King;

that you the wed - ding feast may share."
to come in - to the ban - quet hall.
for ev - er let our prais - es ring.

350 Keep Your Lamps Trimmed and Burning

1 Keep your lamps trimmed and burn - ing; keep your
2 It's our faith makes us hap - py; it's our
3 We are climb - ing Ja - cob's lad - der; we are
4 Ev - ery round goes high - er, high - er; ev - ery

lamps trimmed and burn - ing; keep your lamps
faith makes us hap - py; it's our faith
climb - ing Ja - cob's lad - der; we are climb - ing
round goes high - er, high - er; ev - ery round goes

trimmed and burn - ing, for the time is draw - ing nigh.
makes us hap - py, for the time is draw - ing nigh.
Ja - cob's lad - der, for the time is draw - ing nigh.
high - er, high - er, for the time is draw - ing nigh.

Refrain

Sis - ters, don't grow wea - ry; broth - ers, don't grow wea - ry;

This African American spiritual has a biblical basis in the parable of the ten maidens (Matthew 25:1–13), but the text actually sung could vary greatly. Such variation can be seen here in the annexing of an often freestanding spiritual based on Jacob's vision (Genesis 28:10–17).

TEXT and MUSIC: African American spiritual

KEEP YOUR LAMPS
7.7.7.7 with refrain

chil-dren, don't grow wea-ry, for the time is draw-ing nigh.

All Who Love and Serve Your City 351

| C | G | C | Em | F | Em |

1 All who love and serve your cit - y, all who
2 In your day of wealth and plen - ty, wast - ed
3 For all days are days of judg - ment, and the
4 Ris - en Lord, shall yet the cit - y be the

| Am | Dm7 | G | Em | Am |

bear its dai - ly stress, all who cry for
work and wast - ed play, call to mind the
Lord is wait - ing still, draw - ing near a
cit - y of de - spair? Come to - day, our

| Em | Am | Dm | C | G | G7 | C |

peace and jus - tice, all who curse and all who bless:
word of Je - sus, "You must work while it is day."
world that spurns him, of - fering peace from Cal - vary's hill.
judge, our glo - ry. Be its name "The Lord is there!"

Guitar chords do not correspond with keyboard harmony.

This 20th-century text greatly enriches the neglected genre of urban hymns. The second stanza quotes John 9:4, the third stanza refers to Jesus weeping over Jerusalem (Matthew 23:37/Luke 13:34), and the final line cites the name given to Israel's future holy city (Ezekiel 48:35).

TEXT: Erik Routley, 1966
MUSIC: *The United States Sacred Harmony*, 1799; harm. Carlton R. Young, 1964
Text © 1969 Stainer & Bell, Ltd. (admin. Hope Publishing Company)
Music Harm. © 1965 Abingdon Press (admin. The Copyright Company)

CHARLESTOWN
8.7.8.7

352 My Lord! What a Morning

Refrain

My Lord! what a morn-ing; my Lord! what a morn-ing;

O my Lord! what a morn-ing, when the stars be-gin to

Fine

fall, when the stars be-gin to fall.

1 You will hear the trum-pet
2 You will hear the sin-ner
3 You will hear the Chris-tian

sound
cry, to wake the na-tions un-der ground,
shout,

to Refrain

look-ing to my God's right hand, when the stars be-gin to fall.

This spiritual reflects on Jesus' saying about the endtimes as recorded in Matthew 24:29–30 / Mark 13:24–26. It belongs to the slower, less common style of spirituals with long, sustained phrases and was among those popularized in concerts by the Fisk Jubilee Singers.

TEXT: African American spiritual
MUSIC: African American spiritual; arr. Melva Wilson Costen, 1989
Music Arr. © 1990 Melva Wilson Costen

MY LORD, WHAT A MORNING
Irregular

My Hope Is Built on Nothing Less 353

1 My hope is built on noth-ing less than Je-sus' blood and
2 When dark-ness seems to hide his face, I rest on his un-
3 His oath, his cov-e-nant, his blood sup-port me in the
4 When he shall come with trum-pet sound, O may I then in

righ-teous-ness; I dare not trust the sweet-est frame, but
chang-ing grace; in ev-ery high and storm-y gale, my
whelm-ing flood; when all a-round my soul gives way, he
him be found, dressed in his righ-teous-ness a-lone, fault-

Refrain

whol-ly lean on Je-sus' name.
an-chor holds with-in the veil.
then is all my hope and stay. On Christ, the sol-id Rock, I stand; all
less to stand be-fore the throne.

oth-er ground is sink-ing sand; all oth-er ground is sink-ing sand.

This hymn develops the imagery of Jesus' remark (Matthew 7:24–27 / Luke 6:47–49) that those who believe in him and act on that belief are like someone who builds a house on a rock. The text is set to a tune created for it by a prolific 19th-century American composer and editor.

TEXT: Edward Mote, c. 1834, alt.
MUSIC: William Batchelder Bradbury, 1863, alt.

SOLID ROCK
LM with refrain

354 Mine Eyes Have Seen the Glory

1 Mine eyes have seen the glo-ry of the com-ing of the Lord;
2 God has sound-ed forth the trum-pet that shall nev-er call re-treat
3 In the beau-ty of the lil-ies Christ was born a-cross the sea,

he is tram-pling out the vin-tage where the grapes of wrath are stored;
and is sift-ing out all hu-man hearts be-fore the judg-ment seat;
with a glo-ry in his bos-om that trans-fig-ures you and me;

he has loosed the fate-ful light-ning of his ter-ri-ble swift sword.
O be swift, my soul, to an-swer; O be ju-bi-lant my feet!
as he died to make us ho-ly, let us live to make all free,

Refrain

God's truth is march-ing on.
Our God is march-ing on. Glo-ry, glo-ry hal-le-
while God is march-ing on.

Though its biblical roots are often overlooked, this text incorporates many apocalyptic images such as the coming of the Lord in glory (Matthew 24:30/Mark 13:26/Luke 21:27), the winepress (Isaiah 63:3; Revelation 14:19, 19:15), and the sharp sword (Isaiah 27:1; Revelation 19:15).

TEXT: Julia W. Howe, 1861, alt.
MUSIC: American melody, 19th cent.

BATTLE HYMN
15.15.15.6 with refrain

O Hear Our Cry, O Lord   355
(Psalm 80)

Capo 1: (Bm)   (D)   (A) (C)   (Em)   (Bm)
      Cm   Eb   Bb   Db   Fm   Cm

1 O   hear our cry, O   Lord;   now   hear us   as   we   pray.
2 En-throned a-bove all worlds, you   shine with ho-ly light.
3 O   Lord, the God of Hosts,   turn   not your face a - way.
4 O   Lord, our God, re - turn; bring peace in - to each home.

  (F#m)   (D)   (Bm)   (F#m)   (B7)   (E)
  Gm   Eb   Cm   Gm   C7   F

You guide us   a   shep-herd leads, so   keep us   in your way.
Lord, pour your power up-on us   all   and save us with your might.
Our tears have been both food and drink; foes mock us night and day.
So   let your face shine on   us   all; re - store us as   your own.

(A) (Dm)   (G) (C)   (F) (B)   (F#)   (B)
Bb Ebm   Ab   Db   Gb C   G   C

O   come;   Lord, come;   re - store and save us   now.

Guitar chords do not correspond with keyboard harmony.

The use of a refrain in this paraphrase of Psalm 80 effectively represents both the structure and the spirit of the original prayer for the restoration of God's favor. Even in the midst of feeling cut off from God, there remains a sense of confidence in God's unfailing mercy.

TEXT: Fred R. Anderson, 1986
MUSIC: Richard Wayne Dirksen, 1974
Text © 1986 Fred R. Anderson
Music © 1974, ren. Harold Flammer Music (a div. of Shawnee Press, Inc.)

VINEYARD HAVEN
SM with refrain

356 Sing Praise to God, Whose Mighty Acts
(Psalm 9)

1 Sing praise to God, whose might-y acts still strong in
mem-ory stand to give us hope when e-vil seems to
gain the up-per hand. Give thanks for deeds of
stead-fast love, for won-ders new and old: for fire and
cloud, for dai-ly food, for mer-cies yet un-told.

2 Though mon-u-ments of e-vil rise in mar-ble,
gilt, and stone, time's search will find their boasts un-true, their
mak-ers' names un-known. Mute av-e-nues of
ruins will mark where once proud cit-ies stood, but from de-
struc-tion God will save the faith-ful, just, and good.

3 Rise up, O God, re-claim the power u-surped by
mor-tal pride; de-flate the hol-low pomp of those whom
rank and ti-tles hide. Let not the need-y
cry un-heard, the suf-fering hope in vain; re-store the
fal-len, bless the meek, till peace and jus-tice reign.

Guitar chords do not correspond with keyboard harmony.

This paraphrase of Psalm 9 affirms the ultimate triumph of God's justice, despite the atrocities and boasts of those who wield worldly power. Its resolute and confident tone is reinforced by a sturdy tune, among the most frequently reprinted ones in 19th-century shape note books.

TEXT: Carl P. Daw Jr., 1996
MUSIC: *Kentucky Harmony*, 1816; harm. Kenneth Munson, 1964
Text © 1996 Hope Publishing Company

SALVATION
CMD

The Days Are Surely Coming 357

1 The days are sure-ly com - ing, says God to all the earth,
2 The days are sure-ly com - ing, says Christ, the prom-ised one,
3 The days are sure-ly com - ing when we will know at last

when you will see my prom - ise: sal - va - tion come to birth.
when you will read my warn - ing in moon and stars and sun.
the full - ness of God's pres - ence, God's prom-ise, come to pass.

My righ-teous-ness and jus-tice will spread through-out the land
Though earth and heav - en trem-ble, stand up and do not fear,
Then righ-teous-ness and jus-tice will spread through-out the land

and you will be de - liv - ered by my al - might - y hand.
for I am your re - deem - er, and I am draw-ing near.
and we will be de - liv - ered by God's al - might - y hand.

This text uses imagery from Jeremiah 33:14–16 and Matthew 24:29–36 / Mark 13:24–32 / Luke 21:25–36. These passages are especially associated with the beginning of Advent, a season that looks forward to Christ's second coming while also preparing us to remember his first coming.

TEXT: David Gambrell, 2009
MUSIC: Welsh folk melody; *Llwybrau Moliant*, 1872; harm. *The English Hymnal*, 1906
Text © 2011 David Gambrell (admin. Presbyterian Publishing Corp.)

LLANGLOFFAN
7.6.7.6.D

358 Steal Away

Refrain

Steal a - way, steal a - way, steal a - way to Je - sus!

Fine

Steal a - way, steal a - way home; I ain't got long to stay here.

1 My Lord, he calls me; he calls me by the thun - der.
2 Green trees are bend - ing; poor sin - ners stand a trem - bling.
3 My Lord, he calls me; he calls me by the light - ning.

to Refrain

The trum - pet sounds with - in my soul; I ain't got long to stay here.

This spiritual illustrates the double meanings at work in many African American slave songs: it is both a call for a direct encounter with Jesus and a summons to slip away from servitude to freedom. Nat Turner reportedly used this song to call together his followers in 1831.

TEXT and MUSIC: African American spiritual

STEAL AWAY
5.7.8.7 with refrain

Freedom Is Coming

359

It is widely recognized that music played a highly significant role in the effectiveness of the anti-apartheid movement in South Africa, and this song is an important reminder that oppressed people everywhere experience a close correlation between political and spiritual freedom.

TEXT and MUSIC: South African
Text and Music © 1984 Utryck (admin. Walton Music Corp.)

FREEDOM IS COMING
Irregular

360 Christ Is Coming!

1 Christ is com-ing! Let cre-a-tion from its groans and
2 Earth can now but tell the sto-ry of your bit-ter
3 With that bless-ed hope be-fore us, flutes are tuned and
4 Long your ex-iles have been pin-ing for your prom-ised

la-bor cease; let the glo-rious proc-la-ma-tion
cross and pain; we shall yet be-hold your glo-ry,
harps are strung; let the might-y ad-vent cho-rus
rest and home, but in heaven-ly glo-ry shin-ing,

hope re-store and faith in-crease: Christ is com-ing!
Lord, when you re-turn to reign: Christ is com-ing!
on-ward roll from tongue to tongue: Christ is com-ing!
soon the ris-en Christ shall come. Christ is com-ing!

Christ is com-ing! Come, O bless-ed Prince of peace.
Christ is com-ing! Let each heart re-peat the strain.
Christ is com-ing! Let each heart re-peat the song.
Christ is com-ing! Joy-ful, shout the vic-tory psalm.

This hymn by a 19th-century Scottish pastor is specifically based on Revelation 1:7 and 22:20, with allusions to several other New Testament passages. Unlike medieval hymns that focused on judgment, this text understands the Second Coming as an occasion of triumph and joy.

TEXT: John Ross Macduff, 1853, alt.
MUSIC: Joachim Neander, 1680

UNSER HERRSCHER
8.7.8.7.8.7

O Christ, the Great Foundation 361

1 O Christ, the great foun-da-tion on which your peo-ple stand
2 Bap-tized in one con-fes-sion, one church in all the earth,
3 Where ty-rants' hold is tight-ened, where strong de-vour the weak,
4 This is the mo-ment glo-rious when he who once was dead

to preach your true sal-va-tion in ev-ery age and land:
we bear our Lord's im-pres-sion, the sign of sec-ond birth:
where in-no-cents are fright-ened, the righ-teous fear to speak,
shall lead his church vic-to-rious, their cham-pion and their head.

pour out your Ho-ly Spir-it to make us strong and pure,
one ho-ly peo-ple gath-ered in love be-yond our own,
there let your church a-wak-ing at-tack the powers of sin
The Lord of all cre-a-tion his heaven-ly king-dom brings:

to keep the faith un-bro-ken as long as worlds en-dure.
by grace we were in-vit-ed; by grace we make you known.
and, all their ram-parts break-ing, with you the vic-tory win.
the fi-nal con-sum-ma-tion, the glo-ry of all things.

The text was written by a leading Chinese educator, author, and editor who chaired the commission that prepared an important ecumenical Chinese hymnal, *Hymns of Universal Praise* (1936). This familiar tune invites comparison of these words with its usual text (see no. 321).

TEXT: Timothy T'ingfang Lew, 1933, alt.; trans. Mildred A. Wiant, 1966
MUSIC: Samuel Sebastian Wesley, 1864
Text © 1977 Chinese Christian Literature Council Ltd.

AURELIA
7.6.7.6.D

362 Rejoice! Rejoice, Believers

1 Re - joice! Re - joice, be - liev - ers, and let your lights ap - pear;
2 See that your lamps are burn - ing; re - plen - ish them with oil;
3 Our hope and ex - pec - ta - tion, O Je - sus, now ap - pear;

the eve - ning is ad - vanc - ing and dark - er night is near.
look now for your sal - va - tion, the end of sin and toil.
a - rise, thou Sun so longed for, a - bove this shad - owed sphere!

The Bride - groom is a - ris - ing and soon he will draw nigh.
The mar - riage feast is wait - ing; the gates wide o - pen stand;
With hearts and hands up - lift - ed, we plead, O Lord, to see

Up, watch with ex - pec - ta - tion; at mid - night comes the cry.
a - rise, O heirs of glo - ry; the Bride - groom is at hand!
the day of earth's re - demp - tion, and ev - er be with thee!

The Latin original of this text based on the parable of the wise and foolish maidens (Matthew 25:1–13)
consisted of ten stanzas, but this briefer version is more appropriate for its message of urgency. It is set to a
spirited minor Welsh tune named for a Pembrokeshire village.

TEXT: Laurentius Laurenti, 1700; trans. Sarah Borthwick Findlater, 1854; alt. *The Hymnal 1982*
MUSIC: Welsh folk melody; *Llwybrau Moliant,* 1872; harm. *The English Hymnal,* 1906

LLANGLOFFAN
7.6.7.6.D

Rejoice, the Lord Is King!

363

Descant

4 Re - joice in glo - rious hope! For Christ, the Judge, shall come

1 Re - joice, the Lord is King! Your Lord and King a - dore!
2 Our Sav - ior, Je - sus, reigns, the God of truth and love;
3 His king - dom can - not fail; he rules o'er earth and heaven;
4 Re - joice in glo - rious hope! For Christ, the Judge, shall come

and gath - er all the saints to their e - ter - nal home.

Re - joice, give thanks, and sing, and tri - umph ev - er - more.
when he had purged our stains, he took his seat a - bove.
the keys of death and hell are to our Je - sus given.
and gath - er all the saints to their e - ter - nal home.

Lift up your heart; lift up your voice! Re - joice, a - gain I say, re - joice!

Lift up your heart; lift up your voice! Re - joice, a - gain I say, re - joice!

Each stanza of this enthronement text prepares for the final line of the refrain, based on Philippians 4:4. "Lord" is here a title of Christ rather than a reference to the undivided Trinity. The late 18th-century tune (first used with Psalm 148) captures the mood well.

TEXT: Charles Wesley, 1746, alt.
MUSIC: John Darwall, 1770; desc. Sydney Hugo Nicholson, 20th cent.
Music Desc. © 1985 Hymns Ancient & Modern (admin. Hope Publishing Company)

DARWALL'S 148TH
6.6.6.6.8.8

364 Lift Up the Gates Eternal
(Psalm 24)

Refrain

Lift up the gates e-ter-nal; lift up your voic-es;
the King of glo-ry comes; the na-tion re-joic-es.

1 See, all the earth is God's, its peo-ple and na-tions;
2 Who can go up this moun-tain, who stand in prais-ing?

3 Come, lift your voic-es high; be lift-ed to glo-ry;
4 Who is this glo-rious one, for whom we are wait-ing?

5 Come, lift your heads with joy; come, lift up your tow-er;
6 Who is this King of glo-ry of whom we're sing-ing?

God built it on the deeps and laid its foun-da-tions.
Those who are pure, who come with clean hands up-rais-ing. (R)

the Lord our God ap-proach-es; come, shout the sto-ry.
We wait the might-y Lord, our God cel-e-brat-ing. (R)

the King of glo-ry comes in full might and pow-er.
Our God, the Lord of Hosts, the vic-tory is bring-ing. (R)

Gradually increasing tempo can heighten the sense of joy and power in this psalm.

This engaging paraphrase of Psalm 24 gains much of its energy from the Israeli folk song for which it was written. This territorial connection adds another dimension to a many-layered text that speaks both to the themes of Advent and to those of Christ's entry into Jerusalem.

TEXT: Arlo D. Duba, 1984; ref. Willard F. Jabusch, 1966, alt.
MUSIC: Israeli folk melody; harm. Alfred V. Fedak, 2011
Text © 1986 Arlo D. Duba
Text Ref. © 1967 Rev. Willard F. Jabusch (Published by OCP)
Music Harm. © 2011 Alfred V. Fedak

GILU HAGALILIM
12.12 with refrain

God Reigns! Let Earth Rejoice! 365
(Psalm 97)

1 God reigns! Let earth re - joice! Let o - ceans
2 God's fire ig - nites the clouds with judg - ment
3 False i - dols rise to claim the weak - ness
4 The ra - diance of God's light beams joy in -

shout God's might! Borne up by truth and righ - teous - ness, God's
swift and just; the e - vil find their deeds in vain; God's
of our pride, but can - not touch the faith - ful ones, for
to our days; now filled with God's own peace and love, our

Refrain

throne is our de - light.
foes are brought to dust. Re - joice! Re -
God stands at our side.
hearts re - sound with praise.

Re - joice!

joice! God reigns! Let earth re - joice!

Re - joice!

The theme of rejoicing that unites Psalm 97 is fittingly emphasized here by the refrain that ties together these four stanzas. Instead of the intimacy with God celebrated in other psalms, the primary concern here is to proclaim God's power over all false gods that tempt us.

TEXT: Michael Morgan, 1995, alt.
MUSIC: Arthur Henry Messiter, 1883
Text © 2010 Michael Morgan (admin. Congregational Ministries Publishing, Presbyterian Church (U.S.A.))

MARION
SM with refrain

366 Love Divine, All Loves Excelling

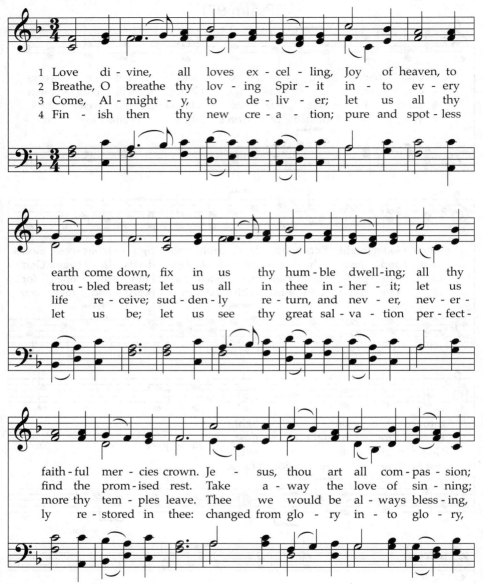

1 Love di - vine, all loves ex - cel - ling, Joy of heaven, to
2 Breathe, O breathe thy lov - ing Spir - it in - to ev - ery
3 Come, Al - might - y, to de - liv - er; let us all thy
4 Fin - ish then thy new cre - a - tion; pure and spot - less

earth come down, fix in us thy hum - ble dwell-ing; all thy
trou - bled breast; let us all in thee in - her - it; let us
life re - ceive; sud - den - ly re - turn, and nev - er, nev - er,
let us be; let us see thy great sal - va - tion per - fect-

faith - ful mer - cies crown. Je - sus, thou art all com - pas - sion;
find the prom - ised rest. Take a - way the love of sin - ning;
more thy tem - ples leave. Thee we would be al - ways bless - ing,
ly re - stored in thee: changed from glo - ry in - to glo - ry,

This text and this tune occur in almost all English-language hymnals (though not always together). The transforming power of love motivates the unending praise of the life to come, and this fine Welsh tune (whose name means "delightful") gives us a foretaste of endless song.

TEXT: Charles Wesley, 1747, alt.
MUSIC: Rowland Hugh Prichard, 1831, alt.

HYFRYDOL
8.7.8.7.D

pure, un - bound - ed love thou art; vis - it us with
Al - pha and O - me - ga be; end of faith, as
serve thee as thy hosts a - bove, pray, and praise thee
till in heaven we take our place, till we cast our

thy sal - va - tion; en - ter ev - ery trem - bling heart.
its be - gin - ning, set our hearts at lib - er - ty.
with - out ceas - ing, glo - ry in thy per - fect love.
crowns be - fore thee, lost in won - der, love, and praise.

367 Come, Ye Thankful People, Come

1 Come, ye thank-ful peo-ple, come; raise the song of har-vest home.
2 All the world is God's own field, fruit in thank-ful praise to yield,
3 For the Lord our God shall come, and shall take the har-vest home;
4 E-ven so, Lord, quick-ly come to thy fi-nal har-vest home.

All is safe-ly gath-ered in, ere the win-ter storms be-gin.
wheat and tares to-geth-er sown, un-to joy or sor-row grown.
from each field shall in that day all of-fens-es purge a-way;
Gath-er thou thy peo-ple in, free from sor-row, free from sin,

God, our Mak-er, doth pro-vide for our wants to be sup-plied.
First the blade, and then the ear, then the full corn shall ap-pear.
give the an-gels charge at last in the fire the tares to cast,
there for-ev-er pu-ri-fied, in thy pres-ence to a-bide:

Come to God's own tem-ple, come; raise the song of har-vest home.
Lord of har-vest, grant that we whole-some grain and pure may be.
but the fruit-ful ears to store in God's gar-ner ev-er-more.
come, with all thine an-gels, come; raise the glo-rious har-vest home!

Despite its familiar Thanksgiving associations, the real concern of this text is to recall the harvest imagery Jesus used to describe the fulfillment of God's sovereignty. The tune name commemorates the royal chapel where the composer was organist for forty-seven years.

TEXT: Henry Alford, 1844, alt.
MUSIC: George Job Elvey, 1858

ST. GEORGE'S WINDSOR
7.7.7.7.D

We Fall Down

368

This praise song is based on the imagery of Revelation 4:8–11, which draws on Isaiah 6:3. This scene of heavenly worship is also part of well-known hymns such as "Holy, Holy, Holy! Lord God Almighty!" (no. 1, stanza 2) and "Love Divine, All Loves Excelling" (no. 366, stanza 4).

TEXT and MUSIC: Chris Tomlin, 1998
Text and Music © 1998 Worshiptogether.com Songs (admin. EMICMGPublishing.com)

WE FALL DOWN
Irregular

369 Blessing and Honor

1 Bless - ing and hon - or and glo - ry and power,
2 Let all the heav - ens sound forth Je - sus' name;
3 Ev - er as - cend - ing the song and the joy,
4 Give we the glo - ry and praise to the Lamb;

wis - dom and rich - es and strength ev - er - more,
let all the earth sing his glo - ry and fame.
ev - er de - scend - ing the love from on high;
take we the robe and the harp and the palm;

be to the Lamb who our bat - tle has won,
O - cean and moun - tain, stream, for - est, and flower
bless - ing and hon - or and glo - ry and praise:
sing we the song of the Lamb that was slain,

whose are the king - dom, the crown, and the throne.
ech - o these prais - es and tell of God's power.
this is the theme of the hymns that we raise.
dy - ing in weak - ness but ris - ing to reign.

Fittingly titled "The Song of the Lamb" by its author, this hymn is a paraphrase and expansion of Revelation 5:12. It is set here to a resonant French tune of a kind that flourished in the transition from the older chant style to the harmonies and rhythms of modern hymns.

TEXT: Horatius Bonar, 1866, alt.
MUSIC: Paris *Antiphoner*, 1681; harm. La Feillée's *Méthode du plain-chant*, 1808

O QUANTA QUALIA
10.10.10.10
(this tune in a lower key, 503)

This Is My Father's World 370

1 This is my Fa-ther's world, and to my lis-tening ears all
2 This is my Fa-ther's world. O, let me ne'er for - get that

na - ture sings, and round me rings the mu - sic of the spheres.
though the wrong seems oft so strong, God is the rul - er yet.

This is my Fa-ther's world; I rest me in the thought of
This is my Fa-ther's world. The bat - tle is not done: Je -

rocks and trees, of skies and seas, his hand the won-ders wrought.
sus who died shall be sat - is - fied, and earth and heaven be one.

When pastor of a Presbyterian church in Lockport, New York, the author of this text referred to his morning walks as "going out to see my Father's world." The tune created for these words is based on an English melody the composer learned from his mother when he was a boy.

TEXT: Maltbie D. Babcock, 1901
MUSIC: Franklin L. Sheppard, 1915; harm. Edward Shippen Barnes, 1926, alt.

TERRA BEATA
SMD

371 New Songs of Celebration Render
(Psalm 98)

1 New songs of cel - e - bra - tion ren - der to God who
2 Joy - ful - ly, heart - i - ly re - sound - ing, let ev - ery
3 Riv - ers and seas and tor - rents roar - ing, hon - or the

has great won - ders done; love sits en - throned in age - less
in - stru - ment and voice peal out the praise of grace a -
Lord with wild ac - claim; moun - tains and stones, look up a -

splen - dor; come and a - dore the might - y One.
bound - ing, call - ing the whole world to re - joice.
dor - ing, and find a voice to praise God's name.

God has made known the great sal - va - tion which all the
Trum - pets and or - gans, set in mo - tion such sounds as
Righ - teous, com - mand - ing, ev - er glo - rious, prais - es be

This Genevan tune (created for Psalm 118 but also used for Psalm 98 in the 1562 edition of the Genevan Psalter) has worked successfully with several English texts. Here it sets a 20th-century paraphrase of Psalm 98 that owes much of its effectiveness to the author's skill with multisyllabic words.

TEXT: Erik Routley, 1972, alt.
MUSIC: Louis Bourgeois, 1543, rev. 1551
Text © 1974 Hope Publishing Company

RENDEZ À DIEU
9.8.9.8.D

O for a World 372

Everything longed for in this text is a reminder of how far our present world is from what God wants. Yet this is not just wishful thinking; it is a call to action, a summons to participate in the fulfillment of God's desire for all earth's people to live in radical *shalom*.

TEXT: Miriam Therese Winter, 1987
MUSIC: Carl Gotthelf Gläser, 1828; arr. Lowell Mason, 1839
Text © 1990 Medical Mission Sisters

AZMON
CM

373 O Day of Peace

1 O day of peace that dim-ly shines through all our
2 Then shall the wolf dwell with the lamb, nor shall the

hopes and prayers and dreams, guide us to jus - tice, truth, and
fierce de - vour the small; as beasts and cat - tle calm-ly

love, de-liv-ered from our self - ish schemes. May swords of hate
graze, a lit-tle child shall lead them all. Then en - e-mies

fall from our hands, our hearts from en - vy find re-lease, till by God's
shall learn to love, all crea-tures find their true ac-cord; the hope of

grace our war-ring world shall see Christ's prom-ised reign of peace.
peace shall be ful - filled, for all the earth shall know the Lord.

Guitar chords do not correspond with keyboard harmony.

This text on peace was created to offer non-nationalistic words for a popular British tune. The first stanza depicts *pax*, a mode of peace focused on ending conflict, and the second (based on Isaiah 11:6–9) describes *shalom*, the condition of living in harmony and mutual good will.

TEXT: Carl P. Daw Jr., 1982
MUSIC: C. Hubert H. Parry, 1916; harm. Charles H. Webb, 1987
Text © 1982 Hope Publishing Company
Music Harm. © 1989 The United Methodist Publishing House (admin. The Copyright Company)

JERUSALEM
LMD

O Holy City, Seen of John 374

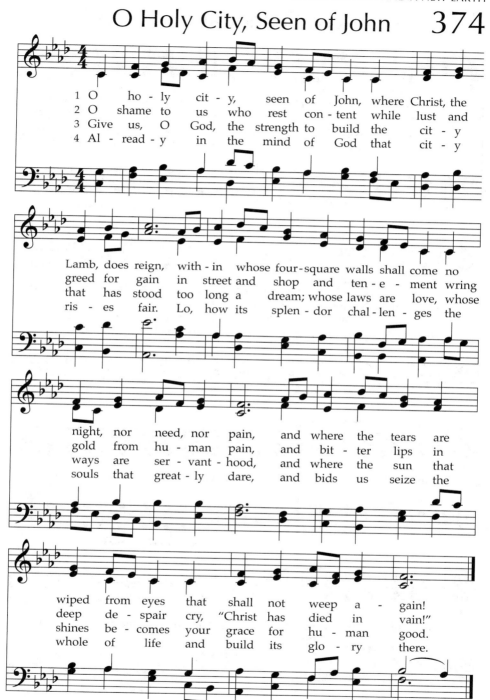

1 O ho-ly cit-y, seen of John, where Christ, the
2 O shame to us who rest con-tent while lust and
3 Give us, O God, the strength to build the cit-y
4 Al-read-y in the mind of God that cit-y

Lamb, does reign, with-in whose four-square walls shall come no
greed for gain in street and shop and ten-e-ment wring
that has stood too long a dream; whose laws are love, whose
ris-es fair. Lo, how its splen-dor chal-len-ges the

night, nor need, nor pain, and where the tears are
gold from hu-man pain, and bit-ter lips in
ways are ser-vant-hood, and where the sun that
souls that great-ly dare, and bids us seize the

wiped from eyes that shall not weep a-gain!
deep de-spair cry, "Christ has died in vain!"
shines be-comes your grace for hu-man good.
whole of life and build its glo-ry there.

Unlike texts that treat the heavenly Jerusalem as a goal for the life to come, this hymn regards John's vision as a challenge to work here and now for the accomplishment of God's purposes on earth. The shape note tune provides an effective setting for this stirring text.

TEXT: Walter Russell Bowie, 1909, alt.
MUSIC: Wyeth's *Repository of Sacred Music*, 1813; harm. C. Winfred Douglas, 1940
Music Harm. © 1943, 1961, 1985 Church Pension Fund

MORNING SONG
8.6.8.6.8.6
(alternate harmonization, 653)

375 Shall We Gather at the River

1 Shall we gath-er at the riv-er, where bright an-gel feet have trod,
2 On the mar-gin of the riv-er, wash-ing up its sil-ver spray,
3 Ere we reach the shin-ing riv-er, lay we ev-ery bur-den down;
4 Soon we'll reach the shin-ing riv-er; soon our pil-grim-age will cease;

with its crys-tal tide for-ev-er flow-ing by the throne of God?
we will walk and wor-ship ev-er, all the hap-py gold-en day.
grace our spir-its will de-liv-er, and pro-vide a robe and crown.
soon our hap-py hearts will quiv-er with the mel-o-dy of peace.

Refrain

Yes, we'll gath-er at the riv-er, the beau-ti-ful, the beau-ti-ful riv-er;

gath-er with the saints at the riv-er that flows by the throne of God.

A Baptist pastor wrote this hymn while seated at his parlor organ. Created as an alternative to gloomy "river of death" hymns, it is a celebration of the "pure river of water of life, clear as crystal, proceeding out of the throne of God and of the Lamb" (Revelation 22:1 KJV).

TEXT and MUSIC: Robert Lowry, 1864

HANSON PLACE
8.7.8.7 with refrain

When All Is Ended

376

Capo 3: (D) (G) (C) (G) (Em) (D) (G)
F Bb Eb Bb Gm F Bb

1 When all is end-ed, time and trou-bles past,
2 As in the night, when light-ning flick-ers free,
3 A-gainst all hope, our wea-ry times have known
4 Then do not cheat the poor, who long for bread,
5 With earth-y faith we sing a song of heaven:
6 With all cre-a-tion, pain and an-ger past,

(D) (Bm) (Em) (B) (Am) (B)
F Dm Gm D Cm D

shall all be mend-ed, sin and death out-cast?
and gives a glimpse of dis-tant hill and tree,
wars end-ed, peace de-clared, com-pas-sion shown,
with dream-worlds in the sky or in the head,
all life ful-filled, all loved, all wrong for-given.
e-vil ex-haust-ed, love su-preme at last,

(Em) (C) (D) (G) (C) (Am) (Em)
Gm Eb F Bb Eb Cm Gm

In hope we sing, and hope to sing at last:
each flash of good dis-clos-es what will be:
great days of free-dom, ty-rants o-ver-thrown:
but sing of slaves set free, and chil-dren fed:
Christ is our sign of hope, for Christ is risen:
a-live in God, we'll sing an un-sur-passed

(D) (G) (D) (Em) (Am7) (Dsus) (D) (G)
F Bb F Gm Cm7 Fsus F Bb

Al-le-lu-ia! Al-le-lu-ia!

Guitar chords do not correspond with keyboard harmony.

This tune, named for Mahatma Gandhi's guru, was created for the text at no. 641, but its melody inspired the present text by evoking an image of God bringing all things to a good end in spite of evil, a hope based on Christ's Resurrection as reflected in acts of peace and justice.

TEXT: Brian Wren, 1988
MUSIC: William P. Rowan, 1985
Text © 1989 Hope Publishing Company
Music © 1993 Selah Publishing Co., Inc.

YOGANANDA
10.10.10 with alleluias
(alternate tune: ENGELBERG)

377 I Want to Walk as a Child of the Light

1 I want to walk as a child of the light. I want to follow
2 I want to see the brightness of God. I want to look at
3 I'm looking for the coming of Christ. I want to be with

Jesus. God set the stars to give light to the world. The
Jesus. Clear Sun of righteousness, shine on my path, and
Jesus. When we have run with patience the race, we

Refrain

star of my life is Jesus.
show me the way to the Father. In him there is no darkness at
shall know the joy of Jesus.

all. The night and the day are both alike. The Lamb is the

The author/composer of this unrhymed hymn regards it as a meditation and prayer deeply rooted in many scriptures, most connected with the theme of light: Genesis 1:17; Psalm 139:12; Isaiah 60:19; Malachi 4:2; John 14:8; Ephesians 5:8; Hebrews 12:1–2; 1 John 1:5; Revelation 21:23.

TEXT and MUSIC: Kathleen Thomerson, 1966
Text and Music © 1970, 1975 Celebration

HOUSTON
10.7.10.8 with refrain

light of the cit-y of God. Shine in my heart, Lord Je - sus.

We Wait the Peaceful Kingdom 378

1 We wait the peace-ful king-dom, when wolf and lamb shall lie
2 Where is the peace-ful king-dom? When will this new day start?
3 When wars of des - o - la - tion and hate come to an end,
4 That lit - tle child shall lead us to walk the cho - sen way,

in gen - tle - ness and friend-ship with-out a fear or sigh,
We long for peace and com - fort to reign with - in each heart.
when na - tion meets with na - tion and calls the oth - er "friend,"
to share the peace - ful king - dom, to greet God's new-born day.

when li - on shall be graz - ing, when snake shall nev - er strike;
Yet not in our lives on - ly, nor sim - ply in our home:
still peace in all its full - ness will on - ly have be - gun;
The child born in a sta - ble is sent to break our chains,

a lit - tle child shall lead us both strong and weak a - like.
we pray that all cre - a - tion will one day find sha - lom.
sha - lom for all cre - a - tion be - gins with jus - tice done.
to bring through word and ta - ble the day when jus - tice reigns.

This text paraphrases Isaiah 11:6–9 in the first stanza, then reflects on that passage in widening frames of reference from self to all creation and identifies its "little child" with one born at Bethlehem. The tune is named for the composer's sister, his first piano teacher.

TEXT: Kathleen R. Moore, 2010
MUSIC: Hal H. Hopson, 1983
Text © 2010 The Hymn Society (admin. Hope Publishing Company)
Music © 1983 Hope Publishing Company

MERLE'S TUNE
7.6.7.6.D

379 We Shall Overcome

1 We shall o-ver-come; we shall o-ver-come;
2 We'll walk hand in hand; we'll walk hand in hand;
3 We shall live in peace; we shall live in peace;
4 We are not a-fraid; we are not a-fraid;
5 God will see us through; God will see us through;

we shall o-ver-come some-day.
we'll walk hand in hand some-day.
we shall live in peace some-day.
we are not a-fraid to-day.
God will see us through to-day.

Refrain

O, deep in my heart I do be-

lieve we shall o-ver-come some-day!

Though now associated primarily with the Civil Rights Movement of the mid-20th century, this spiritual most likely dates from the days of the slave trade; and similarities with the tune SICILIAN MARINERS (see no. 546) suggest that it might have been a worksong aboard slave ships.

TEXT: African American spiritual
MUSIC: African American spiritual; arr. William Farley Smith, 1986
Music Arr. © 1989 The United Methodist Publishing House (admin. The Copyright Company)

WE SHALL OVERCOME
Irregular

God Is Our Help, Refuge, and Strength

380

하나님은 피난처요
(Psalm 46)

Refrain / 후렴

God is our help, ref-uge, and strength. In trou-bling times, we will not fear.
만 군 의 주 하 나 님 이 우 리 함 께 계 시 리 니

God is our help, ref-uge, and strength. In trou-bling times, we will not fear.
야 - 곱 의 하 나 님 은 우 리 들 의 피 난 처 라

PSALM 46

Refrain

1 God is our refuge and strength,
   a very present help in trouble.
2 **Therefore we will not fear, though the earth be moved,**
   and though the mountains be toppled into the depths of the sea;
3 though its waters rage and foam,
   and though the mountains tremble at its tumult.
   The LORD of hosts is with us;
   the God of Jacob is our stronghold. *Refrain*
4 There is a river whose streams make glad the city of God,
   the holy habitation of the Most High.
5 **God is in the midst of the city;**
   it shall not be overthrown;
   God shall help it at the break of day.
6 The nations make much ado, and the realms are shaken;
   God has spoken, and the earth shall melt away.
7 **The LORD of hosts is with us;**
   the God of Jacob is our stronghold. *Refrain*
8 Come now and look upon the works of the LORD,
   what awesome things God has done on earth.
9 **It is the LORD who makes war to cease in all the world,**
   who breaks the bow, and shatters the spear, and burns the shields with fire.
10 "Be still, then, and know that I am God;
   I will be exalted among the nations;
   I will be exalted in the earth."
11 **The LORD of hosts is with us;**
   the God of Jacob is our stronghold. *Refrain*

The English refrain consists of a twice-sung condensed paraphrase of Psalm 46:1–3. It works well, either alone or with a responsive reading, because it states so concisely the general theme illustrated by the list of natural and political calamities making up the rest of the psalm.

MUSIC: Seung Nam Kim, 2000
Music © 2002 Seung Nam Kim
Responsive Reading © 1993 The Order of St. Benedict (admin. The Liturgical Press)

GOD IS OUR HELP
LM

381 Arise, O Lord Our God, Arise

(Psalm 132)

1 A - rise, O Lord our God, a - rise and
2 Your gra - cious cov - enant, Lord, ful - fill; turn
3 Your Zi - on you have cho - sen, Lord, and

en - ter now in - to your rest; O let this house be
not a - way from us your face; es - tab - lish here Mes -
you have said, "I love her well, this is my con - stant

your a - bode, for - ev - er with your pres - ence blest.
si - ah's throne and let him reign with - in this place.
rest - ing place, and here will I de - light to dwell."

This paraphrase uses selected verses from Psalm 132, beginning with a petition for God's presence in the Temple, which in turn becomes the throne of the promised Messiah. The third stanza balances the first with the divine assurance that Jerusalem is the place where God dwells.

TEXT: *The New Metrical Version of the Psalms*, 1909, alt.
MUSIC: Attr. Freeman Lewis, 1814; harm. John Leon Hooker, 1984
Music Harm. © 1984 John Leon Hooker

BOURBON
LM

Heaven Is Singing for Joy

El cielo canta alegría

382

1 Heav - en is sing - ing for joy, al - le - lu - ia,
2 Heav - en is sing - ing for joy, al - le - lu - ia,
3 Heav - en is sing - ing for joy, al - le - lu - ia,

1 El cie - lo can - ta a - le - grí - a, ¡a - le - lu - ya!,

for in your life and in mine is shin - ing the glo - ry of God.
for your life and mine u - nite in the love of our God.
for your life and mine will al - ways bear wit - ness to God.

por-que en tu vi-da y la mí - a bri - lla la glo - ria de Dios.

Refrain / Estribillo

Al - le - lu - ia, al - le - lu - ia!

¡A - le - lu - ya, a - le - lu - ya!

Al - le - lu - ia, al - le - lu - ia!

¡A - le - lu - ya, a - le - lu - ya!

2 *El cielo canta alegría, ¡aleluya!,*
   porque a tu vida y la mía
   las une el amor de Dios. Estribillo

3 *El cielo canta alegría, ¡aleluya!,*
   porque tu vida y la mía
   proclamarán al Señor. Estribillo

Written in 1958 for a picnic of theological students in Argentina, this piece represents the first Christian hymn in the 20th century to use Latin American folk music. The text is based on Jesus' saying that heaven rejoices at the repentance of each sinner (Luke 15:7).

TEXT and MUSIC: Pablo Sosa, 1958
Text and Music © 1958 GIA Publications, Inc.

ALEGRÍA
7.4.6.8 with refrain

383 Dream On, Dream On
꿈을 꾸세 평화의 자녀

Capo 3: (Am) / Cm

1 Dream on, dream on, chil-dren of peace,
2 Hope on, hope on, Eas - ter peo - ple:
3 Mount up, mount up, like an ea - gle,

till on earth God's king - dom come.
beyond the cross, a dawn - ing sun.
to the heights, be - yond the clouds.

Wolf and lamb will feed to - geth - er; lions like
Christ, our peace, broke down all bar - riers: na - tion,
Strife and sor - row shall not stop you; pain and

ox - en will eat straw. Dust shall be the
cul - ture, tribe, and clan. Rec - on - cil - ing
tears shall lose their power. E - ven though the

This future-oriented Korean text draws on the promises of a number of biblical passages. The first stanza is based primarily on Isaiah 11:6–9. The second stanza includes references to Ephesians 2:14–16 and Colossians 1:20, while the third stanza uses the images of Isaiah 40:29–31.

TEXT: Hae Jong Kim, 1992, alt.
MUSIC: Sunkyung Lee, 2001
Text and Music © 2001 The United Methodist Publishing House (admin. The Copyright Company)

DREAM ON
Irregular

KOREAN

1 꿈을 꾸세 평화의 자녀
주의 나라 이르도록
양과 늑대 함-께 놀--고
사자들도 풀-을 뜯으며
독사들도 흙을 먹고
상처주지 않는곳
서로 다른 모-든 백-성
평화롭게 살리라

2 소망하세 부활의 자녀
어둠후에 아침오리
평화주신 구-주 예--수
우리장벽 모-두 허무사
하나님과 화목하며
하나되게 하셨네
정의평화 자-유 주신
참된 소망 주예수

3 올라가세 독수리같이
구름너머 하늘높이
슬픔근심 사-라지--고
눈물고통 모-두 이기리
피곤하여 넘어져도
주가 새 힘 주시리
걸어가세 달-려가-세
쓰러지지 않으리

384 Soon and Very Soon

1 Soon and ver - y soon we are going to see the King.
2 No more cry - ing there: we are going to see the King.
3 No more dy - ing there: we are going to see the King.
4 Soon and ver - y soon we are going to see the King.

Soon and ver - y soon we are going to see the King.
No more cry - ing there: we are going to see the King.
No more dy - ing there: we are going to see the King.
Soon and ver - y soon we are going to see the King.

Soon and ver - y soon we are going to see the King.
No more cry - ing there: we are going to see the King.
No more dy - ing there: we are going to see the King.
Soon and ver - y soon we are going to see the King.

Hal - le - lu - jah, hal - le - lu - jah, we're going to see the King!

This spirited African American gospel hymn draws on John's vision of the new heaven and the new earth in Revelation 21:3–4, with its wonderful promise that God will wipe away the tears from all eyes, that death will be no longer, and that there will be no more mourning or pain.

TEXT and MUSIC: Andraé Crouch, 1976
Text and Music © 1976 Crouch Music and Bud John Songs (admin. EMICMGPublishing.com)

SOON AND VERY SOON
12.12.12 with refrain

All People That on Earth Do Dwell 385
(Psalm 100)

1 All peo-ple that on earth do dwell, sing to the
2 Know that the Lord is God in-deed; with-out our
3 O en-ter then his gates with praise; ap-proach with
4 For why? The Lord our God is good; his mer-cy

Lord with cheer-ful voice; him serve with mirth, his
aid he did us make; we are his folk; he
joy his courts un-to; praise, laud, and bless his
is for-ev-er sure; his truth at all times

praise forth tell. Come ye be-fore him and re-joice.
doth us feed, and for his sheep he doth us take.
name al-ways, for it is seem-ly so to do.
firm-ly stood, and shall from age to age en-dure.

In a pairing that began in 1561, this paraphrase of Psalm 100 by a Scot is set to a tune that a French composer originally created for Psalm 134 in the Genevan Psalter of 1551. They have appeared together in nearly every comprehensive English-language hymnal since then.

TEXT: William Kethe, 1560
MUSIC: Attr. Louis Bourgeois, 1551
OLD HUNDREDTH
LM

386 Come, Worship God
(Psalm 95)

1 Come, wor-ship God, who is wor-thy of hon - or;
2 Ruled by your might are the heights of the moun - tains;
3 We are your peo - ple, the sheep of your pas - ture;
4 Now let us lis - ten, for you speak a - mong us;

en - ter God's pres - ence with thanks and a song!
held in your hands are the depths of the earth.
you are our Mak - er, and to you we pray.
o - pen our hearts to re - ceive what you say.

You are the rock of your peo - ple's sal - va - tion
Yours is the sea, yours the land, for you made them,
Glad - ly we kneel in o - be - dience be - fore you;
Peace be to all who re - mem - ber your good - ness,

to whom our ju - bi - lant prais - es be - long.
God a - bove all gods, who gave us our birth.
great is the one whom we wor - ship this day!
trust in your word, and re - joice in your way!

Psalm 95, often called *Venite* from its first word in Latin, has long served as an opening canticle in the worship of Western Christianity. John Calvin found here two reasons to praise God: for sustaining the created world and for adopting the church into a gracious relationship.

TEXT: Michael Perry, 1980
MUSIC: *Paris Antiphoner*, 1681; harm. La Feillée's *Méthode du plain-chant*, 1808
Text © 1980 The Jubilate Group (admin. Hope Publishing Company)

O QUANTA QUALIA
11.10.11.10
(this tune in a higher key, 369)

Let Us Come to Worship God 387

咱著敬拜主上帝

1 Let us come to wor-ship God; let us come to wor-ship God;
2 Let us sing and praise the Lord; let us sing and praise the Lord;

1 咱 著 敬 拜 主 上 帝, 咱 著 敬 拜 主 上 帝,
2 咱 著 謳 咾 主 上 帝, 咱 著 謳 咾 主 上 帝,

bless the ho - ly name; en - ter God's house with thanks and rev - erence,
make a joy - ful noise; sing to the Rock of our sal - va - tion,

他 聖 名 至 大; 著 用 虔 誠 感 謝 入 聖 殿,
著 歡 喜 唱 歌; 著 稱 讚 拯 救 咱 的 石 磐,

for the Lord is good; God's love en - dures for - e'er.
for the Lord is full of grace and King of all.

因 為 他 大 慈 愛 到 永 遠 無 息.
萬 國 君 王, 主 上 帝, 至 尊 至 大.

This hymn of praise was created to employ a tune shared by three aboriginal Taiwanese tribes. The text is based on Psalm 100:4–5 and Psalm 95:1, 3. This hymn is especially appropriate as a processional incorporating joyful movement and accompanied by drums and small untuned bells.

TEXT: I-to Loh, 1987
MUSIC: Taiwanese melody; transcr. Gadu Masegseg, 1987
Text © 1990 I-to Loh (admin. GIA Publications, Inc.)

HIAO HOIAN
7.7.5.9.11

388 Come All You People

Uyai mose

This short gathering song (based on a text adapted from Psalm 95:6) is a great favorite among children in Zimbabwe, and it is frequently used as a processional song for worship. The choir enters singing, the congregation picks up their excitement, and soon all are singing.

TEXT: Alexander Gondo, 20th cent.; transcr. I-to Loh, 1986
MUSIC: Alexander Gondo, 20th cent.; arr. John L. Bell, 1994
Music Arr. © 1994 WGRG, Iona Community (admin. GIA Publications, Inc.)

UYAI MOSE
5.6.5.6.5.6.7

389 Come and Sing the Praise of the Lord

Hal'luhu b'zilz'le shama (Psalm 150)

Come and sing the praise of the Lord: sing
Ha - l' - lu - hu, ha - l' - lu - hu b' -

hal - le - lu - jah! Come and sing the
zil - z' - le sha - ma. Ha - l' - lu - hu,

praise of the Lord: sing hal - le - lu - jah!
ha - l' - lu - hu b' - zil - z' - le t'ru - ah.

Let all that lives, all that has breath, sing the
Kol ha - n'sha - mah t' - ha - lel yah, ha -

praise of God, hal - le - lu - jah! Let all that lives,
l' - lu - yah, ha - l' - lu - yah. Kol ha - n'sha - mah

all that has breath, sing the praise of God.
t' - ha - lel yah, ha - l' - lu - yah.

HEBREW

הללוהו בצלצלי־שמע הללוהו בצלי תרועה

כל הנשמה תהלל יה הללו־יה

This paraphrase of Psalm 150:6 gains much conviction by being set to an Israeli melody. Similarly, the equivalence of the phrase "Praise the Lord" and the familiar word "Hallelujah" becomes especially obvious when the Hebrew version is heard in alternation with the English text.

TEXT: From Psalm 150
MUSIC: Israeli melody; arr. John L. Bell, 2008
Music Arr. © 2008 WGRG, Iona Community (admin. GIA Publications, Inc.)

HAL'LUHU
Irregular

Praise, Praise, Praise the Lord! 390

Louez le Seigneur!

This song may be repeated, adding a vocal part on each repetition: melody (alto) alone; melody + tenor; melody + lower parts; all voices.

This brief song of praise comes from Cameroon, where it is used primarily as a processional song with rhythmic movement and increasing harmonies. The organizing aesthetic here is repetition, experienced as a means of intensification expressed in multiple languages.

TEXT: Cameroon song
MUSIC: Cameroon melody; arr. Ralph M. Johnson, 1994
Text and Music © 1994 earthsongs

LOUEZ LE SEIGNEUR
Irregular

This Is the Day

Este es el día
(Psalm 118)

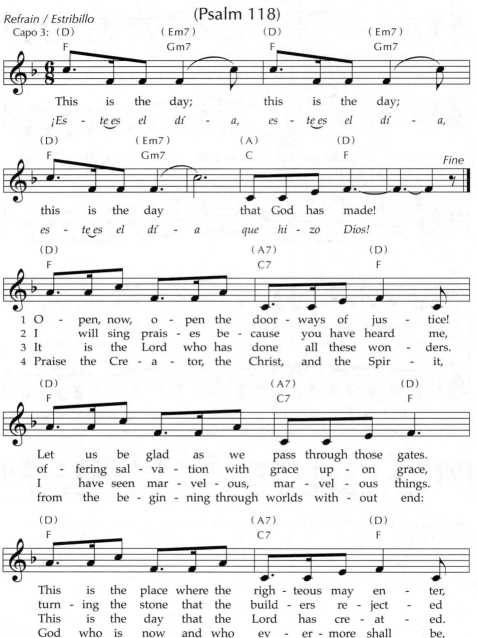

Refrain / Estribillo

Capo 3: (D)

This is the day; this is the day;
¡Es - te es el dí - a, es - te es el dí - a,

this is the day that God has made!
es - te es el dí - a que hi - zo Dios!

1 O - pen, now, o - pen the door - ways of jus - tice!
2 I will sing prais - es be - cause you have heard me,
3 It is the Lord who has done all these won - ders.
4 Praise the Cre - a - tor, the Christ, and the Spir - it,

Let us be glad as we pass through those gates.
of - fering sal - va - tion with grace up - on grace,
I have seen mar - vel - ous, mar - vel - ous things.
from the be - gin - ning through worlds with - out end:

This is the place where the righ - teous may en - ter,
turn - ing the stone that the build - ers re - ject - ed
This is the day that the Lord has cre - at - ed.
God who is now and who ev - er - more shall be,

The author/composer has incorporated elements of his Argentinian culture in this dynamic paraphrase of Psalm 118. In particular, the melodic patterns of the refrain are intended to suggest the way cowboys (*gauchos*) greet each other when they ride out to their work in the morning.

TEXT: Pablo Sosa, 1983; trans. Mary Louise Bringle, 2006
MUSIC: Pablo Sosa, 1983; arr. Alfred V. Fedak, 2012
Text and Music © 1983 GIA Publications, Inc.
English Trans. © 2006 GIA Publications, Inc.

ESTE ES EL DÍA
11.10.11.10 with refrain

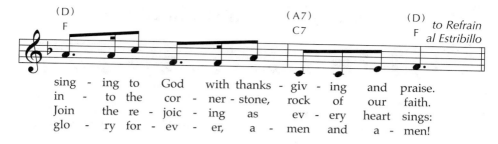

sing - ing to God with thanks - giv - ing and praise.
in - to the cor - ner - stone, rock of our faith.
Join the re - joic - ing as ev - ery heart sings:
glo - ry for - ev - er, a - men and a - men!

SPANISH

1 Ábranme las puertas de la justicia,
y entraré alabando a mi Dios.
Esta es la puerta que Dios nos ha dado,
todos los justos por ella entrarán.

2 Voy a alabarte porque me has oído
y porque fuiste mi gran salvación.
Esa piedra que todos despreciaron
resulta ahora ser fundamental.

3 Es el Señor quien ha hecho todo esto;
¡qué maravilla poder verlo hoy!
Este es el día que el Señor ha hecho,
con alegría gocemos en Él.

4 Al Padre, Hijo y Espíritu Santo
demos la gloria por la eternidad;
como al principio, tal cual es ahora
y lo será para siempre jamás.

Jesus, We Are Here 392

Jesu, tawa pano

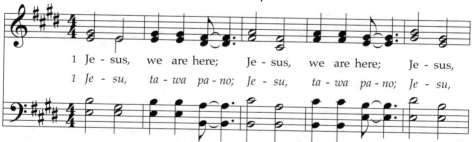

1 Je - sus, we are here; Je - sus, we are here; Je - sus,
1 Je - su, ta - wa pa - no; Je - su, ta - wa pa - no; Je - su,

we are here; we are here for you.
ta - wa pa - no; ta - wa pa - no, mu zi - ta re - nyu.

Leader: Wel - come, Je - sus.
Mam - bo Je - su.

2 Savior,... 3 Teacher,... 4 Spirit,...

When coming to worship involves long and possibly dangerous travel, "we are here" voices a powerful commitment as well as a desire to build community with those who have gathered. Some of that meaning can be grasped if this song is sung in parts, especially in the original Shona.

TEXT and MUSIC: Patrick Matsikenyiri, 1990
Text and Music © 1990, 1996 Patrick Matsikenyiri (admin. General Board of Global Ministries t/a GBGMusik)

JESUS, TAWA PANO
Irregular

393 O Day of Rest and Gladness

1 O day of rest and glad - ness, O day of joy and light,
2 On you, at earth's cre - a - tion the light first had its birth;
3 On you, God's peo - ple, meet - ing, the Ho - ly Scrip-ture hear,

O balm for care and sad - ness, most beau - ti - ful, most bright;
on you, for our sal - va - tion Christ rose from depths of earth;
Christ's liv - ing pres - ence greet - ing, through bread and wine made near.

on you, the high and low - ly, through a - ges joined in tune,
on you, our Lord vic - to - rious sent Spir - it forth from heaven.
New grac - es ev - er gain - ing from this our day of rest,

sing "Ho - ly, ho - ly, ho - ly" to the great God tri - une.
And thus on you, most glo - rious, a tri - ple light was given.
we reach the rest re - main - ing to spir - its of the blest.

In this text the first day of the week represents a threefold commemoration of Creation, Resurrection, and Pentecost—each an encounter with Trinitarian activity centered on one of the Three Persons. The tune name recalls the secular German song adapted for use with several hymns.

TEXT: Stanzas 1–2, Christopher Wordsworth, 1862, alt.; stanza 3, Charles P. Price, 1980, alt.   ES FLOG EIN KLEINS WALDVÖGELEIN
MUSIC: Memmingen ms., 17th cent.; harm. George Ratcliffe Woodward, 1904   7.6.7.6.D
Text St. 3 © 1985 Charles P. Price

Christ Is Made the Sure Foundation 394

1 Christ is made the sure foun-da - tion, Christ the head and
2 To this tem - ple, where we call you, come, O Lord of
3 Here be-stow on all your ser - vants what they seek from
4 Laud and hon - or to the Fa - ther, laud and hon - or

cor - ner - stone, cho - sen of the Lord and pre - cious,
hosts, and stay; come, with all your lov - ing - kind - ness;
you to gain; what they gain from you, for - ev - er
to the Son, laud and hon - or to the Spir - it,

bind - ing all the church in one; ho - ly Zi - on's
hear your peo - ple as we pray, and your full - est
with the bless - ed to re - tain; and here - af - ter
ev - er three and ev - er one: one in might and

help for - ev - er, and our con - fi - dence a - lone.
ben - e - dic - tion shed with - in these walls to - day.
in your glo - ry ev - er - more with you to reign.
one in glo - ry while un - end - ing a - ges run!

Guitar chords do not correspond with keyboard harmony.

Although this ancient text has often been used at church dedications, the first stanza clearly refers to the people of God and the second to the place where they meet. The stately and soaring tune is aptly named for the edifice where the composer served as organist and is buried.

TEXT: Latin, 7th cent.; trans. John Mason Neale, 1851, alt.
MUSIC: Henry Purcell, c. 1680; adapt. Ernest Hawkins, 1843

WESTMINSTER ABBEY
8.7.8.7.8.7
(alternate tune: REGENT SQUARE)

395 Blessed Jesus, at Your Word

1 Bless - ed Je - sus, at your word we have come a -
2 All our knowl - edge, sense, and sight lie in deep - est
3 Glo - rious Lord, your - self im - part, Light of Light, from

gain to hear you; let our thoughts and hearts be stirred
dark - ness shroud - ed, till your Spir - it breaks our night,
God pro - ceed - ing. Touch our lips and ears and heart;

and in glow - ing faith be near you. By your gos - pel
fill - ing us with light un - cloud - ed. All good thoughts and
help us by your Spir - it's plead - ing. Hear the cry your

true and ho - ly, teach us, Lord, to love you sole - ly.
all good liv - ing come but by your gra - cious giv - ing.
church now rais - es; hear, and bless our prayers and prais - es.

Originally conceived to be sung before the sermon, this hymn assumes a congregation that assembles regularly, and it needs to be placed near the beginning rather than the end of worship. The simple repetitive tune reinforces the text's sense of receptivity and expectation.

TEXT: Tobias Clausnitzer, 1663; trans. Catherine Winkworth, 1858, alt.
MUSIC: Johann Rudolph Ahle, 1664; harm. Johann Sebastian Bach, 18th cent., alt.

LIEBSTER JESU
7.8.7.8.8.8

Brethren, We Have Met to Worship 396

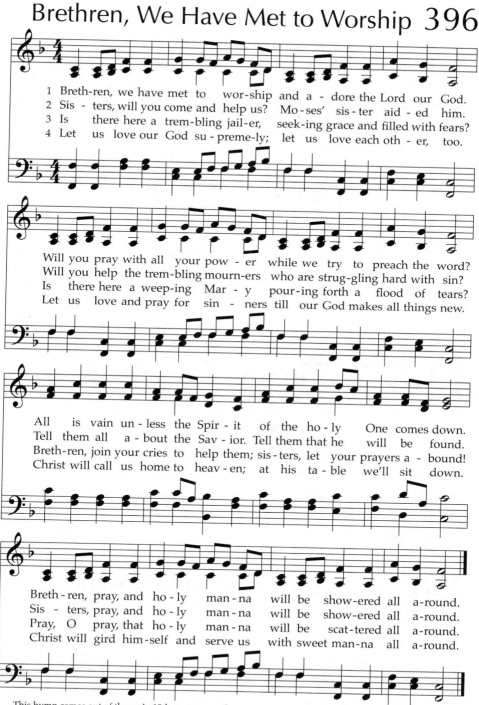

1 Breth-ren, we have met to wor-ship and a-dore the Lord our God.
2 Sis-ters, will you come and help us? Mo-ses' sis-ter aid-ed him.
3 Is there here a trem-bling jail-er, seek-ing grace and filled with fears?
4 Let us love our God su-preme-ly; let us love each oth-er, too.

Will you pray with all your pow-er while we try to preach the word?
Will you help the trem-bling mourn-ers who are strug-gling hard with sin?
Is there here a weep-ing Mar-y pour-ing forth a flood of tears?
Let us love and pray for sin-ners till our God makes all things new.

All is vain un-less the Spir-it of the ho-ly One comes down.
Tell them all a-bout the Sav-ior. Tell them that he will be found.
Breth-ren, join your cries to help them; sis-ters, let your prayers a-bound!
Christ will call us home to heav-en; at his ta-ble we'll sit down.

Breth-ren, pray, and ho-ly man-na will be show-ered all a-round.
Sis-ters, pray, and ho-ly man-na will be show-ered all a-round.
Pray, O pray, that ho-ly man-na will be scat-tered all a-round.
Christ will gird him-self and serve us with sweet man-na all a-round.

This hymn comes out of the early 19th-century southern camp meeting experience, where believers were invited to pray for new converts, often likened to biblical characters such as Paul's jailer (Philippians 1:12–13). As its name shows, the five-note tune was created for this text.

TEXT: George Atkins, 1819, alt.
MUSIC: *Columbian Harmony*, 1825; harm. Alfred V. Fedak, 2011
Music Harm. © 2011 Alfred V. Fedak

HOLY MANNA
8.7.8.7.D
(alternate harmonization, 509)

397 O Look and Wonder

¡Miren qué bueno! (Psalm 133)

Refrain / Estribillo

O look and won - der: how good it is!

¡Mi - ren qué bue - no, qué bue - no es!

1 How good it is when broth-ers dwell in peace with one an - oth - er;
2 How good it is when sis - ters dwell in peace with one an - oth - er,
3 How good it is when all earth's peo - ple dwell in peace to - geth - er:

1 Mi - ren qué bue-no es cuan - do los her - ma - nos es - tán jun - tos,
2 Mi - ren qué bue-no es cuan - do las her - ma - nas es - tán jun - tas,
3 Mi - ren qué bue-no es cuan - do nos reu - ni - mos to - dos jun - tos,

to Refrain / al Estribillo

it is like pre-cious oil when run - ning fresh on Aar - on's beard.
fresh like the morn-ing dew that falls on Zi - on's ho - ly hill.
that is where God will pour the bless - ing, life for - ev - er - more.

es co - mo a - cei - te bue - no de - rra - ma - do so-bre Aa - rón.
se pa - re - ce al ro - cí - o so - bre los mon - tes de Sión.
por - que el Se - ñor ahí man - da vi - da e - ter - na y ben - di - ción.

This infectious song from Argentina paraphrases Psalm 133, with the intention of encouraging a sense of communion among the members of a congregation. The underlying dance/song form is the *chamarrita*, brought to South America in the 1800s by Portuguese settlers from the Azores.

TEXT and MUSIC: Pablo Sosa, 1972
Text and Music © 1972 GIA Publications, Inc.

MIREN QUÉ BUENO
Irregular

398 How Very Good and Pleasant

(Psalm 133)

How ver-y good and pleas-ant when we live in u-ni-ty. It is

This paraphrase draws on Psalm 133, one of the Songs of Ascent sung by pilgrims to Jerusalem. It adapts the original theme of national unity through shared worship on Mount Zion into a celebration of the unity God grants to those who come together in one place for worship.

TEXT and MUSIC: Barbara Boertje, 1997
Text and Music © 1997 Barbara Boertje

HOW VERY GOOD
Irregular

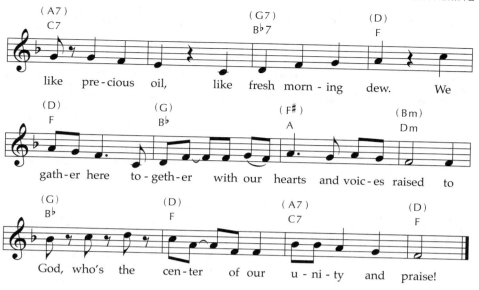

like pre-cious oil, like fresh morn-ing dew. We

gath-er here to-geth-er with our hearts and voic-es raised to

God, who's the cen-ter of our u-ni-ty and praise!

God Welcomes All 399

God wel-comes all, strang-ers and friends;

God's love is strong and it nev-er ends.

This "short song," as the Iona Community calls it, can be especially effective as a means of setting a welcoming tone for a service (especially an ecumenical one). Like most such songs, it needs to be sung several times, adding and improvising harmony with each repetition.

TEXT: John L. Bell, 2008
MUSIC: South African song; transcr. John L. Bell, 2008
Text and Music Transcr. © 2008 WGRG, Iona Community (admin. GIA Publications, Inc.)

THEMBA AMEN
4.4.9

400 I Rejoiced When I Heard Them Say
(Psalm 122)

1 I re-joiced when I heard them say: "Let us
2 Like a tem-ple of u-ni-ty is the
3 It is faith-ful to Is-rael's law, there to
4 For the peace of all na-tions, pray: for God's
5 For the love of my friends and kin I will

go to the house of God." And now our feet are
cit-y, Je-ru-sa-lem. It is there all tribes will
praise the name of God. All the judg-ment seats of
peace with-in your homes. May God's last-ing peace sur-
bless you with signs of peace. For the love of God's own

stand-ing in your gates, O Je-ru-sa-lem!
gath-er, all the tribes of the house of God.
Da-vid were set down in Je-ru-sa-lem.
round us; may it dwell in Je-ru-sa-lem.
peo-ple I will la-bor and pray for you.

Refrain

Sha-lom, sha-lom, the peace of God be here.

Sha-lom, sha-lom, God's jus-tice be ev-er near.

Psalm 122 is among the most joyful of the pilgrimage psalms, because it sings of finally reaching Jerusalem, the home of the Temple. This rejoicing spills over into prayers for peace inspired perhaps by the placename Jerusalem, from roots meaning "to establish peace" (*shalom*).

TEXT and MUSIC: Bernadette Farrell, 1993
Text and Music © 1993 Bernadette Farrell (Published by OCP)

ENGLAND
LM with refrain

Here in This Place
Gather Us In

1 Here in this place the new light is stream-ing; now is the dark-ness
2 We are the young, our lives are a mys-tery. We are the old who
3 Here we will take the wine and the wa-ter; here we will take the
4 Not in the dark of build-ings con-fin-ing, not in some heav-en,

van-ished a - way; see in this space our fears and our dream-ings
yearn for your face. We have been sung through-out all of his - to-ry,
bread of new birth. Here you shall call your sons and your daugh-ters,
light years a - way: here in this place the new light is shin - ing;

brought here to you in the light of this day.
called to be light to the whole hu - man race.
call us a - new to be salt for the earth.
now is the king - dom, and now is the day.

Gath-er us in, the lost and for - sak - en; gath-er us in, the
Gath-er us in, the rich and the haugh-ty; gath-er us in, the
Give us to drink the wine of com - pas-sion; give us to eat the
Gath-er us in and hold us for - ev - er; gath-er us in and

blind and the lame; call to us now, and we shall a - wak - en;
proud and the strong; give us a heart, so meek and so low - ly;
bread that is you; nour-ish us well, and teach us to fash-ion
make us your own; gath - er us in, all peo - ples to-geth - er,

we shall a - rise at the sound of our name.
give us the cour-age to en - ter the song.
lives that are ho - ly and hearts that are true.
fire of love in our flesh and our bone.

The "you/your" mentioned in every stanza is never identified, but this 1979 hymn is clearly a corporate
prayer to God on behalf of the diverse congregation who have assembled for worship, longing to be
transformed and used as God's witnesses and for God's purposes.

TEXT and MUSIC: Marty Haugen, 1979
Text and Music © 1982 GIA Publications, Inc.

GATHER US IN
10.9.10.10.D

402

How Lovely, Lord

(Psalm 84)

1 How love - ly, Lord, how love - ly is your a - bid - ing place;
2 In your blest courts to wor - ship, O God, a sin - gle day
3 A sun and shield for - ev - er are you, O Lord Most High;

my soul is long-ing, faint - ing, to feast up - on your grace.
is bet - ter than a thou - sand if I from you should stray.
you show - er us with bless - ings; no good will you de - ny.

The spar - row finds a shel - ter, a place to build her nest;
I'd rath - er keep the en - trance and claim you as my Lord
The saints, your grace re - ceiv - ing, from strength to strength shall go,

and so your tem - ple calls us with - in its walls to rest.
than rev - el in the rich - es the ways of sin af - ford.
and from their life shall riv - ers of bless - ing o - ver - flow.

The author of this text, a Presbyterian minister and educator, was humming this tune as he began to create a paraphrase of Psalm 84 that would emphasize the beauty and peace of God's house. The tune is named for the composer's oldest sister, who was his first piano teacher.

TEXT: Arlo D. Duba, 1984
MUSIC: Hal H. Hopson, 1983
Text © 1986 Hope Publishing Company
Music © 1983 Hope Publishing Company

MERLE'S TUNE
7.6.7.6.D

Open Now Thy Gates of Beauty 403

1 O - pen now thy gates of beau - ty, Zi - on, let me
2 Gra - cious God, I come be - fore thee; come thou al - so
3 Speak, O Lord, and I will hear thee; let thy will be

en - ter there, where my soul in joy - ful du - ty
un - to me; where we find thee and a - dore thee,
done in - deed; may I un - dis - turbed draw near thee,

waits for God who an - swers prayer; O how bless - ed
there a heaven on earth must be; to my heart O
while thou dost thy peo - ple feed. Here of life the

is this place, filled with so - lace, light, and grace.
en - ter thou; let it be thy tem - ple now.
foun - tain flows; here is balm for all our woes.

In the first stanza "Zion" is not a general synonym for Jerusalem but a reference to the part of the city where
the Temple stood. It prepares the way for the interior temple of the heart in stanza two. The pre-existing tune
is by a prominent German Reformed hymnwriter.

TEXT: Benjamin Schmolck, 1732; trans. Catherine Winkworth, 1863, alt.
MUSIC: Joachim Neander, 1680; harm. *The Chorale Book for England*, 1863, alt.

UNSER HERRSCHER
8.7.8.7.7.7

404 What Is This Place

1 What is this place, where we are meet-ing? On-ly a house, the
2 Words from a-far, stars that are fall-ing. Sparks that are sown in
3 And we ac-cept bread at his ta-ble, bro-ken and shared, a

earth its floor. Walls and a roof, shel-ter-ing peo-ple, win-dows for
us like seed: names for our God, dreams, signs, and won-ders sent from the
liv-ing sign. Here in this world, dy-ing and liv-ing, we are each

light, an o-pen door. Yet it be-comes a bod-y that
past are what we need. We in this place re-mem-ber and
oth-er's bread and wine. This is the place where we can re-

lives when we are gath-ered here, and know our God is near.
speak a-gain what we have heard: God's free re-deem-ing word.
ceive what we need to in-crease: God's jus-tice and God's peace.

This text by a 20th-century Jesuit beautifully captures the fundamental truth that "church" is not primarily the building but the people who come together in order to be nourished by Word and Table so that they may show forth Christ's redeeming presence in the world.

TEXT: Huub Oosterhuis, 1968; trans. David Smith, 1970
MUSIC: Neder-landtsch Gedenck-Clanck, 1626; harm. Bernard Huijbers, 1968
Text and Music Harm. © 1967 Gooi En Sticht, Bv, Baarn, The Netherlands (admin. OCP for English-language countries)

KOMT NU MET ZANG
9.8.9.8.9.6.6

Praise God for This Holy Ground 405

Capo 2: (D)

Hal - le - lu - jah! Hal - le - lu - jah! Hal - le - lu - jah!

God's good - ness is e - ter - nal.

1 Praise God for this ho - ly ground,
2 Praise God in whose word we find
3 Praise God who through Christ makes known
4 Praise God's Spir - it who be - friends,
5 Though praise ends, praise is be - gun

place and peo - ple, sight and sound.
food for bod - y, soul, and mind.
all are loved and called God's own.
rais - es, hum - bles, breaks, and mends.
where God's will is glad - ly done.

Although several passages in the Psalms come close to the wording of this refrain, none matches it exactly. The refrain serves as a summation of the stanzas, each of which is filled with multiple instances of God's providential mercy, and all of them are worth pondering.

TEXT and MUSIC: John L. Bell, 2002
Text and Music © 2002 WGRG, Iona Community (admin. GIA Publications, Inc.)

HEYMONYSTRAAT
7.7.12.7

406 We Are Standing on Holy Ground
Holy Ground

We are stand - ing on ho - ly ground,
and I know that there are an - gels all a -
round; let us praise Je - sus
now; we are stand - ing in his
pres - ence on ho - ly ground.

The phrase "holy ground" resonates with the experience of Moses at the burning bush, where he had an encounter with God (Exodus 3:5; also quoted in the martyr Stephen's sermon, Acts 7:33). The reference to angels may recall Jacob's vision (Genesis 28:12–17) or Hebrews 12:22.

TEXT and MUSIC: Geron Davis, 1983
Text and Music © 1983 Songchannel Music Company and Meadowgreen Music Company
(admin. EMICMGPublishing.com)

HOLY GROUND
Irregular

Spirit Divine, Attend Our Prayers 407

1 Spir - it di - vine, at - tend our prayers, and make this
2 Come as the light. To us re - veal our emp - ti -
3 Come as the fire and purge our hearts like sac - ri -
4 Come as the dove and spread your wings, the wings of
5 Spir - it di - vine, at - tend our prayers. Make a lost

house your home. De - scend with all your
ness and woe. And lead us in those
fi - cial flame. Let our whole soul an
peace - ful love. And let the church on
world your home. De - scend with all your

gra - cious powers. O come, great Spir - it, come!
paths of life where all the righ - teous go.
of - fering be to our Re - deem - er's name.
earth be - come blest as the church a - bove.
gra - cious powers. O come, great Spir - it, come!

The subtle changes between the first and last stanzas here are important; they reveal how the gift of the Holy Spirit transforms and widens our concern from ourselves to the world around us. The tune is named for the text it first set, "Now let all thank and bring honor."

TEXT: Andrew Reed, 1829, alt.
MUSIC: Johann Crüger, c. 1647

NUN DANKET ALL' UND BRINGET EHR'
CM

408 There's a Sweet, Sweet Spirit

1 There's a sweet, sweet Spir-it in this place, and I
2 There are bless-ings you can-not re - ceive till you

know that it's the Spir - it of the Lord; there are
know him in his full - ness and be - lieve; you're the

sweet ex - pres-sions on each face, and I
one to prof - it when you say, "I am

know they feel the pres - ence of the Lord.
going to walk with Je - sus all the way."

This gospel hymn grew out of this African American author and composer's intense experience of prayer with her interracial choir in Los Angeles one Sunday morning before worship. She recalled that sense of "a sweet, sweet Spirit" when she sat down at her piano the next day.

TEXT and MUSIC: Doris Akers, 1962
Text and Music © 1962, ren. 1990 Manna Music, Inc. (admin. ClearBox Rights)

SWEET, SWEET SPIRIT
9.11.9.11 with refrain

Refrain

Sweet Ho-ly Spir-it, sweet heav-en-ly Dove, stay right here with us, fill-ing us with your love; and for these bless-ings we lift our hearts in praise; with-out a doubt we'll know that we have been re-vived when we shall leave this place.

409

God Is Here!

1 God is here! As we your peo-ple meet to
2 Here are sym-bols to re-mind us of our
3 Here our chil-dren find a wel-come in the
4 Lord of all, of church and king-dom, in an

of-fer praise and prayer, may we find in
life-long need of grace; here are ta-ble,
Shep-herd's flock and fold; here as bread and
age of change and doubt keep us faith-ful

full-er mea-sure what it is in Christ we share.
font, and pul-pit; here the cross has cen-tral place.
wine are tak-en, Christ sus-tains us as of old.
to the gos-pel; help us work your pur-pose out.

Commissioned for the dedication of a renovated worship space in Austin, Texas, this text is one of the few to devote attention to how customary church features facilitate worship. The tune was composed in wartime Britain to replace a Haydn tune tainted by Nazi associations.

TEXT: Fred Pratt Green, 1979; rev. 1988
MUSIC: Cyril Vincent Taylor, 1941
Text © 1979 Hope Publishing Company
Music © 1942, ren. 1970 Hope Publishing Company

ABBOT'S LEIGH
8.7.8.7.D

Here, as in the world a - round us, all our
Here in hon - es - ty of preach - ing, here in
Here the ser - vants of the Ser - vant seek in
Here, in this day's ded - i - ca - tion, all we

var - ied skills and arts wait the com - ing
si - lence, as in speech, here, in new - ness
wor - ship to ex - plore what it means in
have to give, re - ceive: we, who can - not

of the Spir - it in - to o - pen minds and hearts.
and re - new - al, God the Spir - it comes to each.
dai - ly liv - ing to be - lieve and to a - dore.
live with - out you, we a - dore you! We be - lieve!

410 God Is Calling through the Whisper

1 God is call-ing through the whis-per of the Spir - it's deep-est sighs,
2 God is call-ing through the voic - es of our neigh-bors' ur - gent prayers,
3 God is call-ing through the mu - sic of sub-lime and hu - man arts,

through the thrill of sud - den beau - ties that can catch us by sur - prise.
through their long - ing for re - demp-tion and for res - cue from de - spair.
through the hymns of earth and an - gels, and the car - ols of our hearts.

Flash of light-ning, crash of thun-der; hush of still - ness, rush of won - der:
Place of hurt or face of need-ing; stri - dent cry or si - lent plead-ing:
Lift of joy and gift of sing - ing; days and nights our prais-es bring-ing:

God is call - ing—can you hear? God is call - ing—can you hear?
God is call - ing—can you hear? God is call - ing—can you hear?
God is call - ing—and we hear! God is call - ing—and we hear!

This wide-ranging text reminds us of the many surprising and urgent ways God calls to us, both to draw us near and to send us forth. In the third line of music it is especially effective at harnessing the momentum of the phrases that are each a note higher than the one before.

TEXT: Mary Louise Bringle, 2003
MUSIC: Polish carol; harm. Wilbur Lee, 1958
Text © 2006 GIA Publications, Inc.
Music Harm. © 1958 Broadman Press (admin. Music Services)

W ŻŁOBIE LEŻY
8.7.8.7.8.8.7.7
(this tune in a higher key, 128)

God Is Here Today

Dios está aquí

God is here to-day; as cer-tain
Dios es-tá a-quí, *tan cier-to co-mo el*

as the air I breathe, as cer-tain
ai-re que res-pi-ro, *tan cier-to co-mo*

as the morn-ing sun that ris - es, as
la ma-ña-na se le-van - ta, *tan*

cer-tain when I sing you'll hear my song.
cier-to co-mo que le can-to y me pue-de o-ír.

Though it is popular throughout Latin America, the conditions of this song's creation have remained obscure. It was once thought to have originated in a Mexican jail but is now known to have been written by an Argentinian who has also lived in the United States and Colombia.

TEXT: Raúl Galeano, 1976; English trans. C. Michael Hawn, 1998
MUSIC: Raúl Galeano, 1976; arr. C. Michael Hawn and Arturo González, 1999
English Trans. and Music Arr. © 1999 Choristers Guild

DIOS ESTÁ AQUÍ
Irregular

412 God, Reveal Your Presence

1 God, re-veal your pres-ence: glad-ly we a-dore you,
2 In God's ho-ly pres-ence, hear the harps re-sound-ing;
3 Foun-tain of all bless-ing, pu-ri-fy my spir-it;

and with awe ap-pear be-fore you. Ho-ly is your tem-
see the crowds the throne sur-round-ing: "Ho-ly, ho-ly, ho-
all my trust is in your mer-it. Like the ho-ly an-

ple: all with-in keep si-lence, hum-bly bow with deep-est
ly!" hear the hymn as-cend-ing, an-gels, saints, their voic-es
gels on your glo-ry gaz-ing, we a-dore, ho-san-nas

rev-erence. You a-lone now we own as our
blend-ing. Turn your ear to us here; hear, O
rais-ing. Let your will ev-er still rule your

Despite multiple layers of translation and revision, this text embodies the mystical piety of one of the
German Reformed Church's greatest hymnists and spiritual leaders of the early 18th century. It is set here to
a slightly earlier tune from that tradition.

TEXT: Gerhard Tersteegen, 1729; trans. Frederick William Foster and John Miller, 1789;
alt. The Presbyterian Church in Canada, 1997
MUSIC: Joachim Neander, 1680
Text © 1997 The Presbyterian Church of Canada

ARNSBERG
6.6.8.6.6.8.3.3.6.6

God and Sav - ior: praise your name for - ev - er!
Christ, the prais - es that your church now rais - es.
church ter - res - trial, as the hosts ce - les - tial.

Come into God's Presence 413

1 Come in - to God's pres-ence sing - ing "Al - le - lu - ia,
2 Come in - to God's pres-ence sing - ing "Je - sus is Lord,
3 Praise the Lord to - geth - er sing - ing "Wor - thy the Lamb,
4 Praise the Lord to - geth - er sing - ing "Glo - ry to God,

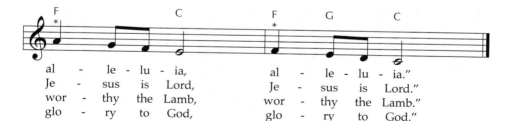

al - le - lu - ia, al - le - lu - ia."
Je - sus is Lord, Je - sus is Lord."
wor - thy the Lamb, wor - thy the Lamb."
glo - ry to God, glo - ry to God."

*May be sung as a canon.

This anonymous worship chorus is thought to have been created extemporaneously during the 1960s and was one of the earliest songs of that kind. The opening line of the text is a paraphrase of Psalm 100:2, and the very act of singing this song fulfills that verse's invitation.

TEXT and MUSIC: Anon.

COME INTO HIS PRESENCE
8.4.4.4

414 Be Still and Know That I Am God

May be sung as a canon.

In many situations, simplicity is more challenging than embellishment. The spiritual life is no exception, as these eight stark monosyllables from Psalm 46:10a make clear. The musical setting is similarly spare, using only five notes to create a sense of melodic spaciousness.

TEXT and MUSIC: John L. Bell, 1989
Text and Music © 1989 WGRG, Iona Community (admin. GIA Publications, Inc.)

PSALM 46
Irregular

415 Come, Ye Sinners, Poor and Needy

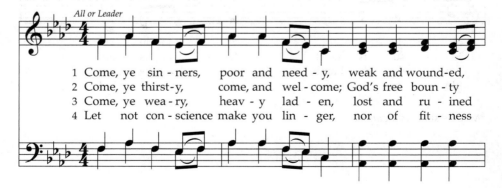

The differing voices of this text indicate that its parts were not created together. The stanzas are cast in the voice of a preacher or exhorter, but the refrain (added later) takes the voice of a penitent heeding that call in language like that of the Prodigal Son (Luke 15:18).

TEXT: Stanzas, Joseph Hart, 1759, alt.; refrain, anon.
MUSIC: Walker's *Southern Harmony,* 1835

RESTORATION
8.7.8.7 with refrain

sick and sore; Je - sus read - y stands to save you,
glo - ri - fy, true be - lief and true re - pen - tance,
by the fall; if you tar - ry till you're bet - ter,
fond - ly dream; all the fit - ness he re - quir - eth

Refrain
All

full of pit - y, love, and power.
ev - ery grace that brings you nigh.
you will nev - er come at all. I will a - rise and
is to feel your need of him.

go to Je - sus; he will em - brace me in his arms. In the

arms of my dear Sav - ior, O there are ten thou - sand charms.

416 O Come unto the Lord

어서 돌아오오

Refrain / 후렴

O come un-to the Lord; O come back to the Lord.
어서 돌 - 아 오 오 어서 돌아 만 오 오

1 No mat - ter how heav-y and how great your sins may
2 Our Sav - ior is wait-ing your re - turn both night and
3 No mat - ter how bur-dened and how beat - en you may

be, there are no sins that Christ our Sav - ior can-not
day. 7 Je - sus anx - ious - ly a - waits you, with
be, 7 the Lord will com - fort you great - ly with

bear, can - not ac - cept. The great depth of Je - sus'
door kept o - pen wide, as one who waits through-
hands that touch and heal. Come un - to Christ, who

This text by a Korean Presbyterian minister is directed to those who have wandered from the ways of God and feel that their sins disqualify them from returning to seek forgiveness. They (and we) are assured that there is no limit to God's love made known through Jesus Christ.

TEXT: Young taik Chun, 1943; English trans. Steve S. Shim, 1976, alt.
MUSIC: Chai Hoon Park, 1943
English Trans. © 1976 The Hymnal Society of Korea

KOREA
Irregular

lov - ing heart is far deep - er than the seas.
out the night for a lost child to come back home.
loves you so. Please come home; please come back home.

KOREAN

1 지은죄가 아무리 무-겁고 크기로
   주- 어찌 못담당하고 못-받으시리요
   우리주의 넓은 가슴은 하늘보다 넓고넓어   후렴

2 우리주는 날마다 기-다리신다오
   밤-마다 문 열어놓고 마-음 졸이시며
   나간 자식 돌아오기만 밤새 기다리신다오   후렴

3 채찍맞아 아파도 주-님의 손으로
   때-리시고 어루만져 위-로해 주시는
   우리주의 넓은 품으로 어서 돌아오오 어서

Lord Jesus, Think on Me   417

1 Lord Je - sus, think on me, and purge a - way my sin. From
2 Lord Je - sus, think on me, a - mid the bat - tle's strife. In
3 Lord Je - sus, think on me, nor let me go a - stray. Through
4 Lord Je - sus, think on me, that, when this life is past, I

earth-born pas-sions set me free, and make me pure with - in.
all my pain and mis-er - y be thou my health and life.
dark - ness and per - plex - i - ty point thou the heaven - ly way.
may the e - ter - nal bright-ness see, and share thy joy at last.

This text is among the oldest hymns in this book; its original Greek version dates from around the beginning of the 5th century. The stanzas used here come from a 19th-century paraphrase, whose simplicity and directness are well complemented by a 16th-century psalm tune.

TEXT: Synesius of Cyrene, 5th cent.; trans. Allen W. Chatfield, 1876, alt.
MUSIC: Daman's *Psalmes*, 1579, alt.

SOUTHWELL
SM

418 Softly and Tenderly Jesus Is Calling

1 Soft - ly and ten - der - ly Je - sus is call - ing, call - ing for
2 Why should we tar - ry when Je - sus is plead - ing, plead - ing for
3 O for the won - der - ful love he has prom - ised, prom - ised for

you and for me. See, on the por - tals he's wait - ing and watch - ing,
you and for me? Why should we lin - ger and heed not his mer - cies,
you and for me! Though we have sinned, he has mer - cy and par - don,

Refrain

watch - ing for you and for me.
mer - cies for you and for me? "Come home, come home!
par - don for you and for me. "Come home, come home!

You who are wea - ry, come home." Ear - nest - ly, ten - der - ly,

Je - sus is call - ing, call - ing, "O sin - ner, come home!"

This 19th-century gospel hymn has often been used as a hymn of invitation at evangelistic services. Its imagery is primarily based on Jesus' parable in Luke 15:11–32, commonly called "The Prodigal Son." Each singer thus becomes a wandering child who is urged to return home.

TEXT and MUSIC: Will L. Thompson, 1880

SOFTLY AND TENDERLY
11.7.11.7 with refrain

Lord, Who May Dwell within Your House

(Psalm 15)

1 Lord, who may dwell with-in your house or
2 Who have no guile up-on their tongues nor
3 Who do no wrong, but keep their word and

on your ho-ly hill? Those who do good and
harm their neigh-bor's life, but hon-or those who
seek no bribe or gain. All those who do such

speak the truth, whose lives are blame-less still;
fear the Lord and turn a-way from strife;
things shall live and safe from harm re-main.

Guitar chords do not correspond with keyboard harmony.

Although Psalm 15 is sometimes said to reflect a ritual for entrance to the Temple, it is better understood as a sketch of how to live in a manner that reflects God's values rather than self-centeredness. Those who faithfully entrust themselves to God will never be disappointed.

TEXT: Christopher L. Webber, 1986
MUSIC: Roy Hopp, 1992
Text © 1986 Christopher L. Webber
Music © 1992 Selah Publishing Co., Inc.

RIDGEMOOR
CM

420 Lord, to You My Soul Is Lifted
(Psalm 25)

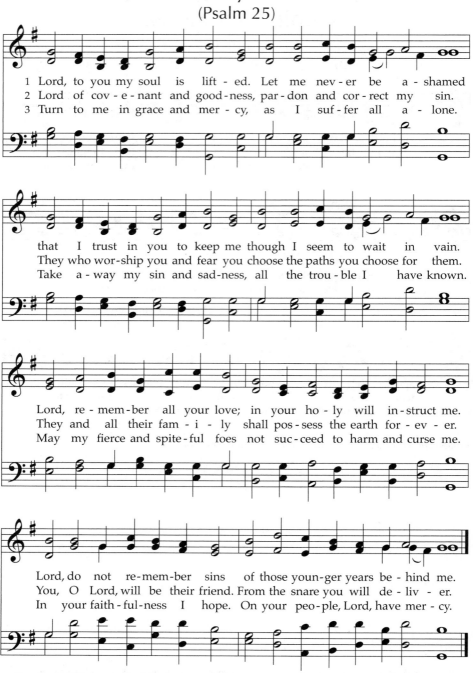

1 Lord, to you my soul is lift - ed. Let me nev - er be a - shamed
2 Lord of cov - e - nant and good - ness, par - don and cor - rect my sin.
3 Turn to me in grace and mer - cy, as I suf - fer all a - lone.

that I trust in you to keep me though I seem to wait in vain.
They who wor - ship you and fear you choose the paths you choose for them.
Take a - way my sin and sad - ness, all the trou - ble I have known.

Lord, re - mem - ber all your love; in your ho - ly will in - struct me.
They and all their fam - i - ly shall pos - sess the earth for - ev - er.
May my fierce and spite - ful foes not suc - ceed to harm and curse me.

Lord, do not re - mem - ber sins of those youn - ger years be - hind me.
You, O Lord, will be their friend. From the snare you will de - liv - er.
In your faith - ful - ness I hope. On your peo - ple, Lord, have mer - cy.

Because this 20th-century English paraphrase of Psalm 25 was created for a 16th-century tune for a French version of the psalm, these lines are organized by meter rather than by rhyme. Combining elements from different eras testifies to the continuity of Reformed tradition.

TEXT: Stanley Wiersma, 1980
MUSIC: Louis Bourgeois, 1551; harm. Howard Slenk, 1985
Text and Music Harm. © 1987 Faith Alive Christian Resources

GENEVAN 25
8.7.8.7.7.8.7.8

Have Mercy, God, upon My Life 421
(Psalm 51)

1 Have mer - cy, God, up - on my life, and
2 My guilt is heav - y on my mind; I
3 Now teach me wis - dom in my soul; I
4 Cre - ate in me a faith - ful heart, a
5 Then I will praise you with my heart, my

make me clean with - in: pour out your ev - er -
know what I have done: a - gainst your jus - tice
long to see your face. Let bones, once bro - ken,
spir - it right and new. Sus - tain me with your
mind, my soul, my voice. You save the least and

faith - ful love and wash a - way my sin.
I have sinned, a - gainst you, God, a - lone.
sing with joy, and heal me by your grace.
sav - ing love and keep me close to you.
seek the lost; let all the world re - joice!

Psalm 51, paraphrased here, has traditionally been known as one of the seven penitential psalms, and it is used annually on Ash Wednesday. But this psalm is not just about human sinfulness; it is also about God's willingness to forgive and restore sinners. That is good news.

TEXT: David Gambrell, 2009
MUSIC: *A Collection of Hymns and Sacred Poems*, 1749
Text © 2011 David Gambrell (admin. Presbyterian Publishing Corp.)

IRISH
CM

422 Create in Me a Clean Heart
(Psalm 51)

Guitar chords do not correspond with keyboard harmony.

This reflective setting of Psalm 51:10–12 uses the first of those verses as an embracing refrain. Because of its penitential tone, a longer version of this psalm is customarily used on Ash Wednesday. In Christian tradition, it is identified as one of the seven penitential psalms.

MUSIC: James M. Capers, 1993; arr. Dennis Friesen-Carper, 1999
Music © 1993, 1999 Augsburg Fortress

CREATE IN ME (Capers)
Irregular

Create in Me a Clean Heart, O God 423

(Psalm 51)

The text here comes from Psalm 51:10–12, three verses that illustrate the pattern of parallels often found in Hebrew poetry. The first verse here centers on positive actions, the second on avoidance of negative actions, and the third on providing an improved spiritual condition.

TEXT: Para. John Carter, 1997
MUSIC: John Carter, 1997
Text and Music © 1997 Hope Publishing Company

SARADAY
Irregular

424 Out of the Depths
(Psalm 130)

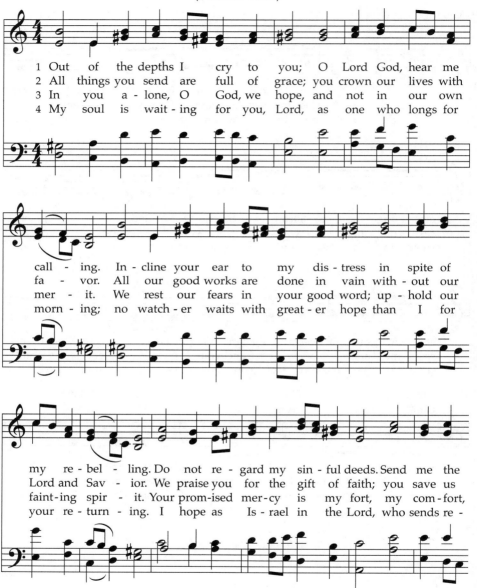

1 Out of the depths I cry to you; O Lord God, hear me
2 All things you send are full of grace; you crown our lives with
3 In you a-lone, O God, we hope, and not in our own
4 My soul is wait-ing for you, Lord, as one who longs for

call - ing. In - cline your ear to my dis - tress in spite of
fa - vor. All our good works are done in vain with - out our
mer - it. We rest our fears in your good word; up - hold our
morn - ing; no watch - er waits with great - er hope than I for

my re - bel - ling. Do not re - gard my sin - ful deeds. Send me the
Lord and Sav - ior. We praise you for the gift of faith; you save us
faint-ing spir - it. Your prom-ised mer-cy is my fort, my com-fort,
your re - turn - ing. I hope as Is - rael in the Lord, who sends re -

In many times and places, human despair has been described as an experience like being in a deep pit or drowning under much water. That is where this paraphrase of Psalm 130 begins. This setting is especially evocative when sung with the original German text.

TEXT: Martin Luther, 1524; trans. composite
MUSIC: Martin Luther, 1524; harm. Johann Sebastian Bach, 1740

AUS TIEFER NOT
8.7.8.7.8.8.7

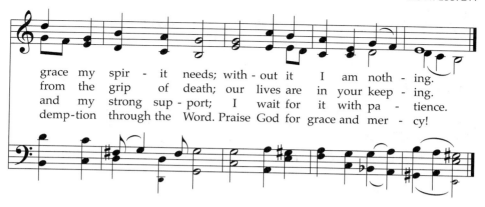

grace my spir - it needs; with - out it I am noth - ing.
from the grip of death; our lives are in your keep - ing.
and my strong sup - port; I wait for it with pa - tience.
demp-tion through the Word. Praise God for grace and mer - cy!

Son of God, Whose Heart Is Peace 425

1 Son of God, whose heart is peace, Son of God, most ho - ly,
2 Take a - way our sin - ful - ness, e - vil that im - pris - ons us;
3 Warm our hearts to love you, Lord, you who died to save us;

to your pres - ence we have come; give us now your love.
free us from what trou - bles us; give our souls re - lease.
gath - er us with - in your arms, Je - sus, on this day.

Even in translation this hymn from the indigenous peoples of New Zealand conveys a stark beauty in its confident address to Christ and its prayer for release from the captivity of sin. Their traditional melody further connects us with these people on the other side of the world.

TEXT: Maori hymn; para. Shirley Erena Murray, 1989
MUSIC: Maori melody
Text © 1990 Christian Conference of Asia (admin. GIA Publications, Inc.)

TAMA NGAKAU MARIE
7.6.7.5

Search Me, O God
主上帝，求祢鑒察我
(Psalm 139)

The two verses that make up this text, Psalm 139:23–24, form a prayer at the conclusion of one of the most remarkably introspective psalms of the Psalter. The distinctive Taiwanese musical setting provided for the words gives them a beautiful sense of mystery and awe.

TEXT: From Psalm 139
MUSIC: I-to Loh, 1990, arr. 2011
Music © 1990 I-to Loh

KÀM-CHHAT
Irregular

Jesus Knows the Inmost Heart 427

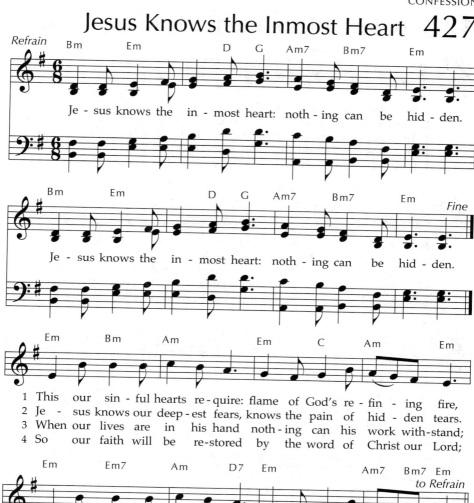

Refrain

Je - sus knows the in - most heart: noth - ing can be hid - den.

Je - sus knows the in - most heart: noth - ing can be hid - den.

Fine

1 This our sin - ful hearts re - quire: flame of God's re - fin - ing fire,
2 Je - sus knows our deep - est fears, knows the pain of hid - den tears.
3 When our lives are in his hand noth - ing can his work with - stand;
4 So our faith will be re - stored by the word of Christ our Lord;

to Refrain

work - ing in us day by day till the dross is burned a - way.
By his words of love and peace ev - ery heart can find re - lease.
his for - give - ness sets us free, saves us for e - ter - ni - ty.
for the warmth his love im - parts melts the ver - y hard - est hearts.

This text was originally created in Pashto, which is the national language of Afghanistan as well as a provincial language of Pakistan and is spoken by more than fifty million people. The refrain seems to be an adaptation of phrases in Psalm 51:6 applied to Jesus.

TEXT: Pashto hymn; trans. Alison Blenkinsop, 1995
MUSIC: Anon.; arr. Geoff Weaver, 1995
Text © 1995 Alison Blenkinsop
Music Arr. © 1995 The Jubilate Group (admin. Hope Publishing Company)

LOE DE ÍSÁ
7.7.7.7 with refrain

428 Before I Take the Body of My Lord

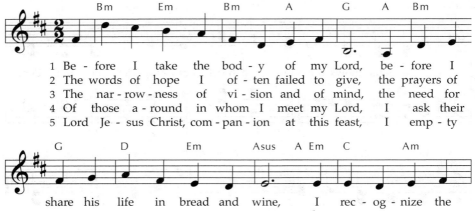

1 Be - fore I take the bod - y of my Lord, be - fore I
2 The words of hope I of - ten failed to give, the prayers of
3 The nar - row - ness of vi - sion and of mind, the need for
4 Of those a - round in whom I meet my Lord, I ask their
5 Lord Je - sus Christ, com - pan - ion at this feast, I emp - ty

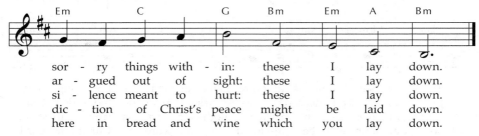

share his life in bread and wine, I rec - og - nize the
kind - ness bur - ied by my pride, the signs of care I
oth - er folk to serve my will, and ev - ery word and
par - don and I grant them mine, that ev - ery con - tra -
now my heart and stretch my hands, and ask to meet you

sor - ry things with - in: these I lay down.
ar - gued out of sight: these I lay down.
si - lence meant to hurt: these I lay down.
dic - tion of Christ's peace might be laid down.
here in bread and wine which you lay down.

As this text acknowledges, the sins that separate us from God and from each other can be both things done and things left undone, as well as attitudes and habits that keep us from living in harmony. Letting go of our self-sufficiency enables us to receive Christ's gracious gifts.

TEXT: John L. Bell and Graham Maule, 1989   LAYING DOWN
MUSIC: John L. Bell, 1989   10.10.10.4
Text and Music © 1989 WGRG, Iona Community (admin. GIA Publications, Inc.)

429 As a Chalice Cast of Gold

1 As a chal - ice cast of gold, bur - nished, bright and
2 Save me from the sooth - ing sin of the emp - ty
3 When I bend up - on my knees, clasp my hands, or
4 When I dance or chant your praise, when I sing a

Guitar chords do not correspond with keyboard harmony.

This prayerful text is based on Mark 7:1–8, 14–15, 21–23, where Jesus teaches that external religious observances are much less important than purity of heart. The tune was composed at the same time as part of a collaborative effort to create new hymns for a seminary community.

TEXT: Thomas H. Troeger, 1984   INWARD LIGHT
MUSIC: Carol Doran, 1984   7.7.7.D
Text and Music © 1985 Oxford University Press

brimmed with wine, make me, Lord, as fit to hold grace and
cul - tic deed and the pi - ous, bab - bling din of the
bow my head, let my spo - ken, pub - lic pleas be di -
psalm or hymn, when I preach your lov - ing ways, let my

truth and love di - vine. Let my praise and
claimed but un - lived creed. Let my ac - tions,
rect - ly, sim - ply said, free of tan - gled
heart add its A - men. Let each cher - ished

wor - ship start with the cleans - ing of my heart.
Lord, ex - press what my tongue and lips pro - fess.
words that mask what my soul would plain - ly ask.
out - ward rite thus re - flect your in - ward light.

Remember Not, O God 430
(Psalm 79)

1 Re - mem - ber not, O God, the sins of long a - go;
2 O Lord, our Sav - ior, help, and glo - ri - fy your name;
3 Then, safe with - in your fold, we will ex - alt your name;

in ten - der mer - cy vis - it us, dis - tressed and hum - bled low.
de - liv - er us from all our sins and take a - way our shame.
our thank - ful hearts with songs of joy your good - ness will pro - claim.

This paraphrase of selected verses from Psalm 79 distills the tone of communal lament that runs through that psalm. Because the sense of shame and the longing for restoration extend to the whole community, this psalm is usually associated with the Jewish exile in Babylon.

TEXT: *The New Metrical Version of the Psalms*, 1909, alt.
MUSIC: Daman's *Psalmes*, 1579, alt.

SOUTHWELL
SM

431

Forgive Us, Lord

Perdón, Señor

1 For grievance and injustice:
2 For weakness and transgression:
3 In your eternal mercy:

1 Por tantas injusticias:
2 Por todas nuestras faltas:
3 En tu misericordia:

Forgive us, Lord.
Perdón, Señor.

Capo 3: (G) (A) (Bm) (Bm) (Dmaj7)
B♭ C Dm Dm Fmaj7

for-
per-

Aloofness and indifference:
Resistance and rebellion:
In your sustaining grace:

Por tanta indiferencia:
Por nuestra rebeldía:
En tu divina gracia:

(G) (A) (Bm) (Em) (Bm) (G) (A) (Bm)
B♭ C Dm Gm Dm B♭ C Dm

give us, Lord. forgive us, Lord.
dón, Señor. perdón, Señor.

Because the congregation's response remains constant throughout this sung confession, the leader may (with appropriate preparation) adapt or enlarge the various petitions to suit a particular occasion or emphasis, as long as the present third stanza always forms the conclusion.

TEXT: Jorge Lockward, 1995; English trans. Raquel Mora Martínez, 1995
MUSIC: Jorge Lockward, 1995
Text and Music © 1996 Abingdon Press (admin. The Copyright Company)

CONFESIÓN
Irregular

How Clear Is Our Vocation, Lord 432

Capo 1: (D)

1 How clear is our vo - ca - tion, Lord, when once we heed your call
2 But if, for-get - ful, we should find your yoke is hard to bear;
3 We mar - vel how your saints be-came in hin-dranc-es more sure:
4 In what you give us, Lord, to do, to - geth - er or a - lone,

to live ac-cord-ing to your word and dai - ly learn, re-freshed, re -
if world-ly pres-sures fray the mind and love it - self can - not un -
whose joy - ful vir-tues put to shame the ca-sual way we wear your
in old rou-tines or ven-tures new, may we not cease to look to

stored, that you are Lord of all and will not let us fall.
wind its tan-gled skein of care: our in-ward life re - pair.
name, and by our faults ob - scure your power to cleanse and cure.
you: the cross you hung up - on, all you en - deav-ored, done.

Guitar chords do not correspond with keyboard harmony.

This reflection on Christian vocation was written to provide a new text for a pre-existing tune, and the poet has crafted his words so well that the two parts mesh smoothly. The tune is named for a noted British boarding school, whose music director was a friend of the composer.

TEXT: Fred Pratt Green, 1981
MUSIC: C. Hubert H. Parry, 1888
Text © 1982 Hope Publishing Company

REPTON
8.6.8.8.6.6

433 Sign Us with Ashes

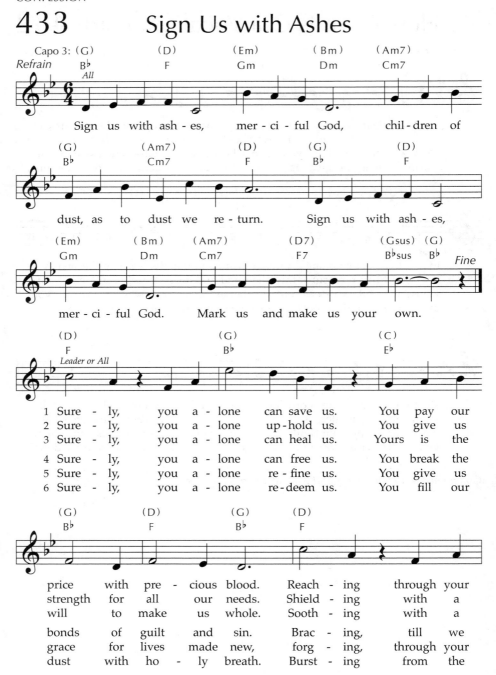

Capo 3: (G)

The refrain here recalls the imposition of ashes, a ritual based on Genesis 3:19, which has been a part of Christian worship on Ash Wednesday since the 9th century. As *The Book of Common Worship* states, "This ancient sign speaks of the frailty and uncertainty of human life."

TEXT: Mary Louise Bringle, 2003
MUSIC: William P. Rowan, 2003
Text and Music © 2006 GIA Publications, Inc.

PHOENIX
LM with refrain

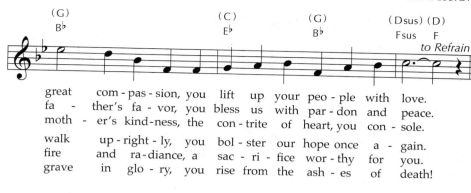

great com-pas-sion, you lift up your peo-ple with love.
fa - ther's fa - vor, you bless us with par-don and peace.
moth - er's kind-ness, the con-trite of heart, you con - sole.

walk up-right-ly, you bol-ster our hope once a - gain.
fire and ra-diance, a sac-ri-fice wor-thy for you.
grave in glo - ry, you rise from the ash-es of death!

Restore in Us, O God 434

1 Re - store in us, O God, the splen-dor of your love;
2 O Spir - it, wake in us the won-der of your power;
3 Bring us, O Christ, to share the full-ness of your joy;
4 Three-per-soned God, ful - fill the prom-ise of your grace,

re - new your im-age in our hearts, and all our sins re-move.
from fruit-less fear un-furl our lives like spring-time bud and flower.
bap - tize us in the ris - en life that death can-not de-stroy.
that we, when all our search-ing ends, may see you face to face.

This text reflects the historic understanding of Lent as a time to prepare catechumens for Baptism and penitents for reconciliation at the Easter Vigil. The first three stanzas address one of the three divine Persons, while the fourth stanza implores the help of the full Trinity.

TEXT: Carl P. Daw Jr., 1987
MUSIC: Hal H. Hopson, 1985
Text © 1989 Hope Publishing Company
Music © 1985 Hope Publishing Company

BAYLOR
SM

435 There's a Wideness in God's Mercy

1 There's a wide-ness in God's mer-cy, like the wide-ness
2 For the love of God is broad-er than the mea-sures

of the sea. There's a kind-ness in God's jus-tice,
of the mind. And the heart of the E-ter-nal

which is more than lib-er-ty. There is no place where earth's
is most won-der-ful-ly kind. If our love were but more

sor-rows are more felt than up in heaven. There is no place
faith-ful, we would glad-ly trust God's Word, and our lives re-

where earth's fail-ings have such kind-ly judg-ment given.
flect thanks-giv-ing for the good-ness of our Lord.

These stanzas, excerpted from quite a few more, offer a reminder that the model for our dealings with others should be God's generosity rather than limited human tolerance. The text is effectively set to a broad and sturdy Dutch folk melody, probably from the 17th century.

TEXT: Frederick William Faber, 1854, alt.
MUSIC: Dutch melody; arr. Julius Röntgen, c. 1906

IN BABILONE
8.7.8.7.D

God of Compassion, in Mercy Befriend Us 436

1 God of com-pas-sion, in mer-cy be-friend us,
2 Though we are lost, you have sought us and found us,
3 How shall we stray, with your hand to di-rect us,

giv-er of grace for our needs all-a-vail-ing.
stilled our rude hearts with your word of con-sol-ing.
you who the stars in their cours-es are guid-ing?

Wis-dom and strength for each day ev-er send us,
Wrap now your peace, like a man-tle, a-round us,
What shall we fear, with your power to pro-tect us,

pa-tience un-tir-ing and cour-age un-fail-ing.
guard-ing our thoughts and our pas-sions con-trol-ling.
we who walk forth in your great-ness con-fid-ing?

By ending with questions rather than simple affirmations, this text conveys a strong sense of faith in God's presence and guidance without ignoring how much of the future remains unknown. The confidence of the text is well matched by its sturdy 17th-century French tune.

TEXT: John J. Moment, 1933, alt.
MUSIC: Paris *Antiphoner*, 1681; harm. La Feillée's *Méthode du plain-chant*, 1808

O QUANTA QUALIA
11.11.11.11
(this tune in a lower key, 503)

437 You Are the Lord, Giver of Mercy!

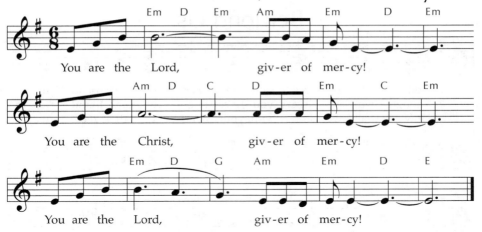

You are the Lord, giv-er of mer-cy!

You are the Christ, giv-er of mer-cy!

You are the Lord, giv-er of mer-cy!

This adaptation of the traditional *Kyrie eleison* text transforms a series of petitions into a series of acclamations. With harsher music these might have seemed bold or rash, but this plaintive setting derived from an Appalachian melody preserves a sense of humility and trust.

TEXT: Trad. liturgical text; rev. *The Worshipbook*, 1970
MUSIC: Appalachian folk melody; arr. Richard D. Wetzel, 1972
Text © 1970 The Westminster Press (admin. Westminster John Knox Press)
Music © 1972 The Westminster Press (admin. Westminster John Knox Press)

WAYFARING STRANGER
9.9.9

438 Rock of Ages, Cleft for Me

1 Rock of A - ges, cleft for me, let me hide my - self in thee.
2 Not the la - bors of my hands can ful - fill thy law's de-mands.
3 Noth-ing in my hand I bring; sim - ply to thy cross I cling;
4 While I draw this fleet-ing breath, when my eye - lids close in death,

Let the wa - ter and the blood from thy wound-ed side which flowed
Could my zeal no res - pite know, could my tears for - ev - er flow,
na - ked, come to thee for dress, help - less, look to thee for grace;
when I soar to worlds un-known, see thee on thy judg-ment throne,

Though scholars discredit the story that this hymn was written when the author found shelter under a large rock during a thunderstorm, the popular appeal of that conjecture perhaps lies in the energy of this plea and the vividness of its imagery drawn from many biblical sources.

TEXT: Augustus M. Toplady, 1776, alt.
MUSIC: Thomas Hastings, 1830, alt.

TOPLADY
7.7.7.7.7.7

be   of   sin   the   dou - ble cure, cleanse from guilt and make me pure.
all   for sin   could not   a - tone. Thou must save, and thou a - lone.
foul, I   to   the foun-tain fly; wash me, Sav - ior, or   I   die.
Rock of A - ges, cleft for me,   let   me hide my - self in   thee.

O My Soul, Bless Your Redeemer 439
(Psalm 103)

1 O   my soul, bless your Re - deem - er; all with-in me bless God's name;
2 God for-gives all your trans-gres-sions, all dis - eas - es gent - ly heals;
3 Far as east from west is   dis - tant, God has put a - way our   sin;
4 As   it   was with-out be - gin - ning, so   it lasts with-out an   end;

bless the Sav - ior, and for - get not all God's mer - cies to   pro-claim.
God re-deems you from de-struc-tion, and with you so   kind-ly deals.
like the pit - y   of   a   fa - ther has the Lord's com - pas-sion been.
to   their chil-dren's chil-dren ev - er shall God's righ - teous-ness ex - tend:

5 Unto such as keep God's cov'nant
  and are steadfast in God's way;
  unto those who still remember
  the commandments and obey.

6 Bless your Maker, all you creatures,
  ever under God's control,
  all throughout God's vast dominion;
  bless the Lord of all, my soul!

These stanzas are selected from sixteen that originally made up this paraphrase of Psalm 103, the second of two versions in the volume where they were first published. The tune used here was probably created as a German psalm tune but later came to be used with hymn texts.

TEXT: The Book of Psalms, 1871, alt.
MUSIC: Witt's Psalmodia Sacra, 1715; harm. William Henry Havergal, 1847, alt.

STUTTGART
8.7.8.7

440 Jesus, Lover of My Soul

1 Je - sus, lov - er of my soul, let me to thy bos - om fly,
2 Oth - er ref - uge have I none; hangs my help-less soul on thee.
3 Thou, O Christ, art all I want; more than all in thee I find.
4 Plen - teous grace with thee is found, grace to cov - er all my sin.

while the near - er wa - ters roll, while the temp-est still is high.
Leave, ah! leave me not a - lone; still sup - port and com - fort me.
Raise the fall - en, cheer the faint, heal the sick, and lead the blind.
Let the heal - ing streams a - bound; make and keep me pure with - in.

Hide me, O my Sav - ior, hide, till the storm of life is past.
All my trust on thee is stayed; all my help from thee I bring.
Just and ho - ly is thy name; I am all un - righ - teous-ness.
Thou of life the foun - tain art; free - ly let me take of thee.

Safe in - to the ha - ven guide. O re - ceive my soul at last!
Cov - er my de-fense-less head with the shad - ow of thy wing.
False and full of sin I am; thou art full of truth and grace.
Spring thou up with - in my heart. Rise to all e - ter - ni - ty.

Originally titled "In Temptation," these four stanzas (of five) call to mind how a spiritual and emotional
tempest can move from turmoil to tranquility. This tune was first used with this text in a cantata by the
composer in 1910, and since then has become the standard one.

TEXT: Charles Wesley, 1740
MUSIC: Joseph Parry, 1876

ABERYSTWYTH
7.7.7.7.D

Hear the Good News of Salvation 441

Wotanin waste nahon po

1 Hear the good news of sal-va-tion: Je-sus died to show God's love.
2 All the sins I have com-mit-ted, to my Sav-ior now I bring.

1 Wo-tan-in wa-ste na-hon po, Je-sus he wa-i-hdu-sna:
2 Wo-a-hta-ni kin e-ca-mon, hdu-ha Je-sus si-ha en,

Such great kind-ness! Such great mer-cy! Come to us from heaven a-bove.
I bow down with tears of an-guish; Christ for-gives and so I sing:

to-wa-o-si-da kin tan-ka, he de-han i-yo-ma-hi.
kun i-wa-hpa-mda wa-ce-ya, Je-sus on-śi-ma-da ce.

Je-sus Christ, how much I love you! Je-sus Christ, you save from sin!

Je-sus Christ wa-ste-wa-da-ka, Je-sus Christ ni-ma-yan: han, wa-

How I love you! Look up-on me. Love me still and cleanse with-in.

ste-wa-da-ke a-ma-ton-we is e-ya wa-ste-ma-da.

This text, originally appearing in four stanzas, was written by the first Native American Dakota to be ordained to the Presbyterian ministry and was published in the Dakota hymnal he edited. Both the Dakota and English versions have been associated with this shape note tune.

TEXT: Native American (Dakota); John B. Renville, 1879; trans. Emma Tibbets, 1955; vers. Jane Parker Huber, 1989
MUSIC: Wyeth's *Repository of Sacred Music, Part Second,* 1813
English Trans. Metrical Version © 1989 Jane Parker Huber (admin. Westminster John Knox Press)

NETTLETON
8.7.8.7.D

442 Just as I Am, without One Plea

1 Just as I am, with-out one plea but that thy
2 Just as I am, though tossed a-bout with man-y a
3 Just as I am, thou wilt re-ceive, wilt wel-come,
4 Just as I am, thy love un-known has bro-ken

blood was shed for me, and that thou biddest me
con - flict, man - y a doubt, fight-ings and fears with -
par - don, cleanse, re - lieve; be - cause thy prom - ise
ev - ery bar - rier down; now to be thine, yea,

come to thee,
in, with - out, O Lamb of God, I come; I come!
I be - lieve,
thine a - lone,

SPANISH

1 *Tal como soy de pecador,*
   sin más confianza que tu amor;
   a tu llamada vengo a ti,
   ¡Cordero de Dios, heme aquí!

KOREAN

1 큰-죄에 빠-진 날 위해
   주 보-혈 흘려 주시고
   또-나를 오-라 하시니-
   주께로 거-저 갑니다

When illness limited her involvement in a bustling household, the author wrote this hymn that helped her both to achieve and to express a renewed sense of worth grounded in Christ's self-giving. Its simple, direct, and deeply felt language has made it a source of comfort to many.

TEXT: Charlotte Elliott, 1834, alt.; Spanish trans. Tomás M. Westrup, alt; Korean trans. anon.
MUSIC: William Batchelder Bradbury, 1849; harm. *The Hymnbook*, 1955
Korean Trans. © The Hymnal Society of Korea
Music Harm. © 1955, ren. 1983 John Ribble (admin. Westminster John Knox Press)

WOODWORTH
LM

There Is a Redeemer

1 There is a Re - deem - er, Je - sus, God's own Son;
2 Je - sus, my Re - deem - er, name a - bove all names,
3 When I stand in glo - ry, I will see his face;

pre - cious Lamb of God, Mes - si - ah, Ho - ly One.
pre - cious Lamb of God, Mes - si - ah, hope for sin - ners slain.
there I'll serve my King for - ev - er in that ho - ly place.

Thank you, O my Fa - ther, for giv - ing us your Son, and

leav - ing your Spir - it till the work on earth is done.

Although the refrain of this piece names all three Persons of the Trinity, the stanzas emphasize references to Jesus Christ under various titles. There is also a shift in tone between the stanzas and the refrain: the former speak about God and the latter speaks to God.

TEXT and MUSIC: Melody Green, 1982
Text and Music © 1982 Birdwing Music, BMG Songs, Ears to Hear Music (admin. EMICMGPublishing.com)

Forgive Our Sins as We Forgive

Capo 5: (Am)

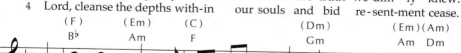

1 "For - give our sins as we for - give," you taught us, Lord, to pray,
2 How can your par - don reach and bless the un - for - giv - ing heart
3 In blaz - ing light your cross re - veals the truth we dim - ly knew:
4 Lord, cleanse the depths with - in our souls and bid re - sent - ment cease.

but you a - lone can grant us grace to live the words we say.
that broods on wrongs and will not let old bit - ter - ness de - part?
what triv - ial debts are owed to us, how great our debt to you!
Then, by your mer - cy rec - on - ciled, our lives will spread your peace.

Few petitions of the Lord's Prayer are as difficult to pray as this one, and we would not dare to pray it if we had to depend on ourselves rather than the example of forgiveness we are given in Jesus Christ. The shape note tune sets these words with appropriate spareness.

TEXT: Rosamond E. Herklots, 1969, 1983, alt.
MUSIC: *Supplement to Kentucky Harmony*, 1820; harm. Margaret W. Mealy, 1985
Text © 1969, 1983 Rosamond E. Herklots (admin. Oxford University Press)
Music Harm. © 1985 GIA Publications, Inc.

445 God, How Can We Forgive

1 God, how can we for-give when bonds of love are torn?
2 When we have missed the mark, and tears of an-guish flow,
3 Who dares to throw the stone to damn an-oth-er's sin,

How can we rise and start a-new, our trust re-born?
how can you still re-lease our guilt, the debt we owe?
when you, while know-ing all our past, for-give a-gain?

When hu-man lov-ing fails and ev-ery hope is gone,
The o-cean depth of grace sur-pass-es all our needs.
No more we play the judge, for by your grace we live.

your love gives strength be-yond our own to face the dawn.
A priest who shares our hu-man pain, Christ in-ter-cedes.
As you, O God, for-give our sin, may we for-give.

This text reflects both the struggle to deal with a deep personal hurt and a keen awareness of biblical language and content. The opening line of stanza two, for example, draws on the root meaning of the Greek word for sin, and the beginning of stanza three alludes to John 8:3–8.

TEXT: Ruth Duck, 1994
MUSIC: Jewish melody, 17th cent.; adapt. Meyer Lyon and Thomas Olivers, 1770
Text © 1996 The Pilgrim Press

LEONI
6.6.8.4.D

How Blest, Those Whose Transgressions 446
(Psalm 32)

1 How blest, those whose trans-gres-sions have free-ly been for-given;
2 While I kept guilt-y si-lence, my strength was spent with grief.
3 So let the god-ly seek you, when trou-bling times are near;

whose guilt is whol-ly cov-ered be-fore the sight of heaven.
Your hand was heav-y on me; my life found no re-lief.
no storm or flood shall reach them, nor cause their hearts to fear.

Blest, those to whom our Lord God will not im-pute their sin:
But when I made con-fes-sion and hid no sin from you,
In you, O Lord, I hide me; you save me from all ill.

whose guilt has been for-giv-en; whose hearts, made true a-gain.
when I re-vealed my fail-ings, you gave me life a-new.
And songs of your sal-va-tion my heart with rap-ture fill.

Although this is one of the traditional seven penitential psalms, it could equally well be called a psalm of
thanksgiving for forgiveness. It bears witness to the desirability of confession as well as to God's gracious
and forgiving nature, encouraging the faithful to seek God.

TEXT: *The New Metrical Version of the Psalms*, 1909, alt.
MUSIC: William Lloyd, 1840

MEIRIONYDD
7.6.7.6.D

447 We Are Forgiven

To sing, rather than simply say, a response to the Declaration of Forgiveness has the effect of making the moment both more affirmative and more corporate. The musical repetition of the two sentences also strengthens awareness of what it means to be assured of God's pardon.

TEXT: Trad. liturgical text
MUSIC: Hal H. Hopson, 1995
Music © 1995 Hal H. Hopson

WE ARE FORGIVEN
10.8.10.8

448 Peace of God Be with You
As-salaamu lakum

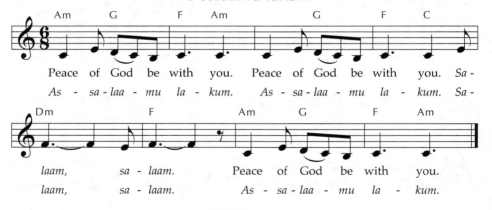

ARABIC

السلامُ لكم .
السلامُ لكم .
سلام ، سلام .
السلامُ لكم .

Both being Semitic languages, Arabic and Hebrew have many similar words, as can be heard here in *Salaam*, which sounds much like *Shalom*. This setting uses the same words and music in all but one phrase, making this brief song easy to learn in either English or Arabic.

TEXT: Arabic greeting
MUSIC: Richard Bruxvoort Colligan, 2004
Music © 2004 Local Church Ministries, United Church of Christ (admin. The Pilgrim Press)

AS-SALAAMU LAKUM
6.6.4.6

Show Us, O Lord, Your Steadfast Love 449
(Psalm 85)

1 Show us, O Lord, your stead - fast love, and let your
2 Mer - cy and truth at last have met; jus - tice and
3 Lord, you will grant pros - per - i - ty; our land will

sav - ing grace be near; when we re - turn with o - pen
peace are rec - on - ciled. Truth has a - ris - en from the
yield its full in - crease. Jus - tice shall go be - fore your

hearts the Lord speaks peace and we will hear.
earth; jus - tice looked down from heaven and smiled.
face; the path - way for your feet is peace.

This paraphrase of the latter part of Psalm 85 includes some remarkable signs of God's reign: that mercy, truth, justice, and peace exist simultaneously and that the fruits of creation will be abundant. Because we still await that day, this psalm is often associated with Advent.

TEXT: Christopher L. Webber, 2008
MUSIC: German melody; harm. Lowell Mason, 1831
Text © 2008 Christopher L. Webber

MENDON
LM

450   Be Thou My Vision

1 Be thou my vi - sion, O Lord of my heart;
2 Be thou my wis - dom, and thou my true Word;
3 Rich - es I heed not, nor vain, emp - ty praise;
4 High King of Heav - en, my vic - to - ry won,

naught be all else to me, save that thou art;
I ev - er with thee and thou with me, Lord;
thou mine in - her - i - tance, now and al - ways;
may I reach heav - en's joys, O bright heaven's Sun!

thou my best thought, by day or by night,
thou my soul's shel - ter, and thou my high tower;
thou and thou on - ly, first in my heart,
Heart of my own heart, what - ev - er be - fall,

wak - ing or sleep - ing, thy pres - ence my light.
raise thou me heaven - ward, O Power of my power.
High King of Heav - en, my trea - sure thou art.
still be my vi - sion, O Rul - er of all.

Guitar chords do not correspond with keyboard harmony.

These stanzas are selected from a 20th-century English poetic version of an Irish monastic prayer dating to the 10th century or before. They are set to an Irish folk melody that has proved popular and easily sung despite its lack of repetition and its wide range.

TEXT: Irish poem; trans. Mary E. Byrne, 1905; vers. Eleanor Hull, 1912, alt.
MUSIC: Irish ballad; harm. David Evans, 1927
Music Harm. © 1927 Oxford University Press

SLANE
10.10.10.10

Open My Eyes, That I May See 451

1 O-pen my eyes, that I may see glimps-es of truth thou hast for me.
2 O-pen my ears, that I may hear voic-es of truth thou send-est clear.
3 O-pen my mouth, and let me bear glad-ly the warm truth ev-ery-where.

Place in my hands the won-der-ful key that shall un-clasp and
And while the wave notes fall on my ear, ev-ery-thing false will
O-pen my heart, and let me pre-pare love with thy chil-dren

set me free. Si-lent-ly now I wait for thee, read-y, my God, thy
dis-ap-pear. Si-lent-ly now I wait for thee, read-y, my God, thy
thus to share. Si-lent-ly now I wait for thee, read-y, my God, thy

will to see. O-pen my eyes; il-lu-mine me, Spir-it di-vine!
will to see. O-pen my ears; il-lu-mine me, Spir-it di-vine!
will to see. O-pen my heart; il-lu-mine me, Spir-it di-vine!

The first woman to publish a collection of her own anthems, this author/composer has created in this hymn a sung prayer for illumination. It not only asks God to help us understand Scripture but also prays for the strength and courage to make God's love known to others.

TEXT and MUSIC: Clara H. Scott, 1895

OPEN MY EYES
8.8.9.8.8.8.8.4

452 Open the Eyes of My Heart

The initial petition of this song is based on the language of Ephesians 1:18, while the second part draws on the account of Isaiah's vision in Isaiah 6:1–5. That event, in turn, is the basis of the threefold *Sanctus* that has become a traditional element in Christian worship.

TEXT and MUSIC: Paul Baloche, 1997
Text and Music © 1997 Integrity's Hosanna! Music (admin. EMICMGPublishing.com)

OPEN THE EYES
Irregular

Open Your Ears, O Faithful People 453

1 O - pen your ears, O faith - ful peo - ple; o - pen your
2 They who have ears to hear the mes - sage, they who have

ears and hear God's word. O - pen your hearts, O
ears, now let them hear; they who would learn the

roy - al priest - hood; God has come to you.
way of wis - dom, let them hear God's word.

Refrain

God has spo - ken to the peo - ple, hal - le - lu - jah!
To - rah o - ra, To - rah o - ra, hal - le - lu - jah!

God has spo - ken words of wis - dom, hal - le - lu - jah!
To - rah o - ra, To - rah o - ra, hal - le - lu - jah!

God has spo - ken to the peo - ple, hal - le - lu - jah!
To - rah o - ra, To - rah o - ra, hal - le - lu - jah!

God has spo - ken words of wis - dom, hal - le - lu - jah!
To - rah o - ra, To - rah o - ra, hal - le - lu - jah!

In the writings of the prophets, the ear is valued above other senses, and the essential declaration of Jewish faith is *shema Ysrael*, "Hear, O Israel" (Deuteronomy 5:1, 6:4–9; Jeremiah 2:4). "To hear" is no small thing, for this verb assumes what is truly heard will also be obeyed.

TEXT: Willard F. Jabusch, 1966; rev. 1982
MUSIC: Hasidic melody; arr. *Evangelical Lutheran Worship*, 2006
Text © 1966, 1982 Willard F. Jabusch (Published by OCP)
Music Arr. © 2006 Augsburg Fortress

YISRAEL V'ORAITA
9.8.9.5 with refrain

454 Take the Saving Word of God

Dawk'yah towgyah thawy báht-awm

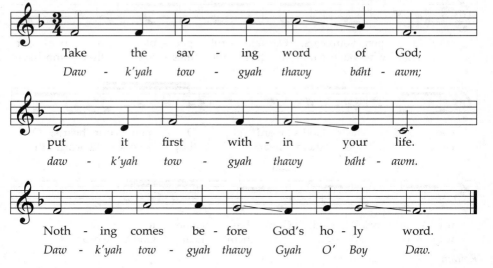

Take the sav - ing word of God;
Daw - k'yah tow - gyah thawy báht - awm;

put it first with - in your life.
daw - k'yah tow - gyah thawy báht - awm.

Noth - ing comes be - fore God's ho - ly word.
Daw - k'yah tow - gyah thawy Gyah O' Boy Daw.

This brief sacred song comes from a Native American tradition now centered in Oklahoma and the Texas panhandle. As often happens when moving between languages, the English text cannot retain the structure of the original but tries to convey its essential spirit and intention.

TEXT: Pawltay (Kiowa); English vers. John Thornburg, 2008
MUSIC: Kiowa melody; transcr. Carlton R. Young, 2008
English Vers. and Transcr. © 2008 General Board of Global Ministries t/a GBGMusik

DAWK'YAH TOWGYAH
7.7.9

455 Listen to the Word That God Has Spoken

Lis-ten to the word that God has spo-ken; lis-ten to the

One who is close at hand; lis-ten to the voice that be -

gan cre - a - tion; lis-ten e-ven if you don't un - der-stand.

May be sung as a round, successive voices entering ad lib.

Like "Open Your Ears, O Faithful People" (see no. 453), this short song from Canada is an encouragement to pay attention to what God is saying. The significance of the text is enhanced by singing this piece as a round, allowing the overlapping phrases to yield a single message.

TEXT: Anon. Canadian, alt.
MUSIC: Anon. Canadian; adapt. Church Hymnary, 4th Edition, 2005

LISTEN
10.10.11.10

Listen, God Is Calling

Neno lake Mungu

Refrain

Leader ... *All*

Lis - ten, lis - ten, God is call-ing, through the Word in - vit-ing,
Ne - no, ne - no la - ke Mu-ngu la - ku - i - ta we - we,

of - fer - ing for - give-ness, com - fort, and joy. joy.
ne - no la wo - ko - vu, te - na je - ma. ma.

Leader ... *All*

1 Je - sus gave his man-date: share the good news
2 Let none be for - got - ten through - out the world.
3 Help us to be faith - ful, stand - ing stead - fast,

Leader ... *All* ... *to Refrain*

that he came to save us and set us free.
In the tri - une name of God go and bap - tize.
walk - ing in your pre - cepts, led by your Word.

This anonymous Swahili hymn from Kenya follows a pattern of traditional African music (refrain, call-and-response stanzas, refrain) also common in African American spirituals. This text affirms that God's inviting and forgiving call can still be heard through the written Word.

TEXT: Kenyan; trans. Howard S. Olson, 1987
MUSIC: Kenyan; arr. Austin C. Lovelace, 1987
English Trans. © 1987 Lutheran Theological College, Makumira (admin. Augsburg Fortress)
Music Arr. © 1987 Austin C. Lovelace (admin. Augsburg Fortress)

NENO LAKE MUNGU
6.4.6.4 with refrain

457 How Happy Are the Saints of God
(Psalm 1)

1 How hap-py are the saints of God who do not
2 Like deep-ly root-ed trees, they stand be-side an
3 While wick-ed ones are whisked a-way like straw be-

heed the wick-ed way; de-light-ing in the
ev-er-flow-ing stream. Their fruit is plen-ti-
fore the driv-ing wind, the saints are firm-ly

ho-ly Word they seek God's wis-dom night and day.
ful and good; their leaves are al-ways grow-ing green.
plant-ed still, and God will keep them to the end.

This paraphrase of Psalm 1 celebrates the permanence of God's way in contrast with the transience of wickedness. While the wicked are dried up and scattered, the holy people of God are rooted and nourished. They bear much good fruit and are blessed with an enduring legacy.

TEXT: David Gambrell, 2009
MUSIC: William Knapp, 1738
Text © 2011 David Gambrell (admin. Presbyterian Publishing Corp.)

WAREHAM
LM
(alternate harmonization, 665)

Thy Word Is a Lamp unto My Feet 458

Thy word is a lamp un-to my feet and a light un-to my path. Thy word is a lamp un-to my feet and a light un-to my path. When I feel a-fraid, and I think I've lost my way, still you're there right be-side me. Noth-ing will I fear as long as you are near. Please be near me to the end.

The refrain of this 20th-century song is a quotation of Psalm 119:105 in the King James Version. That longest of all psalms celebrates the gift of God's law by accumulating many synonyms for it. In Christian practice, this verse has been used to give thanks for all Scripture.

TEXT: Amy Grant, 1984
MUSIC: Michael W. Smith, 1984; arr. John Sharber
Text and Music © 1984 Meadowgreen Music Company (admin. EMICMGPublishing.com)/Word Music

THY WORD
Irregular

459 O Word of God Incarnate

1 O Word of God in-car-nate, O Wis-dom from on high,
2 The church from you, dear Sav-ior, re-ceived this gift di-vine;
3 O make your church, dear Sav-ior, a lamp of pur-est gold

O Truth un-changed, un-chang-ing, O Light of our dark sky:
and still that light is lift-ed on all the earth to shine.
to bear be-fore the na-tions your true light, as of old;

we praise you for the ra-diance that from the hal-lowed page,
It is the chart and com-pass that, all life's voy-age through,
O teach your wan-dering pil-grims by this our path to trace,

a lan-tern to our foot-steps, shines on from age to age.
a-mid the rocks and quick-sands still guides, O Christ, to you.
till, clouds and storms thus end-ed, we see you face to face.

The opening four lines of this hymn celebrate attributes of Christ that are revealed through holy Scripture, which serves as a lantern, a chart, and a compass for the church in seeking to know Christ better. The setting of the tune comes from Felix Mendelssohn's *Elijah*.

TEXT: William Walsham How, 1867, alt.
MUSIC: *Neuvermehrtes Meiningisches Gesangbuch,* 1693; adapt. Felix Mendelssohn, 1847

MUNICH
7.6.7.6.D

Break Thou the Bread of Life   460

1 Break thou the bread of life, dear Lord, to me,
2 Bless thou the truth, dear Lord, now un - to me,

as thou didst break the loaves be - side the sea.
as thou didst bless the bread by Gal - i - lee.

Be - yond the sa - cred page I seek thee, Lord.
Then shall all bond - age cease, all fet - ters fall.

My spir - it pants for thee, O liv - ing Word!
And I shall find my peace, my all in all.

The phrase "bread of life" as a metaphor for scripture has misled many people into thinking of this hymn as being connected with the Lord's Supper, when its true subject is Bible study. Both the author and the composer were active in the work of the Chautauqua Assembly.

TEXT: Mary Ann Lathbury, 1877, alt.
MUSIC: William Fisk Sherwin, 1877, alt.

BREAD OF LIFE
6.4.6.4.D

461 As Dew Falls Gently at Dawn

1 As dew falls gent-ly at dawn, speak to us your
2 As rain falls feed-ing the earth, send the bless-ings
3 As light shines forth from the sun, shed on us your

beau-ti-ful word. Je-sus, Lord, when you send your word,
of your great love. Je-sus, Lord, when you send your grace,
spir-it of joy. Sav-ior, Je-sus, send us your peace,

word of life and lamp to our feet, all we who wan-der in
grace un-bound-ed, fill-ing our souls, all we who hun-ger and
peace that calms our souls from with-in. All we who suf-fer and

This gentle Korean hymn interweaves several patterns through its three stanzas. First are nurturing natural phenomena: dew, rain, sun. These are paralleled by spiritual gifts: word, grace, peace. Both patterns are united by a recurring sixth line conveying the theme of the text.

TEXT: Hee Bo Kim; trans. Edward Poitras, alt.
MUSIC: Soon Sae Kim
English Trans. © The Korean Hymnal Society
Music © 1982 Soon Sae Kim

AS DEW FALLS
7.8.8.8.7.7.8.8

sin   find   strength   and   new-ness   of   life.   Je - sus, Lord,   when
thirst   find   strength   and   new-ness   of   life.   Je - sus, Lord,   when
sigh   find   strength   and   new-ness   of   life.   Je - sus, Lord,   when

you   send   your word   morn - ing breaks and   we   walk   in   light.
you   send   your love   we   a - rise   and   fol - low   your way.
you   send   your peace,   we   are filled   with   heav - en - ly   love.

462 I Love to Tell the Story

1 I love to tell the sto - ry of un-seen things a-bove,
2 I love to tell the sto - ry; 'tis pleas-ant to re-peat
3 I love to tell the sto - ry, for those who know it best

of Je - sus and his glo - ry, of Je - sus and his love.
what seems, each time I tell it, more won-der-ful - ly sweet!
seem hun-ger-ing and thirst-ing to hear it, like the rest.

I love to tell the sto - ry, be-cause I know 'tis true;
I love to tell the sto - ry, for some have nev-er heard
And when, in scenes of glo - ry, I sing the new, new song,

it sat-is-fies my long-ings as noth-ing else could do.
the mes-sage of sal-va - tion from God's own ho - ly Word.
'twill be the old, old sto - ry that I have loved so long.

This text is drawn from the second part of a fifty-stanza poem on the life of Christ written in 1866, during the author's recovery from a serious illness. The tune named for her first appeared three years later, and the composer was responsible for the creation of the refrain.

TEXT: Katherine Hankey, 1866; ref. William G. Fischer, 1869
MUSIC: William G. Fischer, 1869

HANKEY
7.6.7.6.D with refrain

Refrain

463 How Firm a Foundation

1 How firm a foun-da-tion, ye saints of the Lord,
2 "Fear not, I am with thee, O be not dis-mayed,
3 "When through the deep wa-ters I call thee to go,
4 "When through fi-ery tri-als thy path-way shall lie,
5 "The soul that on Je-sus hath leaned for re-pose,

is laid for your faith in God's ex-cel-lent Word!
for I am thy God, and will still give thee aid;
the riv-ers of sor-row shall not o-ver-flow;
my grace, all suf-fi-cient, shall be thy sup-ply;
I will not, I will not de-sert to its foes;

What more can be said than to you God hath said,
I'll strength-en thee, help thee, and cause thee to stand,
for I will be near thee, thy trou-bles to bless,
the flame shall not hurt thee; I on-ly de-sign
that soul, though all hell should en-deav-or to shake,

to you who for ref-uge to Je-sus have fled?
up-held by my righ-teous, om-nip-o-tent hand.
and sanc-ti-fy to thee thy deep-est dis-tress.
thy dross to con-sume, and thy gold to re-fine.
I'll nev-er, no, nev-er, no, nev-er for-sake."

It seems odd now to think of singing this text to ADESTE FIDELES, but mainline churches did so well into
the 20th century because of a cultural bias against shape note music. The vigor of the present tune seems
especially right for the final line's reference to Hebrews 13:5.

TEXT: "K" in John Rippons's *A Selection of Hymns,* 1787, alt.
MUSIC: American folk melody; Funk's *Genuine Church Music,* 1832, alt.

FOUNDATION
11.11.11.11

Our Father, Which Art in Heaven 464

1 Our Fa - ther, which art in heav - en:
2 On earth as it is in heav - en:
3 And for - give us all our debts:
4 And lead us not in - to temp - ta - tion:
5 For thine is the king - dom, the power, and the glo - ry:

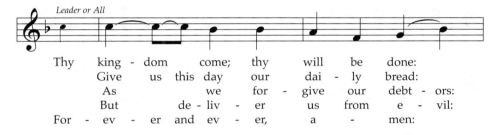

hal - low - ed - a be thy name.

Leader or All

Thy king - dom come; thy will be done:
Give us this day our dai - ly bread:
As we for - give our debt - ors:
But de - liv - er us from e - vil:
For - ev - er and ev - er, a - men:

hal - low - ed - a be thy name.

This lively call-and-response setting of the Lord's Prayer, based on the King James Version, uses the opening blessing as the congregation's refrain. This repetition is more than a convenience; it is a reminder of our abiding hope that all people will come to honor God's name.

TEXT: Trad. liturgical text
MUSIC: West Indian folk melody; transcr. Olive Pattison, 1945; harm. *The Presbyterian Hymnal*, 1989
Music Transcr. © 1945 Boosey & Co., Ltd.
Music Harm. © 1990 Westminster John Knox Press

WEST INDIAN
Irregular

465 What a Friend We Have in Jesus

죄짐 맡은 우리구주

1 What a friend we have in Je - sus, all our sins and griefs to bear!
2 Have we tri - als and temp-ta - tions? Is there trou-ble an - y-where?
3 Are we weak and heav - y lad - en, cum-bered with a load of care?

What a priv-i-lege to car - ry ev-ery-thing to God in prayer!
We should nev-er be dis-cour-aged; take it to the Lord in prayer!
Pre - cious Sav-ior, still our ref - uge; take it to the Lord in prayer!

O what peace we of-ten for - feit; O what need-less pain we bear,
Can we find a friend so faith-ful who will all our sor-rows share?
Do thy friends de-spise, for-sake thee? Take it to the Lord in prayer!

all be - cause we do not car - ry ev-ery-thing to God in prayer!
Je - sus knows our ev-ery weak-ness; take it to the Lord in prayer!
In his arms he'll take and shield thee; thou wilt find a so-lace there.

This text was written by an Irish-born immigrant to Canada to comfort his mother in Ireland when she was going through a time of special sorrow. The role of prayer as a source of strength and consolation is underscored by its repeated use as a rhyme word in all three stanzas.

TEXT: Joseph Scriven, 1855; Korean trans. The United Methodist Korean Hymnal Committee, 2001
MUSIC: Charles C. Converse, 1868
Korean Trans. © 2001 The United Methodist Publishing House (admin. The Copyright Company)

CONVERSE
8.7.8.7.D

KOREAN

1 죄짐맡은 우리구주 어찌좋은 친군지
걱정근심 무거운짐 우리주께 맡기세
아픈상처 위로하며 평화내려 주시니
우리주께 기도하여 모든짐을 맡기세

2 시험걱정 모든괴롬 없는사람 누군가
우리낙심 하지말고 기도드려 아뢰세
이런진실 하신친구 어디다시 있을까
우리약함 아시오니 주께기도 드리세

3 근심걱정 무거운짐 아니진자 누군가
피난처는 우리예수 주께기도 드리세
세상친구 멸시하고 너를조롱 하여도
예수품에 안기어서 참된위로 받겠네

Come and Fill Our Hearts 466
Confitemini Domino

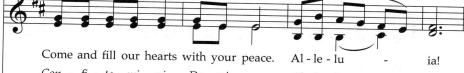

Come and fill our hearts with your peace. You a-lone, O Lord, are ho-ly.
Con - fi - te - mi - ni Do - mi - no quo - ni - am bo - nus.

Come and fill our hearts with your peace. Al - le - lu - ia!
Con - fi - te - mi - ni Do - mi - no. Al - le - lu - ia!

This prayer chant—intended for repeated singing—was originally created for a Latin text (Psalm 106:1a and Psalm 118:1a, 29a) on which the present English text is loosely based. Chants at Taizé often use Latin because it is a language free of political overtones.

TEXT and MUSIC: Jacques Berthier, 1982
Text and Music © 1991 Les Presses de Taizé (admin. GIA Publications, Inc.)

CONFITEMINI DOMINO
Irregular

467

Give Us Light
Jyothi dho Prabhu

1 Give us light; give us light; give us light, O Lord.
2 Give us life; give us life; give us life, O Lord.
3 Grant us peace; grant us peace; grant us peace, O Lord.
4 Save us now; save us now; save us now, O Lord.
5 Give us grace; give us grace; give us grace, O Lord.

HINDI

1 *Jyothi dho Prabhu.*

2 *Jiivan dho Prabhu.*

3 *Shanthi dho Prabhu.*

4 *Mukthi dho Prabhu.*

5 *Aasish dho Prabhu.*

From northern India comes this refrain from a typical *bhajan,* a kind of spiritual song praising the attributes of God. The Indian tradition of repeating important words and phrases (often even more than here) can be seen in this text drawn from images appearing in John 1:9–17.

TEXT: Charles Vas
MUSIC: Charles Vas, alt.
Text and Music © 1990 Christian Conference of Asia (admin. GIA Publications, Inc.)

JYOTHI DHO
Irregular

468

In My Life
Lord, Be Glorified

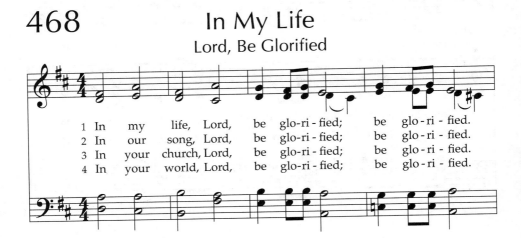

1 In my life, Lord, be glo-ri-fied; be glo-ri-fied.
2 In our song, Lord, be glo-ri-fied; be glo-ri-fied.
3 In your church, Lord, be glo-ri-fied; be glo-ri-fied.
4 In your world, Lord, be glo-ri-fied; be glo-ri-fied.

This praise song can be understood as a sung version of the first part of the answer to the first question of the Westminster Catechism: that a human being's "chief end is to glorify God." Numerous related Scriptures can be cited, including 1 Corinthians 6:20 and 10:31.

TEXT and MUSIC: Bob Kilpatrick, 1978
Text and Music © 1978, 1986 Prism Tree Music, assigned 1998 to The Lorenz Corp.

LORD, BE GLORIFIED
4.4.4.4.6

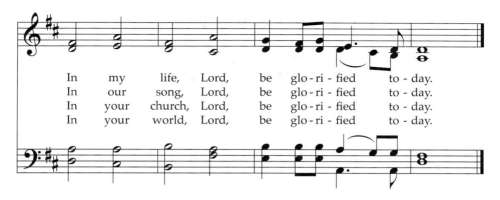

In my life, Lord, be glo-ri-fied to-day.
In our song, Lord, be glo-ri-fied to-day.
In your church, Lord, be glo-ri-fied to-day.
In your world, Lord, be glo-ri-fied to-day.

Lord, Listen to Your Children Praying 469

Lord, lis-ten to your chil-dren pray-ing. Lord, send your Spir-it in this place. Lord, lis-ten to your chil-dren pray-ing. Send us love; send us power; send us grace.

This chorus from a longer song has become a popular sung prayer for the presence of the Holy Spirit. Easily memorized, it makes a very suitable sung response at appropriate points during a series of prayer concerns or with repeated singing can open or close a time of prayer.

TEXT and MUSIC: Ken Medema, 1970
Text and Music © 1973 Hope Publishing Company

CHILDREN PRAYING
Irregular

470 There Is a Longing in Our Hearts

Refrain

There is a long-ing in our hearts, O Lord, for
you to re-veal your-self to us.
There is a long-ing in our hearts for love we
on-ly find in you, our God.

Leader or All

1 For jus-tice, for free-dom, for mer-cy:
2 For wis-dom, for cour-age, for com-fort:
3 For heal-ing, for whole-ness, for new life:
4 Lord save us, take pit-y, Light in our

hear our prayer. In sor-row, in grief:
hear our prayer. In weak-ness, in fear:
hear our prayer. In sick-ness, in death:
dark-ness. We call you; we wait:

be near; hear our prayer, O God.

The refrain that frames this sung prayer describes why we pray, and the stanzas indicate what we pray for. These requests are not for possessions but for qualities and conditions we hope for in the world around us, and they emerge from the changing circumstances of our lives.

TEXT and MUSIC: Anne Quigley, 1992
Text and Music © 1992 Anne Quigley (Published by OCP)

LONGING
Irregular

O Lord, Hear My Prayer

The Lord Is My Song

O Lord, hear my prayer. O Lord, hear my prayer.
Or The Lord is my song; the Lord is my praise:

When I call, an-swer me. O Lord, hear my prayer. O
all my hope comes from God. The Lord is my song; the

Lord, hear my prayer. Come and lis-ten to me.
Lord is my praise: God, the well-spring of life.

This chant from the Taizé Community in France is provided with two sets of words, either of which can be used as best suits the occasion. The first text is based on Psalm 102:1–2, and the second is an amalgam of phrases drawn from Psalms 118:14, 25:5, 36:9, and John 4:14.

TEXT: Taizé Community, 1982, 1991
MUSIC: Jacques Berthier, 1982
Text and Music © 1982 Les Presses de Taizé (admin. GIA Publications, Inc.)

HEAR MY PRAYER
5.5.6.D

472

Kum ba Yah

1 *Kum ba yah, my Lord, kum ba yah! Kum ba
2 Some-one's cry - ing, Lord, kum ba yah! Some-one's
3 Some-one's sing - ing, Lord, kum ba yah! Some-one's
4 Some-one's pray - ing, Lord, kum ba yah! Some-one's

yah, my Lord, kum ba yah! Kum ba yah, my Lord,
cry - ing, Lord, kum ba yah! Some-one's cry - ing, Lord,
sing - ing, Lord, kum ba yah! Some-one's sing - ing, Lord,
pray - ing, Lord, kum ba yah! Some-one's pray - ing, Lord,

kum ba yah! O Lord, kum ba yah!

*Come by here

This African American spiritual, first recorded in the 1920s, seems to have originated somewhere in the southern United States. It enjoyed renewed popularity during the folk revival of the 1960s and became a standard campfire song, eventually traveling throughout the world.

TEXT and MUSIC: African American spiritual

KUM BA YAH
8.8.8.5

Shepherd Me, O God
(Psalm 23)

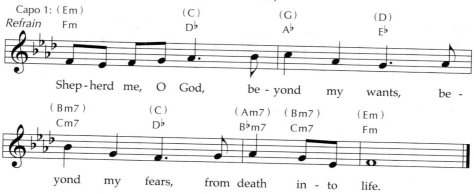

Leader stanzas included in Accompaniment Edition

PSALM 23

Refrain

1 The LORD is my shepherd;
   I shall not want.
2 **He makes me lie down in green pastures.**
   He leads me beside still waters.

   Refrain

3 He restores my soul.
   He leads me in paths of righteousness
   for his name's sake.
4 **Even though I walk through the valley**
   of the shadow of death, I fear no evil,
   for thou art with me;
   thy rod and thy staff, they comfort me.

   Refrain

5 Thou preparest a table before me
   in the presence of my enemies;
   thou anointest my head with oil;
   my cup overflows.
6 **Surely goodness and mercy shall**
   follow me all the days of my life,
   and I shall dwell in the house
   of the LORD forever. *Refrain*

PSALM PRAYER

Lord Jesus Christ, our good shepherd,
in the waters of Baptism you give us
   birth,
and at your table you nourish us with
   heavenly food.
In your goodness and mercy,
lead us along safe paths,
beyond the terrors of evil and death,
to the house of the Lord
where we may rest securely in you
   forever.
Amen.

For centuries no psalm has been better known or more beloved than Psalm 23. Although most people now have little occasion to encounter actual shepherds in daily life, this image remains a cherished and meaningful expression of reliance on God's faithful protection and provision.

TEXT and MUSIC: Marty Haugen, 1986
Text and Music © 1986 GIA Publications, Inc.
Responsive Reading © 1952, rev. 1971 Division of Christian Education
   of the National Council of the Churches of Christ in the U.S.A.

SHEPHERD ME
Irregular

474

As a Child Rests
(Psalm 131)

Refrain

As a child rests in its moth-er's arms, so will I rest in you.

As a child rests in its moth-er's arms, so will I rest in you.

Fine

to Refrain

1 My God, I am not proud. I do not look for things too great.
2 My God, I trust in you. You care for me, you give me peace.
3 O Is - rael, trust in God, now and al - ways trust in God.

Guitar chords do not correspond with keyboard harmony.

The image of the resting child in this paraphrase of Psalm 131 seems even more remarkable when this psalm is put in context. It is one of the Songs of Ascent sung by pilgrims on the way to Jerusalem. To be still in God in the midst of such activity is indeed a blessed condition.

TEXT: Christopher Walker, 1988, alt.
MUSIC: Christopher Walker, 1988
Text and Music © 1988, 1989 Christopher Walker (Published by OCP)

AS A CHILD RESTS
Irregular

Come, Thou Fount of Every Blessing 475

1 Come, thou Fount of ev-ery bless-ing; tune my heart to sing thy grace;
2 Here I raise my Eb-e-ne-zer; hith-er by thy help I'm come;
3 O to grace how great a debt-or dai-ly I'm con-strained to be!

streams of mer-cy, nev-er ceas-ing, call for songs of loud-est praise.
and I hope, by thy good plea-sure, safe-ly to ar-rive at home.
Let that grace now, like a fet-ter, bind my wan-dering heart to thee.

Teach me some me-lo-dious son-net, sung by flam-ing tongues a-bove;
Je-sus sought me when a strang-er, wan-dering from the fold of God;
Prone to wan-der, Lord, I feel it, prone to leave the God I love;

praise the mount! I'm fixed up-on it, mount of God's un-chang-ing love!
he, to res-cue me from dan-ger, in-ter-posed his pre-cious blood.
here's my heart; O take and seal it; seal it for thy courts a-bove.

Written for Pentecost by a British Baptist pastor, this text is full of biblical terms like "Ebenezer" (1 Samuel 7:12), Hebrew for "a stone of help" set up to give thanks for God's assistance. The tune name honors hymnal compiler Asahel Nettleton, who probably did not compose it.

TEXT: Robert Robinson, 1758, alt.
MUSIC: Wyeth's *Repository of Sacred Music, Part Second,* 1813

NETTLETON
8.7.8.7.D

476 Crashing Waters at Creation

1 Crash - ing wa - ters at cre - a - tion, or - dered
2 Part - ing wa - ter stood and trem - bled as the
3 Cleans - ing wa - ter once at Jor - dan closed a -
4 Liv - ing wa - ter, nev - er end - ing, quench the

by the Spir - it's breath, first to wit - ness
cap - tives passed on through, wash - ing off the
round the One fore - told, o - pened to re -
thirst and flood the soul. Well - spring, Source of

day's be - gin - ning from the bright - ness of night's death.
chains of bond - age: chan - nel to a life made new.
veal the glo - ry ev - er new and ev - er old.
life e - ter - nal, drench our dry - ness; make us whole.

Like the Thanksgiving Over the Water in the rite of Baptism, this text by a United Church of Canada minister recalls significant events in salvation history involving water. The final stanza is a prayer to Christ, the Living Water (John 4:10, 14), to quench our spiritual thirst.

CRASHING WATERS
8.7.8.7

TEXT: Sylvia G. Dunstan, 1987
MUSIC: William A. Cross, 1992
Text © 1991 GIA Publications, Inc.
Music © 1994 William A. Cross

Thy Mercy and Thy Truth, O Lord 477
(Psalm 36)

1 Thy mer - cy and thy truth, O Lord, tran -
2 Lord, all thy crea - tures thou wilt save. Since
3 With the a - bun - dance of thy house we
4 The foun - tain of e - ter - nal life is
5 From those that know thee, may thy love and

scend the loft - y sky; thy judg - ments are a
thou art ev - er kind, be - neath the shad - ow
shall be sat - is - fied; from riv - ers of un -
found a - lone with thee. And in the bright - ness
mer - cy ne'er de - part, and may thy jus - tice

might - y deep, and as the moun - tains high.
of thy wings we may a ref - uge find.
fail - ing joy our thirst shall be sup - plied.
of thy light we clear - ly light shall see.
still pro - tect and bless the up - right heart.

These five stanzas celebrating God's merciful care for all creation correspond to Psalm 36:5–10 and were prepared by a joint committee of nine North American churches in the Reformed tradition. They are set here to a simple but memorable tune from the mid-16th century.

TEXT: *The New Metrical Version of the Psalms*, 1909, alt.
MUSIC: Thomas Tallis, c. 1567, alt.

TALLIS' ORDINAL
CM
(this tune in a lower key, 776)

478 Save Me, O God; I Sink in Floods

(Psalm 69)

1 Save me, O God; I sink in floods, plunged in- to mis- er- y. My con- stant weep- ing brings no help; Lord, hear and an- swer me. In full as- sur- ance of your grace I turn to you in prayer. De- liv- er me from surg- ing floods; draw near; reach out in care.

2 Your stead- fast mer- cy, Lord, is good; hide not your face from me. Hear my dis- tress and an- swer, Lord; make haste and set me free. You know of my re- proach and shame; my heart de- spairs from grief. I looked for pit- y, but I found no com- fort or re- lief.

3 Though I am poor and sor- row- ful, O Lord, at- tend my cry. Let your sal- va- tion come to me, and lift me up on high. Let heaven and earth and seas re- joice; let all that move give praise. All those that love God's name shall live in Zi- on all their days.

Guitar chords do not correspond with keyboard harmony.

Because Hebrew thought identified large, uncontrolled bodies of water with chaos, this flood imagery is an effective way to express overwhelming distress. In Christian practice Psalm 69 has been second only to Psalm 22 in its use as a foreshadowing of the sufferings of Christ.

SALVATION
CMD

TEXT: Marie J. Post, 1985
MUSIC: *Kentucky Harmony*, 1816; harm. Kenneth Munson, 1964
Text Para. © 1987 Faith Alive Christian Resources

Ho, All Who Thirst
Come Now to the Water

This song brings together many biblical references that help to enlarge an appreciation of the water of baptism. The refrain is based on Isaiah 55:1, stanza one adapts Jeremiah 2:13, stanza two draws on Revelation 7:17, and the third stanza condenses the imagery of John 4:10–14.

TEXT and MUSIC: Alexander M. Peters, 1997
Text and Music © 1997 Alexander M. Peters

JACOB'S WELL
5.7.5.5 with refrain

480 Take Me to the Water

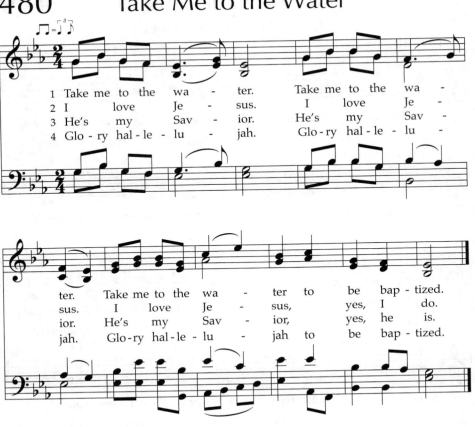

1 Take me to the wa - ter.   Take me to the wa -
2 I love Je - sus.   I love Je -
3 He's my Sav - ior.   He's my Sav -
4 Glo - ry hal - le - lu - jah.   Glo - ry hal - le - lu -

ter.   Take me to the wa - ter to be bap - tized.
sus.   I love Je - sus,   yes, I do.
ior.   He's my Sav - ior,   yes, he is.
jah.   Glo - ry hal - le - lu - jah to be bap - tized.

This African American spiritual sums up the commitment of a candidate for baptism: the request for the rite, an expression of motivation, and a succinct affirmation of faith. The widening melodic lines build anticipation and give weight to the final phrase of each stanza.

TEXT and MUSIC: African American spiritual

TAKE ME TO THE WATER
Irregular

I Believe in God the Father

1 I be-lieve in God the Fa - ther, mer - ci - ful and might-y Lord,
2 Un-der Pi - late, Je - sus suf - fered, faith-ful to his fi - nal breath.
3 I be-lieve in God the Spir - it, and the church in ev - ery place;

mak - er of the earth and heav - ens, whom we wor-ship and a - dore;
He was cru - ci - fied and bur - ied, and de-scend-ed in - to death.
saints in glo - ri - ous com - mu - nion, all for-giv - en, full of grace;

and in Je - sus Christ the Son, on - ly Sav - ior, sov - ereign one,
From the grave he did a - rise; he as-cend-ed through the skies;
flesh and blood will live a - gain; life in Christ will nev - er end.

by the Ho - ly Spir-it giv - en, born of Mar - y, bless - ed vir-gin.
now en-throned with God in heav-en, he will judge the dead and liv-ing.
Ho - ly Spir - it, Son and Fa-ther: I will praise your name for - ev - er.

This text is a 21st-century metrical paraphrase of the Apostles' Creed (in the manner of Calvin's Strasbourg liturgy). Its connections with Reformed tradition are further strengthened by being set to the tune created for Psalm 42 in the 1551 Genevan Psalter (see also no. 87).

TEXT: David Gambrell, 2009
MUSIC: Genevan Psalter, 1551
Text © 2011 David Gambrell (admin. Presbyterian Publishing Corp.)

GENEVAN 42
8.7.8.7.7.7.8.8

482 Baptized in Water

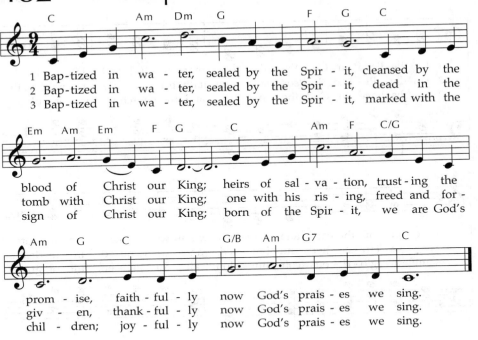

1 Bap-tized in wa - ter, sealed by the Spir - it, cleansed by the
2 Bap-tized in wa - ter, sealed by the Spir - it, dead in the
3 Bap-tized in wa - ter, sealed by the Spir - it, marked with the

blood of Christ our King; heirs of sal - va - tion, trust - ing the
tomb with Christ our King; one with his ris - ing, freed and for -
sign of Christ our King; born of the Spir - it, we are God's

prom - ise, faith - ful - ly now God's prais - es we sing.
giv - en, thank - ful - ly now God's prais - es we sing.
chil - dren; joy - ful - ly now God's prais - es we sing.

Each stanza of this compact and carefully constructed text about baptism begins with allusions to John 3:5 and Ephesians 1:13. The interplay of constant and changing lines accentuates each added image. It is set here to a Gaelic tune first transcribed in the 19th century.

TEXT: Michael J. Saward, 1981
MUSIC: Gaelic melody; arr. Dale Grotenhuis, 1985
Text © 1982 The Jubilate Group (admin. Hope Publishing Company)
Music Arr. © 1987 Faith Alive Christian Resources

BUNESSAN
5.5.8.5.5.9

Dearest Jesus, We Are Here 483

1 Dear-est Je-sus, we are here, glad-ly your com-
2 Your com-mand is clear and plain, and we would o-
3 This is why we come to you, in our arms this
4 Gra-cious Head, your mem-ber own; Shep-herd, take your

mand o - bey - ing. With this child we now draw near
bey it du - ly: "You must all be born a - gain,
in - fant bear - ing. Tru - ly, here your grace we view.
lamb and feed it; Prince of Peace, make here your throne;

in re-sponse to your own say - ing that to you it
heart and life re-new-ing tru - ly, born of wa - ter
Let this child, your mer-cy shar - ing, in your arms be
Way of life, to heav-en lead it; pre-cious Vine, let

shall be giv-en as a child and heir of heav - en.
and the Spir-it, and my king-dom thus in-her - it."
shield-ed ev - er, yours on earth and yours for-ev - er.
noth-ing sev-er from your side this branch for-ev - er.

As the similarity of their opening lines suggests (they are identical in German), this text for the baptism of a child was written in imitation of the sermon hymn "Blessed Jesus, at Your Word" (no. 395), which is the text usually associated with the tune they share.

TEXT: Benjamin Schmolck, 1704; trans. Catherine Winkworth, 1858, alt.
MUSIC: Johann Rudolph Ahle, 1664; harm. Johann Sebastian Bach, alt.

LIEBSTER JESU
7.8.7.8.8.8

484 Out of Deep, Unordered Water

1 Out of deep, un-or-dered wa-ter God cre-
2 Wa-ter on the hu-man fore-head, birth-mark
3 Stand-ing round the font re-minds us of the

at-ed light and land, world of bird and beast and,
of the love of God, is the sign of death and
He-brews' climb a-shore. Life is hal-lowed by the

lat-er, in God's im-age, wom-an, man.
ris-ing; through the seas there runs a road.
knowl-edge God has been this way be-fore.

There is wa-ter in the riv-er bring-ing life to tree and plant.

By connecting the water in the font with the waters of creation, the parted waters through which the Israelites were set free, and the rivers that sustain life everywhere, this hymn reminds us that baptism incorporates us into God's creative, redemptive, and sustaining activity.

TEXT: Fred Kaan, 1965
MUSIC: C. Hubert H. Parry, 1897
Text © 1968 Hope Publishing Company

RUSTINGTON
8.7.8.7.D

Let cre - a - tion praise its giv - er: there is wa - ter in the font.

We Know That Christ Is Raised   485

Capo 3: (D)

1 We know that Christ is raised and dies no more.
2 We share by wa - ter in his sav - ing death.
3 The Fa - ther's splen - dor clothes the Son with life.
4 A new cre - a - tion comes to life and grows

Em - braced by death he broke its fear - ful hold,
Re - born we share with him an Eas - ter life
The Spir - it's pow - er shakes the church of God.
as Christ's new bod - y takes on flesh and blood.

and our de - spair he turned to blaz - ing joy.
as liv - ing mem - bers of a liv - ing Christ.
Bap - tized we live with God the Three in One.
The u - ni - verse, re - stored and whole, will sing:

1–3   Al - le - lu - ia!   4   Al - le - lu - ia!

Guitar chords do not correspond with keyboard harmony.

Beginning with an allusion to Romans 6:9, this exuberant baptismal hymn unfolds the implications of our incorporation into Christ's new life, making us "a new creation" (2 Corinthians 5:17). The text was written to fit this expansive tune by a distinguished British composer.

TEXT: John Brownlow Geyer, 1967, alt.
MUSIC: Charles Villiers Stanford, 1904
Text © 1972 John Brownlow Geyer

ENGELBERG
10.10.10.4
(this tune in a higher key, 641)

486 Child of Blessing, Child of Promise

1 Child of bless - ing, child of prom - ise, bap - tized
2 Child of love, our love's ex - pres - sion, love's cre -
3 Child of joy, our dear - est trea - sure, God's you
4 Child of God, your lov - ing Par - ent, learn to

with the Spir - it's sign, with this wa - ter God has
a - tion, loved in - deed! Fresh from God, re - fresh our
are, from God you came. Back to God we hum - bly
lis - ten for God's call. Grow to laugh and sing and

sealed you un - to love and grace di - vine.
spir - its; in - to joy and laugh - ter lead.
give you: live as one who bears Christ's name.
wor - ship; trust and love God more than all.

This hymn addressed to a newly-baptized child begins each stanza with a facet of the child's identity, culminating in "child of God." By being directed to one person rather than the whole congregation, this text occupies a special category among the "songs of encouragement."

TEXT: Ronald S. Cole-Turner, 1980
MUSIC: V. Earle Copes, 1959
Text © 1981 Ronald S. Cole-Turner

KINGDOM
8.7.8.7
(alternate tune: STUTTGART)

These Treasured Children

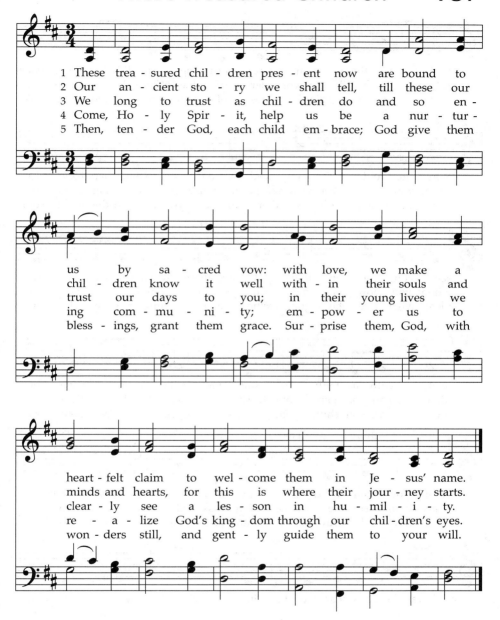

1 These trea-sured chil-dren pres-ent now are bound to
2 Our an-cient sto-ry we shall tell, till these our
3 We long to trust as chil-dren do and so en-
4 Come, Ho-ly Spir-it, help us be a nur-tur-
5 Then, ten-der God, each child em-brace; God give them

us by sa-cred vow: with love, we make a
chil-dren know it well with-in their souls and
trust our days to you; in their young lives we
ing com-mu-ni-ty; em-pow-er us to
bless-ings, grant them grace. Sur-prise them, God, with

heart-felt claim to wel-come them in Je-sus' name.
minds and hearts, for this is where their jour-ney starts.
clear-ly see a les-son in hu-mil-i-ty.
re-a-lize God's king-dom through our chil-dren's eyes.
won-ders still, and gent-ly guide them to your will.

This text emphasizes the covenantal dimensions of baptism, most obvious in the baptism of children (though also present in the baptism of adults), including the worshiping community's commitment to acquaint children with salvation history and to learn from their humble trust.

TEXT: Jacque B. Jones, 2009
MUSIC: Trier ms. 15th cent.; adapt. Michael Praetorius, 1609
Text © 2010 GIA Publications, Inc.

PUER NOBIS NASCITUR
LM
(alternate harmonization, 67)

488 I Was There to Hear Your Borning Cry

1 "I was there to hear your born-ing cry; I'll be there when
2 "When you heard the won-der of the Word, I was there to
3 "In the mid-dle a-ges of your life, not too old, no

you are old. I re-joiced the day you were bap-tized to
cheer you on. You were raised to praise the liv-ing Lord to
lon-ger young, I'll be there to guide you through the night, com-

see your life un-fold. I was there when you were but a
whom you now be-long. If you find some-one to share your
plete what I've be-gun. When the eve-ning gent-ly clos-es

child with a faith to suit you well; in a blaze of
time and you join your hearts as one, I'll be there to
in and you shut your wea-ry eyes, I'll be there as

light you wan-dered off to find where de-mons dwell."
make your vers-es rhyme from dusk till ris-ing sun."
I have al-ways been with just one more sur-prise."

4 "I was there to hear your born-ing cry; I'll be there when you are old.

I re-joiced the day you were bap-tized to see your life un-fold."

Originally created to accompany a video series on baptism, this hymn speaks in the imagined conversational voice of God, assuring the person being baptized of God's presence throughout the changing stages of life. It offers a reminder that baptism is a once-in-a-lifetime event.

TEXT and MUSIC: John C. Ylvisaker, 1985
Text and Music © 1985 John C. Ylvisaker

WATERLIFE
9.7.9.6.D

Wonder of Wonders, Here Revealed 489

1 Won-der of won-ders, here re-vealed: God's cov-e-
2 Here in this sac-ra-ment we see God's grace un-
3 This child of God, though young or old, we wel-come
4 Now we our vow of faith re-new, stretch wide our

nant with us is sealed, and long be-fore we
bound, for all, for me! May we re-spond with
now in-to Christ's fold, to know with us God's
sights to glo-bal view, and claim with Chris-tians

know or pray, God's love en-folds us ev-ery day.
joy-ful praise in lov-ing ser-vice all our days.
lov-ing care, and all our joys and sor-rows share.
far and near a larg-er fam-i-ly held dear.

In creating this text (for which she chose this existing tune as its setting), the author wished to emphasize two themes: that God loves us before we know how to love in return, and that through baptism we become part of a worldwide family unbounded by space or time.

TEXT: Jane Parker Huber, 1980, alt.
MUSIC: William Boyd, 1864
Text © 1980 Jane Parker Huber (admin. Westminster John Knox Press)

PENTECOST (Boyd)
LM

490

Wash, O God, Your Sons and Daughters

Capo 3: (D)   (Bm)   (G)
F   Dm   B♭

1 Wash, O God, your sons and daugh-ters, new-born crea-tures
2 Ev-ery day we need your nur-ture; by your milk may
3 O how deep your ho-ly wis-dom! Un-i-mag-ined,

(D)   (Bm)
F   Dm

of your womb. Num-ber them a-mong your peo-ple, raised like
we be fed. Let us join your feast, par-tak-ing cup of
all your ways! To your name be glo-ry, hon-or! With our

(G)   (D)   (A)
B♭   F   C

Christ from death and tomb. Weave them gar-ments bright and
bless-ing, liv-ing bread. God, re-new us; guide our
lives we wor-ship, praise! We your peo-ple stand be-

(Bm)   (F♯m)   (Bm)   (G)   (A)   (D)
Dm   Am   Dm   B♭   C   F

spark-ling; com-pass them with love and light. Fill, a-noint them;
foot-steps, free from sin and all its snares, one with Christ in
fore you, wa-ter-washed and Spir-it-born. By your grace, our

(Bm)   (G)   (D)
Dm   B♭   F

send your Spir-it, ho-ly dove and heart's de-light.
liv-ing, dy-ing, by your Spir-it, chil-dren, heirs.
lives we of-fer. Re-cre-ate us; God, trans-form!

Guitar chords do not correspond with keyboard harmony.

This text incorporates many of the images associated with the water of baptism in the Thanksgiving Over the Water in *The Book of Common Worship,* especially nourishment, the calling forth of life, cleansing and renewal, freedom from bondage, and sharing in Christ's resurrection.

TEXT: Ruth Duck, 1987, rev.   BEACH SPRING
MUSIC: *The Sacred Harp,* 1844; harm. James H. Wood, 1958   8.7.8.7.D
Text © 1989 The United Methodist Publishing House (admin. The Copyright Company)
Music Harm. © 1958, ren. 1986 Broadman Press/Van Ness Press, Inc. (admin. Music Services)

You Have Put On Christ

1 You have put on Christ; in Christ you have been bap-tized.
2 We have put on Christ; in Christ we have been bap-tized.

Al - le - lu - ia! Al - le - lu - ia!

May be sung as a canon.

This brief, easily sung congregational response is appropriate for use at baptism, either of children or adults, as well as at occasions including the Reaffirmation of the Baptismal Covenant. It was created by the International Commission on English in the Liturgy.

TEXT: From the Rite of Baptism for Children, ICEL
MUSIC: Howard Hughes, SM, 1977
Text © 1969 International Commission on English in the Liturgy
Music © 1977 International Commission on English in the Liturgy

BAPTIZED IN CHRIST
Irregular

You Belong to Christ

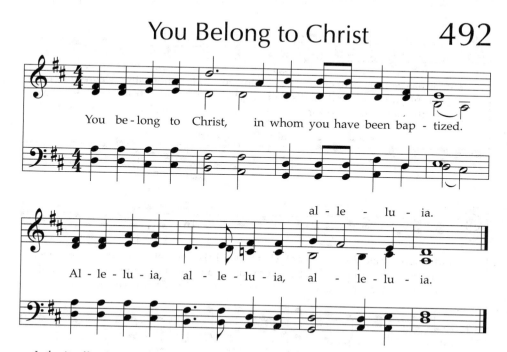

You be-long to Christ, in whom you have been bap - tized.

al - le - lu - ia.

Al - le - lu - ia, al - le - lu - ia, al - le - lu - ia.

In the rite of baptism provided in *Evangelical Lutheran Worship* this text appears as one of the optional congregational responses after each person is baptized. It represents an adaptation of recurring scriptural images and closely resembles the language of Galatians 3:27 and 29.

TEXT: *Holy Baptism and Related Rites, Renewing Worship,* vol. 3, 2002
MUSIC: Robert A. Hobby, 2003
Text © 2002 Augsburg Fortress
Music © 2003 Augsburg Fortress

YOU BELONG TO CHRIST
Irregular

493 Now There Is No Male or Female

1 Now there is no male or fe-male; now there is no free or slave;
2 Cru - ci - fied with Christ the Sav-ior, bap-tized in his ho - ly death,
3 Death has no do - min-ion o'er him, so for us death holds no power;

now there is no Jew or Gen-tile in the earth Christ died to save.
and as Christ was raised to glo - ry we have new life on this earth.
life's own wa-ters now have marked us, born to God this ver - y hour.

Christ has set us free for free-dom: we no more sing slav-ery's creed;
Power of wa-ter and God's nam-ing, turn-ing us from dark to light,
From this mo-ment and for - ev - er dead to sin, a - live in Christ,

old sub - mis-sions can-not claim us; Christ has set us free in - deed.
joins us to those who, be - fore us, ran the race and fought the fight.
born of wa - ter and the Spir - it, now in Christ we find our life.

Opening with an allusion to Galatians 3:28 and closing with one to John 3:5, this text is filled with specific scriptural phrases related to baptism. It also includes larger themes like the parallels with the deliverance of Israel from slavery through the waters of the Red Sea.

TEXT: Lynette Miller, 1985
MUSIC: *Gesangbuch*, 1695
Text © 1986 Lynette Miller

OMNI DIE (Trier)
8.7.8.7.D

Jesus, Thou Joy of Loving Hearts 494

1 Je - sus, thou joy of lov - ing hearts, thou fount of
2 Thy truth un-changed hath ev - er stood; thou sav - est
3 We taste thee, O thou liv - ing bread, and long to
4 Our rest - less spir - its yearn for thee, wher-e'er our
5 O Je - sus, ev - er with us stay; make all our

life, thou light of all, from the best bliss that
those that on thee call; to them that seek thee
feast up - on thee still; we drink of thee, the
change - ful lot is cast, glad when thy gra - cious
mo - ments calm and bright. O chase the night of

earth im - parts we turn, un - filled, to heed thy call.
thou art good, to them that find thee, all in all.
foun - tain-head, and thirst our souls from thee to fill.
smile we see, blest when our faith can hold thee fast.
sin a - way; shed o'er the world thy ho - ly light.

This 19th-century American translation of stanzas from a longer Latin poem is so well shaped that it sounds like an original meditation on Christian experience centered on the Lord's Supper. The North American tune name seems not to have originated with the English composer.

TEXT: Latin, 12th cent.; trans. Ray Palmer, 1858, alt.
MUSIC: Henry Baker, 1854

QUEBEC
LM

495 Thee We Adore, O Hidden Savior, Thee

1 Thee we a - dore, O hid - den Sav - ior, thee,
2 O blest me - mo - rial of our dy - ing Lord,
3 Foun - tain of good - ness, Je - sus, Lord and God,
4 O Christ, whom now be - neath a veil we see,

who at this bless - ed feast art pleased to be;
who liv - ing bread to all doth here af - ford!
cleanse us, un - clean, with thy most cleans - ing blood;
may what we thirst for soon our por - tion be,

both flesh and spir - it in thy pres - ence fail,
O may our souls for - ev - er feed on thee,
in - crease our faith and love, that we may know
to gaze on thee un - veiled, and see thy face,

yet here thy pres - ence we de - vout - ly hail.
and thou, O Christ, for - ev - er pre - cious be!
the hope and peace which from thy pres - ence flow.
the vi - sion of thy glo - ry and thy grace.

Originally conceived as a private prayer of preparation and set out in seven four-line stanzas in Latin, this text has been the inspiration for many English hymn versions, including this one by an English bishop. The fairly late plainsong tune moves toward modern tonalities.

TEXT: Attr. Thomas Aquinas, 13th cent.; trans. James Russell Woodford, 1850
MUSIC: *Processionale*, 1697

ADORO TE DEVOTE
10.10.10.10

Bread of Heaven, on Thee We Feed 496

1 Bread of heaven, on thee we feed, for thou art our
food in - deed. Ev - er may our souls be fed
with this true and liv - ing Bread, day by day with
strength sup - plied through the life of Christ who died.

2 Vine of heaven, thy love sup - plies this blest cup of
sac - ri - fice. 'Tis thy wounds our heal - ing give;
to thy cross we look and live. Thou our life! O
let us be root - ed, graft - ed, built on thee.

Both the names used to address Christ in this eucharistic hymn appear only in the Fourth Gospel. Jesus refers to himself as the Bread of Heaven in John 6:51 and as the True Vine in John 15:1. The text is set to a tune with diverse roots, Welsh and French, sacred and secular.

TEXT: Josiah Conder, 1824, alt.
MUSIC: French and Welsh melody; arr. Hugh Davies, 1906

ARFON
7.7.7.7.7.7

497 Bread of Life from Heaven

Refrain

Bread of life from heav-en, your blood and bod-y giv-en, we
eat this bread and drink this cup un-til you come a-gain.

Last time

1 Break now the bread of Christ's sac-ri-fice; giv-ing thanks,
2 Seek not the food that will pass a-way; set your hearts
3 Love as the One who, in love for you, gave him-self
4 Dwell in the One who now dwells in you; make your home
5 Drink of this cup and de-clare his death; eat this bread

hun-gry ones, gath-er round. Eat, all of you, and be
on the food that en-dures. Come, learn the true and the
for the life of the world. Come to the One who is
in the life-giv-ing Word. Know on-ly Christ, ho-ly
and be-lieve Eas-ter morn; trust his re-turn and, with

to Refrain

sat-is-fied; in Christ's pres-ence the loaves will a-bound.
liv-ing way, that the full-ness of life may be yours.
food for you, that your hun-ger and thirst be no more.
One of God, and be-lieve in the truth you have heard.
ev-ery breath, praise the One in whom you are re-born.

This Lord's Supper hymn began with the music of the refrain, an Argentine melody for the *Sanctus*. Then the refrain text was written to fit that music, followed by stanzas based on themes from John 6. Finally, a melody for the stanzas was composed in the style of the refrain.

TEXT: Susan R. Briehl, 2001
MUSIC: Refrain, Argentine melody; stanzas, Marty Haugen, 2001
Text and Music © 2001 GIA Publications, Inc.

ARGENTINE SANTO | BREAK NOW THE BREAD
9.9.9.9 with refrain

Loaves Were Broken, Words Were Spoken

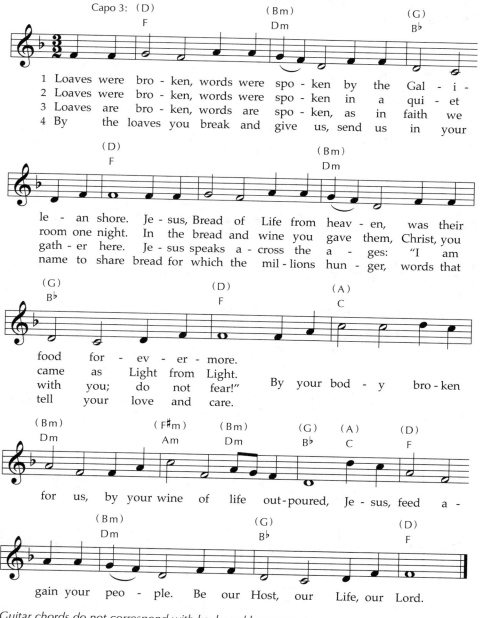

1 Loaves were bro - ken, words were spo - ken by the Gal - i -
2 Loaves were bro - ken, words were spo - ken in a qui - et
3 Loaves are bro - ken, words are spo - ken, as in faith we
4 By the loaves you break and give us, send us in your

le - an shore. Je - sus, Bread of Life from heav - en, was their
room one night. In the bread and wine you gave them, Christ, you
gath - er here. Je - sus speaks a - cross the a - ges: "I am
name to share bread for which the mil - lions hun - ger, words that

food for - ev - er - more.
came as Light from Light.
with you; do not fear!" By your bod - y bro - ken
tell your love and care.

for us, by your wine of life out - poured, Je - sus, feed a -

gain your peo - ple. Be our Host, our Life, our Lord.

Guitar chords do not correspond with keyboard harmony.

The first two stanzas of this text deal with events in the past (the feeding of the multitude and the Last Supper) and the final two with events in the present. The recurring last four lines of each stanza serve as an affirmation of Christ's continuing presence at all times.

TEXT: Herman G. Stuempfle Jr., 2005
MUSIC: *The Sacred Harp*, 1844; harm. James H. Wood, 1958
Text © 2006 GIA Publications, Inc.
Music Harm. © 1958, ren. 1986 Broadman Press/Van Ness Press, Inc. (admin. Music Services)

BEACH SPRING
8.7.8.7.D

499 Bread of the World in Mercy Broken

Bread of the world in mer-cy bro-ken, Wine of the soul in mer-cy shed, by whom the words of life were spo-ken, and in whose death our sins are dead: look on the heart by sor-row bro-ken; look on the tears by sin-ners shed; so may your feast be-come the to-ken that by your grace our souls are fed.

This prayer-text divides into distinct halves, the first four lines being an extended address to Christ, and the last four being a series of petitions. These carefully crafted words are set to one of the most majestic tunes to emerge from the tradition of Reformed psalmody.

TEXT: Reginald Heber, 1827, alt.
MUSIC: Louis Bourgeois, 1543; rev. 1551; harm. *The Hymnal 1940*

RENDEZ À DIEU
9.8.9.8.D

Be Known to Us in Breaking Bread 500

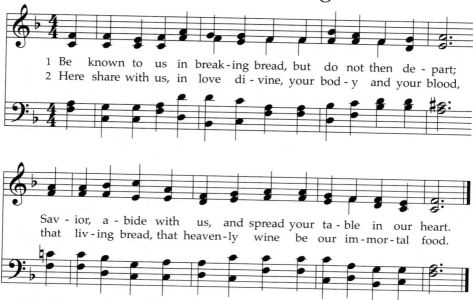

1 Be known to us in break-ing bread, but do not then de-part;
2 Here share with us, in love di-vine, your bod-y and your blood,

Sav-ior, a-bide with us, and spread your ta-ble in our heart.
that liv-ing bread, that heaven-ly wine be our im-mor-tal food.

Not all communion texts refer to the Last Supper: this brief hymn is based on the meal at Emmaus shared by the Risen Christ and his two companions on the road (Luke 24:13–35). It is set to a 16th-century psalm tune that carries the text with appropriate simplicity.

TEXT: James Montgomery, 1825
MUSIC: Day's *Psalter*, 1562

ST. FLAVIAN
CM

Feed Us, Lord 501

1 Feed us, Lord. Feed us, Lord. In the bro-ken bread,
2 Quench us, Lord. Quench us, Lord. On this thirst-y ground,
3 Fill us, Lord. Fill us, Lord, with the bread and wine
4 Lead us, Lord. Lead us, Lord, nour-ished here by Christ,

be re-vealed a-gain. Come and feed our hearts, O Lord.
may your love flow down. Come and quench our hearts, O Lord.
of the ris-en Christ. Come and fill our hearts, O Lord.
giv-en strength for life. Come and lead our hearts, O Lord.

Not many Lord's Supper hymns call attention to the post-Resurrection meals Christ shared with his disciples, but the first stanza here alludes to the meal at Emmaus, when he was made known in the breaking of the bread (Luke 24:13–35), and stanza three refers to "the risen Christ."

TEXT and MUSIC: Greg Scheer, 2007
Text and Music © 2007 Greg Scheer

FEED US
3.3.5.5.7

502 We Who Once Were Dead

1 We who once were dead now live, ful - ly know-ing Je - sus
2 We were lost in night, but you sought and found us. Give us
3 He be - came our bread; Je - sus died to save us. On him
4 Let us share the pain you en - dured in dy - ing; we shall
5 Je - sus, you were dead, but you rose and, liv - ing, made your-
6 This is your de - sign; in this meal we meet you. Be our

as our head. Life is o - ver - flow - ing when he breaks the bread.
strength to fight; death is all a - round us. Je - sus, be our light.
we are fed, eat - ing what he gave us, ris - ing from the dead.

then re - main liv - ing; death de - fy - ing, we shall rise a - gain.
self our bread, in your good-ness giv - ing life though we were dead.
bread and wine, Je - sus, we en - treat you. This shall be our sign.

This 20th-century Dutch hymn could well be understood as an expansion of the imagery of death and life in Romans 6:1–11, interpreted from a eucharistic perspective. Such short lines and exact rhymes are a challenge to maintain; the art of this text is a measure of its conviction.

TEXT: Muus Jacobse, 1961; trans. composite
MUSIC: Rik Veelenturf, 1960
Text and Music © 1967 Gooi En Sticht, Bv, Baarn, The Netherlands (admin. OCP for English-language countries)

MIDDEN IN DE DOOD
5.6.5.6.5

Lord, We Have Come
at Your Own Invitation

1 Lord, we have come at your own in-vi-ta-tion,
2 Here, at your ta-ble, con-firm our in-ten-tion;
3 When, at your ta-ble, each time of re-turn-ing,

cho-sen by you, to be count-ed your friends;
give it your seal of for-give-ness and grace;
vows are re-newed and our cour-age re-stored,

yours is the strength that sus-tains ded-i-ca-tion;
teach us to serve with-out pride or pre-ten-sion,
may we in-creas-ing-ly glo-ry in learn-ing

ours, a com-mit-ment we know nev-er ends.
Lord, in your king-dom, what-ev-er our place.
all that it means to ac-cept you as Lord.

St. Augustine spoke of eucharist as "the repeatable part of baptism," and this hymn reminds us that each time we share in the Lord's Supper we are renewing our baptismal vows. The text is set to a tune that dates to the transition between plainchant and modern tonalities.

TEXT: Fred Pratt Green, 1977, alt.
MUSIC: Paris Antiphoner, 1681; harm. La Feillée's Méthode du plain-chant, 1808
Text © 1979 Hope Publishing Company

O QUANTA QUALIA
11.10.11.10
(this tune in a higher key, 369)

504 We Come as Guests Invited

1 We come as guests in - vit - ed when Je - sus bids us dine,
2 We eat and drink, re - ceiv - ing from Christ the grace we need,
3 One bread is ours for shar - ing, one sin - gle fruit - ful vine,

his friends on earth u - nit - ed to share the bread and wine;
and in our hearts be - liev - ing on him by faith we feed;
our fel - low-ship de - clar - ing re - newed in bread and wine:

the bread of life is bro - ken; the wine is free - ly poured
with won - der and thanks-giv - ing for love that knows no end,
re - newed, sus-tained, and giv - en by to - ken, sign, and word,

for us, in sol - emn to - ken of Christ our dy - ing Lord.
we find in Je - sus liv - ing our ev - er - pres - ent friend.
the pledge and seal of heav - en, the love of Christ our Lord.

Without attempting to unravel the mystery of Christ's presence in the bread and wine, the central stanza of this text affirms that we are nourished by faith rather than by understanding. This hopeful text is reinforced by a gentle 16th-century tune created for a secular text.

TEXT: Timothy Dudley-Smith, 1975
MUSIC: Johann Steurlein, 1575
Text © 1984 Hope Publishing Company

WIE LIEBLICH IST DER MAIEN
7.6.7.6.D

The Trumpets Sound, the Angels Sing 505
The Feast Is Ready

1 The trum-pets sound; the an - gels sing; the feast is
2 Ta - bles are la - den with good things; O taste the
3 The hun-gry heart he sat - is - fies, of - fers the

read - y to be - gin. The gates of heaven are o - pen wide,
peace and joy he brings. He'll fill you up with love di - vine;
poor his par - a - dise. Now hear all heaven and earth ap-plaud

and Je - sus wel - comes you in - side.
he'll turn your wa - ter in - to wine.
the a - maz - ing good - ness of the Lord.

Refrain

Sing with thank - ful - ness songs of pure de - light.

Come and rev - el in heav - en's love and light.

Take your place at the ta - ble of the King.

The feast is read - y to be - gin;

the feast is read - y to be - gin.

This celebratory gathering song is cast in a highly rhythmic praise and worship style and brings together many images associated with the eucharistic feast. Despite its new sound, its emphasis on communion as a foretaste of the Heavenly Banquet is a very traditional theme.

TEXT and MUSIC: Graham Kendrick, 1989
Text and Music © 1989 Make Way Music (admin. Music Services)

THE FEAST IS READY
LM with refrain

506 Look Who Gathers at Christ's Table!

1 Look who gath-ers at Christ's ta-ble! Hear the sto-ries
2 Clouds of light sur-round the ta-ble; an-cient fol-low-
3 Their sad sto-ries are re-peat-ed in a thou-sand
4 Bring your joy and bring your sad-ness, and pre-pare to

that they bring. Some are weep-ing; some are laugh-ing;
ers ap-pear, saints con-fess-ing how they wres-tled
dif-ferent ways, but they share one thing in com-mon:
be sur-prised by the host whose hands are wound-ed,

some have songs they want to sing. Oth-ers ask why they're in-
with their guilt, their doubt and fear. Pe-ter tells of his de-
they all end in thanks and praise for the host who has in-
who will o-pen wide your eyes when he bless-es bread and

vit-ed, bur-dened by the wrong they've done. Christ in-sists they
ny-ing Christ was ev-er in his sight; Paul re-lates his
vit-ed north and south and east and west to con-verge a-
breaks it— truth and man-na from a-bove!—and then pass-es

This text celebrates the radical hospitality that characterizes Christ's welcome, which transcends time and
reaches in all directions (Matthew 8:11 / Luke 13:29). Saints of old are, like us, people in need of forgiveness,
and the response to such pardon is "thanks and praise."

TEXT: Thomas H. Troeger, 2000
MUSIC: Michael Corzine, 2000
Text © 2002 Oxford University Press
Music © 2000 Michael Corzine

COPELAND
8.7.8.7.D

all   are   wel - come.   There is   room   for   ev - ery - one.
fruit - less ef - forts   to   ob - lit - er - ate   the   light.
round   this ta - ble,   where all   life   is   fed   and   blest.
wine   that wak - ens   in   your heart the   taste of   love.

Come to the Table of Grace   507

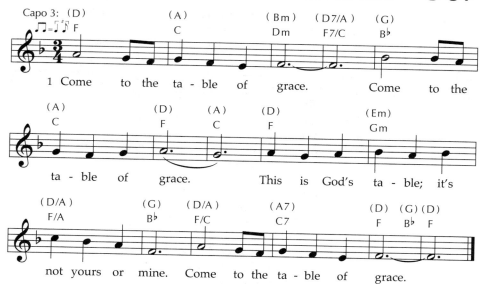

1 Come to the ta - ble of grace. Come to the ta - ble of grace. This is God's ta - ble; it's not yours or mine. Come to the ta - ble of grace.

2 Come to the table of peace...
3 Come to the table of love...
4 Come to the table of hope...
5 Come to the table of joy...

The simple, formulaic nature of this song makes it especially suitable for use during the communion portion of the Lord's Supper. Because it can be learned readily and does not require reference to a printed source, it frees people to sing before and after receiving the elements.

TEXT and MUSIC: Barbara Hamm, 2008
Text and Music © 2008 Hope Publishing Company

TABLE OF GRACE
7.7.10.7

508

Come to the Table

식탁에 와서

G   Em7   Am7

*1 Come to the ta - ble, all you who praise God.
2 Come eat this bread now, my bro - ken bod - y.
3 All is now read - y, like the first ta - ble.

G   Em   A7   Dsus   D

Laid in a sta - ble, God's gift of love:
My vow re - mem - ber: I am your Lord.
Pray for the Spir - it; lift up your hearts.

G   G7   C   Cm

Je - sus our Sav - ior poured out his life's blood.
Drink of this wine, the cup of sal - va - tion,
Christ has a - ris - en, our Lord and Sav - ior.

G   D7   G

Our sins for - giv - en, God's gift of love.
for you are mine, and I am your Lord.
With great thanks - giv - ing, lift up your hearts.

KOREAN

1 식탁에 와서 찬양드리세,
   사랑의 선물 나누시네,
   주님의 몸과 주님의 피를
   우리를 위해 주시었네

2 너희를 위한 나의 몸이니
   받아서 먹고 기념하라
   이 잔은 나의 새 언약이니
   죄사함 위해 흘린 피라

3 주님의 성령 임-하시네,
   거룩한 주의 살-과 피
   나를 새롭게 바꿔 주시네
   새생명 주심 감사하세

*Stanza 1 may be sung by a leader.

This Korean text accomplishes a rare feat in a Lord's Supper hymn by dealing with the full range of Christ's life from the Nativity to the Resurrection. The first and third stanzas are in the voice of the congregation, while the middle stanza recalls Christ's words of institution.

TEXT: Paul Junggap Huh, 2007; English trans. Paul Junggap Huh, 2011, alt.
MUSIC: Hyun Chul Lee, 2007
Text © 2007 and English Trans. © 2011 Paul Junggap Huh
Music © 2007 Hyun Chul Lee

COME TO THE TABLE
5.5.5.4.D

All Who Hunger, Gather Gladly 509

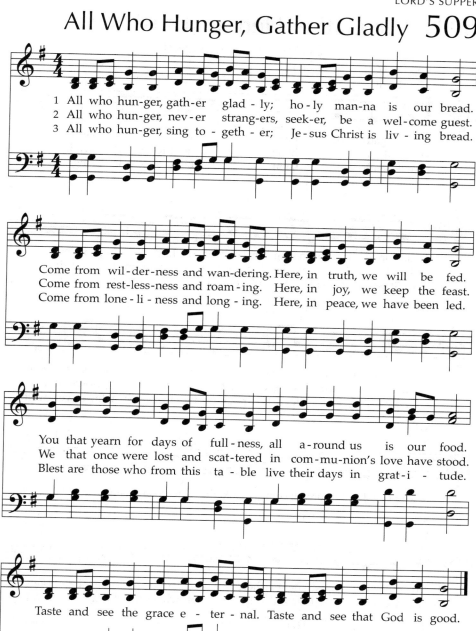

1 All who hun-ger, gath-er glad - ly; ho - ly man-na is our bread.
2 All who hun-ger, nev - er strang-ers, seek-er, be a wel-come guest.
3 All who hun-ger, sing to - geth - er; Je-sus Christ is liv - ing bread.

Come from wil-der-ness and wan-dering. Here, in truth, we will be fed.
Come from rest-less-ness and roam-ing. Here, in joy, we keep the feast.
Come from lone - li - ness and long - ing. Here, in peace, we have been led.

You that yearn for days of full - ness, all a-round us is our food.
We that once were lost and scat-tered in com-mu-nion's love have stood.
Blest are those who from this ta - ble live their days in grat-i - tude.

Taste and see the grace e - ter - nal. Taste and see that God is good.

The United Church of Canada minister who wrote this text was introduced to shape note tunes at the 1990 Hymn Society conference in Charleston, South Carolina. Afterwards she vacationed with friends nearby and worked out this text while humming this tune as she walked up and down the beach.

TEXT: Sylvia G. Dunstan, 1990
MUSIC: William Moore's *Columbian Harmony*, 1825
Text © 1991 GIA Publications, Inc.

HOLY MANNA
8.7.8.7.D
(alternate harmonization, 396)

510 We Gather Here in Jesus' Name
Come, Share the Lord

The center of this text recalls Christ's post-Resurrection meal at Emmaus (Luke 24:13–35), a reminder that the Risen Christ is in our midst when two or three gather in his name (Matthew 18:20) and share a foretaste of the Heavenly Feast (Matthew 26:29/Luke 22:18/Mark 14:25).

TEXT and MUSIC: Bryan Jeffery Leech, 1984
Text and Music © 1984 Fred Bock Music Co., Inc.

COME, SHARE THE LORD
Irregular

Come, Behold! the Feast of Heaven 511

1 Come, be-hold! the feast of heaven
2 All is read-y, come at-tend
3 All who trust in God be-long
4 As the Lord our God has willed,

Al - le - lu - ia!

has to mor-tal flesh been given.
as the Lord's in-vit-ed friend;
at this ban-quet with this throng.
here the hun-gry soul is filled;

Al - le - lu - ia!

Hear the Word of God de-clared:
come from north, west, south, and east;
Share the mys-tic ho-ly food;
here the wea-ry are re-freshed.

Al - le - lu - ia!

"Come! the ban-quet is pre-pared."
cel-e-brate the joy-ful feast.
taste and see: the Lord is good.
All who share God's feast are blessed.

Al - le - lu - ia!

Though rightly viewed as a meal of remembrance, the Lord's Supper is also an occasion of anticipation. This text draws on abundant biblical imagery to evoke the fulfillment of Jesus' promise to share the feast anew "in the kingdom of God" (Matthew 26:29/Mark 14:25/Luke 22:16).

TEXT: John F. Underwood, 1993
MUSIC: Robert Williams, 1817; harm. David Evans, 1927
Text © 1993 John F. Underwood
Music Harm. © 1927 Oxford University Press

LLANFAIR
7.7.7.7 with alleluias

512 The Bread and the Wine Are Here

The bread and the wine are here; (The feast is here.)

come now, all who hun-ger and thirst.

Come need-y; come now with-out fear.

Drink joy, as the last be-come first! (The last are first!)

Refrain

Come in; sit down; there's room at the ta-ble;

There are many dimensions to the celebration of the Lord's Supper, and this song focuses on the important theme of hospitality, with reference to Jesus' table ministry and his teaching about the reversal of social distinctions (Matthew 19:30 / Mark 10:31 / Luke 13:30 / Matthew 20:16).

TEXT and MUSIC: Daniel Charles Damon, 1993
Text and Music © 1993 Hope Publishing Company

LOVE FEAST
7.8.8.8 with refrain

en - joy   the feast love has   spread   for   you.

This Is the Feast of Victory 513

This is the feast of vic-to-ry for our God. Al-le-

lu - ia! Al-le-lu-ia! Al - le - lu - ia! lu - ia!

1 Wor - thy is Christ, the Lamb who was slain, whose
2 Pow - er, rich - es, wis - dom, and strength, and
3 Sing with all the peo - ple of God, and
4 Bless - ing, hon - or, glo - ry, and might be to
5 For the Lamb who was slain has be -

blood set us free to be peo - ple of God.
hon - or, bless - ing, and glo - ry are his.
join in the hymn of all cre - a - tion.
God and the Lamb for - ev - er. A - men.
gun his reign. Al - le - lu - ia!

This exuberant unrhymed paraphrase is especially well suited for use at celebrations of the Lord's Supper in Easter Season. The stanzas are derived from several passages in Revelation (5:9–10, 12–14; 7:10b, 12), while the refrain possibly refers to 1 Corinthians 15:54b–56.

TEXT: John W. Arthur, 1970
MUSIC: Richard Hillert, 1975, alt.
Text © 1978 Lutheran Book of Worship (admin. Augsburg Fortress)
Music © 1975, 1988 Richard Hillert (Published by OCP)

FESTIVAL CANTICLE
Irregular

514 Soul, Adorn Yourself with Gladness

1 Soul, a - dorn your - self with glad - ness; leave the gloom - y haunts of
2 Sun, who all my life does bright - en; light, who does my soul en -
3 Je - sus, source of last - ing plea - sure, tru - est friend and dear - est

sad - ness. Come in - to the day - light's splen - dor; there with
light - en; joy, your won - drous gift be - stow - ing; fount, from
trea - sure, peace be - yond all un - der - stand - ing, joy in -

joy your prais - es ren - der. Bless the one whose grace un - bound - ed
which all good is flow - ing: at your feet I cry, my Mak - er,
to all life ex - pand - ing: hum - bly now, I bow be - fore you,

this a - maz - ing ban - quet found - ed; Christ, though heaven - ly,
let me be a fit par - tak - er of this bless - ed
love in - car - nate, I a - dore you; wor - thi - ly let

Although the celebration of the Lord's Supper is a solemn occasion, it is not a sad or somber one, but one evoking a deep joy. That tone also characterizes this chorale setting created for the original German text and notable for its support of the numerous two-syllable rhymes.

TEXT: Johann Franck, c. 1649; stanzas 1–2, trans. Catherine Winkworth, 1858; rev. 1863, alt.;
    stanza 3, trans. John Caspar Mattes, 1913, alt.
MUSIC: Johann Crüger, 1649
Text © 1978 Lutheran Book of Worship (admin. Augsburg Fortress)

SCHMÜCKE DICH
LMD

high, and ho - ly, deigns to dwell with you most low - ly.
food from heav - en, for our good, your glo - ry giv - en.
me re - ceive you and, so fa - vored, nev - er leave you.

I Come with Joy

515

Capo 3: (D) (G) (A) (D) (Bm)
F B♭ C F Dm

1 I come with joy, a child of God, for - giv - en, loved, and
2 I come with Chris-tians far and near to find, as all are
3 As Christ breaks bread and bids us share, each proud di - vi - sion
4 The Spir - it of the ris - en Christ, un - seen, but ev - er
5 To - geth - er met, to - geth - er bound by all that God has

(Asus) (Am) (G) (F♯m) (D)
Csus Cm B♭ Am F

free, the life of Je - sus to re - call, in
fed, the new com - mu - ni - ty of love in
ends. The love that made us, makes us one, and
near, is in such friend - ship bet - ter known, a -
done, we'll go with joy, to give the world the

(Em) (D/F♯) (G) (A) (Am7) (D)
Gm F/A B♭ C Cm7 F

love laid down for me, in love laid down for me.
Christ's com - mu - nion bread, in Christ's com - mu - nion bread.
strang - ers now are friends, and strang - ers now are friends.
live a - mong us here, a - live a - mong us here.
love that makes us one, the love that makes us one.

Guitar chords do not correspond with keyboard harmony.

This text affirms that Christian unity is not achievement but gift, one renewed each time we gather for the Lord's Supper. Each of us enters as an "I" and leaves as part of "we." The unadorned language of this text is well matched to the simple shape note tune that sets it here.

TEXT: Brian Wren, 1968; rev. 1993
MUSIC: American folk melody; arr. Austin C. Lovelace, 1977
Text © 1971, rev. 1995 Hope Publishing Company
Music Arr. © 1977 Hope Publishing Company

DOVE OF PEACE
8.6.8.6.6

516 For the Bread Which You Have Broken

1 For the bread which you have bro - ken, for the
2 By this prom - ise that you love us, by your
3 With the saints who now a - dore you seat - ed
4 In your ser - vice, Lord, de - fend us; in our

wine which you have poured, for the words which you have
gift of peace re - stored, by your call to heaven a -
at the heaven - ly board, may the church still wait - ing
hearts keep watch and ward; in the world to which you

spo - ken, now we give you thanks, O Lord.
bove us, hal - low all our lives, O Lord.
for you keep love's tie un - bro - ken, Lord.
send us let your king - dom come, O Lord.

The author of this text, the editor of several Presbyterian hymnals, was the foremost American hymnologist of the early 20th century. Although some of his language in this text echoes early hymns of the church, he is writing here not as a scholar but as a person of deep faith.

TEXT: Louis FitzGerald Benson, 1924, alt.
MUSIC: V. Earle Copes, 1959

KINGDOM
8.7.8.7

Here, O Our Lord, We See You 517

1 Here, O our Lord, we see you face to face.
2 Here would we feed up - on the bread of God,
3 This is the hour of ban - quet and of song;
4 Too soon we rise; the sym - bols dis - ap - pear.
5 Feast af - ter feast thus comes and pass - es by,

Here would we touch and han - dle things un - seen,
here drink with you the roy - al cup of heaven;
this is the heaven - ly ta - ble for us spread.
The feast, though not the love, is past and gone;
yet, pass - ing, points to that glad feast a - bove,

here grasp with firm - er hand e - ter - nal grace,
here would we lay a - side each earth - ly load,
Here let us feast and, feast - ing, still pro - long
the bread and wine re - move, but you are here,
giv - ing sweet fore - taste of the fes - tal joy,

and all our wea - ri - ness up - on you lean.
and taste a - fresh the calm of sin for - given.
the fel - low - ship of liv - ing wine and bread.
near - er than ev - er, still our shield and sun.
the Lamb's great brid - al feast of bliss and love.

These stanzas are selected from a ten-stanza hymn written in 1855 to serve as a monthly post-communion reflection for the members of St. Andrew's Free Church, Greenock, Scotland. They are set to a tune named for both a coastal town and a large bay in northwest England.

TEXT: Horatius Bonar, 1855, alt.
MUSIC: Frederick Cook Atkinson, 1870

MORECAMBE
10.10.10.10

518

Your Only Son
Lamb of God

1 Your on - ly Son, no sin to hide, but you have
2 Your gift of love, we cru - ci - fied; we laughed and
3 I was so lost, I should have died, but you have

sent him from your side to walk up - on this guilt - y
scorned him as he died; the hum - ble King we named a
brought me to your side to be led by your staff and

sod, and to be - come the Lamb of God.
fraud, and sac - ri - ficed the Lamb of God.
rod, and to be called a lamb of God.

Refrain

O Lamb of God, sweet Lamb of God, I love the

ho - ly Lamb of God! O wash me in his pre - cious

blood, my Je - sus Christ, the Lamb of God.

John the Baptist calls Jesus "the Lamb of God" when he sees Jesus coming for baptism at the Jordan River (John 1:29, 36). Sacrificial lamb references appear in Acts 8:32 (quoting Isaiah 53:7) and 1 Peter 1:19 as well as in twenty-eight triumphant "Lamb" mentions in Revelation.

TEXT and MUSIC: Twila Paris, 1985
Text and Music © 1985 Mountain Spring Music and Straightway Music (admin. EMICMGPublishing.com)

LAMB OF GOD
LM with refrain

You Are My Strength When I Am Weak 519
You Are My All in All

You are my strength when I am weak; you are the trea-sure that I

seek; you are my all in all. When I fall down, you pick me

up; when I am dry, you fill my cup; you are my all in all.

Je - sus, Lamb of God, wor-thy is your name!

Je - sus, Lamb of God, wor-thy is your name!

*May be sung as a canon.

The expression "all in all," meaning "everything," owes much of its endurance in English usage to its appearance in 1 Corinthians 15:28, though many phrases leading up to it here have parallels in Hebrew Scripture. The second section echoes the song to the Lamb in Revelation 5:12.

TEXT and MUSIC: Dennis L. Jernigan, 1990
Text and Music © 1991 Shepherd's Heart Music, Inc. (admin. PraiseCharts.com)

JERNIGAN
8.8.6.D with refrain

520

Taste and See
(Psalm 34)

Because the first half of verse 8 is the emotional high point of Psalm 34, this paraphrase fittingly uses it as a refrain. In the Christian context of the Lord's Supper, the invitation to participate ("taste") is joined with the promise of blessing ("see that the Lord is good").

TASTE AND SEE
Irregular

521 In Remembrance of Me

This text is built on four familiar words of Christ at the Last Supper, as recorded in Luke 22:19 and 1 Corinthians 11:24–25. Radiating from that corporate memory of the church, additional actions are encouraged in Christ's voice using allusions to other passages of Scripture.

TEXT: Ragan Courtney, 1972
MUSIC: Buryl Red, 1972
Text and Music © 1972 Broadman Press (admin. Music Services)

RED
Irregular

pre - cious blood shed for you, shed for you.

3 In re - mem - brance of me, search for truth. In re-

mem-brance of me, al-ways love. In re-mem-brance of

me, don't look a-bove, but in your heart, look for

God. Do this in re-mem-brance of me.

522 I Am the Bread of Life

Leader or All

1 "I am the bread of life. You who
2 "The bread that I will give is my
3 "Un - less you eat of the
4 "I am the res - ur - rec - tion;
5 Yes, Lord, I be - lieve that

come to me shall not hun - ger, and who be -
flesh for the life of the world, and if you
flesh of the Son of Man and
I am the life. If you be -
you are the Christ, the

lieve in me shall not thirst. No one can come to
eat of this bread, you shall live for -
drink of his blood, and drink of his
lieve in me, e - ven though you
Son of God, who has

me un - less the Fa - ther beck - ons."
ev - er; you shall live for - ev - er."
blood, you shall not have life with - in you."
die, you shall live for - ev - er."
come in - to the world.

Refrain

All

"And I will raise you up, and I will raise you up,

As the quotation marks suggest, the first four stanzas and refrain are quoted from Jesus (John 6:35, 44, 51, 53; 11:25), while the fifth stanza draws on the words of Martha (John 11:27), voicing our response also. Being mindful of these differences allows more prayerful singing.

TEXT: Suzanne Toolan, RSM, 1966, rev.
MUSIC: Suzanne Toolan, RSM, 1966
Text and Music © 1966, 1970, 1986, 1993 GIA Publications, Inc.

I AM THE BREAD
Irregular

and I will raise you up on the last day."

You Satisfy the Hungry Heart 523

Refrain

You sat-is-fy the hun-gry heart with gift of fin-est wheat;

come give to us, O sav-ing Lord, the bread of life to eat.

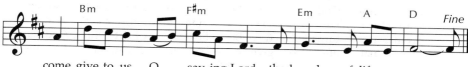

1 As when the shep-herd calls his sheep, they know and heed his voice,
2 With joy-ful lips we sing to you our praise and grat-i-tude
3 Is not the cup we bless and share the blood of Christ out-poured?
4 The mys-tery of your pres-ence, Lord, no mor-tal tongue can tell:
5 You give your-self to us, O Lord; then self-less let us be,

to Refrain

so when you call your fam-i-ly, Lord, we fol-low and re-joice.
that you should count us wor-thy, Lord, to share this heaven-ly food.
Do not one cup, one loaf, de-clare our one-ness in the Lord?
whom all the world can-not con-tain comes in our hearts to dwell.
to serve each oth-er in your name in truth and char-i-ty.

Guitar chords do not correspond with keyboard harmony.

Submitted together, this text and tune were chosen from about two hundred entries to be the official hymn for the 41st International Eucharistic Congress held at Philadelphia in 1976. At the center of its many biblical images, the third stanza draws on 1 Corinthians 10:16–17.

TEXT: Omer Westendorf, 1976
MUSIC: Robert E. Kreutz, 1976
Text and Music © 1977 Archdiocese of Philadelphia (Published by International Liturgy Publications)

BICENTENNIAL
CM with refrain

524 The Rice of Life

1 The rice of life from heav-en came to bring true
2 True rice the hun-gry world has fed, the rice re-
3 The rice of God for all is meant; no one who
4 The liv-ing rice, for all a sign, came down e-

life from God a-bove. Re-ceive this gift; God's mer-cy
quired for life be-low. Pro-vide this gift; God's mer-cy
comes is turned a-way. Be-lieve in Christ whom God has
ter-nal life to give. A-bide in Christ, the liv-ing

claim; in joy and pain give thanks for love.
spread; in weak-ness God's com-pas-sion show.
sent; in hum-ble trust God's will o-bey.
vine; in Christ, with peo-ple die and live.

Indicating up glide (‿) and down glide (‵), typical of Bunun singing style.

For the rice-based peoples of Asia, Jesus' self-disclosure as the Bread of Life (John 6:35, 51) does not relate to daily experience as it does in Western societies. This hymn seeks to bridge that gap and to alert us to such assumptions. The tune name is Taiwanese for "rice-food."

TEXT: J. Andrew Fowler, 1983
MUSIC: I-to Loh, 1984
Text © 1990 Christian Conference of Asia (admin. GIA Publications, Inc.)
Music © 1990 GIA Publications, Inc.

BÍ–NÎU
LM

Let Us Break Bread Together 525

1 Let us break bread to-geth-er on our knees; (on our knees)
2 Let us drink wine to-geth-er on our knees; (on our knees)
3 Let us praise God to-geth-er on our knees; (on our knees)

let us break bread to-geth-er on our knees. (on our knees)
let us drink wine to-geth-er on our knees. (on our knees)
let us praise God to-geth-er on our knees. (on our knees)

Refrain

When I fall on my knees, with my face to the ris-ing sun,

O Lord, have mer-cy on me. (on me)

This African American spiritual quite possibly reflects the circumstances of slaves attending early morning communion services in colonial Anglican churches, but its combination of hope ("rising sun") and supplication ("Lord, have mercy") speaks to many worshipers' experience.

TEXT: African American spiritual
MUSIC: African American spiritual; arr. Melva Wilson Costen, 1988
Music Arr. © 1990 Melva Wilson Costen

LET US BREAK BREAD
10.10 with refrain

526 Let Us Talents and Tongues Employ

1 Let us tal-ents and tongues em-ploy, reach-ing out with a
2 Christ is a-ble to make us one; at the ta-ble he
3 Je-sus calls us in, sends us out bear-ing fruit in a

shout of joy: bread is bro-ken; the wine is poured;
sets the tone, teach-ing peo-ple to live to bless,
world of doubt, gives us love to tell, bread to share:

Refrain

Christ is spo-ken and seen and heard.
love in word and in deed ex-press. Je-sus lives a-gain;
God (Im-man-u-el) ev-ery-where!

earth can breathe a-gain; pass the Word a-round: loaves a-bound!

Guitar chords do not correspond with keyboard harmony.

Maracas and other rhythm instruments may be used.

This "communion calypso" (as the author called it) affirms the continuing presence of Christ both in the sacramental meal and in the lives of Christians. Because this text was written to fit a pre-existing tune, it has a rather telegraphic style that encourages pondering.

TEXT: Fred Kaan, 1975
MUSIC: Jamaican folk melody; adapt. Doreen Potter, 1975
Text and Music © 1975 Hope Publishing Company

LINSTEAD
LM with refrain

Eat This Bread

Opt. A "Eat this bread; drink this cup; come to me and
Opt. B Eat this bread; drink this cup; come to Christ and

nev - er be hun - gry. Eat this bread;
nev - er be hun - gry. Eat this bread;

drink this cup; trust in me and you will not thirst."
drink this cup; trust in Christ and you will not thirst.

This text from the Taizé Community is based on John 6:35, which is paraphrased here in two styles. The more immediate first version maintains the second-person invitation spoken by Jesus, while the alternative version provides a more general statement in the third person.

TEXT: Robert J. Batastini and the Taizé Community, 1984, alt.
MUSIC: Jacques Berthier, 1984
Text and Music © 1984 Les Presses de Taizé (admin. GIA Publications, Inc.)

BERTHIER
Irregular

528 Come, Let Us Eat

1 Come, let us eat, for now the feast is spread;
2 Come, let us drink, for now the wine is poured;
3 In Je - sus' pres - ence now we meet and rest;
4 Rise, then, to spread a - broad God's might - y word;

come, let us eat, for now the feast is spread.
come, let us drink, for now the wine is poured.
in Je - sus' pres - ence now we meet and rest.
rise, then, to spread a - broad God's might - y word.

Our Lord's bod - y let us take to - geth - er;
Je - sus' blood poured, let us drink to - geth - er;
In the pres - ence of our Lord we gath - er;
Je - sus ris - en will bring in the king - dom;

our Lord's bod - y let us take to - geth - er.
Je - sus' blood poured, let us drink to - geth - er.
in the pres - ence of our Lord we gath - er.
Je - sus ris - en will bring in the king - dom.

This Lord's Supper hymn in a call-and-response style comes from Liberia, where it was first sung in the Loma language by an indigenous literacy teacher and evangelist. The words and music were taken down then and were later published in a hymnal of the Lutheran World Federation.

TEXT: Stanzas 1–3, Billema Kwillia, 1960s; trans. Margaret D. Miller, 1969, alt.; stanza 4, Gilbert E. Doan, 1978
MUSIC: Billema Kwillia, 1960s; adapt. Leland B. Sateren, 1972, alt.
Text Sts. 1–3 and Music © 1970 The Lutheran World Federation
Text St. 4 and Music Adapt. © 1972 Contemporary Worship 4 (admin. Augsburg Fortress)

A VA DE
10.10.10.10

Draw Us in the Spirit's Tether 529

1 Draw us in the Spir-it's teth - er, for when hum - bly
2 As dis - ci - ples used to gath - er in the name of
3 All our meals and all our liv - ing make as sac - ra -

in your name two or three are met to-geth - er,
Christ to sup, then with thanks to God the giv - er
ments of you, that by car - ing, help-ing, giv - ing,

you are in the midst of them. Al - le - lu - ia! Al - le -
break the bread and bless the cup, Al - le - lu - ia! Al - le -
we may be dis - ci - ples true. Al - le - lu - ia! Al - le -

lu - ia! Here we touch your gar - ment's hem.
lu - ia! so now bind our friend - ship up.
lu - ia! We will serve with faith a - new.

Guitar chords do not correspond with keyboard harmony.

This communion text calls attention to the inherent sacramental nature of all meals and the communal dimensions of all human interaction. The tune, originally composed for an anthem setting of this text, honors the institution where the composer was trained and later taught.

TEXT: Percy Dearmer, 1931, alt.
MUSIC: Harold Friedell, 1957
Text © 1931 Oxford University Press
Music © 1957, ren. H. W. Gray Company (admin. Alfred Publishing Co., Inc.)

UNION SEMINARY
8.7.8.7.4.4.7

530 One Bread, One Body

Refrain

One bread, one bod-y, one Lord of all, one cup of bless-ing which we bless.

And we, though man-y, through-out the earth, we are one bod-y in this one Lord. *(C) Fine*

1 Gen - tile or Jew, ser - vant or free, wom - an or man, no more.
2 Man - y the gifts, man - y the works, one in the Lord of all.
3 Grain for the fields, scat-tered and grown, gath-ered to one, for all.

to Refrain

This Lord's Supper text is based on various Scriptures (1 Corinthians 10:16–17, Galatians 3:28, and 1 Corinthians 12:1–31) as well as imagery from the *Didache*, a significant Christian document from the early 2nd century, about scattered grain united in the eucharistic bread.

TEXT and MUSIC: John B. Foley, SJ, 1978
Text and Music © 1978 John B. Foley, SJ (Published by OCP)

ONE BREAD, ONE BODY
Irregular

Seed, Scattered and Sown

531

Seed, scat-tered and sown; wheat, gath-ered and grown;
bread, bro-ken and shared as one, the liv-ing bread of God.
Vine, fruit of the land; wine, work of our hands; one cup that is
shared by all, the liv-ing cup, the liv-ing bread of God.

1 Is not the bread we break a shar-ing in our Lord?
2 The seed which falls on rock will with-er and will die.
3 As wheat up-on the hills was gath-ered and was grown,

Is not the cup we bless the blood of Christ out-poured?
The seed with-in good ground will flow-er and have life.
so may the church of God be gath-ered in-to one.

This hymn draws on very old Christian materials, the earliest being Jesus' parables about sowers and seed (Matthew 13/Mark 4/Luke 8). Stanza one paraphrases 1 Corinthians 10:16, and stanza three uses imagery from the *Didache*, a major Christian document from the early 2nd century.

TEXT: Dan Feiten, 1987
MUSIC: Dan Feiten, 1987; arr. Eric Gunnison and R. J. Miller, alt.
Text and Music © 1987 International Liturgy Publications

SEED SCATTERED
Irregular

532

Sheaves of Wheat

Una espiga

1 Sheaves of wheat turned by sun - light in - to gold,
2 Here we gath - er to share a com - mon meal.
3 As each grain blends to form a sin - gle loaf,
4 At the ta - ble of God we join to eat,

1 U - na es - pi - ga do - ra - da por el sol,
2 Com - par - ti - mos la mis - ma com - mu - nión,
3 Co - mo gra - nos que han he - cho el mis - mo pan,
4 En la me - sa de Dios se sen - ta - rán,

grapes in clus - ters, like ru - bies on the vine,
We are har - vest by God the Sow - er sown,
or as notes weave to shape a sin - gle song,
and as sis - ters and broth - ers break the bread.

el ra - ci - mo que cor - ta el vi - ña - dor,
so - mos tri - go del mis - mo sem - bra - dor,
co - mo no - tas que te - jen un can - tar,
co - mo hi - jos su pan com - part - ti - rán,

feed our hearts as the pre - cious blood and bod - y of our
brought to - geth - er to share the joys and sor - rows that we
or as drop - lets u - nite with - in the o - cean's depth and
Fed by faith, hope, and love, we sing our joy to all we

se con - vier - ten a - ho - ra en pan y vi - no de a -
un mo - li - no a la vi - da, nos tri - tu - ra con do -
co - mo go - tas de a - gua que se fun - den en el
u - na mis - ma es - pe - ran - za ca - mi - nan - do can - ta -

This text by a leading Spanish author/composer expands vivid images of grain and grape used to provide bread and wine for the celebration of the Lord's Supper into symbols of the interconnection of all human experience, but especially of the shared life in Christian community.

TEXT: Cesáreo Gabaráin, 1973; trans. Mary Louise Bringle, 2008
MUSIC: Cesáreo Gabaráin, 1973; harm. Skinner Chávez-Melo, 1987
Text and Music © 1973 Cesáreo Gabaráin (Published by OCP)
Music Harm. © 1987 OCP

UNA ESPIGA
10.10.13.10

Lord: gifts of heav - en from earth - ly bread and wine.
feel, all re - fined by life's com - mon grind - ing stone.
foam, to each oth - er as Chris - tians we be - long.
meet, as the bod - y of Christ, our liv - ing head.

mor, en el cuer - po y la san - gre del Se - ñor.
lor, Dios nos ha - ce pue - blo nue - vo en el a - mor.
mar, los cris - tia - nos un cuer - po for - ma - rán.
rán, en la vi - da co - mo her - ma - nos se a - ma - rán.

In the Singing 533

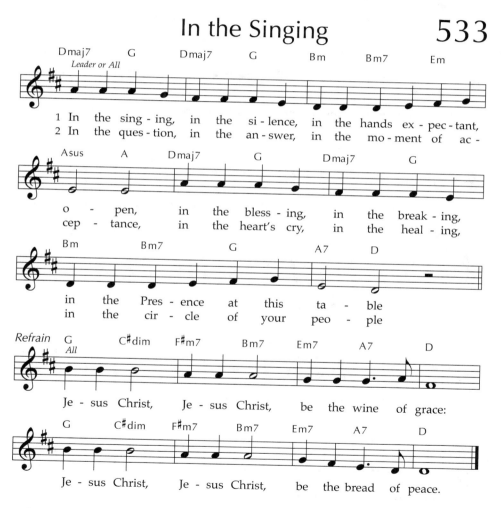

1 In the sing - ing, in the si - lence, in the hands ex - pec - tant,
2 In the ques - tion, in the an - swer, in the mo - ment of ac -

o - pen, in the bless - ing, in the break - ing,
cep - tance, in the heart's cry, in the heal - ing,

in the Pres - ence at this ta - ble
in the cir - cle of your peo - ple

Refrain

Je - sus Christ, Je - sus Christ, be the wine of grace:

Je - sus Christ, Je - sus Christ, be the bread of peace.

In its vivid and carefully observed details this profoundly simple text evokes the interplay of present awareness and timeless meaning that accompanies the celebration of the Lord's Supper. Its unifying tone of solemn joy is aptly conveyed by the chantlike musical setting.

TEXT: Shirley Erena Murray, 1994
MUSIC: Carlton R. Young, 1996
Text and Music © 1996 Hope Publishing Company

BREAD OF PEACE
LM with refrain

534 Now the Silence

Lacking punctuation and rhyme in the text and bar lines in the music, this meditative Lord's Supper hymn may at first seem like random musings. But both parts of the hymn are made up of careful patterns that combine to waken memory and to evoke a strong sense of God's presence.

TEXT: Jaroslav J. Vajda, 1968
MUSIC: Carl F. Schalk, 1969
Text and Music © 1969 Hope Publishing Company

NOW
Irregular

Bless the Lord, O My Soul   535

This responsive adaptation of Psalm 103:1–2 is the first option provided to follow communion in the Service for the Lord's Day. The setting is arranged from an easily learned Appalachian folk melody and lends itself to accompaniment by guitars or other suitable instruments.

TEXT: Trad. liturgical text; rev. *The Worshipbook*, 1970
MUSIC: Appalachian folk melody; *The Worshipbook*, 1972; arr. Richard D. Wetzel, 1972
Music Arr. © 1972 The Westminster Press (admin. Westminster John Knox Press)

BLESS THE LORD
Irregular

536 Rise, O Church, like Christ Arisen

1 Rise, O church, like Christ a - ris - en, from this
2 Rise, trans - formed, and choose to fol - low af - ter
3 Rise, re - mem - ber well the fu - ture God has
4 Ser - vice be our sure vo - ca - tion; cour - age

meal of love and grace; may we through such love en -
Christ, though wound - ed, whole; bro - ken, shared, our lives are
called us to re - ceive; pres - ent by God's lov - ing
be our dai - ly breath; mer - cy be our des - ti -

vi - sion whose we are, and whose, our praise. Al - le -
hal - lowed to re - lease and to con - sole. Al - le -
nur - ture, Spir - it - ed then let us live. Al - le -
na - tion from this day and un - to death. Al - le -

lu - ia, al - le - lu - ia: God, the won - der of our days.
lu - ia, al - le - lu - ia: Christ, our pres - ent, past, and goal.
lu - ia, al - le - lu - ia: Spir - it, grace by whom we live.
lu - ia, al - le - lu - ia. Rise, O church, a liv - ing faith.

Guitar chords do not correspond with keyboard harmony.

The second line of the first stanza shows that this hymn is meant for use in the context of the Lord's Supper, but the last stanza further clarifies its special purpose as a sending hymn celebrating the values guiding the work of the church in the world: service, courage, mercy.

TEXT: Susan Palo Cherwien, 1997
MUSIC: Timothy J. Strand, 1997
Text © 1997 Susan Palo Cherwien (admin. Augsburg Fortress)
Music © 1997 Augsburg Fortress

SURGE ECCLESIA
8.7.8.7.8.7

When at This Table

1 When at this ta-ble I re-ceive a bless-ing,
2 If at this ta-ble I have need of heal-ing,
3 If at this ta-ble I for-get the hun-gry,
4 If at this ta-ble I make ded-i-ca-tion
5 What faith I have, I bring to join this ta-ble,

the bro-ken bread, the wine of life for me,
un-bid-den grief, re-la-tion-ship gone wrong,
the dis-pos-sessed and war-fare's spread-ing stain,
to give my life in serv-ing what is good,
what hope I hold, in Christ is taught and true;

then let me share the peace with you, my neigh-bor,
then let me know the hands of God en-fold-ing,
then let this bread be-come the bread of judg-ment,
then let my cen-ter be where God in-vites me,
with broth-ers, sis-ters, I will share the bless-ing,

and let the Spir-it set our spir-its free.
and let la-ment be-come be-liev-ing song.
this wine the sharp a-ware-ness of that pain.
and show the words of Je-sus un-der-stood.
the feast where God is mak-ing all things new.

Though cast in an individual's voice, this prayerful text shows a strong communal awareness of the people gathered around the Lord's Table, their personal burdens, and matters of both local and global concern. The final two stanzas reflect renewed spiritual strength and resolve.

TEXT: Shirley Erena Murray, 2004
MUSIC: Jane Marshall, 2005
Text © 2004 Hope Publishing Company
Music © 2006 Hope Publishing Company

FEASTDAY
11.10.11.10

538 Hallelujah! We Sing Your Praises

Haleluya! Pelo tsa rona

Refrain, *sung twice each time*

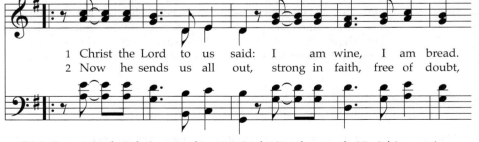

Hal - le - lu - jah! We sing your prais - es; all our
Ha - le - lu - ya! Pe - lo tsa ro - na, di tha -

hearts are filled with glad - ness. Hal - le - lu - jah! We sing your
bi - le ka - o - fe - la. Ha - le - lu - ya! Pe - lo tsa

Fine

prais - es; all our hearts are filled with glad - ness.
ro - na, di tha - bi - le ka - o - fe - la.

1 Christ the Lord to us said: I am wine, I am bread.
2 Now he sends us all out, strong in faith, free of doubt,

Originally created in the Sotho language, this ecstatic South African hymn reached English by way of a
Swedish translation and is now found in numerous hymnals. It can serve as a powerful sending hymn for
connecting what happens at the Lord's Table with our mission in the world.

TEXT: South African; trans. Gracia Grindal, 1984
MUSIC: South African; arr. *Freedom Is Coming*, 1984
English Trans. and Music Arr. © 1984 Utryck (admin. Walton Music Corp.)

HALELUYA! PELO TSA RONA
6.6.6.8 with refrain

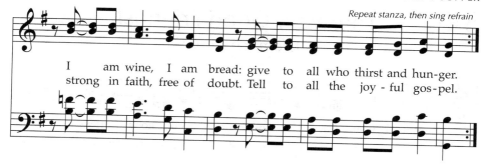

Repeat stanza, then sing refrain

I am wine, I am bread: give to all who thirst and hun-ger.
strong in faith, free of doubt. Tell to all the joy - ful gos-pel.

SENDING

We Will Go Out with Joy

539

1 We will go out with joy   in the Spir - it; we will go out with God.
2 Now an - y - one who's born   of the Spir - it, sing a new song of joy.
3 We will go out with joy   in the Spir - it; we will go out with God.

Fine

We will go out with joy   in the Spir-it; we will go out with God.
Now an - y - one who's born   of the Spir - it, sing a new song of joy.
We will go out with joy   in the Spir-it; we will go out with God.

Refrain

Al - le - lu - ia! We will go out with joy.

to Stanzas

Al - le - lu - ia! Al - le - lu - ia!

Drawing on the phrasing of Isaiah 55:12, this joyful sending hymn was created by a musical Canadian father and daughter, beginning with the tune that emerged from a four-hand piano improvisation. The completed hymn later served as the recessional music for her wedding.

TEXT and MUSIC: Andrew Donaldson and Hilary Seraph Donaldson, 2003
Text and Music © 2003 Andrew Donaldson and Hilary Seraph Donaldson

WE WILL GO OUT WITH JOY
10.6.10.6 with refrain

540

Farewell, Good Friends!

Shalom, chaverim!

Fare - well, good friends! Fare - well, good friends! Sha -
Sha - lom, cha - ve - rim! Sha - lom, cha - ve - rot! Sha -

lom, sha - lom! Till we meet a - gain, till we
lom, sha - lom! Le - hit - ra - ot, le -

meet a - gain, sha - lom, sha - lom.
hit - ra - ot, sha - lom, sha - lom.

May be sung as a canon.

HEBREW

שלום חברים
שלום חברות
שלום שלום
להתראות
להתראות
שלום שלום

While it is true that the Hebrew word *shalom* means "peace" and that it is used to greet people and bid them farewell, its larger sense is a feeling of contentment, wholeness, and harmony. Singing this round in the original language is one way to share in that fuller meaning.

TEXT: Hebrew blessing
MUSIC: Israeli melody

SHALOM, CHAVERIM
Irregular

God Be with You Till We Meet Again 541

Unison   *Harmony*

1 God be with you till we meet a-gain; lov - ing coun - sels
2 God be with you till we meet a-gain; un - seen wings pro-
3 God be with you till we meet a-gain; when life's per - ils
4 God be with you till we meet a-gain; keep love's ban - ner

guide, up-hold you, with a shep-herd's care en - fold you:
tect - ing hide you, dai - ly man - na still pro-vide you:
thick con-found you, put un - fail - ing arms a - round you:
float - ing o'er you; smite death's threat-ening wave be - fore you:

Unison

God be with you till we meet a - gain.

A North American Congregational minister wrote this text as a Christian expansion of the root sense of
"good-bye": God be [with] ye/you. The tune, named for a cousin, was composed by one of the few 20th-
century British composers to make a major contribution to hymnody.

TEXT: Jeremiah Eames Rankin, 1880, alt.   RANDOLPH
MUSIC: Ralph Vaughan Williams, 1906   9.8.8.9
                                                              (alternate tune: GOD BE WITH YOU, 542)

542 God Be with You Till We Meet Again

1 God be with you till we meet a - gain; lov - ing
2 God be with you till we meet a - gain; un - seen
3 God be with you till we meet a - gain; when life's
4 God be with you till we meet a - gain; keep love's

coun - sels guide, up - hold you, with a shep - herd's care en -
wings pro - tect - ing hide you, dai - ly man - na still pro -
per - ils thick con - found you, put un - fail - ing arms a -
ban - ner float - ing o'er you; smite death's threat - ening wave be -

fold you:
vide you:
round you: God be with you till we meet a - gain.
fore you:

After writing the first stanza of his "Christian Good-bye," the author sent it to two composers, one celebrated
and one unknown, to see how each would set it. This is the second person's tune, which the author found
more effective and used for the hymn's first publication.

TEXT: Jeremiah Eames Rankin, 1880, alt.
MUSIC: William G. Tomer, 1880

GOD BE WITH YOU
9.8.8.9
(alternate tune: RANDOLPH, 541)

God, Be the Love to Search and Keep Me

O Christ, Surround Me

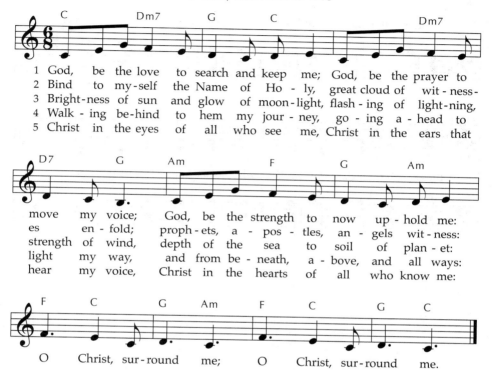

1 God, be the love to search and keep me; God, be the prayer to
2 Bind to my-self the Name of Ho-ly, great cloud of wit-ness-
3 Bright-ness of sun and glow of moon-light, flash-ing of light-ning,
4 Walk-ing be-hind to hem my jour-ney, go-ing a-head to
5 Christ in the eyes of all who see me, Christ in the ears that

move my voice; God, be the strength to now up-hold me:
es en-fold; proph-ets, a-pos-tles, an-gels wit-ness:
strength of wind, depth of the sea to soil of plan-et:
light my way, and from be-neath, a-bove, and all ways:
hear my voice, Christ in the hearts of all who know me:

O Christ, sur-round me; O Christ, sur-round me.

This hymn is a 21st-century adaptation of the traditional Celtic prayer style known as a *lorica* (Latin for "armor" or "breastplate"). Many such petitions for God's presence and protection were never written down, but this one is based on an example attributed to St. Patrick.

TEXT and MUSIC: Richard Bruxvoort Colligan, 2004
Text and Music © 2004 This Here Music, Worldmaking.net

GREEN TYLER
9.8.9.5.5

544

Bless the Lord

Bless the Lord, my soul, and bless God's ho - ly name.

Bless the Lord, my soul, who leads me in - to life.

This refrain based on Psalm 103:1 is meant for repeated singing. To "bless God's holy name" (which could not be spoken by observant Jews) is a reminder to be grateful even for what we cannot comprehend, trusting that God's providence will show us "the path of life" (Psalm 16:11).

TEXT: Taizé Community, 1984
MUSIC: Jacques Berthier, 1984
Text and Music © 1984, 1998 Les Presses de Taizé (admin. GIA Publications, Inc.)

BLESS THE LORD (Taizé)
Irregular

Lord, Bid Your Servant Go in Peace 545
Song of Simeon

1 Lord, bid your ser - vant go in peace; your
2 This is the Sav - ior of the world, the

word is now ful - filled. These eyes have seen sal -
Gen - tiles' prom - ised light, God's glo - ry dwell - ing

va - tion's dawn, this child so long fore - told.
in our midst, the joy of Is - ra - el.

This unrhymed 20th-century paraphrase by a Scottish Jesuit gives fresh immediacy to the Song of Simeon (Luke 2:29–32) and recaptures something of that aged priest's sense of wonder in beholding the infant Christ. The shape note tune enhances the text's down-to-earth quality.

TEXT: James Quinn, SJ, 1969
MUSIC: American folk melody; arr. Annabel Morris Buchanan, 1938
Text © 1969 James Quinn, SJ
Music Arr. © 1938, ren. H. W. Gray Company (admin. Alfred Music Publishing)

LAND OF REST
CM
(alternate harmonization, 691)

546 Lord, Dismiss Us with Your Blessing

1 Lord, dis-miss us with your bless-ing; fill our hearts with
2 Thanks we give and ad-o-ra-tion for your gos-pel's
3 Sav-ior, when your love shall call us, from our strug-gling

joy and peace; let us each, your love pos-sess-ing,
joy-ful sound; may the fruits of your sal-va-tion
pil-grim way, let no fear of death ap-pall us,

tri-umph in re-deem-ing grace. O re-fresh us,
in our hearts and lives a-bound. Ev-er faith-ful,
glad your sum-mons to o-bey. May we ev-er,

O re-fresh us, trav-el-ing through this wil-der-ness.
ev-er faith-ful to your truth may we be found.
may we ev-er reign with you in end-less day.

This hymn of corporate benediction is one of several using the same first line. It was written by a Baptist pastor who dedicated his entire ministry to a small church in rural Yorkshire. The tune used here was first transcribed from Sicilian sailors in the late 18th century.

TEXT: Attr. John Fawcett, 1773, alt.; stanza 3, alt. Geoffrey Thring, 1880, alt.
MUSIC: Sicilian melody, 18th cent.

SICILIAN MARINERS
8.7.8.7.8.7

Go, My Children, with My Blessing 547

1 "Go, my chil-dren, with my bless-ing, nev-er a-lone.
2 "Go, my chil-dren, sins for-giv-en, at peace and pure.
3 "Go, my chil-dren, fed and nour-ished, clos-er to me.

Wak-ing, sleep-ing, I am with you, you are my own.
Here you learned how much I love you, what I can cure.
Grow in love and love by serv-ing, joy-ful and free.

In my love's bap-tis-mal riv-er I have made you mine for-
Here you heard my dear Son's sto-ry; here you touched him, saw his
Here my Spir-it's pow-er filled you; here my ten-der com-fort

ev-er. Go, my chil-dren, with my bless-ing, you are my own."
glo-ry. Go, my chil-dren, sins for-giv-en, at peace and pure."
stilled you. Go, my chil-dren, fed and nour-ished, joy-ful and free."

Because this Welsh melody usually sets evening texts, the author was asked to create one for use in daytime. His recasting of the Aaronic blessing in Numbers 6:22–27 imagines that passage as a benediction that might be spoken by God at the conclusion of a worship service.

TEXT: Jaroslav J. Vajda, 1983
MUSIC: Welsh melody
Text © 1983 Concordia Publishing House

AR HYD Y NOS
8.4.8.4.8.8.8.4

548 May God Support You All Your Days
(Psalm 20)

1 May God sup-port you all your days, in times of
2 May God con-firm your heart's de-sire and bring to
3 May God be near you when you pray, to help you
4 Our hope is in the Ho-ly One. The swift and

glad-ness and in need. May God re-mem-ber you with
full-ness all your plans. May God's sus-tain-ing love in-
with a gen-tle hand. May God for-ev-er guide your
strong will sure-ly fall, but you will stand with God a-

grace and bless your ev-ery word and deed.
spire your shouts of praise and joy-ful dance.
way and lead you to the prom-ised land.
lone, who hears and an-swers when you call.

This text is loosely based on Psalm 20, the first of the psalms for the welfare of the king in battle. This royal psalm is here adapted as a sung blessing and prayer for those setting out on any new venture, making it appropriate for ordinations, weddings, or other such services.

TEXT: David Gambrell, 2009
MUSIC: Lee Hastings Bristol Jr., 1962
Text © 2011 David Gambrell (admin. Presbyterian Publishing Corp.)
Music © 1962 Theodore Presser Co. (admin. Carl Fischer, Inc.)

DICKINSON COLLEGE
LM

May the Love of the Lord
唯願神的愛撫慰你的靈

May the love of the Lord rest up-on your soul.
唯　　願　神　的　愛　撫　慰　你　的　靈.

May God's love dwell in you, through-out ev-ery day.
每　時　刻　他　的　愛　住　在　你　心　裡,

May God's coun-te-nance shine up-on you and be gra-cious to you.
他　的　榮　光　照　耀　你,　慈　愛　伴　隨　你,

May God's Spir-it be up-on you as you leave this place.
無　論　何　處　他　的　靈　都　永　遠　伴　隨　你.

The tune ("pure knowledge of God"), named for the son of the composer, was created to be a lullaby. The infant stopped breathing at one day old but was revived by the prompt action of nurses. The thankful mother wrote the English version of the Aaronic blessing (Numbers 6:24–26).

TEXT: Maria Ling, 1990; Chinese trans. Li Dong, 1990
MUSIC: Swee Hong Lim, 1990
Text and Music © 2000 Maria Ling and Swee Hong Lim (admin. General Board of Global Ministries t/a GBGMusik)

SOON TI
Irregular

550 Give Praise to the Lord

(Psalm 149)

1 Give praise to the Lord, and sing a new song;
2 With tim-brel and harp and joy-ful ac-claim,
3 In glo-ry ex-ult, all saints of the Lord;
4 For this is God's word: the saints shall not fail,

a-mid all the saints God's prais-es pro-long;
with glad-ness, O God, we praise your great name;
with song in the night high prais-es ac-cord;
but o-ver the earth their power shall pre-vail;

a song to your Mak-er and Rul-er now raise,
for now in your peo-ple good plea-sure you seek;
go forth in God's ser-vice and strong in God's might
all king-doms and na-tions shall yield to their sway.

all chil-dren of Zi-on: re-joice and give praise.
with robes of sal-va-tion you cov-er the meek.
to con-quer all e-vil and stand for the right.
To God give the glo-ry; sing prais-es for aye.

This adaptation of Psalm 149 is organized by themes of praise and service, with a strong implication that they are not really separable but are two aspects of the same God-centered impulse. This text is set to a jubilant tune derived from a late 19th-century English anthem.

TEXT: *The New Metrical Version of the Psalms*, 1909, alt.
MUSIC: C. Hubert H. Parry, 1894

LAUDATE DOMINUM
10.10.11.11

Lord, Have Mercy

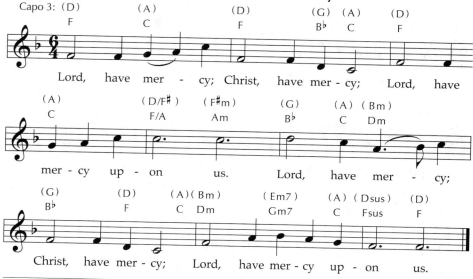

Lord, have mer - cy; Christ, have mer - cy; Lord, have
mer - cy up - on us. Lord, have mer - cy;
Christ, have mer - cy; Lord, have mer - cy up - on us.

TEXT: Trad. liturgical text
MUSIC: American folk melody; arr. Richard Proulx, 1984
Music Arr. © 1986 GIA Publications, Inc.

LAND OF REST

Holy, Holy, Holy

552

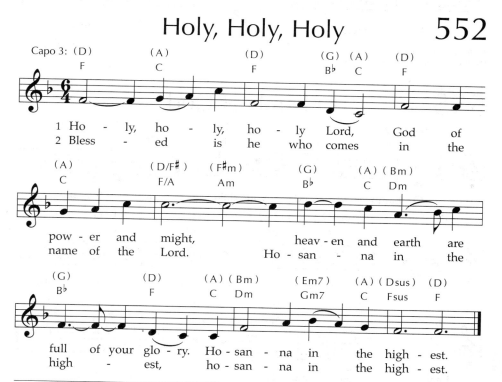

1 Ho - ly, ho - ly, ho - ly Lord, God of
2 Bless - ed is he who comes in the

pow - er and might, heav - en and earth are
name of the Lord. Ho - san - na in the

full of your glo - ry. Ho - san - na in the high - est.
high - est, ho - san - na in the high - est.

TEXT: Trad. liturgical text
MUSIC: American folk melody; adapt. Marcia Pruner, 1980; arr. Richard Proulx, 1984
Music Adapt. © 1980 Church Pension Fund
Music Arr. © 1986 GIA Publications, Inc.

LAND OF REST

553 Christ Has Died; Christ Is Risen

Christ has died; Christ is ris-en; Christ will come a-gain.

Christ has died; Christ is ris-en; Christ will come a-gain.

TEXT: Trad. liturgical text
MUSIC: American folk melody; arr. Richard Proulx, 1984
Music Arr. © 1986 GIA Publications, Inc.

LAND OF REST

554 Amen

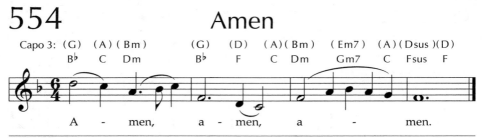

A - men, a - men, a - men.

TEXT: Trad. liturgical text
MUSIC: American folk melody; arr. Richard Proulx, 1995
Music Arr. © 1995 GIA Publications, Inc.

LAND OF REST

555 O Lamb of God

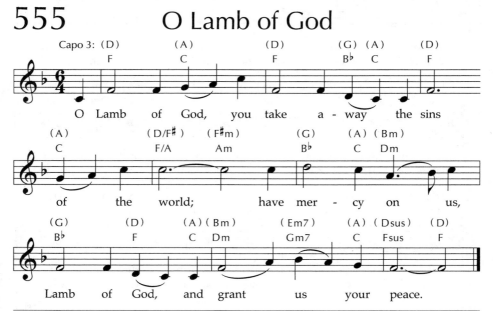

O Lamb of God, you take a - way the sins

of the world; have mer - cy on us,

Lamb of God, and grant us your peace.

TEXT: Trad. liturgical text
MUSIC: American folk melody; arr. Richard Proulx, 1995
Music Arr. © 1995 GIA Publications, Inc.

LAND OF REST

Holy, Holy, Holy

Ho - ly, ho - ly, ho - ly Lord,

God of power and might,

heaven and earth are full of your glo - ry. Ho -

san - na in the high - est.

Blessed is the One who comes in the Lord's name. Ho -

san - na in the high - est.

Blessed is the One who comes in the Lord's name. Ho -

san - na in the high - est.

TEXT: Trad. liturgical text
MUSIC: Leon Roberts, 1981; arr. Hanan Yaqub, 1998
Music © 1981 GIA Publications, Inc.

SANCTUS (Roberts)

557 Christ Has Died; Christ Is Risen

Christ has died; Christ is ris - en;
Christ will come a - gain.
Christ has died; Christ is ris - en;
Christ will come a - gain.

TEXT: Trad. liturgical text
MUSIC: Leon Roberts, 1981; arr. Hanan Yaqub, 1998
Music © 1981 GIA Publications, Inc.

MEMORIAL ACCLAMATION (Roberts)

558 Amen

A - men, a - men, a - men, a - men,
a - men, a - men, a -
men, a - men, a - men.

TEXT: Trad. liturgical text
MUSIC: Leon Roberts, 1981; arr. Hanan Yaqub, 1998
Music © 1981 GIA Publications, Inc.

AMEN (Roberts)

Holy, Holy, Holy

Ho - ly, ho - ly, ho - ly Lord, God of pow-er and might, heav-en and earth are full of your glo - ry. Ho - san - na in the high - est. Bless-ed is he who comes in the name of the Lord. Ho - san - na in the high - est, ho - san - na in the high - est.

TEXT: Trad. liturgical text
MUSIC: Per Harling, 2004
Music © 2004 Augsburg Fortress

SANCTUS (Harling)

560 Christ Has Died; Christ Is Risen

Christ has died; Christ is ris - en; Christ will come a - gain.

TEXT: Trad. liturgical text
MUSIC: Per Harling, 2004
Music © 2004 Augsburg Fortress

MEMORIAL ACCLAMATION (Harling)

561 Amen

A - men, a - men, a - men.

TEXT: Trad. liturgical text
MUSIC: Per Harling, 2004
Music © 2004 Augsburg Fortress

AMEN (Harling)

562 Holy, Holy, Holy

Ho - ly, ho - ly, ho - ly Lord, God of power and might,

TEXT: Trad. liturgical text
MUSIC: *Deutsche Messe,* Franz Schubert, 1827; adapt. Richard Proulx, 1985
Music Adapt. © 1985, 1989 GIA Publications, Inc.

SANCTUS (Schubert)

563 Christ Has Died; Christ Is Risen

Christ has died; Christ is risen; Christ will come a-gain.

TEXT: Trad. liturgical text
MUSIC: *Deutsche Messe*, Franz Schubert, 1827; adapt. Richard Proulx, 1995
Music Adapt. © 1985, 1995 GIA Publications, Inc.

MEMORIAL ACCLAMATION (Schubert)

564 Amen

A - men, a - men, a - men. A - men, a - men.

TEXT: Trad. liturgical text
MUSIC: *Deutsche Messe*, Franz Schubert, 1827; adapt. Richard Proulx, 1985
Music Adapt. © 1985, 1989 GIA Publications, Inc.

AMEN (Schubert)

565 Holy, Holy, Holy

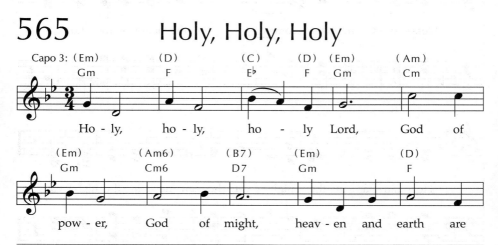

Ho - ly, ho - ly, ho - ly Lord, God of pow - er, God of might, heav - en and earth are

TEXT: Trad. liturgical text
MUSIC: Marty Haugen, 1984
Music © 1984 GIA Publications, Inc.

SANCTUS (Haugen)

full of your glo-ry. Ho-san-na in the high-est. Bless-ed is he who comes in the name of the Lord. Ho-san-na in the high-est, ho-san-na in the high - est.

Christ Has Died; Christ Is Risen 566

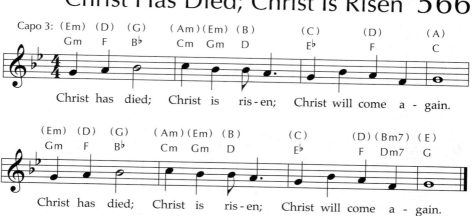

Christ has died; Christ is ris-en; Christ will come a-gain.

Christ has died; Christ is ris-en; Christ will come a-gain.

TEXT: Trad. liturgical text
MUSIC: Marty Haugen, 1984
Music © 1984 GIA Publications, Inc.

MEMORIAL ACCLAMATION 1 (Haugen)

567 Dying You Destroyed Our Death

TEXT: Trad. liturgical text
MUSIC: Marty Haugen, 1990
Music © 1990 GIA Publications, Inc.

MEMORIAL ACCLAMATION 2 (Haugen)

568 Amen

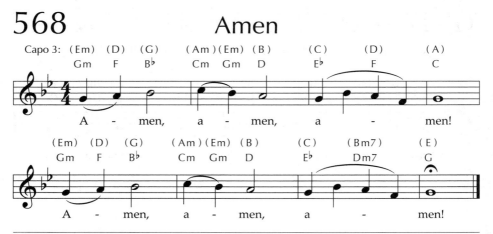

TEXT: Trad. liturgical text
MUSIC: Marty Haugen, 1984
Music © 1984 GIA Publications, Inc.

AMEN (Haugen)

Holy, Holy, Holy

Ho - ly, ho - ly, ho - ly Lord, God of pow-er and might,

heav-en and earth are full of your glo-ry. Ho-san-na in the

high - est. Blessed is the One who comes in the name of the

Lord. Ho - san - na in the high - est.

TEXT: Trad. liturgical text
MUSIC: Curt Oliver, 1997
Music © 1997 Curt Oliver

SANCTUS (Oliver)

Dying You Destroyed Our Death 570

Dy - ing you de-stroyed our death; ris - ing you re -

stored our life. Lord Je - sus, come in glo - ry.

TEXT: Trad. liturgical text
MUSIC: Curt Oliver, 1997
Music © 1997 Curt Oliver

MEMORIAL ACCLAMATION (Oliver)

571 Amen

A - men, a - men, a - men.

TEXT: Trad. liturgical text
MUSIC: Curt Oliver, 1997
Music © 1997 Curt Oliver

AMEN (Oliver)

572 Holy, Holy, Holy

Ho - ly, ho - ly, ho - ly Lord, God of

pow - er and might, heav - en and earth are

full of your glo - ry. Ho - san - na in the high - est.

Blessed is he who comes in the name of the

Lord. Ho - san - na in the high - est.

TEXT: Trad. liturgical text
MUSIC: Thomas Pavlechko, 2006
Music © 2006 Augsburg Fortress

SANCTUS (Pavlechko)

Christ Has Died; Christ Is Risen 573

Christ has died; Christ is ris-en; Christ will come a-gain.

TEXT: Trad. liturgical text
MUSIC: Thomas Pavlechko, 2006
Music © 2006 Augsburg Fortress

MEMORIAL ACCLAMATION (Pavlechko)

Amen 574

A - men, a - men, a - men.

TEXT: Trad. liturgical text
MUSIC: Thomas Pavlechko, 2006
Music © 2006 Augsburg Fortress

AMEN (Pavlechko)

Lord, Have Mercy upon Us 575

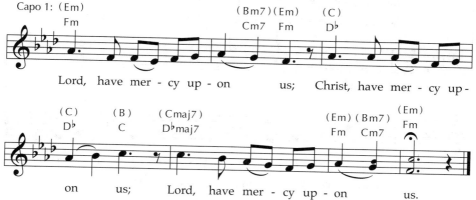

Lord, have mer-cy up-on us; Christ, have mer-cy up-on us; Lord, have mer-cy up-on us.

Guitar chords do not correspond with keyboard harmony.

TEXT: Trad. liturgical text
MUSIC: J. Christopher Pardini, 2005
Music © 2011 Birnamwood Publications (a div. of MorningStar Music Publishers, Inc.)

KYRIE ELEISON (Pardini)

576   Lord, Have Mercy

Lord, have mer - cy.

Christ, have mer - cy. Lord, have mer - cy on us.

TEXT: Trad. liturgical text
MUSIC: Swee Hong Lim, 1990
Music © 1990 Swee Hong Lim (admin. General Board of Global Ministries t/a GBGMusik)

SINGAPURA

577   Lord, Have Mercy

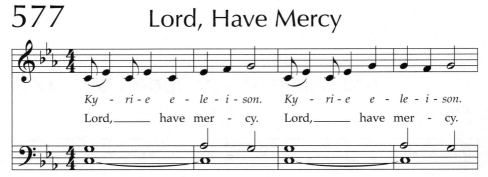

Ky - ri - e e - le - i - son. Ky - ri - e e - le - i - son.

Lord,____ have mer - cy. Lord,____ have mer - cy.

Note: Lower voices may hum.

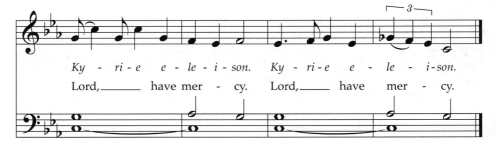

Ky - ri - e e - le - i - son. Ky - ri - e e - le - i - son.

Lord,____ have mer - cy. Lord,____ have mer - cy.

TEXT: Trad. liturgical text
MUSIC: Dinah Reindorf, 1987
Music © 1987 Dinah Reindorf

KYRIE ELEISON (Reindorf)

O Lord, Have Mercy

Kyrie eleison
Oré poriajú verekó

TEXT: Trad. liturgical text
MUSIC: Guarani melody; harm. Carlton R. Young, 1996
Music Harm. © 1996 General Board of Global Ministries t/a GBGMusik

ORÉ PORIAJÚ VEREKÓ

579 Lord, Have Mercy

Kyrie eleison

1 Lord, have mer - cy. Lord, have mer - cy.
2 Christ, have mer - cy. Christ, have mer - cy.
3 Lord, have mer - cy. Lord, have mer - cy.

1 Ky - ri - e e - lei - son. Ky - ri - e e - lei - son.
2 Chris - te e - lei - son. Chris - te e - lei - son.
3 Ky - ri - e e - lei - son. Ky - ri - e e - lei - son.

Lord, have mer - cy.
Christ, have mer - cy.
Lord, have mer - cy.

Ky - ri - e e - le - i - son.
Chris - te e - le - i - son.
Ky - ri - e e - le - i - son.

TEXT: Trad. liturgical text
MUSIC: Russian Orthodox chant

KYRIE ELEISON (Orthodox)

580 Glory Be to the Father

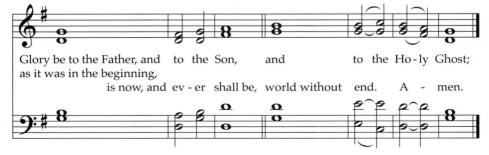

Glory be to the Father, and to the Son, and to the Ho - ly Ghost;
as it was in the beginning, is now, and ev - er shall be, world without end. A - men.

TEXT: Trad. liturgical text
MUSIC: Scottish chant

GLORIA PATRI (Scottish)

Glory Be to the Father

Glo - ry be to the Fa - ther, and to the Son, and to the Ho - ly Ghost; as it was in the be - gin - ning, is now, and ev - er shall be, world with - out end. A - men, a - men.

TEXT: Trad. liturgical text
MUSIC: Henry W. Greatorex, 1851

GLORIA PATRI (Greatorex)

582

Glory to God,
Whose Goodness Shines on Me

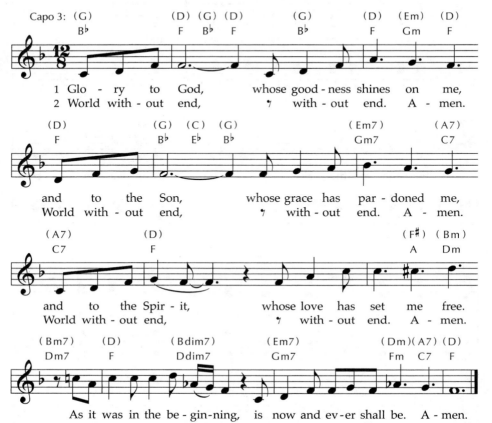

TEXT: Trad. liturgical text; adapt. Paul M. Vasile, 2008
MUSIC: Paul M. Vasile, 2008
Text Adapt. and Music © 2008 Paul M. Vasile

GLORY TO GOD (Vasile)

Glory to God
Gloria, gloria

Glo - ry to God, glo - ry to God, glo - ry in the high - est!
Glo - ri - a, glo - ri - a, in ex - cel - sis De - o!

Glo - ry to God, glo - ry to God, al - le - lu - ia, al - le - lu - ia!
Glo - ri - a, glo - ri - a, al - le - lu - ia, al - le - lu - ia!

May be sung as a canon.

TEXT: Trad. liturgical text
MUSIC: Jacques Berthier, 1979
Music © 1979, 1981 Les Presses de Taizé (admin. GIA Publications, Inc.)

GLORIA (Taizé)

Glory, Glory, Glory
584

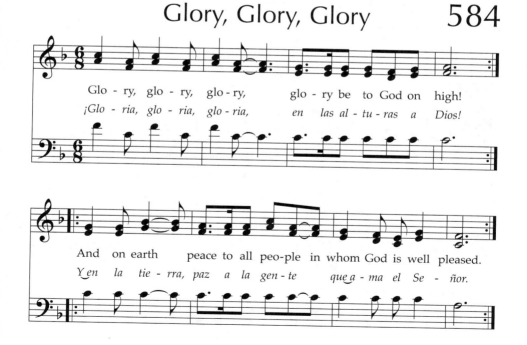

Glo - ry, glo - ry, glo - ry, glo - ry be to God on high!
¡Glo - ria, glo - ria, glo - ria, en las al - tu - ras a Dios!

And on earth peace to all peo - ple in whom God is well pleased.
Y en la tie - rra, paz a la gen - te que a - ma el Se - ñor.

TEXT: Based on Luke 2:14; Pablo Sosa, 1989
MUSIC: Pablo Sosa, 1989
Text and Music © 1989 GIA Publications, Inc.

CUEQUITA

585

Glory to God
Gloria a Dios

1 Glory to God, glory to God, glory in the high - est!
2 Glory to God, glory to God, glory to Christ Je - sus!
3 Glory to God, glory to God, glory to the Spir - it!

1 ¡Glo-ria a Dios, glo-ria a Dios, glo-ria en los cie - los!
2 ¡Glo-ria a Dios, glo-ria a Dios, glo-ria a Je - su-cris - to!
3 ¡Glo-ria a Dios, glo-ria a Dios, glo-ria al Es - pí - ri - tu!

To God be glo-ry for - ev - er! Al-le-lu-ia, A - men!

¡A Dios la glo-ria por siem - pre! ¡A-le-lu-ya, A - mén!

Al-le-lu-ia, A - men! Al-le-lu-ia, A - men!

¡A - le-lu-ya, A - mén! ¡A - le-lu-ya, A - mén!

May be sung in call and response pattern.

TEXT: Anon.
MUSIC: Peruvian melody

MACHU-PICHU

586

Alleluia

Al-le-lu - ia, al-le-lu - ia, al-le-lu - ia.

Al-le-lu - ia, al-le-lu - ia, al-le-lu - ia.

TEXT: Trad. liturgical text
MUSIC: Jacques Berthier, 1984
Music © 1984 Les Presses de Taizé (admin. GIA Publications, Inc.)

ALLELUIA 7

Alleluia!

Al - le - lu - ia! Al - le - lu - ia!

Al - le - lu - ia! Al - le - lu - ia!

TEXT: Trad. liturgical text
MUSIC: Fintan O'Carroll, 1981; harm. Christopher Walker, 1985
Music © 1985 Fintan O'Carroll and Christopher Walker (Published by OCP)

CELTIC ALLELUIA

Alleluia

Al - le-lu - ia, al - le - lu - ia! Al - le-lu - ia, al - le-lu - ia!

Al - le-lu - ia, al - le - lu - ia! Al - le - lu - ia, al - le-lu - ia!

Al - le-lu - ia, al - le - lu - ia! Al - le - lu - ia, al - le - lu - ia!

Al - le-lu - ia, al - le - lu - ia! Al - le-lu - ia, al - le-lu - ia!

TEXT: Trad. liturgical text
MUSIC: Howard Hughes, SM, 1973
Music © 1973, 1979 GIA Publications, Inc.

JOYFUL ALLELUIA

589

Alleluia
Aleluya

Al - le - lu - ia, al - le - lu - ia. Al - le - lu - ia, al - le - lu - ia.
A - le - lu - ya, a - le - lu - ya. A - le - lu - ya, a - le - lu - ya.

Al - le - lu - ia, al - le - lu - ia. Now the Lord is risen in - deed.
A - le - lu - ya, a - le - lu - ya. El Se - ñor re - su - ci - tó.

TEXT: Trad. liturgical text
MUSIC: Honduran melody

HONDURAS ALLELUIA

Hallelujah

Hal - le - lu - jah, hal - le - lu - jah,

Hal - le - lu - jah, hal - le - lu,

Hal - le - lu - jah, hal - le - lu - jah,

hal - le - lu - jah, hal - le - lu - jah.

hal - le - lu - jah, hal - le - lu - jah.

hal - le - lu - jah, hal - le - lu - jah.

Repeat as desired.

TEXT: Trad. liturgical text
MUSIC: Abraham Maraire, 20th cent.; arr. Patrick Matsikenyiri, 2004
Music © United Methodist Music Service

HALLELUJAH (Maraire)

591 Halle, Halle, Hallelujah!

TEXT: Ref., trad. liturgical text; stanzas, Marty Haugen, 1990
MUSIC: Caribbean melody; arr. John L. Bell, 1990; stanzas, Marty Haugen, 1990
Text and Music © 1990 WGRG, Iona Community (admin. GIA Publications, Inc.)
Music Arr. © 1993 GIA Publications, Inc.

HALLE, HALLE
Irregular

Leader/All (sung over or in alternation with refrain)

1 O God, to whom shall we go? You a - lone have the
2 My sheep hear my voice, says the Lord. When I call them they

words of life. Let your words be our prayer and the song we
fol - low me. I will lead them to rest by the peace - ful

to Refrain

sing: hal - le - lu - jah, hal - le - lu - jah!
streams: hal - le - lu - jah, hal - le - lu - jah!

592

Holy, Holy, Holy

TEXT: Trad. liturgical text
MUSIC: Paul M. Vasile, 2008
Music © 2008 Paul M. Vasile

SANCTUS (Vasile)

Holy, Holy

Guitar chords do not correspond with keyboard harmony.

TEXT: Trad. liturgical text
MUSIC: David E. Poole, 2007
Music © 2007 David E. Poole

SANCTUS (Poole)

594 Holy, Holy, Holy, Holy

Santo, santo, santo, santo

Capo 3: (D)   (A)

Refrain/Estribillo   F   C

Ho-ly, ho-ly, ho-ly, ho-ly, ho-ly, ho-ly is our God,
San-to, san-to, san-to, san-to, san-to, san-to es nues-tro Dios,

(A7)
C7   (D) F

God, the Lord of earth and heav-en. Ho-ly, ho-ly is our God.
Se-ñor de to-da la tie-rra. San-to, san-to es nues-tro Dios.

(D) F   (A) C

Ho-ly, ho-ly, ho-ly, ho-ly, ho-ly, ho-ly is our God.
San-to, san-to, san-to, san-to, san-to, san-to es nues-tro Dios,

(A7)
C7   (D) F   Fine

God, the Lord of all of his-tory. Ho-ly, ho-ly is our God.
Se-ñor de to-da la his-to-ria. San-to, san-to es nues-tro Dios.

(D7)
F7   (G) B♭   (A) C   (D) F

Who ac-com-pa-nies our peo-ple, who lives with-in our strug-gles,
Que a-com-pa-ña a nues-tro pue-blo, que vi-ve en nues-tras lu-chas,

(D) F   (A) C   (A7) C7   (D) F

of all the earth and heav-en the one and on-ly Lord.
del u-ni-ver-so en-te-ro el ú-ni-co Se-ñor.

TEXT: Guillermo Cuéllar, 1977; trans. Linda McCrae, 1988
MUSIC: Guillermo Cuéllar, 1977; arr. Raquel Mora Martínez, 1996
Text and Music © 1988, 1993, 1994 GIA Publications, Inc.

CUÉLLAR
Irregular

Holy, Holy, Holy

Santo, santo, santo

595

TEXT and MUSIC: Trad. Argentine

ARGENTINE SANTO
6.7.8.5

596

You Are Holy

Eres santo

*May be sung as a canon.

TEXT: Per Harling, 1990; Spanish trans. Raquel Gutiérrez-Achon, 1991, alt.
MUSIC: Per Harling, 1990
Text and Music © 1990 Ton Vis Produktion AB (admin. Augsburg Fortress)
Spanish Trans. © Raquel Gutiérrez-Achon

DU ÄR HELIG
Irregular

597 Holy, Most Holy Lord

Sanna, sannanina

San-na, san-na-ni-na, san-na, san-na, san-na. Ho-san-na
Ho-ly, most ho-ly Lord, Lord God of power and might, Most ho-ly

San-na, san-na-ni-na, san-na, san-na, san-na. Ho-san-na
heav-en and earth are filled, filled with your ho-ly light. Most bless-ed

San-na, san-na, san-na, san-na-ni-na, san-na,
O bless-ed is the One, the One who comes, comes in

san-na, san-na. Ho-san-na San-na, san-na, san-
the name of God. Ho-san-na Ho-san-na in the

na, san-na-ni-na, san-na, san-na, san-na. San-na-ni-na
high-est, ho-san-na, san-na, san-na, san-na. Most ho-ly Lord

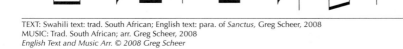

TEXT: Swahili text: trad. South African; English text: para. of *Sanctus*, Greg Scheer, 2008
MUSIC: Trad. South African; arr. Greg Scheer, 2008
English Text and Music Arr. © 2008 Greg Scheer

SANNANINA
Irregular

Amen, We Praise Your Name 598
Amen siakudumisa

TEXT: South African
MUSIC: S. C. Molefe, c. 1976; transcr. David Dargie, 1983
Text and Music © Lumko Institute, South Africa
Music Transcr. © 1983 David Dargie (admin. Choristers Guild)

AMEN SIAKUDUMISA
Irregular

599 Amen

A - men. A - men.

TEXT: Trad. liturgical text
MUSIC: Attr. Johann G. Naumann, 18th cent.

DRESDEN AMEN

600 Amen

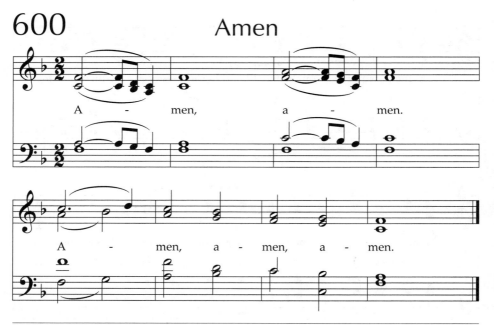

A - men, a - men.

A - men, a - men, a - men.

TEXT: Trad. liturgical text
MUSIC: African American; arr. Nelsie T. Johnson, 1988

AMEN

601 Amen

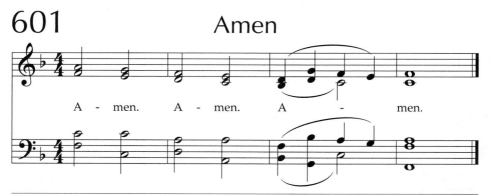

A - men. A - men. A - men.

TEXT: Trad. liturgical text
MUSIC: Anon. Danish

DANISH AMEN

Holy Lamb of God

Ya hamalallah

Ho - ly Lamb of God, you take a - way the
Ya ha - ma - lal - lah al - ha - mel kha - ta - yal

sin of the world. Have mer - cy on us.
'a - lam: ir - ham - na.

Ho - ly Lamb of God, you take a - way the
Ya ha - ma - lal - lah al - ha - mel kha - ta - yal

sin of the world. Grant us your peace;
'a - lam: im - nah - nas - sa - lam, im -

grant us your peace; grant us your peace.
nah - nas - sa - lam, im - nah - nas - sa - lam.

ARABIC

يا حملَ الله

يا حملَ الله الحامل خطايا العالم : ارحمنا.
يا حملَ الله الحامل خطايا العالم : ارحمنا.
يا حملَ الله الحامل خطايا العالم : امنحنا السلام ، امنحنا السلام.

TEXT: Trad. liturgical text
MUSIC: Yusuf Khill, 1956
Music © 2003 Yusuf Khill

YA HAMALALLAH
Irregular

603 Lamb of God

Lamb of God, you take a-way the sin of the world: have mer - cy, have mer - cy on us. Lamb of God, you take a-way the sin of the world: grant us, O grant us your peace.

TEXT: Trad. liturgical text
MUSIC: Paul M. Vasile, 2008
Music © 2008 Paul M. Vasile

AGNUS DEI (Vasile)

604 Lamb of God

Lamb of God, you take a - way the sin of the world; have mer - cy on us. Lamb of God, you take a - way the sin of the

Guitar chords do not correspond with keyboard harmony.

TEXT: Trad. liturgical text
MUSIC: Robert Buckley Farlee, 2006
Music © 2006 Augsburg Fortress

AGNUS DEI (Farlee)

world; have mer - cy on us. Lamb of God, you take a - way the

sin of the world; grant us peace; grant us peace.

Praise to God the Father 605

Da n'ase

Praise to God the Fa - ther; praise to God the Son;
Da n'a - se! Da n'a - se! Da On - ya - me a - se!

praise to God the Spir - it: praise to the Three - in - One.
Da n'a - se! Da n'a - se! Da On - ya - me a - se!

Sing praise, sing praise to the Lord on high.
Ef - ia - se o - ye n'a n'a - do - e do - e so.

Praise to God Al - might - y; praise to the Ho - ly One.
Da n'a - se! Da n'a - se! Da On - ya - me a - se!

TEXT: Anon.
MUSIC: Ghanaian melody; arr. Alfred V. Fedak, 2011
Music Arr. © 2011 Alfred V. Fedak

DA N'ASE
Irregular

606
Praise God, from Whom All Blessings Flow
Doxology

Praise God, from whom all bless-ings flow; praise *him, all crea-tures
here be-low; praise *him a-bove, ye heaven-ly host; praise
Fa-ther, Son, and Ho-ly Ghost. A-men.

*Or "God"

TEXT: Thomas Ken, 1695, 1709
MUSIC: Genevan Psalter, 1551

OLD HUNDREDTH
LM

607
Praise God, from Whom All Blessings Flow
Doxology

Praise God, from whom all bless-ings flow; praise Christ, all peo-ple

TEXT: Neil Weatherhogg, 1988
MUSIC: Genevan Psalter, 1551
Text © 1990 Neil Weatherhogg

OLD HUNDREDTH
LM

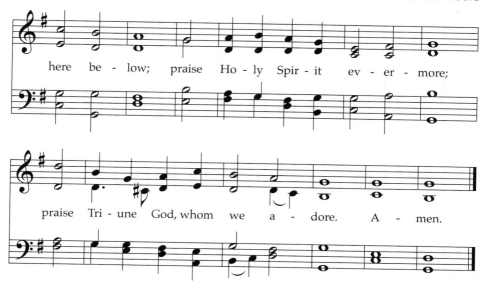

here be - low; praise Ho - ly Spir - it ev - er - more;

praise Tri - une God, whom we a - dore. A - men.

Praise God, from Whom All Blessings Flow

608

Praise God, from whom all bless-ings flow; praise Christ, all

peo - ple here be - low; praise Ho - ly Spir - it ev - er -

more; praise Tri - une God, whom we a - dore.

TEXT: Neil Weatherhogg, 1988
MUSIC: Hal H. Hopson, 2008
Text © 1990 Neil Weatherhogg
Music © 2008 Hal H. Hopson

PRAISE GOD (Hopson)
LM

609 Praise God, from Whom All Blessings Flow

Praise God, from whom all bless-ings flow. Praise God, all crea-tures

high and low. Al - le - lu - ia, al - le - lu - ia! Praise

God, in Je - sus ful - ly known: Cre - a - tor, Word, and Spir - it

one. Al - le - lu - ia, al - le - lu - ia! Al - le -

lu - ia, al - le - lu - ia, al - le - lu - ia!

TEXT: Brian Wren, 1989
MUSIC: *Geistliche Kirchengesäng*, 1623; harm. Hal H. Hopson, 1998
Text © 1989 Hope Publishing Company
Music Harm. © 1998 Hope Publishing Company

LASST UNS ERFREUEN
LM with alleluias
(alternate harmonization, 10)

O for a Thousand Tongues to Sing 610

1 O for a thou - sand tongues to sing my
2 The name of Je - sus charms our fears, and
3 Christ speaks, and lis - tening to his voice new
4 My gra - cious Mas - ter and my God, as -
5 To God all glo - ry, praise, and love be

dear Re - deem - er's praise, the glo - ries of my
bids our sor - rows cease, sings mu - sic in the
life the dead re - ceive; the mourn - ful wak - en
sist me to pro - claim, to spread through all the
now and ev - er given by saints be - low and

God and King, the tri - umphs of God's grace!
sin - ner's ears, brings life, and health, and peace.
to re - joice; the poor in heart be - lieve.
earth a - broad the hon - ors of thy name.
saints a - bove, the church in earth and heaven.

SPANISH

1 Mil voces para celebrar
a mi Libertador,
las glorias de su majestad,
los triunfos de su amor.

KOREAN

1 만 입이 내게 있으면
그 입 다 가지고
내 구주 주신 은총을
늘 찬송하겠네

This text comes from an eighteen-stanza hymn the author wrote to mark the first anniversary of his life-changing conversion experience. It is now customarily the first hymn in Methodist hymnals worldwide. This tune, adapted from a German composer, is the usual North American setting.

TEXT: Charles Wesley, 1739, alt.; Spanish trans. Federico J. Pagura;
Korean trans. The United Methodist Korean Hymnal Committee, 2001
MUSIC: Carl Gotthelf Gläser, 1828; arr. Lowell Mason, 1839
Spanish Trans. © 1989 The United Methodist Publishing House (admin. The Copyright Company)
Korean Trans. © 2001 The United Methodist Publishing House (admin. The Copyright Company)

AZMON
CM

611 Joyful, Joyful, We Adore Thee

1 Joy-ful, joy-ful, we a-dore thee, God of glo-ry, Lord of love!
2 All thy works with joy sur-round thee; earth and heaven re-flect thy rays;
3 Mor-tals, join the hap-py cho-rus which the morn-ing stars be-gan.

Hearts un-fold like flowers be-fore thee, o-pening to the sun a-bove.
stars and an-gels sing a-round thee, cen-ter of un-bro-ken praise.
Love di-vine is reign-ing o'er us, join-ing all in heav-en's plan.

Melt the clouds of sin and sad-ness; drive the dark of doubt a-way.
Field and for-est, vale and moun-tain, flower-y mead-ow, flash-ing sea,
Ev-er sing-ing, march we on-ward, vic-tors in the midst of strife.

Giv-er of im-mor-tal glad-ness, fill us with the light of day.
chant-ing bird and flow-ing foun-tain, call us to re-joice in thee.
Joy-ful mu-sic leads us sun-ward in the tri-umph song of life.

This well-known melody was created to provide a choral setting for J. C. F. von Schiller's poem, "An die Freude" (To Joy), as the final movement of the composer's *Ninth Symphony*. The author, a prominent Presbyterian pastor and author, wrote the words with this tune in mind.

TEXT: Henry van Dyke, 1907, alt.
MUSIC: Ludwig van Beethoven, 1824; adapt. Edward Hodges, 1842, alt.

HYMN TO JOY
8.7.8.7.D

We Praise You, O God

1 We praise you, O God, our Re - deem - er, Cre - a - tor;
2 We wor - ship you, God of our fa - thers and moth - ers;
3 With voic - es u - nit - ed our prais - es we of - fer

in grate - ful de - vo - tion our trib - ute we bring.
through tri - al and tem - pest our guide you have been.
and glad - ly our songs of thanks - giv - ing we raise.

We lay it be - fore you; we kneel and a - dore you;
When per - ils o'er - take us, you will not for - sake us,
With you, Lord, be - side us, your strong arm will guide us.

we bless your ho - ly name; glad prais - es we sing.
and with your help, O Lord, our strug - gles we win.
To you, our great Re - deem - er, for - ev - er be praise!

The author wrote this text when only nineteen years old in response to a request from the organist of the
Brick Presbyterian Church in New York City, who wanted another Thanksgiving text to sing to this Dutch
tune. He regarded the usual text (see no. 336) as too full of conflict.

TEXT: Julia C. Cory, 1902, alt.
MUSIC: *Neder-landtsch Gedenck-Clanck*, 1626; harm. Eduard Kremser, 1877

KREMSER
12.11.12.11
(this tune in a lower key, 336)

613 O Lord, Our Lord

How Majestic Is Your Name

O Lord, our Lord, how ma-jes-tic is your name in all the

earth. O earth. O Lord, we praise your name. O

Lord, we mag-ni-fy your name: Prince of Peace, might-y

God; O Lord God Al-might - y.

The repeated opening sentence here quotes Psalm 8:1 (identical with Psalm 8:9), and the Messianic title
"Prince of Peace" comes from Isaiah 9:6. The recurring musical patterns make this piece easy to sing, and
it appropriately assigns its highest note to the phrase "mighty God."

TEXT and MUSIC: Michael W. Smith, 1981
Text and Music © 1981 Meadowgreen Music Company (admin. EMICMGPublishing.com)

HOW MAJESTIC
Irregular

Great Are You, Lord

614

Great Is the Lord

Great are you, Lord: you are ho-ly and just; by your pow-er we trust in your

love.   Great are you, Lord: you are faith-ful and true;   by your

mer - cy   you prove   you are love.   Great are you, Lord,   and

wor-thy   of glo - ry!   Great are you, Lord,   and   wor-thy   of praise.

Great are you, Lord.   We   lift   up   our voice;   we   lift   up   our voice:

great   are you, Lord!   Great   are you, Lord!

Although it is not a direct paraphrase of any particular psalm, this text echoes "great is the Lord and greatly to be praised," found in three of them (Psalms 48:1; 96:4; 145:3). Such songs of adoration lift up the heart and mind to God, asking nothing but to enjoy God's presence.

TEXT and MUSIC: Michael W. Smith and Deborah D. Smith, 1982, alt.
Text and Music © 1982 Meadowgreen Music Company (admin. EMICMGPublishing.com)

GREAT IS THE LORD
Irregular

615 Praise to the Lord

하나님을 찬양하세

1 Praise to the Lord and glo - ry to God. We gath - er in
2 Be with us, Lord, as we come to you. You are the

1 하 나 님 을 찬 양 하 세 무 릎
2 평 화 의 왕 임 하 소 서 사 랑

wor - ship and fall up-on our knees. Raise high your voic-es; sing to the
King of peace, the God of love. U - nite us, Lord, that we would be

꿇 어 경 배 해 그 의 사 랑 그 의
의 주 오 소 서 우 리 모 두 주 안

Lord; give thanks for God's love and grace. Praise to the Lord!
one; your love is the bond of peace. Praise to the Lord!

은 혜 소 리 높 여 찬 양 해
에 서 하 나 되 게 하 소 서

This text from Korea affirms that the shared adoration of God fosters a sense of common purpose. The
second stanza ends with an allusion to Ephesians 4:3, a further reminder of Christian unity, reinforced
earlier by an echo of Christ's prayer that "all may be one" (John 17:21).

TEXT: Sung Mo Moon and Seung-Won Park, 1989; English trans. Edward Poitras
MUSIC: Sung Mo Moon, 1989
Text and Music © Kyung Dong Presbyterian Church (admin. Sung Mo Moon and Seung-Won Park)

PRAISE TO THE LORD
Irregular

Our God Is an Awesome God 616
Awesome God

Our God is an awe-some God who reigns from heav-en a-bove
with wis - dom, power, and love; our God is an awe-some God!

This is a contemporary worship song that first gained recognition on Christian radio and later became a popular congregational song. "Awesome" here is not a trivial expression but carries the meaning of "awe-inspiring" and is based on Scripture (e.g. Daniel 9:4).

TEXT: Rich Mullins, 1988, alt.
MUSIC: Rich Mullins, 1988
Text and Music © 1988 Universal Music - Brentwood Benson Publishing

AWESOME GOD
Irregular

Blest Be God, Praised Forever 617
Rab ki hove sanaa hameshaa (Psalm 150)

Refrain

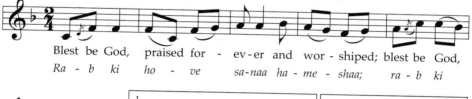

Blest be God, praised for - ev-er and wor - shiped; blest be God,
Ra - b ki ho - ve sa-naa ha - me - shaa; ra - b ki

praised for - ev - er.
ho - ve sa - naa.

ev - er.
sa - naa.

PSALM 150

Refrain

1 Hallelujah!
Praise God in the holy temple;
give praise in the firmament of heaven.

2 **Praise God who is mighty in deed;
give praise for God's excellent
greatness.** *Refrain*

3 Praise God with the blast of the ram's-horn;
give praise with lyre and harp.

4 **Praise God with timbrel and dance;
give praise with strings and pipe.**

5 Praise God with resounding cymbals;
give praise with loud-clanging
cymbals.

6 **Let everything that has breath
praise the LORD.
Hallelujah!** *Refrain*

This refrain comes from a longer Punjabi song of praise paraphrasing Psalm 150, which was recorded in Lahore in 1989. As the psalm encourages, singing is customarily accompanied by various small instruments, including the paired (high- and low-toned) hand drums called *tabla*.

TEXT: Ref., anon.; English para., James Minchin, 1990
MUSIC: Punjabi melody; transcr. I-to Loh, 1989
Text and Music © 1990, 2000 Christian Conference of Asia (admin. GIA Publications, Inc.)
Responsive Reading © 1993 The Order of St. Benedict (admin. The Liturgical Press)

SANAA
Irregular

618 O Love, How Deep, How Broad, How High

1 O love, how deep, how broad, how high, be - yond all
2 For us bap - tized, for us he bore his ho - ly
3 For us by wick - ed - ness be - trayed, for us, in
4 For us he rose from death a - gain; for us he
5 All glo - ry to our Lord and God, for love so

thought and fan - ta - sy, that God, the Son of
fast and hun - gered sore; for us temp - ta - tions
crown of thorns ar - rayed, he bore the shame - ful
went on high to reign; for us he sent the
deep, so high, so broad: the Trin - i - ty whom

God, should take our mor - tal form for mor - tals' sake.
sharp he knew, for us, the tempt - er o - ver - threw.
cross and death; for us gave up his dy - ing breath.
Spir - it here to guide, to strength - en, and to cheer.
we a - dore for - ev - er and for - ev - er - more.

Reducing a twenty-three-stanza Latin text to these five English stanzas intensifies this survey of the mystery of the Incarnation and strengthens the repeated reminder that all was done "for us." A comparable tone of proclamation animates this 15th-century song celebrating a military victory.

TEXT: Thomas à Kempis, 15th cent.; trans. Benjamin Webb, 1854, alt.
MUSIC: "The Agincourt Song," c. 1415; harm. Alfred V. Fedak, 1993
Music Harm. © 1993 Selah Publishing Co., Inc.

DEO GRACIAS
LM
(alternate harmonization, 189)

Praise, My Soul, the God of Heaven 619
(Psalm 103)

1 Praise, my soul, the God of heav - en; glad of heart your
2 Praise God for the grace and fa - vor shown our fore - bears
3 Like a lov - ing par - ent car - ing, God knows well our
4 An - gels, teach us ad - o - ra - tion; you be - hold God

car - ols raise; ran - somed, healed, re - stored, for - giv - en,
in dis - tress; God is still the same for - ev - er,
fee - ble frame, glad - ly all our bur - dens bear - ing,
face to face. Sun and moon and all cre - a - tion,

who, like me, should sing God's praise? Al - le - lu - ia!
slow to chide, and swift to bless. Al - le - lu - ia!
still to count - less years the same. Al - le - lu - ia!
dwell - ers all in time and space: Al - le - lu - ia!

Al - le - lu - ia! Praise the Mak - er all your days!
Al - le - lu - ia! Sing our Mak - er's faith - ful - ness!
Al - le - lu - ia! All with - in me, praise God's name!
Al - le - lu - ia! Praise with us the God of grace!

This adaptation of an older paraphrase of Psalm 103 (see no. 620) is informed by an awareness that much of the received language of religious traditions enshrines social values that obscure the goodness of God, which far transcends all our labels and categories and hierarchies.

TEXT: Henry Francis Lyte, 1834; adapt. Ecumenical Women's Center, 1974
MUSIC: John Goss, 1869
Text Adapt. © 1974 Ecumenical Women's Center

LAUDA ANIMA
8.7.8.7.8.7

620 Praise, My Soul, the King of Heaven
(Psalm 103)

1 Praise, my soul, the King of heav - en; to his
2 Praise him for his grace and fa - vor to his
3 Fa - ther - like, he tends and spares us; well our
4 An - gels, help us to a - dore him; you be -

feet your trib - ute bring; ran - somed, healed, re - stored, for -
peo - ple in dis - tress; praise him still the same as
fee - ble frame he knows; in his hands he gent - ly
hold him face to face. Sun and moon, bow down be -

giv - en, ev - er - more his prais - es sing: Al - le - lu - ia!
ev - er, slow to chide, and swift to bless: Al - le - lu - ia!
bears us, res - cues us from all our foes. Al - le - lu - ia!
fore him, dwell - ers all in time and space: Al - le - lu - ia!

Al - le - lu - ia! Praise the ev - er - last - ing King.
Al - le - lu - ia! Glo - rious in his faith - ful - ness.
Al - le - lu - ia! Wide - ly yet his mer - cy flows.
Al - le - lu - ia! Praise with us the God of grace.

This free paraphrase of Psalm 103 gains much energy and conviction by including the double "Alleluia!" before the final line of text. That repeated four-note figure descending from the tune's highest note gives voice to the praise that the rest of the hymn evokes.

TEXT: Henry Francis Lyte, 1834, alt.
MUSIC: John Goss, 1869

LAUDA ANIMA
8.7.8.7.8.7

I Will Call upon the Lord

Part 1 (melody)

I will call up-on the Lord who is wor-thy to be

Part 2 (echo)

I will call up-on the Lord

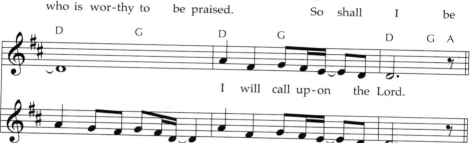

praised. So shall I be saved from my en-e-mies.

who is wor-thy to be praised. So shall I be

I will call up-on the Lord.

saved from my en-e-mies. I will call up-on the Lord.

Refrain

The Lord liv-eth, and bless-ed be the Rock, and let the God of my sal-

va-tion be ex-alt-ed. The Lord liv-eth, and bless-ed be the Rock,

and let the God of my sal-va-tion be ex-alt-ed.

This text is based on Psalm 18:3 and 46 in the King James Version and uses musical repetition to give weight to each verse. The earlier verse is treated as a canon with a concluding unison phrase, and the later one is sung through twice in unison to a nearly identical melody.

TEXT and MUSIC: Michael O'Shields, 1994
Text and Music © 1981 Universal Music Corp. and Sound III, Inc. (admin. Hal Leonard Corporation)

I WILL CALL
Irregular

622 I Will Exalt My God, My King

Te exaltaré, mi Dios, mi Rey
(Psalm 145)

Capo 5:

1 I will ex-alt my God, my King; I will praise your
2 Each gen-er-a-tion to the next will pro-claim your

1 Te e-xal-ta-ré, mi Dios, mi Rey, y ben-de-ci-
2 Ge-ne-ra-ción a ge-ne-ra-ción ce - le-bra-

name for-ev - er. I will ex-alt your name for -
works of splen - dor, and cel-e-brate your might-y

ré tu nom - bre. E - ter-na-men-te y pa - ra
rá tus o - bras y a-nun-cia-rá tus po-de-ro-sos

ev - er. Ev-ery day I'll praise your ho-ly name.
deeds. Ev-ery day I'll praise your ho-ly name.

siem - pre, ca-da dí-a te ben-de-ci-ré.
he - chos; ca-da dí-a te ben-de-ci-ré.

Refrain / Estribillo

I will praise your name for-ev - er; I will ex-alt your
Y a-la-ba-ré tu nom - bre e-ter-na-men-te y

Even in translation, this Ecuadoran paraphrase of Psalm 145:1–7 communicates a blend of love and praise
that feels more intimate than more formal paraphrases. It may actually be truer to the spirit of the original
text, which is an acrostic on the letters of the Hebrew alphabet.

TEXT: Casiodoro Cárdenas, 1975; stanza 1 and ref., trans. composite;
  stanza 2 trans., Mary Louise Bringle, 2011
MUSIC: Casiodoro Cárdenas, 1975; arr. Raquel Mora Martínez, 1979
Music Arr. © 1979 Raquel Mora Martínez

TE EXALTARÉ, MI DIOS
Irregular

name for - ev - er. Lord our God, you are great and wor-thy
pa - ra siem - pre. Gran - de es Je - ho - vá y dig - no

of the high-est praise and hon - or, for your great-ness is
de su - pre - ma a - la - ban - za; y su gran - de - za_es in -

far be - yond us; ev-ery day I'll praise your ho - ly name.
es - cru - ta - ble; ca - da dí - a te ben - de - ci - ré.

623 I've Got Peace like a River

1 I've got peace like a river; I've got peace like a
2 I've got joy like a fountain; I've got joy like a
3 I've got love like an ocean; I've got love like an

riv-er; I've got peace like a riv-er, in my
foun-tain; I've got joy like a foun-tain, in my
o-cean; I've got love like an o-cean, in my

soul.   I've got riv-er, in my soul.
soul.   I've got foun-tain, in my soul.
soul.   I've got o-cean, in my soul.

In the King James Version, the promise of "peace like a river" is twice mentioned in Isaiah (48:18; 66:12) as a blessing that comes from doing God's will. The water imagery of this African American spiritual also provides reminders of Christians' baptismal identity.

TEXT and MUSIC: African American spiritual

PEACE LIKE A RIVER
7.7.10

I Greet Thee, Who My Sure Redeemer Art 624

1 I greet thee, who my sure Re-deem-er art,
  my on-ly trust and Sav-ior of my heart,
  who pain didst un-der-go for my poor sake;
  I pray thee from our hearts all cares to take.

2 Thou art the King of mer-cy and of grace,
  reign-ing om-ni-po-tent in ev-ery place:
  so come, O King, and our whole be-ing sway;
  shine on us with the light of thy pure day.

3 Thou art the life, by which a-lone we live,
  and all our sub-stance and our strength re-ceive;
  sus-tain us by thy faith and by thy power,
  and give us strength in ev-ery try-ing hour.

4 Thou hast the true and per-fect gen-tle-ness;
  no harsh-ness hast thou and no bit-ter-ness.
  O grant to us the grace we find in thee,
  that we may dwell in per-fect u-ni-ty.

5 Our hope is in no oth-er save in thee;
  our faith is built up-on thy prom-ise free;
  Lord, give us peace, and make us calm and sure,
  that in thy strength we ev-er-more en-dure.

The original French text, sometimes attributed to John Calvin, seems to be a Protestant reworking of a Roman Catholic hymn, not a typical practice for him. Yet this text and tune (adapted from GENEVAN 124) clearly date from the early years of the Reformed tradition.

TEXT: *Psalms,* Strasbourg, 1545; trans. Elizabeth Lee Smith, 1868
MUSIC: Genevan Psalter, 1551

TOULON
10.10.10.10

625

O Lord My God

How Great Thou Art

1 O Lord my God, when I in awe-some won-der con - sid - er
2 When through the woods and for-est glades I wan-der and hear the
3 And when I think that God, his Son not spar-ing, sent him to
4 When Christ shall come with shout of ac - cla - ma - tion and take me

all the *worlds thy hands have made, I see the stars, I
birds sing sweet - ly in the trees, when I look down from
die, I scarce can take it in, that on the cross, my
home, what joy shall fill my heart! Then *I shall bow in

hear the *roll - ing thun - der, thy power through - out the
loft - y moun-tain gran - deur and hear the brook and
bur - den glad - ly bear - ing, he bled and died to
hum - ble ad - o - ra - tion, and there pro - claim, "My

*Author's original words are "works," "mighty," and "shall I bow."

This tuneful retelling of the salvation story began in Swedish and was translated into German and then into Russian before reaching its English form. Despite such linguistic and musical revisions, it continues to be a meaningful source of comfort to many people.

TEXT: Stuart K. Hine, 1953; Spanish trans. Arturo W. Hotton Rives, alt.; Korean trans. anon.
MUSIC: Swedish folk melody; adapt. Stuart K. Hine, 1949
Text and Music © 1949 and 1953 The Stuart Hine Trust (U.S.A. print rights admin. Hope Publishing Company.
All other U.S.A. rights admin. EMICMGPublishing.com)

HOW GREAT THOU ART
11.10.11.10 with refrain

Refrain

u - ni - verse dis - played:
feel the gen - tle breeze:
take a - way my sin:
God, how great thou art!"

Then sings my soul, my Sav - ior God, to thee: How great thou art! How great thou art! Then sings my soul, my Sav - ior God, to thee: How great thou art! How great thou art!

KOREAN

1 주 하나님 지으신 모든세계
   내마음 속에 그리어 볼때
   하늘의 별 울려 퍼지는 뇌성
   주님의 권능 우주에 찼네

후렴 주님의 높고 위대하심을
   내영혼이 찬양하네
   주님의 높고 위대하심을
   내영혼이 찬양하네

2 숲속이나 험한산 골짝에서
   지저귀는 저 새소리들과
   고요하게 흐르는 시냇물은
   주님의 솜씨 노래하도다   후렴

3 주하나님 독생자 아낌없이
   우리를 위해 보내주셨네
   십자가에 피흘려 죽으신 주
   내모든 죄를 대속하셨네   후렴

4 내주 예수 세상에 다시 올 때
   저천국으로 날 인도하리
   나 겸손히 엎드려 경배하며
   영원히 주를 찬양하리라   후렴

SPANISH

1 *Señor, mi Dios, al contemplar los cielos,*
   el firmamento y las estrellas mil,
   al oír tu voz en los potentes truenos
   y ver brillar al sol en su cenit,

Estribillo *Mi corazón se llena de emoción.*
   ¡Cuán grande es Él! ¡Cuán grande es Él!
   Mi corazón se llena de emoción.
   ¡Cuán grande es Él! ¡Cuán grande es Él!

2 *Al recorrer los montes y los valles*
   y ver las bellas flores al pasar,
   al escuchar el canto de las aves
   y el murmurar del claro manantial, Estribillo

3 *Cuando recuerdo de tu amor divino*
   que desde el cielo al Salvador envió,
   al buen Jesús, que por salvarme vino
   y en una cruz por mí sufrió y murió, Estribillo

4 *Cuando me lleves, Dios a tu presencia,*
   al dulce hogar, al cielo de esplendor;
   te adoraré, cantando la grandeza
   de tu poder y tu infinito amor. Estribillo

626 As the Deer

As the deer pants for the wa - ter, so my
soul longs af - ter you. You a - lone are my
heart's de - sire, and I long to wor - ship you.
You a - lone are my strength, my shield; to you a - lone
may my spir - it yield. You a - lone are my
heart's de - sire, and I long to wor - ship you.

This praise chorus begins as a paraphrase of Psalm 42:1 and later incorporates parts of Psalm 28:7. In some early Christian communities, people chanted or sang Psalm 42 on their way to be baptized, and many early Christian baptisteries were decorated with deer drinking water.

TEXT and MUSIC: Martin J. Nystrom, 1984
Text and Music © 1984 Universal Music - Brentwood Benson Publishing

AS THE DEER
Irregular

I Love You, Lord

I love you, Lord, and I lift my voice to wor - ship you; O my soul, re - joice. Take joy, my King, in what you hear; may it be a sweet, sweet sound in your ear.

This simple song of adoration provides a significant blend of individual and communal considerations, for although the text is written in the voice of one person, the music involves multiple voices singing in harmony. The resulting experience seems more shared than solitary.

TEXT and MUSIC: Laurie Klein, 1978
Text and Music © 1978 House of Mercy Music (admin. Universal Music - Brentwood Benson Publishing)

I LOVE YOU, LORD
Irregular

628 Praise, I Will Praise You, Lord

Je louerai l'Éternel

1 Praise, I will praise you, Lord, with all my heart. O
2 Love, I will love you, Lord, with all my heart. O
3 Serve, I will serve you, Lord, with all my heart. O

God, I will tell the won-ders of your ways, and glo-ri-fy your name.

Praise, I will praise you, Lord, with all my heart. In
Love, I will love you, Lord, with all my heart. In
Serve, I will serve you, Lord, with all my heart. In

you I will find the source of all my joy. Al - le - lu - ia!

FRENCH
Je louerai l'Éternel de tout mon coeur,
je raconterai toutes tes merveilles,
je chanterai ton nom.
Je louerai l'Éternel de tout mon coeur,
je ferai de toi le sujet de ma joie.
Alleluia!

This simple song based on Psalm 9:1–2 was created in the mid-1970s for a morning devotional of a group touring in the picturesque high Alps. Later it was incorporated into their programs and soon spread throughout Europe and the world, being translated into many languages.

TEXT: Claude Frayssé, 1975; English trans. Kenneth I. Morse, 1988
MUSIC: Claude Frayssé, 1975; harm. Alain Bergèse, 1976
Text and Music © 1975 Claude Frayseé
English Trans. © 1989 The Hymnal Project (admin. Brethren Press)

JE LOUERAI L'ÉTERNEL
Irregular

Jesus, the Very Thought of Thee 629

1 Je - sus, the ver - y thought of thee
2 Nor voice can sing, nor heart can frame,
3 O hope of ev - ery con - trite heart,
4 But what to those who find? Ah, this
5 Je - sus, our on - ly joy be thou,

with sweet - ness fills my breast. But sweet - er far thy
nor can the mind re - call a sweet - er sound than
O joy of all the meek, to those who fall, how
nor tongue nor pen can show. The love of Je - sus,
as thou our prize wilt be. Je - sus, be thou our

face to see, and in thy pres - ence rest.
thy blest name, O Sav - ior of us all.
kind thou art! How good to those who seek!
what it is none but his loved ones know.
glo - ry now, and through e - ter - ni - ty.

The sweetness celebrated in this anonymous 12th-century Latin poem is not cloying or sentimental; it is more like an antidote to bitterness and a source of hope and healing. The best-known 19th-century translation is set here to a tune composed especially for these words.

TEXT: Latin hymn, 12th cent.; trans. Edward Caswall, 1849, alt.
MUSIC: John Bacchus Dykes, 1866, alt.

ST. AGNES
CM

630

Fairest Lord Jesus

1 Fair - est Lord Je - sus, Rul - er of all
2 Fair are the mead - ows, fair - er still the
3 Fair is the sun - shine, fair - er still the
4 Beau - ti - ful Sav - ior, Rul - er of the

na - ture, O thou of God to earth come
wood - lands, robed in the bloom - ing garb of
moon - light, and all the twink - ling, star - ry
na - tions, Son of God and Son of

down, thee will I cher - ish, thee will I
spring. Je - sus is fair - er; Je - sus is
host. Je - sus shines bright - er; Je - sus shines
Man! Glo - ry and hon - or, praise, ad - o -

hon - or, thou, my soul's glo - ry, joy, and crown.
pur - er, who makes the woe - ful heart to sing.
pur - er, than all the an - gels heaven can boast.
ra - tion, now and for - ev - er - more be thine!

Franz Liszt used this melody for a "Crusaders' March" in an oratorio, but this hymn had nothing to do with the Crusades. No record of the German text exists before the middle of the 17th century or of the Silesian folk melody before the first half of the 19th century.

TEXT: Münster *Gesangbuch*, 1677; stanzas 1–3, trans. *Church Chorals and Choir Studies*, 1850, alt.; stanza 4, trans. Joseph August Seiss, 1873, alt.
MUSIC: Silesian folk melody; *Schlesische Volkslieder*, 1842

CRUSADERS' HYMN
5.6.8.5.5.8

In the Presence of Your People 631

(Psalm 22)

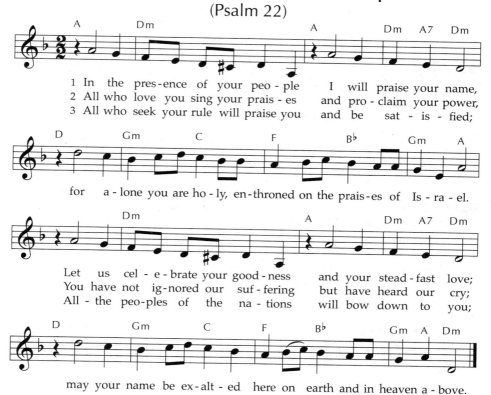

1 In the pres-ence of your peo-ple I will praise your name,
2 All who love you sing your prais-es and pro-claim your power,
3 All who seek your rule will praise you and be sat - is - fied;

for a - lone you are ho - ly, en-throned on the prais-es of Is - ra - el.

Let us cel - e - brate your good-ness and your stead-fast love;
You have not ig-nored our suf - fering but have heard our cry;
All - the peo-ples of the na - tions will bow down to you;

may your name be ex-alt - ed here on earth and in heaven a - bove.

This text based on the affirmative later parts of Psalm 22 (especially verses 3, 22–28) has an unusual structure, with alternating lines of stanza and refrain. It also has an uncommon history, as the first stanza was written in New Zealand and the remaining stanzas in Canada.

TEXT: Stanza 1, Brent Sinclair Chambers, 1977; stanzas 2–3, Bert Polman, 1986
MUSIC: Brent Sinclair Chambers, 1977
Text and Music © 1977 Broadman Press (admin. Music Services)

CELEBRATION
Irregular

632
People of the Lord
(Psalm 78)

1 Peo - ple of the Lord, lis - ten to my voice.
2 Tell of God's great deeds. Teach God's lov - ing law
3 Tell the news till each gen - er - a - tion knows.
4 May we trust in God, rest in God's strong hand,

Hear the an - cient words. Once a - gain re - joice!
that faith's pre - cious seed in each heart may grow.
They, in turn, will teach those yet to be born.
live in God's strong love, fol - low God's com - mands.

Refrain

What we have heard, what we have known, let our tongues

tell our sons and daugh - ters the won - ders of our liv - ing God,

Stanzas may be sung as a canon.

This paraphrase of the first seven verses of Psalm 78 represents the introduction to a long narrative history, with special emphasis on the mighty acts of God on Israel's behalf. This retelling is also intended to prevent the hearers from repeating their ancestors' mistakes.

TEXT: Greg Scheer, 2010, alt.
MUSIC: Greg Scheer, 2010
Text and Music © 2010 Greg Scheer

JENNY VAN TSCHEGG
5.5.5.5.8.9.8.9

that they may join us in the cho - rus.

Praise Ye the Lord

633

(Psalm 150)

Refrain

Praise ye the Lord, Hal-le-lu-jah! Ev-ery-bod-y praise the Lord.

1 Praise God with the sound of the trum - pet. Praise God with the
2 Praise God with ho - ly cym - bals. Praise God with
3 Praise God in the ho - ly tem - ple. Praise God for al -
4 Praise God on top of the moun-tains. Praise God both

lute and the harp. Praise God with tim - brel and danc -
strings and with pipes. Praise God with clash - ing cym -
might - y deeds. Praise God for those boun - ti - ful mer -
day and night. Praise God down in the low val -

- ing. Praise God wher - ev - er you are.
- bals. Praise God with all of your might.
- cies, for God ful - fills our needs.
- leys. Praise God be - cause it's all right.

Like the original psalm, this paraphrase of Psalm 150 ranges widely through lists of how, why, and where to praise God. Couched in a syncopated African American gospel style, the setting invites the addition of instruments, though the voices of singers remain most important.

TEXT and MUSIC: J. Jefferson Cleveland, 1981
Text and Music © 1981 J. Jefferson Cleveland

CLEVELAND
Irregular

634 To God Be the Glory

1 To God be the glo-ry; great things he has done!
2 Great things he has taught us; great things he has done,

So loved he the world that he gave us his Son,
and great our re-joic-ing through Je-sus the Son;

who yield-ed his life an a-tone-ment for sin,
but pur-er and high-er and great-er will be

and o-pened the life-gate that all may go in.
our won-der, our trans-port, when Je-sus we see.

This American gospel song became popular in England in the late 19th century, then returned to this country in the mid-20th century with the Billy Graham crusades. Its continuing popularity may well be due to the freedom from subjective considerations in its praise of God.

TEXT: Fanny Jane Crosby, 1875
MUSIC: William Howard Doane, 1875

TO GOD BE THE GLORY
11.11.11.11 with refrain

Refrain

Praise the Lord, praise the Lord; let the earth hear his voice!

Praise the Lord, praise the Lord; let the peo - ple re - joice!

O come to the Fa - ther through Je - sus the Son,

and give him the glo - ry: great things he has done!

635 Sing, Praise, and Bless the Lord
Laudate Dominum

Sing, praise, and bless the Lord. Sing, praise, and bless the Lord.
Lau - da - te Do - mi - num, lau - da - te Do - mi - num,

Peo - ples! Na - tions! Al - le - lu - ia!
om - nes gen - tes, al - le - lu - ia!

Sing, praise, and bless the Lord. Sing, praise, and bless the Lord.
Lau - da - te Do - mi - num, lau - da - te Do - mi - num,

Peo - ples! Na - tions! Al - le - lu - ia!
om - nes gen - tes, al - le - lu - ia!

By the way the notes fall on the syllables, repeated singing reveals that this refrain based on Psalm 117:1 originally set the Latin text. The refrains of the ecumenical community at Taizé, France, often use Latin because it is not the language of any current political power.

TEXT: Taizé Community, 1980
MUSIC: Jacques Berthier, 1980
Text and Music © 1991 Les Presses de Taizé (admin. GIA Publications, Inc.)

LAUDATE DOMINUM (Taizé)
6.6.8.6.6.8

Let All the World in Every Corner Sing 636

Let all the world in ev-ery cor-ner sing, my God and King!

1 The heavens are not too high, God's praise may thith-er
2 The church with psalms must shout: no door can keep them

fly; the earth is not too low, God's prais-es there may grow.
out. But, more than all, the heart must bear the long-est part.

Let all the world in ev-ery cor-ner sing, my God and King!

The 20th-century tune used here is among the few to honor the intention of the author, a 17th-century
Anglican pastor and poet, to sing the refrain before, between, and after the two stanzas. The mention of
"psalms" in the second stanza is a clue that hymns were not yet common.

TEXT: George Herbert, 17th cent., alt.
MUSIC: Erik Routley, 1964
Music © 1976 Hinshaw Music, Inc.

AUGUSTINE
10.4.6.6.6.6.10.4

637

O Sing to the Lord
Cantai ao Senhor

1 O sing to the Lord; O sing God a
2 For God is the Lord, and God has done
3 So dance for our God and blow all the
4 O shout to our God, who gave us the
5 For Je - sus is Lord! A - men! Al - le -

new song. O sing to the Lord; O sing God a
won - ders. For God is the Lord, and God has done
trum - pets. So dance for our God and blow all the
Spir - it. O shout to our God, who gave us the
lu - ia! For Je - sus is Lord! A - men! Al - le -

new song. O sing to the Lord; O sing God a new song.
won - ders. For God is the Lord, and God has done won - ders.
trum - pets. So dance for our God and blow all the trum - pets.
Spir - it. O shout to our God, who gave us the Spir - it.
lu - ia! For Je - sus is Lord! A - men! Al - le - lu - ia!

O sing to our God; O sing to our God.

PORTUGUESE

1 *Cantai ao Senhor um cântico novo, (3x)*
   cantai ao Senhor, cantai ao Senhor.

2 *Porque ele fez, ele fez maravilhas, (3x)*
   cantai ao Senhor, cantai ao Senhor.

3 *Cantai ao Senhor, bendizei o seu nome, (3x)*
   cantai ao Senhor, cantai ao Senhor.

4 *É ele quem dá o Espírito Santo, (3x)*
   cantai ao Senhor, cantai ao Senhor.

5 *Jesus é o Senhor! Amém, aleluia! (3x)*
   cantai ao Senhor, cantai ao Senhor.

SPANISH

1 *Cantad al Señor un cántico nuevo. (3x)*
   ¡Cantad al Señor, cantad al Señor!

2 *Pues nuestro Señor ha hecho prodigios. (3x)*
   ¡Cantad al Señor, cantad al Señor!

3 *Cantad al Señor, alabadle con arpa. (3x)*
   ¡Cantad al Señor, cantad al Señor!

4 *Es él quien nos da el Espíritu Santo. (3x)*
   ¡Cantad al Señor, cantad al Señor!

5 *¡Jesús es Señor! ¡Amén, aleluya! (3x)*
   ¡Cantad al Señor, cantad al Señor!

A Lutheran missionary musician heard this song at a pastors' conference in southern Brazil in 1982, then went home to Argentina (where he was then serving) and translated it from Portuguese into Spanish. Later, when back in the U.S.A. on furlough, he translated it into English.

TEXT: Brazilian folk song; trans. Spanish, 1982, and English, 1986, Gerhard M. Cartford
MUSIC: Brazilian folk melody; arr. Gerhard M. Cartford, 1982
English and Spanish Trans. and Music Arr. © Gerhard M. Cartford (admin. Augsburg Fortress)

CANTAI AO SENHOR
5.6.5.6.5.6.5.5

O Come and Sing unto the Lord 638

(Psalm 95)

1 O come and sing unto the Lord; to God our voices raise; let us in our most joy - ful songs the Lord, our Sav - ior, praise.

2 Be - fore God's pres - ence let us come with praise and thank - ful voice; let us sing psalms to God with grace; with grate - ful hearts, re - joice.

3 The Lord our God is King of kings, a - bove all gods en-throned; the depths of earth and moun - tains high by God a - lone are owned.

4 To God the spa - cious sea be - longs; God made its waves and tides, and by God's hand the ris - ing land was formed, and still a - bides.

5 O come, and bow - ing down to God our wor - ship let us bring; yea, let us kneel be - fore the Lord, our Mak - er and our King.

This selection of paraphrased verses from Psalm 95 was prepared by a joint committee of nine North American churches in the Reformed tradition. It is set here to an anonymous and originally nameless tune, eventually named to reflect that its first publication was in Dublin.

TEXT: *The New Metrical Version of the Psalms*, 1909, alt.
MUSIC: *A Collection of Hymns and Sacred Poems*, 1749

IRISH
CM

639 O Sing a New Song
(Psalm 96)

Refrain

O sing a new song to the Lord;
sing to the Lord; sing all the earth.

1 O sing a new song to the Lord;
2 Proclaim God's salvation day by day;

3 The Lord is great and worthy of all praise,
4 For the Lord made the heavens!

5 Let the heavens be glad; let the earth re - joice;
6 Shout for joy, all trees of the woods,

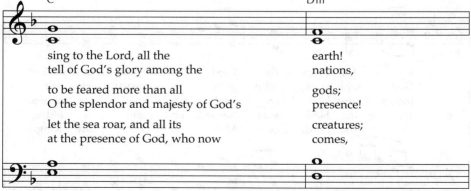

sing to the Lord, all the earth!
tell of God's glory among the nations,

to be feared more than all gods;
O the splendor and majesty of God's presence!

let the sea roar, and all its creatures;
at the presence of God, who now comes,

This setting of Psalm 96 provides a refrain for singing before the chanting of the psalm's verses, at designated intervals between the verses, and at the conclusion of the psalm. In our praise of God we are made new, and that change in us is what makes our songs new.

TEXT: Helen L. Wright, 1983, alt.
MUSIC: Hal H. Hopson, 1983
Text © 1986 Helen L. Wright
Music © 1986 Hope Publishing Company

O SING A NEW SONG
Irregular

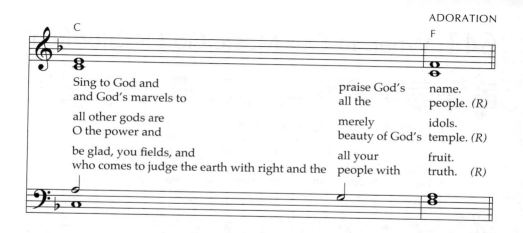

Sing to God and praise God's name.
and God's marvels to all the people. *(R)*

all other gods are merely idols.
O the power and beauty of God's temple. *(R)*

be glad, you fields, and all your fruit.
who comes to judge the earth with right and the people with truth. *(R)*

Open Your Mouth and Praise the Lord! 640

Leader

1 O - pen your mouth and praise the Lord!
2 Clap your hands; O clap your hands!
3 Dance to God; O dance to God!
4 Praise the Lord; O praise the Lord!

People

Mmmm, mmmm.

All

Praise the Lord: the Lord is good!
Clap your hands: the Lord is good!
Dance to God: the Lord is good!
Praise the Lord: the Lord is good!

Clapping pattern

Drawing on a number of verses from Psalms (47:1; 51:15; 135:3; 150:4), this song joins an English text to a Yoruba melody that clearly uses the call-and-response pattern heard in many African traditions and in African American spirituals (and encourages improvised additions).

TEXT: Godwin Sadoh, 2005
MUSIC: Yoruba folk melody; adapt. Godwin Sadoh, 2005; arr. Greg Scheer, 2008
Text and Music © 2005 Wayne Leupold Editions, Inc.
Music Arr. © 2008 Greg Scheer

OPEN YOUR MOUTH (Yoruba)
Irregular

641 When in Our Music God Is Glorified

1 When in our mu - sic God is glo - ri - fied,
2 How of - ten, mak - ing mu - sic, we have found
3 So has the church, in lit - ur - gy and song,
4 And did not Je - sus sing a psalm that night
5 Let ev - ery in - stru - ment be tuned for praise!

and ad - o - ra - tion leaves no room for pride,
a new di - men - sion in the world of sound,
in faith and love, through cen - tu - ries of wrong,
when ut - most e - vil strove a - gainst the light?
Let all re - joice who have a voice to raise!

it is as though the whole cre - a - tion cried:
as wor - ship moved us to a more pro - found
borne wit - ness to the truth in ev - ery tongue:
Then let us sing, for whom he won the fight:
And may God give us faith to sing al - ways:

Al - le - lu - ia!   Al - le - lu - ia!

Guitar chords do not correspond with keyboard harmony.

Written to supply this tune with words suitable for occasions celebrating music, this text explores how human song gives voice to creation, how music can convey new insight, how sung faith has kept the church authentic, how Jesus relied on the psalms, and how sound can be praise.

TEXT: Fred Pratt Green, 1972, alt.
MUSIC: Charles Villiers Stanford, 1904, alt.
Text © 1972 Hope Publishing Company

ENGELBERG
10.10.10.4
(this tune in a lower key, 485)

Heleluyan, We Are Singing

This Muscogee hymn is a Trail of Tears song, a testimony that their Christian faith was more powerful than their mistreatment by those who took away their ancestral homelands. Revered and cherished, it remains the most popular Muscogee hymn sung in churches in Oklahoma.

TEXT: Muscogee (Creek) hymn; English vers. Brian Wren, 2008
MUSIC: Muscogee (Creek) melody; transcr. Carlton R. Young, 2008
English Vers. and Music Transcr. © 2008 General Board of Global Ministries t/a GBGMusik

HELELUYAN
Irregular

643 Now Thank We All Our God

1 Now thank we all our God with heart and hands and voic - es,
2 O may this boun - teous God through all our life be near us,
3 All praise and thanks to God, who reigns in high - est heav - en,

who won - drous things hath done, in whom this world re - joic - es;
with ev - er joy - ful hearts and bless - ed peace to cheer us;
to Fa - ther and to Son and Spir - it now be giv - en:

who, from our moth - ers' arms, hath blessed us on our way
and keep us in God's grace, and guide us when per - plexed,
the one e - ter - nal God, whom heaven and earth a - dore,

with count - less gifts of love, and still is ours to - day.
and free us from all ills in this world and the next.
the God who was, and is, and shall be ev - er - more.

Although this hymn is often used on large and festive occasions, its first two stanzas had much humbler beginnings: they originated as a family table prayer during the Thirty Years' War (1618–1648). These words have been associated with this tune since the mid-17th century.

TEXT: Martin Rinkart, c. 1636; trans. Catherine Winkworth, 1858, alt.
MUSIC: Johann Crüger, 1647; harm. Felix Mendelssohn, 1840

NUN DANKET ALLE GOTT
6.7.6.7.6.6.6.6

Give Thanks, O Christian People 644

1 Give thanks, O Chris-tian peo - ple, for work-ers of our day
2 Give thanks, O Chris-tian peo - ple, for lead-ers of our years
3 Give thanks, O Chris-tian peo - ple, for all who love the Lord,
4 Give thanks, O Chris-tian peo - ple, for life in fel-low-ship

who heed the call to ser - vice and make it their life's way
who live to share with oth - ers our joy when Christ ap-pears,
who live each day be - liev - ing in God's e - ter-nal Word:
with all who trust our Sav - ior their serv-ing to e - quip:

to go to feed the hun - gry, to tend to those in need,
to teach the ones who seek light, to guide the fal - tering feet,
to share Christ's love in liv - ing, to wit-ness with each deed,
to ease an - oth-er's bur-dens, to cope in joy and stress,

to work for e - qual jus - tice, till all God's folk are freed.
to lead the fol - lowers for - ward our liv - ing Lord to meet.
to use the tal - ents giv - en to plant the gos - pel seed.
to mag - ni - fy God's mes - sage and Christ's great love con - fess.

This text was written by a Presbyterian director of Christian education in Washington, DC, to honor the ministry of a colleague who was leaving the area. It is an effective reminder that God's people serve in many vocations and ministries. The tune adapts a secular German song.

TEXT: Mary Jackson Cathey, 1984
MUSIC: Memmingen ms., 17th cent.; harm. George Ratcliffe Woodward, 1904
Text © 1986 Fresh Winds of the Spirit by Lavon Bayler (admin. The Pilgrim Press)

ES FLOG EIN KLEINS WALDVÖGELEIN
7.6.7.6.D

645 Sing Praise to God Who Reigns Above

1 Sing praise to God who reigns a-bove, the God of all
2 What God's al-might-y power has made God's gra-cious mer-
3 The Lord is nev-er far a-way, but, through all grief
4 Thus all my toil-some way a-long I sing a-loud

cre-a-tion, the God of power, the God of love,
cy keep-eth; by morn-ing glow or eve-ning shade
dis-tress-ing, an ev-er-pres-ent help and stay,
thy prais-es, that all may hear the grate-ful song

the God of our sal-va-tion. With
God's watch-ful eye ne'er sleep-eth. With-
our peace and joy and bless-ing, as
my voice un-wea-ried rais-es. Be

heal-ing balm my soul is filled, and ev-ery faith-less
in the king-dom of God's might, lo! all is just and
with a moth-er's ten-der hand God gent-ly leads the
joy-ful in the Lord, my heart; both soul and bod-y,

The regal divine imagery here will not be new to most singers, but some may not expect the third stanza's image of God as mother. Yet it is part of God's self-description in Isaiah 66:13. This Bohemian Brethren tune resembles both Genevan psalm tunes and French folk songs.

TEXT: Johann Jacob Schütz, 1675; trans. Frances Elizabeth Cox, 1864, alt.
MUSIC: Bohemian Brethren's *Kirchengesang,* 1566; harm. Maurice F. Bell, 1906, alt.

MIT FREUDEN ZART
8.7.8.7.8.8.7

mur - mur stilled:
all is right:
cho - sen band: to God all praise and glo - ry!
take your part:

Sing Out, My Soul
Magnificat

646

Sing out, my soul. Sing out, my soul. Sing out and
Ma - gni - fi - cat. Ma - gni - fi - cat. Ma - gni - fi -

glo - ri - fy the Lord who sets us free. Sing out, my soul.
cat a - ni - ma me - a Do - mi - num. Ma - gni - fi - cat.

Sing out, my soul. Sing out and glo - ri - fy the Lord God!
Ma - gni - fi - cat. Ma - gni - fi - cat a - ni - ma me - a!

May be sung as a canon.

This canonic chant from the Taizé Community is based on the opening phrase of Mary's song when she visited her relative Elizabeth, mother of John the Baptist (Luke 1:39–56). Both Eastern and Western churches have used the full text for many centuries as part of daily prayers.

TEXT: Taizé Community, 1978
MUSIC: Jacques Berthier, 1978
Text and Music © 1979 Les Presses de Taizé (admin. GIA Publications, Inc.)

MAGNIFICAT (Taizé)
Irregular

647

Give Thanks

Give thanks with a grate-ful heart; give thanks to the Ho-ly One;

give thanks be-cause we're giv-en Je-sus Christ, the Son. Give

Son. And now let the weak say, "We are strong"; let the

poor say, "We are rich be-cause of what the Lord has done for

us!" And us!" Give thanks. Give thanks.

Drawing on language from 2 Corinthians 6:10 and 12:10 as well as Psalm 126:3, this short and repetitive song can be easily memorized. The simple vocabulary makes it suitable for multigenerational use, reminding all ages how gratitude for God's goodness changes our perspective.

Thankful Hearts and Voices Raise 648

Thank-ful hearts and voic-es raise; tell ev-ery-one what
God has done. Let ev-ery-one who seeks the Lord re-
joice and bear the name of Christ. Send us with your
prom-is-es and lead your peo-ple forth in joy with shouts of
thanks-giv-ing. Al-le-lu-ia, al-le-lu-ia.

This canticle for use at the close of worship comes from *Evangelical Lutheran Worship* (2006) and is included here in honor of the full communion agreement between the Presbyterian Church (U.S.A.) and the Evangelical Lutheran Church in America. It concludes with echoes of Isaiah 55:12.

TEXT: John W. Arthur, 1970, alt.
MUSIC: Ronald A. Nelson, 1970
Text and Music © 1978, 1995 Augsburg Fortress

THANKFUL HEARTS
Irregular

649 Amazing Grace, How Sweet the Sound

1 A - maz - ing grace, how sweet the sound, that
2 'Twas grace that taught my heart to fear, and
3 Through man - y dan - gers, toils, and snares, I
4 The Lord has prom - ised good to me; his
5 When we've been there ten thou - sand years, bright

saved a wretch like me! I once was lost, but
grace my fears re - lieved. How pre - cious did that
have al - read - y come. 'Tis grace has brought me
word my hope se - cures. He will my shield and
shin - ing as the sun, we've no less days to

now am found, was blind, but now I see.
grace ap - pear the hour I first be - lieved!
safe thus far, and grace will lead me home.
por - tion be as long as life en - dures.
sing God's praise than when we'd first be - gun.

CHOCTAW

Shilombish holitopa ma!
Ishmminti pulla cha
hatak ilbusha pia ha
is pi yukpalashke.

CREEK

Po ya fek cha he thlat ah tet
ah non ah cha pa kas
cha fee kee o funnan la kus
um e ha ta la yus.

NAVAHO

Nizhóníígo joobá diits' a'
yisdáshíítinigíí,
lah yóóiiyá, k'ad
*   shénáhoosdzin,*
doo eesh'íí da ńt'éé.

As was his custom, the author wrote this hymn to accompany his sermon on 1 Chronicles 17:16–17, preached on January 1, 1773; he called it "Faith's Review and Expectation." Much of its current popularity comes from this now-familiar tune, an association that began in 1835.

TEXT: Stanzas 1–4, John Newton, 1772; stanza 5, *A Collection of Sacred Ballads*, 1790; Navaho, Albert Tsosie
MUSIC: *Columbian Harmony*, 1829; arr. Edwin O. Excell, 1910, alt.
Text Phonetic Transcr. Cherokee, Kiowa, Creek, and Choctaw © Oklahoma Indian Missionary Conference;
*   Phonetic Transcr. Navaho © Albert Tsosie*

AMAZING GRACE
CM

CHEROKEE

Ooh nay thla nah, hee oo way gee'.
E gah gwoo yah hay ee.
Naw gwoo joe sah, we you low say,
e gah gwoo yah ho nah.

KIOWA

Daw k'ee da ha dawtsahy he tsow'haw
daw k'ee da ha dawtsahy hee.
Bay dawtsahy taw, gaw aym ow thah t'aw,
daw k'ee da ha dawtsahy h'ee.

O Beauty Ever Ancient 650

1 O beau-ty ev-er an-cient, O beau-ty ev-er new,
2 O beau-ty in cre-a-tion, in world of sound and sight,
3 O beau-ty that is move-ment in liq-uid line of grace,
4 O beau-ty of the Spir-it where love is shin-ing through,

di-vine and Ho-ly Pres-ence, my be-ing sings to you,
O beau-ty in the si-lence, in dark-ness as in light,
O beau-ty that is still-ness in love-ly form or face,
O beau-ty ev-er an-cient, O beau-ty ev-er new,

in grat-i-tude, in wor-ship my be-ing sings to you!

Guitar chords do not correspond with keyboard harmony.

Both Psalms 29:2b and 96:6a encourage us to "worship the Lord in the beauty of holiness," yet celebrating the beauty of the holy God is not an end in itself but involves a call to oppose unjust ugliness. The beauty that draws us to God also urges us to work for mercy and justice.

TEXT: Shirley Erena Murray, 2000
MUSIC: Alfred V. Fedak, 2007
Text © 2000 Hope Publishing Company
Music © 2009 Selah Publishing Co., Inc.

ANCIENT BEAUTY
7.6.7.6 with refrain

651 I Waited Patiently for God
(Psalm 40)

1 I waited patiently for God, for
2 God raised me from a miry pit, from
3 And on my lips a song was put, a
4 Great wonders you have done, O Lord, all

God to hear my prayer; and God bent down to
mud and sinking sand, and set my feet up-
new song to the Lord. Many will marvel
purposed for our good. Unable every

where I sank and listened to me there.
on a rock where I can firmly stand.
o- pen-eyed and put their trust in God.
one to name, I bow in gratitude.

Psalm 40 is generally understood to be in two parts, an opening section of thanksgiving and a concluding section of lament. This 20th-century paraphrase is based on the earlier portion, and the third stanza is a significant testimony to the importance of singing God's praise.

TEXT: The Iona Community, 1993
MUSIC: William Billings, 1794; arr. Donald Busarow, 1978, alt.
Text © 1993 WGRG, Iona Community (admin. GIA Publications, Inc.)
Music Arr. © 1978 Lutheran Book of Worship (admin. Augsburg Fortress)

LEWIS-TOWN
CM

A Grateful Heart

(Psalm 111)

1 A grate-ful heart is what I bring, a song of
2 Your name is known in all the lands. You feed the
3 With sav-ing love you set us free, and still you

praise, my of-fer-ing. A-mong the saints I
poor with gen-tle hands. Your word is true, your
dwell in mys-ter-y with wis-dom none can

lift my voice: in you, O God, I will re-joice.
works are just; in you, O God, the faith-ful trust.
com-pre-hend. Your praise, O God, will nev-er end.

This paraphrase of Psalm 111 preserves the psalm's quality of providing a general list of God's praiseworthy characteristics rather than giving thanks for a particular act of deliverance. In the original text these attributes are organized as an acrostic on the Hebrew alphabet.

TEXT: David Gambrell, 2009
MUSIC: *Second Supplement to Psalmody in Miniature*, 1783; harm. Edward Miller, 1790
Text © 2011 David Gambrell (admin. Presbyterian Publishing Corp.)

ROCKINGHAM
LM

653 Give Thanks to God Who Hears Our Cries

(Psalm 107)

1 Give thanks to God who hears our cries and saves in
2 If you have ev - er wan - dered where no hu - man
3 If you have ev - er lived in - side the pris - on
4 If you drew near the gates of death, too sick to

trou - bled days with won - drous works to hu - man - kind that
help was near, and in your trou - ble cried to God, who
of your gloom and cried to God, who broke your bonds and
eat or dress, and cried to God, who heard your voice and

call for high - est praise. Let all who know God's
res - cued you from fear, then thank the God of
raised you from your tomb, then praise the One who
healed all your dis - tress, then sing with sounds of

The singing of psalm paraphrases is the most long-standing musical practice in Reformed tradition, dating from John Calvin's own congregation in Geneva in the 16th century. This recent paraphrase of Psalm 107 illustrates the interpretive flexibility that is a hallmark of the form.

TEXT: Ruth Duck, 2007
MUSIC: Wyeth's *Repository of Sacred Music, Part Second*, 1813; harm. Richard Proulx, 1975
Text © 2011 GIA Publications, Inc.
Music Harm. © 1975 GIA Publications, Inc.

MORNING SONG
8.6.8.6.8.6
(alternate harmonization, 374)

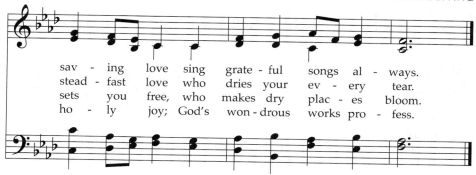

sav - ing love sing grate - ful songs al - ways.
stead - fast love who dries your ev - ery tear.
sets you free, who makes dry plac - es bloom.
ho - ly joy; God's won - drous works pro - fess.

5 If you have felt your courage fail
before a violent sea
and cried to God, who stilled the storm,
and made the wild wind flee,
then in the congregation praise
the One who heard your plea.

6 So praise the One whose love is great,
whose kindness is well-known.
Consider well the healing hand
and help you have been shown,
and tell the world what God has done.
Praise God and God alone!

In the Lord I'll Be Ever Thankful 654

In the Lord I'll be ev - er thank - ful; in the Lord I will re -

joice! Look to God; do not be a - fraid. Lift up your

voic - es; the Lord is near. Lift up your voic - es; the Lord is near.

This refrain from the ecumenical monastic community at Taizé, France, is meant for repeated singing. A wonderful quilt of psalm-like phrases, it would be appropriate at any time but the concluding emphasis on the nearness of the Lord makes it especially fitting for use in Advent.

TEXT: Taizé Community, 1986
MUSIC: Jacques Berthier, 1986
Text and Music © 1991 Les Presses de Taizé (admin. GIA Publications, Inc.)

IN THE LORD I'LL BE EVER THANKFUL
Irregular

655 What Shall I Render to the Lord
(Psalm 116)

1 What shall I ren - der to the Lord; what
2 Sal - va - tion's cup my soul shall take while
3 Not light - ly dost thou, Lord, per - mit thy
4 With - in God's house, the house of prayer, my

shall my of - fering be, for all the gra - cious
to the Lord I pray, and with God's peo - ple
cho - sen saints to die; from death thou hast de -
soul shall bless the Lord, and prais - es to God's

ben - e - fits God hath be - stowed on me?
I will meet, my thank - ful vows to pay.
liv - ered me; thy ser - vant, Lord, am I.
ho - ly name let all the saints ac - cord.

Selecting these four stanzas from eleven that formed a second paraphrase of Psalm 116 in their original volume has made the theme of gratitude for God's protection and bounty more apparent. The tune that sets them may have its origins in an 18th-century Scottish folk song.

TEXT: *The New Metrical Version of the Psalms*, 1909, alt.
MUSIC: Hugh Wilson, c. 1800; adapt. and harm. Robert Smith, 1825

MARTYRDOM
CM

We've Come This Far by Faith 656

We've come this far by faith, lean-ing on the Lord,

trust-ing in the ho-ly Word; God's nev-er failed us yet.

O, can't turn a-round, we've come this

far by faith. We've come this far by faith.

This refrain from a longer hymn could well be understood as a black gospel reflection on several biblical passages: 2 Corinthians 5:7, 1 Samuel 7:12, and 1 Chronicles 17:16. All these texts bear witness to God's faithfulness toward all who are engaged in the pilgrimage of faith.

TEXT and MUSIC: Albert A. Goodson, 1956
Text and Music © 1965, ren.1993 Manna Music, Inc. (admin. ClearBox Rights)

THIS FAR BY FAITH
Irregular

657 Sing to God, with Joy and Gladness
(Psalm 147)

Refrain

Sing to God, with joy and glad-ness, hymns and psalms of grat-i-tude; with the voice of praise dis-cov-er that to wor-ship God is good. *Fine*

1 God u-nites the scat-tered peo-ple, gath-ers those who wan-dered far, heals the hurt and bro-ken
2 Such is God's great power and wis-dom, none can cal-cu-late or tell; keen is God to ground the
3 God with clouds the sky has cur-tained, thus en-sur-ing rain shall fall; earth, re-spond-ing, grows to
4 God's dis-cern-ment nev-er fa-vors strength or speed to lift or move; God de-lights in those who

The five songs of praise that conclude the biblical psalter (Psalms 146–150) all begin and end with "Hallelujah!" That ecstatic Hebrew word is expanded here into the refrain that opens and closes this paraphrase of Psalm 147, an appropriate frame for its theme of thanksgiving.

TEXT: John L. Bell, 1993, alt.
MUSIC: John L. Bell, 1993
Text and Music © 1993 WGRG, Iona Community (admin. GIA Publications, Inc.)

GLENDON
8.7.8.7.D

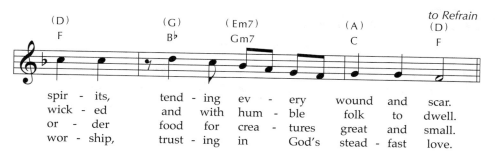

(D) (G) (Em7) (A) to Refrain
F B♭ Gm7 C (D)
F

spir - its, tend - ing ev - ery wound and scar.
wick - ed and with hum - ble folk to dwell.
or - der food for crea - tures great and small.
wor - ship, trust - ing in God's stead - fast love.

God Is So Good 658

1 God is so good; God is so good;
2 God cares for me; God cares for me;
3 God loves me so; God loves me so;
4 God is so good; God is so good;

God is so good; God's so good to me.
God cares for me; God's so good to me.
God loves me so; God's so good to me.
God is so good; God's so good to me.

The exact origins of this chorus celebrating God's providential care are not clear, but it seems to have arisen during the 1970s. Because the text changes so little, the slowly rising four-note pattern of the tune provides the primary source of energy within its five-note range.

TEXT and MUSIC: Anon.

GOD IS SO GOOD
4.4.4.5

659 Know That God Is Good

Mungu ni mwema

1 Know that God is good. Know that
2 Hal - le, hal - le - lu - jah. Hal - le,
Mu - ngu ni mwe - ma. Mu - ngu

God is good. Know that God is good;
hal - le - lu - jah. Hal - le, hal - le - lu - jah,
ni mwe - ma. Mu - ngu ni mwe - ma,

God is good; God is good.
hal - le - lu - jah, hal - le - lu - jah.
ni mwe - ma, ni mwe - ma.

This engaging song from central Africa is based on an affirmation that recurs in numerous psalms (34:8; 73:1; 100:5; 135:3; 145:9) as well as several other books of the Hebrew Scriptures. Both the brief text (in English, Hebrew, and Shona) and the musical parts are easily learned.

TEXT: Democratic Republic of Congo
MUSIC: Democratic Republic of Congo; arr. Edo Bumba, 1997
Music Arr. © Edo Bumba

MUNGU NI MWEMA
5.5.5.3.3

Lord, We Thank You for This Food 660

*Simulation of pounding rice; the tenor may be sung by two groups interlocking ♪♪ ♪♪ etc.

This sung table grace provides words for a melody from the Bunun people of Taiwan. Because the "tom tom" lines in the lower voices of this setting are intended to imitate the sounds made when pounding rice, this sung prayer is also a way of remembering all whose labors feed us.

TEXT: I-to Loh, 1990
MUSIC: Bunun melody
Text © 1990 I-to Loh (admin. GIA Publications, Inc.)

MOTOMASE
Irregular

661 Why Should I Feel Discouraged?

His Eye Is on the Sparrow

1 Why should I feel dis-cour-aged? Why should the shad-ows come?
2 "Let not your heart be trou-bled," his ten-der word I hear,
3 When-ev-er I am tempt-ed, when-ev-er clouds a-rise,

Why should my heart be lone-ly and long for heaven and home,
and rest-ing on his good-ness, I lose my doubts and fears;
when song gives place to sigh-ing, when hope with-in me dies,

when Je-sus is my por-tion? My con-stant friend is he:
though by the path he lead-eth but one step I may see:
I draw the clos-er to him; from care he sets me free:

his eye is on the spar-row, and I know he watch-es me;

his eye is on the spar-row, and I know he watch-es me.

Refrain

I sing be-cause I'm hap-py, (I'm hap-py) I sing be-cause I'm free, (I'm free)

This hymn based on Jesus' saying about God's care for all creatures (Matthew 10:29–30 / Luke 12:6–7) began with the refrain's last line, inspired by a woman who had endured much illness. It was first sung in public at the Royal Albert Hall, London, during evangelistic services in 1905.

TEXT: Civilla Durfee Martin, 1905
MUSIC: Charles H. Gabriel, 1905

SPARROW
Irregular

for his eye is on the spar-row, and I know he watch-es me.

Christ, Whose Glory Fills the Skies 662

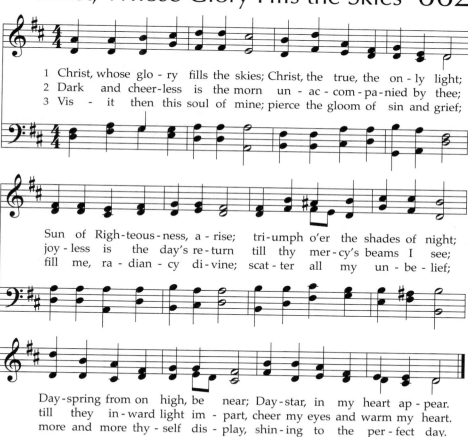

1 Christ, whose glo - ry fills the skies; Christ, the true, the on - ly light;
2 Dark and cheer-less is the morn un - ac - com - pa-nied by thee;
3 Vis - it then this soul of mine; pierce the gloom of sin and grief;

Sun of Righ-teous-ness, a - rise; tri-umph o'er the shades of night;
joy - less is the day's re-turn till thy mer-cy's beams I see;
fill me, ra - dian-cy di - vine; scat - ter all my un - be - lief;

Day-spring from on high, be near; Day-star, in my heart ap - pear.
till they in - ward light im - part, cheer my eyes and warm my heart.
more and more thy - self dis - play, shin - ing to the per - fect day.

This well-crafted morning hymn opens by celebrating daylight as an image of Christ, the true Light, then
ponders life without light, and culminates in a prayer for inward light. The tune's name honors its German
roots: Ratisbon is the former English name for Regensburg.

TEXT: Charles Wesley, 1740
MUSIC: German folk melody; adapt. Johann Werner, 1815; harm. William Henry Havergal, 1847

RATISBON
7.7.7.7.7.7

663 Awake, My Soul, and with the Sun

1 A - wake, my soul, and with the sun your dai - ly
2 Lord, I my vows to you re - new. Dis - perse my
3 Di - rect, con - trol, sug - gest, this day, all I de -

stage of du - ty run; shake off dull sloth, and
sins as morn - ing dew; guard my first springs of
sign or do or say, that all my powers, with

joy - ful rise to pay your morn - ing sac - ri - fice.
thought and will, and with your - self my spir - it fill.
all their might, in your sole glo - ry may u - nite.

These three stanzas (of the original fifteen) convey the essence of the morning hymn that was paired with "All Praise to Thee, My God, This Night" (no. 675) in the daily devotions of the boys at Winchester College. This tune was later composed especially for these words.

TEXT: Thomas Ken, 1695, alt.
MUSIC: François Hippolyte Barthélémon, 1785; harm. The Church Hymnal for the Christian Year, 1917

MORNING HYMN
LM

Morning Has Broken

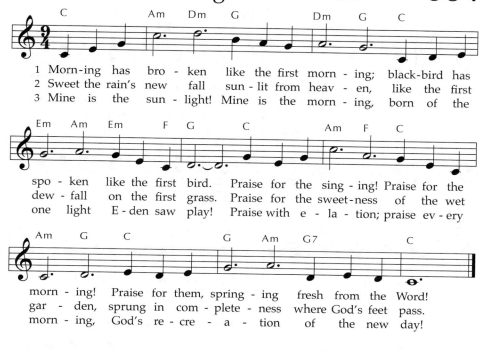

1 Morn-ing has bro - ken like the first morn - ing; black-bird has
2 Sweet the rain's new fall sun - lit from heav - en, like the first
3 Mine is the sun - light! Mine is the morn - ing, born of the

spo - ken like the first bird. Praise for the sing - ing! Praise for the
dew - fall on the first grass. Praise for the sweet-ness of the wet
one light E - den saw play! Praise with e - la - tion; praise ev - ery

morn - ing! Praise for them, spring - ing fresh from the Word!
gar - den, sprung in com - plete - ness where God's feet pass.
morn - ing, God's re - cre - a - tion of the new day!

This 20th-century text was created to provide words for this traditional tune named for a small village on the Isle of Mull, off the west coast of Scotland. Through repeated use of "new" and "first," each morning is treated as a re-creation of the promise of the original day.

TEXT: Eleanor Farjeon, 1931, alt.
MUSIC: Gaelic melody; arr. Beverly A. Howard, 2012
Text © David Higham Assoc., Ltd.
Music Arr. © 2012 Beverly A. Howard

BUNESSAN
5.5.5.4.D

665

As Morning Dawns
(Psalm 5)

1 As morn-ing dawns, Lord, hear our cry. O sov-ereign
2 Be-fore you, Lord, the wick-ed fall, and none shall
3 Your stead-fast love shall wel-come all who seek your
4 Let all who seek you then re-joice, and sing to

God, now hear our sigh. As first light brings the
dwell with-in your hall. The proud shall nev-er
house and on you call. O lead us, Lord, in
you with joy-ful voice. For you shall bless the

sun's warm rays, ac-cept our sac-ri-fice of praise.
gain a place, nor e-vil live to see your face.
righ-teous-ness, as through this day your name we bless.
righ-teous, Lord. For-ev-er be your name a-dored.

This paraphrase of Psalm 5 emphasizes shared human experience by beginning with the common hope that a new day offers new opportunities and by recasting the lone psalmist's voice into plural expressions. The tune is named for the composer's birthplace in Dorset, England.

TEXT: Fred R. Anderson, 1986
MUSIC: William Knapp, 1738
Text © 1986 Fred R. Anderson

WAREHAM
LM
(alternate harmonization, 320)

O Splendor of God's Glory Bright 666

1 O Splen - dor of God's glo - ry bright, from light e -
2 Come, Ho - ly Sun of heaven - ly love, rain down your
3 O joy - ful be the pass - ing day with thoughts as
4 O Lord, with each re - turn - ing morn, your im - age

ter - nal bring - ing light; O Light of Light, light's
ra - diance from a - bove, and to our in - ward
clear as morn - ing's ray, with faith like noon - tide
to our heart is born; O may we ev - er

liv - ing spring, true Day, all days il - lu - min - ing:
hearts con - vey the Ho - ly Spir - it's cloud - less ray.
shin - ing bright, our souls un - shad - owed by the night.
clear - ly view our Sav - ior and our God in you.

This morning hymn is based on a Latin text attributed to a 4th-century bishop. It weaves various images of Christ as Light with light-based descriptions of each day's passing. It is set to a dance-like tune from at least the 15th century that enhances the energy in the text.

TEXT: Ambrose of Milan, c. 374; trans. composite
MUSIC: Trier ms., 15th cent.; adapt. Michael Praetorius, 1609

PUER NOBIS NASCITUR
LM
(alternate harmonization, 67)

667 When Morning Gilds the Skies

1 When morn-ing gilds the skies, my heart a-wak-ing cries: may Je-sus Christ be praised! A-like at work and prayer to Je-sus I re-pair: may Je-sus Christ be praised!

2 Does sad-ness fill my mind? A so-lace here I find: may Je-sus Christ be praised! Or fades my earth-ly bliss? My com-fort still is this: may Je-sus Christ be praised!

3 Let earth's wide cir-cle round in joy-ful notes re-sound: may Je-sus Christ be praised! Let air and sea and sky from depth to height re-ply: may Je-sus Christ be praised!

4 Be this, while life is mine, my can-ti-cle di-vine: may Je-sus Christ be praised! Be this the e-ter-nal song through all the a-ges long: may Je-sus Christ be praised!

This is not just a morning hymn, though this excerpt from an English translation of an early 19th-century German text may not convey how thoroughly the original deals with different kinds of time throughout the day. The tune was composed as a setting for this English text.

TEXT: German hymn, c. 1800; trans. Edward Caswall, 1853, 1858, alt.
MUSIC: Joseph Barnby, 1868

LAUDES DOMINI
6.6.6.D

Golden Breaks the Dawn 668

1 Gold-en breaks the dawn; comes the east-ern sun
2 Ho-ly, liv-ing God, keep me safe to-day;
3 Give me dai-ly bread, while I do my part,

like a rid-er strong, set the course to run.
though I wea-ry plod, make me kind, I pray.
bright skies o-ver-head, glad-ness in my heart.

Birds a-bove me fly; flow-ers bloom be-low;
Let me guide our youth, hon-or weak and old;
Sim-ple wants pro-vide; e-vil let me shun,

through the earth and sky God's great mer-cies flow.
let me serve with truth, and God's love un-fold.
Je-sus at my side, till the day is done.

In ways reminiscent of the imagery of Lamentations 3:22–23, this popular Chinese text skillfully layers short phrases to create a picture of the dawning day as a context for affirming God's mercies and for seeking God's protection and provision. The tune name means "happy peace."

TEXT: Tzu-chen Chao, 1931; para. Frank W. Price, 1953
MUSIC: Te-ngai Hu, 1934; arr. Bliss Wiant, 1934
Text and Music © 1977 Chinese Christian Literature Council Ltd.

LE P'ING
5.5.5.5.D

669 Let's Sing unto the Lord *Cantemos al Señor*

1 Let's sing un-to the Lord a hymn of glad re-joic-ing.
2 Let's sing un-to the Lord a hymn of ad-o-ra-tion,

Let's sing a hymn of love, at the new day's fresh be-gin-ning.
which shows our love and faith and the hope of all cre-a-tion.

God made the sky a-bove, the stars, the sun, the o-ceans;
Through all that has been made, the Lord is praised for great-ness,

and God saw it was good, for those works were filled with beau-ty.
and so we sing to God, who be-stows such love-ly bless-ings.

Refrain / Estribillo

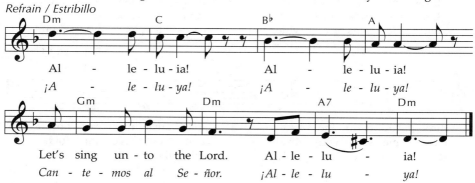

Al - le - lu - ia! Al - le - lu - ia!
¡A - le - lu - ya! ¡A - le - lu - ya!

Let's sing un-to the Lord. Al-le-lu - ia!
Can-te-mos al Se-ñor. ¡Al-le-lu - ya!

SPANISH

1 *Cantemos al Señor*
  un himno de alegría,
  un cántico de amor
  al nacer el nuevo día.
  Él hizo el cielo, el mar,
  el sol y las estrellas,
  y vio en ellos bondad,
  pues sus obras eran bellas.   Estribillo

2 *Cantemos al Señor*
  un himno de alabanza
  que exprese nuestro amor,
  nuestra fe y nuestra esperanza.
  En toda la creación
  pregona su grandeza,
  así nuestro cantar
  va anunciando su belleza.   Estribillo

Showing the apparent influence of Genesis 1 and Psalm 19, this cheerful hymn was created as the entrance hymn for a mass setting by the author/composer. The joyful tone of this music needs not to be rushed but savored, more like an accentuated dance than a hasty gallop.

TEXT: Carlos Rosas, 1976; English trans. Roberto Escamilla, Elise S. Eslinger,
  and George Lockwood, 1983, 1987
MUSIC: Carlos Rosas, 1976; arr. Raquel Mora Martínez, 1980
Text and Music © 1976 OCP
English Trans. © 1989 OCP
Music Arr. © 1983 OCP

CANTEMOS AL SEÑOR
6.7.6.8.D with refrain

From the Rising of the Sun   670
(Psalm 113)

This paraphrase of Psalm 113:3 concisely represents the psalm beginning the group called the Egyptian *Hallel* (113–118) used at all major Jewish festivals. One of these may have been what Jesus and his disciples sang at the conclusion of the Last Supper (Matthew 26:30/Mark 14:26).

TEXT and MUSIC: Anon.

RISING SUN
Irregular

671 O Radiant Light, O Sun Divine

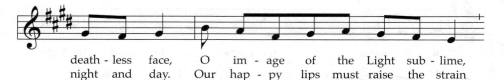

1 O ra-diant Light, O Sun di - vine, of God the Fa-ther's
2 O Son of God, the source of life, praise is your due by
3 Lord Je - sus Christ, as day - light fades, as shine the lights of

death - less face, O im - age of the Light sub - lime,
night and day. Our hap - py lips must raise the strain
e - ven - tide, we praise the Fa - ther with the Son,

that fills the heaven - ly dwell - ing place:
of your es - teemed and splen - did name.
the Spir - it blest and with them one. A - men.

This text is a 20th-century metrical paraphrase of one of the oldest Christian hymns, *Phos hilaron* (gladdening light), dating from at least the 3rd century (see also nos. 672 and 673). It is associated with an evening service, held both in churches and in homes, when lamps or candles are lighted.

TEXT: *Phos hilaron*, 3rd cent.; trans. William G. Storey, c. 1970
MUSIC: Sarum plainsong, Mode IV, 9th cent.; harm. C. Winfred Douglas, 1943
Text © 1979 William G. Storey
Music Harm. © 1943, 1961 Church Pension Fund

CONDITOR ALME SIDERUM
LM
(alternate harmonization, 84)

O Gladsome Light

1 O glad-some light, O grace of our Cre - a - tor's face,
2 As fades the day's last light, we see the lamps of night
3 To you of right be - longs all praise of ho - ly songs,

the e - ter - nal splen-dor wear - ing: ce - les - tial, ho - ly, blest,
our com - mon hymn out - pour - ing, O God of might un-known,
O Son of God, Life - giv - er; you, there - fore, O Most High,

our Sav - ior Je - sus Christ, joy - ful in your ap - pear - ing.
you, the in - car - nate Son, and Spir - it blest a - dor - ing.
the world does glo - ri - fy and shall ex - alt for - ev - er.

This paraphrase of a 3rd-century Christian lamplighting hymn (see also nos. 671 and 673) was created by an English poet who, as a former parish choirmaster, had developed a keen musical sensitivity. He wrote with this Genevan tune in mind, which initiated this continuing pairing of words and music.

TEXT: *Phos hilaron*, 3rd cent.; para. Robert Seymour Bridges, 1899, alt.
MUSIC: Genevan Psalter, 1551; harm. Claude Goudimel, 1565

LE CANTIQUE DE SIMÉON
6.6.7.6.6.7

673

Jesus, Light of Joy

1 Je - sus, light of joy, sur - round us; let your splen - did
2 Now the shad - ows fall a - round us; now the eve - ning
3 With the saints we lift our voic - es, God of pow - er,

glo - ry shine: source of ev - ery earth - ly bles - sing,
has be - gun: still your gra - cious light is with us,
God of might. All cre - a - tion shines with glo - ry,

heav - en's ev - er - last - ing sign. Al - le - lu - ia,
bright - er than the morn - ing sun. Al - le - lu - ia,
sing - ing prais - es day and night: al - le - lu - ia,

al - le - lu - ia, we a - dore you, light di - vine.
al - le - lu - ia, God of glo - ry, Three - in - One.
al - le - lu - ia, ho - ly, ho - ly, ho - ly light.

The images of light in this text are drawn from the ancient Christian vesper hymn *Phos hilaron*, which dates
from at least the 3rd century. (For other versions, see nos. 671 and 672.) That rather brief original hymn is
augmented here in the third stanza by language based on the *Sanctus*.

TEXT: David Gambrell, 2009
MUSIC: John Goss, 1869
Text © 2011 David Gambrell (admin. Presbyterian Publishing Corp.)

LAUDA ANIMA
8.7.8.7.8.7

I Call, O Lord, on You

(Psalm 141)

674

1 I call, O Lord, on you: come quick-ly to my aid;
2 Lord, let my prayer as-cend like in-cense in your sight;
3 Set, Lord, a guard to keep close watch up-on my mouth;
4 Have pit-y, Lord, on me; you are my strength, my shield:

hear from your throne in heaven a-bove my cry of deep dis-tress.
see in my hands to heaven a-bove my eve-ning sac-ri-fice.
let no re-bel-lious word es-cape your seal up-on my lips.
you are my ref-uge in all ills; I turn in trust to you.

This paraphrase of Psalm 141 is held together by the simple dignity of its language rather than by rhyme.
There is a surprising immediacy in this private prayer, offered at the end of a tiring and trying day and
seeking strength to avoid saying things that are untrue or hurtful.

TEXT: James Quinn, SJ, 1994
MUSIC: Samuel Howard, 1762
Text © 1994 James Quinn, SJ (admin. in North America Selah Publishing Co., Inc.)

ST. BRIDE
SM

675 All Praise to Thee, My God, This Night

1 All praise to thee, my God, this night, for all the
2 For-give me, Lord, through Christ, I pray, the wrong that
3 O may my soul on thee re-pose, and with sweet
4 Praise God, from whom all bless-ings flow; praise God, all

bless-ings of the light! Keep me, O keep me
I have done this day, that I, be-fore I
sleep mine eye-lids close. Re-fresh my strength, for
crea-tures here be-low; praise God a-bove, ye

safe from harm with-in the shel-ter of thine arm!
sleep, may be at peace with neigh-bor, self, and thee.
thine own sake, to serve thee well when I a-wake.
heaven-ly host; praise Fa-ther, Son, and Ho-ly Ghost.

*May be sung as a canon.

Originally consisting of twelve stanzas, this was the bedtime hymn of the boys at Winchester School in England. Now it is one of the best-known evening hymns in English (usually matched with this tune and sung in canon), and its final stanza has taken on a life of its own.

TEXT: Thomas Ken, 1674, alt.
MUSIC: Thomas Tallis, 1567, adapt.

TALLIS' CANON
LM

Day Is Done

1 Day is done, but love un-fail-ing dwells ev - er here;
2 Dark de-scends, but light un-end-ing shines through our night;
3 Eyes will close, but you un-sleep-ing watch by our side.

shad - ows fall, but hope, pre - vail-ing, calms ev - ery fear.
you are with us, ev - er lend-ing new strength to sight:
Death may come; in love's safe - keep-ing still we a - bide.

God, our Mak - er, none for - sak-ing, take our hearts, of love's own
one in love, your truth con - fess-ing, one in hope of heav - en's
God of love, all e - vil quell-ing, sin for - giv - ing, fear dis -

mak - ing; watch our sleep-ing; guard our wak-ing; be al - ways near.
bless-ing, may we see, in love's pos-sess-ing, love's end - less light!
pel - ling, stay with us, our hearts in-dwell-ing, this e - ven - tide.

This 20th-century hymn by a Scottish Jesuit paraphrases several traditional evening prayers and takes its shape from the familiar Welsh tune to which it is set. Its rhyme pattern requires considerable poetic skill, as only three rhymes serve for the eight lines of text.

TEXT: James Quinn, SJ, 1969, alt.
MUSIC: Welsh melody, c. 1784
Text © 1969 James Quinn, SJ (admin. Continuum, a div. of Bloomsbury Publishing Plc.)

AR HYD Y NOS
8.4.8.4.8.8.8.4

677 The Day Thou Gavest, Lord, Is Ended

1 The day thou gav - est, Lord, is end - ed; the dark - ness
2 We thank thee that thy church un - sleep - ing, while earth rolls
3 As o'er each con - ti - nent and is - land the dawn leads
4 The sun that bids us rest is wak - ing thy chil - dren
5 So be it, Lord; thy throne shall nev - er, like earth's proud

falls at thy be - hest. To thee our morn - ing
on - ward in - to light, through all the world a
on an - oth - er day, the voice of prayer is
'neath the west - ern sky, and hour by hour fresh
em - pires, pass a - way; thy king - dom stands, and

hymns as - cend - ed; thy praise shall hal - low now our rest.
watch is keep - ing and rests not now by day or night.
nev - er si - lent, nor dies the song of praise a - way.
lips are mak - ing thy won - drous do - ings heard on high.
grows for - ev - er un - til there dawns thy glo - rious day.

Written as a confident expression of missionary expansion, this text has become a humbler evening reflection concerning the rest of the world and humanity's place in God's universe. The tune name honors both the composer's given name and the church where he was baptized.

TEXT: John Ellerton, 1870, alt.
MUSIC: Clement Cottewill Scholefield, 1874

ST. CLEMENT
9.8.9.8

Our Darkness Is Never Darkness in Your Sight

678

La ténèbre n'est point ténèbre devant toi

Like other chants from the Taizé Community in France, this paraphrase of Psalm 139:12 is meant for repeated singing. It is most effective at evening services and works well with other Taizé chants such as "Within Our Darkest Night" (no. 294) and "The Lord Is My Light" (no. 842).

TEXT: Taizé Community, 1991
MUSIC: Jacques Berthier, 1991
Text and Music © 1991 Les Presses de Taizé (admin. GIA Publications, Inc.)

LA TÉNÈBRE
Irregular

679 Let the Whole Creation Cry

(Psalm 148)

1 Let the whole cre - a - tion cry, "Glo - ry to the Lord on high."
2 Men and wom-en, young and old, raise the an-them loud and bold;

Heaven and earth, a - wake and sing, "Praise to our al - might-y King."
join with chil - dren's songs of praise; wor-ship God through length of days.

Praise God, an - gel hosts a - bove, ev - er bright and fair in love;
From the north to south-ern pole let the might-y cho - rus roll:

sun and moon, up - lift your voice; night and stars, in God re - joice!
"Ho - ly, ho - ly, ho - ly One, glo - ry be to God a - lone!"

Originally this text was more than twice as long as the present version because it followed Psalm 148 in directing additional parts of the created order to praise God. This wide-ranging text is set here to a suitably expansive and well-crafted 17th-century chorale melody.

TEXT: Stopford A. Brooke, 1881, alt.
MUSIC: Jakob Hintze, 1678; harm. Johann Sebastian Bach

SALZBURG
7.7.7.7.D

Soft Rains of Spring Flow

1 Soft rains of spring flow through the fields; earth a-wakes and
2 Ten-der young shoots, green in the sun, glis-ten with the
3 Our hearts are filled: God gives us grace; o-ver-flow-ing

greets a new year. Deep with-in the soil of our hearts seeds of
beau-ty of spring. God will watch and care for each one, bring the
we give our praise. We come hum-bly bring-ing our thanks, bring our

love be-gin to take root. Sum-mer brings floods, tem-pest and
growth and strength to bear fruit, speak-ing the word, quench-ing their
hearts and of-fer them back. Our har-vest here on God's rich

storm; sun breaks forth; birds tend their young. Then the day of
thirst, hear-ing their prayer, feed-ing their souls. God will love and
earth, all is a gift God free-ly makes. Lord and Sav-ior,

har-vest will come, when we gath-er all that God gives.
care for each one, till the bright day har-vest will come.
we sing your praise, thank and bless you all of our days.

This gentle text celebrates the changing seasons as testimony to God's care for all creation, and meditating on that theme inspires thanks. The tune name is pronounced "peacocks," and commemorates the Presbyterian Committee on Congregational Song, who compiled this hymnal.

TEXT: Jong Rack Im, 1993; trans. Edward Poitras, 2001, alt.
MUSIC: Seung Nam Kim, 2001; adapt. Paul Junggap Huh, 2011; arr. Alfred V. Fedak, 2011
Text © The Korean Hymnal Society
Music © 2011 Paul Junggap Huh and Seung Nam Kim
Music Arr. © 2011 Alfred V. Fedak

PCOCS
LMD

681 This Is the Day the Lord Hath Made
(Psalm 118)

1 This is the day the Lord hath made; the hours are all God's own. Let heaven re - joice; let earth be glad, and praise sur - round the throne.

2 Ho - san - na to the a - noint - ed King, to Da - vid's ho - ly Son! Help us, O Lord; de - scend and bring sal - va - tion from the throne.

3 Blest be the Lord, who comes in power with mes - sag - es of grace, who comes in this ac - cept - ed hour to save our sin - ful race.

4 Ho - san - na in the high - est strains the church on earth can raise! The high - est heavens in which God reigns shall now re - sound with praise.

These stanzas provide Watts's paraphrase of Psalm 118:24–29 (minus a stanza he inserted about Easter and Pentecost as part of his effort to Christianize the Psalms). They are set to a tune composed for and named by a Paul Gerhardt text, "Now Let All Thank and Bring Honor."

TEXT: Isaac Watts, 1719, alt.
MUSIC: Johann Crüger, c. 1647

NUN DANKET ALL' UND BRINGET EHR'
CM

It Is Good to Sing Your Praises 682
(Psalm 92)

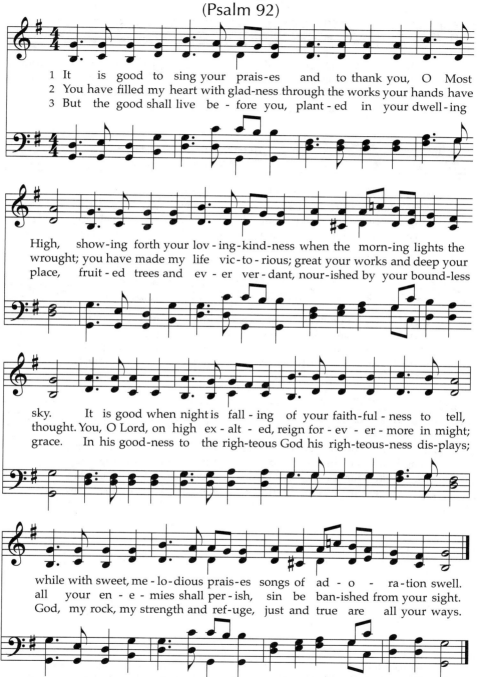

1 It is good to sing your prais-es and to thank you, O Most
2 You have filled my heart with glad-ness through the works your hands have
3 But the good shall live be - fore you, plant - ed in your dwell-ing

High, show-ing forth your lov - ing-kind-ness when the morn-ing lights the
wrought; you have made my life vic - to - rious; great your works and deep your
place, fruit - ed trees and ev - er ver - dant, nour-ished by your bound-less

sky. It is good when night is fall - ing of your faith-ful - ness to tell,
thought. You, O Lord, on high ex - alt - ed, reign for - ev - er - more in might;
grace. In his good-ness to the right-teous God his right-teous-ness dis-plays;

while with sweet, me - lo-dious prais-es songs of ad - o - ra -tion swell.
all your en - e - mies shall per - ish, sin be ban-ished from your sight.
God, my rock, my strength and ref-uge, just and true are all your ways.

Psalm 92, paraphrased here, is the only psalm that the Bible assigns to a specific day: the Sabbath. This may
be because of the mention of "works" in stanza two, recalling that, after six days of creation, God rested on
the Sabbath (Genesis 2:2–3), when the faithful do the same.

TEXT: *The New Metrical Version of the Psalms,* 1909, alt.
MUSIC: Leavitt's *Christian Lyre,* 1830/31

ELLESDIE
8.7.8.7.D

683   Lord of All Hopefulness

1 Lord of all hope-ful-ness, Lord of all joy, whose
2 Lord of all ea-ger-ness, Lord of all faith, whose
3 Lord of all kind-li-ness, Lord of all grace, your
4 Lord of all gen-tle-ness, Lord of all calm, whose

trust, ev-er child-like, no cares could de-stroy: be
strong hands were skilled at the plane and the lathe: be
hands swift to wel-come, your arms to em-brace: be
voice is con-tent-ment, whose pres-ence is balm: be

there at our wak-ing and give us, we pray, your
there at our la-bors and give us, we pray, your
there at our hom-ing and give us, we pray, your
there at our sleep-ing and give us, we pray, your

bliss in our hearts, Lord, at the break of the day.
strength in our hearts, Lord, at the noon of the day.
love in our hearts, Lord, at the eve of the day.
peace in our hearts, Lord, at the end of the day.

When first published in 1931, this "All-Day Hymn" (as it was titled) seemed very daring for not using traditional archaic pronouns to address Christ. Current pronouns no longer disturb, but the comforting Jesus portrayed here needs to be balanced by his call to discipleship.

TEXT: Jan Struther, 1931
MUSIC: David Schwoebel, 2008
Text © 1931 Oxford University Press
Music © 2008 Celebrating Grace, Inc.

COURTNEY
10.11.11.12
(alternate tune: SLANE)

Faith Begins by Letting Go 684

1 Faith be - gins by let - ting go, giv - ing up what
2 Faith en - dures by hold - ing on, keep - ing mem - ory's
3 Faith ma - tures by reach - ing out, stretch - ing minds, en -

had seemed sure, tak - ing risks and press - ing on,
roots a - live so that hope may bear its fruit;
larg - ing hearts, shar - ing strug - gles, liv - ing prayer,

though the way feels less se - cure: pil - grim - age both
prom - ise - fed, our souls will thrive, not through mer - it
bind - ing up the bro - ken parts; till we find the

right and odd, trust - ing all our life to God.
we pos - sess but by God's great faith - ful - ness.
com - mon - place ripe with wit - ness to God's grace.

This text affirms that faith is not a state of being but a process of becoming what we are called to be in relationship to God, other people, and the world. The movement from one stage of faith to another is suggested by gestures of the hand: letting go, holding on, reaching out.

TEXT: Carl P. Daw Jr., 1995
MUSIC: Charles F. Gounod, 1872
Text © 1996 Hope Publishing Company

LUX PRIMA
7.7.7.7.7.7

685 Unseen God, Your Hand Has Guided

1 Un - seen God, your hand has guid - ed these two
2 You have made them in your im - age, formed them
3 May their fin - gers, in - ter - twin - ing, weave a
4 Shape their hands, O God, for shar - ing: o - pen,
5 God, through all the years be - fore them, let your

lives on sep - arate ways till they heard your
for com - mu - ni - ty. Bless their hands, now
stron - ger bond to bear bur - dens fu - ture
reach - ing out to give. Make their hearts, as
hand their hands up - hold. On their un - seen

call to trav - el hand in hand through all their days.
linked to - geth - er, yoked in love that sets them free.
years may bring them: stress of du - ty, weight of care.
you have shown us, quick, when wound - ed, to for - give.
way be - friend them; with your love their love en - fold.

This wedding or anniversary text effectively weaves together metaphorical and literal references to hands. The metaphors, referring to God's providential care, are always singular, while the human references all involve more than one hand and evoke visual and tactile images.

MERTON
8.7.8.7

TEXT: Herman G. Stuempfle Jr., 1998
MUSIC: William Henry Monk, 1850
Text © 2000 GIA Publications, Inc.

God of Our Life

1 God of our life, through all the cir-cling years, we trust in thee.
2 God of the past, our times are in thy hand. With us a-bide.
3 God of the com-ing years, through paths un-known we fol-low thee.

In all the past, through all our hopes and fears, thy hand we see.
Lead us by faith to hope's true prom-ised land. Be thou our guide.
When we are strong, Lord, leave us not a-lone. Our ref-uge be.

With each new day, when morn-ing lifts the veil,
With thee to bless, the dark-ness shines as light,
Be thou for us in life our dai-ly bread,

we own thy mer - cies, Lord, which nev-er fail.
and faith's fair vi - sion chang-es in-to sight.
our heart's true home when all our years have sped.

This text was created for the celebration of the fiftieth anniversary of the Shadyside Presbyterian Church in Pittsburgh, Pennsylvania, by its pastor. He wrote these words especially for this tune, originally composed for John Henry Newman's text "Lead, Kindly Light."

TEXT: Hugh Thomson Kerr, 1916, alt.
MUSIC: Charles Henry Purday, 1860; harm. John Weaver, 1986
Text © 1928 F. M. Braselman, ren. 1956 Presbyterian Board of Christian Education
  (admin. Westminster John Knox Press)
Music Harm. © 1990 Hope Publishing Company

SANDON
10.4.10.4.10.10

687 Our God, Our Help in Ages Past

(Psalm 90)

1 Our God, our help in a - ges past, our
2 Be - neath the shad - ow of thy throne thy
3 Be - fore the hills in or - der stood, or
4 A thou - sand a - ges in thy sight are

hope for years to come, our shel - ter from the
saints have dwelt se - cure; suf - fi - cient is thine
earth re - ceived its frame, from ev - er - last - ing
like an eve - ning gone, short as the watch that

storm - y blast, and our e - ter - nal home:
arm a - lone, and our de - fense is sure.
thou art God, to end - less years the same.
ends the night be - fore the ris - ing sun.

5 Time, like an ever rolling stream,
bears all our years away;
they fly forgotten, as a dream
dies at the opening day.

6 Our God, our help in ages past,
our hope for years to come,
be thou our guard while life shall last,
and our eternal home.

Many people sing this hymn unaware that it paraphrases Psalm 90, partly because this text speaks so immediately to the human condition. Since the middle of the 19th century, it has usually been joined to this tune named for the London parish where the composer was organist.

TEXT: Isaac Watts, 1719, alt.
MUSIC: Attr. William Croft, 1708

ST. ANNE
CM

Spirit of God, Descend upon My Heart 688

1 Spir - it of God, de - scend up - on my heart;
2 I ask no dream, no proph - et ec - sta - sies,
3 Hast thou not bid us love thee, God and King;
4 Teach me to feel that thou art al - ways nigh.
5 Teach me to love thee as thine an - gels love,

wean it from earth; through all its puls - es move;
no sud - den rend - ing of the veil of clay,
all, all thine own, soul, heart, and strength, and mind?
Teach me the strug - gles of the soul to bear,
one ho - ly pas - sion fill - ing all my frame;

stoop to my weak - ness, might - y as thou art,
no an - gel vis - i - tant, no o - pening skies;
I see thy cross; there teach my heart to cling.
to check the ris - ing doubt, the reb - el sigh.
the bap - tism of the heaven - de - scend - ed Dove,

and make me love thee as I ought to love.
but take the dim - ness of my soul a - way.
O let me seek thee, and O let me find!
Teach me the pa - tience of un - an - swered prayer.
my heart an al - tar, and thy love the flame.

This reflection on Galatians 5:25 was written by a literary Anglican clergyman whose preaching drew people of many social classes to one of the formerly poorer London churches. The tune was created for "Abide with Me" (no. 836) but more often appears with the present text.

TEXT: George Croly, 1867
MUSIC: Frederick Cook Atkinson, 1870

MORECAMBE
10.10.10.10

689 When the Morning Stars Together

1 When the morn-ing stars to - geth - er their Cre - a - tor's
2 When in syn - a - gogue and tem - ple voic - es raised the
3 Voice and in - stru - ment in un - ion through the a - ges
4 Lord, we bring our gift of mu - sic; touch our lips and

glo - ry sang, and the an - gel host all shout-ed till with
psalm-ists' songs, of - fering up the ad - o - ra - tion which a -
spoke your praise. Plain-song, tune - ful hymns, and an - thems told your
fire our hearts. Teach our minds and train our sens - es; fit us

joy the heav-ens rang, then your wis - dom and your great-ness
lone to you be - longs; when the sing - ers, trum - pets, cym - bals
faith - ful, gra - cious ways. Choir and or - ches - tra and or - gan
for these sa - cred arts. Then with skill and con - se - cra - tion

Opening with imagery from Job 38:7, this text celebrates the role of music in worship from earliest times to the present. It is set to a German tune that may have originated as a folk melody. The tune name, German for "white flags," comes from one of the early texts set to it.

TEXT: Albert F. Bayly, 1966, alt.
MUSIC: German melody; harm. *Tochter Sion*, 1741
Text © 1966 Oxford University Press

WEISSE FLAGGEN
8.7.8.7.D

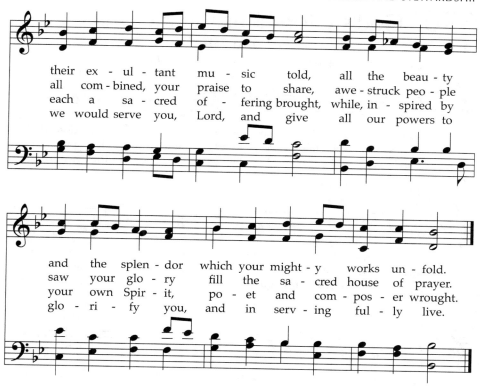

their ex - ul - tant mu - sic told, all the beau - ty
all com - bined, your praise to share, awe - struck peo - ple
each a sa - cred of - fering brought, while, in - spired by
we would serve you, Lord, and give all our powers to

and the splen - dor which your might - y works un - fold.
saw your glo - ry fill the sa - cred house of prayer.
your own Spir - it, po - et and com - pos - er wrought.
glo - ri - fy you, and in serv - ing ful - ly live.

690 God's Glory Fills the Heavens
(Psalm 19)

Guitar chords do not correspond with keyboard harmony.

This paraphrase of Psalm 19 was part of a longer work commissioned by the Associate Reformed Presbyterian Church for its Bicentennial Anniversary in 1982. The three stanzas reflect the psalm's three themes: creation, the giving of the Law, and the human response to these gifts.

TEXT: Carl P. Daw Jr., 1982
MUSIC: Irish melody; arr. Charles Villiers Stanford, 1902
Text © 1989 Hope Publishing Company

ST. PATRICK
LMD

strength and grace from far - thest heaven comes forth the sun.
found so fine, no hon - ey in the comb more sweet.
make me whole, O Lord, my ref - uge and my might.

Lord, When I Came into This Life 691

1 Lord, when I came in - to this life you
2 With - in the cir - cle of the faith, as
3 In all the ten - sions of my life, be -
4 So help me in my un - be - lief and

called me by my name; to - day I come, com -
mem - ber of your cast, I take my place with
tween my faith and doubt, let your great Spir - it
let my life be true: feet firm - ly plant - ed

mit my - self, re - spond - ing to your claim.
all the saints of fu - ture, pres - ent, past.
give me hope, sus - tain me, lead me out.
on the earth, my sights set high on you.

Written for the confirmation of the author's son, this text of self-dedication also voices our recurring
individual need to recommit ourselves in less formal ways. The familiar shape note tune enhances a sense
of finding our place among God's people from all times and places.

TEXT: Fred Kaan, 1976
MUSIC: American folk melody; harm. Charles H. Webb, 1988
Text © 1979 The Hymn Society (admin. Hope Publishing Company)
Music Harm. © 1989 The United Methodist Publishing House (admin. The Copyright Company)

LAND OF REST
CM
(alternate harmonization, 545)

692 Spirit, Open My Heart

The pace and diversity of modern life often hinder us from remaining vulnerable to our emotions and to the humanness of other people. This prayerful text to be open to such joys and pains draws on Ezekiel 11:19 and 36:26 in stanza one and echoes Jeremiah 31:33 in stanza two.

TEXT: Ruth Duck, 1994
MUSIC: Irish melody; arr. Alfred V. Fedak, 2011
Text © 1996 The Pilgrim Press
Music Harm. © 2011 Alfred V. Fedak

WILD MOUNTAIN THYME
Irregular

Though I May Speak

The Gift of Love

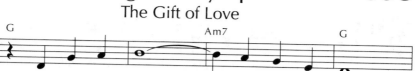

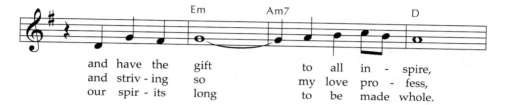

1 Though I may speak with brav - est fire,
2 Though I may give all I pos - sess,
3 Come, Spir - it, come, our hearts con - trol;

and have the gift to all in - spire,
and striv - ing so my love pro - fess,
our spir - its long to be made whole.

and have not love, my words are vain,
but not be given by love with - in,
Let in - ward love guide ev - ery deed;

as sound - ing brass, and hope - less gain.
the prof - it soon turns strange - ly thin.
by this we wor - ship, and are freed.

As paraphrases of 1 Corinthians 13:1, 3 the first two stanzas here are in the first person singular, yet they lead into a plural prayer for the gift of such love, for it thrives in community. These words are especially poignant with this adaptation of an English folk melody.

TEXT: Hal H. Hopson, 1972
MUSIC: English folk melody; adapt. Hal H. Hopson, 1972
Text and Music © 1972 Hope Publishing Company

GIFT OF LOVE
LM

694 Great God of Every Blessing

1 Great God of ev-ery bless-ing, of faith-ful, lov-ing care,
2 Your Word is our sal-va-tion, the source of end-less grace,
3 Your Spir-it is our teach-er, the light that guides our search,

you are the fount of good-ness, the dai-ly bread we share.
in death and life ex-tend-ing your cov-e-nant em-brace.
trans-form-ing bro-ken peo-ple in-to the ho-ly church.

How can we hope to thank you? Our praise is but a start:
In Christ we are one bod-y; each mem-ber has a part:
For feed-ing us with mer-cy, for wis-dom you im-part:

sin-cere-ly and com-plete-ly I of-fer you my heart.

Written for the 500th anniversary of John Calvin's birth, this text sums up his liturgical theology, ending each stanza with his motto: *Cor meum tibi offero, Domine, prompte et sincere.* By moving from plural to singular the stanzas show how corporate faith becomes personal piety.

TEXT: David Gambrell, 2009
MUSIC: Samuel Sebastian Wesley, 1864
Text © 2011 David Gambrell (admin. Presbyterian Publishing Corp.)

AURELIA
7.6.7.6.D

Change My Heart, O God   695

Cámbiame, Señor 항상진실케

The central image of the potter and the clay in this text comes from Isaiah 64:8 (and there is a similar reference in Jeremiah 18:1–6), while the petition for a changed heart is similar to Psalm 51:10. Such readiness to do God's will is a significant feature of the spiritual life.

TEXT: English and Spanish, Eddie Espinosa, 1982;
   Korean trans., The United Methodist Korean Hymnal Committee, 2001
MUSIC: Eddie Espinosa, 1982
Text and Music © 1982 Mercy/Vineyard Publishing (admin. in North America Music Services)

CHANGE MY HEART
Irregular

696 O God, You Are My God Alone

(Psalm 63)

1 O God, you are my God a-lone, whom ea-ger-ly I seek,
2 Your faith-ful love sur-pass-es life, e-vok-ing all my praise.
3 Through-out the night I lie in bed and call you, Lord, to mind;

though long-ing fills my soul with thirst and leaves my bod-y weak.
Through ev-ery day, to bless your name, my hands in joy I'll raise.
in dark-est hours I med-i-tate how God, my strength, is kind.

Just as a dry and bar-ren land a-waits a fresh-ening shower,
My deep-est needs you sat-is-fy as with a sump-tuous feast.
Be-neath the shad-ow of your wing, I live and feel se-cure;

I long with-in your house to see your glo-ry and your power.
So, on my lips and in my heart, your praise has nev-er ceased.
and dai-ly as I fol-low close, your right hand keeps me sure.

Given its wide range of references, scholars have proposed many occasions and uses for Psalm 63. Because of the imagery that opens stanza three in this paraphrase, for example, the great Reformed theologian and scholar Theodore Beza regularly recited this psalm at night.

TEXT: The Iona Community, 1993
MUSIC: Mary Kay Beall, 1991
Text © 1993 WGRG, Iona Community (admin. GIA Publications, Inc.)
Music © 1991 Hope Publishing Company

GRATUS
CMD

Take My Life

1 Take my life and let it be con-se-crat-ed, Lord, to thee;
2 Take my hands and let them move at the im-pulse of thy love;
3 Take my voice and let me sing al-ways, on-ly, for my King;
4 Take my sil-ver and my gold; not a mite would I with-hold;

take my mo-ments and my days; let them flow in
take my feet and let them be swift and beau-ti-
take my lips and let them be filled with mes-sa-
take my in-tel-lect and use ev-ery power as

cease-less praise; let them flow in cease-less praise.
ful for thee, swift and beau-ti-ful for thee.
ges from thee, filled with mes-sa-ges from thee.
thou shalt choose, ev-ery power as thou shalt choose.

5 Take my will and make it thine;
it shall be no longer mine.
Take my heart, it is thine own;
it shall be thy royal throne,
it shall be thy royal throne.

6 Take my love; my Lord, I pour
at thy feet its treasure store;
take myself and I will be
ever, only, all for thee,
ever, only, all for thee.

This hymn of consecration radiates from the repeated word "take," resulting in a remarkably full survey of a person's attributes and possessions and giving weight to the "all" at the end. The composer of the tune was influential in the renewal of Reformed hymnody in French.

TEXT: Frances Ridley Havergal, 1874
MUSIC: H. A. César Malan, 1827

HENDON
7.7.7.7

698 Take, O Take Me as I Am

Take, O take me as I am; sum-mon out what I shall be; set your seal up-on my heart and live in me.

The brevity of this text and tune invite repeated singing, either as a sustained chain of sound or as a sung response in a series of prayers. It offers a more reflective approach to the same theme of self-dedication evident in older hymns such as "Just as I Am" (see no. 442).

TEXT and MUSIC: John L. Bell, 1995
Text and Music © 1995 WGRG, Iona Community (admin. GIA Publications, Inc.)

TAKE ME AS I AM
7.7.7.4

699 Fill My Cup

Refrain

Fill my cup; let it o-ver-flow; fill my cup; let it o-ver-flow; fill my cup; let it

The refrain of this gospel song by a well-known Presbyterian pastor and musician can be understood as a meditation on Psalm 23:5, while the stanzas reflect an updated and easily accessible interpretation of the prayer often attributed to St. Francis of Assisi (see no. 753).

TEXT and MUSIC: Isaiah Jones Jr., 1969
Text and Music © 1970 Davike Music Company, assigned 1986 Fricout Music Company

FILL MY CUP
8.7.8.7 with refrain

o - ver-flow; let it o - ver - flow with love. *Fine*

1 Lord, let me be   your in - stru-ment,   spread-ing
2 It's   my de - sire   to live for you   and to

sun - shine   in the land;   let peo - ple   see   your
al - ways   walk up - right;   give me the strength   to

works in me;   help me   live   the best   I   can.
face each day;   stay with   me   through each   dark   night.

700 I'm Gonna Live So God Can Use Me

1 I'm gon-na live so (live so)
2 I'm gon-na work so (work so)
3 I'm gon-na pray so (pray so)
4 I'm gon-na sing so (sing so)

God can use me an-y-

where, Lord, an-y-time!

(an-y-time!)

I'm gon-na
I'm gon-na
I'm gon-na
I'm gon-na

live so (live so)
work so (work so)
pray so (pray so)
sing so (sing so)

God can use me an-y-

where, Lord, an-y-time!
(my Lord,) (an-y-time!)

This African American spiritual has more depth than may at first appear: for people who are bound in slavery to sing about dedicating themselves to God's use shows a profound awareness of God-given self-worth despite circumstances that would deny their human or spiritual value.

TEXT: African American spiritual
MUSIC: African American spiritual; arr. Wendell P. Whalum, 1984
Music Arr. © Estate of Wendell P. Whalum

I'M GONNA LIVE
Irregular

Lord, Prepare Me
Sanctuary
701

Lord, pre - pare me to be a sanc - tu - ar - y, pure and

ho - ly, tried and true. With thanks - giv - ing,

I'll be a liv - ing sanc - tu - ar - y for you.

The lines given here convey the central message of the longer song for which they form the refrain. The principal Scripture reference is 1 Corinthians 3:16–17, Paul's reminder to the Christians at Corinth that "[they] are God's temple and that God's Spirit dwells in [them]."

TEXT: John Thompson and Randy Scruggs, 1982
MUSIC: John Thompson and Randy Scruggs, 1982; arr. Nylea L. Butler-Moore
Text and Music © 1982 Full Armor Music Publishing Co.
Music Arr. © 2013 Full Armor Music Publishing Co. (admin. in the U.S.A. Peermusic III, Ltd./Hal Leonard Corp.)

SANCTUARY
Irregular

Christ Be Beside Me
702

1 Christ be   be - side   me; Christ be   be - fore   me; Christ   be   be -
2 Christ on   my right   hand, Christ on   my left   hand, Christ   all   a -
3 Christ be   in   all   hearts think - ing   a - bout   me; Christ be   on

hind   me, King of my   heart. Christ be with - in   me; Christ be   be -
round   me, shield in the   strife. Christ in   my sleep - ing, Christ in   my
all   tongues tell - ing of   me.   Christ be   the vi - sion   in eyes that

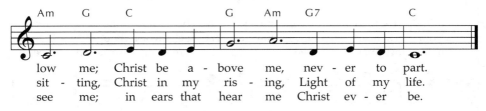

low   me; Christ be   a - bove   me, nev - er   to   part.
sit - ting,   Christ in my   ris - ing, Light   of my   life.
see   me;   in ears that   hear   me Christ ev - er   be.

This text adapts part of a traditional Irish prayer associated with St. Patrick (see also no. 6). Such a prayer for protection is known as a *lorica*, from a Latin word for "breastplate" or "armor." It is set to a Gaelic melody that gained wide popularity in the 1970s.

TEXT: James Quinn, SJ, 1969
MUSIC: Gaelic melody; arr. Dale Grotenhuis, 1985
Music Arr. © 1987 Faith Alive Christian Resources

BUNESSAN
5.5.5.4.D

703 Jesus, Thy Boundless Love to Me

1 Je - sus, thy bound - less love to me no thought can
2 O grant that noth - ing in my soul may dwell, but
3 O Love, how gra - cious is thy way! All fear be -

reach, no tongue de - clare; O knit my thank - ful heart to
thy pure love a - lone; O may thy love pos - sess me
fore thy pres - ence flies; care, an - guish, sor - row melt a -

thee, and reign with - out a ri - val there! Thine whol - ly,
whole, my joy, my trea - sure, and my crown! All cold - ness
way wher - e'er thy heal - ing beams a - rise. O Je - sus,

thine a - lone, I'd live; my - self to thee en - tire - ly give.
from my heart re - move; may ev - ery act, word, thought be love.
noth - ing may I see, noth - ing de - sire, or seek, but thee.

John Wesley learned the original German hymn from the Moravians during his time in Savannah, Georgia, and translated all sixteen stanzas. The tune, named for a 4th-century martyr, comes out of the Roman Catholic revival movement of the mid-19th century.

TEXT: Paul Gerhardt, 1653; trans. John Wesley, c. 1739, alt.
MUSIC: Henri Frederick Hemy, 1864; alt. James George Walton, 1874

ST. CATHERINE
8.8.8.8.8.8

To My Precious Lord

내게있는향유옥합

Refrain

To my pre-cious Lord I bring my flask of fra-grant oil;
내 게 있 는 향 유 옥 합 주 께 가 져 와

kneel-ing down, I kiss his feet, a-noint them with the oil.
그 발 위 에 입 맞 추 고 깨 뜨 립 니 다

Harmony

1 Je - sus, who for my sake walked the road to Cal - va - ry,
2 Je - sus, who for my sake had his feet nailed to the cross,
3 When in clouds of glo - ry you come back to earth a - gain,

with each step has marked the im - print of his love for me.
with his blood has washed and healed me, paid the heav - y cost.
Je - sus, with your love, em - brace and claim me as your friend.

KOREAN

1 나를위해험한산길오르신그발
   걸음마다크신사랑새겨놓았네

2 나를위해십자가에오르신그발
   흘린피로나의죄를대속하셨네

3 주님다시이땅위에임하실그때
   주의크신사랑으로날받아주소서

This popular Korean praise and worship song speaks in the voice of the penitent woman who washes Christ's feet in Luke 7:36–50. It is a remarkable devotional text, both for inviting singers to identify with a woman's experience and for exploring neglected imagery.

TEXT: Chung Kwan Park, 1983; English trans. Edward Poitras, 2001; rev. Mary Louise Bringle, 2011
MUSIC: Chung Kwan Park, 1983; arr. Paul Junggap Huh and Alfred V. Fedak, 2012
Text and Music © Chung Kwan Park (admin. KCMCA)
English Trans. © 2001, alt. 2013 The United Methodist Publishing House (admin. The Copyright Company)

TO MY PRECIOUS LORD
8.5.8.5 with refrain

705

You Are Holy
Prince of Peace

Songs of personal devotion to Christ have long formed part of congregational song, a tradition continued in this contemporary praise and worship song. The two parts suggest the voices of heart and mind, the latter being distinguished by familiarity with many scriptural images.

TEXT and MUSIC: Marc Imboden and Tammi Rhoton, 1994
Text and Music © 1994 Imboden Music and Martha Jo Music (admin. Music Services)

YOU ARE HOLY
Irregular

continued

Commit Your Way to God the Lord 706
(Psalm 37)

1 Com - mit your way to God the Lord: your cause will
2 Be still be - fore the Lord and wait, and do not
3 Sal - va - tion comes from God a - lone: the faith - ful
4 Com - mit your way to God the Lord; to peace and

shine as bright as fire; de - light to do God's
fret when wrong suc - ceeds; re - frain from an - ger,
know their help is sure; to heav - en, all our
truth and grace as - pire; then mer - cy shall be

ho - ly word and you shall find what you de - sire.
turn from hate, for God will pun - ish e - vil deeds.
needs are known, and in God's strength we are se - cure.
your re - ward; God's prom - is - es, your heart's de - sire.

John Calvin summarized Psalm 37 by saying, "It enjoins us to confide in the providence of God." This compact paraphrase maintains that perspective by drawing mainly on the psalm's promises and assurances rather than on its descriptions of the activities of the wicked.

TEXT: Michael Perry, 1989
MUSIC: Thurlow Weed, 2009
Text © 1989 The Jubilate Group (admin. Hope Publishing Company)
Music © 2009 Thurlow Weed

GUILSBOROUGH
LM

707 Take Thou Our Minds, Dear Lord

1 Take thou our minds, dear Lord, we hum-bly pray;
2 Take thou our hearts, O Christ; they are thine own;
3 Take thou our wills, Most High! Hold thou full sway;
4 Take thou our-selves, O Lord, heart, mind, and will;

give us the mind of Christ each pass-ing day;
come thou with-in our souls and claim thy throne;
have in our in-most souls thy per-fect way;
through our sur-ren-dered souls thy plans ful-fill.

teach us to know the truth that sets us free;
help us to shed a-broad thy death-less love;
guard thou each sa-cred hour from self-ish ease;
We yield our-selves to thee: time, tal-ents, all;

grant us in all our thoughts to hon-or thee.
use us to make the earth like heaven a-bove.
guide thou our or-dered lives as thou dost please.
we hear, and hence-forth heed, thy sov-ereign call.

This hymn began with the tune, which the composer hummed to the author with a request for a text that would challenge the hearts and minds of young people. The text of the first three stanzas was written that day, and the fourth stanza later emerged at a youth conference.

TEXT: William H. Foulkes, stanzas 1–3, 1918, stanza 4, c. 1920
MUSIC: Calvin Weiss Laufer, 1918

HALL
10.10.10.10

We Give Thee but Thine Own 708

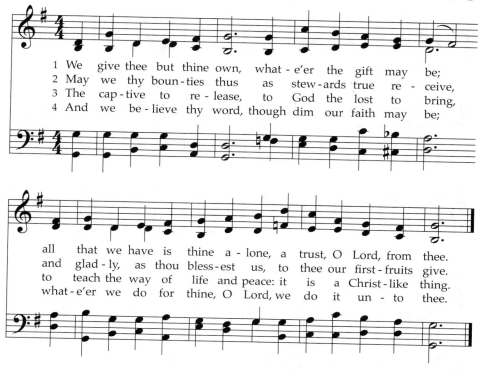

1 We give thee but thine own, what-e'er the gift may be;
2 May we thy boun-ties thus as stew-ards true re-ceive,
3 The cap-tive to re-lease, to God the lost to bring,
4 And we be-lieve thy word, though dim our faith may be;

all that we have is thine a-lone, a trust, O Lord, from thee.
and glad-ly, as thou bless-est us, to thee our first-fruits give.
to teach the way of life and peace: it is a Christ-like thing.
what-e'er we do for thine, O Lord, we do it un-to thee.

Each successive stanza here expands the implications of the familiar affirmation of the first one. Much more than a concern with money, stewardship shapes our relationship with God and with other people. Despite this tune's name, no source has been found in Schumann's works.

TEXT: William Walsham How, c. 1858
MUSIC: Mason and Webb's *Cantica Laudis*, 1850

SCHUMANN
SM

709

God, We Honor You

God, we hon - or you. God, we trust in you.

God, we wor - ship and a - dore you.

Take what we bring, of - fered to you.

Teach us to show your a - bun - dant bless - ings.

Al - le - lu - ia, al - le - lu - ia,

al - le - lu - ia, a - men.

May be sung as a canon.

This offertory acclamation was created by a Mennonite musician and draws on the simplicity and strength of a tradition accustomed to unaccompanied singing. When sung as a canon, this acclamation simultaneously voices praises of God, prayers to God, and alleluias.

TEXT and MUSIC: James E. Clemens, 2008
Text and Music © 2008 James E. Clemens

ABUNDANT BLESSINGS
Irregular

We Lift Our Voices

We Are an Offering

This praise and worship song can best be understood as reflecting on and expanding 1 Chronicles 29:14b: "For all things come of you, [O Lord,] and of your own have we given you." There are also echoes of Paul's appeal for Christians to be living sacrifices (Romans 12:1).

TEXT and MUSIC: Dwight Liles, 1984
Text and Music © 1984 Word Music, LLC

OFFERING
Irregular

711 Lord of All Good

1 Lord of all good, our gifts we bring to you;
2 We give our minds to un-der-stand your ways;
3 Fa-ther, whose boun-ty all cre-a-tion shows;

use them your ho-ly pur-pose to ful-fill,
hands, eyes, and voice to serve your great de-sign;
Christ, by whose will-ing sac-ri-fice we live;

to-kens of love and pledg-es brought a-new,
heart with the flame of your own love a-blaze,
Spir-it, from whom all life in full-ness flows:

that our whole life is of-fered to your will.
till for your glo-ry all our powers com-bine.
to you with grate-ful hearts our-selves we give.

A pastor wrote this text for a Christmas fair, which perhaps added echoes to the words "gifts" and "give" in the first two stanzas. But no hints are needed to grasp the full meaning of this hymn's final line. The text is set to a shortened form of a widely used Genevan tune.

TEXT: Albert F. Bayly, 1962, alt.
MUSIC: Genevan Psalter, 1551; adapt. from GENEVAN 124
Text © 1962 Oxford University Press

TOULON
10.10.10.10

As Those of Old Their Firstfruits Brought 712

1 As those of old their first-fruits brought of vine-yard, flock, and field
2 A world in need now sum-mons us to la-bor, love, and give,
3 In grat-i-tude and hum-ble trust we bring our best to-day,

to God, the giv-er of all good, the source of boun-teous yield,
to make our life an of-fer-ing that all may tru-ly live.
to serve your cause and share your love with all a-long life's way.

so we to-day our first-fruits bring, the wealth of this good land:
The church of Christ is call-ing us to make the dream come true:
O God who gave your-self to us in Je-sus Christ your Son,

of farm and mar-ket, shop and home, of mind and heart and hand.
a world re-deemed by Christ-like love, all life in Christ made new.
help us to give our-selves each day un-til life's work is done.

This text by a Presbyterian pastor in California expresses the conviction that being a good steward is an essential part of the Christian life, for self-giving is God's own nature. The tune is named for the village in Surrey where the arranger collected this tune in 1903.

TEXT: Frank von Christierson, 1960, alt.
MUSIC: English folk melody; arr. Ralph Vaughan Williams, 1906
Text © 1961, ren. 1989 The Hymn Society (admin. Hope Publishing Company)

FOREST GREEN
CMD

713 Touch the Earth Lightly

1 Touch the earth light - ly, use the earth gent - ly,
2 We who en - dan - ger, who cre - ate hun - ger,
3 Let there be green - ing, birth from the burn - ing,
4 God of all liv - ing, God of all lov - ing,

nour - ish the life of the world in our care:
a - gents of death for all crea - tures that live,
wa - ter that bless - es and air that is sweet,
God of the seed - ling, the snow, and the sun,

gift of great won - der, ours to sur - ren - der,
we who would fos - ter clouds of di - sas - ter,
health in God's gar - den, hope in God's chil - dren,
teach us, de - flect us, Christ re - con - nect us,

trust for the chil - dren to - mor - row will bear.
God of our plan - et, fore - stall and for - give!
re - gen - er - a - tion that peace will com - plete.
us - ing us gent - ly and mak - ing us one.

An Australian aboriginal saying opens this gentle hymn from New Zealand on the stewardship of creation. "Clouds of disaster" in the second stanza refers to the testing of nuclear devices then occurring in the Pacific Ocean, but the concern for all created things is timeless.

TEXT: Shirley Erena Murray, 1991
MUSIC: Colin Gibson, 1992
Text and Music © 1992 Hope Publishing Company

TENDERNESS
5.5.10.D

God of the Fertile Fields

714

1 God of the fer - tile fields, shap - er of
2 We would be stew - ards true, hold - ing in
3 As grows the hid - den seed to fruit that
4 God of the coun - try - side, dear to the

earth that yields our dai - ly bread: forth from your
trust from you all that you give; help us in
serves our need, so your reign grows. Let all our
Christ who died to make us one: we pledge our

boun - teous hand come gifts your love has planned,
love to share, teach us like you to care
toil be used, no gift of yours a - bused,
lives a - new in faith - ful love to you.

that all in ev - ery land be clothed and fed.
for peo - ple ev - ery - where, that all may live.
no hum - ble task re - fused your love be - stows.
Guide all we say and do. Your will be done.

Greater awareness has enlarged Christian stewardship to develop new dimensions of concern for people in all parts of the world. Because we believe that it is God's will that the gifts we have received should be shared, this hymn concludes with that phrase from the Lord's Prayer.

TEXT: Georgia Harkness, 1955, alt.
MUSIC: Felice de Giardini, 1769, alt.
Text © 1955, ren. 1983 The Hymn Society (admin. Hope Publishing Company)

ITALIAN HYMN
6.6.4.6.6.6.4

715 The Earth Belongs to God Alone

1 The earth be - longs to God a - lone; hard
2 The fer - tile ground through years of toil has
3 All life be - longs to God a - lone, in
4 Till God en - dows the earth once more with

clay, rich soil, fine sand. Give thanks wher - ev - er
cried for Sab - bath rest— a time of peace for
wil - der - ness and fields. From fal - low land, or
E - den's state of grace, may we en - deav - or

food is grown on bor - rowed ho - ly land.
worn - out soil so land can be re - freshed.
plowed and sown, God gives the good it yields.
to re - store all land as sa - cred space.

This text emerged from a study of the attention in Levitical laws to the well-being of the land, especially by calling for fallow periods, or "land sabbaths," to preserve the soil. 2 Chronicles 36:21 even suggests that the Babylonian exile may have resulted from abusing the land.

God, Whose Giving Knows No Ending 716

Capo 3: (D) (Bm) (G)
F Dm B♭

1 God, whose giv - ing knows no end - ing, from your rich and
2 Skills and time are ours for press - ing toward the goals of
3 Trea - sure, too, you have en - trust - ed, gain through powers your

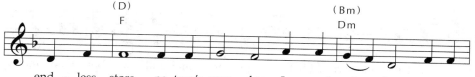

(D) (Bm)
F Dm

end - less store, na - ture's won - der, Je - sus' wis - dom, cost - ly
Christ, your Son: all at peace in health and free - dom, rac - es
grace con - ferred: ours to use for home and kin - dred, and to

(G) (D) (A)
B♭ F C

cross, grave's shat - tered door: gift - ed by you, we turn
joined, the church made one. Now di - rect our dai - ly
spread the gos - pel word. O - pen wide our hands in

(Bm) (F♯m) (Bm) (G) (A) (D)
Dm Am Dm B♭ C F

to you, of - fering up our - selves in praise; thank - ful song shall
la - bor, lest we strive for self a - lone. Born with tal - ents,
shar - ing, as we heed Christ's age - less call, heal - ing, teach - ing,

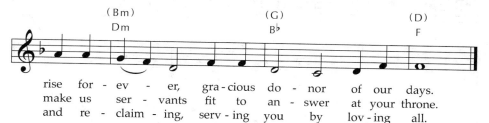

(Bm) (G) (D)
Dm B♭ F

rise for - ev - er, gra - cious do - nor of our days.
make us ser - vants fit to an - swer at your throne.
and re - claim - ing, serv - ing you by lov - ing all.

Guitar chords do not correspond with keyboard harmony.

This text on stewardship was one of about 450 submissions in a search for such hymns conducted by the Hymn Society of America in 1961. These words are well grounded by their musical setting, an early American shape note tune named for a Baptist church in Harris County, Georgia.

TEXT: Robert L. Edwards, 1961, alt.
MUSIC: *The Sacred Harp*, 1844; harm. James H. Wood, 1958
Text © 1961, ren. 1989 The Hymn Society (admin. Hope Publishing Company)
Music Harm. © 1958, ren. 1986 Broadman Press (admin. Music Services)

BEACH SPRING
8.7.8.7.D

717 For the Life That You Have Given

For the life that you have giv-en, for the love in

Christ made known, with these fruits of time and la-bor, with these

gifts that are your own: here we of-fer, Lord, our prais-es;

heart and mind and strength we bring; give us grace to

love and serve you, liv-ing what we pray and sing.

The text was commissioned in 1987 by Fourth Presbyterian Church in Chicago, where it has continued to be used each Sunday as the offertory response. The triune activity of God as Creator (line 1), Savior (line 2), and Sustainer (line 7) enables and inspires our thanks and praise.

TEXT: Carl P. Daw Jr., 1987
MUSIC: Leavitt's *Christian Lyre*, 1830/31
Text © 1990 Hope Publishing Company

PLEADING SAVIOR
8.7.8.7.D
(alternate harmonization, 23)

Take Up Your Cross, the Savior Said 718

1 Take up your cross, the Sav - ior said, if
2 Take up your cross; let not its weight fill
3 Take up your cross; heed not the shame, and
4 Take up your cross, then, in Christ's strength, and

you would my dis - ci - ple be; take up your cross with
your weak spir - it with a - larm; Christ's strength shall bear your
let your fool - ish pride be still; the Lord for you ac -
calm - ly ev - ery dan - ger brave: it guides you to a -

will - ing heart, and hum - bly fol - low af - ter me.
spir - it up and brace your heart and nerve your arm.
cept - ed death up - on a cross, on Cal - vary's hill.
bun - dant life and leads to vic - tory o'er the grave.

Written by a nineteen-year-old in Connecticut, this challenging text has been widely printed on both sides of the Atlantic. It is strengthened by its resolute repetition of the same four words at the beginning of each stanza and by the appropriately stark shape note tune.

TEXT: Charles William Everest, 1833, alt.
MUSIC: Attr. Freeman Lewis, 1814; harm. John Leon Hooker, 1984
Music Harm. © 1984 John Leon Hooker

BOURBON
LM

719 Come, Labor On

Capo 1: (G) (C)   (G) (Em) (C)   (G)   (C)   (D)   (G)

1 Come, la - bor on. Who dares stand i - dle on the har - vest plain
2 Come, la - bor on. Claim the high call - ing an - gels can - not share;
3 Come, la - bor on. Cast off all gloom - y doubt and faith - less fear!
4 Come, la - bor on. No time for rest, till glows the west - ern sky,

while all   a - round us waves the gold - en grain? And   to each
to young and old the gos - pel glad - ness bear.   Re - deem the
No arm so weak but may do ser - vice here. Though fee - ble
till the long shad - ows o'er our path - way lie,   and   a glad

ser - vant does the Mas - ter say, "Go work   to - day."
time; its hours too swift - ly fly. The night   draws nigh.
a - gents, may we all ful - fill God's righ - teous will.
sound comes with the set - ting sun, "Well done,   well   done!"

Guitar chords do not correspond with keyboard harmony.

Using Jesus' harvest imagery in John 4:35–38 and Matthew 9:37–38 / Luke 10:2, this urgent text sounds a compelling call to Christian service. The words gain energy from the strong unison tune in the English cathedral style, whose name echoes the Benedictine motto "Prayer is work."

TEXT: Jane Laurie Borthwick, 1859; rev. 1863, alt.
MUSIC: Thomas Tertius Noble, 1918

ORA LABORA
4.10.10.10.4

Jesus Calls Us

1 Je - sus calls us: o'er the tu - mult of our
2 Je - sus calls us from the wor - ship of the
3 In our joys and in our sor - rows, days of
4 Je - sus calls us: by thy mer - cies, Sav - ior,

life's wild, rest - less sea; day by day his sweet voice
vain world's gold - en store, from each i - dol that would
toil and hours of ease, still he calls, in cares and
may we hear thy call, give our hearts to thine o -

sound - eth say - ing, "Chris - tian, fol - low me."
keep us, say - ing, "Chris - tian, love me more."
plea - sures, "Chris - tian, love me more than these."
be - dience, serve and love thee best of all.

Like many hymns that adults have come to cherish, this text based on Jesus' calling of the disciple Andrew was written for a 19th-century collection of hymns for children. The popular tune used here was composed for these words more than a quarter of a century later.

TEXT: Cecil Frances Alexander, 1852
MUSIC: William H. Jude, 1887

GALILEE
8.7.8.7

721 Lord, You Have Come to the Lakeshore

Tú has venido a la orilla

1 Lord, you have come to the lake-shore look-ing
2 You know so well my pos-ses-sions; my boat
3 You need my hands, full of car - ing, through my
4 You, who have fished oth - er o - ceans, ev - er

nei - ther for wealth-y nor wise ones; you on - ly
car - ries no gold and no weap - ons; ? you will
la - bors to give oth-ers rest and con - stant
longed for by souls who are wait - ing, my lov - ing

asked me to fol - low hum - bly.
find there my nets and la - bor.
love that keeps on lov - ing.
friend, as thus you call me:

Refrain / Estribillo

O Lord, with your eyes you have searched me, and while
Se - ñor, me has mi - ra - do a los o - jos, son - ri -

smil - ing have spo - ken my name; now my
en - do has di - cho mi nom - bre, en la a -

This is one of the most popular songs to emerge from the 1970s revival of religious song in Spain. It asks singers to become like the fishermen who left boats and nets to follow Jesus, first as disciples learning his way of love, then as apostles carrying that love to others.

TEXT: Cesáreo Gabaráin, 1979; English trans. Gertrude Suppe, George Lockwood,
and Raquel Gutiérrez-Achon, 1988, alt.
MUSIC: Cesáreo Gabaráin, 1979; harm. Skinner Chávez-Melo, 1987
Text, English Trans., and Music © 1979, 1987, 1989 Cesáreo Gabaráin (Published by OCP)
Music Harm. © 1987 OCP

PESCADOR DE HOMBRES
8.10.10 with refrain

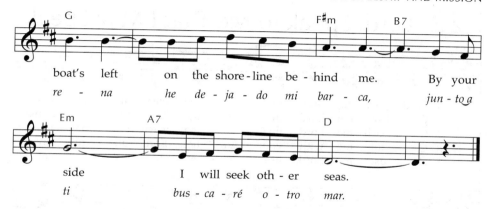

boat's left on the shore-line be-hind me. By your

re - na he de - ja - do mi bar - ca, jun - to a

side I will seek oth - er seas.

ti bus - ca - ré o - tro mar.

SPANISH

1 *Tú has venido a la orilla,*
  no has buscado ni a sabios, ni a ricos,
  tan sólo quieres que yo te siga.   Estribillo

2 *Tú sabes bien lo que tengo:*
  en mi barca no hay oro ni espadas,
  tan solo redes y mi trabajo.   Estribillo

3 *Tú necesitas mis manos,*
  mi cansancio que a otros descanse,
  amor que quiera seguir amando.   Estribillo

4 *Tú, pescador de otros lagos,*
  ansia eterna de almas que esperan,
  amigo bueno, que así me llamas.   Estribillo

722 Lord, Speak to Me That I May Speak

1 Lord, speak to me that I may speak in liv - ing
2 O lead me, Lord, that I may lead the wan-dering
3 O teach me, Lord, that I may teach the pre - cious
4 O fill me with your full - ness, Lord, un - til my
5 O use me, Lord, use e - ven me, just as you

ech - oes of your tone. As you have sought, so
and the wa - vering feet. O feed me, Lord, that
truths which you im - part. And wing my words that
ver - y heart o'er - flow in kin - dling thought and
will, and when, and where un - til your bless - ed

let me seek your err - ing chil - dren, lost and lone.
I may feed your hun-gering ones with man - na sweet.
they may reach the hid - den depths of man - y a heart.
glow - ing word, your love to tell, your praise to show.
face I see, your rest, your joy, your glo - ry share.

Two great truths inform this text: first, that the testimony of experience is powerful and persuasive; and second, that no one should venture to minister on one's own strength rather than God's. The tune reflects a 19th-century practice of adapting piano pieces as hymn tunes.

TEXT: Frances Ridley Havergal, 1872, alt.
MUSIC: Robert Schumann, 1839, alt.

CANONBURY
LM

Lord, Speak for Me, for I Am Yours 723
(Psalm 26)

1 Lord, speak for me, for I am yours, and
2 I do not sit with those who cheat, the
3 I wash my hands in in - no - cence and
4 I love your house, O might - y Lord; I
5 I walk in my in - teg - ri - ty; re -

test my mind and heart. I walk with stead - y
false who love pre - tense. I do not fol - low
seek your al - tar, Lord, and, sing - ing there with
love the ho - ly place where you in your great
deem me, Lord, in grace. Se - cure - ly now I

trust in you, nor from your ways de - part.
where they go, nor count them as my friends.
thank - ful voice, your might - y works re - cord.
glo - ry dwell; you vis - it us in grace.
stand, O Lord; in wor - ship I bring praise.

Despite the concerns it shares with Psalm 1, Psalm 26 is not a declaration of blessing on those who live faithfully but the prayer of such a person to be vindicated by God. There is no prideful desire to seem holier than other people, only to appear before God without pretense.

TEXT: Marie J. Post, 1983
MUSIC: Leo Sowerby, 1962
Text © 1987 Faith Alive Christian Resources
Music © 1964 Abingdon Press (admin. The Copyright Company)

PERRY
CM

724 O Jesus, I Have Promised

1 O Je - sus, I have prom - ised to serve thee to the end;
2 O let me feel thee near me! The world is ev - er near:
3 O let me hear thee speak - ing in ac - cents clear and still,
4 O Je - sus, thou hast prom - ised to all who fol - low thee

be thou for - ev - er near me, my Mas - ter and my friend;
I see the sights that daz - zle; the tempt - ing sounds I hear.
a - bove the storms of pas - sion, the mur - murs of self - will;
that where thou art in glo - ry there shall thy ser - vant be.

I shall not fear the bat - tle if thou art by my side,
My foes are ev - er near me, a - round me and with - in;
O speak to re - as - sure me, to has - ten or con - trol;
And, Je - sus, I have prom - ised to serve thee to the end;

nor wan - der from the path - way if thou wilt be my guide.
but, Je - sus, draw thou near - er and shield my soul from sin.
O speak, and make me lis - ten, thou guard - ian of my soul.
O give me grace to fol - low, my Mas - ter and my friend.

Written to highlight the promises made by the author's daughter and two sons at their confirmation, this
text equally well recalls the promises of discipleship made in Baptism and in the Reaffirmation of the
Baptismal Covenant. The tune was written for a text now unused.

TEXT: John Ernest Bode, 1866, alt.
MUSIC: Arthur Henry Mann, 1881

ANGEL'S STORY
7.6.7.6.D
(alternate tune: NYLAND, 725)

O Jesus, I Have Promised

1 O Je-sus, I have prom-ised to serve you to the end;
2 O let me feel you near me! The world is ev-er near:
3 O let me hear you speak-ing in ac-cents clear and still,
4 O Je-sus, you have prom-ised to all who fol-low you

be now and al-ways near me, my Mas-ter and my friend;
I see the sights that daz-zle; the tempt-ing sounds I hear.
a-bove the storms of pas-sion, the mur-murs of self-will;
that where you are in glo-ry your ser-vant shall be too.

I shall not fear the bat-tle if you are by my side,
My foes are ev-er near me, a-round me and with-in;
O speak to re-as-sure me, to has-ten or con-trol;
And, Je-sus, I have prom-ised to serve you to the end;

nor wan-der from the path-way if you will be my guide.
but, Je-sus, draw still near-er and shield my soul from sin.
O speak, and make me lis-ten, true guard-ian of my soul.
now give me grace to fol-low, my Mas-ter and my friend.

Guitar chords do not correspond with keyboard harmony.

This hymn written by an Anglican clergyman for the confirmation of his children in Victorian times appears here in updated language that may help to make its challenging commitments more immediate. The tune is named for the province in Finland from which it comes.

TEXT: John Ernest Bode, 1866, alt.
MUSIC: Finnish folk melody; adapt. and harm. David Evans, 1927
Music Adapt. and Harm.© 1927 Oxford University Press

NYLAND
7.6.7.6.D
(alternate tune: ANGEL'S STORY, 724)

726 Will You Come and Follow Me

The Summons

1 "Will you come and fol-low me if I but call your name?
2 "Will you leave your-self be-hind if I but call your name?
3 "Will you let the blind-ed see if I but call your name?
4 "Will you love the 'you' you hide if I but call your name?
5 Lord, your sum-mons ech-oes true when you but call my name.

Will you go where you don't know and nev-er be the same?
Will you care for cruel and kind and nev-er be the same?
Will you set the pris-oners free and nev-er be the same?
Will you quell the fear in-side and nev-er be the same?
Let me turn and fol-low you and nev-er be the same.

Will you let my love be shown; will you let my name be known;
Will you risk the hos-tile stare should your life at-tract or scare?
Will you kiss the lep-er clean, and do such as this un-seen,
Will you use the faith you've found to re-shape the world a-round,
In your com-pa-ny I'll go where your love and foot-steps show.

will you let my life be grown in you and you in me?"
Will you let me an-swer prayer in you and you in me?"
and ad-mit to what I mean in you and you in me?"
through my sight and touch and sound in you and you in me?"
Thus I'll move and live and grow in you and you in me.

The first four stanzas of this ballad-like hymn are understood to be in the voice of Christ, with the fifth reflecting the individual singer's response. Created for this traditional Scottish tune, the text was written to mark the conclusion of a youth volunteer's time of ministry.

TEXT: John L. Bell and Graham Maule, 1987
MUSIC: Scottish melody; arr. John L. Bell, 1987
Text and Music Arr. © 1987 WGRG, Iona Community (admin. GIA Publications, Inc.)

KELVINGROVE
13.13.7.7.13

Will You Let Me Be Your Servant 727
The Servant Song

1,6 Will you let me be your ser-vant, let me
2 We are pil-grims on a jour-ney; we're to-
3 I will hold the Christ-light for you in the
4 I will weep when you are weep-ing; when you
5 When we sing to God in heav-en, we shall

be as Christ to you? Pray that I may have the
geth-er on the road. We are here to help each
night-time of your fear. I will hold my hand out
laugh I'll laugh with you. I will share your joy and
find such har-mo-ny, born of all we've known to-

grace to let you be my ser - vant too.
oth-er walk the mile and bear the load.
to you, speak the peace you long to hear.
sor-row till we've seen this jour - ney through.
geth-er of Christ's love and ag - o - ny.

(repeat stanza 1)

The opening and closing stanza expresses the essence of this folk-style song about the mutuality of servant ministry: those who serve must also be willing to be served. This is what Christ intended when he commanded the disciples to "wash one another's feet" (John 13:14).

TEXT: Richard Gillard, 1977, alt.
MUSIC: Richard Gillard, 1977; arr. Betty Pulkingham
Text and Music © 1977 Universal Music - Brentwood Benson Publishing

THE SERVANT SONG
8.7.8.7

728 Somebody's Knocking at Your Door

Some-bod-y's knock-ing at your door; some-bod-y's

knock-ing at your door; O sin-ner, why don't you

an-swer? Some-bod-y's knock-ing at your door.

1 Knocks like Je-sus.
2 Can't you hear him? Some-bod-y's knock-ing at your
3 An-swer Je-sus.

The description of the Son of Man as standing at the door and knocking (Revelation 3:20) has given rise to many visual and verbal representations of that figure. This African American spiritual uses its repeated phrases to imitate knocking and to give immediacy to this encounter.

TEXT: African American spiritual
MUSIC: African American spiritual; arr. Joy F. Patterson, 1989
Music Arr. © 1990 Joy F. Patterson

SOMEBODY'S KNOCKIN'
Irregular

729 Lord, I Want to Be a Christian

1 Lord, I want to be a Chris-tian in my heart, in my heart;
2 Lord, I want to be more lov-ing in my heart, in my heart;
3 Lord, I want to be more ho-ly in my heart, in my heart;
4 Lord, I want to be like Je-sus in my heart, in my heart;

Lord, I want to be a Chris-tian in my heart.
Lord, I want to be more lov-ing in my heart.
Lord, I want to be more ho-ly in my heart.
Lord, I want to be like Je-sus in my heart.

In my heart, in my heart,
In my heart, in my heart,

Lord, I want to be a Chris-tian in my heart.
Lord, I want to be more lov-ing in my heart.
Lord, I want to be more ho-ly in my heart.
Lord, I want to be like Je-sus in my heart.

Through its recurring phrase, "in my heart," this poignant African American spiritual expresses the desire that our professed faith will not be superficial or hypocritical but will permeate the very center of our being, so that we may truly be the people God calls us to be.

TEXT and MUSIC: African American spiritual

I WANT TO BE A CHRISTIAN
Irregular

I Sing a Song of the Saints of God 730

1 I sing a song of the saints of God, pa - tient and brave and true, who toiled and fought and lived and died for the Lord they loved and knew. And one was a doc - tor, and one was a queen, and one was a shep - herd - ess on the green: they were all of them saints of God, and I mean, God help - ing, to be one too.

2 They loved their Lord so dear, so dear, and God's love made them strong; and they fol - lowed the right, for Je - sus' sake, the whole of their good lives long. And one was a sol - dier, and one was a priest, and one was slain by a fierce wild beast: and there's not an - y rea - son, no, not the least, why I should - n't be one too.

3 They lived not on - ly in a - ges past; there are hun - dreds of thou - sands still; the world is bright with the joy - ous saints who love to do Je - sus' will. You can meet them in school, or in lanes, or at sea, in church, or in trains, or in shops, or at tea; for the saints of God are just folk like me, and I mean to be one too.

Guitar chords do not correspond with keyboard harmony.

Despite the quaintness of some of the language in this text, it has an important message to communicate about the down-to-earth ordinariness of the holy people of God at all times and places. The tune name honors the island in Vermont's Lake Champlain where the composer lived.

TEXT: Lesbia Scott, 1929, alt.
MUSIC: John Henry Hopkins, 1940
Text © 1929 Lesbia Scott (admin. Church Publishing, Inc.)

GRAND ISLE
Irregular

731
Give Thanks for Those Whose Faith Is Firm

1 Give thanks for those whose faith is firm when all around seems bleak: on God's good prom-ise they re-ly, so while they live and when they die how force-ful-ly they speak: the strong, who once were weak!

2 Give thanks for those whose hope is clear, be-yond mere mor-tal sight: who seek the cit-y God has planned, the true, e-ter-nal prom-ised land, and steer on toward that light, a bea-con ev-er bright.

3 Give thanks for those whose love is pure, a spar-kling pre-cious stone: they show by what they say and do an in-ward beau-ty, warm and true, for God's con-cerns they own: God's love through them is known.

4 Give thanks for saints of a-ges past and saints a-live to-day: though of-ten by this world de-spised, their hearts by God are rich-ly prized. Give thanks that we may say we share their pil-grim way.

Guitar chords do not correspond with keyboard harmony.

The first three stanzas of this text are organized around the three great virtues—faith, hope, and love—mentioned in 1 Corinthians 13:13. These have indeed been the marks of the faithful people of God always and everywhere, and the final stanza sums up our gratitude for them.

TEXT: Martin E. Leckebusch, 1998
MUSIC: C. Hubert H. Parry, 1888
Text © 2003 Kevin Mayhew Ltd.

REPTON
8.6.8.8.6.6

Rejoice in God's Saints

732

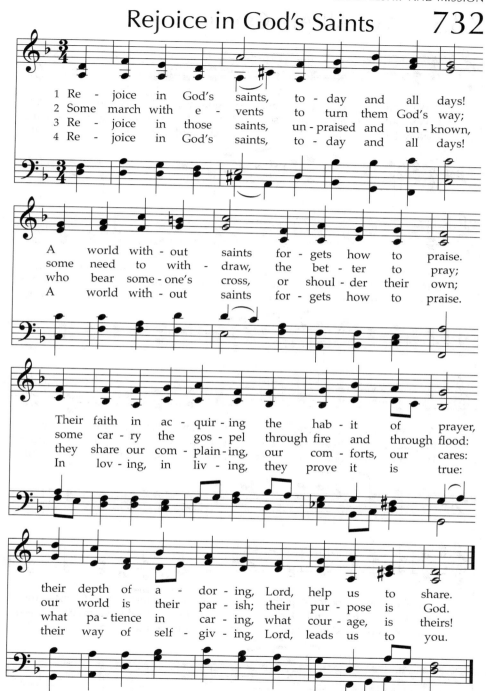

1 Re - joice in God's saints, to - day and all days!
2 Some march with e - vents to turn them God's way;
3 Re - joice in those saints, un - praised and un - known,
4 Re - joice in God's saints, to - day and all days!

A world with - out saints for - gets how to praise.
some need to with - draw, the bet - ter to pray;
who bear some - one's cross, or shoul - der their own;
A world with - out saints for - gets how to praise.

Their faith in ac - quir - ing the hab - it of prayer,
some car - ry the gos - pel through fire and through flood:
they share our com - plain - ing, our com - forts, our cares:
In lov - ing, in liv - ing, they prove it is true:

their depth of a - dor - ing, Lord, help us to share.
our world is their par - ish; their pur - pose is God.
what pa - tience in car - ing, what cour - age, is theirs!
their way of self - giv - ing, Lord, leads us to you.

A more generally applicable version of a text written for the 600th anniversary of Julian of Norwich's *Revelations of Divine Love* in 1973, this hymn uses a tune created for the Scotsman William Kethe's paraphrase of Psalm 104, which appeared in several 16th-century psalters.

TEXT: Fred Pratt Green, 1973; rev. 1977
MUSIC: Ravenscroft's *Whole Booke of Psalmes*, 1621; harm. Alfred V. Fedak, 1997
Text © 1973, 1980 Hope Publishing Company
Music Harm. © 1997 Selah Publishing Co., Inc.

OLD 104TH
10.10.11.11
(alternate tune: LAUDATE DOMINUM)

733 We All Are One in Mission

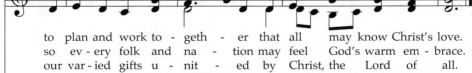

1 We all are one in mis - sion; we all are one in call,
2 We all are called for ser - vice to wit - ness in God's name.
3 Now let us be u - nit - ed and let our song be heard.

our var - ied gifts u - nit - ed by Christ, the Lord of all.
Our min - is - tries are dif - ferent; our pur - pose is the same:
Now let us be a ves - sel for God's re - deem - ing word.

A sin - gle, great com - mis - sion com - pels us from a - bove
to touch the lives of oth - ers by God's sur - pris - ing grace,
We all are one in mis - sion; we all are one in call,

to plan and work to - geth - er that all may know Christ's love.
so ev - ery folk and na - tion may feel God's warm em - brace.
our var - ied gifts u - nit - ed by Christ, the Lord of all.

A Lutheran pastor wrote this text in response to a bishop's letter that said, "Our mission is to touch the lives of others with Christ's love." This theme is made stronger by recognizing that shared purposes do not require the denial of diversity but are enriched by it.

TEXT: Rusty Edwards, 1985, alt.
MUSIC: Memmingen ms., 17th cent.; harm. George Ratcliffe Woodward, 1904
Text © 1986 Hope Publishing Company

ES FLOG EIN KLEINS WALDVÖGELEIN
7.6.7.6.D

Hope of the World

1 Hope of the world, thou Christ of great com - pas - sion:
2 Hope of the world, God's gift from high - est heav - en,
3 Hope of the world, a - foot on dust - y high - ways,
4 Hope of the world, who by thy cross didst save us
5 Hope of the world, O Christ, o'er death vic - to - rious,

speak to our fear - ful hearts by con - flict rent;
bring - ing to hun - gry souls the bread of life:
show - ing to wan - dering souls the path of light:
from death and deep de - spair, from sin and guilt:
who by this sign didst con - quer grief and pain:

save us, thy peo - ple, from con - sum - ing pas - sion,
still let thy Spir - it un - to us be giv - en
walk thou be - side us lest the tempt - ing by - ways
we ren - der back the love thy mer - cy gave us;
we would be faith - ful to thy gos - pel glo - rious;

who by our own false hopes and aims are spent.
to heal earth's wounds and end our bit - ter strife.
lure us a - way from thee to end - less night.
take thou our lives and use them as thou wilt.
thou art our Lord! Thou dost for - ev - er reign!

This winning entry by a groundbreaking woman theologian was selected from over five hundred others in a search for a hymn to be used at the Second Assembly of the World Council of Churches in Evanston, Illinois, in October 1954. The theme of the assembly was "Jesus Christ, Hope of the World."

TEXT: Georgia Harkness, 1954
MUSIC: Genevan Psalter, 1551
Text © 1954, ren. 1982 The Hymn Society (admin. Hope Publishing Company)

DONNE SECOURS
11.10.11.10

735 I Need Thee Every Hour

1 I need thee ev-ery hour, most gra - cious Lord;
2 I need thee ev-ery hour; stay thou near by;
3 I need thee ev-ery hour; teach me thy will,
4 I need thee ev-ery hour, Most Ho - ly One;

no ten - der voice like thine can peace af - ford.
temp - ta - tions lose their power when thou art nigh.
and thy rich prom - is - es in me ful - fill.
O make me thine in - deed, thou bless - ed Son.

Refrain

I need thee, O I need thee, ev - ery hour I need thee!

O bless me now, my Sav - ior— I come to thee!

Encouraged by her pastor in Brooklyn, New York, the author of this text wrote over four hundred hymn texts. This is the only one to receive wide use, but it has been translated into many languages. Her pastor composed this tune and, with her consent, added the text of the refrain.

TEXT: Annie S. Hawks, 1872; ref., Robert Lowry, 1872
MUSIC: Robert Lowry, 1872

NEED
6.4.6.4 with refrain

I Want to Be as Close to You 736

1 I want to be as close to you as
2 I want to be as close to you as
3 I want to be as close to you as
4 You want to be as close to me as
5 Like Mar - y, John, and Mag - da - lene, make

she who gave you birth. Christ Je - sus, let my
was be - lov - ed John. Christ, let me fol - low
Mag - da - lene who went, pro - claim - ing news of
moth - er, broth - er, friend. Christ, keep me faith - ful
us dis - ci - ples true. Like moth - er, broth - er,

"yes," like hers, bring bless - ings on our earth.
where you lead, by trust and friend - ship drawn.
death's de - feat, your first a - pos - tle sent.
to your love, a love that has no end.
sis - ter, friend, Christ, keep us close to you.

Guitar chords do not correspond with keyboard harmony.

This text centers on three significant people in Christ's earthly life, Mary his mother, John the beloved disciple, and Mary Magdalene, the first witness to his Resurrection. With these models to guide us, we can learn much about how to live out our desire to be near to Christ.

TEXT: Delores Dufner, OSB, 2006; rev. 2009
MUSIC: Hal H. Hopson, 1985
Text © 2006, 2009 Delores Dufner, OSB
Music © 1985 Hope Publishing Company

DAVIDSON
CM

737 Lord Jesus, You Shall Be My Song

Jésus, je voudrais te chanter

1 Lord Je - sus, you shall be my song as I jour - ney;
2 Lord Je - sus, I'll praise you as long as I jour - ney.
3 As long as I live, Je - sus, make me your ser - vant,
4 I fear in the dark and the doubt of my jour - ney;

I'll tell ev - ery - bod - y a - bout you wher - ev - er I go:
May all of my joy be a faith - ful re - flec - tion of you.
to car - ry your cross and to share all your bur - dens and tears.
but cour - age will come with the sound of your steps by my side.

you a - lone are our life and our peace and our love.
May the earth and the sea and the sky join my song.
For you saved me by giv - ing your bod - y and blood.
And with all of the fam - ily you saved by your love,

Originally created in French, this text reflects the ministry of a Roman Catholic religious community, the Little Sisters of Jesus, who work with people on the margins of society. This hymn is also beloved by the Ark (*L'Arche*) communities who minister to adults with disabilities.

TEXT: Les Petites Soeurs de Jésus and L'Arche Community, 1961; English trans. Stephen Somerville, 1970
MUSIC: Les Petites Soeurs de Jésus and L'Arche Community, 1961
Text and Music © Les Petites Soeurs de Jésus (admin. Augsburg Fortress)
English Trans.© 1970 Stephen Somerville (admin. Augsburg Fortress)

LES PETITES SOEURS
12.14.12.12

Lord Je - sus, you shall be my song as I jour - ney.
Lord Je - sus, I'll praise you as long as I jour - ney.
As long as I live, Je - sus, make me your ser - vant.
we'll sing to your dawn at the end of our jour - ney.

FRENCH

1 Jésus, je voudrais te chanter sur ma route;
Jésus, je voudrais t'annoncer à mes voisins partout,
car toi seul es la vie et la paix et l'amour:
Jésus, je voudrais te chanter sur ma route.

2 Jésus, je voudrais te louer sur ma route;
Jésus, je voudrais que ma voix soit l'écho de ta joie,
et que chante la terre et que chante le ciel;
Jésus, je voudrais te louer sur ma route.

3 Jésus, je voudrais te servir sur ma route;
Jésus, je voudrais partager les souffrances de ta croix,
car tu livres pour moi et ton corps et ton sang;
Jésus, je voudrais te servir sur ma route.

4 Jésus, je voudrais tout au long de ma route
entendre tes pas résonner dans la nuit près de moi,
jusqu'à l'aube du jour où ton peuple sauvé,
Jésus, chantera ton retour sur ma route.

738 O Master, Let Me Walk with Thee

1 O Master, let me walk with thee
2 Help me the slow of heart to move
3 Teach me thy patience, still with thee
4 In hope that sends a shining ray

in lowly paths of service free;
by some clear, winning word of love;
in closer, dearer company,
far down the future's broadening way;

tell me thy secret; help me bear the
teach me the wayward feet to stay, and
in work that keeps faith sweet and strong, in
in peace that only thou canst give, with

strain of toil, the fret of care.
guide them in the homeward way.
trust that triumphs over wrong.
thee, O Master, let me live.

In honestly admitting the limits of human ability, this prayerful hymn does not seek a sense of God's presence for self-comfort but for strength and companionship in pursuing the tasks that God sets before us. The author specifically chose this tune to accompany his words.

TEXT: Washington Gladden, 1879
MUSIC: Henry Percy Smith, 1874

MARYTON
LM

O for a Closer Walk with God 739

1 O for a clos - er walk with God, a
2 Re - turn, O ho - ly Dove, re - turn, sweet
3 The dear - est i - dol I have known, what -
4 So shall my walk be close with God, calm

calm and heaven - ly frame, a light to shine up -
mes - sen - ger of rest! I hate the sins that
e'er that i - dol be, help me to tear it
and se - rene my frame; so pur - er light shall

on the road that leads me to the Lamb!
made thee mourn and drove thee from my breast.
from thy throne, and wor - ship on - ly thee.
mark the road that leads me to the Lamb.

Merely longing for a restored relationship with God is not enough; real repentance requires amendment of life (stanza 3). The similarity of stanzas 1 and 4 suggests both continuity and improvement. This tune was one of the new common tunes in the Scottish Psalter of 1635.

TEXT: William Cowper, 1769
MUSIC: Scottish Psalter, 1635; harm. *The English Hymnal*, 1906, alt.

CAITHNESS
CM

740 Lead Me, Guide Me

Guitar chords do not correspond with keyboard harmony.

This African American gospel hymn can well be understood as an updated adaptation of Psalm 5:8, with the "enemies" of the psalm treated as the pressures and temptations of daily life. As with the psalms, the "I" here is understood to express a shared communal experience.

TEXT: Doris Akers, 1953
MUSIC: Doris Akers, 1953; arr. Richard Smallwood
Text and Music © 1953, ren. Doris Akers (admin. Chappell & Co., Inc./Alfred Publishing Co., Inc.)

LEAD ME, GUIDE ME
Irregular

Guide My Feet

1 Guide my feet while I run this race;
(yes, my Lord!)
guide my feet while I run this race;
(yes, my Lord!)
guide my feet while I run this race, for I
don't want to run this race in vain! (race in vain!)

2 Hold my hand ...
3 Stand by me ...
4 I'm your child ...

5 Search my heart ...
6 Guide my feet ...

This African American spiritual is based on the imagery of "the race that is set before us" in Hebrews 12:1–2. Its call-and-response structure allows for the improvisation and addition of stanzas related to an athletic metaphor that is as vivid today as it was centuries ago.

TEXT: African American spiritual
MUSIC: African American spiritual; harm. Wendell P. Whalum, c. 1984
Music Harm. © Estate of Wendell P. Whalum

GUIDE MY FEET
8.8.8.10

742 We Will Walk with God

Sizohamba naye

We will walk with God, my broth-ers; we will walk with God.
Si - zo-ham - ba na - ye, wo wo wo, si - zo-ham - ba na - ye.

We will walk with God, my sis-ters; we will walk with God.
Si - zo-ham - ba na - ye, wo wo wo, si - zo-ham - ba na - ye.

We will go re - joic-ing till the king-dom has come.
Ngom-hla wen-ja - bu - la, si - zo-ham - ba na - ye.

We will go re - joic-ing till the king-dom has come.
Ngom-hla wen-ja - bu - la, si - zo-ham - ba na - ye.

With its themes of commitment and sending, this energetic song from Swaziland works well for ending a time together, either an occasion of worship or some other gathering. The simple tune does not require supporting instruments but invites percussion and improvisation.

TEXT: Swaziland text; English trans. John L. Bell, 2002
MUSIC: Swaziland melody; arr. John L. Bell, 2008
English Trans. © 2002 WGRG, Iona Community (admin. GIA Publications, Inc.)
Music Arr. © 2008 WGRG, Iona Community (admin. GIA Publications, Inc.)

SIZOHAMBA NAYE
Irregular

O God, You Are My God

Step by Step

743

O God, you are my God, and I will ev-er praise you. O God, you are my God, and I will ev-er praise you. I will seek you in the morn - ing, and I will learn to walk in your ways. And step by step you'll lead me, and I will fol - low you all of my days.

Though this refrain from a longer song is not a paraphrase of any particular psalm, the language in the first six lines has definite scriptural overtones (such as Psalms 31:14, 5:3; Deuteronomy 26:17). The final two lines sound more spontaneous and lead to a confident conclusion.

TEXT and MUSIC: David Strasser (Beaker), 1991

STEP BY STEP
Irregular

744 Arise, Your Light Is Come!

1 A - rise, your light is come! The Spir - it's call o - bey;
2 A - rise, your light is come! Fling wide the pris - on door;
3 A - rise, your light is come! All you in sor - row born,
4 A - rise, your light is come! The moun - tains burst in song!

show forth the glo - ry of your God, which shines on you to - day.
pro - claim the cap - tives' lib - er - ty, good ti - dings to the poor.
bind up the bro - ken-heart-ed ones and com - fort those who mourn.
Rise up like ea - gles on the wing; God's power will make us strong.

Echoing imagery from Isaiah 61:1–2 and other passages, this text was created as an inclusive-language
alternative to an older hymn using this late 19th-century tune. Because it is a song of encouragement rather
than a song of praise, it is not directed to God but to people.

TEXT: Ruth Duck, 1974
MUSIC: William H. Walter, 1894
Text © 1992 GIA Publications, Inc.

FESTAL SONG
SM
(this tune in a lower key, 815)

745 Now Go in Joy

Now go in joy to spread the Word till all peo - ple have

heard: God em - brac - es all! Fol - low, then, the dis -

*May be sung as a canon.

With its themes of bearing witness in the world, this lively sending song works especially well when sung in
canon. The tune name refers to a street parade with music that occurs in many Bahamian towns on Boxing
Day (December 26), New Year's Day, and sometimes in the summer.

TEXT: Mary Louise Bringle, 2004
MUSIC: Caribbean folk melody; arr. Jorge Lockward, 2001
Text © 2006 GIA Publications, Inc.
Music Arr. © 2001 Jorge Lockward

JUNKANOO
Irregular

Send Me, Jesus

Thuma mina

746

Because such a sending song has a place in many Christian traditions, several versions of both this text (based on Isaiah 6:8) and tune can be found throughout South Africa. When desired, additional English stanzas can be improvised in alternation with the original Zulu text.

TEXT: South African; English trans. *Freedom Is Coming*, 1984
MUSIC: South African; arr. *Freedom Is Coming*, 1984
Text and Music © 1984 Walton Music Corp.

THUMA MINA
4.4.4.3

747 The Lord Now Sends Us Forth

Enviado soy de Dios

The Lord now sends us forth with hands to serve and give, to
En - via - do soy de Dios, mi ma - no lis - ta es - tá pa-

make of all the earth a bet - ter place to live.
ra cons - truir con él un mun - do fra - ter - nal.

The an - gels are not sent in - to our world of pain to
Los án - ge - les no son en - via - dos a cam - biar un

do what we were meant to do in Je - sus' name; that
mun - do de do - lor por un mun - do me - jor; me

falls to you and me and all who are made free. Help
ha to - ca - do a mí ha - cer - lo rea - li - dad. A-

us, O Lord, we pray, to do your will to - day.
yú - da - me, Se - ñor, a ha - cer tu vo - lun - tad.

This text by a Cuban Pentecostal pastor is plural here in English and singular in the original Spanish version;
singing both languages helps to show how the call to action in the world is both corporate and individual.
The minor tune suggests the resolve needed to do God's work.

TEXT: José Aguiar, 20th cent.; English trans. Gerhard M. Cartford, 1998
MUSIC: Pedro Infante, 20th cent.; arr. *Evangelical Lutheran Worship*, 2006
English Trans. © 1998 Augsburg Fortress
Music Arr. © 2003 Augsburg Fortress

ENVIADO
12.12.12.12.12.12

Go with Us, Lord

Go with us, Lord, and guide the way through this and
ev - ery com - ing day, that in your Spir - it
strong and true our lives may be our gift to you.

May be sung as a canon.

This very accessible sung prayer was created by the director of children's ministry at the National Presbyterian Church in Washington, DC, for use by their children's choir, but it is suitable for people of all ages. The familiar tune makes it easy to learn and to memorize.

TEXT: Mary Jackson Cathey, 1986
MUSIC: Thomas Tallis; adapt. Parker's *Whole Psalter*, c. 1561
Text © 1990 Hope Publishing Company

TALLIS' CANON
LM

749 Come! Live in the Light!

We Are Called

1 Come! Live in the light! Shine with the joy and the love of the Lord! We are called to be light for the king-dom, to live in the free-dom of the cit-y of God.

2 Come! O-pen your heart! Show your mer-cy to all those in fear! We are called to be hope for the hope-less so ha-tred and vio-lence will be no more.

3 Sing! Sing a new song! Sing of that great day when all will be one! God will reign, and we'll walk with each oth-er as sis-ters and broth-ers u-nit-ed in love.

Refrain

We are called to act with jus-tice; we are called to love ten-der-ly; we are called to serve one an-oth-er, to walk hum-bly with God.

The thematic and musical center of this hymn on the vocation of all believers is found in the refrain, which is based on the well-known challenge of Micah 6:8, "What does the Lord require of you but to do justice, and to love kindness, and to walk humbly with your God?"

TEXT and MUSIC: David Haas, 1988
Text and Music © 1988 GIA Publications, Inc.

WE ARE CALLED
Irregular

Goodness Is Stronger than Evil 750

Good-ness is stron-ger than e - vil; love is stron-ger than hate;

light is stron-ger than dark - ness; life is stron-ger than death.

Vic - tory is ours; vic - tory is ours

Oh, vic - tory is ours; vic - tory is

through God who loves us. us.

ours through God who loves us. us.

Recognizing that this text arose from the years of apartheid in South Africa adds depth and resonance to its already confident language. Yet these words can also be read as a summary of Christ's death and resurrection, the true basis of our hope that good will triumph over evil.

TEXT: Desmond Tutu, c. 1994
MUSIC: John L. Bell, 1996
Text © 1995 Desmond Tutu
Music © 1996 WGRG, Iona Community (admin. GIA Publications, Inc.)

GOODNESS IS STRONGER
8.6.7.6.4.4.5

751 From the Nets of Our Labor

We Will Rise Up and Follow

1 From the nets of our la - bors, through the noise and con -
2 When we faint and grow wea - ry from the bear - ing of
3 In the eyes of the strang-er— tear - ful, joy - ous, or
4 When we hear words of ha - tred spread-ing fear or false
5 In each mo-ment of cour - age, stead - fast e - ven through
6 Like dis - ci - ples be - fore us, from the cit - y or

fu - sion, from the cit - y or sea - shore,
bur - dens, with a mes - sage of com - fort,
fright - ened— in the face of each neigh - bor,
wit - ness, words that cry to be chal - lenged,
trem - bling; in the yearn - ing for jus - tice,
sea - shore, risk - ing self - less com - pas - sion:

Refrain
Je - sus sum-mons us all. We will rise up and fol - low,

Christ be - fore and be - side us, lov - ing pat-tern to

guide us, as we an - swer the call.

This text effectively evokes the call of the disciples who were fishermen (Matthew 4:18–22 / Mark 1:16–20 / Luke 5:1–11), while also describing the circumstances of our daily lives through which Jesus continues to summon us to be responsive to the needs and challenges of our own day.

TEXT: Mary Louise Bringle, 2004
MUSIC: John R. Kleinheksel Sr., 2004
Text and Music © 2006 GIA Publications, Inc.

HAMILTON
7.7.7.6 with refrain

Dona nobis pacem

752

Sim shalom
Rabbu habna salamann tamman

*May be sung as a canon.

HEBREW

שים שלום עלינו

ARABIC

رُبُّ هِبْنَا سَلاماً تَاماً.
رُبُّ هِبْنَا السَلام.

Whether sung in Latin, Hebrew, Arabic, or any other language, there is no common human prayer deeper than the longing for peace: peace among people and peace in our hearts. The style of this familiar musical setting suggests that it dates from the late 18th or early 19th century.

TEXT: Trad. liturgical text
MUSIC: Anon.; arr. Eric T. Myers, 2012
Music Arr. © 2012 Eric T. Myers

DONA NOBIS PACEM
Irregular

753 Make Me a Channel of Your Peace
Prayer of St. Francis

1 Make me a chan-nel of your peace. Where
2 Make me a chan-nel of your peace. Where
4 Make me a chan-nel of your peace. It

there is ha-tred, let me bring your love. Where
there's de-spair in life, let me bring hope. Where
is in par-don-ing that we are par-doned, in

there is in-ju-ry, your par-don, Lord, and
there is dark-ness, on-ly light, and
giv-ing of our-selves that we re-ceive, and in

where there's doubt, true faith in you.
where there's sad-ness, ev-er joy.
dy-ing that we're born to e-ter-nal life.

3 O, Mas-ter, grant that I may nev-er seek so

much to be con-soled, as to con-sole, to be

Guitar chords do not correspond with keyboard harmony.

Though popular opinion credits this prayer to Francis of Assisi, the earliest known printing was in a French religious magazine in 1912. Yet that gentle saint's spirit seems evident in these words, a quality that has spurred many paraphrases and musical settings such as this one.

TEXT: Anon., c. 1912; adapt. Sebastian Temple, 1967
MUSIC: Sebastian Temple, 1963; arr. Alfred V. Fedak, 2011
Text and Music © 1967 OCP

PRAYER OF ST. FRANCIS
Irregular

un-der-stood, as to un-der-stand, to be

to Stanza 4

loved, as to love, with all my soul.

Help Us Accept Each Other   754

1 Help us ac-cept each oth-er as Christ ac-cept-ed us;
2 Teach us, O Lord, your les-sons, as in our dai-ly life
3 Let your ac-cep-tance change us, so that we may be moved
4 Lord, for to-day's en-coun-ters with all who are in need,

teach us as sis-ter, broth-er, each per-son to em-brace.
we strug-gle to be hu-man and search for hope and faith.
in liv-ing sit-u-a-tions to do the truth in love;
who hun-ger for ac-cep-tance, for jus-tice and for bread,

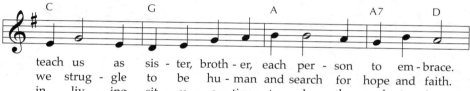

Be pres-ent, Lord, a-mong us and bring us to be-lieve
Teach us to care for peo-ple, for all, not just for some,
to prac-tice your ac-cep-tance un-til we know by heart
we need new eyes for see-ing, new hands for hold-ing on:

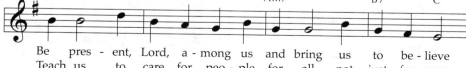

we are our-selves ac-cept-ed, and meant to love and live.
to love them as we find them, or as they may be-come.
the ta-ble of for-give-ness, and laugh-ter's heal-ing art.
re-new us with your Spir-it; Lord, free us; make us one!

Guitar chords do not correspond with keyboard harmony.

The scriptural basis of this text is Romans 15:7, recast as a prayer in the opening two lines of the first stanza. The many implications of living as people who have been accepted by Christ fill the remaining stanzas. This tune was composed for the first publication of this text.

TEXT: Fred Kaan, 1974
MUSIC: Doreen Potter, 1974
Text and Music © 1975 Hope Publishing Company

BARONITA
7.6.7.6.D

755 Alleluia! Laud and Blessing
(Psalms 111 and 112)

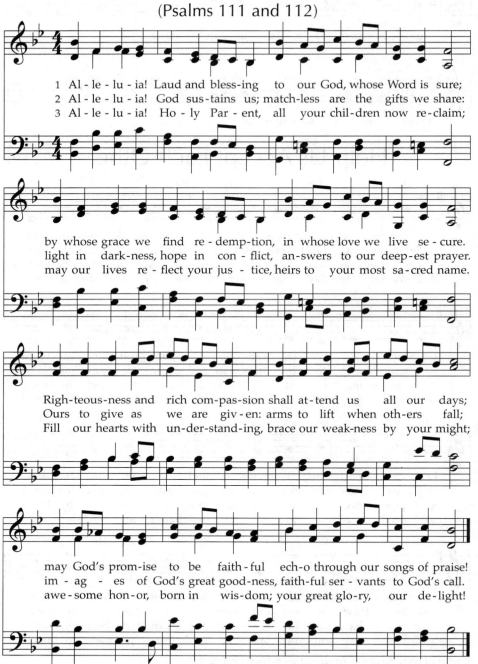

1 Al - le - lu - ia! Laud and bless-ing to our God, whose Word is sure;
2 Al - le - lu - ia! God sus-tains us; match-less are the gifts we share:
3 Al - le - lu - ia! Ho - ly Par - ent, all your chil-dren now re-claim;

by whose grace we find re - demp-tion, in whose love we live se - cure.
light in dark-ness, hope in con - flict, an-swers to our deep-est prayer.
may our lives re - flect your jus - tice, heirs to your most sa-cred name.

Righ-teous-ness and rich com-pas-sion shall at-tend us all our days;
Ours to give as we are giv - en: arms to lift when oth-ers fall;
Fill our hearts with un-der-stand-ing, brace our weak-ness by your might;

may God's prom-ise to be faith - ful ech-o through our songs of praise!
im - ag - es of God's great good-ness, faith-ful ser - vants to God's call.
awe-some hon-or, born in wis-dom; your great glo-ry, our de-light!

Psalms 111 and 112 are appropriately brought together in this paraphrase. Both form acrostics: each poetic line begins with a letter of the Hebrew alphabet in order. In addition, both psalms begin with "hallelujah," and they share much vocabulary as well as a theme of praise.

TEXT: Michael Morgan, 2011
MUSIC: Tochter Sion, 1741
Text © 2011 Michael Morgan (admin. Faith Alive Christian Resources)

WEISSE FLAGGEN
8.7.8.7.D

O God of Every Nation

756

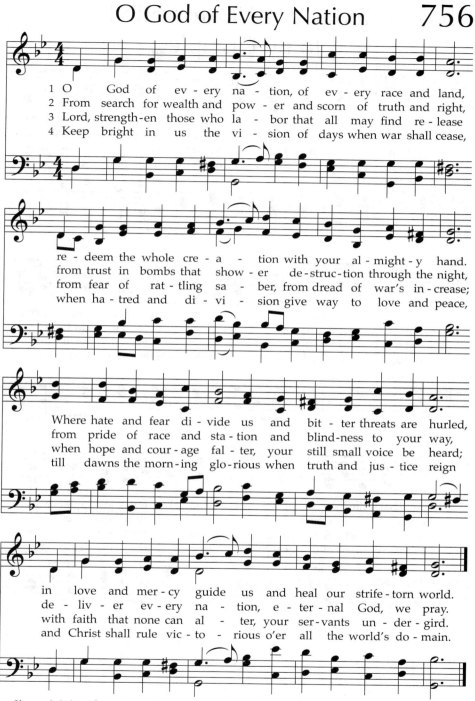

1 O God of every nation, of every race and land,
2 From search for wealth and power and scorn of truth and right,
3 Lord, strength-en those who labor that all may find re-lease
4 Keep bright in us the vision of days when war shall cease,

re-deem the whole cre-a-tion with your al-might-y hand.
from trust in bombs that show-er de-struc-tion through the night,
from fear of rat-tling sa-ber, from dread of war's in-crease;
when ha-tred and di-vi-sion give way to love and peace,

Where hate and fear di-vide us and bit-ter threats are hurled,
from pride of race and sta-tion and blind-ness to your way,
when hope and cour-age fal-ter, your still small voice be heard;
till dawns the morn-ing glo-rious when truth and jus-tice reign

in love and mer-cy guide us and heal our strife-torn world.
de-liv-er ev-ery na-tion, e-ter-nal God, we pray.
with faith that none can al-ter, your ser-vants un-der-gird.
and Christ shall rule vic-to-rious o'er all the world's do-main.

If we truly believe that God cares for all people, we cannot limit our prayers and songs for peace to the
welfare of our own nation, no matter how much we may love it. This challenging text is set to a stirring
Welsh tune, named for a hamlet with a prominent Baptist chapel.

TEXT: William W. Reid Jr., 1958, alt.
MUSIC: Welsh folk melody; *Llwybrau Moliant*, 1872; harm. *The English Hymnal*, 1906
Text © 1958, ren. 1986 The Hymn Society (admin. Hope Publishing Company)

LLANGLOFFAN
7.6.7.6.D

757 Today We All Are Called to Be Disciples

1 To - day we all are called to be dis - ci - ples of the
2 God made the world and at its birth or - dained our hu - man
3 Pray jus - tice may come roll - ing down as in a might - y
4 May we in ser - vice to our God act out the liv - ing

Lord, to help to set the cap - tive free, make
race to live as stew - ards of the earth, re -
stream, with righ - teous - ness in field and town to
word, and walk the road the saints have trod till

plow - share out of sword, to feed the hun - gry, quench their
spond - ing to God's grace. But we are vain and sad - ly
cleanse us and re - deem. For God is long - ing to re -
all have seen and heard. As stew - ards of the earth may

This text placing stewardship in the context of faithful witness was written by a retired Presbyterian minister to be part of the 1986 stewardship campaign titled "Called to Be Disciples." The tune name recalls the Sussex village where the arranger first heard the melody.

TEXT: H. Kenn Carmichael, 1985
MUSIC: *English County Songs*, 1893; harm. Ralph Vaughan Williams, 1906
Text © 1989 H. Kenn Carmichael

KINGSFOLD
CMD

thirst, make love and peace our fast, to serve the
proud; we sow not peace but strife. Our dis - cord
store an earth where con - flicts cease, a world that
we give thanks in one ac - cord to God who

poor and home - less first, our ease and com - fort last.
spreads a dead - ly cloud that threat - ens all of life.
was cre - at - ed for a har - mo - ny of peace.
calls us all to be dis - ci - ples of the Lord.

758 Why Do Nations Rage Together
(Psalm 2)

1 Why do na-tions rage to-geth - er; why in vain do
2 To the chil-dren of the prom-ise God shall give the

they con-spire? Rul - ers of earth's vast do - min - ions light
throne this day. With a scep - ter forged of i - ron, they

the skies with mar - tyrs' fire. Truth mis - tak - en, God for -
shall dash their foes as clay: faith re - veal-ing, hum - bly

sak - en, banes of righ - teous - ness a - rise; yet shall
kneel - ing, quench the fire and sheathe the sword, for God's

In this concise paraphrase of Psalm 2, the first stanza describes a political struggle from a human perspective, while the second stanza describes how the matter is resolved through God's power. The frequent three-note figures in this Welsh tune help to convey a sense of turmoil.

TEXT: Michael Morgan, 1995
MUSIC: Thomas John Williams, 1890
Text © 2010 Michael Morgan (admin. Congregational Ministries Publishing, Presbyterian Church (U.S.A.))

EBENEZER
8.7.8.7.D

they reap sore dis - plea-sure, sure de - feat be - fore God's eyes.
wrath is quick-ly kin - dled; blest are they who serve the Lord.

O God, We Bear the Imprint 759

1 O God, we bear the im-print of your face: the col - ors
2 Where we are torn and pulled a - part by hate be - cause our
3 O God, we share the im - age of the One whose flesh and

of our skin are your de - sign, and what we have of
race, our skin is not the same, while we are judged un -
blood are ours, what-ev - er skin; in Christ's hu - man - i -

beau - ty in our race as man or wom - an, you a -
e - qual by the state and vic - tims made be - cause we
ty we find our own, and in his fam - i - ly our

lone de - fine, who stretched a liv - ing fab - ric on our
own our name, hu - man - i - ty re - duced to lit - tle
prop - er kin: Christ is the broth - er we still cru - ci -

frame and gave to each a lan - guage and a name.
worth, dis - hon - ored is your liv - ing face on earth.
fy, his love the lan - guage we must learn, or die.

Rather than treating racism as a societal problem, this text considers the issue from a theological point of view. When we distance ourselves from other people merely because of the color of their skin, we fail to honor their God-likeness and to see Christ's image in them.

TEXT: Shirley Erena Murray, 1987
MUSIC: Margaret R. Tucker, 1998
Text © 1987 Hope Publishing Company
Music © 1998 Hope Publishing Company

TODOS LOS COLORES
10.10.10.10.10.10

760 Bring Many Names

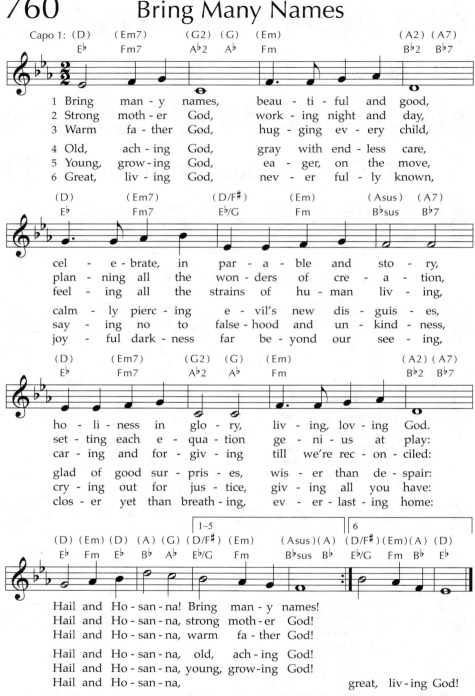

This text affirms that the images we use for God can be inspired by either gender because both males and females reflect the image and likeness of God (Genesis 1:27). Similarly, since God is with us at all stages of life, all ages hold the potential to reveal something about God.

TEXT: Brian Wren, 1986, rev.
MUSIC: Carlton R. Young, 1987
Text and Music © 1989 Hope Publishing Company

WESTCHASE
9.10.11.9

Called as Partners in Christ's Service 761

1 Called as part-ners in Christ's ser-vice, called to min-is-tries of grace,
2 Christ's ex-am-ple, Christ's in-spir-ing, Christ's clear call to work and worth,
3 Thus new pat-terns for Christ's mis-sion, in a small or glob-al sense,
4 So God grant us for to-mor-row ways to or-der hu-man life

we re-spond with deep com-mit-ment fresh new lines of faith to trace.
let us fol-low, nev-er fal-tering, rec-on-cil-ing folk on earth.
help us bear each oth-er's bur-dens, break-ing down each wall or fence.
that sur-round each per-son's sor-row with a calm that con-quers strife.

May we learn the art of shar-ing, side by side and friend with friend,
Men and wom-en, rich-er, poor-er, all God's peo-ple, young and old,
Words of com-fort, words of vi-sion, words of chal-lenge, said with care,
Make us part-ners in our liv-ing, our com-pas-sion to in-crease,

e-qual part-ners in our car-ing to ful-fill God's cho-sen end.
blend-ing hu-man skills to-geth-er gra-cious gifts from God un-fold.
bring new power and strength for ac-tion, make us col-leagues, free and fair.
mes-sen-gers of faith, thus giv-ing hope and con-fi-dence and peace.

This hymn is a celebration of mutuality and diversity as well as a challenge to the Christian community to live out a ministry of reconciliation and inclusion. This 20th-century text is set to a 19th-century tune named for the noted pastor and preacher Henry Ward Beecher.

TEXT: Jane Parker Huber, 1981
MUSIC: John Zundel, 1870
Text © 1981 Jane Parker Huber (admin. Westminster John Knox Press)

BEECHER
8.7.8.7.D
(alternate tune: EBENEZER)

762 When the Poor Ones
Cuando el pobre

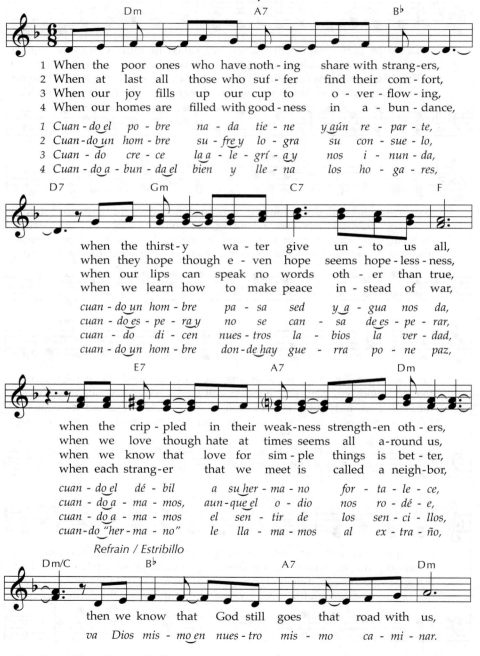

1 When the poor ones who have noth-ing share with strang-ers,
2 When at last all those who suf-fer find their com-fort,
3 When our joy fills up our cup to o - ver - flow-ing,
4 When our homes are filled with good-ness in a - bun - dance,

1 Cuan-do el po - bre na - da tie - ne y aún re - par - te,
2 Cuan-do un hom - bre su - fre y lo - gra su con - sue - lo,
3 Cuan - do cre - ce la a - le - grí - a y nos i - nun - da,
4 Cuan - do a - bun - da el bien y lle - na los ho - ga - res,

when the thirst-y wa - ter give un - to us all,
when they hope though e - ven hope seems hope - less - ness,
when our lips can speak no words oth - er than true,
when we learn how to make peace in - stead of war,

cuan - do un hom - bre pa - sa sed y a - gua nos da,
cuan - do es - pe - ra y no se can - sa de es - pe - rar,
cuan - do di - cen nues - tros la - bios la ver - dad,
cuan - do un hom - bre don - de hay gue - rra po - ne paz,

when the crip - pled in their weak-ness strength-en oth - ers,
when we love though hate at times seems all a-round us,
when we know that love for sim - ple things is bet - ter,
when each strang-er that we meet is called a neigh-bor,

cuan - do el dé - bil a su her - ma - no for - ta - le - ce,
cuan - do a - ma - mos, aun-que el o - dio nos ro - dé - e,
cuan - do a - ma - mos el sen - tir de los sen - ci - llos,
cuan - do "her - ma - no" le lla - ma - mos al ex - tra - ño,

Refrain / Estribillo

then we know that God still goes that road with us,
va Dios mis - mo en nues - tro mis - mo ca - mi - nar.

Drawing on the parable revealing Christ's presence in "the least of these" (Matthew 25:31–46), the stanzas here give examples (the "when") while the refrain affirms the promise (the "then"). The journey imagery of the refrain may be based on the Emmaus story (Luke 24:13–35).

TEXT: José Antonio Olivar and Miguel Manzano, 1970; trans. George Lockwood, 1980, alt.
MUSIC: José Antonio Olivar and Miguel Manzano, 1970; arr. Alvin Schutmaat, 1971
Text and Music © 1971 José Antonio Olivar and Miguel Manzano (Published by OCP)

EL CAMINO
12.11.12 with refrain

then we know that God still goes that road with us.
Va Dios mis - mo en nues-tro mis - mo ca - mi - nar.

The Lord Hears the Cry of the Poor 763
(Psalm 82)

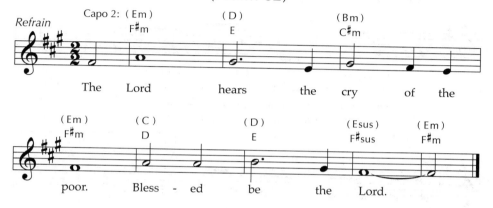

The Lord hears the cry of the

poor. Bless - ed be the Lord.

PSALM 82

Refrain

1 God arises in the council of heaven
   and gives judgment in the midst of the gods:

2 **"How long will you judge unjustly,**
   and show favor to the wicked?

3 Save the weak and the orphan;
   defend the humble and needy;

4 **rescue the weak and the poor;**
   deliver them from the power of the wicked. *Refrain*

5 They do not know, neither do they understand;
   they go about in darkness;
   all the foundations of the earth are shaken.

6 **Now I say to you, 'You are gods,**
   and all of you children of the Most High;

7 nevertheless, you shall die like mortals,
   and fall like any leader.'"

8 **Arise, O God, and rule the earth,**
   for you shall take all nations for your own. *Refrain*

The first part of this antiphon for Psalm 82 is based on Psalm 69:33a, and the second part is a benediction
found throughout Hebrew Scripture. It fittingly frames a psalm describing God's indignation that lesser
deities reward the wicked but treat the weak and needy unjustly.

TEXT and MUSIC: John B. Foley, SJ, 1978
Text and Music © 1978, 1991 John B. Foley, SJ, and OCP
Responsive Reading © 1993 The Order of St. Benedict (admin. The Liturgical Press)

THE CRY OF THE POOR
Irregular

764 For the Troubles and the Sufferings
Pelas dores deste mundo

1 For the trou - bles and the suf - fer - ings of the world,
2 Lend an ear to the ris - ing cry for help

1 *Pe - las do - res des - te mun - do, ó Se - nhor,*
2 *Teus ou - vi - dos se in - cli - nem ao cla - mor*

God, we call up - on your mer - cy: the
from op - pressed and hope - less peo - ple: Come!

im - plo - ra - mos pi - e - da - de. A
des - sa gen - te o - pri - mi - da. A -

whole cre - a - tion's la - bor - ing in pain!
Has - ten your sal - va - tion, heal - ing love!

um só tem - po ge - me a cri - a - ção.
pres - sa - te com tu - a sal - va - ção.

We pray for peace, the bless - ed peace that
We pray for power, the power that will sus -

A tu - a pax, ben - di - ta e ir - ma -
O teu po - der sus - ten - te o tes - te -

comes from mak - ing jus - tice, to cov - er and em -
tain your peo - ple's wit - ness: un - til your King - dom

na - da co'a jus - ti - ça a - bra - ce o mun - do in -
mu - nho do teu po - vo. Teu Rei - no ve - nha a

This Brazilian hymn was prominently used at the 9th Assembly of the World Council of Churches in Porto Alegre, Brazil, in 2006, for which the theme was "God, in Your Grace, Transform the World." The image of creation being in labor until God's will is done echoes Romans 8:19–23.

TEXT: Rodolfo Gaede Neto, 1998; trans. Simei Monteiro and Jorge Lockward, 2004
MUSIC: Rodolfo Gaede Neto, 1998; harm. Jorge Lockward, 2004
Text and Music © 1998 Rodolfo Gaede Neto
English Trans. and Music Harm. © 2004 General Board of Global Ministries t/a GBGMusik

PELAS DORES DESTE MUNDO
Irregular

brace   us.   Have mer - cy, Lord!   come, Ky - ri - e e - le - i - son!
tei - ro.   Tem com - pai - xão!   nos!   Ky - ri - e e - le - i - son!

May the God of Hope Go with Us 765
Song of Hope / Canto de esperanza

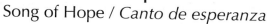

May the God of hope go with us ev - ery day,   fill - ing all our
¡Dios de la es - pe - ran - za, da - nos go - zo y paz!   Al mun - do en

lives with love and joy and peace.   May the God of jus - tice speed us
cri - sis, ha - bla tu ver - dad.   Dios de la jus - ti - cia, mán - da -

on   our way,   bring - ing light and hope to ev - ery land and race.
nos   tu luz,   luz y es - pe - ran - za en la os - cu - ri - dad.

Pray - ing,   let us work for peace; sing - ing,   share our joy with all;
O - re - mos   por la paz,   can - te - mos   de tu a - mor.

work - ing   for a world that's new,   faith - ful when we hear Christ's call.
Lu - che - mos   por   la paz,   fie - les   a   ti, Se - ñor.

This Argentine folk melody sets Spanish and English words, both created by a PC(USA) missionary with much Latin American experience. The two versions complement each other: the Spanish text offering a prayer to God, and the English one providing inspiration for the singers.

TEXT: Alvin Schutmaat, 1984   ARGENTINA
MUSIC: Argentine folk melody   11.11.11.11 with refrain

766 The Church of Christ Cannot Be Bound

1 The church of Christ can - not be bound by
2 True faith will o - pen up the door and
3 True love will not sit i - dly by when
4 If what we have we free - ly share to
5 The church of Christ can - not be bound by

walls of wood or stone. Where char - i - ty and
step in - to the street. True ser - vice will seek
jus - tice is de - nied. True mer - cy hears the
meet our neigh - bor's need, then we ex - tend the
walls of wood or stone. Where char - i - ty and

love are found, there can the church be known.
out the poor and ask to wash their feet.
home - less cry and wel - comes them in - side.
Spir - it's care through ev - ery self - less deed.
love are found, there can the church be known.

This text was the winning entry in a hymnwriting competition seeking new texts dealing with poverty and homelessness, but as the stanza sung at the beginning and end of the hymn makes clear, such specific ministries grow out of an understanding of the church as love in action.

TEXT: Adam M. L. Tice, 2005
MUSIC: African American spiritual; *Jubilee Songs*, 1884; adapt. Harry T. Burleigh, 1940
Text © 2005 GIA Publications, Inc.

MC KEE
CM

Together We Serve

Capo 3: (G) (D) (Em) (Bm7)
B♭ F Gm Dm7

1 To - geth - er we serve, u - nit - ed by love,
2 We seek to be - come a bea - con of hope,
3 We wel - come the scarred, the wealth - y, the poor,
4 To - geth - er, by grace, we wit - ness and work,

(C) (G) (Am7) (Dsus) (D)
E♭ B♭ Cm7 Fsus F

in - vit - ing God's world to the glo - ri - ous feast.
a lamp for the heart and a light for the feet.
the bus - y, the lone - ly, and all who need care.
re - mem - ber - ing Je - sus, in whom we grow strong.

(G) (D) (C) (Bm)
B♭ F E♭ Dm

We work and we pray through sor - row and joy,
We learn, year by year, to let love shine through
We of - fer a home to those who will come,
To - geth - er we serve in Spir - it and truth,

(G) (C) (G) (Am) (D7) (G)
B♭ E♭ B♭ Cm F7 B♭

ex - tend - ing God's love to the last and the least.
un - til we see Christ in each per - son we meet.
our hands quick to help, our hearts read - y to dare.
re - mem - ber - ing love is the strength of our song.

The first three words of this text appear in the website address for First Presbyterian Church of San Anselmo, California, for whose centennial the hymn was commissioned. The text draws on Ephesians 4:11–16, a passage describing the many gifts and ministries within the body of Christ.

TEXT and MUSIC: Daniel Charles Damon, 1996
Text and Music © 1998 Hope Publishing Company

SAN ANSELMO
5.5.11.D

768 Somos el cuerpo de Cristo/
We Are the Body of Christ

In this bilingual hymn the leader and the congregation sing both Spanish and English, so that the very act of singing becomes the beginning of mutual understanding as each language endeavors to mirror the other, highlighting words that are similar and words that are different.

TEXT: Jaime Cortez and Bob Hurd, 1994
MUSIC: Jaime Cortez, 1994; arr. Jeffrey Honoré, 1994
Text and Music © 1994 Jaime Cortez (Published by OCP)

SOMOS EL CUERPO DE CRISTO
Irregular

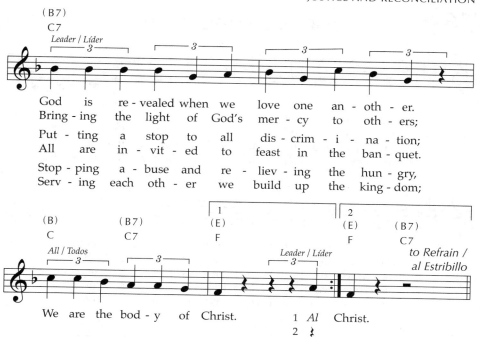

(B7)
C7
Leader / Líder

God   is   re - vealed when we   love   one   an - oth - er.
Bring - ing   the   light   of   God's   mer - cy   to   oth - ers;
Put - ting   a   stop   to   all   dis - crim - i - na - tion;
All   are   in - vit - ed   to   feast   in   the   ban - quet.
Stop - ping   a - buse   and   re - liev - ing   the   hun - gry,
Serv - ing   each   oth - er   we   build   up   the   king - dom;

(B)   (B7)   1   (E)   2   (E)   (B7)
C   C7   F   F   C7
All / Todos   Leader / Líder   to Refrain /
                                                                 al Estribillo

We   are   the   bod - y   of   Christ.   1 Al   Christ.
                                               2 𝄽
                                               3 𝄽

769 For Everyone Born

1 For ev-ery-one born, a place at the ta-ble,
2 For wom-an and man, a place at the ta-ble,
3 For young and for old, a place at the ta-ble,
4 For just and un-just, a place at the ta-ble,
5 For ev-ery-one born, a place at the ta-ble,

for ev-ery-one born, clean wa-ter and bread,
re-vis-ing the roles, de-cid-ing the share,
a voice to be heard, a part in the song,
a-bus-er, a-bused, with need to for-give,
to live with-out fear, and sim-ply to be,

a shel-ter, a space, a safe place for grow-ing,
with wis-dom and grace, di-vid-ing the pow-er,
the hands of a child in hands that are wrin-kled,
in an-ger, in hurt, a mind-set of mer-cy,
to work, to speak out, to wit-ness and wor-ship,

for ev-ery-one born, a star o-ver-head,
for wom-an and man, a sys-tem that's fair,
for young and for old, the right to be-long,
for just and un-just, a new way to live,
for ev-ery-one born, the right to be free,

This hymn from a noted New Zealand hymnwriter affirms that God's hospitality transcends the barriers erected by human society and that we who have been created in God's image are called to live in ways that reflect our Creator's values: justice and joy, compassion and peace.

TEXT: Shirley Erena Murray, 1998
MUSIC: Brian Mann, 2006
Text © 1998 Hope Publishing Company
Music © 2006 Brian Mann (admin. General Board of Global Ministries t/a GBGMusik)

FOR EVERYONE BORN
11.10.11.10 with refrain

Refrain

and God will de-light when we are cre - a - tors of jus - tice and

joy, com-pas - sion and peace: yes,

God will de-light when we are cre - a - tors of jus - tice,

jus-tice and joy!

770 I'm Gonna Eat at the Welcome Table

1 I'm gon-na eat at the wel-come ta - ble;
2 I'm gon-na eat and drink with my Je - sus;
3 I'm gon-na join with sis - ters, broth - ers;
4 Here all the world will find a wel - come;
5 We're gon-na feast on milk and hon - ey;

I'm gon-na eat at the wel-come ta - ble, Al - le - lu - ia.
I'm gon-na eat and drink with my Je - sus, Al - le - lu - ia.
I'm gon-na join with sis - ters, broth - ers, Al - le - lu - ia.
here all the world will find a wel - come, Al - le - lu - ia.
we're gon-na feast on milk and hon - ey, Al - le - lu - ia.

I'm gon-na eat at the wel-come ta - ble; I'm gon - na
I'm gon-na eat and drink with my Je - sus; I'm gon - na
I'm gon-na join with sis - ters, broth - ers; I'm gon - na
Here all the world will find a wel - come; here all the
We're gon-na feast on milk and hon - ey; we're gon - na

eat at the wel - come ta - ble, Al - le - lu - ia.
eat and drink with my Je - sus, Al - le - lu - ia.
join with sis - ters, broth - ers, Al - le - lu - ia.
world will find a wel - come, Al - le - lu - ia.
feast on milk and hon - ey, Al - le - lu - ia.

The image of a great feast showing God's welcome of all people was part of Jewish tradition (Isaiah 25:6–9)
and underlies Jesus' parable of the Great Banquet (Luke 14:15–24). Such equality remains as unknown to
many people today as it was to the slaves who created this spiritual.

TEXT: African American spiritual, alt.
MUSIC: African American spiritual; arr. Carl Diton, 1980, alt.
Music Arr. © 1930, ren. G. Schirmer, Inc.

WELCOME TABLE
Irregular

What Is the World Like

1 What is the world like when God's will is done?
2 What is the world like when God's will is done?
3 What is the world like when God's will is done?
4 What is the world like when God's will is done?
5 These are the sto - ries that Je - sus im - parts,

Mus - tard seeds grow more than we can con - ceive:
Wit - ness the wan - der - ing child com - ing home;
No more is neigh - bor just al - ly or friend;
Read - y for feast - ing, we watch through the night,
filled with the Spir - it who joins us as one.

roots thread the soil; branch - es reach for the sun.
watch as the par - ent breaks in - to a run.
peace thrives in plac - es where once there was none.
tend - ing our lamps till the new day's be - gun.
Born through our voic - es, our hands, and our hearts,

This is how God moves us each to be - lieve.
This is how God longs for us when we roam.
This is how God works when ri - val - ries end.
This is how God read - ies us for the light.
this is a new world where God's will is done.

Guitar chords do not correspond with keyboard harmony.

This text and tune were written to conclude a hymn festival at the 2009 Annual Conference of The Hymn Society in the United States and Canada. Four parables framed both the festival and the hymn: the Mustard Seed, the Prodigal Son, the Good Samaritan, and the Ten Bridesmaids.

TEXT: Adam M. L. Tice, 2009
MUSIC: Sally Ann Morris, 2009
Text and Music © 2009 GIA Publications, Inc.

NEW WORLD
10.10.10.10

772

Live into Hope

1 Live in-to hope of cap-tives freed, of sight re-
2 Live in-to hope! The blind shall see with in-sight
3 Live in-to hope of lib-er-ty, the right to
4 Live in-to hope of cap-tives freed from chains of

gained, the end of greed. The op-pressed shall be the
and with clar-i-ty, re-mov-ing shades of
speak, the right to be, the right to have one's
fear or want or greed. God now pro-claims our

first to see the year of God's own ju-bi-lee!
pride and fear, a vi-sion of our God brought near.
dai-ly bread, to hear God's word and thus be fed.
full re-lease to faith and hope and joy and peace.

This text on Luke 4:16–20, the author's first, was written for the United Presbyterian Women's National Meeting in July 1976 because the team planning worship could not find a suitable hymn on that passage. She wrote the words with this vigorous 18th-century tune in mind.

TEXT: Jane Parker Huber, 1976
MUSIC: Musica Sacra, c. 1778
Text © 1980 Jane Parker Huber (admin. Westminster John Knox Press)

TRURO
LM

Heaven Shall Not Wait

773

1 Heaven shall not wait for the poor to lose their pa-tience,
2 Heaven shall not wait for the rich to share their for-tunes,
3 Heaven shall not wait for the dawn of great i - de - as,
4 Heaven shall not wait for tri - um - phant Hal - le - lu - jahs,

the scorned to smile, the de - spised to find a friend:
the proud to fall, the e - lite to tend the least:
thoughts of com - pas - sion di - vorced from cries of pain:
when earth has passed and we reach an - oth - er shore:

Je - sus is Lord; he has cham - pioned the un - want - ed;
Je - sus is Lord; he has shown the mas - ter's priv - ilege:
Je - sus is Lord; he has mar - ried word and ac - tion;
Je - sus is Lord in our pres - ent im - per - fec - tion;

in him in - jus - tice con - fronts its time - ly
to kneel and wash ser - vants' feet be - fore they
his cross and com - pa - ny make his pur - pose
his power and love are for now and then for

1–3
end.
feast.
plain.

4
ev - er - more.

This stirring, prophetic hymn is organized around two recurring four-syllable phrases, the first of which introduces an idealized scenario of what Dietrich Bonhoeffer would call "cheap grace," while the second announces the "costly grace" of God's redeeming work in Jesus Christ.

TEXT: John L. Bell and Graham Maule, 1987
MUSIC: John L. Bell, 1987
Text and Music © 1987 WGRG, Iona Community (admin. GIA Publications, Inc.)

HEAVEN SHALL NOT WAIT
12.11.12.11

774 There Is Now a New Creation

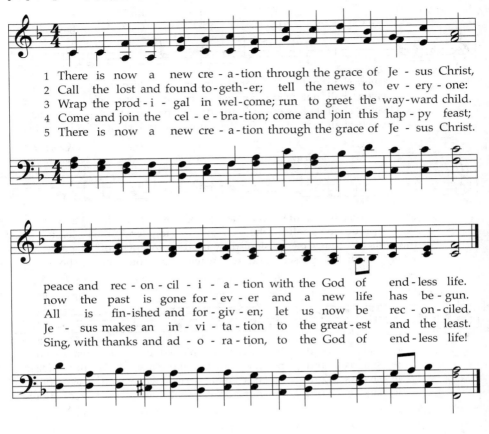

1 There is now a new cre - a - tion through the grace of Je - sus Christ,
2 Call the lost and found to - geth - er; tell the news to ev - ery - one:
3 Wrap the prod - i - gal in wel - come; run to greet the way - ward child.
4 Come and join the cel - e - bra - tion; come and join this hap - py feast;
5 There is now a new cre - a - tion through the grace of Je - sus Christ.

peace and rec - on - cil - i - a - tion with the God of end - less life.
now the past is gone for - ev - er and a new life has be - gun.
All is fin - ished and for - giv - en; let us now be rec - on - ciled.
Je - sus makes an in - vi - ta - tion to the great - est and the least.
Sing, with thanks and ad - o - ra - tion, to the God of end - less life!

At the center of this text stands a reference to the well-known parable of the Prodigal Son (Luke 15:11–32), and the fourth stanza forms an effective bridge between that gospel story and the celebration of the Lord's Supper. The first and last stanzas draw on 2 Corinthians 5:17.

TEXT: David Gambrell, 2009
MUSIC: Witt's *Psalmodia Sacra*, 1715, alt.
Text © 2011 David Gambrell (admin. Presbyterian Publishing Corp.)

STUTTGART
8.7.8.7

I Want Jesus to Walk with Me 775

1 I want Je - sus to walk with me;
2 In my tri - als, Lord, walk with me;
3 When I'm in trou - ble, Lord, walk with me;

I want Je - sus to walk with me;
in my tri - als, Lord, walk with me;
when I'm in trou - ble, Lord, walk with me;

all a - long my pil - grim jour - ney,
when my heart is al - most break - ing,
when my head is bowed in sor - row,

Lord, I want Je - sus to walk with me.
Lord, I want Je - sus to walk with me.
Lord, I want Je - sus to walk with me.

The two equal phrases in each line suggest that this African American spiritual shares some characteristics of work or field songs that were used to coordinate the efforts of slaves involved in tasks (road clearing, ditch digging, etc.) that needed combined rhythmic strokes.

TEXT: African American spiritual
MUSIC: African American spiritual; arr. Nolan Williams Jr., 2000
Music Arr. © 2000 GIA Publications, Inc.

WALK WITH ME
8.8.8.9

776 O God, Be Gracious

(Psalm 4)

1 O God, be gra - cious; hear my prayer, and
2 How long, O God, will li - ars boast while
3 When ter - ror wakes me from my dreams and
4 Some fear that you will not pro - vide; they
5 Now lay me down to sleep in peace; in

an - swer when I cry. You give me hope in
I am smeared with shame? Come, set your faith - ful
shakes me through and through, teach me to pray with
cry, "Show us your face!" But you have sat - is -
safe - ty let me rest. O God, with - in your

my dis - tress; you will not pass me by.
ser - vant free; I call up - on your name!
con - fi - dence and put my trust in you.
fied my heart with good - ness, joy, and grace.
lov - ing care I am for - ev - er blessed.

This paraphrase of Psalm 4 speaks to us across the ages with a problem we also know: lack of sleep caused by worry and fear. Yet there is hope, because God is gracious and calms our fearful hearts, giving us the peace that allows us to find rest even in the midst of trying times.

TEXT: David Gambrell, 2009
MUSIC: Thomas Tallis, c. 1567, alt.
Text © 2011 David Gambrell (admin. Presbyterian Publishing Corp.)

TALLIS' ORDINAL
CM
(this tune in a higher key, 477)

How Long, O Lord

777

(Psalm 13)

1 How long, O Lord, will you for-get an an-swer to my prayer? No to-kens of your love I see; your face is turned a - way from me; I wres - tle with de - spair!

2 How long, O Lord, will you for-sake and leave me in this way? When will you come to my re - lief? My heart is o - ver-whelmed with grief, by e - vil night and day!

3 How long, O Lord? But you for-give with mer - cy from a - bove. I find that all your ways are just; I learn to praise you and to trust in your un - fail - ing love!

Guitar chords do not correspond with keyboard harmony.

This paraphrase of Psalm 13 convincingly captures the psalm's initial sense of self-centered desperation. Then, like sunlight breaking through clouds of despair, this mood is suddenly dispelled by an awareness of God's mercy and love, which is so much greater than we can imagine.

TEXT: Barbara Woollett, 1990
MUSIC: Christopher Norton, 1990
Text © 1990 The Jubilate Group (admin. Hope Publishing Company)
Music © 1993 HarperCollins Religious (admin. U.S.A. and Canada Music Services)

HOW LONG, O LORD
8.6.8.8.6

778 As Pants the Deer for Living Streams

(Psalms 42 and 43)

1 As pants the deer for liv - ing streams, in dry or des - ert space,
2 Tears are my bread both night and day; fools crush me, soul and bone.
3 Deep calls to deep, the bil - lows roar; they cov - er me with pain.
4 O send your light to guide me home; my Sav - ior, guide me still.

I thirst for you, O liv - ing God; I long to see your face!
They laugh and ask, "Where is your God?" I hope in you a - lone.
I cry for heal - ing and for home; God, show your love a - gain!
With shout-ing pil - grims I will come to climb your ho - ly hill.

O how I miss the hap - py days when with the throng I'd praise!
Why cast me off? Where have you gone? Why is your grace with-drawn?
With - out your peo - ple, who am I? With - out you I will die.
Then with the harp I'll sing your praise; my hap - py voice I'll raise.

Refrain

Take cour - age now, my trem - bling heart, for God will take your part!

Guitar chords do not correspond with keyboard harmony.

Because they share vocabulary, themes, and a refrain, Psalms 42 and 43 are regarded as one extended prayer for help. Although cast as the voice of one person, this is really the plea of the whole Jewish people longing to return from exile and to worship once more in Jerusalem.

TEXT: Ruth Duck, 1985
MUSIC: John D. Horman, 2003
Text © 1992 GIA Publications, Inc.
Music © 2003 Zimbel Press

SEACHRIST
CMD

How Long, O God, Will My Prayers Be in Vain?

779

1 How long, O God, will my prayers be in vain? Why must I
2 When e - vil pros-pers and hope is long gone, do not for-
3 Ear - ly and late will my tongue sing your praise; you will up -

lan - guish in sor - row and pain? Do not a - ban - don a
sake me, your pres-ence with-drawn. Shield and pro - tect those who
hold me the length of my days. You are a strong-hold for

child you have made; you are my shel - ter, my so - lace and shade.
call on your name; you are my God, and your bless-ing I claim.
all the op-pressed; hear us, O God! Let your peo - ple be blessed.

This text does not paraphrase any specific psalm, but it adopts the vocabulary and the structure of many psalms. The first two stanzas begin with a sense of abandonment and despair, which is countered by remembrance of God's nature. This memory leads to a final stanza of praise.

TEXT and MUSIC: Barbara Hamm, 2009
Text and Music © 2009 Hope Publishing Company

LAND OF MERCY
10.10.10.10

780 Come Quickly, Lord, to Rescue Me
(Psalm 70)

1 Come quick - ly, Lord, to res - cue me, and
2 May all who seek your name re - joice, your
3 Yet I am poor and need - y, Lord; be

has - ten to my help, I pray. May all who seek to
praise in grat - i - tude re - cord. May those who love your
quick to hear my ur - gent plea. You are my help, my

take my life be put to shame with - out de - lay.
sav - ing power say ev - er - more, "Ex - alt the Lord!"
Sav - ior God! Do not de - lay; re - mem - ber me.

While this paraphrase is short, so is Psalm 70, which has only five verses and is almost identical to Psalm 40:13–17. This brief prayer for deliverance from enemies and blessing on the faithful is often used during Holy Week because of its parallels with Christ's suffering.

TEXT: Bert Polman, 1983
MUSIC: Walker's *Southern Harmony*, 1835; harm. Erik Routley, 1985
Text © 1987 Faith Alive Christian Resources
Music Harm. © 1985 Hope Publishing Company

DISTRESS
LM
(alternate harmonization, 210)

Hear My Cry, O God, and Save Me! 781
(Psalm 77)

1 Hear my cry, O God, and save me! Trou-bles
2 You, O God, once walked be-side me. In the
3 All cre - a - tion bows be - fore you; saints in

and dis - tress en - slave me. Day and night I
night your songs re - vived me. Were your prom - is -
earth and heaven a - dore you. Thun - der roars and

seek your face, yearn - ing for your light and grace.
es in vain? Will you smile on me a - gain?
tor - rents fall at your word, O God of all!

But these eyes: they can - not see you; out - stretched
Long a - go you brought re - demp - tion; your right
In our grief, you stand be - side us, there to

arms: they can - not feel you. My heart breaks in
hand won our sal - va - tion. I re - mem - ber
lift us, and to guide us, un - seen sav - ior

deep de - spair; my soul longs to hold you here.
deeds of old: now, re - mem - ber me, O Lord!
of our days, heir to end - less songs of praise!

The growing confidence in this paraphrase of Psalm 77 is signaled by the movement from "me" to "us";
recalling the shared history of God's people is a source of comfort and hope. Such remembering is also
evident in the musical setting that uses the Genevan tune for this psalm.

TEXT: Michael Morgan, 2011
MUSIC: Genevan Psalter, 1551; arr. Alfred V. Fedak, 2011
Text © 2011 Michael Morgan (admin. Faith Alive Christian Resources)
Music Arr. © 2011 Faith Alive Christian Resources

GENEVAN 77
8.8.7.7.D

782 Hear My Prayer, O God
(Psalm 143)

1 Hear my prayer, O God, and lis-ten to my plea;
2 Hound-ed by a foe who crushed me to the ground,
3 An-swer soon, O God; my spir-it faints in me;
4 Keep me safe, O God, and help me learn your will;

faith-ful, righ-teous One, give ear and an-swer me.
I am like the dead or those in pris-on bound.
do not hide your face, or I will cease to be.
let your Spir-it lead through lev-el path-ways still.

Judge me not, I pray; no mer-it dare I claim;
Hope-less, numbed by fear, I pon-der all your care;
When the morn-ing dawns, make known your love a-new;
For your great Name's sake, my griefs and fears dis-pel;

know-ing my own faults, I trust in your just Name.
thirst-y as parched earth, I lift my hands in prayer.
show me how to walk, for I will trust in you.
free me from my foes, that I may serve you well.

This text is a 21st-century paraphrase of Psalm 143, the last of the seven penitential psalms. Internal references suggest that the original psalm was associated with a night of prayer in the Temple. It is set to a chant-like tune composed especially for these words.

TEXT: Carl P. Daw Jr., 2005
MUSIC: Hal H. Hopson, 2006
Text © 2005 Hope Publishing Company
Music © 2006 Hope Publishing Company

HYMN CHANT
5.6.5.6.D

When We Are Tested

1 When we are test-ed and wres-tle a-lone,
2 When in the des-ert we cry for re-lief,
3 When we are tempt-ed to bar-ter our souls,
4 When we have strug-gled and searched through the night,

fam-ished for bread when the world of-fers stone,
plead-ing for paths marked by cer-tain be-lief,
trad-ing the truth for the power to con-trol,
sort-ing and sift-ing the wrong from the right,

nour-ish us, God, by your word and your way,
lift us to love you be-yond sign and test,
teach us to wor-ship and praise on-ly you,
Sav-ior, sur-round us with cir-cles of care,

food that sus-tains us by night and by day.
trust-ing your pres-ence, our on-ly true rest.
seek-ing your will in the work that we do.
an-gels of heal-ing, of hope, and of prayer.

Although the Temptation of Christ is mentioned in all three synoptic gospels (Matthew 4:1–11 / Mark 1:12–13 / Luke 4:1–13), this hymn is based on the Lukan version. It is notable that each stanza begins "when," not "if"; temptation is not an optional feature of the spiritual life.

TEXT: Ruth Duck, 1996
MUSIC: Carlton R. Young, 1996
Text © 1996 Hope Publishing Company
Music © 1996 Abingdon Press (admin. The Copyright Company)

ANGELS OF HEALING
10.10.10.10

784 By the Waters of Babylon
(Psalm 137)

By the wa - ters, the wa - ters of Bab - y - lon,

we sat down and wept, and wept for Zi - on.

We re-mem - ber, we re-mem - ber, we re-mem - ber Zi - on.

*May be sung as a canon.

This canonic setting of a paraphrase of Psalm 137:1 gains much of its power from simple but profound patterns, especially the first two lines that descend like vocal tears. By contrast the phrases of the final line move upward, affirming that memory rebuilds what has fallen.

TEXT: Psalm 137:1
MUSIC: Jewish melody

BY THE WATERS OF BABYLON
Irregular

785 In Deepest Night

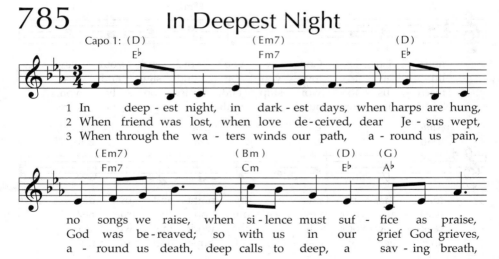

Capo 1: (D) (Em7) (D)
Eb Fm7 Eb

1 In deep - est night, in dark - est days, when harps are hung,
2 When friend was lost, when love de - ceived, dear Je - sus wept,
3 When through the wa - ters winds our path, a - round us pain,

(Em7) (Bm) (D) (G)
Fm7 Cm Eb Ab

no songs we raise, when si - lence must suf - fice as praise,
God was be - reaved; so with us in our grief God grieves,
a - round us death, deep calls to deep, a sav - ing breath,

(D) (Dmaj7)(E) (Em7) (G) (A7)(Dsus) (D)
Eb Ebmaj7 F Fm7 Ab Bb7 Ebsus Eb

yet sound - ing in us qui - et - ly there is the song of God.
and round a - bout us mourn - ful - ly there are the tears of God.
and found be - side us faith - ful - ly there is the love of God.

If we are honest about the range of human experience, not everything we sing in church can be loud or joyful. The author describes this hymn as "a song of quiet hope in the middle of intense sorrow." It speaks eloquently of God's presence with us through our most difficult times.

TEXT: Susan Palo Cherwien, 1995
MUSIC: David Schwoebel, 2008
Text © 1995 Susan Palo Cherwien (admin. Augsburg Fortress)
Music © 2008 Celebrating Grace, Inc.

ROSE MARY
8.8.8.8.6

Why Stand So Far Away, My God? 786
(Psalm 10)

1 Why stand so far a - way, my God? Why
2 Why do you hide when, full of lies, they
3 The weak are crushed and fall to earth; the
4 In a - ges past you heard the voice of
5 A - rise, O God, and lift your hand; bring

hide in times of need? The proud, un - bri - dled,
mur - der and be - tray? They wait to pounce up -
wick - ed strut and preen. Why in these cruel, cha -
those the proud op - press. Re - mem - ber those who
jus - tice to the poor. Come, help us stop the

chase the poor, and curse you in their greed.
on the weak as li - ons stalk their prey.
ot - ic times can - not your face be seen?
suf - fer now, who cry in deep dis - tress.
flow of blood! Let ter - ror reign no more!

This paraphrase of Psalm 10 is striking in its timeless questions and its keen sense of being abandoned by God. The injustice, oppression, and fear it describes resonate with the state of the world in our own day. Like the ancient psalmist, we pray for God to end the reign of terror.

TEXT: Ruth Duck, 1985
MUSIC: Wyeth's *Repository of Sacred Music, Part Second*, 1813; harm. C. Winfred Douglas, 1940
Text © 1992 GIA Publications, Inc.
Music Harm. © 1940 C. Winfred Douglas (admin. Church Pension Fund)

MORNING SONG
CM

787 God Weeps with Us Who Weep and Mourn

1 God weeps with us who weep and mourn; God's
2 Through tears and sor - row, God, we share a
3 And yet be - cause, like us, you weep, we

tears flow down with ours, and God's own heart is
sense of your vast grief: the weight of bear - ing
trust you will re - ceive and in your ten - der

bruised and worn from all the heav - y hours
ev - ery prayer for heal - ing and re - lief,
heart will keep the ones for whom we grieve,

of watch - ing while the soul's bright fire burned
the bur - den of our ques - tions why, the
while with your tears our hearts will taste the

low - er day by day, and pulse and breath and
doubts that they en - gage, and as our friends and
deep, dear core of things from which both life and

Guitar chords do not correspond with keyboard harmony.

This hymn especially appropriate for funerals began as a wordless tune composed upon reading the obituary of Thomas Layton Moshier, a friend who died from AIDS. Several months later the tune was sent to the author, who created this text incorporating a reference to Romans 12:15.

TEXT: Thomas H. Troeger, 1996, alt.
MUSIC: Sally Ann Morris, 1995
Text © 2002 Oxford University Press
Music © 1998 GIA Publications, Inc.

MOSHIER
CMD

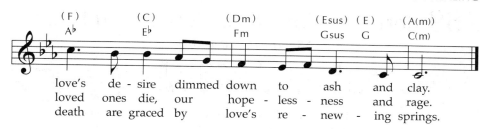

love's de - sire dimmed down to ash and clay.
loved ones die, our hope - less - ness and rage.
death are graced by love's re - new - ing springs.

To You, O Lord, We Lift Our Eyes 788
(Psalm 123)

1 To you, O Lord, we lift our eyes, to you en-
2 Have mer - cy on us now, O Lord; con - tempt has

throned in heaven a - bove; as ser - vants wait for
been our lot too long. Too long have we been

those they serve, so we look up and wait God's love.
mocked and scorned, de - rid - ed by the proud and strong.

Psalm 123 is one of several "songs of ascents," likely sung by Jewish pilgrims on their way to Jerusalem for one of the three great annual feasts: Passover, Weeks, and Booths. As this paraphrase suggests, these were short psalms that could be easily memorized and sung together.

TEXT: Christopher L. Webber, 2008
MUSIC: Adapt. from George Frederick Handel, c. 1750
Text © 2008 Christopher L. Webber

CANNONS
LM

789 Jesus, Savior, Lord, Now to You I Come

Saranam, saranam

Refrain

Je - sus, Sav - ior, Lord, now to you I come. Sa - ra -
You're my rock, my ref - uge, my heaven - ly home. Sa - ra -

Fine

nam, sa-ra-nam, sa-ra-nam.
1 From the earth wher-ev-er I may be,
2 In your heart give me a hid-ing place,
3 Then with joy to you my vows I'll pay,

out of des - per - a - tion and through ag - o - ny, I cry in
and be - neath your wings let me find shel - tering grace; O let me
and give thanks for all your mer - cy ev - ery day. I'll hum - bly

to Refrain

help-less-ness: O an-swer me. Sa-ra-nam, sa-ra-nam, sa-ra-nam.
see the sun-shine of your face. Sa-ra-nam, sa-ra-nam, sa-ra-nam.
fol-low in your per-fect way. Sa-ra-nam, sa-ra-nam, sa-ra-nam.

Claimed by both Pakistanis and Indians, this is one of the most popular South Asian hymns. The text
represents a Christian adaptation of Psalm 61, and the psalm's theme is reinforced by the mantra-like
repetition of the word "saranam," meaning "I take refuge" or "surrender."

TEXT: D. T. Niles, 1963, rev.
MUSIC: Punjabi melody; arr. Geoff Weaver, 1995
Text © 1963 Christian Conference of Asia (admin. GIA Publications, Inc.)
Music Arr. © 1995 The Jubilate Group (admin. Hope Publishing Company)

SARANAM
Irregular

In Silence My Soul Thirsts

(Psalm 62)

790

1 In si - lence my soul thirsts for God; for
2 In still - ness I pour out my fears; the
3 In qui - et - ness my Lord con - ferred two

God a - lone I wait. My en - e - mies may
sol - i - tude builds trust. My ref - uge rests in
truths I now de - clare: no great - er love than

chase me down; love shields me from their hate.
God's great grace. My anx - ious thoughts are hushed.
God's is known; no pow - er can com - pare.

Refrain

God is my rock; God is my strength; God is

my sal - va - tion, my ref - uge, my a -

bid - ing peace. I shall not be shak - en.

Psalm 62 is usually described as a song of confidence or trust, and that emphasis is made especially clear by the recurring refrain of this paraphrase. Its affirmations also serve as a testimony intended to lead others to make the same commitment to rely on God's steadfast love.

TEXT: Sheldon W. Sorge and Tammy Wiens, 2000
MUSIC: Sheldon W. Sorge, 2000
Text and Music © 2000 Sheldon W. Sorge

MY SOUL THIRSTS
CM with refrain

791

For You, My God, I Wait
(Psalms 130 and 131)

1 For you, my God, I wait with hope born
2 Lord, hear my plead - ing voice, and let me
3 If you should list my faults, the sins of

4 For e - ven from the deep I know you
5 And once my soul is still, in you I
6 O God, you are my hope; I know that

of the Word. Like sleep - less ones who
know you hear! As sleep - less ones feel
heart and hand, like sleep - less ones who

hear my cries. Like sleep - less ones who
find my rest, at peace as though a
you for - give. Your love re - deems me

long to dream I wait and call my Lord.
rest ap - proach, I know my God is near.
groan at dawn I know I could not stand!

dream at last, I ease my wea - ry eyes.
child up - on a gen - tle moth - er's breast.
from the depths so I may rise and live.

Unlike most paraphrases of Psalm 130, this one begins in the thematic center of the psalm and works backwards to the familiar "out of the depths" language of the opening verse. This focus on waiting allows the paraphrase to incorporate the imagery of the brief related Psalm 131.

TEXT: Adam M. L. Tice, 2003
MUSIC: David Ward, 2011
Text © 2011 GIA Publications, Inc.
Music © 2011 David Ward (admin. Faith Alive Christian Resources)

SPRINGTIME
SM

There Is a Balm in Gilead

792

Refrain

There is a balm in Gil-e-ad to make the wound-ed whole;

Fine

there is a balm in Gil-e-ad to heal the sin-sick soul.

1 Some-times I feel dis-cour-aged, and think my work's in vain, but
2 Don't ev-er feel dis-cour-aged, for Je-sus is your friend, and
3 If you can-not preach like Pe-ter, if you can-not pray like Paul, you can

to Refrain

then the Ho-ly Spir-it re-vives my soul a-gain. There is a
if you lack for knowl-edge, he'll not re-fuse to lend. There is a
tell the love of Je-sus and say, "He died for all." There is a

This African American spiritual offers a long-delayed answer to the prophet Jeremiah's question, "Is there no balm in Gilead?" (Jeremiah 8:22). No earthly remedy can compare with the healing that comes from a sense of God's presence; nothing else can heal "the sin-sick soul."

TEXT: African American spiritual
MUSIC: African American spiritual; arr. Melva Wilson Costen, 1989, alt.
Music Arr. © 1990 Melva Wilson Costen

BALM IN GILEAD
7.6.7.6 with refrain

793   O Christ, the Healer

1 O Christ, the heal-er, we have come to pray for
2 From ev-ery ail-ment flesh en-dures our bod-ies
3 How strong, O Lord, are our de-sires, how weak our
4 In con-flicts that de-stroy our health we rec-og-
5 Grant that we all, made one in faith, in your com-

health, to plead for friends. How can we fail to
clam-or to be freed; yet in our hearts we
knowl-edge of our-selves! Re-lease in us those
nize the world's dis-ease; our com-mon life de-
mu-ni-ty may find the whole-ness that, en-

be re-stored when reached by love that nev-er ends?
would con-fess that whole-ness is our deep-est need.
heal-ing truths un-con-scious pride re-sists or shelves.
clares our ills. Is there no cure, O Christ, for these?
rich-ing us, shall reach the whole of hu-man-kind.

Guitar chords do not correspond with keyboard harmony.

This prayer for wholeness of body, mind, and spirit considers not only the infirmities of individuals but also those of localities, societies, and nations. In the midst of such widespread need, worshiping communities are called to continue Christ's healing work in the world.

TEXT: Fred Pratt Green, 1967, alt.   ERHALT UNS, HERR
MUSIC: Klug's *Geistliche Lieder*, 1543; harm. Johann Sebastian Bach, 1725   LM
Text © 1969 Hope Publishing Company

O Savior, in This Quiet Place 794

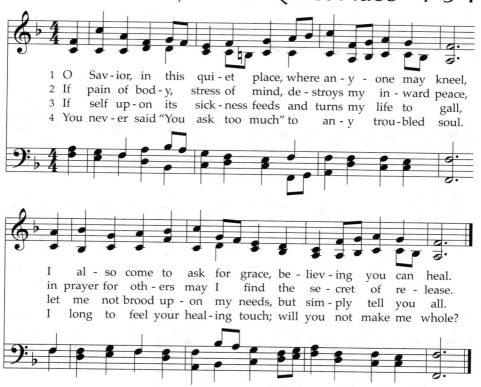

1 O Sav-ior, in this qui-et place, where an-y-one may kneel,
2 If pain of bod-y, stress of mind, de-stroys my in-ward peace,
3 If self up-on its sick-ness feeds and turns my life to gall,
4 You nev-er said "You ask too much" to an-y trou-bled soul.

I al-so come to ask for grace, be-liev-ing you can heal.
in prayer for oth-ers may I find the se-cret of re-lease.
let me not brood up-on my needs, but sim-ply tell you all.
I long to feel your heal-ing touch; will you not make me whole?

5 But if the thing I most desire
   is not your way for me,
   may faith, when tested in the fire,
   prove its integrity.

6 Of all my prayers, may this be chief:
   till faith is fully grown,
   Lord, disbelieve my unbelief,
   and claim me as your own.

This prayer for healing was written for the ecumenical St. Barnabas Counseling Centre in Norwich, England. As hymns often do, it provides a model for how to pray honestly but not selfishly. It is set to a tune by an Anglican clergyman who wrote on scientific and musical matters.

TEXT: Fred Pratt Green, 1974, alt.
MUSIC: William Jones, 1789
Text © 1974 Hope Publishing Company

ST. STEPHEN
CM

795 Healer of Our Every Ill

Refrain

Heal-er of our ev-ery ill, light of each to-mor-row,

give us peace be-yond our fear, and hope be-yond our sor-row.

1 You who know our fears and sad-ness, grace us with your peace and
2 In the pain and joy be-hold-ing how your grace is still un-
3 Give us strength to love each oth-er, ev - ery sis - ter, ev - ery
4 You who know each thought and feel-ing, teach us all your way of

to Refrain

glad - ness; Spir - it of all com - fort, fill our hearts.
fold - ing, give us all your vi - sion, God of love.
broth - er; Spir - it of all kind - ness, be our guide.
heal - ing; Spir - it of com-pas - sion, fill each heart.

As soon becomes apparent, this sung prayer is not limited to personal physical healing. It deals with the larger and intangible gifts of peace and hope to vanquish fear and sorrow, and it is cast in the plural because it is concerned with the healing of a wounded community.

TEXT and MUSIC: Marty Haugen, 1986
Text and Music © 1987 GIA Publications, Inc.

HEALER OF OUR EVERY ILL
8.8.9 with refrain

We Come to You for Healing, Lord 796

1 We come to you for heal - ing, Lord, of
2 As once you walked through an - cient streets and
3 You touch us through phy - si - cians' skills, through
4 Through nights of pain and wake - ful - ness, through
5 We come to you, O lov - ing Lord, in

bod - y, mind, and soul, and pray that by your
reached toward those in pain, we know you come a -
nurs - es' gifts of care, and through the love of
days when strength runs low, grant us your gift of
our dis - tress and pain, in trust that through our

Spir - it's touch we may a - gain be whole.
mong us still with power to heal a - gain.
faith - ful friends who lift our lives in prayer.
pa - tience, Lord, your calm - ing peace to know.
nights and days your grace will heal, sus - tain.

Unlike many hymns on the theme of healing, this text appropriately includes the ministry of medical personnel as instruments of God's healing activity. It also acknowledges that illness is not limited to physical symptoms, but involves mental, emotional, and spiritual dimensions.

TEXT: Herman G. Stuempfle Jr., 2002
MUSIC: American folk melody; arr. Annabel Morris Buchanan, 1938
Text © 2006 GIA Publications, Inc.
Music Arr. © 1938, ren. The H. W. Gray Company (admin. Alfred Music Publishing)

LAND OF REST
CM
(alternate harmonization, 691)

797 We Cannot Measure How You Heal

1 We can - not mea - sure how you heal or
2 The pain that will not go a - way, the
3 So some have come who need your help and

an - swer ev - ery suf - ferer's prayer, yet
guilt that clings from things long past, the
some have come to make a - mends, as

we be - lieve your grace re - sponds where
fear of what the fu - ture holds, are
hands which shaped and saved the world are

faith and doubt u - nite to care. Your
pres - ent as if meant to last. But
pres - ent in the touch of friends. Lord,

This 20th-century text from the Iona Community grapples with the realities of illness and pain, not only as they afflict the body but even more as they lay waste to mind and soul. The traditional folk melody helps to convey the sort of communal experience assumed in the last stanza.

TEXT: John L. Bell and Graham Maule, 1989
MUSIC: Scottish melody; arr. John L. Bell, 1989
Text and Music © 1989 WGRG, Iona Community (admin. GIA Publications, Inc.)

YE BANKS AND BRAES
LMD

hands, though blood - ied on the cross, sur -
pres - ent too is love which tends the
let your Spir - it meet us here to

vive to hold and heal and warn, to
hurt we nev - er hoped to find, the
mend the bod - y, mind, and soul, to

car - ry all through death to life and
pri - vate ag - o - nies in - side, the
dis - en - tan - gle peace from pain, and

cra - dle chil - dren yet un - born.
mem - o - ries that haunt the mind.
make your bro - ken peo - ple whole.

798 All with Joyful Exultation
(Psalm 30)

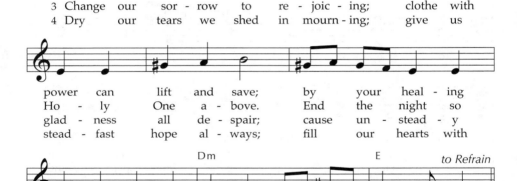

Refrain

All with joy-ful ex-ul-ta-tion let us sing to God our praise;
to the rock of our sal-va-tion loud ho-san-nas raise.

1 Lord, we sing with joy-ful voic-es; your great
2 Praise to you, our sure sal-va-tion, you, the
3 Change our sor-row to re-joic-ing; clothe with
4 Dry our tears we shed in mourn-ing; give us

power can lift and save; by your heal-ing
Ho-ly One a-bove. End the night so
glad-ness all de-spair; cause un-stead-y
stead-fast hope al-ways; fill our hearts with

touch, re-vive us; life re-store be-yond the grave.
dimmed by an-guish, with your light of peace and love.
feet that stum-ble now to dance be-neath your care.
ex-pec-ta-tion; fill our songs with thanks and praise.

This joyful paraphrase of Psalm 30 could well illustrate how to fulfill the first question of the Westminster Catechism: that a human being's "chief end" is "to glorify God, and to enjoy him forever." It is set to a Hasidic melody that suggests the ties with Jewish tradition.

TEXT: Ref. Hal H. Hopson, 2008; stanzas Michael Morgan, 1999; rev. 2011
MUSIC: Hasidic melody; arr. *Evangelical Lutheran Worship*, 2006
Text Ref. © 2008 Birnamwood/MorningStar Music
Text Sts. © 1999, 2011 Michael Morgan (admin. Faith Alive Christian Resources)
Music Arr. © 2006 Augsburg Fortress

YISRAEL V'ORAITA
8.7.8.7 with refrain

I Love the Lord, Who Heard My Cry 799
(Psalm 116)

1 I love the Lord, who heard my cry
2 I love the Lord, who heard my cry

and pit - ied ev - ery groan.
and chased my grief a - way.

Long as I live and trou - bles rise,
O let my heart no more de - spair

I'll has - ten to God's throne.
while I have breath to pray.

This setting of stanzas from a metrical psalm draws on an African American singing tradition marked by a slow pace and individual improvisation. Vestiges of that practice appear here in the pattern of extended syllables occurring at regular intervals without regard to meaning.

TEXT: Isaac Watts, 1719, alt.
MUSIC: African American spiritual; arr. Richard Smallwood, 1975
Music Arr. © 1975 Richard Smallwood (admin. Conexion Entertainment Group LLC)

I LOVE THE LORD
CM

800 Sometimes a Light Surprises

1 Some - times a light sur - pris - es the child of God who sings;
2 In ho - ly con - tem - pla - tion we sweet - ly then pur - sue
3 It can bring with it noth - ing but he will bear us through;
4 Though vine nor fig tree nei - ther their longed-for fruit should bear,

it is the Lord who ris - es with heal - ing in his wings;
the theme of God's sal - va - tion and find it ev - er new;
who gives the lil - ies cloth - ing will clothe his peo - ple, too;
though all the fields should with - er, nor flocks nor herds be there,

when com - forts are de - clin - ing, he grants the soul a - gain
set free from pres - ent sor - row, we cheer - ful - ly can say,
be - neath the spread-ing heav - ens no crea - ture but is fed;
yet God the same a - bid - ing, his praise shall tune my voice;

a sea - son of clear shin - ing to cheer it af - ter rain.
"Let the un - known to - mor - row bring with it what it may."
and he who feeds the ra - vens will give his chil - dren bread.
for while in him con - fid - ing, I can - not but re - joice.

This is one of the few hymns rooted in what can happen during worship, and that experience—gaining a spiritual insight while singing—is no less possible now than when this text was written in the 18th century. It is set here to a folk song variously labeled Irish or English.

TEXT: William Cowper, 1779, alt.
MUSIC: Irish folk melody; arr. Alfred V. Fedak, 2011
Music Arr. © 2011 Alfred V. Fedak

SALLEY GARDENS
7.6.7.6.D

The Lord's My Shepherd, I'll Not Want 801
(Psalm 23)

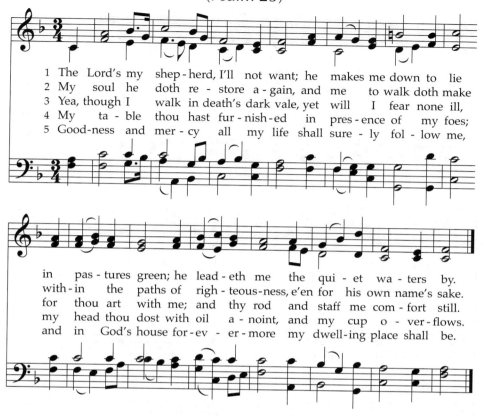

1 The Lord's my shep-herd, I'll not want; he makes me down to lie
2 My soul he doth re-store a-gain, and me to walk doth make
3 Yea, though I walk in death's dark vale, yet will I fear none ill,
4 My ta-ble thou hast fur-nish-ed in pres-ence of my foes;
5 Good-ness and mer-cy all my life shall sure-ly fol-low me,

in pas-tures green; he lead-eth me the qui-et wa-ters by.
with-in the paths of righ-teous-ness, e'en for his own name's sake.
for thou art with me; and thy rod and staff me com-fort still.
my head thou dost with oil a-noint, and my cup o-ver-flows.
and in God's house for-ev-er-more my dwell-ing place shall be.

KOREAN

1 주 나의 목자 되시니 부족함 없도다
  푸른 풀밭 호숫가로 날 인도하시네

2 내 영혼 소생시키며 그 이름 위하여
  늘 의로운 길 걷도록 날 인도하시네

3 나 어둠 골짝 지나도 두려움 없겠네
  주 막대기 와 지팡이 날 안위하시네

4 주 나의 원수 앞에서 내 상을 베푸사
  머리에 기름 부으니 내 잔이 넘치네

5 선함과 인자하심이 내 평생 따르리
  여호와 전에 영원히 나 거하리로다

SPANISH

1 Es el Señor mi buen pastor y nada faltará;
  por verdes prados con amor Él me conducirá.

2 Al lado de aguas de quietud haráme reposar;
  por sendas justas y de paz su mano me guiará.

3 Y cuando en valle de dolor o muerte deba andar,
  no sentiré ningún temor, pues Él me guardará.

4 Es sabio y fiel mi buen pastor, jamás me dejará;
  con su cayado, mi Señor, aliento me dará.

5 Hasta el final me seguirán misericordia y bien;
  y de mi Padre en el hogar por siempre moraré.

This paraphrase of Psalm 23 comes from the so-called Scottish Psalter of 1650, actually produced by the Westminster Assembly and intended for use by all Presbyterians in the British Isles, in place of the Sternhold and Hopkins "Old Version" of the Church of England.

TEXT: Scottish Psalter, 1650; Korean trans. The United Methodist Korean Hymnal Committee, 2001;
 Spanish trans. Federico J. Pagura
MUSIC: Jessie Seymour Irvine, 1872; harm. T. C. L. Pritchard, 1929
Korean Trans. © 2001 The United Methodist Publishing House (admin. The Copyright Company)
Spanish Trans. © Federico J. Pagura
Music Harm. © 1929 Oxford University Press

CRIMOND
CM

802 The King of Love My Shepherd Is

(Psalm 23)

1 The King of love my shep-herd is, whose good-ness
2 Where streams of liv-ing wa-ter flow my ran-somed
3 Per-verse and fool-ish oft I strayed, but yet in
4 In death's dark vale I fear no ill with thee, dear

fail - eth nev - er; I noth - ing lack if
soul he lead - eth, and where the ver - dant
love he sought me, and on his shoul - der
Lord, be - side me; thy rod and staff my

I am his and he is mine for - ev - er.
pas - tures grow, with food ce - les - tial feed - eth.
gent - ly laid, and home, re - joic - ing, brought me.
com - fort still, thy cross be - fore to guide me.

5 Thou spread'st a table in my sight;
   thy unction grace bestoweth;
   and O what transport of delight
   from thy pure chalice floweth!

6 And so through all the length of days
   thy goodness faileth never;
   Good Shepherd, may I sing thy praise
   within thy house forever.

Since its creation in the mid-19th century, this text has been one of the favorite paraphrases of Psalm 23 in the English-speaking world. That popularity increased in the early 20th century when *The English Hymnal*, 1906, first joined these words to this flowing Irish melody.

TEXT: Henry Williams Baker, 1868
MUSIC: Irish melody; harm. *The English Hymnal*, 1906, alt.

ST. COLUMBA
8.7.8.7

My Shepherd Will Supply My Need 803
(Psalm 23)

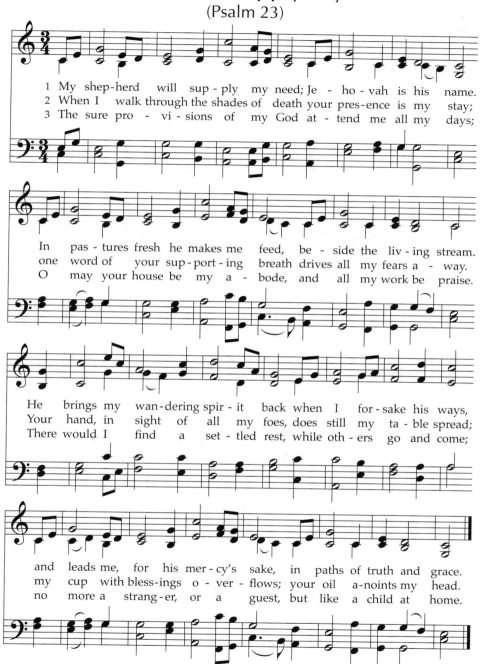

1 My shep-herd will sup-ply my need; Je - ho-vah is his name.
2 When I walk through the shades of death your pres-ence is my stay;
3 The sure pro - vi - sions of my God at - tend me all my days;

In pas - tures fresh he makes me feed, be - side the liv - ing stream.
one word of your sup-port-ing breath drives all my fears a - way.
O may your house be my a - bode, and all my work be praise.

He brings my wan-dering spir - it back when I for-sake his ways,
Your hand, in sight of all my foes, does still my ta - ble spread;
There would I find a set - tled rest, while oth - ers go and come;

and leads me, for his mer - cy's sake, in paths of truth and grace.
my cup with bless-ings o - ver - flows; your oil a-noints my head.
no more a strang - er, or a guest, but like a child at home.

The effectiveness of this beloved paraphrase of Psalm 23 owes much to the flowing shape note melody that serves as a "living stream" to carry the text, which in turn has been given a remarkable clarity and lightness through the poet's masterful use of single-syllable words.

TEXT: Isaac Watts, 1719, alt.
MUSIC: U.S.A. folk melody; Lewis's *Beauties of Harmony,* 1828; harm. Dale Grotenhuis, 1986
Music Harm. © 1990 Dale Grotenhuis

RESIGNATION
CMD
(alternate harmonization, 74)

804 Rejoice, Ye Pure in Heart!

1 Re - joice, ye pure in heart! Re - joice, give thanks, and sing!
2 With voice as full and strong as o - cean's surg - ing praise,
3 Yes, on through life's long path, still chant-ing as ye go,
4 At last the march shall end; the wea - ried ones shall rest;
5 Then on, ye pure in heart! Re - joice, give thanks, and sing!

Your fes - tal ban-ner wave on high, the cross of Christ your King.
send forth the stur-dy hymns of old, the psalms of an - cient days.
from youth to age, by night and day, in glad-ness and in woe:
the pil - grims find their home at last, Je - ru - sa-lem the blest.
Your fes - tal ban-ner wave on high, the cross of Christ your King.

Refrain

Re - joice! Re - joice! Re - joice, give thanks, and sing!

Re - joice! Re - joice!

These stanzas are drawn from a much longer hymn created for the processional at an English choir festival in 1865. The original text lacked the refrain that gives the hymn so much of its energy and interest. That feature was added by the composer of this tune in 1883.

TEXT: Edward Hayes Plumptre, 1865
MUSIC: Arthur Henry Messiter, 1883

MARION
SM with refrain

Come Sing to God

(Psalm 30)

805

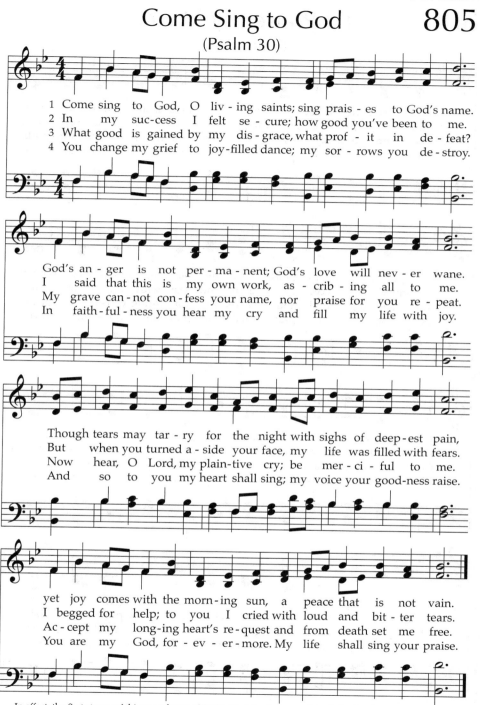

1 Come sing to God, O liv-ing saints; sing prais-es to God's name.
2 In my suc-cess I felt se-cure; how good you've been to me.
3 What good is gained by my dis-grace, what prof-it in de-feat?
4 You change my grief to joy-filled dance; my sor-rows you de-stroy.

God's an-ger is not per-ma-nent; God's love will nev-er wane.
I said that this is my own work, as-crib-ing all to me.
My grave can-not con-fess your name, nor praise for you re-peat.
In faith-ful-ness you hear my cry and fill my life with joy.

Though tears may tar-ry for the night with sighs of deep-est pain,
But when you turned a-side your face, my life was filled with fears.
Now hear, O Lord, my plain-tive cry; be mer-ci-ful to me.
And so to you my heart shall sing; my voice your good-ness raise.

yet joy comes with the morn-ing sun, a peace that is not vain.
I begged for help; to you I cried with loud and bit-ter tears.
Ac-cept my long-ing heart's re-quest and from death set me free.
You are my God, for-ev-er-more. My life shall sing your praise.

In effect, the first stanza of this paraphrase of Psalm 30 states the general truth that has been learned from the personal experience described in the last three stanzas. It is set to an 18th-century German tune brought into use with English hymnody in the 19th century.

TEXT: Fred R. Anderson, 1986
MUSIC: *Gesangbuch der Herzogl. Wirtembergischen Katholischen Hofkapelle*, 1784; alt. 1868
Text © 1986 Fred R. Anderson

ELLACOMBE
CMD

806 I'll Praise My Maker

(Psalm 146)

1 I'll praise my Mak-er while I've breath; and when my voice
2 How hap-py they whose hopes re-ly on Is-rael's God,
3 The Lord pours eye-sight on the blind; the Lord sup-ports
4 I'll praise my Mak-er while I've breath; and when my voice

is lost in death, praise shall em-ploy my no-bler powers.
who made the sky and earth and seas with all their train;
the faint-ing mind and sends the la-boring con-science peace.
is lost in death, praise shall em-ploy my no-bler powers.

My days of praise shall ne'er be past while life and thought
whose truth for-ev-er stands se-cure, who saves the op-pressed
God helps the strang-er in dis-tress, the wid-owed and
My days of praise shall ne'er be past while life and thought

and be-ing last, or im-mor-tal-i-ty en-dures.
and feeds the poor, and none shall find God's prom-ise vain.
the par-ent-less, and grants the pris-oner sweet re-lease.
and be-ing last, or im-mor-tal-i-ty en-dures.

This paraphrase of Psalm 146 was a great favorite of John Wesley: it appeared in his first hymn collection in 1737 (published in Charleston, South Carolina) and was on his lips when he died. The 16th-century tune to which it is set here is the one Watts had in mind for it.

TEXT: Isaac Watts, 1719; adapt. John Wesley, 1736, alt.
MUSIC: Attr. Matthäus Greiter, 1525; harm. V. Earle Copes, 1963
Music Harm. © 1964 Abingdon Press (admin. The Copyright Company)

OLD 113TH
8.8.8.8.8.8

When We Must Bear Persistent Pain 807

1 When we must bear per - sis - tent pain and suf - fer
2 Sup - port us as we learn new ways to care for
3 We thank you for the bet - ter days when we may
4 In ease or pain, in life and death, to you our

with no cure in sight, come, Ho - ly Pres - ence,
bod - ies new - ly frail. Help us en - dure, and
smile to greet the sun, to do your work with
frag - ile lives be - long, and so we trust you

breathe your peace with gifts of warmth and heal - ing light.
live and love. Hear our com - plaint when pa - tience fails.
clear - ing mind, and bless your name when day is done.
in all things. You are our hope, our health, our song.

Reflecting the author's own experience of debilitating migraine headaches, this sung prayer speaks for many people whose lives involve constant pain, often without hope of lasting relief. This text is effectively set to a shape note tune using only five tones of the scale.

TEXT: Ruth Duck, 2004
MUSIC: Walker's *Southern Harmony*, 1835; harm. David N. Johnson, 1968
Text © 2005 GIA Publications, Inc.
Music © 1968 Augsburg Fortress

PROSPECT
LM

808   When Memory Fades

1 When mem-ory fades and rec-og-ni-tion fal-ters,
2 As frail-ness grows and youth-ful strengths di-min-ish
3 With-in your Spir-it, good-ness lives un-fad-ing.

when eyes we love grow dim, and minds, con-fused,
in wea-ry arms that worked their ear-nest fill,
The past and fu-ture min-gle in-to one.

speak to our souls of love that nev-er al-ters;
your ag-ing ser-vants la-bor now to fin-ish
All joys re-main, un-shad-owed light per-vad-ing.

speak to our hearts by pain and fear a-bused.
their earth-ly tasks, as fits your mys-ter-y's will.
No val-ued deed will ev-er be un-done.

Especially in developed countries, people are living longer than in earlier eras, yet many abilities do not endure through these added years. This text affirms that although our human memories fade and our human arms weaken, the memory and arms of God uphold us everlastingly.

TEXT: Mary Louise Bringle, 2000
MUSIC: Jean Sibelius, 1899; arr. The Hymnal, 1933, alt.
Text © 2002 GIA Publications, Inc.
Music Arr. © 1933, ren. 1961 Presbyterian Board of Christian Education (admin. Westminster John Knox Press)

FINLANDIA
11.10.11.10.11.10

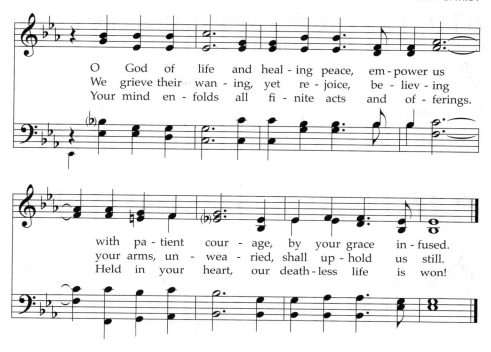

O God of life and heal - ing peace, em - power us
We grieve their wan - ing, yet re - joice, be - liev - ing
Your mind en - folds all fi - nite acts and of - ferings.

with pa - tient cour - age, by your grace in - fused.
your arms, un - wea - ried, shall up - hold us still.
Held in your heart, our death - less life is won!

Why Has God Forsaken Me? 809

1 "Why has God for - sak - en me?" cried our Sav - ior from the cross
2 At the tomb of Laz - a - rus Je - sus wept with o - pen grief:
3 As his life ex - pired, our Lord placed him - self with - in God's care:
4 Mys - tery shrouds our life and death but we need not be a - fraid,

as he shared the lone - li - ness of our deep - est grief and loss.
grant us, Lord, the tears which heal all our pain and un - be - lief.
at our dy - ing, Lord, may we trust the love which con - quers fear.
for the mys - tery's heart is love, God's great love which Christ dis - played.

To offer an answer to this hymn's opening question, this New Zealand author leads us through events at the end of Jesus' life that help us grasp "the love which conquers fear." The tune, whose name is Japanese for "mystery," uses a five-tone Japanese scale to convey that quality.

TEXT: Bill Wallace, 1980
MUSIC: Taihei Sato, 1981
Text © 1981 W. L. Wallace
Music © 1983 Christian Conference of Asia (admin. GIA Publications, Inc.)

SHIMPI
7.7.7.7

810 When in the Night I Meditate
(Psalm 16)

1 When in the night I med - i - tate on
2 For - ev - er in my thought, the Lord be -
3 My in - most be - ing thrills with joy and
4 I know that I shall not be left for -
5 The path of life you show to me; of

mer - cies mul - ti - plied, my grate - ful heart in -
fore my face shall stand; se - cure, un - moved I
glad - ness fills my breast; be - cause on God my
got - ten in the grave, and from cor - rup - tion,
joy a bound - less store is ev - er found at

spires my tongue to bless the Lord, my guide.
shall re - main, with God at my right hand.
trust is stayed, my flesh in hope shall rest.
you, O Lord, your ho - ly one will save.
your right hand, and plea - sures ev - er - more.

Corresponding to Psalm 16:7–11, these five stanzas celebrating God's guidance and protection formed the second half of a paraphrase of the full psalm in their original publication. These words are set to a 16th-century psalm tune that has been effective with many texts.

TEXT: *The New Metrical Version of the Psalms,* 1909, alt.
MUSIC: Day's *Psalter,* 1562

ST. FLAVIAN
CM

Make Your Face to Shine

Haz resplandecer tu rostro

(Psalm 31)

These selected verses of Psalm 31 are slightly reordered here (as 16, 14–15) to give initial emphasis to the petition for God's favor, expressed in the typical Hebraic image of a radiant face. That plea is then reinforced by affirmations of the psalmist's unwavering trust in God.

TEXT and MUSIC: Jay Weldon Wilkey, 2002
Text and Music © 2002 Jay Weldon Wilkey

GLÁUCIA
Irregular

812 O Save Me, God, and Hear My Cry
(Psalm 54)

1 O save me, God, and hear my cry: my prayer to you as-cends.
2 You, Lord, my help shall ev - er be, though e - vil powers as-sail.
3 My sac - ri - fice I of - fer you as thanks for all your grace.

And vin - di - cate me by your might; on you my hope de-pends.
From their de-signs, my life re-deem through grace which can-not fail.
Let me so live that I in death may greet you face to face.

The three stanzas of this paraphrase nicely condense all seven verses of Psalm 54 and trace its movement from an appeal for help, through a statement of hope amid adversity, to a vow of thanksgiving. The words are set to an early American shape note tune that gives them urgency.

TEXT: Michael Morgan, 1995
MUSIC: *Supplement to Kentucky Harmony*, 1820; harm. Margaret W. Mealy, 1985
Text © 2010 Michael Morgan (admin. Congregational Ministries Publishing, Presbyterian Church (U.S.A.))
Music Harm. © 1985 GIA Publications, Inc.

DETROIT
CM

813 God, My Help and Hiding Place
(Psalm 71)

1 God, my help and hid - ing place, res - cue me from shame.
2 From my youth I praised your name, trust - ing you to save.
3 Let me live to teach the young what your love can do,

Be my strength as I grow old; come and clear my name.
Now that I am turn - ing gray, lift me from the grave.
so may peo - ple yet to come place their trust in you.

The delicacy of the Japanese melody adds to the sense of isolation and vulnerability in this 21st-century paraphrase of Psalm 71. Yet the prayerful tone shows that a lifetime of trust has taught the psalmist to be confident of God's steadfast care, a theme worth singing about.

TEXT: Ruth Duck, 2011
MUSIC: Isao Koizumi, 1958
Text © 2011 GIA Publications, Inc.
Music © 1958 Isao Koizumi

TOKYO
7.5.7.5.D

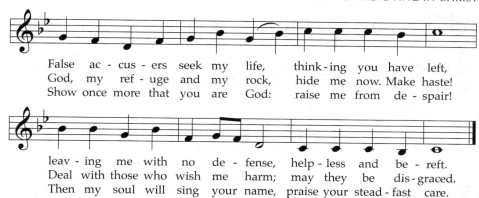

False ac-cus-ers seek my life, think-ing you have left,
God, my ref-uge and my rock, hide me now. Make haste!
Show once more that you are God: raise me from de-spair!

leav-ing me with no de-fense, help-less and be-reft.
Deal with those who wish me harm; may they be dis-graced.
Then my soul will sing your name, praise your stead-fast care.

In God Alone 814
Mon âme se repose

In God a-lone my soul can find rest and peace, in
Mon â - me se re - po - se en paix sur Dieu seul: de

God my peace and joy. On - ly in God my
lui vient mon sa - lut. Oui, sur Dieu seul mon

soul can find its rest, find its rest and peace.
â - me se re - po - se, se re - po - se en paix.

This prayer response based on Psalm 62:1, 5 comes from the ecumenical community in Taizé, France (see also no. 843). It is intended for repeated singing in either language (or both). It can also be used effectively as a recurring congregational response in a series of prayers.

TEXT: Taizé Community, 1991   MON ÂME SE REPOSE
MUSIC: Jacques Berthier, 1991   Irregular
Text and Music © 1991 Les Presses de Taizé (admin. GIA Publications, Inc.)

815 Give to the Winds Thy Fears

1 Give to the winds thy fears; hope, and be
2 Through waves and clouds and storms God gent - ly
3 Leave to God's sov - ereign sway to choose and
4 Let us in life, in death, thy stead - fast

un - dis - mayed. God hears thy sighs and
clears the way. Wait pa - tient - ly; so
to com - mand. So shalt thou, won - dering,
truth de - clare, and pub - lish with our

counts thy tears; God shall lift up thy head.
shall this night soon end in joy - ous day.
own God's way, how wise, how strong God's hand!
fi - nal breath thy love and guard - ian care.

This text uses selected stanzas from sixteen four-line English stanzas based on the original German text, which was twice as long. The German hymn was constructed as an acrostic on Martin Luther's translation of Psalm 37:5, and much of the spirit of that psalm is retained here.

TEXT: Paul Gerhardt, 1653; trans. John Wesley, 1737, alt.
MUSIC: William H. Walter, 1872

FESTAL SONG
SM
(this tune in a higher key, 744)

If Thou but Trust in God to Guide Thee 816

1 If thou but trust in God to guide thee, with hope-ful heart through all thy ways, God will give strength, what-e'er be-tide thee, to bear thee through the e - vil days. Who trusts in God's un-chang-ing love builds on the rock that nought can move.

2 On - ly be still, and wait God's lei - sure in cheer-ful hope, with heart con-tent to take what-e'er thy Keep-er's plea-sure and all - dis - cern - ing love hath sent. No doubt our in - most wants are clear to One who holds us al - ways dear.

3 Sing, pray, and swerve not from God's ways, but do thine own part faith - ful - ly. Trust the rich prom - is - es of grace; so shall they be ful - filled in thee. God nev - er yet for - sook at need the soul se - cured by trust in - deed.

This hymn is a testimony of experience. The original seven-stanza German text (based on Psalm 55:22) and its tune were created by the author/composer at the age of twenty in thanksgiving for finding employment many weeks after being left almost penniless following a robbery.

TEXT: Georg Neumark, 1641; trans. Catherine Winkworth, 1855, 1863, alt.
MUSIC: Georg Neumark, 1641

WER NUR DEN LIEBEN GOTT
9.8.9.8.8.8

817 We Walk by Faith and Not by Sight

1 We walk by faith and not by sight; with
2 We may not touch your hands and side, nor
3 Help then, O Lord, our un - be - lief; and
4 And when our life of faith is done, in

gra - cious words draw near, O Christ, who spoke as
fol - low where you trod; but in your prom - ise
may our faith a - bound to call on you when
realms of clear - er light may we be - hold you

none e'er spoke: "My peace be with you here."
we re - joice and cry, "My Lord and God!"
you are near and seek where you are found.
as you are, with full and end - less sight.

Guitar chords do not correspond with keyboard harmony.

The opening line here is essentially a quotation of 2 Corinthians 5:7, but that affirmation is fleshed out by references to the appearance of the risen Christ to Thomas (John 20:19–29). The shape note tune, named for a stream in Fayette County, Pennsylvania, adds resolution to the words.

TEXT: Henry Alford, 1844, alt.
MUSIC: Samuel McFarland, c. 1814; harm. Richard Proulx, 1986
Music Harm. © 1986 GIA Publications, Inc.

DUNLAP'S CREEK
CM

By Gracious Powers

818

1 By gra - cious powers so won - der - ful - ly shel - tered,
2 Yet is this heart by its old foe tor - ment - ed,
3 And when this cup you give is filled to brim - ming
4 Yet when a - gain in this same world you give us

and con - fi - dent - ly wait - ing, come what may,
still e - vil days bring bur - dens hard to bear;
with bit - ter suf - fering, hard to un - der - stand,
the joy we had, the bright - ness of your sun,

we know that God is with us night and morn - ing
O give our fright - ened souls the sure sal - va - tion
we take it thank - ful - ly and with - out trem - bling,
we shall re - mem - ber all the days we lived through,

and nev - er fails to greet us each new day.
for which, O Lord, you taught us to pre - pare.
out of so good and so be - loved a hand.
and our whole life shall then be yours a - lone.

This text (made from the author's last poem) turns in the middle of stanza two, where broad affirmations yield to a prayer continuing through the rest of the hymn, a prayer that testifies to deep confidence. The minor tune helps to convey such tensions in the life of faith.

TEXT: Dietrich Bonhoeffer, 1944; trans. Fred Pratt Green, 1972
MUSIC: C. Hubert H. Parry, 1904
Text © 1974 Hope Publishing Company

INTERCESSOR
11.10.11.10

819

Be Still, My Soul

1 Be still, my soul: the Lord is on thy side.
2 Be still, my soul: thy God doth un-der-take
3 Be still, my soul: the hour is has-tening on

Bear pa-tient-ly the cross of grief or pain.
to guide the fu-ture sure-ly as the past.
when we shall be for-ev-er with the Lord;

Leave to thy God to or-der and pro-vide,
Thy hope, thy con-fi-dence let noth-ing shake;
when dis-ap-point-ment, grief, and fear are gone,

who through all chang-es faith-ful will re-main.
all now mys-te-rious shall be bright at last.
sor-row for-got, love's pur-est joys re-stored.

This meditative text seems to be rooted in Psalm 46:10, "Be still and know that I am God," while also reaching forward to 1 Thessalonians 4:17b, "we will be with the Lord forever." Much of the appeal of this hymn comes from its tune, named for the tone poem on which it is based.

TEXT: Katharina von Schlegel, 1752; trans. Jane Laurie Borthwick, 1855, alt.
MUSIC: Jean Sibelius, 1899; arr. *The Hymnal*, 1933, alt.
Music Arr. © 1933, ren. 1961 Presbyterian Board of Christian Education (admin. Westminster John Knox Press)

FINLANDIA
10.10.10.10.10.10

Be still, my soul: thy best, thy heaven-ly Friend
Be still, my soul: the waves and winds still know
Be still, my soul: when change and tears are past

through thorn-y ways leads to a joy-ful end.
his voice who ruled them while he dwelt be-low.
all safe and bless-ed we shall meet at last.

Nothing Can Trouble 820
Nada te turbe

Noth-ing can trou-ble; noth-ing can fright-en. Those who seek
Na - da te tur-be, na - da te es-pan - te. Quien a Dios

God shall nev-er go want-ing. God a-lone fills us.
tie - ne na - da le fal - ta. So - lo Dios bas - ta.

This meditative refrain from Taizé is based on a saying attributed to Teresa of Avila: "Let nothing trouble you; let nothing frighten you. All things are passing; God never changes. Patience obtains all things. Whoever possesses God lacks nothing: God alone suffices."

TEXT: Attr. Teresa of Avila, 16th cent.; para. Taizé Community: Spanish, 1986; English, 1995
MUSIC: Jacques Berthier, 1986
Text and Music © 1991 Les Presses de Taizé (admin. GIA Publications, Inc.)

NADA TE TURBE
Irregular

821 My Life Flows On

How Can I Keep from Singing?

1 My life flows on in end-less song, a-bove earth's lam-en-ta-tion.
2 Through all the tu-mult and the strife, I hear that mu-sic ring-ing.
3 What though my joys and com-forts die? I know my Sav-ior liv-eth.
4 The peace of Christ makes fresh my heart, a foun-tain ev-er spring-ing!

I hear the clear, though far-off hymn that hails a new cre-a-tion.
It finds an ech-o in my soul. How can I keep from sing-ing?
What though the dark-ness gath-er round? Songs in the night he giv-eth.
All things are mine since I am his! How can I keep from sing-ing?

Refrain

No storm can shake my in-most calm while to that Rock I'm cling-ing.

Since Christ is Lord of heaven and earth, how can I keep from sing-ing?

In the *New York Observer* of August 7, 1868, this text was titled "Always Rejoicing," and was attributed to "Pauline T." This may well be where the Baptist pastor and musician to whom it is usually credited encountered the words that he later published with his tune.

TEXT and MUSIC: Robert Lowry, 1869

HOW CAN I KEEP FROM SINGING
8.7.8.7 with refrain

When We Are Living

Pues si vivimos

822

1 When we are liv - ing, it is in Christ Je - sus,
2 Through all our liv - ing, we our fruits must give.
3 'Mid times of sor - row and in times of pain,
4 A - cross this wide world, we shall al - ways find

1 *Pues si vi - vi - mos, pa - ra Él vi - vi - mos,*
2 *En es - ta vi - da fru - tos hay que dar*
3 *En la tris - te - za y en el do - lor,*
4 *En es - te mun - do por do - quier ha - brá*

and when we're dy - ing, it is in the Lord.
Good works of ser - vice are for of - fer - ing.
when sens - ing beau - ty or in love's em - brace,
those who are cry - ing with no peace of mind,

y si mo - ri - mos pa - ra Él mo - ri - mos.
y bue - nas o - bras he - mos de o - fren - dar.
en la be - lle - za y en el a - mor,
gen - te que llo - ra y sin con - so - lar.

Both in our liv - ing and in our dy - ing,
When we are giv - ing, or when re - ceiv - ing,
wheth - er we suf - fer, or sing re - joic - ing,
but when we help them, or when we feed them,

Sea que vi - va - mos o que mu - ra - mos,
Sea ya que de - mos o que re - ci - ba - mos,
sea que su - fra - mos o que go - ce - mos,
Sea que a - yu - de - mos o que a - li - men - te - mos,

we be - long to God; we be - long to God.
so - mos del Se - ñor, so - mos del Se - ñor.

This hymn began as an orally transmitted stanza reflecting on Romans 14:7–8 and was expanded by a Spanish-language hymnal committee to offer additional examples of the many dimensions of life, thereby strengthening the recurring affirmation that we belong to God through them all.

TEXT: Stanza 1, anon.; English trans. Elise S. Eslinger, 1983;
    stanzas 2–4, Roberto Escamilla, 1983; English trans. George Lockwood, 1987
MUSIC: Spanish melody; arr. Barbara C. Mink, 1988
English Trans. © 1989 The United Methodist Publishing House (admin. The Copyright Company)
Spanish Text Sts. 2–4 © 1983 Abingdon Press (admin. The Copyright Company)
Music Arr. © 1988 Barbara C. Mink (admin. Community of Christ)

SOMOS DEL SEÑOR
10.10.10.10

823 Shall Tribulation or Distress

1 Shall trib-u-la-tion or dis-tress, shall per-se-
2 Shall ill-ness, hun-ger, or de-spair, shall lone-ly
3 No, nei-ther an-gel hosts nor thrones, nor height nor

cu-tion, fire, or sword, or an-y per-il of this
grief or anx-ious fears, or deeds of ha-tred and dis-
depth of e-vil's reach, nor pres-ent things, nor things to

world— or e-ven death, or e-ven death— shall an-y
dain— or e-ven death, or e-ven death— shall an-y
come— not e-ven death, not e-ven death— not an-y

power of earth or heaven di-vide us from your love, O Christ?
power of earth or heaven di-vide us from your love, O Christ?
power of earth or heaven can part us from your love, O Christ.

Guitar chords do not correspond with keyboard harmony.

Reversing the usual pattern, the tune came first in this hymn; the tune name was assigned only after the text was written. The author first heard the repeated phrase "or/not even death" implied by the melody, which sent her to the passage from Romans 8:31–39 paraphrased here.

TEXT: Mary Louise Bringle, 2006
MUSIC: Sally Ann Morris, 2006
Text and Music © 2006 GIA Publications, Inc.

ROMANS 8
8.8.8.4.4.8.8

There Is a Place of Quiet Rest 824
Near to the Heart of God

1 There is a place of qui - et rest, near to the heart of God,
2 There is a place of com - fort sweet, near to the heart of God,
3 There is a place of full re - lease, near to the heart of God,

a place where sin can-not mo - lest, near to the heart of God.
a place where we our Sav - ior meet, near to the heart of God.
a place where all is joy and peace, near to the heart of God.

Refrain

O Je - sus, blest Re - deem - er, sent from the heart of God,

hold us, who wait be - fore thee, near to the heart of God.

A Presbyterian campus pastor and choir director in Missouri wrote this simple but moving hymn in response to the death of two young nieces from diphtheria. By distilling such personal grief into the shared assurances of faith, these words have brought comfort to many.

TEXT and MUSIC: Cleland Boyd McAfee, 1901

MC AFEE
CM with refrain

825 Swing Low, Sweet Chariot

Refrain

Swing low, sweet char - i - ot, com-ing for to car-ry me home.

Swing low, sweet char - i - ot, com-ing for to car-ry me home. *Fine*

1 I looked o-ver Jor-dan, and what did I see   com-ing for to car-ry me home?
2 If   you get there be - fore   I   do,   com-ing for to car-ry me home,
3 The bright-est day that ev - er   I   saw,   com-ing for to car-ry me home,
4 I'm some-times up and some-times down, com-ing for to car-ry me home,

to Refrain

A   band of an-gels com-ing af-ter me, com-ing for to car-ry me home. O,
tell   all my friends I'm com - ing   too, com-ing for to car-ry me home. O,
when Je - sus washed my sins   a - way, com-ing for to car-ry me home. O,
but   still my soul feels heaven-ly bound, com-ing for to car-ry me home. O,

While ostensibly based on Elijah's ascent into heaven (2 Kings 2:11), this African American spiritual also communicates the enslaved people's hope that they might find deliverance across a river (i.e. in the free states beyond the Ohio). Call-and-response singing enhances this piece.

TEXT: African American spiritual
MUSIC: African American spiritual; arr. Robert Nathaniel Dett, 1936
Music Arr. © 1936, ren. Belwin-Mills Publishing Corp. (admin. Alfred Publishing Co., Inc.)

SWING LOW
Irregular

Lift High the Cross

Refrain
Descant

This majestic hymn celebrates the paradox that for Christians a means of painful death has been transformed into a symbol of renewed life; a sign of defeat has become an emblem of victory. With the cross traced on our foreheads at Baptism we are marked as Christ's own forever.

TEXT: George William Kitchin, 1887; rev. Michael Robert Newbolt, 1916, alt.
MUSIC: Sydney Hugo Nicholson, 1916; desc. Richard Proulx, 1985
Text and Music © 1974 Hope Publishing Company
Music Desc. © 1985 Hope Publishing Company

CRUCIFER
10.10 with refrain

827 O Morning Star, How Fair and Bright

1 O Morn - ing Star, how fair and bright! You shine with
2 Lord, when you look on us in love, at once there
3 What joy to know, when life is past, the Lord we

God's own truth and light, a - glow with grace and mer - cy!
falls from God a - bove a ray of pur - est plea - sure.
love is first and last, the end and the be - gin - ning!

Of Ja - cob's line, King Da - vid's son, our Lord and Sav - ior,
Your word and Spir - it, flesh and blood re - fresh our souls with
He will one day, O glo - rious grace, trans - port us to that

This "Queen of Chorales" (see no. 349 for the "King") is often associated with Epiphany because of the star imagery, but the text is really addressed to Christ as the Morning Star (Revelation 22:16), who guides and sustains us in this life and is our hope for the life to come.

TEXT: Philipp Nicolai, 1597; trans. *Lutheran Book of Worship*, 1978
MUSIC: Philipp Nicolai, 1599; harm. Johann Sebastian Bach, 1740
Text © 1978 Lutheran Book of Worship (admin. Augsburg Fortress)

WIE SCHÖN LEUCHTET
Irregular

you   have won our hearts to   serve you   on - ly!   Low - ly,
heaven-ly   food. You   are   our   dear - est   trea - sure!   Let your
hap - py   place be - yond   all   tears and   sin - ning!   A - men!

ho - ly!   Great   and   glo - rious,   all   vic - to - rious, rich   in
mer - cy   warm   and   cheer us!   O   draw near us!   For   you
A - men!   Come, Lord Je - sus!   Crown of   glad - ness!   We   are

bless - ing!   Rule   and   might o'er   all   pos - sess - ing!
teach   us   God's own   love through you   has   reached   us.
yearn - ing   for   the   day   of   your   re - turn - ing.

828 More Love to Thee, O Christ

1 More love to thee, O Christ, more love to thee!
2 Once earth-ly joy I craved, sought peace and rest.
3 Then shall my lat-est breath whis-per thy praise;

Hear thou the prayer I make on bend-ed knee.
Now thee a-lone I seek; give what is best.
this be the part-ing cry my heart shall raise.

This is my ear-nest plea: more love, O Christ, to thee;
This all my prayer shall be: more love, O Christ, to thee;
This still its prayer shall be: more love, O Christ, to thee;

more love to thee, more love to thee!

Perhaps because this prayer-poem by the wife of a leading 19th-century Presbyterian minister grew out of her own physical and emotional suffering, it has continued to speak to many people in similar distress. It is set here to the tune created for its first printing in a hymnal.

TEXT: Elizabeth Payson Prentiss, 1856
MUSIC: William Howard Doane, 1870

MORE LOVE TO THEE
6.4.6.4.6.6.4.4

My Faith Looks Up to Thee 829

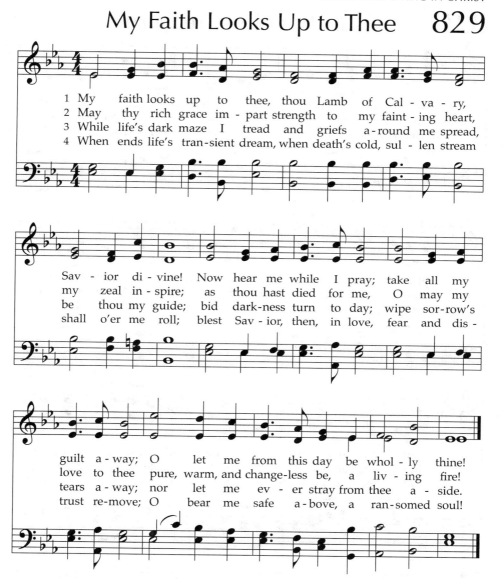

1 My faith looks up to thee, thou Lamb of Cal - va - ry,
2 May thy rich grace im - part strength to my faint - ing heart,
3 While life's dark maze I tread and griefs a - round me spread,
4 When ends life's tran-sient dream, when death's cold, sul - len stream

Sav - ior di - vine! Now hear me while I pray; take all my
my zeal in - spire; as thou hast died for me, O may my
be thou my guide; bid dark-ness turn to day; wipe sor-row's
shall o'er me roll; blest Sav - ior, then, in love, fear and dis -

guilt a - way; O let me from this day be whol - ly thine!
love to thee pure, warm, and change-less be, a liv - ing fire!
tears a - way; nor let me ev - er stray from thee a - side.
trust re-move; O bear me safe a - bove, a ran-somed soul!

Originally a poem of private reflection, this text was offered to the composer when he asked the author if he had written anything that could be set to music for a new hymn and tune collection. This was the first tune written for these words and has proved the most enduring.

TEXT: Ray Palmer, 1830
MUSIC: Lowell Mason, 1831, alt.

OLIVET
6.6.4.6.6.6.4

830   Jesus, Priceless Treasure

1 Je - sus, price-less trea - sure, source of pur - est
2 In thine arm I rest me; foes who would op -
3 Hence, all fears and sad - ness! For the Lord of

plea - sure, tru - est friend to me; ah, how long I've
press me can - not reach me here. Though the earth be
glad - ness, Je - sus, en - ters in: God, who dear - ly

pant - ed, and my heart has faint - ed, thirst-ing, Lord, for
shak - ing, ev - ery heart be quak - ing, Je - sus calms my
loves us, from all tri - al saves us; gives sweet peace with -

thee! Thine I am, O spot - less Lamb: noth - ing in the
fear; light-nings flash and thun - ders crash: yet, though sin and
in; I have borne this world - ly scorn; still in thee lies

The classic marriage of words and music that characterizes German chorales can be seen well in this simple
but intense text voiced by an already elegant tune that Bach burnishes in his harmonization. Text and tune
evoke each other and reinforce the ardor of those who sing.

TEXT: Johann Franck, 1650; trans. Catherine Winkworth, 1863, alt.   JESU, MEINE FREUDE
MUSIC: Johann Crüger, 1653; harm. Johann Sebastian Bach, 1723   6.6.5.6.6.5.7.8.6

world can hide thee; naught I ask be - side thee.
hell as - sail me, Je - sus will not fail me.
pur - est plea - sure, Je - sus, price - less trea - sure!

I Depend upon Your Faithfulness 831
Tu fidelidad

I de - pend up - on your faith - ful - ness.
Tu fi - de - li - dad es gran - de,

I can jour - ney on, for you are al - ways there.
tu fi - de - li - dad in - com - pa - ra - ble es.

None com - pares with you, O bless - ed One;
Na - die co - mo tú, ben - di - to Dios.

O how great your faith - ful - ness.
Gran - de tu fi - de - li - dad.

This short song's derivation from Lamentations 3:23 is somewhat more obvious in the original Spanish text than in the English version, so it is desirable to sing both languages whenever feasible. Like chants from Taizé, this piece benefits from being sung more than once.

TEXT: Miguel Cassina, 1994; English trans. Andrew Donaldson, 2001
MUSIC: Miguel Cassina, 1994; arr. Andrew Donaldson, 2008
Text, English Trans., and Music © 1994 Balsamo Producciones (admin. EMICMGPublishing.com)

TU FIDELIDAD
Irregular

832 Here on Jesus Christ I Will Stand

Kwake Yesu Nasimama

Refrain

Here on Je-sus Christ I will stand. He's the sol-id rock of my
Kwa-ke Ye-su na - si-ma-ma, ndi-ye mwam-ba ni sa-la-

life. He's the sol-id rock of my life. He's the sol-id rock
ma. Ndi-ye mwam-ba ni sa-la-ma, ndi-ye mwam-ba ni

Fine

of my life. 1 There's no oth-er place I can hide
sa - la - ma. 2 It is not the work of my hands
3 When my days on this earth are done,

till the storm that rag - es sub - sides. My voice cries to God
that has washed a - way all my sins. I'm re-deemed, and all
and I stand at God's ho - ly throne, my heart will not have

This hymn represents a Kenyan adaptation of the gospel hymn, "My Hope Is Built on Nothing Less" (see no. 353), a connection that is most obvious in their similar refrains. Both the original and derived texts affirm that our hope is not in ourselves but in Christ's redeeming work.

TEXT: Kenyan hymn; adapt. Greg Scheer, 2007
MUSIC: Kenyan melody; arr. Greg Scheer, 2007
Text © 2007 East Africa Annual Conference (admin. General Board of Global Ministries t/a GBGMusik)
English Adapt. and Music Arr. © 2007 Greg Scheer (admin. General Board of Global Ministries t/a GBGMusik)

KWAKE YESU NASIMAMA
LM

to Refrain

from the flood, and I'm saved be - cause of his blood.
of my days, Je - sus Christ will be my heart's praise.
an - y fear; in Christ's righ - teous - ness I am here.

O Love That Wilt Not Let Me Go 833

1 O Love that wilt not let me go, I rest my
2 O Light that fol - lowest all my way, I yield my
3 O Joy that seek - est me through pain, I can - not
4 O Cross that lift - est up my head, I dare not

wea - ry soul in thee; I give thee back the life I owe, that
flick - ering torch to thee; my heart re - stores its bor - rowed ray, that
close my heart to thee; I trace the rain - bow through the rain, and
ask to fly from thee; I lay in dust life's glo - ry dead, and

in thine o - cean depths its flow may rich - er, full - er be.
in thy sun - shine's blaze its day may bright - er, fair - er be.
feel the prom - ise is not vain that morn shall tear - less be.
from the ground there blos - soms red life that shall end - less be.

This intense hymn of commitment to God (addressed as Love, Light, and Joy) closes with an invocation of
the ultimate testimony to those attributes (the Cross). The composer, a Scotsman, named this specially-
composed tune for the 11th-century patroness of Scotland.

TEXT: George Matheson, 1881, alt.
MUSIC: Albert Lister Peace, 1884, alt.

ST. MARGARET
8.8.8.8.6

834 Precious Lord, Take My Hand

1 Pre - cious Lord, take my hand; lead me on, help me
2 When my way grows drear, pre - cious Lord, lin - ger

stand; I am tired, I am weak, I am worn.
near; when my life is al - most gone,

Through the storm, through the night, lead me on to the
hear my cry, hear my call, hold my hand lest I

light; take my hand, pre - cious Lord, lead me home.
fall; take my hand, pre - cious Lord, lead me home.

This black gospel song, like much hymnody, sprang out of the author's deep personal loss (the death of his wife and newborn son), yet it has brought solace to many. He thought his fingers were playing new music, but they unlocked a deep memory of a tune almost a century old.

TEXT: Thomas A. Dorsey, 1938
MUSIC: George N. Allen, 1844; arr. Thomas A. Dorsey, 1938
Text and Music Arr. © 1938, ren. Warner-Tamerlane Publishing Corp. (admin. Alfred Publishing Co., Inc.)

PRECIOUS LORD
6.6.9.D

Just a Closer Walk with Thee 835

Refrain Just a clos-er walk with thee, grant it,
1 I am weak, but thou art strong; Je - sus,
2 Through this world of toil and snares, if I
3 When my fee - ble life is o'er, time for

Je - sus, is my plea, dai - ly walk-ing close to
keep me from all wrong; I'll be sat - is - fied as
fal - ter, Lord, who cares? Who with me my bur - den
me will be no more; guide me gent - ly, safe - ly

thee: let it be, dear Lord, let it be.
long as I walk, let me walk close to thee. *Ref.*
shares? None but thee, dear Lord, none but thee. *Ref.*
o'er to thy shore, dear Lord, to thy shore. *Ref.*

The chromatic musical style of this anonymous short hymn suggests that it probably dates from the early 20th century. It also seems to owe much of its popularity to radio broadcasts and recordings as well as to evangelistic meetings and singing conventions of that era.

TEXT and MUSIC: Trad. North American hymn

CLOSER WALK
Irregular

836 Abide with Me

1 A - bide with me: fast falls the e - ven - tide.
2 Swift to its close ebbs out life's lit - tle day;
3 I need thy pres - ence ev - ery pass - ing hour;
4 I fear no foe, with thee at hand to bless;
5 Hold thou thy cross be - fore my clos - ing eyes;

The dark - ness deep - ens; Lord, with me a - bide!
earth's joys grow dim; its glo - ries pass a - way;
what but thy grace can foil the tempt - er's power?
ills have no weight, and tears no bit - ter - ness.
shine through the gloom and point me to the skies.

When oth - er help - ers fail and com - forts flee,
change and de - cay in all a - round I see.
Who, like thy - self, my guide and stay can be?
Where is death's sting? Where, grave, thy vic - to - ry?
Heaven's morn - ing breaks, and earth's vain shad - ows flee;

help of the help - less, O a - bide with me.
O thou who chang - est not, a - bide with me.
Through cloud and sun - shine, Lord, a - bide with me.
I tri - umph still, if thou a - bide with me.
in life, in death, O Lord, a - bide with me.

By blending end of day and end of life, the imagery of this well-known Victorian hymn has made it valuable for both evening services and funerals. Although the author wrote his own music for it, the present tune has been firmly associated with this text for over 150 years.

TEXT: Henry Francis Lyte, 1847
MUSIC: William Henry Monk, 1861

EVENTIDE
10.10.10.10

What a Fellowship, What a Joy Divine 837
Leaning on the Everlasting Arms

1 What a fel-low-ship, what a joy di-vine, lean-ing on the ev-er-
2 O how sweet to walk in this pil-grim way, lean-ing on the ev-er-
3 What have I to dread, what have I to fear, lean-ing on the ev-er-

last-ing arms; what a bless-ed-ness, what a peace is mine,
last-ing arms; O how bright the path grows from day to day,
last-ing arms? I have bless-ed peace with my Lord so near,

lean-ing on the ev-er-last-ing arms.

Refrain

Lean - ing,
Lean-ing on Je - sus,

lean - ing,
lean-ing on Je - sus, safe and se-cure from all a-larms; lean -
lean-ing on

ing, lean - ing,
Je - sus, lean-ing on Je - sus, lean-ing on the ev-er-last-ing arms.

The composer of the tune (and creator of the refrain) asked the author of the stanzas to write a hymn based on the latter part of Deuteronomy 33:27 (as worded in the King James Version): "Underneath are the everlasting arms." Their joint effort has proved very popular.

TEXT: Elisha A. Hoffman, 1887
MUSIC: Anthony J. Showalter, 1887

SHOWALTER
10.9.10.9 with refrain

838 Standing on the Promises

1 Stand - ing on the prom - is - es of Christ my king,
2 Stand - ing on the prom - is - es that can - not fail,
3 Stand - ing on the prom - is - es of Christ the Lord,
4 Stand - ing on the prom - is - es I can - not fall,

through e - ter - nal a - ges let his prais - es ring;
when the howl - ing storms of doubt and fear as - sail,
bound to him e - ter - nal - ly by love's strong cord,
lis - tening ev - ery mo - ment to the Spir - it's call,

glo - ry in the high - est, I will shout and sing,
by the liv - ing Word of God I shall pre - vail,
o - ver - com - ing dai - ly with the Spir - it's sword,
rest - ing in my Sav - ior as my all in all,

stand - ing on the prom - is - es of God.
stand - ing on the prom - is - es of God.
stand - ing on the prom - is - es of God.
stand - ing on the prom - is - es of God.

Perhaps because this hymn is so well known, its language sounds vaguely scriptural; but while there are various biblical uses of "stand" and "promise(s)," the two words are never combined. The confidence here is similar to that of "My Hope Is Built on Nothing Less" (see no. 353).

TEXT and MUSIC: R. Kelso Carter, 1886

PROMISES
11.11.11.9 with refrain

839 Blessed Assurance, Jesus Is Mine!

1 Bless-ed as-sur-ance, Je-sus is mine! O what a fore-taste of glo-ry di-vine! Heir of sal-va-tion, pur-chase of God, born of his Spir-it, washed in his blood.

2 Per-fect sub-mis-sion, per-fect de-light, vi-sions of rap-ture now burst on my sight; an-gels de-scend-ing, bring from a-bove ech-oes of mer-cy, whis-pers of love.

3 Per-fect sub-mis-sion, all is at rest; I in my Sav-ior am hap-py and blest, watch-ing and wait-ing, look-ing a-bove, filled with his good-ness, lost in his love.

Refrain

This is my sto-ry; this is my song, prais-ing my Sav-ior

Sometimes this prolific 19th-century hymnwriter wrote texts for others to set, and sometimes she created words for tunes others had composed. This text was of the second kind, and the resulting close fit between words and music has made them both popular and inseparable.

TEXT: Fanny Jane Crosby, 1873; Korean trans. The United Methodist Korean Hymnal Committee, 2001
MUSIC: Phoebe Palmer Knapp, 1873
Korean Trans. © 2001 The United Methodist Publishing House (admin. The Copyright Company)

ASSURANCE
9.10.9.9 with refrain

all the day long; this is my sto - ry; this is my

song, prais - ing my Sav - ior all the day long.

KOREAN

1 예수를 내가 주로 믿어
    성령과 피로써 거듭나니
    이세상에서 내 영혼이
    하늘의 영광 누리도다

후렴   이것이 나의 간증이요
      이것이 나의 찬송일세
      나사는 동안 끊임없이
      예수 내 구주 찬송하리

2 온전히 주께 맡긴 내영
    온전한 기쁨을 누리면서
    자비와 사랑 속삭이는
    하늘의 천사 보리로다 후렴

3 예수께 맡긴 나의 영혼
    주안에 복되고 평안하니
    세상도 없고 나도 없고
    사랑의 주만 보이도다 후렴

840　When Peace like a River

It Is Well with My Soul

1 When peace like a riv-er at-tend-eth my way, when
2 Though Sa-tan should buf-fet, though tri-als should come, let
3 He lives: O the bliss of this glo-ri-ous thought. My
4 Lord, has-ten the day when our faith shall be sight, the

sor-rows like sea bil-lows roll, what-ev-er my lot, thou hast
this blest as-sur-ance con-trol, that Christ hath re-gard-ed my
sin, not in part, but the whole, is nailed to the cross and I
clouds be rolled back as a scroll, the trum-pet shall sound and the

taught me to say, it is well, it is well with my soul.
help-less es-tate, and hath shed his own blood for my soul.
bear it no more. Praise the Lord, praise the Lord, O my soul!
Lord shall de-scend; e-ven so it is well with my soul.

Refrain

It is well with my soul;
It is well with my soul;

This text is a remarkable expression of faith born of grief. The author, an active Presbyterian layman who had just lost four daughters in a tragic shipwreck, wrote it while sailing to Paris to meet his wife, who had survived. The tune was named for the ship that sank.

TEXT: Horatio G. Spafford, 1876, alt.
MUSIC: Philip P. Bliss, 1876

VILLE DU HAVRE
11.8.11.9 with refrain

it is well; it is well with my soul.

God Is My Strong Salvation 841
(Psalm 27)

Capo 1: (Em) (Bm) (Em) (Bm) (Em) (Bm) (G)
Fm Cm Fm Cm Fm Cm A♭

1 God is my strong sal - va - tion; what foe have I to fear?
2 Place on the Lord re - li - ance; my soul, with cour-age wait;

(Em) (Bm) (D) (G) (Bm) (Em) (Bm) (Em)
Fm Cm E♭ A♭ Cm Fm Cm Fm

In per - il and temp - ta - tion my light, my help, is near.
God's truth be thine af - fi - ance, when faint and des - o - late.

(Bm) (G) (D) (Em) (Bm) (Em) (Bm) (G)
Cm A♭ E♭ Fm Cm Fm Cm A♭

Though hosts en - camp a - round me, firm to the fight I stand;
God's might thy heart shall strength - en; God's love thy joy in - crease;

(Em) (Bm) (D) (G) (Bm) (Em) (Bm) (Em)
Fm Cm E♭ A♭ Cm Fm Cm Fm

what ter - ror can con - found me, with God at my right hand?
mer - cy thy days shall length - en; the Lord will give thee peace.

Guitar chords do not correspond with keyboard harmony.

Preserving the author's intention, his abbreviated paraphrase of Psalm 27 appears here in two eight-line stanzas, the first containing general affirmations and the second assurances to his fainting soul. This sense of resolution is strengthened by the sturdy shape note tune.

TEXT: James Montgomery, 1822, alt.
MUSIC: *The Sacred Harp*, 1844; harm. Austin C. Lovelace, 1964
Music Harm. © 1964 Abingdon Press (admin. The Copyright Company)

WEDLOCK
7.6.7.6.D

842   The Lord Is My Light

(Psalm 27)

*Each of the two themes can be sung separately, either in unison or as a round.
The two themes can also be sung together.*

PSALM 27

Refrain

1 The LORD is my light and my salvation;
  whom then shall I fear?
    the LORD is the strength of my life;
    of whom then shall I be afraid?

2 **When evildoers came upon me to eat up my flesh,**
  it was they, my foes and my adversaries, who stumbled and fell.

3 Though an army should encamp against me,
  yet my heart shall not be afraid;

  and though war should rise up against me,
    yet will I put my trust in the LORD.

4 One thing have I asked of the LORD;
  one thing I seek;
    that I may dwell in the house of the LORD all the days of my life;

  to behold the fair beauty of the LORD,
    to seek God in the temple. *Refrain*

This adaptation of Psalm 27:1 from the Taizé Community provides an effective refrain for a responsive
reading of the whole psalm. The two melodies can be sung either in harmony or as a round. The refrain can
also be used on its own during congregational candlelighting services.

TEXT: Taizé Community, 1991   THE LORD IS MY LIGHT
MUSIC: Jacques Berthier, 1991   Irregular
Text and Music © 1991 Les Presses de Taizé (admin. GIA Publications, Inc.)
Responsive Reading of Psalm 27 © 1993 The Order of St. Benedict (admin. The Liturgical Press)

5 For on the day of trouble the LORD shall shelter me in safety;
the LORD shall hide me in the secrecy of the holy place
and set me high upon a rock.

6 **Even now the LORD lifts up my head**
above my enemies round about me.

Therefore I will offer in the holy place an oblation
with sounds of great gladness;
I will sing and make music to the LORD. *Refrain*

7 Hearken to my voice, O LORD, when I call;
have mercy on me and answer me.

8 **You speak in my heart and say, "Seek my face."**
Your face, LORD, will I seek.

9 Hide not your face from me,
nor turn away your servant in displeasure.

You have been my helper;
cast me not away;
do not forsake me, O God of my salvation.

10 Though my father and my mother forsake me,
the LORD will sustain me. *Refrain*

11 Show me your ways, O LORD;
lead me on a level path, because of my enemies.

12 **Deliver me not into the hand of my adversaries,**
for false witnesses have risen up against me,
and also those who speak malice.

13 What if I had not believed
that I should see the goodness of the LORD
in the land of the living!

14 **O tarry and await the LORD's pleasure;**
be strong, and the LORD shall comfort your heart;
wait patiently for the LORD. *Refrain*

843 My Soul Is at Rest
(Psalm 62)

My soul is at rest in God a-lone; my sal-va-tion comes from God.

PSALM 62

Refrain

1 For God alone my soul in silence waits;
   from God comes my salvation.

2 **God alone is my rock and my salvation,**
   my stronghold, so that I shall not be greatly shaken. *Refrain*

3 How long will you assail me to crush me, all of you together,
   as you would a leaning fence, a toppling wall?

4 **They seek only to bring me down from my place of honor;**
   lies are their chief delight.

   They bless with their lips,
   but in their hearts they curse. *Refrain*

5 For God alone my soul in silence waits;
   truly, my hope is in God.

6 **God alone is my rock and my salvation,**
   my stronghold, so that I shall not be shaken.

7 In God is my safety and my honor;
   God is my strong rock and my refuge. *Refrain*

8 Put your trust in God always, O people;
   pour out your hearts before God, who is our refuge.

9 **Those of high degree are but a fleeting breath;**
   even those of low estate cannot be trusted.

   On the scales they are lighter than a breath,
   all of them together.

10 **Put no trust in extortion; in robbery take no empty pride;**
    though wealth increase, set not your heart upon it. *Refrain*

11 God has spoken once, twice have I heard it,
    that power belongs to God.

12 **Steadfast love is yours, O Lord,**
    for you repay all people according to their deeds. *Refrain*

This briefer version of a refrain based on Psalm 62:1, 5 (compare with no. 814) also comes from the
ecumenical community at Taizé, France. It can be used alone for repeated singing or as a prayer response,
but it appears here as a refrain that ties together the entire psalm.

TEXT: Taizé Community, 1984
MUSIC: Jacques Berthier, 1981
Text and Music © 1991 Les Presses de Taizé (admin. GIA Publications, Inc.)
Responsive Reading of Psalm 62 © 1993 The Order of St. Benedict (admin. The Liturgical Press)

MY SOUL IS AT REST
9.7

Incline Your Ear, O Lord, to Me 844
(Psalm 86)

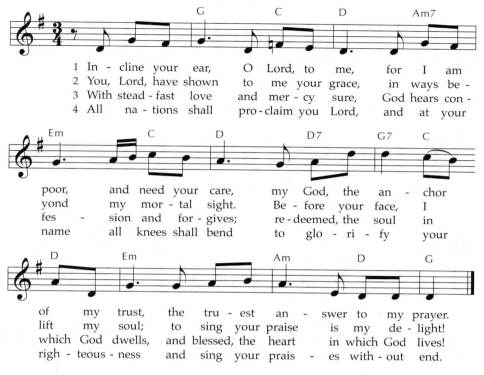

1 In - cline your ear, O Lord, to me, for I am
2 You, Lord, have shown to me your grace, in ways be -
3 With stead - fast love and mer - cy sure, God hears con -
4 All na - tions shall pro - claim you Lord, and at your

poor, and need your care, my God, the an - chor
yond my mor - tal sight. Be - fore your face, I
fes - sion and for - gives; re - deemed, the soul in
name all knees shall bend to glo - ri - fy your

of my trust, the tru - est an - swer to my prayer.
lift my soul; to sing your praise is my de - light!
which God dwells, and blessed, the heart in which God lives!
righ - teous - ness and sing your prais - es with - out end.

Guitar chords do not correspond with keyboard harmony.

This paraphrase of Psalm 86 begins as an individual lament, but it gradually moves into general affirmations and concludes with the declaration that all people will one day worship God. The tune is based on a traditional English ballad air named for a village in North Yorkshire.

TEXT: Michael Morgan, 1995
MUSIC: English folk melody; harm. Arthur Hutchings, 1981
Text © 2010 Michael Morgan (admin. Congregational Ministries Publishing, Presbyterian Church (U.S.A.))
Music Harm. © 1969 International Committee on English in the Liturgy

DANBY
LM

845 To the Hills I Lift My Eyes

내가 산을 향하여
(Psalm 121)

To the hills I lift my eyes long - ing to know
내 가 산 을 향 하 여 눈 을 드 니

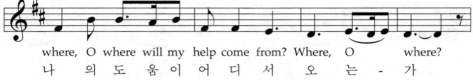

where, O where will my help come from? Where, O where?
나 의 도 움 이 어 디 서 오 는 - 가

My help comes from the Lord, who made heaven and earth.
나 의 도 움 이 천 지 를 지 으 - 신

God the Cre - a - tor will keep my life. God is my help.
여 호 와 하 나 님 에 게 서 오 - 네

This paraphrase of Psalm 121:1–2 speaks to a recurring human condition, represented here by the song of a pilgrim gazing up at the hills around Jerusalem. When we find ourselves surrounded by overwhelming problems, where do we turn for help? The Korean tune name means "my help."

TEXT: Song-suk Im, 1990; English trans. Emily R. Brink, 2011
MUSIC: Song Lee, 1990
Text, English Trans., and Music © 1990, 2011 Christian Conference of Asia (admin. GIA Publications, Inc.)

NA-UI DO-UM
7.4.8.3

Fight the Good Fight

846

1 Fight the good fight with all thy might.
2 Run the straight race through God's good grace;
3 Cast care a - side; lean on thy guide.
4 Faint not nor fear: God's arms are near.

Christ is thy strength and Christ thy right.
lift up thine eyes, and seek Christ's face.
God's bound - less mer - cy will pro - vide.
God chang - eth not, and thou art dear.

Lay hold on life, and it shall be
Life with its way be - fore us lies;
Trust, and thy trust - ing soul shall prove
On - ly be - lieve, and thou shalt see

thy joy and crown e - ter - nal - ly.
Christ is the path, and Christ the prize.
Christ is its life, and Christ its love.
that Christ is all in all to thee.

The opening phrase here (based on 1 Timothy 6:12) is not a military image but an athletic one, from a Greek verb meaning "struggle" or "grapple" or "wrestle." The sports context continues in later stanzas reflecting the experience of a runner (recalling Hebrews 12:1–2).

TEXT: John Samuel Bewley Monsell, 1863, alt.
MUSIC: Attr. John Hatton, c. 1793

DUKE STREET
LM

847 Our Hope, Our Life
(Psalm 49)

1 Our hope, our life are in the Lord, the God we
2 Some flaunt their gold; some trust its power, but what they
3 Though wealth or learn - ing may be ours, or fame that
4 Be - yond this age of shame and sham we glimpse a

hon - or and con - fess. Why crave re - nown or
cher - ish will de - cay; and still the ran - som
spreads through-out the land, the shack - les of mor -
bet - ter des - ti - ny: the Lord will lift us

op - u - lence? They fade, those things we now pos - sess.
for a soul re - mains a price too great to pay.
tal - i - ty pre - vent so much that we have planned.
free from death to dwell in praise e - ter - nal - ly.

Guitar chords do not correspond with keyboard harmony.

As this recent paraphrase of Psalm 49 illustrates, human beings have long been tempted to put their trust in earthly assets, especially wealth and fame. But these are not enduring possessions, and they cannot save us. Only in God can we find unfailing hope and eternal life.

TEXT: Martin E. Leckebusch, 2006, alt.
MUSIC: English folk melody; harm. John Weaver, 1988
Text © 2006 Kevin Mayhew Ltd.
Music Harm. © 1990 Hope Publishing Company

O WALY WALY
LM

Trust in God

(Psalm 125)

848

1 Trust in God and you will be shel-tered for e - ter - ni - ty;
2 Lift your eyes to see the hills, through the a - ges stand-ing still,
3 In the prom-ised, ho - ly land may the wick-ed nev - er stand;

like a moun-tain, strong and sure, by God's grace you will en - dure.
wrapped a-round the cit - y walls: so our God sur-rounds us all.
but where good and kind - ness reign, may the peace of God re - main.

Psalm 125 is one of the songs that would have been sung by Jewish pilgrims going to Jerusalem. As the imagery of this paraphrase suggests, it was probably reserved for use during the final ascent to the city, closing with a prayer for peace wherever God's faithful people dwell.

TEXT: David Gambrell, 2009
MUSIC: Orlando Gibbons, 1623, alt.
Text © 2011 David Gambrell (admin. Presbyterian Publishing Corp.)

SONG 13
7.7.7.7

849 Everyone Who Longs for the Boundless Love of God

하나님의 사랑을 사모하는 자

Ev-ery-one who longs for the bound-less love of God,
Ev-ery-one who wor-ships God and sings glad songs of praise,
하 나 님 의 사 랑 을 사 모 하 는 자
하 나 님 께 찬 양 과 경 배 하 는 자

ev-ery-one who hopes for the com-ing of God's peace,
ev-ery-one who fol-lows God's good and ho-ly way,
하 나 님 의 평 안 을 바 라 보 는 자
하 나 님 의 선 하 심 을 닮 아 가 는 자

the Lord God who cre-at-ed all things beau-ti-ful and good
너 의 모 든 것 창 조 하 신 우 리 주 님 이

1
loves you more than you can ev-er ful-ly know.
너 를 얼 마 나 사 랑 하 시 는 지

2
now as one of God's own. God is al-ways watch-ing
자 녀 삼 으 셨 네 하 나 님 사 랑 의

The first stanza of this Korean hymn identifies how to "prepare the way of the Lord," in other words, how to be receptive to God's activity. The second stanza moves into active engagement: worship and obedience. The final section offers many assurances of God's presence and care.

TEXT: Sung-ho Park, 2001; English trans. Edward Poitras, 2001, alt.
MUSIC: Sung-ho Park, 2001; arr. Alfred V. Fedak, 2012
Text and Music © 2001 Sung-ho Park
Music Arr. © 2011 Alfred V. Fedak

EVERYONE WHO LONGS
Irregular

850 In a Deep, Unbounded Darkness

1 In a deep, un-bound-ed dark - ness, long be - fore the first
2 Though our world is ev - er - chang-ing, you are con-stant, firm,
3 Joy trans-forms our lips to boast - ing on - ly in your match-
4 God of Ha - gar, God of Sa - rah, God of no - mad A -

light shone, you, O God, be - yond all mer - it worked a
and sure, faith - ful to your cov-enant prom - ise. Trust - ing
less grace, send - ing Christ to dwell a - mong us, Word made
bra - ham; God of Mir - yam, God of Mo - ses, Fi - ery

won - der faith makes known: in your mer - cy, in your
you, we live, se - cure: sing - ing prais - es, sing - ing
flesh in time and space: Friend and Sav - ior, Friend and
Pil - lar, great I AM: lead us home-ward, lead us

mer - cy, you em-braced us as your own,
prais - es, long as heart and breath en - dure,
Sav - ior, in whose life we glimpse your face,
home - ward, to the love - feast of the Lamb,

ev - er - more and ev - er - more.

Setting this translation of a Chinese hymn to Western plainsong enhances the universal context of the opening stanza. The familiar pattern of creation, covenant, and incarnation in the first three stanzas leads to a far-reaching final stanza that looks both backward and forward.

TEXT: Anon. Chinese; trans. Francis P. Jones, 1953; adapt. Mary Louise Bringle, 2012
MUSIC: Plainsong, Mode V; harm. C. Winfred Douglas, 1940
Text © 2012 GIA Publications, Inc.
Music Harm. © 1943, 1961, 1985 Church Pension Fund

DIVINUM MYSTERIUM
8.7.8.7.8.7.7

Come, Bring Your Burdens to God 851
Woza nomthwalo wakho

A great strength of music from southeastern Africa is that it usually emerges from communal life, and in singing such songs we unite our sung prayers with those of the people who created them. This one is based on the singing of the Mooiplaas congregation in South Africa.

TEXT: South African; English trans. Barbara Clark, Mairi Munro, and Martine Stemerick, 2008
MUSIC: South African melody; arr. Welile Sigobi, 2008
English Trans. and Music Arr. © 2008 WGRG, Iona Community (admin. GIA Publications, Inc.)

WOZA NOMTHWALO WAKHO
7.7.7.8

852 When the Lord Redeems the Very Least

1 When the Lord re-deems the ver-y least,
2 When the Lord re-stores the sick and weak, we will re-
3 When the Lord re-vives the world from death, we will re-joice, will re-
4 When the Lord re-turns in vic-to-ry,

joice.
joice, will re-joice.

When the hun-gry gath-er for the feast,
When the earth is giv-en to the meek,
When the word of God fills ev-ery breath,
When we live in glo-rious lib-er-ty,

Refrain

we will re-joice. We will re-
we will re-joice, will re-joice, will re-joice. We will re-joice, will re-

What does it mean to pray "thy kingdom come"? This text (loosely modeled on Psalm 126) sketches out some of the features that help us to know when God's reign has truly come. The energy of the gospel song tune adds to the sense of rejoicing repeatedly promised in this text.

TEXT: Sylvia G. Dunstan, c. 1991
MUSIC: Albert E. Brumley, 1932; arr. Evelyn Simpson-Curenton, c. 2001
Text © 1991 GIA Publications, Inc.
Music © 1932 Hartford Music Co., ren. 1960 Albert E. Brumley & Sons (admin. ClearBox Rights)

I'LL FLY AWAY
9.4.9.4 with refrain

joice with glad-ness. We will re-joice.
joice with glad-ness. We will re-joice, will re-joice with glad-ness. All our

We will re-joice!
days we'll sing to God in praise. We will re-joice, will re-joice, will re-joice!

853 We Are Marching in the Light of God

Siyahamba

We are march-ing in the light of God; we are march-ing in the
Si - ya - hamb' e - ku - kha - nyen' kwen - khos', si - ya - hamb' e - ku - kha -

light of God. We are march - ing in the light of God;
nyen' kwen - khos'. Si - ya - hamb' e - ku - kha - nyen' kwen - khos',

we are march-ing in the light of God.
si - ya - hamb' e - ku - kha - nyen' kwen - khos'.

we are march-ing in the light of, the light of God.
si - ya - hamb' e - ku - kha - nyen' kwen -, kha - nyen' kwen - khos'.

we are march-ing in the light of God.
si - ya - hamb' e - ku - kha - nyen' kwen - khos'.

This lively Zulu/Xhosa freedom song originated in a Methodist young men's group in South Africa and has gone on to become popular in many other languages around the globe. Some additional stanzas are suggested, but others may be improvised as appropriate to the occasion.

TEXT: South African; English trans. Gracia Grindal, 1984
MUSIC: South African; arr. *Freedom Is Coming*, 1984
English Trans. and Music Arr. © 1984 Utryck (admin. Walton Music Corp.)

SIYAHAMBA
Irregular

Additional stanzas ad lib.:
We are dancing…
We are praying…
We are singing…

Appendix 1

THEOLOGICAL VISION STATEMENT

Collections of hymns, psalms, and spiritual songs give voice to the church's core beliefs and theological convictions. Their texts are "compact theology,"[1] and the selection of hymns and songs, the order in which they are presented, and even the ways in which they are indexed shape the theological thinking and ultimately the faith and practices of the church.

Previous hymnals have responded to the needs of the church and the world by highlighting the rhythms of the church year, the centrality of the psalms in the prayer and praise of Reformed churches, the corporate witness of the church to the world, the seeking of God's peace and God's justice, and the rich musical and poetic resources of world Christianity. All these motifs remain important and should be retained, in one way or another, in this collection.

This collection of hymns and songs, however, will be published amid different conditions than those that molded previous hymnals. It will be offered in a world in which trust in human progress has been undermined and where eclectic spiritualities often fail to satisfy deep spiritual hungers. It will be used by worshipers who have not had life-long formation by Scripture and basic Christian doctrine, much less Reformed theology. It is meant for a church marked by growing diversity in liturgical practice. Moreover, it addresses a church divided by conflicts but nonetheless, we believe, longing for healing and the peace that is beyond understanding.

To inspire and embolden a church facing these formidable challenges, the overarching theme of this collection will be God's powerful acts of creation, redemption, and final transformation. It will also bespeak the human responses that God's gracious acts make possible. In other words, the framework for this collection of congregational song will be the history of salvation.

This theme of salvation history answers the needs of the church and the world in the following ways:

- The priority placed on God's acts offers hope to those whose faith in human efforts has been undermined.

- A focus on salvation history reminds a church and world riddled with anxiety, frustration, and conflict that love has come to earth and that the risen and ascended Christ is alive and active.

---

[1] "Compact theology" is a phrase used by the late David Allan Hubbard, biblical scholar and president of Fuller Seminary, to describe hymn texts.

- The emphasis on God's provision for us invites our grateful response. It makes a place for expressions of corporate commitment as well as personal devotion.

- The framework of salvation history is widely inclusive. It has places for existing hymns and invites the writing of new words and music to supply major omissions. It makes room for the whole of the biblical witness, not only psalms and the Gospels that are already well reflected in hymn texts, but also the segments of the Scriptures that are not. It incorporates the events of the Christian year, the sacraments, and the mission of the church throughout the world as Christ's living body.

- As such, this framework both encompasses and enriches the liturgical practices that exist in the church. It includes the christological rhythm of the liturgical year, from Advent to the Reign of Christ, but also places the liturgical year in the wider framework of God's covenantal acts in creation and toward Israel. It challenges all users, whatever liturgical patterns they use, to shape their worship by the full extent of the biblical narrative.

- The rich narrative of salvation history—with the life stories of people like Abraham and Sarah, Eli and Samuel, Boaz and Ruth, Philip and the Ethiopian eunuch—makes audible the manifold ways in which God engages people of different ages, nationalities, races, and genders.

- The framework of the history of salvation offers a theological rationale for asking us to learn songs that come from cultures different from our own: Pentecost teaches us to speak and hear the gospel in many tongues and languages and only thus, "with all the saints," to comprehend the breadth and length and height and depth of the love of Christ (Eph. 3:18). We do not sing hymns and songs because they were birthed in our culture; we sing them because they teach us something about the richness that is in God.

- Likewise, the notion of salvation history invites us to bridge the divide between different musical styles and traditions. As scribes who have been trained for God's reign will bring out of their treasures "what is new and what is old" (Matt. 13:52), so musicians are invited to lead us in songs both old and new, in praise of a God who is the first and the last, the ancient of everlasting days, and the Lord of the new creation.

—Ratified by the Presbyterian Committee on Congregational Song (PCOCS), February 2009

Appendix 2

A STATEMENT ON LANGUAGE

Language is close to the heart of Christian faith. As befits a faith community called into being by a God we know as the Word made flesh, we pray, proclaim, teach, comfort, admonish, serve, and administer justice with words woven in and through all our actions. Language used in worship has great power. Therefore the language used in collections of hymns, psalms, and spiritual songs matters a great deal. Worshipful words joined to worshipful music deeply shape the faith and practices of the church.

The church has been enriched by several decades of conversations about language used for God and for the people of God. Christians in denominations like the Presbyterian Church (U.S.A.) have become aware that our language can exclude and stereotype, but also that carefully chosen language can embrace and include people who have been separated from the centers of power. A commitment to inclusive language for the people of God reflects the consensus of the church.[1] When it comes to language used for God, however, the conversation is still ongoing. While many are deeply nurtured and comforted by traditional imagery for God, many others are concerned about associations of patriarchy and other forms of domination and are looking for other and more diverse language.

In negotiating these different convictions, the Presbyterian Committee on Congregational Song is guided by the theological framework of this new collection of songs: salvation history. Scripture uses an abundantly rich array of prose and poetry to tell us about God's powerful acts of creation, redemption, and final transformation. Much biblical imagery is indeed masculine, but there is also a wide variety of other metaphors that are either feminine or gender-neutral. Most important, behind all biblical narrative lies the deep and prevailing sense that God is the one whose ways and thoughts are as beyond human speech as the heaven is higher than the earth (Isa. 55:8–9). Our lips need to be cleansed by a burning coal before we speak or sing any word about the holy God (Isa. 6:5).

The framework of salvation history requires a collection of songs that reflects the full extent of the biblical narrative and also the full array of biblical language used for God—even if that leads us to using words and imagery that go beyond our natural comfort.

---

[1] Cf. the *Book of Order*, the PC(USA) "Report and Recommendations in Response to Referral on Inclusive Language" (1985), and the "Report to the Church on Issues of Language and Gender" (2000).

Given these commitments, the committee seeks a songbook that is characterized, as a church document formulates it, by "inclusive language with reference to the people of God, and expansive language with reference to God."[2] Thus the committee uses the following guidelines:

Language used for the people of God

- Language that stereotypes persons according to categories such as gender, race, ethnicity, socioeconomic class, sexual orientation, age, or disabilities will be avoided.

- The "generic masculine" is no longer universally understood to include persons of both genders and will therefore be avoided. Texts that employ the generic masculine will be evaluated individually to determine what alterations, if any, are poetically appropriate.

- Salvation history invites us to sing joyfully of the creative and healing presence of our God. We will be sensitive, however, to potentially denigrating implications of poetic metaphors in our songs, especially with respect to persons of color or with disabilities.

Language used for God

- The collection will draw from the full reservoir of biblical imagery for God and God's gracious acts. The final product will include both metaphors that are comfortable in their familiarity and those that are enriching in their newness.

- The collection will emphasize that the God who meets us so graciously and intimately in salvation history is at the same time one who is wholly other and beyond gender.[3] Therefore, texts will reflect a strong preference for avoiding the use of male pronouns for God. In evaluating each hymn or song, issues of tradition, theological integrity, poetic quality, and copyright will all be considered. The goal is a collection in which traditional hymns and songs are balanced with others that are more gender-neutral or expansive in their reference to God.

- Two references to God should be preserved in the collection:

  1. In the biblical narrative both the God of Israel and Christ are called "Lord." The practice of calling God "Lord" goes back to Greek-speaking Jews who sought to avoid pronouncing God's holy name, YHWH, by using a replacement term: Lord (*Kyrios*). The practice has since been followed by virtually all Christian Bible translations. Rather than being an expression of domination or masculinity, "Lord" stands in for the name by which God chose to disclose Godself in Hebrew Scripture (Exod. 3:15).

---

[2] *Well Chosen Words!* Published and revised by the Women's Ministries, National Ministries Division, and the Advocacy Committee for Women's Concerns, a ministry of the Presbyterian Mission Agency of the PC(USA), 2012. Cf. also the *Book of Order*.

[3] Cf. the 1998 PC(USA) *The Study Catechism*, questions 11–13.

That "Jesus Christ is Lord (*Kyrios*)" is one of the oldest confessions concerning Jesus. It has both a Roman and a Jewish background. On the one hand, "Lord" (*Kyrios*) was the title of the Roman emperor. When the writers of the New Testament confess Jesus to be Lord, they thereby proclaim that not Caesar, but Christ rules this world. On the other hand, in applying the reference to the name of Israel's God to Jesus, the New Testament makes a startling identity statement: that in Jesus this very God has become present among us.

Were we no longer to use "Lord" for Israel's God, we would no longer understand what we claim about Jesus' identity when we confess him Lord. Were we no longer to use "Lord" for Jesus, we would lose the strongest defense we have against empire: that Christ is Lord, and not Caesar.

2. The church confesses a Trinitarian God: one God, in Father, Son, and Holy Spirit. This is the formula by which we are baptized; this is the name that unites us with each other and with all Christian communities beyond our denomination (Matt. 28:19). This threefold name will not be eliminated. At the same time, many other images and metaphors for the Trinity will be welcomed, as long as they express the principles of Trinitarian theology:

   a. God exists in three persons, but there is nevertheless only one God who knows and loves and acts;

   b. in salvation history, no person of the Trinity acts alone; every act is an act of all three persons in the one God;

   c. each person of the Trinity is not a part of God, but fully God.

—Ratified by the Presbyterian Committee on Congregational Song (PCOCS), October 2009

ACKNOWLEDGMENTS

Services of Worship

Musical setting of the Service for the Lord's Day by Hal H. Hopson. Music © 2013 Birnamwood Publications (admin. MorningStar Music Publishers, Inc.). Used by permission.

Prayer ("God of All Glory," p. 2) based on a prayer written by Susan J. White and James F. White. Used by permission.

Prayer for Illumination (p. 5) from *The United Methodist Hymnal*, 1989. Used by permission of the United Methodist Publishing House.

Prayer Over the Gifts and *Post-Communion Prayer* (pp. 8, 12) from *Evangelical Lutheran Worship* © 2006 Evangelical Lutheran Church in America (admin. Augsburg Fortress). Reproduced by permission. All rights reserved.

Prayer ("Holy God, Let the Incense of Our Prayer," p. 29) from *Morning Praise and Evensong* by William G. Storey, D.M.S., Franck C. Quinn, OP, and David F. Wright, OP. © 1973 Fides Publishers, Inc. (alt.). Used by permission.

Other Texts for Worship

The New Revised Standard Version of the Bible © 1989 Division of Christian Education of the National Council of Churches of Christ in the United States of America.

Materials prepared by the Consultation on Common Texts (CCT), published in *Revised Common Lectionary* © 1992.

Materials prepared by the English Language Liturgical Consultation (ELLC), published in *Praying Together* © 1988: the preface dialogue, the Lord's Prayer, the texts "Glory to God in the Highest," "Holy, Holy, Holy," "Lamb of God," and Apostles' Creed (common text). Used by permission.

The Apostles' Creed, the Nicene Creed, and the Brief Statement of Faith published in *Book of Confessions* © 1996 Office of the General Assembly, Presbyterian Church (U.S.A.). Used by permission.

Spanish texts of the Lord's Prayer, Law of God, and Summary of the Law are taken from *Reina Valera 1995* © Sociedades Bíblicas Unidas, 1995. Used by permission.

Spanish versions of the creeds © 2004 Office of the General Assembly, Presbyterian Church (U.S.A.). Used by permission.

Korean versions of the creeds © 1993 Office of the General Assembly, Presbyterian Church (U.S.A.). Used by permission.

Grateful Acknowledgment

Presbyterian Publishing Corporation (PPC), Presbyterian Association of Musicians (PAM), and the Office of Theology and Worship (TAW) would like to express their appreciation to the members of the Presbyterian Committee on Congregational Song (PCOCS), their families, and the churches and institutions they serve, for their many hours of devoted service to this important project.

PPC, PAM, and TAW also thank their colleagues in the Presbyterian Center for the support and encouragement they have given the project, including Linda Valentine and Gradye Parsons and their staffs.

With deep gratitude we thank all those who assisted with the development and production of this resource for worship, especially the following:

Production:
Gwen Stamm, interior design
Lisa Buckley, cover design
James Clemens and Andrew Parks, engraving
Carl P. Daw Jr., informational notes
Judith Muck, indexing
Julie Tonini, Director of Production
Erika Lundbom, Production Specialist
Jessie Clark, Production Assistant
David Dobson, Editorial Director
Alicia Samuels, Director of Electronic Resources
Scott Shorney and Hope Publishing Company
Presbyterian Publishing Corporation staff

Worship Consultants:
Kimberly Bracken Long
Teresa Lockhart Stricklen
Harold M. Daniels
Arlo D. Duba

Language Advisers:
Arabic: Amgad Beblawi; Raafat Girgis; Victor Makari
Hebrew: Marianne Blickenstaff
Korean: Paul Junggap Huh; Grace Kim; Janice Kim
Mandarin and Taiwanese: Chi Yi Chen Wolbrink
Portuguese: Gláucia Vasconcelos Wilkey
Spanish: Marissa Galvan-Valle; Norma Sayago

Copyright Advice and Assistance:
Colleagues from various publishing companies, especially Kyle Cothern (GIA), Susan Gilbert (Hope Publishing Co.), Martin Seltz (Augsburg Fortress), and Diane Dykgraaf (Faith Alive Christian Resources)

Other Consultants:
Robert Batastini, Joyce Borger, Melva Costen, John Dull, Michael Hawn, Jorge Lockward, I-to Loh, Ron Rienstra, Greg Scheer, Martin Tel, Eric Wall, Paul Westermeyer, Presbyterians for Disability Concerns, staff of Racial Ethnic & Women's Ministries, staff of Research Services, congregations across the country that volunteered to be test sites, and colleagues from *Evangelical Lutheran Worship* and *Lift Up Your Hearts* hymnal projects

COPYRIGHT HOLDER ACKNOWLEDGMENTS

179 *Text* © 2003 John Thornburg (admin. Wayne Leupold Editions). *Music* © 1994 Hope Publishing Company, Carol Stream, IL 60188. All rights reserved. Used by permission.

180 *Text and Music* © 1986 Oxford University Press, Inc. Assigned © 2010 to Oxford University Press. Reproduced by permission. All rights reserved.

181 *Text* © 1986 Oxford University Press, Inc. Assigned © 2010 to Oxford University Press. Reproduced by permission. All rights reserved.

183 *Text* © 1991 GIA Publications, Inc. All rights reserved. Used by permission. *Music* © 1993 Selah Publishing Co., Inc. www.selahpub.com. All rights reserved. Used by permission.

184 *Text* © 2002 GIA Publications, Inc. All rights reserved. Used by permission. *Music* © 2002 Selah Publishing Co., Inc. www.selahpub.com. All rights reserved. Used by permission.

185 *English Trans.* © 1980 The Hymnal Society of Korea. *English Vers. and Music* © 1967, 1989 The United Methodist Publishing House (admin. The Copyright Company, Nashville, TN). All rights reserved. International copyright secured. Used by permission.

186 *Text* © 1992 GIA Publications, Inc. All rights reserved. Used by permission. *Music* © 1995 Jeeva Sam. All rights reserved. Used by permission. *Music Arr.* © 1995 Ron Klusmeier (admin. Musiklus klus@musiklus.com). All rights reserved. Used by permission.

190 *Text* © 1985 Oxford University Press, Inc. Assigned © 2010 to Oxford University Press. Reproduced by permission. All rights reserved. *Music* © 1943, 1961, 1985 Church Pension Fund. Used by permission.

191 *Text* © 1988 Hope Publishing Company, Carol Stream, IL 60188. All rights reserved. Used by permission. *Music* © 1991 Selah Publishing Co., Inc. www.selahpub.com. All rights reserved. Used by permission.

192 *Text and Music* © 1987 Make Way Music (admin. Music Services in the Western Hemisphere). ASCAP. All rights reserved.

193 *Text* © 1991 Concordia Publishing House. Used by permission. www.cph.org.

195 *English Trans.* © 1990 James Minchin (admin. Asian Institute for Liturgy and Music). *Music* © 1990 Francisco F. Feliciano (admin. Asian Institute for Liturgy and Music). All rights reserved. *Music Arr.* © 2006 Augsburg Fortress.

199 *Text and Music* © 1972 The United Methodist Publishing House (admin. The Copyright Company, Nashville, TN). *English Trans.* © 1979 The United Methodist Publishing House (admin. The Copyright Company, Nashville, TN). All rights reserved. International copyright secured. Used by permission.

200 *Text* © 1985 Oxford University Press, Inc. Assigned © 2010 to Oxford University Press. Reproduced by permission. All rights reserved. *Music* © 1960 World Library Publications, www.wlpmusic.com. All rights reserved. Used by permission.

201 *Text* © 1993 Hope Publishing Company, Carol Stream, IL 60188. All rights reserved. Used by permission.

202 *Text* © 1974 Hope Publishing Company. *Music Harm.* © 1990 Hope Publishing Company, Carol Stream, IL 60188. All rights reserved. Used by permission.

203 *Text and Music* © 1969 Hope Publishing Company. *Music Arr.* © 1982 Hope Publishing Company, Carol Stream, IL 60188. All rights reserved. Used by permission.

204 *Text and Music* © 1984 Les Presses de Taizé (admin. GIA Publications, Inc.). All rights reserved. Used by permission.

205 *Text and Music* © 1979 Les Presses de Taizé (admin. GIA Publications, Inc.). All rights reserved. Used by permission.

206 *Text* © 1990 Stainer & Bell, Ltd. (admin. Hope Publishing Company). *Music* © 1998 Hope Publishing Company, Carol Stream, IL 60188. All rights reserved. Used by permission.

207 *Text and Music* © 2006 GIA Publications, Inc. All rights reserved. Used by permission.

208 *Text* © 2010 Michael Morgan from *Psalter for Christian Worship*. Used by permission of Congregational Ministries Publishing, Presbyterian Church (U.S.A.). *Music* © 2009 Thurlow Weed. Used by permission.

209 *Music* © 1924 Trustees of the John Ireland Charitable Trust. Used by permission.

210 *Text* © 1986 Christopher L. Webber. Used by permission.

211 *Text* © 2010 Michael Morgan from *Psalter for Christian Worship*. Used by permission of Congregational Ministries Publishing, Presbyterian Church (U.S.A.). *Music Harm.* © 1965 Abingdon Press (admin. The Copyright Company, Nashville, TN). All rights reserved. International copyright secured. Used by permission.

214 *Text* © 2011 David Gambrell (admin. Presbyterian Publishing Corp.). All rights reserved. Used by permission. *Music Harm.* © 1943, 1961, 1985 Church Pension Fund. Used by permission.

215 *Music Harm.* © 1965 Abingdon Press (admin. The Copyright Company, Nashville, TN). All rights reserved. International copyright secured. Used by permission.

217 *Text* © 2008 Faith Alive Christian Resources. Used by permission. *Music* © 1925 from *Enlarged Songs of Praise*. Reproduced by permission of Oxford University Press. All rights reserved.

222 *Text* © 2002 GIA Publications, Inc. All rights reserved. Used by permission. *Music* © 1993 Selah Publishing Co., Inc. www.selahpub.com. All rights reserved. Used by permission.

225 *Music* © 1967 Concordia Publishing House. Used by permission. www.cph.org.

226 *Text* © 1976 Hinshaw Music, Inc. Reprinted by permission. *Music* © 1987 Birnamwood Publications (a div. of MorningStar Music Publishers, Inc.). Used by permission.

227 *Text and Music* © 1981 Les Presses de Taizé (admin. GIA Publications, Inc.). All rights reserved. Used by permission.

228 *Music Arr.* © 1990 Melva Wilson Costen. All rights reserved. Used by permission.

229 *Text* © 2009 GIA Publications, Inc. *Music Harm.* © 1995 GIA Publications, Inc. All rights reserved. Used by permission.

230 *Text* © 1989 Hope Publishing Company. *Music* © 1990 Hope Publishing Company, Carol Stream, IL 60188. All rights reserved. Used by permission.

293 *Text* © 1987 The Hymn Society (admin. Hope Publishing Company, Carol Stream, IL 60188). All rights reserved. Used by permission.

294 *Text and Music* © 1991 Les Presses de Taizé (admin. GIA Publications, Inc.). All rights reserved. Used by permission.

295 *Text* © 1991 GIA Publications, Inc. All rights reserved. Used by permission.

296 *Text* © 2002 GIA Publications, Inc. *Music* © 1999 William P. Rowan (admin. GIA Publications, Inc.). All rights reserved. Used by permission.

297 *Text* © 1995 The Pilgrim Press. All rights reserved. Used by permission.

298 *Text* © 1978 Hope Publishing Company. *Music* © 1942, ren. 1970 Hope Publishing Company, Carol Stream, IL 60188. All rights reserved. Used by permission.

300 *Text and Music* © 1966 F. E. L. Publications, assigned 1991 to The Lorenz Corporation. All rights reserved. Used by permission.

301 *Text and Music* © 1994 GIA Publications, Inc. All rights reserved. Used by permission.

302 *Text* © 2001 Carolyn Winfrey Gillette. All rights reserved. Used by permission. *Music Harm.* © 1990 Hope Publishing Company, Carol Stream, IL 60188. All rights reserved. Used by permission.

303 *Text* © 1989 Hope Publishing Company, Carol Stream, IL 60188. All rights reserved. Used by permission. *Music* © 1989 Selah Publishing Co, Inc. www.selahpub.com. All rights reserved. Used by permission.

305 *Text* © 1989 Brian Dill. All rights reserved. Used by permission.

308 *Text* © 1990 Hope Publishing Company, Carol Stream, IL 60188. All rights reserved. Used by permission.

309 *Text* © 1990 Hope Publishing Company. *Music* © 1942, ren. 1970 Hope Publishing Company, Carol Stream, IL 60188. All rights reserved. Used by permission.

311 *Text* © 1958 The United Methodist Publishing House (admin. The Copyright Company, Nashville, TN). All rights reserved. International copyright secured. Used by permission. *Music* Used by permission of Hiroshi Koizumi.

312 *Text* © 1995 Hope Publishing Company, Carol Stream, IL 60188. All rights reserved. Used by permission. *Music* © 1995 Selah Publishing Co., Inc. www.selahpub.com. All rights reserved. Used by permission.

314 *Text and Music* © 1993 Bernadette Farrell. Published by OCP, 5536 NE Hassalo, Portland, OR 97213. All rights reserved. Used by permission.

315 *Text and Music* © 1994 Julian B. Rush. All rights reserved. Used by permission.

316 *Text* © 1960, ren. 1988 World Library Publications, wlpmusic.com. All rights reserved. Used by permission.

319 *Text and Music* © 1995 Curious? Music UK (PRS) (admin. in the U.S.A. and Canada EMICMGPublishing.com). All rights reserved. Used by permission.

320 *Text* © 1971 Hope Publishing Company, Carol Stream, IL 60188. All rights reserved. Used by permission.

322 *English Trans.* © 1996 Abingdon Press (admin. The Copyright Company, Nashville, TN). All rights reserved. International copyright secured. Used by permission. *Music Arr.* © 1992 Celebremos/Libros Alianza. All rights reserved. Used by permission.

323 *Text* © 2000 Bill Wallace (admin. General Board of Global Ministries t/a GBGMusik). *Music* © 2000 I-to Loh (admin. General Board of Global Ministries t/a GBGMusik, 475 Riverside Dr., New York, NY 10115). Used by permission.

324 *Text* © 1993 GIA Publications, Inc. All rights reserved. Used by permission. *Music Harm.* © 1927 Oxford University Press. Used by permission.

328 *Music Arr.* © 2011 Alfred V. Fedak. Used by permission.

330 *Text* © 2011 Martin Tel (admin. Faith Alive Christian Resources). All rights reserved. Used by permission.

332 *Text and Music* © 1981 Caribbean Conference of Churches (CCC). All rights reserved. Used by permission of the CCC.

333 *Text* © 2010 Michael Morgan from *Psalter for Christian Worship*. Used by permission of Congregational Ministries Publishing, Presbyterian Church (U.S.A.).

335 *Text and Music* © 1987 Faith Alive Christian Resources. All rights reserved. Used by permission.

340 *Text Sts. 1–2* © 1934, 1962 The Lorenz Corporation. *St. 3* © 1964 The Lorenz Corporation. All rights reserved. Used by permission. *Music Arr.* © 1933, ren. 1961 Presbyterian Board of Christian Education. Used by permission of Westminster John Knox Press.

344 *Text and Music* © 1996 World Library Publications, wlpmusic.com. All rights reserved. Used by permission.

345 *Text* © 1995 Kevin Mayhew Ltd. All rights reserved. Used by permission. *Music* © 1989 Selah Publishing Co., Inc. www.selahpub.com. All rights reserved. Used by permission.

346 *Text* © 1968 Hope Publishing Company, Carol Stream, IL 60188. All rights reserved. Used by permission.

349 *Text* © 1982 Hope Publishing Company, Carol Stream, IL 60188. All rights reserved. Used by permission.

351 *Text* © 1969 Stainer & Bell, Ltd. (admin. Hope Publishing Company, Carol Stream, IL 60188). All rights reserved. Used by permission. *Music Harm.* © 1965 Abingdon Press (admin. The Copyright Company, Nashville, TN). All rights reserved. International copyright secured. Used by permission.

352 *Music Arr.* © 1990 Melva Wilson Costen. All rights reserved. Used by permission.

355 *Text* © 1986 Fred R. Anderson from *Singing Psalms of Joy and Praise*. Used by permission. *Music* © 1974, ren. Harold Flammer Music (a div. of Shawnee Press, Inc.). International copyright secured. All rights reserved. Reprinted by permission.

356 *Text* © 1996 Hope Publishing Company, Carol Stream, IL 60188. All rights reserved. Used by permission.

357 *Text* © 2011 David Gambrell (admin. Presbyterian Publishing Corp.). All rights reserved. Used by permission.

359 *Text and Music* © 1984 Utryck (admin. Walton Music Corp.). All rights reserved. Used by permission.

524 *Text* © 1990 Christian Conference of Asia (admin. GIA Publications, Inc.). *Music* © 1990 GIA Publications, Inc. All rights reserved. Used by permission.

525 *Music Arr.* © 1990 Melva Wilson Costen. All rights reserved. Used by permission.

526 *Text and Music* © 1975 Hope Publishing Company, Carol Stream, IL 60188. All rights reserved. Used by permission.

527 *Text and Music* © 1984 Les Presses de Taizé (admin. GIA Publications, Inc.). All rights reserved. Used by permission.

528 *Text Sts. 1–3 and Music* © 1970 The Lutheran World Federation. Used by permission of Augsburg Fortress. *Text St. 4 and Music Adapt.* © 1972 *Contemporary Worship 4* (admin. Augsburg Fortress). All rights reserved. Used by permission.

529 *Text* From *Enlarged Songs of Praise*, 1931. Reproduced by permission of Oxford University Press. All rights reserved. *Music* © 1957, ren. H. W. Gray Company. All rights controlled and admin. Alfred Publishing Co., Inc. All rights reserved. Used by permission of Alfred Publishing Co., Inc.

530 *Text and Music* © 1978 John B. Foley, SJ. Published by OCP, 5536 NE Hassalo, Portland, OR 97213. All rights reserved. Used by permission.

531 *Text and Music* © 1987 International Liturgy Publications, P. O. Box 50476, Nashville, TN 37205. www.ilpmusic.org. All rights reserved.

532 *Text and Music* © 1973 Cesáreo Gabaráin. Published by OCP. *Music Harm.* © 1987 OCP, 5536 NE Hassalo, Portland, OR 97213. All rights reserved. Used by permission.

533 *Text and Music* © 1996 Hope Publishing Company, Carol Stream, IL 60188. All rights reserved. Used by permission.

534 *Text and Music* © 1969 Hope Publishing Company, Carol Stream, IL 60188. All rights reserved. Used by permission.

535 *Music Arr.* © 1972 The Westminster Press from *The Worshipbook—Services and Hymns.* Used by permission of Westminster John Knox Press.

536 *Text* © 1997 Susan Palo Cherwien (admin. Augsburg Fortress). *Music* © 1997 Augsburg Fortress. All rights reserved. Used by permission.

537 *Text* © 2004 Hope Publishing Company. *Music* © 2006 Hope Publishing Company, Carol Stream, IL 60188. All rights reserved. Used by permission.

538 *English Trans. and Music Arr.* © 1984 Utryck (admin. Walton Music Corp.). Used by permission.

539 *Text and Music* © 2003 Andrew Donaldson and Hilary Seraph Donaldson. Used by permission.

543 *Text and Music* © 2004 This Here Music (ASCAP) Worldmaking.net. Used by permission.

544 *Text and Music* © 1984, 1998 Les Presses de Taizé (admin. GIA Publications, Inc.). All rights reserved. Used by permission.

545 *Text* © 1969 James Quinn, SJ. Used by permission of Continuum, an imprint of Bloomsbury Publishing Plc. *Music Arr.* © 1938, ren. The H. W. Gray Company. All rights controlled and admin. Belwin-Mills Publishing Corp., a div. of Alfred Music Publishing. All rights reserved. Used by permission of Alfred Publishing Co., Inc.

547 *Text* ©1983 Concordia Publishing House. Used by permission. www.cph.org.

548 *Text* © 2011 David Gambrell (admin. Presbyterian Publishing Corp.). All rights reserved. Used by permission. *Music* © 1962 Theodore Presser Co. All rights reserved. Used by permission of Carl Fischer, Inc.

549 *Text and Music* © 2000 Maria Ling and Swee Hong Lim (admin. General Board of Global Ministries t/a GBGMusik, 475 Riverside Dr., New York, NY 10115). Used by permission.

551 *Music Arr.* © 1986 GIA Publications, Inc. All rights reserved. Used by permission.

552 *Music Adapt.* © 1980 Church Pension Fund. Used by permission. *Music Arr.* © 1986 GIA Publications, Inc. All rights reserved. Used by permission.

553 *Music Arr.* © 1986 GIA Publications, Inc. All rights reserved. Used by permission.

554 *Music Arr.* © 1995 GIA Publications, Inc. All rights reserved. Used by permission.

555 *Music Arr.* © 1995 GIA Publications, Inc. All rights reserved. Used by permission.

556 *Music* © 1981 GIA Publications, Inc. All rights reserved. Used by permission.

557 *Music* © 1981 GIA Publications, Inc. All rights reserved. Used by permission.

558 *Music* © 1981 GIA Publications, Inc. All rights reserved. Used by permission.

559 *Music* © 2004 Augsburg Fortress. All rights reserved. Used by permission.

560 *Music* © 2004 Augsburg Fortress. All rights reserved. Used by permission.

561 *Music* © 2004 Augsburg Fortress. All rights reserved. Used by permission.

562 *Music Adapt.* © 1985, 1989 GIA Publications, Inc. All rights reserved. Used by permission.

563 *Music Adapt.* © 1985, 1995 GIA Publications, Inc. All rights reserved. Used by permission.

564 *Music Adapt.* © 1985, 1989 GIA Publications, Inc. All rights reserved. Used by permission.

565 *Music* © 1984 GIA Publications, Inc. All rights reserved. Used by permission.

566 *Music* © 1984 GIA Publications, Inc. All rights reserved. Used by permission.

567 *Music* © 1990 GIA Publications, Inc. All rights reserved. Used by permission.

568 *Music* © 1984 GIA Publications, Inc. All rights reserved. Used by permission.

569 *Music* © 1997 Curt Oliver. All rights reserved. Used by permission.

570 Music © 1997 Curt Oliver. All rights reserved. Used by permission.

571 *Music* © 1997 Curt Oliver. All rights reserved. Used by permission.

572 *Music* © 2006 Augsburg Fortress. All rights reserved. Used by permission.

573 *Music* © 2006 Augsburg Fortress. All rights reserved. Used by permission.

574 *Music* © 2006 Augsburg Fortress. All rights reserved. Used by permission.

575 *Music* © 2011 Birnamwood Publications, a div. of MorningStar Music Publishers, Inc., St. Louis, MO. Used by permission.

576 *Music* © 1990 Swee Hong Lim (admin. General Board of Global Ministries t/a GBGMusik, 475 Riverside Dr., New York, NY 10015). Used by permission.

577 *Music* © 1987 Dinah Reindorf. All rights reserved. Used by permission.

578 *Music Harm.* © 1996 General Board of Global Ministries t/a GBGMusik, 475 Riverside Dr., New York, NY 10115. Used by permission.

582 *Text Adapt. and Music* © 2008 Paul M. Vasile. All rights reserved. Used by permission.

583 *Music* © 1979, 1981 Les Presses de Taizé (admin. GIA Publications, Inc.). All rights reserved. Used by permission.

584 *Text and Music* © 1989 GIA Publications, Inc. All rights reserved. Used by permission.

586 *Music* © 1984 Les Presses de Taizé (admin. GIA Publications, Inc.). All rights reserved. Used by permission.

587 *Music* © 1985 Fintan O'Carroll and Christopher Walker. Published by OCP, 5536 NE Hassalo, Portland, OR 97213. All rights reserved. Used by permission.

588 *Music* © 1973, 1979 GIA Publications, Inc. All rights reserved. Used by permission.

590 *Music* © United Methodist Music Service. All rights reserved. Used by permission.

591 *Text and Music* © 1990 WGRG, Iona Community (admin. GIA Publications, Inc.). *Music Arr.* © 1993 GIA Publications, Inc. All rights reserved. Used by permission.

592 *Music* © 2008 Paul M. Vasile. All rights reserved. Used by permission.

593 *Music* © 2007 David E. Poole. All rights reserved. Used by permission. www.davidepoole.com.

594 *Text and Music* © 1988, 1993, 1994 GIA Publications, Inc. All rights reserved. Used by permission.

596 *Text and Music* © 1990 Ton Vis Produktion AB (admin. Augsburg Fortress). *Spanish Trans.* © Raquel Gutiérrez-Achon. All rights reserved. Used by permission.

597 *English Text* and *Music Arr.* © 2008 Greg Scheer. Used by permission.

598 *Text and Music* © Lumko Institute, South Africa. *Music Transcr.* © 1983 David Dargie (admin. Choristers Guild). All rights reserved. Used by permission.

602 *Music* © 2003 Yusuf Khill. Used by permission.

603 *Music* © 2008 Paul M. Vasile. All rights reserved. Used by permission.

604 *Music* © 2006 Augsburg Fortress. All rights reserved. Used by permission.

605 *Music Arr.* © 2011 Alfred V. Fedak. Used by permission.

607 *Text* © 1990 Neil Weatherhogg. All rights reserved. Used by permission.

608 *Text* © 1990 Neil Weatherhogg. All rights reserved. Used by permission. *Music* © 2008 Hal H. Hopson. Used by permission.

609 *Text* © 1989 Hope Publishing Company. *Music Harm.* © 1998 Hope Publishing Company, Carol Stream, IL 60188. All rights reserved. Used by permission.

610 *Spanish Trans.* © 1989 The United Methodist Publishing House (admin. The Copyright Company). *Korean Trans.* © 2001 The United Methodist Publishing House (admin. The Copyright Company, Nashville, TN). All rights reserved. International copyright secured. Used by permission.

613 *Text and Music* © 1981 Meadowgreen Music Company (ASCAP) (admin. EMICMGPublishing.com). All rights reserved. Used by permission.

614 *Text and Music* © 1982 Meadowgreen Music Company (ASCAP) (admin. EMICMGPublishing.com). All rights reserved. Used by permission.

615 *Text and Music* © Kyung Dong Presbyterian Church. Used by permission of Sung Mo Moon and Seung-Won Park.

616 *Text and Music* © 1988 Universal Music - Brentwood Benson Publishing (ASCAP). All rights reserved. Used by permission.

617 *Text and Music* © 1990, 2000 Christian Conference of Asia (admin. GIA Publications, Inc.). All rights reserved. Used by permission. *Responsive Reading* of Psalm 150 from *An Inclusive-Language Psalter of the Christian People* © 1993 The Order of St. Benedict (admin. The Liturgical Press, Collegeville, Minnesota).

618 *Music Harm.* © 1993 Selah Publishing Co., Inc. www.selahpub.com. All rights reserved. Used by permission.

619 *Text Adapt.* © 1974 Ecumenical Women's Center. All rights reserved.

621 *Text and Music* © 1981 Universal Music Corp. and Sound III, Inc. This *Arr.* © 2013 Universal Music Corp. and Sound III, Inc. All rights controlled and admin. Universal Music Corp. Used by permission of Hal Leonard Corporation.

622 *Music Arr.* © 1979 Raquel Mora Martínez. Used by permission.

625 *Text and Music* © 1949 and 1953 The Stuart Hine Trust (U.S.A. print rights admin. Hope Publishing Company, Carol Stream, IL 60188). All rights reserved. Used by permission. All other U.S.A. rights admin. EMICMGPublishing.com.

626 *Text and Music* © 1984 Universal Music - Brentwood Benson Publishing (ASCAP). All rights reserved. Used by permission.

627 *Text and Music* © 1978 House of Mercy Music (ASCAP) (admin. Universal Music - Brentwood Benson Publishing/Universal Music - Brentwood Benson Publishing (ASCAP)). All rights reserved. Used by permission.

628 *Text and Music* © 1975 Claude Fraysée. All rights reserved. Used by permission. *English Trans.* © 1989 The Hymnal Project (admin. Brethren Press). Used by permission.

631 *Text and Music* © 1977 Broadman Press (admin. Music Services). All rights reserved. Used by permission.

632 *Text and Music* © 2010 Greg Scheer. All rights reserved. Used by permission.

633 *Text and Music* © 1981 J. Jefferson Cleveland. All rights reserved. Used by permission.

635 *Text and Music* © 1991 Les Presses de Taizé (admin. GIA Publications, Inc.). All rights reserved. Used by permission.

636 *Music* © 1976 Hinshaw Music, Inc. Reprinted by permission.

637 *English and Spanish Trans. and Music Arr.* © Gerhard M. Cartford. Used by permission of Augsburg Fortress.

639 *Text* © 1986 Helen L. Wright from *A Psalm Sampler. Music* © 1986 Hope Publishing Company, Carol Stream, IL 60188. All rights reserved. Used by permission.

640 *Text and Music* © 2005 Wayne Leupold Editions, Inc. Used by permission. *Music Arr.* © 2008 Greg Scheer. All rights reserved. Used by permission.

641 *Text* © 1972 Hope Publishing Company, Carol Stream, IL 60188. All rights reserved. Used by permission.

642 *English Vers. and Music Transcr.* © 2008 General Board of Global Ministries t/a GBGMusik, 475 Riverside Dr., New York, NY 10115. All rights reserved. Used by permission.

644 *Text* © 1986 *Fresh Winds of the Spirit* by Lavon Bayler (admin. The Pilgrim Press). All rights reserved. Used by permission.

646 *Text and Music* © 1979 Les Presses de Taizé (admin. GIA Publications, Inc.). All rights reserved. Used by permission.

647 *Text and Music* © 1978 Integrity's Hosanna! Music (admin. EMICMGPublishing.com). All rights reserved. Used by permission.

648 *Text and Music* © 1978, 1995 Augsburg Fortress. All rights reserved. Used by permission.

649 *Text Phonetic Transcr. Cherokee, Kiowa, Creek, and Choctaw* © Oklahoma Indian Missionary Conference. *Phonetic Transcr. Navaho* © Albert Tsosie.

650 *Text* © 2000 Hope Publishing Company, Carol Stream, IL 60188. All rights reserved. Used by permission. *Music* © 2009 Selah Publishing Co., Inc. www.selahpub.com. All rights reserved. Used by permission.

651 *Text* © 1993 WGRG, Iona Community (admin. GIA Publications, Inc.). All rights reserved. Used by permission. *Music Arr.* © 1978 *Lutheran Book of Worship* (admin. Augsburg Fortress). All rights reserved. Used by permission.

652 *Text* © 2011 David Gambrell (admin. Presbyterian Publishing Corp.). All rights reserved. Used by permission.

653 *Text* © 2011 GIA Publications, Inc. *Music Harm.* © 1975 GIA Publications, Inc. All rights reserved. Used by permission.

654 *Text and Music* © 1991 Les Presses de Taizé (admin. GIA Publications, Inc.). All rights reserved. Used by permission.

656 *Text and Music* © 1965, ren. 1993 Manna Music, Inc. (admin. ClearBox Rights). All rights reserved. Used by permission.

657 *Text and Music* © 1993 WGRG, The Iona Community (admin. GIA Publications, Inc.). All rights reserved. Used by permission.

659 *Music Arr.* © Edo Bumba. All rights reserved. Used by permission.

660 *Text* © 1990 I-to Loh (admin. GIA Publications, Inc.). All rights reserved. Used by permission.

664 *Text* © David Higham Associates, Ltd. All rights reserved. Used by permission. *Music Arr.* © 2012 Beverly A. Howard. All rights reserved. Used by permission.

665 *Text* © 1986 Fred R. Anderson from *Singing Psalms of Joy and Praise.* All rights reserved. Used by permission.

668 *Text and Music* © 1977 Chinese Christian Literature Council Ltd., Hong Kong. All rights reserved. Used by permission.

669 *Text and Music* © 1976 OCP. *English Trans.* © 1989 OCP. *Music Arr.* © 1983 OCP, 5536 NE Hassalo, Portland, OR 97213. All rights reserved. Used by permission.

671 *Text* © 1979 William G. Storey. All rights reserved. Used by permission. *Music Harm.* © 1943, 1961 Church Pension Fund. Used by permission.

673 *Text* © 2011 David Gambrell (admin. Presbyterian Publishing Corp.). All rights reserved. Used by permission.

674 *Text* © 1994 James Quinn, SJ (admin. in North America Selah Publishing Co., Inc.). All rights reserved. Used by permission. www.selahpub.com.

676 *Text* © 1969 James Quinn, SJ (admin. Continuum, a div. of Bloomsbury Publishing Plc.). All rights reserved. Used by permission.

678 *Text and Music* © 1991 Les Presses de Taizé (admin. GIA Publications, Inc.). All rights reserved. Used by permission.

680 *Text* © The Korean Hymnal Society. Used by permission. *Music* © 2011 Paul Junggap Huh and Seung Nam Kim. All rights reserved. Used by permission. *Music Arr.* © 2011 Alfred V. Fedak. Used by permission.

683 Text © 1931 Oxford University Press. Reproduced by permission. All rights reserved. *Music* © 2008 Celebrating Grace, Inc., Macon, GA. www.celebrating-grace.com. All rights reserved. Used by permission.

684 *Text* © 1996 Hope Publishing Company, Carol Stream, IL 60188. All rights reserved. Used by permission.

685 *Text* © 2000 GIA Publications, Inc. All rights reserved. Used by permission.

686 *Text* © 1928 F. M. Braselman, ren. 1956 Presbyterian Board of Christian Education (admin. Westminster John Knox Press). *Music Harm.* © 1990 Hope Publishing Company, Carol Stream, IL 60188. All rights reserved. Used by permission.

689 *Text* © 1966 Oxford University Press. Reproduced by permission. All rights reserved.

690 *Text* © 1989 Hope Publishing Company, Carol Stream, IL 60188. All rights reserved. Used by permission.

691 *Text* © 1979 The Hymn Society (admin. Hope Publishing Company, Carol Stream, IL 60188). All rights reserved. Used by permission. *Music Harm.* © 1989 The United Methodist Publishing House (admin. The Copyright Company, Nashville, TN). All rights reserved. Used by permission.

692 *Text* © 1996 The Pilgrim Press. All rights reserved. Used by permission. *Music Harm.* © 2011 Alfred V. Fedak. All rights reserved. Used by permission.

693 *Text and Music* © 1972 Hope Publishing Company, Carol Stream, IL 60188. All rights reserved. Used by permission.

TOPICAL INDEX

LECTIONARY INDEX

Psalm entries that appear in italics represent full settings of psalms (such as metrical paraphrases and responsorial versions) that are appropriate for use when singing the psalm for the day from the Revised Common Lectionary. For an exhaustive listing of these psalm citations, see the Psalm Index (pp. 989–990).

Year A

First Sunday of Advent
See also 82–107, 347–369
Isa. 2:1–5   95, 103, 663, 757, 795, 830
Ps. 122   301, *400*, 752
Rom. 13:11–14   97, 353, 663, 667
Matt. 24:36–44   88, 102, 104, 352, 384

Second Sunday of Advent
See also 82–107, 347–369
Isa. 11:1–10   77, 85, 88, 129, 138, 278, 384, 407, 827
Ps. 72:1–7, 18–19   *149*, 265, 320, 327, 342, 634
Rom. 15:4–13   102, 265, 372, 623, 624, 629, 734, 827
Matt. 3:1–12   82, 83, 96, 163, 292, 407

Third Sunday of Advent
See also 82–107, 347–369
Isa. 35:1–10   107, 123, 213, 302
Ps. 146:5–10   149, 390, *806*
Luke 1:46b–55   99, 100
Jas. 5:7–10   82, 83, 92, 97, 213, 351, 819
Matt. 11:2–11   95, 106, 107, 140, 249, 349

Fourth Sunday of Advent
See also 82–107, 347–369
Isa. 7:10–16   88, 91, 98, 123, 129
Ps. 80:1–7, 17–19   *355*, 434, 740, 811
Rom. 1:1–7   117, 118, 120, 145
Matt. 1:18–25   100, 119, 127, 136, 146, 189

Nativity of the Lord /
Christmas Eve / Proper I
See also 108–156
Isa. 9:2–7   86, 119, 123, 127, 130, 143, 158, 233, 765
Ps. 96   299, *304*, 539, 634, *639*, 676
Titus 2:11–14   110, 112, 409, 515, 852
Luke 2:1–14 (15–20)   102, 111, 113, 114, 115, 116, 117, 118, 119, 120, 121, 122, 123, 124, 125, 126, 127, 128, 130, 131, 132, 133, 135, 136, 141, 142, 143, 144, 145, 147, 155, 291

Nativity of the Lord /
Christmas (at dawn) / Proper II
See also 108–156
Isa. 62:6–12   69, 432, 697, 746
Ps. 97   1, *365*
Titus 3:4–7   187, 437, 532
Luke 2:(1–7) 8–20   86, 97, 102, 108, 116, 117, 118, 119, 122, 123, 127, 128, 130, 132, 135, 136, 138, 139, 140, 141, 142, 145, 147, 291, 634

Year B

First Sunday of Advent
See also 82–107, 347–369
Isa. 64:1–9   39, 95, 442, 695, 756
Ps. 80:1–7, 17–19   81, *355*, 740
1 Cor. 1:3–9   6, 12, 23, 39, 84
Mark 13:24–37   105, 354, 357, 384

Second Sunday of Advent
See also 82–107, 347–369
Isa. 40:1–11   77, 85, 88, 129, 138, 384, 407, 627
Ps. 85:1–2, 8–13   93, 364, *449*, 643, 795, 818
2 Pet. 3:8–15a   93, 313, 359, 376, 687, 729
Mark 1:1–8   88, 143, 165, 541, 542

Third Sunday of Advent
See also 82–107, 347–369
Isa. 61:1–4, 8–11   82, 83, 96, 401, 852
Ps. 126   *73, 74*, 149, 634
Luke 1:46b–55   99, 100
1 Thess. 5:16–24   12, 265, 392, 418, 541, 542, 668, 804
John 1:6–8, 19–28   12, 96, 99, 102, 455, 673, 749

Fourth Sunday of Advent
See also 82–107, 347–369
2 Sam. 7:1–11, 16   39, 88, 109, 139
Ps. 89:1–4, 19–26   21, *67*, 681
Luke 1:46b–55   99, 100
Rom. 16:25–27   12, 108, 123, 265
Luke 1:26–38   98, 99, 101, 119, 127, 144, 275

Nativity of the Lord /
Christmas Eve / Proper I
See also 108–156
Isa. 9:2–7   86, 119, 123, 127, 130, 143, 158, 233, 765
Ps. 96   299, *304*, 539, 634, *639*, 676
Titus 2:11–14   110, 112, 409, 515, 852
Luke 2:1–14 (15–20)   102, 111, 113, 114, 115, 116, 117, 118, 119, 120, 121, 122, 123, 124, 125, 126, 127, 128, 130, 131, 132, 133, 135, 136, 141, 142, 143, 144, 145, 147, 155, 291

Nativity of the Lord /
Christmas (at dawn) / Proper II
See also 108–156
Isa. 62:6–12   69, 432, 697, 746
Ps. 97   1, *365*
Titus 3:4–7   187, 437, 532
Luke 2:(1–7) 8–20   86, 97, 102, 108, 116, 117, 118, 119, 122, 123, 127, 128, 130, 132, 135, 136, 138, 139, 140, 141, 142, 145, 147, 291, 634

Year C

First Sunday of Advent
See also 82–107, 347–369
Jer. 33:14–16   88, 95, 129, 357, 681
Ps. 25:1–10   93, *420*, 471
1 Thess. 3:9–13   84, 103, 313, 348
Luke 21:25–36   354, 463, 832

Second Sunday of Advent
See also 82–107, 347–369
Mal. 3:1–4   77, 82, 83, 85, 88, 129, 134, 138, 266, 282, 366, 384, 407
Luke 1:68–79, 3:1–6   96, 106, 122, 132, 163, 292
Phil. 1:3–11   36, 366, 427, 761, 767, 828
Luke 3:1–6   95, 96, 106, 163

Third Sunday of Advent
See also 82–107, 347–369
Zeph. 3:14–20   82, 83, 628, 645, 756
Isa. 12:2–6   71, 299, 610, 634, 739
Phil. 4:4–7   363, 465, 634, 667, 668, 701, 824
Luke 3:7–18   96, 144, 163, 164, 403, 476

Fourth Sunday of Advent
See also 82–107, 347–369
Mic. 5:2–5a   69, 119, 121, 127
Ps. 80:1–7   *355*, 434
Luke 1:46b–55   99, 100
Heb. 10:5–10   312, 761, 817
Luke 1:39–45 (46–55)   89, 98, 119, 127, 153, 646

Nativity of the Lord /
Christmas Eve / Proper I
See also 108–156
Isa. 9:2–7   86, 119, 123, 127, 130, 143, 158, 233, 765
Ps. 96   299, *304*, 539, 634, *639*, 676
Titus 2:11–14   110, 112, 409, 515, 852
Luke 2:1–14 (15–20)   102, 111, 113, 114, 115, 116, 117, 118, 119, 120, 121, 122, 123, 124, 125, 126, 127, 128, 130, 131, 132, 133, 135, 136, 141, 142, 143, 144, 145, 147, 155, 291

Nativity of the Lord /
Christmas (at dawn) / Proper II
See also 108–156
Isa. 62:6–12   69, 432, 697, 746
Ps. 97   1, *365*
Titus 3:4–7   187, 437, 532
Luke 2:(1–7) 8–20   86, 97, 102, 108, 116, 117, 118, 119, 122, 123, 127, 128, 130, 132, 135, 136, 138, 139, 140, 141, 142, 145, 147, 291, 634

Nativity of the Lord /
Christmas Day / Proper III
See also 108–156
Isa. 52:7–10   20, 134, 136, 141, 174, 266, 349, 697

Year A

**Nativity of the Lord /
Christmas Day / Proper III**
See also 108–156
Isa. 52:7–10   20, 134, 136, 141, 174,
                266, 349, 697
Ps. 98   1, 80, *276, 371,* 435, 539,
                611, 641
Heb. 1:1–4 (5–12)   4, 49, 119, 123,
                126, 127, 143, 145,
                147, 213, 265, 630, 666
John 1:1–14   9, 12, 86, 102, 108,
                113, 119, 127, 128, 130, 132,
                133, 158, 171, 231, 440, 459,
                634, 666, 673, 749, 818

First Sunday after Christmas Day
See also 108–156
Isa. 63:7–9   14, 39, 354, 436
Ps. 148   14, 16, *17, 18,* 26, 33, 42,
                80, 538, 642, 669, *679*
Heb. 2:10–18   4, 130, 220, 275,
                326, 634, 759
Matt. 2:13–23   119, 127, 134, 153,
                154, 220, 231, 266

**Second Sunday after
Christmas Day**
See also 108–156
Jer. 31:7–14   12, 20, 174, 319, 375,
                401, 486, 772
Ps. 147:12–20   440, *657,* 676, 804
Eph. 1:3–14   132, 134, 147, 266,
                307, 321, 394, 435,
                486, 489, 700, 840
John 1:(1–9)10–18   12, 96, 102, 108,
                119, 127, 130, 132, 133, 141, 150,
                171, 231, 440, 666, 673, 818

Epiphany of the Lord
See also 150–156
Isa. 60:1–6   86, 94, 107, 130, 265,
                744
Ps. 72:1–7, 10–14   *149,* 320, 327,
                342
Eph. 3:1–12   96, 265, 299, 395, 465,
                618, 662, 677, 700, 827
Matt. 2:1–12   117, 118, 131, 133,
                135, 138, 141, 142, 145,
                146, 147, 151, 152, 853

Baptism of the Lord
See also 163–164, 475–493
Isa. 42:1–9   265, 286, 320, 543, 629,
                757, 765
Ps. 29   *10,* 21, *259,* 634, 650
Acts 10:34–43   96, 317, 318, 399,
                447
Matt. 3:13–17   164, 317, 318, 407,
                408, 480, 688

Second Sunday after Epiphany
Isa. 49:1–7   3, 39, 488, 853
Ps. 40:1–11   353, 451, *651,* 841
1 Cor. 1:1–9   39, 494, 625, 649, 724,
                725, 827, 837
John 1:29–42   86, 279, 408, 688

Third Sunday after Epiphany
Isa. 9:1–4   14, 130, 169, 463, 662
Ps. 27:1, 4–9   12, *90,* 620, *841, 842*

Year B

**Nativity of the Lord /
Christmas Day / Proper III**
See also 108–156
Isa. 52:7–10   20, 134, 136, 141, 174,
                266, 349, 697
Ps. 98   1, 80, *276, 371,* 435, 539,
                611, 641
Heb. 1:1–4 (5–12)   4, 49, 119, 123,
                126, 127, 143, 145,
                147, 213, 265, 630, 666
John 1:1–14   9, 12, 86, 102, 108,
                113, 119, 127, 128, 130, 132,
                133, 158, 171, 231, 440, 459,
                634, 666, 673, 749, 818

First Sunday after Christmas Day
See also 108–156
Isa. 61:10–62:3   8, 14, 353, 514
Ps. 148   14, 16, *17, 18,* 26, 33, 42,
                80, 538, 642, 669, 679
Gal. 4:4–7   4, 119, 127, 215, 482,
                490, 734
Luke 2:22–40   114, 115, 119, 127,
                157, 148, 545, 546

**Second Sunday after
Christmas Day**
See also 108–156
Jer. 31:7–14   12, 20, 174, 319, 375,
                401, 486, 772
Ps. 147:12–20   440, *657,* 676, 804
Eph. 1:3–14   132, 134, 147, 266,
                307, 321, 394, 435,
                486, 489, 700, 840
John 1:(1–9)10–18   12, 96, 102, 108,
                119, 127, 130, 132, 133, 141, 150,
                171, 231, 440, 666, 673, 818

Epiphany of the Lord
See also 150–156
Isa. 60:1–6   86, 94, 107, 130, 265,
                744
Ps. 72:1–7, 10–14   *149,* 320, 327,
                342
Eph. 3:1–12   96, 265, 299, 395, 465,
                618, 662, 677, 700, 827
Matt. 2:1–12   117, 118, 131, 133,
                135, 138, 141, 142, 145,
                146, 147, 151, 152, 853

Baptism of the Lord
See also 163–164, 475–493
Gen. 1:1–5   7, 9, 24, 230, 476, 484,
                664, 850
Ps. 29   *10,* 21, *259,* 634, 650
Acts 19:1–7   286, 293, 401, 482
Mark 1:4–11   292, 408, 476, 480,
                483, 493

Second Sunday after Epiphany
1 Sam. 3:1–10 (11–20)   69, 663,
                686, 722, 741
Ps. 139:1–6, 13–18   *28, 29,* 426,
                488, 686
1 Cor. 6:12–20   27, 187, 468, 492,
                697, 701, 702
John 1:43–51   69, 450, 634, 720

Third Sunday after Epiphany
Jonah 3:1–5, 10   14, 109, 169, 438,
                463
Ps. 62:5–12   89, 463, *790,* 814, 832,
                843

Year C

Ps. 98   1, 80, *276, 371,* 435, 539,
                611, 641
Heb. 1:1–4 (5–12)   4, 49, 119, 123,
                126, 127, 143, 145,
                147, 213, 265, 630, 666
John 1:1–14   9, 12, 86, 102, 108,
                113, 119, 127, 128, 130, 132,
                133, 158, 171, 231, 440, 459,
                634, 666, 673, 749, 818

First Sunday after Christmas Day
See also 108–156
1 Sam. 2:18–20, 26   14, 69, 629
Ps. 148   14, 16, *17, 18,* 26, 33, 42,
                80, 538, 642, 669, *679*
Col. 3:12–17   4, 265, 315, 345, 654,
                689, 692, 737, 821
Luke 2:41–52   5, 119, 126, 127, 140,
                158

**Second Sunday after
Christmas Day**
See also 108–156
Jer. 31:7–14   12, 20, 174, 319, 375,
                401, 486, 772
Ps. 147:12–20   440, *657,* 676, 804
Eph. 1:3–14   132, 134, 147, 266,
                307, 321, 394, 435,
                486, 489, 700, 840
John 1:(1–9)10–18   12, 96, 102, 108,
                119, 127, 130, 132, 133, 141, 150,
                171, 231, 440, 666, 673, 818

Epiphany of the Lord
See also 150–156
Isa. 60:1–6   86, 94, 107, 130, 265,
                744
Ps. 72:1–7, 10–14   *149,* 320, 327,
                342
Eph. 3:1–12   96, 265, 299, 395, 465,
                618, 662, 677, 700, 827
Matt. 2:1–12   117, 118, 131, 133,
                135, 138, 141, 142, 145,
                146, 147, 151, 152, 853

Baptism of the Lord
See also 163–164, 475–493
Isa. 43:1–7   177, 463, 547, 612, 732,
                816, 840
Ps. 29   *10,* 21, *259,* 634, 650
Acts 8:14–17   108, 293, 480, 482
Luke 3:15–17, 21–22   96, 164, 408,
                480, 688

Second Sunday after Epiphany
Isa. 62:1–5   39, 263, 347, 773
Ps. 36:5–10   12, 81, 435, 440, *477,*
                833
1 Cor. 12:1–11   12, 292, 297, 300,
                302, 717, 733
John 2:1–11   292, 349, 395, 830

Third Sunday after Epiphany
Neh. 8:1–3, 5–6, 8–10   14, 20, 39,
                50
Ps. 19   14, 20, 39, *61,* 370, 625,
                627, *690*
1 Cor. 12:12–31a   265, 306, 409,
                495, 717, 768
Luke 4:14–21   301, 317, 318, 634,
                757, 772, 792

Year A

| 1 Cor. 1:10–18 | 213, 316, 321, 322, 846 |
| Matt. 4:12–23 | 170, 343, 721, 724, 725, 738, 751 |

Fourth Sunday after Epiphany

Mic. 6:1–8	70, 418, 739, 749
Ps. 15	364, 419, 700
1 Cor. 1:18–31	213, 223, 224, 372, 630, 754
Matt. 5:1–12	172, 643

Fifth Sunday after Epiphany

Isa. 58:1–9a (9b–12)	65, 70, 74, 287, 314, 346, 361, 658, 663
Ps. 112:1–9 (10)	86, 667, 755
1 Cor. 2:1–12 (13–16)	349, 629, 694, 722
Matt. 5:13–20	377, 395, 700, 733, 753, 757

Sixth Sunday after Epiphany

Deut. 30:15–20	410, 688
Ps. 119:1–8	61, 64, 815
1 Cor. 3:1–9	285, 441
Matt. 5:21–37	444, 472

Seventh Sunday after Epiphany

Lev. 19:1–2, 9–18	62, 203, 313, 377, 463, 729
Ps. 119:33–40	64, 385, 458
1 Cor. 3:10–11, 16–23	27, 321, 403, 463, 492
Matt. 5:38–48	203, 722, 753, 771

Eighth Sunday after Epiphany

Isa. 49:8–16a	3, 6, 71, 177, 227
Ps. 131	282, 474, 791, 815, 819
1 Cor. 4:1–5	320, 409, 716
Matt. 6:24–34	175, 683, 802

Ninth Sunday after Epiphany

Deut. 11:18–21, 26–28	61, 64, 549
Ps. 31:1–5, 19–24	11, 214, 811
Rom. 1:16–17; 3:22b–28 (29–31)	2, 649
Matt. 7:21–29	245, 320, 793

Transfiguration of the Lord

See also 189–193

Exod. 24:12–18	11, 12
Ps. 2	758
Ps. 99	57, 635
2 Pet. 1:16–21	258, 452, 662, 683
Matt. 17:1–9	156, 189, 190, 191, 193, 274

Ash Wednesday

See also 165–167, 415–434

Joel 2:1–2, 12–17	416, 435, 619, 620, 738, 757
Isa. 58:1–12	433, 762, 802
Ps. 51:1–17	421, 422, 423, 427, 436, 451, 640, 688, 710, 739
2 Cor. 5:20b–6:10	212, 215, 269, 366, 441, 629, 722, 817
Matt. 6:1–6, 16–21	165, 167, 218, 292, 450, 649, 683, 708, 817, 824

First Sunday in Lent

See also 165–167, 415–434

| Gen. 2:15–17; 3:1–7 | 225, 226, 757, 833 |
| Ps. 32 | 41, 440, 446 |

Year B

| 1 Cor. 7:29–31 | 306, 695, 734, 814, 836 |
| Mark 1:14–20 | 151, 170, 410, 721, 724, 725, 751 |

Fourth Sunday after Epiphany

Deut. 18:15–20	65, 174, 722
Ps. 111	440, 634, 755, 820
1 Cor. 8:1–13	12, 15, 169, 316, 450
Mark 1:21–28	180, 181, 662

Fifth Sunday after Epiphany

Isa. 40:21–31	30, 43, 315, 327, 331, 461, 686, 744, 829, 846
Ps. 147:1–11, 20c	12, 440, 645, 657
1 Cor. 9:16–23	12, 157, 287, 305, 753
Mark 1:29–39	793, 795, 796, 797, 834

Sixth Sunday after Epiphany

2 Kgs. 5:1–14	415, 438
Ps. 30	4, 654, 798, 805
1 Cor. 9:24–27	4, 741, 846
Mark 1:40–45	242, 353, 793

Seventh Sunday after Epiphany

Isa. 43:18–25	157, 177, 425
Ps. 41	172, 208, 793
2 Cor. 1:18–22	303, 735, 816, 826, 838
Mark 2:1–12	157, 343, 475

Eighth Sunday after Epiphany

Hos. 2:14–20	77, 169, 378, 435
Ps. 103:1–13, 22	35, 76, 439, 619, 620
2 Cor. 3:1–6	192, 292, 363
Mark 2:13–22	192, 292, 435

Ninth Sunday after Epiphany

Deut. 5:12–15	157, 393, 396,
Ps. 81:1–10	56, 58, 611
2 Cor. 4:5–12	1, 409, 666
Mark 2:23–3:6	325, 662, 719

Transfiguration of the Lord

See also 189–193

2 Kings 2:1–12	11, 825
Ps. 50:1–6	13, 370, 403, 668
2 Cor. 4:3–6	12, 86, 192, 409, 666
Mark 9:2–9	156, 189, 190, 192, 193, 406

Ash Wednesday

See also 165–167, 415–434

Joel 2:1–2, 12–17	416, 435, 619, 620, 738, 757
Isa. 58:1–12	433, 762, 802
Ps. 51:1–17	421, 422, 423, 427, 436, 451, 640, 688, 710, 739
2 Cor. 5:20b–6:10	212, 215, 269, 366, 441, 629, 722, 817
Matt. 6:1–6, 16–21	165, 167, 218, 292, 450, 649, 683, 708, 817, 824

First Sunday in Lent

See also 165–167, 415–434

Gen. 9:8–17	22, 157, 713, 833
Ps. 25:1–10	89, 339, 420
1 Pet. 3:18–22	218, 626, 634
Mark 1:9–15	165, 166, 231, 242, 292, 775, 783

Year C

Fourth Sunday after Epiphany

Jer. 1:4–10	463, 691, 697
Ps. 71:1–6	275, 326, 440, 813
1 Cor. 13:1–13	205, 370, 629, 693, 808, 833
Luke 4:21–30	162, 722

Fifth Sunday after Epiphany

Isa. 6:1–8 (9–13)	1, 4, 12, 49, 68, 69, 169, 282, 287, 368, 369, 392, 452, 746
Ps. 138	334, 694, 801, 802
1 Cor. 15:1–11	4, 232, 236, 245, 369, 485
Luke 5:1–11	170, 282, 649, 720, 726, 751

Sixth Sunday after Epiphany

Jer. 17:5–10	680, 743
Ps. 1	454, 457, 806, 816
1 Cor. 15:12–20	644, 852
Luke 6:17–26	234, 249, 815

Seventh Sunday after Epiphany

Gen. 45:3–11, 15	71, 661, 815
Ps. 37:1–11, 39–40	410, 425, 706, 820
1 Cor. 15:35–38, 42–50	236, 240, 247, 274, 306
Luke 6:27–38	346, 756, 795

Eighth Sunday after Epiphany

Isa. 55:10–13	80, 237, 539, 648, 663
Ps. 92:1–4, 12–15	621. 634, 675, 677, 682
1 Cor. 15:51–58	237, 245, 321, 505, 846
Luke 6:39–49	312, 718

Ninth Sunday after Epiphany

1 Kgs. 8:22–23, 41–43	346, 394
Ps. 96:1–9	236, 304, 539, 639, 650
Gal. 1:1–12	366, 783
Luke 7:1–10	634, 795

Transfiguration of the Lord

See also 189–193

Exod. 34:29–35	12, 66
Ps. 99	57, 327, 329, 635
2 Cor. 3:12–4:2	278, 288, 495, 666
Luke 9:28–36 (37–43)	156, 189, 190, 192, 193, 411

Ash Wednesday

See also 165–167, 415–434

Joel 2:1–2, 12–17	416, 435, 619, 620, 738, 757
Isa. 58:1–12	433, 762, 802
Ps. 51:1–17	421, 422, 423, 427, 436, 451, 640, 688, 710, 739
2 Cor. 5:20b–6:10	212, 215, 269, 366, 441, 629, 722, 817
Matt. 6:1–6, 16–21	165, 167, 218, 292, 450, 649, 683, 708, 817, 824

First Sunday in Lent

See also 165–167, 415–434

Deut. 26:1–11	8, 336, 712
Ps. 91:1–2, 9–16	43, 168, 326
Rom. 10:8b–13	481, 510, 621
Luke 4:1–13	165, 166, 167, 292, 618, 783

Year A

Rom. 5:12–19   223, 224, 275, 649
Matt. 4:1–11   165, 166, 167, 618,
                783, 819

Second Sunday in Lent
See also 165–167, 415–434
Gen. 12:1–4a   37, 50, 486
Ps. 121   12, *45*, 645, *845*
Rom. 4:1–5, 13–17   12, 440, 829
Matt. 17:1–9   191, 274, 539, 634
John 3:1–17   137, 189, 190, 292, 483

Third Sunday in Lent
See also 165–167, 415–434
Exod. 17:1–7   8, 53, 65, 81, 438,
                494
Ps. 95   21, 32, *386*, 387, 388, 451,
          638, 817
Rom. 5:1–11   123, 451, 688, 707,
                833
John 4:5–42   81, 242, 440, 479,
                494, 666, 719

Fourth Sunday in Lent
See also 165–167, 415–434
1 Sam. 16:1–13   30, 32, 39, 288,
                  663, 834
Ps. 23   *473, 801, 802, 803*, 816
Eph. 5:8–14   377, 739, 748, 749,
                827, 853
John 9:1–41   314, 351, 490, 684,
                719, 793

Fifth Sunday in Lent
See also 165–167, 415–434
Ezek. 37:1–14   53, 286
Ps. 130   424, 681, *791*, 832
Rom. 8:6–11   53, 66, 288, 407, 634
John 11:1–45   250, 292, 728, 785,
                793, 809

Passion/Palm Sunday
(Sixth Sunday in Lent):
Liturgy of the Palms
See also 196–228
Ps. 118:1–2, 19–29   200, *391*, 403,
                      466, 514, *681*
Matt. 21:1–11   160, 196, 197, 198,
                  199, 200, 514, 618, 736

Passion/Palm Sunday
(Sixth Sunday in Lent):
Liturgy of the Passion
See also 196–228
Isa. 50:4–9a   291, 686, 750
Ps. 31:9–16   *214*, 275, 686, *811*
Phil. 2:5–11   49, 84, 108, 119, 127,
                140, 215, 220, 228, 262, 263,
                299, 497, 514, 630, 727
Matt. 26:14–27:66 or
Matt. 27:11–54   7, 84, 161, 171, 195,
                  202, 204, 218, 223, 224, 226,
                  495, 501, 504, 506, 534, 672

Monday of Holy Week
Isa. 42:1–9   53, 265, 286, 320, 409,
                450, 757, 765
Ps. 36:5–11   12, 39, 43, 65, 440,
                475, 477, 833
Heb. 9:11–15   223, 224, 264, 321,
                435, 475, 495, 625
John 12:1–11   201, 203, 216, 435,
                629, 630

Year B

Second Sunday in Lent
See also 165–167, 415–434
Gen. 17:1–7, 15–16   39, 49
Ps. 22:23–31   49, *210, 631*
Rom. 4:13–25   240, 742, 819, 838
Mark 8:31–38   220, 231, 245, 320,
                726
Mark 9:2–9   189, 190, 191

Third Sunday in Lent
See also 165–167, 415–434
Exod. 20:1–17   20, 39, 88, 625, 681
Ps. 19   14, 24, 39, *61*, 625, *690*
1 Cor. 1:18–25   213, 225, 265, 307,
                  826
John 2:13–22   5, 157, 225, 394, 402,
                432

Fourth Sunday in Lent
See also 165–167, 415–434
Num. 21:4–9   14, 223, 224, 416, 610
Ps. 107:1–3, 17–22   14, 643, *653*,
                      803
Eph. 2:1–10   225, 345, 383, 624,
                634, 700, 742
John 3:14–21   119, 127, 137, 377,
                634, 749

Fifth Sunday in Lent
See also 165–167, 415–434
Jer. 31:31–34   69, 692, 833
Ps. 51:1–12   *421, 422, 423*
Ps. 119:9–16   *64*
Heb. 5:5–10   3, 209, 223, 224, 264
John 12:20–33   171, 242, 531, 718,
                  724, 725, 767

Passion/Palm Sunday
(Sixth Sunday in Lent):
Liturgy of the Palms
See also 196–228
Ps. 118:1–2, 19–29   200, *391*, 403,
                      466, 514, *681*
Mark 11:1–11   160, 196, 197, 198,
                199, 200, 514, 618, 736
John 12:12–16   196

Passion/Palm Sunday
(Sixth Sunday in Lent):
Liturgy of the Passion
See also 196–228
Isa. 50:4–9a   291, 686, 750
Ps. 31:9–16   *214*, 275, 686, *811*
Phil. 2:5–11   49, 84, 108, 119, 127,
                140, 215, 220, 228, 262, 263,
                299, 497, 514, 630, 727
Mark 14:1–15:47 or
Mark 15:1–39 (40–47)   7, 84, 161,
                171, 195, 202, 204, 220, 223, 224,
                227, 495, 501, 504, 534, 672, 704, 809

Monday of Holy Week
Isa. 42:1–9   53, 265, 286, 320, 409,
                450, 757, 765
Ps. 36:5–11   12, 39, 43, 65, 440,
                475, 477, 833
Heb. 9:11–15   223, 224, 264, 321,
                435, 475, 495, 625
John 12:1–11   201, 203, 216, 435,
                629, 630

Year C

Second Sunday in Lent
See also 165–167, 415–434
Gen. 15:1–12, 17–18   49, 258, 260
Ps. 27   12, *90*, 282, 440, *841, 842*
Phil. 3:17–4:1   12, 213, 221, 846
Luke 9:28–36   189, 190, 191, 193,
                282
Luke 13:31–35   35, 194, 487, 512

Third Sunday in Lent
See also 165–167, 415–434
Isa. 55:1–9   65, 78, 79, 416, 435,
                739, 792
Ps. 63:1–8   440, *696*, 743, 808, 814,
                816
1 Cor. 10:1–13   65, 438, 484, 783
Luke 13:1–9   307, 427, 429, 441,
                442, 649, 800

Fourth Sunday in Lent
See also 165–167, 415–434
Josh. 5:9–12   73, 416, 509, 643
Ps. 32   440, *446*, 447, 804
2 Cor. 5:16–21   23, 119, 127, 231,
                  634, 774, 821
Luke 15:1–3, 11b–32   119, 127, 231,
                      382, 416, 649, 771

Fifth Sunday in Lent
See also 165–167, 415–434
Isa. 43:16–21   463, 645
Ps. 126   31, *73, 74*, 674
Phil. 3:4b–14   216, 223, 224, 634,
                846
John 12:1–8   161, 201, 629, 630, 830

Passion/Palm Sunday
(Sixth Sunday in Lent):
Liturgy of the Palms
See also 196–228
Ps. 118:1–2, 19–29   200, *391*, 403,
                      466, 514, *681*
Luke 19:28–40   160, 196, 197, 198,
                199, 200, 514, 618, 736

Passion/Palm Sunday
(Sixth Sunday in Lent):
Liturgy of the Passion
See also 196–228
Isa. 50:4–9a   291, 686, 750
Ps. 31:9–16   *214*, 275, 686, *811*
Phil. 2:5–11   49, 84, 108, 119, 127,
                140, 215, 220, 228, 262, 263,
                299, 497, 514, 630, 727
Luke 22:14–23:56 or
Luke 23:1–49   7, 84, 161, 171, 195,
                204, 218, 220, 221, 228, 291, 294,
                495, 497, 501, 504, 506, 534, 672

Monday of Holy Week
Isa. 42:1–9   53, 265, 286, 320, 409,
                450, 757, 765
Ps. 36:5–11   12, 39, 43, 65, 440,
                475, 477, 833
Heb. 9:11–15   223, 224, 264, 321,
                435, 475, 495, 625
John 12:1–11   201, 203, 216, 435,
                629, 630

Tuesday of Holy Week
Isa. 49:1–7   265, 662
Ps. 71:1–14   275, 326, 434, 438,
                450, 471, *813*

Year A

Tuesday of Holy Week
Isa. 49:1–7   265, 662
Ps. 71:1–14   275, 326, 434, 438,
                          450, 471, *813*
1 Cor. 1:18–31   81, 213, 216, 223,
    224, 225, 274, 372, 450, 630, 826
John 12:20–36   182, 209, 225, 377,
              718, 724, 725, 738, 826

Wednesday of Holy Week
Isa. 50:4–9a   216, 221, 225, 455
Ps. 70   775, *780*
Heb. 12:1–3   4, 220, 232, 321, 326,
                        624, 718, 741
John 13:21–32   215, 223, 224

Maundy Thursday
See also 202–208, 494–538
Exod. 12:1–4 (5–10), 11–14   30, 50,
                    218, 233, 789
Ps. 116:1–2, 12–19   655, 699, *799,*
                           818
1 Cor. 11:23–26   495, 497, 504, 507,
    508, 511, 514, 516, 521, 523,
      525, 527, 532, 537, 770
John 13:1–17, 31b–35   30, 187, 202,
    203, 206, 207, 300, 316, 343,
    428, 464, 490, 498, 499, 506,
      514, 727, 738, 757, 818

Good Friday
See also 209–228
Isa. 52:13–53:12   39, 212, 215, 219,
          221, 222, 228, 299
Ps. 22   49, *210,* 326, *631*
Heb. 4:14–16; 5:7–9   187, 213, 217,
    220, 307, 393, 465, 518, 824
Heb. 10:16–25   39, 829
John 18:1–19:42   171, 194, 213, 216,
    220, 223, 224, 228, 245, 809, 818

Holy Saturday
Job 14:1–14   836
Lam. 3:1–9, 19–24   39, 59, 435, 668,
                            831
Ps. 31:1–4, 15–16   *214,* 326, 686,
                           811
1 Pet. 4:1–8   209, 307
Matt. 27:57–66   220, 228
John 19:38–42   171, 200

Easter Vigil*
See also 229, 230
Exod. 14:10–31; 15:20–21   65, 234,
                        476, 740
Ps. 114   57, *58,* 81, 359, 438
Rom. 6:3–11   233, 234, 246, 482,
    485, 489, 490, 491, 499, 502, 826
Matt. 28:1–10   6, 132, 229, 232,
    233, 235, 241, 243, 245, 249,
    251, 254, 255, 295, 618, 681

**Resurrection of the Lord /
Easter Sunday**
See also 229–257, 277
Acts 10:34–43   96, 234, 317, 318,
                            725
Jer. 31:1–6   724, 833
Ps. 118:1–2, 14–24   35, 280, 332,
                       391, 403, *681*

Year B

Tuesday of Holy Week
Isa. 49:1–7   265, 662
Ps. 71:1–14   275, 326, 434, 438,
                          450, 471, *813*
1 Cor. 1:18–31   81, 213, 216, 223,
    224, 225, 274, 372, 450, 630, 826
John 12:20–36   182, 209, 225, 377,
              718, 724, 725, 738, 826

Wednesday of Holy Week
Isa. 50:4–9a   216, 221, 225, 455
Ps. 70   775, *780*
Heb. 12:1–3   4, 220, 232, 321, 326,
                        624, 718, 741
John 13:21–32   215, 223, 224

Maundy Thursday
See also 202–208, 494–538
Exod. 12:1–4 (5–10), 11–14   30, 50,
                    218, 233, 789
Ps. 116:1–2, 12–19   655, 699, *799,*
                           818
1 Cor. 11:23–26   495, 497, 504, 507,
    508, 511, 514, 516, 521, 523,
      525, 527, 532, 537, 770
John 13:1–17, 31b–35   30, 187, 202,
    203, 206, 207, 300, 316, 343,
    428, 464, 490, 498, 499, 506,
      514, 727, 738, 757, 818

Good Friday
See also 209–228
Isa. 52:13–53:12   39, 212, 215, 219,
           221, 222, 228, 299
Ps. 22   49, *210,* 326, *631*
Heb. 4:14–16; 5:7–9   187, 213, 217,
    220, 307, 393, 465, 518, 824
Heb. 10:16–25   39, 829
John 18:1–19:42   171, 194, 213, 216,
    220, 223, 224, 228, 245, 809, 818

Holy Saturday
Job 14:1–14   836
Lam. 3:1–9, 19–24   39, 59, 435, 668,
                            831
Ps. 31:1–4, 15–16   *214,* 326, 686,
                           811
1 Pet. 4:1–8   209, 307
Matt. 27:57–66   220, 228
John 19:38–42   171, 200

Easter Vigil*
See also 229, 230
Exod. 14:10–31; 15:20–21   65, 234,
                        476, 740
Ps. 114   57, *58,* 81, 359, 438
Rom. 6:3–11   233, 234, 246, 482,
    485, 489, 490, 491, 499, 502, 826
Mark 16:1–8   6, 132, 229, 232,
    233, 234, 235, 241, 245, 249,
    251, 253, 255, 295, 618, 681

**Resurrection of the Lord /
Easter Sunday**
See also 229–257, 277
Acts 10:34–43   96, 234, 317, 318
Isa. 25:6–9   242, 294, 532
Ps. 118:1–2, 14–24   35, 280, 332,
                       391, 403, *681*

Year C

1 Cor. 1:18–31   81, 213, 216, 223,
    224, 225, 274, 372, 450, 630, 826
John 12:20–36   182, 209, 225, 377,
            718, 724, 725, 738, 826

Wednesday of Holy Week
Isa. 50:4–9a   216, 221, 225, 455
Ps. 70   775, *780*
Heb. 12:1–3   4, 220, 232, 321, 326,
                        624, 718, 741
John 13:21–32   215, 223, 224

Maundy Thursday
See also 202–208, 494–538
Exod. 12:1–4 (5–10), 11–14   30, 50,
                    218, 233, 789
Ps. 116:1–2, 12–19   655, 699, *799,*
                           818
1 Cor. 11:23–26   495, 497, 504, 507,
    508, 511, 514, 516, 521, 523,
      525, 527, 532, 537, 770
John 13:1–17, 31b–35   30, 187, 202,
    203, 206, 207, 300, 316, 343,
    428, 464, 490, 498, 499, 506,
      514, 727, 738, 757, 818

Good Friday
See also 209–228
Isa. 52:13–53:12   39, 212, 215, 219,
          221, 222, 228, 299
Ps. 22   49, *210,* 326, *631*
Heb. 4:14–16; 5:7–9   187, 213, 217,
    220, 307, 393, 465, 518, 824
Heb. 10:16–25   39, 829
John 18:1–19:42   171, 194, 213, 216,
    220, 223, 224, 228, 245, 809, 818

Holy Saturday
Job 14:1–14   836
Lam. 3:1–9, 19–24   39, 59, 435, 668,
                            831
Ps. 31:1–4, 15–16   *214,* 326, 686,
                           811
1 Pet. 4:1–8   209, 307
Matt. 27:57–66   220, 228
John 19:38–42   171, 200

Easter Vigil*
See also 229, 230
Exod. 14:10–31; 15:20–21   65, 234,
                        476, 740
Ps. 114   57, *58,* 81, 359, 438
Rom. 6:3–11   233, 234, 246, 482,
    485, 489, 490, 491, 499, 502, 826
Luke 24:1–12   6, 121, 132, 119,
    231, 232, 233, 234, 235, 236,
    238, 240, 241, 245, 253, 251,
    255, 255, 295, 618, 681

**Resurrection of the Lord /
Easter Sunday**
See also 229–257, 277
Acts 10:34–43   96, 234, 317, 318
Isa. 65:17–25   373, 376
Ps. 118:1–2, 14–24   35, 280, 332,
                       391, 403, *681*
1 Cor. 15:19–26   232, 237, 248, 361,
                   370, 485, 634

---

*Full list of readings for the Easter Vigil: Gen. 1:1–2:4a; Ps. 136:1–9, 23–26; Gen. 7:1–5, 11–18; 8:6–18; 9:8–13; Ps. 46; Gen. 22:1–18; Ps. 16; Exod. 14:10–31; 15:20–21; Exod. 15:1b–13, 17–18; Isa. 55:1–11; Isa. 12:2–6; Prov. 8:1–8, 19–21; 9:4b–6; Ps. 19; Ezek. 36:24–28; Pss. 42 and 43; Ezek. 37:1–14; Ps. 143; Zeph. 3:14–20; Ps. 98; Rom. 6:3–11; Ps. 114; Matt 28:1–10 (A); Mark 16:1–8 (B); Luke 24:1–12 (C).

Year A

Col. 3:1–4   232, 258, 361, 363, 485, 634

Acts 10:34–43   96, 149, 159, 317, 318, 319, 399, 405, 447

John 20:1–18   171, 220, 238, 242, 245, 251, 254, 255

Matt. 28:1–10   232, 235, 243, 248, 249, 253

Easter Evening

Isa. 25:6–9   236, 238, 242, 245, 292, 532,

Ps. 114   *58*, 359

1 Cor. 5:6b–8   235, 237, 255, 497

Luke 24:13–49   252, 254, 257, 510, 762

Second Sunday of Easter

See also 229–257, 277

Acts 2:14a, 22–32   238, 244, 277, 463

Ps. 16   338, 450, 535, 544, 629, *810*, 814, 837

1 Pet. 1:3–9   232, 290, 326, 437, 463, 629, 634, 734, 817

John 20:19–31   86, 200, 231, 235, 238, 242, 245, 254, 255, 256, 257, 286, 311, 317, 318, 467, 678, 752, 817

Third Sunday of Easter

See also 229–257, 277

Acts 2:14a, 36–41   404, 506, 525, 526, 737

Ps. 116:1–4, 12–19   393, 643, *655*, 799, 828

1 Pet. 1:17–23   232, 482, 629, 729, 830, 839

Luke 24:13–35   231, 252, 257, 500, 737, 818

Fourth Sunday of Easter

See also 229–257, 277

Acts 2:42–47   39, 515, 526, 528

Ps. 23   39, 81, 187, 327, 407, 440, *473*, 718, *801, 802, 803*

1 Pet. 2:19–25   213, 220, 226, 231, 408, 504, 718, 724, 725, 741, 748, 801, 802

John 10:1–10   119, 127, 187, 220, 410, 506, 541, 542,

Fifth Sunday of Easter

See also 229–257, 277

Acts 7:55–60   50, 79, 169, 463, 686

Ps. 31:1–5, 15–16   *214*, 275, 326, 327, 625, *811*

1 Pet. 2:2–10   4, 321, 327, 361, 409, 463, 645

John 14:1–14   431, 444, 483, 624, 634, 645, 671, 724, 725, 820

Sixth Sunday of Easter

See also 229–257, 277

Acts 17:22–31   624, 686, 735, 739, 824

Ps. 66:8–20   *54*, 275, 388, 642

1 Pet. 3:13–22   12, 372, 490, 624, 634, 804

John 14:15–21   242, 282, 317, 318, 366, 395, 407, 425, 828

Year B

1 Cor. 15:1–11   232, 233, 236, 361, 399, 634

Acts 10:34–43   96, 149, 159, 317, 318, 319, 399, 405, 447

John 20:1–18   171, 220, 238, 242, 245, 251, 254, 255

Mark 16:1–8   232, 242, 245, 248, 249, 253

Easter Evening

Isa. 25:6–9   236, 238, 242, 245, 292, 532,

Ps. 114   *58*, 359

1 Cor. 5:6b–8   235, 237, 255, 497

Luke 24:13–49   252, 254, 257, 510, 762

Second Sunday of Easter

See also 229–257, 277

Acts 4:32–35   169, 239, 762

Ps. 133   306, 317, 318, 372, *397*, *398*, 408, 440, 624, 754

1 John 1:1–2:2   9, 12, 108, 192, 377, 428, 440, 624, 745

John 20:19–31   86, 200, 231, 235, 238, 242, 245, 254, 255, 256, 257, 286, 311, 317, 318, 467, 678, 752, 817

Third Sunday of Easter

See also 229–257, 277

Acts 3:12–19   209, 218, 247, 494

Ps. 4   547, 675, 676, 740, *776*

1 John 3:1–7   251, 549, 629, 630, 676, 703

Luke 24:36b–48   231, 234, 248, 295, 296, 630

Fourth Sunday of Easter

See also 229–257, 277

Acts 4:5–12   39, 187, 624, 834

Ps. 23   39, 81, 187, 327, 407, 440, *473*, 718, *801, 802, 803*

1 John 3:16–24   215, 280, 308, 343, 394, 549, 624, 629, 748, 754, 757, 836

John 10:11–18   11, 353, 396, 541, 542, 801, 802

Fifth Sunday of Easter

See also 229–257, 277

Acts 8:26–40   157, 222, 278, 480, 518

Ps. 22:25–31   *210*, 611, *631*, 641, 809

1 John 4:7–21   22, 205, 286, 450, 624, 685

John 15:1–8   231, 245, 285, 479, 450, 483, 526, 703

Sixth Sunday of Easter

See also 229–257, 277

Acts 10:44–48   134, 266, 288, 346, 480

Ps. 98   *276, 371*, 539

1 John 5:1–6   306, 379, 438, 629, 754, 761

John 15:9–17   205, 231, 311, 317, 318, 465, 526, 703

Ascension of the Lord

See also 258–277

Acts 1:1–11   258, 265, 268, 277, 282, 407, 462, 662, 826

Ps. 47   41, *261*, 616, 640, 645

Ps. 93   *271, 272*, 677

Year C

Acts 10:34–43   96, 149, 159, 317, 318, 319, 399, 405, 447

John 20:1–18   171, 220, 238, 242, 245, 251, 254, 255

Luke 24:1–12   231, 232, 236, 242, 248, 253

Easter Evening

Isa. 25:6–9   236, 238, 242, 245, 292, 532,

Ps. 114   *58*, 359

1 Cor. 5:6b–8   235, 237, 255, 497

Luke 24:13–49   252, 254, 257, 510, 762

Second Sunday of Easter

See also 229–257, 277

Acts 5:27–32   159, 462, 536

Ps. 118:14–29   *391*, 681

Ps. 150   33, *389*, 617, *633*, 637, 640, 709

Rev. 1:4–8   1, 35, 108, 232, 260, 280, 299, 348, 514

John 20:19–31   86, 200, 231, 235, 238, 242, 245, 254, 255, 256, 257, 286, 311, 317, 318, 467, 678, 752, 817

Third Sunday of Easter

See also 229–257, 277

Acts 9:1–6 (7–20)   240, 325, 662, 761

Ps. 30   4, 390, 451, 667, *798, 805*

Rev. 5:11–14   4, 265, 369, 513, 614, 667, 826

John 21:1–19   242, 257, 314, 483, 720, 828

Fourth Sunday of Easter

See also 229–257, 277

Acts 9:36–43   39, 65, 247, 324, 793

Ps. 23   39, 81, 187, 327, 407, 440, *473*, 718, *801, 802, 803*

Rev. 7:9–17   81, 215, 265, 299, 326, 327, 369, 412, 440, 518, 748

John 10:22–30   182, 187, 221, 801, 802, 824

Fifth Sunday of Easter

See also 229–257, 277

Acts 11:1–18   14, 282, 288, 610

Ps. 148   *17, 18*, 26, 33, 669, *679*

Rev. 21:1–6   81, 269, 362, 374, 517, 833

John 13:31–35   203, 205, 300, 316, 317, 318, 343, 529, 738, 757

Sixth Sunday of Easter

See also 229–257, 277

Acts 16:9–15   295, 307, 490, 733

Ps. 67   327, *341*, 547, 765

Rev. 21:10, 22–22:5   79, 265, 362, 375, 377, 403, 517

John 5:1–9   796

John 14:23–29   282, 351, 395, 448, 461, 540, 688

Ascension of the Lord

See also 258–277

Acts 1:1–11   258, 265, 268, 277, 282, 407, 462, 662, 826

Ps. 47   41, *261*, 616, 640, 645

Ps. 93   *271, 272*, 677

Year A

Ascension of the Lord
See also 258–277
Acts 1:1–11   258, 265, 268, 277, 282, 407, 462, 662, 826
Ps. 47   41, *261*, 616, 640, 645
Ps. 93   *271, 272,* 677
Eph. 1:15–23   4, 35, 245, 249, 263, 264, 321, 353, 451, 644
Luke 24:44–53   237, 260, 268, 277, 282, 395, 662

Seventh Sunday of Easter
See also 229–257, 277
Acts 1:6–14   258, 407, 463, 662
Ps. 68:1–10, 32–35   *55,* 183, 616, 851
1 Pet. 4:12–14; 5:6–11   220, 246, 463, 468, 740, 742, 823, 846
John 17:1–11   220, 282, 317, 318, 492, 733

Day of Pentecost
See also 277–294
Acts 2:1–21   66, 123, 280, 281, 283, 284, 288, 289, 290, 291, 292, 297, 404, 406, 539, 745, 769
Num. 11:24–30   407, 612
Ps. 104:24–34, 35b   14, 16, 20, 21, *34,* 41, 81, 323, 370
1 Cor. 12:3b–13   280, 285, 317, 318, 322, 537, 629, 733
John 20:19–23   231, 246, 705
John 7:37–39   81, 311, 317, 318, 649, 817

Trinity Sunday
See also 1–11
Gen. 1:1–2:4a   7, 9, 14, 20, 24, 32, 230, 476, 484, 664, 681, 850
Ps. 8   14, 15, 21, *25,* 245, 451, 613, 625, 713, 757
2 Cor. 13:11–13   299, 379, 408, 432, 716, 745
Matt. 28:16–20   242, 252, 292, 296, 297, 298, 320, 456, 716, 747, 757

Proper 3 (May 24–28)
Isa. 49:8–16a   263, 307, 734
Ps. 131   282, *474, 791,* 819
1 Cor. 4:1–5   351, 352, 394, 395, 541, 542, 761
Matt. 6:24–34   20, 175, 462, 475, 649, 697, 819, 839

Proper 4 (May 29–June 4)
Gen. 6:9–22; 7:24; 8:14–19   15, 462
Ps. 46   *329, 380,* 414, 819
Deut. 11:18–21, 26–28   6
Ps. 31:1–5, 19–24   *214, 666, 811*
Rom. 1:16–17; 3:22b–28, (29–31)   6, 326, 691, 739
Matt. 7:21–29   541, 542, 621, 731, 793

Proper 5 (June 5–June 11)
Gen. 12:1–9   49, 51, 331
Ps. 33:1–12   *40,* 48, 337, 339, 340, 539
Hos. 5:15–6:6   149
Ps. 50:7–15   *13*
Rom. 4:13–25   49, 240, 305, 838
Matt. 9:9–13, 18–26   157, 161, 515

Year B

Eph. 1:15–23   4, 35, 245, 249, 263, 264, 321, 353, 451, 644
Luke 24:44–53   237, 260, 268, 277, 282, 395, 662

Seventh Sunday of Easter
See also 229–257, 277
Acts 1:15–17, 21–26   303, 719, 722, 839
Ps. 1   *457,* 741, 765
1 John 5:9–13   89, 374, 443, 451, 454, 465, 472, 481, 847
John 17:6–19   460, 465, 492, 634, 734, 775

Day of Pentecost
See also 277–294
Acts 2:1–21   66, 123, 280, 281, 283, 284, 288, 289, 290, 291, 292, 297, 404, 406, 539, 612, 745, 769
Ezek. 37:1–14   285, 286, 407
Ps. 104:24–34, 35b   14, 16, 20, 21, *34,* 41, 81, 323, 370
Rom. 8:22–27   280, 285, 360, 629, 734, 817, 849
John 15:26–27; 16:4b–15   235, 255, 278, 282, 283, 286, 288, 462

Trinity Sunday
See also 1–11
Isa. 6:1–8   1, 4, 12, 68, 69, 287, 347, 368, 486, 746
Ps. 29   *2,* 8, *10,* 41, *259,* 610, 634
Rom. 8:12–17   1, 4, 12, 300, 317, 318, 369, 482
John 3:1–17   119, 127, 137, 225, 282, 292, 317, 318, 483, 490, 634

Proper 3 (May 24–28)
Hos. 2:14–20   4, 260, 351, 435
Ps. 103:1–13, 22   35, *439,* 615, *619, 620*
2 Cor. 3:1–6   37, 192, 288, 450, 735, 822
Mark 2:13–22   382, 415, 422, 423, 446, 739, 851

Proper 4 (May 29–June 4)
1 Sam. 3:1–10 (11–20)   69, 746
Ps. 139:1–6, 13–18   *28, 29, 426*
Deut. 5:12–15   663
Ps. 81:1–10   11, *56,* 451
2 Cor. 4:5–12   409, 666, 671, 672, 710
Mark 2:23–3:6   719, 793, 796, 797

Proper 5 (June 5–June 11)
1 Sam. 8:4–11 (12–15), 16–20 (11:14–15)   344
Ps. 138   *334,* 681, 694
Gen. 3:8–15   130, 370
Ps. 130   344, *424, 791*
2 Cor. 4:13–5:1   376, 829, 846
Mark 3:20–35   700, 736, 771

Proper 6 (June 12–June 18)
1 Sam. 15:34–16:13   263, 663
Ps. 20   *548,* 804
Ezek. 17:22–24   22, 36
Ps. 92:1–4, 12–15   634, 641, *682*
2 Cor. 5:6–10 (11–13), 14–17   434, 656, 748, 774, 792, 817, 822
Mark 4:26–34   171, 293, 684, 714

Year C

Eph. 1:15–23   4, 35, 245, 249, 263, 264, 321, 353, 451, 644
Luke 24:44–53   237, 260, 268, 277, 282, 395, 662

Seventh Sunday of Easter
See also 229–257, 277
Acts 16:16–34   358, 359, 661, 814
Ps. 97   1, 81, *365,* 827
Rev. 22:12–14, 16–17, 20–21   81, 226, 242, 418, 615, 630, 662, 817
John 17:20–26   103, 242, 300, 362, 495, 504

Day of Pentecost
See also 277–294
Acts 2:1–21   66, 123, 280, 281, 283, 284, 288, 289, 290, 291, 292, 297, 388, 404, 406, 539, 612, 745, 769
Gen. 11:1–9   407, 833
Ps. 104:24–34, 35b   14, 16, 20, 21, *34,* 41, 81, 323, 370
Rom. 8:14–17   278, 280, 293, 317, 318, 629, 839
John 14:8–17 (25–27)   279, 282, 285, 317, 318, 351, 395, 407, 688

Trinity Sunday
See also 1–11
Prov. 8:1–4, 22–31   12, 88, 91, 102, 174, 818
Ps. 8   14, 15, 21, *25,* 245, 451, 613, 625, 713, 757
Rom. 5:1–5   281, 284, 353, 451, 623, 688, 707
John 16:12–15   9, 245, 267, 278, 279, 280, 283, 285, 287

Proper 3 (May 24–28)
Isa. 55:10–13   77, 78, 80, 308
Ps. 92:1–4, 12–15   625, 641, 675, *682*
1 Cor. 15:51–58   236, 237, 238, 353, 366, 369
Luke 6:39–49   104, 353, 738, 832, 835, 836, 838

Proper 4 (May 29–June 4)
1 Kgs. 18:20–21 (22–29), 30–39   463, 645
Ps. 96   299, *304,* 402, 614, 634, *639*
1 Kgs. 8:22–23, 41–43   394
Ps. 96:1–9   299, *304,* 402, 614, 634, *639*
Gal. 1:1–12   307, 416, 441, 768
Luke 7:1–10   704, 736, 738

Proper 5 (June 5–June 11)
1 Kgs. 17:8–16 (17–24)   201, 610
Ps. 146   4, *806*
1 Kgs. 17:17–24   795
Ps. 30   4, 667, *798, 805*
Gal. 1:11–24   4, 250, 691
Luke 7:11–17   343, 372, 459, 793

Proper 6 (June 12–June 18)
1 Kgs. 21:1–10 (11–14), 15–21a   434
Ps. 5:1–8   1, *665,* 667
2 Sam. 11:26–12:10, 13–15   417, 434, 663
Ps. 32   440, *446,* 804
Gal. 2:15–21   1, 223, 224, 231, 240, 497, 649, 703
Luke 7:36–8:3   171, 182, 201, 834

Year A

Rom. 8:26–39   30, 445, 823, 833, 846
Matt. 13:31–33, 44–52   5, 714, 771, 830

Proper 13 (July 31–August 6)
Gen. 32:22–31   760, 833
Ps. 17:1–7, 15   *211*, 470, 816
Isa. 55:1–5   78, 479, 528
Ps. 145:8–9, 14–21   4, *42*, 270, 622
Rom. 9:1–5   4, 49, 50, 51, 453, 463, 649
Matt. 14:13–21   343, 460, 497, 498, 532

Proper 14 (August 7–August 13)
Gen. 37:1–4, 12–28   8, 754
Ps. 105:1–6, 16–22, 45b   *59*, 634, 648
1 Kgs. 19:9–18   22, 169, 698
Ps. 85:8–13   *449*, 795, 818
Rom. 10:5–15   175, 264, 462, 481, 621, 634, 648
Matt. 14:22–33   8, 159, 184, 185, 353, 444, 463, 834

Proper 15 (August 14–August 20)
Gen. 45:1–15   30, 250
Ps. 133   *397, 398*, 408
Isa. 56:1, 6–8   8, 299
Ps. 67   119, 327, *341*, 398, 765
Rom. 11:1–2a, 29–32   265, 432, 435, 624, 826
Matt. 15:(10–20) 21–28   119, 127, 317, 318, 343, 649, 754

Proper 16 (August 21–August 27)
Exod. 1:8–2:10   269, 817
Ps. 124   *330*, 709
Isa. 51:1–6   51, 87, 765
Ps. 138   81, *334*
Rom. 12:1–8   310, 320, 700, 710, 716, 727, 748, 768
Matt. 16:13–20   81, 317, 318, 683, 718, 726

Proper 17 (August 28–September 3)
Exod. 3:1–15   49, 52, 331, 405
Ps. 105:1–6, 23–26, 45b   *59*, 275, 634
Jer. 15:15–21   69, 460
Ps. 26:1–8   93, 723
Rom. 12:9–21   14, 265, 310, 316, 372, 724, 725, 727, 823
Matt. 16:21–28   220, 718, 826, 833

Proper 18 (September 4–September 10)
Exod. 12:1–14   233
Ps. 149   232, 539, *550*, 637
Ezek. 33:7–11   663, 722
Ps. 119:33–40   64
Rom. 13:8–14   203, 232, 377, 744, 771
Matt. 18:15–20   203, 394, 472, 529

Proper 19 (September 11–September 17)
Exod. 14:19–31   65, 174, 476, 484
Ps. 114   58
Exod. 15:1b–11, 20–21   234, 324, 616

Year B

Proper 14 (August 7–August 13)
2 Sam. 18:5–9, 15, 31–33   12, 267
Ps. 130   *424*, 791, 832
1 Kgs. 19:4–8   69, 169, 509
Ps. 34:1–8   65, 427, *520*
Eph. 4:25–5:2   15, 407, 444, 698, 734, 738, 739
John 6:35, 41–51   65, 401, 496, 504, 522, 524, 541, 542, 734

Proper 15 (August 14–August 20)
1 Kgs. 2:10–12; 3:3–14   65, 174
Ps. 111   440, *652, 755*
Prov. 9:1–6   174, 738
Ps. 34:9–14   *520*, 659
Eph. 5:15–20   308, 361, 533, 654, 689, 734
John 6:51–58   407, 495, 504, 541, 542, 719, 734, 747

Proper 16 (August 21–August 27)
1 Kgs. 8:(1, 6, 10–11) 22–30, 41–43   230, 394, 636
Ps. 84   *402*, 626, 849
Josh. 24:1–2a, 14–18   47, 62
Ps. 34:15–22   *520*, 786
Eph. 6:10–20   269, 275, 307, 629, 756, 838, 846
John 6:56–69   541, 542, 724, 725, 765, 839

Proper 17 (August 28–September 3)
Song 2:8–13   14
Ps. 45:1–2, 6–9   *333*, 630
Deut. 4:1–2, 6–9   32, 39, 301, 729
Ps. 15   93, *419*
Jas. 1:17–27   12, 14, 32, 39, 340, 708, 717
Mark 7:1–8, 14–15, 21–23   351, 429, 442, 630

Proper 18 (September 4–September 10)
Prov. 22:1–2, 8–9, 22–23   660, 773
Ps. 125   394, *848*
Isa. 35:4–7a   20, 610
Ps. 146   390, 645, *806*
Jas. 2:1–10 (11–13), 14–17   317, 318, 343, 762, 771
Mark 7:24–37   203, 317, 318, 495, 610

Proper 19 (September 11–September 17)
Prov. 1:20–33   174, 453, 707
Ps. 19   14, *61*, 625, *690*
Isa. 50:4–9a   455, 722, 841
Ps. 116:1–9   393, *655*, 799
Jas. 3:1–12   265, 693, 722, 723, 737
Mark 8:27–38   157, 220, 718

Proper 20 (September 18–September 24)
Prov. 31:10–31   174, 201, 324
Ps. 1   12, *457*, 840
Jer. 11:18–20   342, 373
Ps. 54   471, *812*
Jas. 3:13–4:3, 7–8a   702, 714, 839
Mark 9:30–37   188, 320, 351, 459

Year C

Ps. 33:12–22   *40*, 48, 317, 318, 338, 815
Heb. 11:1–3, 8–16   65, 326, 339, 656, 684, 730, 817
Luke 12:32–40   242, 307, 317, 318, 320, 350, 362, 716, 771

Proper 15 (August 14–August 20)
Isa. 5:1–7   5, 342, 354
Ps. 80:1–2, 8–19   *355*, 740
Jer. 23:23–29   28, 49
Ps. 82   340, 708, *763*
Heb. 11:29–12:2   326, 656, 718, 730, 817, 846
Luke 12:49–56   30, 51, 136, 718, 724, 725, 817

Proper 16 (August 21–August 27)
Jer. 1:4–10   69, 70, 691
Ps. 71:1–6   *813*
Isa. 58:9b–14   35, 287, 435
Ps. 103:1–8   35, *439, 619, 620*
Heb. 12:18–29   374, 405, 406, 407, 435, 442, 514
Luke 13:10–17   242, 343, 795, 797

Proper 17 (August 28–September 3)
Jer. 2:4–13   14, 453, 463, 479
Ps. 81:1, 10–16   *56*, 667
Prov. 25:6–7   70, 174
Ps. 112   611, *755*
Heb. 13:1–8, 15–16   14, 49, 108, 411, 463, 645, 710, 762
Luke 14:1, 7–14   282, 343, 722

Proper 18 (September 4–September 10)
Jer. 18:1–11   5, 695
Ps. 139:1–6, 13–18   *28, 29*, 302, *426, 686*
Deut. 30:15–20   663
Ps. 1   *457*
Phlm. 1–21   213, 754, 761
Luke 14:25–33   213, 220, 223, 224, 718, 742

Proper 19 (September 11–September 17)
Jer. 4:11–12, 22–28   335, 342, 739
Ps. 14   *335*, 773
Exod. 32:7–14   278, 434
Ps. 51:1–10   *421, 422, 423*, 427, 688
1 Tim. 1:12–17   12, 132, 212, 619, 620, 634
Luke 15:1–10   173, 382, 442, 649

Proper 20 (September 18–September 24)
Jer. 8:18–9:1   738, 739, 792
Ps. 79:1–9   *430*
Amos 8:4–7   70, 331, 343
Ps. 113   299, 327, *670*, 677
1 Tim. 2:1–7   103, 340, 346, 634
Luke 16:1–13   697, 698, 700, 708

Proper 21 (September 25–October 1)
Jer. 32:1–3a, 6–15   8, 70, 321
Ps. 91:1–6, 14–16   *43, 168*, 275, 764
Amos 6:1a, 4–7   415, 434, 740
Ps. 146   326, *806*

Year A

1 John 3:1–3   104, 326, 369, 412, 630, 730, 760, 804

Matt. 5:1–12   172, 487, 630, 718, 823

Proper 26
(October 30–November 5)

Josh. 3:7–17   65, 69, 741

Ps. 107:1–7, 33–37   643, *653*

Mic. 3:5–12   70, 756

Ps. 43   35, *778*, 792

1 Thess. 2:9–13   729, 749

Matt. 23:1–12   320, 374, 712, 775

Proper 27
(November 6–November 12)

Josh. 24:1–3a, 14–25   47, 62, 347

Ps. 78:1–7   453, 624, *632*

Amos 5:18–24   342, 503, 757

Ps. 70   625, *780*

1 Thess. 4:13–18   352, 357, 358, 363, 819, 839

Matt. 25:1–13   85, 175, 349, 350, 362, 771

Proper 28
(November 13–November 19)

Judg. 4:1–7   363, 611

Ps. 123   *788*

Zeph. 1:7, 12–18   342, 453, 663

Ps. 90:1–8 (9–11), 12   4, 12, *687*

1 Thess. 5:1–11   4, 12, 305, 384, 494, 716

Matt. 25:14–30   242, 249, 612, 716, 719

Christ the King / Reign of Christ
Proper 29

See also 258–276

Ezek. 34:11–16, 20–24   123, 187, 274, 279, 681, 802

Ps. 100   81, *385*, 643

Ps. 95:1–7a   *386*, 387, 388, 413, *638*

Eph. 1:15–23   4, 245, 268, 321, 363, 451, 514, 677

Matt. 25:31–46   186, 320, 323, 343, 541, 542, 660, 757, 766

New Year's Day

Eccl. 3:1–13   14, 21, 30, 39, 250, 488, 645

Ps. 8   *25*, 36, 81, 625, 687

Rev. 21:1–6a   346, 362, 374

Matt. 25:31–46   44, 79, 245, 343, 364, 612, 664, 816

Thanksgiving Day

Deut. 8:7–18   327, 643

Ps. 65   15, 32, *38*, 41, 81, 514

2 Cor. 9:6–15   48, 315, 345, 644, 711, 714, 717

Luke 17:11–19   15, 36, 41, 179, 367, 612, 643, 649

Year B

Heb. 9:24–28   92, 102, 260, 262, 363

Mark 12:38–44   70, 316, 697, 708, 762

Proper 28
(November 13–November 19)

1 Sam. 1:4–20   39, 99, 324, 540

1 Sam. 2:1–10   535, 837

Dan. 12:1–3   41, 258

Ps. 16   332, 544, *810*

Heb. 10:11–14 (15–18), 19–25   39, 352, 629, 824, 846

Mark 13:1–8   215, 292, 357, 618

Christ the King / Reign of Christ
Proper 29

See also 258–276

2 Sam. 23:1–7   265

Ps. 132:1–12 (13–18)   149, 227, *381*, 394

Dan. 7:9–10, 13–14   12, 41, 368, 675

Ps. 93   81, *271*, *272*, 363

Rev. 1:4b–8   1, 12, 35, 108, 232, 264, 265, 705

John 18:33–37   159, 171, 220, 264, 269, 274, 307

New Year's Day

Eccl. 3:1–13   14, 21, 30, 39, 250, 645

Ps. 8   *25*, 36, 81, 625, 687

Rev. 21:1–6a   346, 362, 374

Matt. 25:31–46   44, 79, 245, 343, 364, 612, 664, 816

Thanksgiving Day

Joel 2:21–27   336, 367

Ps. 126   31, *73*, *74*, 149, 610, 634

1 Tim. 2:1–7   48, 169, 331, 346, 794

Matt. 6:25–33   20, 36, 175, 611, 643, 683, 802

Year C

Proper 28
(November 13–November 19)

Isa. 65:17–25   77, 91, 373

Isa. 12   645

Mal. 4:1–2a   119, 127, 174, 611, 666

Ps. 98   *276*, *371*, 435, 641

2 Thess. 3:6–13   295, 719, 757, 761, 767

Luke 21:5–19   119, 127, 352, 353, 738

Christ the King / Reign of Christ
Proper 29

See also 258–276

Jer. 23:1–6   88, 222, 268, 463, 625

Luke 1:68–79   41, 109, 122, 132

Ps. 46   275, *329*, *380*, 463

Col. 1:11–20   4, 108, 213, 216, 305, 307, 309, 624, 634

Luke 23:33–43   132, 171, 200, 220, 227, 228, 274

New Year's Day

Eccl. 3:1–13   14, 21, 30, 39, 250, 645

Ps. 8   *25*, 36, 81, 625, 687

Rev. 21:1–6a   346, 362, 374

Matt. 25:31–46   44, 79, 245, 343, 364, 612, 664, 816

Thanksgiving Day

Deut. 26:1–11   65, 541, 542, 650

Ps. 100   41, 37, *385*, 387, 413, 643, 645

Phil. 4:4–9   363, 448, 472, 685, 697, 734

John 6:25–35   14, 36, 346, 496, 497, 523, 712

Scriptural Index

Psalm entries that appear in italics represent full settings of psalms (such as metrical paraphrases and responsorial versions) that are appropriate for use when singing the psalm for the day from the Revised Common Lectionary. For an exhaustive listing of these psalm citations, see the Psalm Index (pp. 989–990).

This index provides a list of full settings of psalms (such as metrical paraphrases and responsorial versions) appropriate for use when singing the psalm for the day from the Revised Common Lectionary. For a more exhaustive listing of psalm citations in Glory to God, including passing references and short refrains based on verses from psalms, see the Scriptural Index (pp. 979–988).

INDEX OF AUTHORS, COMPOSERS, AND SOURCES

ALPHABETICAL INDEX OF TUNES

First Lines and Common Titles